OPERATING SYSTEMS:

Design
and
Implementation

ANDREW S. TANENBAUM

Vrije Universiteit
Amsterdam, The Netherlands

PRENTICE-HALL, INC., Englewood Cliffs, New Jersey 07632

Library of Congress Cataloging-in-Publication Data

Tanenbaum, Andrew S., (date)
    Operating systems.

    Bibliography: p. 337.
    Includes index.
    1. Operating systems (Computers)   I. Title.
QA76.76.O63T36   1986   005.4′3   86-18752
ISBN   0-13-637406-9

Editorial/production supervision
    and interior design by Margaret Rizzi
Cover design by Lundgren Graphics, Ltd.
Cover cartoon by Jos Collignon
Manufacturing buyer: Ed O'Dougherty

© 1987 by Prentice-Hall, Inc.
A Division of Simon & Schuster
Englewood Cliffs, New Jersey 07632

LIMITS OF LIABILITY AND DISCLAIMER OF WARRANTY
The author and publisher of this book have used their best efforts in preparing this book.
These efforts include the development, research and testing of the theories and programs
to determine their effectiveness. The author and publisher make no warranty of any kind,
expressed or implied, with regard to these programs or the documentation contained in
this book. The author and publisher shall not be liable in any event for incidental or con-
sequential damages in connection with, or arising out of, the furnishing, performance, or
use of these programs.

Printed in the United States of America

10 9 8 7 6 5 4 3 2

ISBN   0-13-637406-9   025

Prentice-Hall International (UK) Limited, *London*
Prentice-Hall of Australia Pty. Limited, *Sydney*
Prentice-Hall Canada Inc., *Toronto*
Prentice-Hall Hispanoamericana, S.A., *Mexico*
Prentice-Hall of India Private Limited, *New Delhi*
Prentice-Hall of Japan, Inc., *Tokyo*
Prentice-Hall of Southeast Asia Pte. Ltd., *Singapore*
Editora Prentice-Hall do Brasil, Ltda., *Rio de Janeiro*

To Suzanne, Barbara, Marvin and the memory of Sweetie π

CONTENTS

5 FILE SYSTEMS   251

Prentice-Hall Software Series
Brian W. Kernighan, Advisor

OPERATING SYSTEMS:
Design
and
Implementation

PREFACE

Most books on operating systems are strong on theory and weak on practice. This one aims to provide a better balance between the two. It covers all the fundamental principles in detail, including processes, interprocess communication, semaphores, monitors, message passing, remote procedure call, scheduling algorithms, input/output, deadlocks, device drivers, memory management, paging algorithms, file system design, network file servers, atomic transactions, security and protection mechanisms. But it also discusses one particular system—MINIX, a UNIX-compatible operating system—in detail, and even provides a complete source code listing for study. This arrangement allows the reader to not only learn the principles, but also to see how they are applied in a real operating system.

An operating system has four major components: process management, input/output, memory management, and the file system. After an introductory chapter, the book contains a chapter about each of these topics. Each chapter contains a lengthy discussion of the relevant principles, illustrated with examples taken from a variety of systems, including UNIX, MS-DOS, CP/M, MULTICS, and other operating systems.

Having taught operating systems courses for 15 years, and having been the principal architect of three different operating systems for three different computers (PDP-11, 68000, and IBM PC), I have come to realize that just studying the theory (deadlocks, scheduling algorithms, etc.) leaves the student with a very distorted view of the subject. Most books and courses devote an enormous amount of time to scheduling algorithms, for example, which in practice are usually less than a page of code, while completely ignoring I/O, which is often 30 percent of the system, or more.

To correct this imbalance I have written a new operating system, MINIX, from scratch. MINIX has the same system calls as Version 7 UNIX (except for the omission of a small number of unimportant ones). I have also supplied a shell that is functionally identical to the UNIX shell, along with more than 60 other programs that are similar to their UNIX counterparts (e.g., *cat, cc, cp, grep, ls,* and *make*). In short, to the user, MINIX looks very much like UNIX.

On the inside, however, the system is completely new. I have taken great pains to structure the system carefully, to make it easy to understand, and easy for students to modify. The major pieces of the system are written as separate modules that communicate by message passing. Procedures are generally short, and structured programming practice is used throughout. The code contains more than 3000 separate comments.

Like all operating systems, MINIX is divided into four major parts: process management, input/output (device drivers), memory management, and the file system. As mentioned above, each of these topics is the subject of a whole chapter in the book. Each chapter first discusses the general principles, and then tells how the subject is handled in MINIX.

The complete MINIX source code is available in several forms and can be used in various ways. One version is for the IBM PC, XT, or AT (and true compatibles) and is distributed on diskette (binaries and sources). If a sufficient number of PCs are available for a course, each student can be given a copy of the software to modify and test on his own PC. A good configuration is 640K RAM and two 360K floppy disks, although smaller configurations are also possible. A hard disk is not necessary.

An alternative way to use the software is to give each student a copy of the MINIX sources on a VAX or other time-shared computer (the host machine). The student can then modify them and compile them on the host, producing a runnable binary image that can be downloaded to an IBM PC for testing. This arrangement has the advantage that only a few IBM PCs are needed, even for a large group of students. It does, however, require a C compiler for the IBM PC running on the host. Such a compiler, based on the Amsterdam Compiler Kit (see the article by Tanenbaum et al. in the *Communications of the ACM*, Sept. 1983, pp. 654-660) is available from the companies listed on page xvi.

The software can also be used for courses, even when no IBM PCs are available. Two possibilities have been provided. First, an IBM PC simulator is included on the magnetic tape available from Prentice-Hall. The simulator interprets the 8088 instructions one at a time, examining and executing them just as a real 8088 does. It also simulates those I/O devices needed to run MINIX.

The other possibility is to have the students work with only the file system. The MINIX file system is actually just a big C program that runs outside the operating system as a user program. It is really a UNIX-compatible remote file server that communicates with the rest of MINIX by message passing on the same machine (although it is easy to set it up to run as a true network file server).

To have a student experiment with the file system on the host computer, the file system and the student's test program should be compiled separately. A main program is needed to set up pipes, fork, and execute the test program and file system, which communicate by passing messages over the pipes. The necessary software for doing all of this on a VAX running UNIX is on the Prentice-Hall tape. Since the file system, set up program, and IBM PC simulator are all written in C, porting them to non-VAX systems should be straightforward.

For those situations in which modifying and experimenting with MINIX is not possible (or not desired), students can still learn about MINIX by reading the source code listing provided in this book.

Finally, for those readers who are only interested in the principles and not at all interested in MINIX, the sections dealing with the MINIX implementation have been clearly marked as such, and can be skipped without loss of continuity. In this mode, the book can be used as a conventional operating systems text, without reference to MINIX at all.

Those readers having access to USENET and wishing to contribute more software, suggest improvements, etc., can do so in comp.os.minix.

For classroom use, a problem solutions manual is available. It can be ordered from Prentice-Hall.

I have been extremely fortunate in having the help of many people during the course of this project. I would especially like to thank Dick Grune, Wiebren de Jonge, Jan Looyen, Jim van Keulen, Hans van Staveren, Jennifer Steiner, and Peter Weinberger for reading parts of the manuscript and making many helpful suggestions. Special thanks also go to Brian Kernighan for 1.4 readings and constantly reminding me about rule 13.

Although I personally wrote the entire 12,000 lines of the operating system proper, a number of other people have contributed utility programs that are included in the distribution. Without their help, MINIX would have been far less useful. In particular, I would like to thank Martin Atkins, Erik Baalbergen, Charles Forsyth, Richard Gregg, Paul Polderman, and Robbert van Renesse. Paul Ogilvie ported the system to MS-DOS. Michiel Huisjes, Patrick van Kleef, and Adri Koppes provided immensely valuable help with many aspects of the software, far above and beyond the call of duty.

Finally, I would like to thank Suzanne for her endless patience while I spent untold hours hiding in front of my PC. Without her support and understanding I would never have made it. I also want to thank Barbara and Marvin for using Suzanne's computer, instead of mine, thus making this book possible. I am better at *jove*, but they are better at *Donald Duck's Playground*.

Andrew S. Tanenbaum

AVAILABILITY OF THE MINIX SOFTWARE

The MINIX software is available from Prentice-Hall in the following forms:

1. A set of diskettes for the IBM PC (or true compatible) with 640K RAM. These diskettes contain a bootable system that can be inserted into the PC and run, as well as the system sources. The source diskettes contain the complete operating system sources, and the sources for all the utility programs except the C compiler, which is also available as described below. This package can also be used with 512K, although the user will have to adjust some program sizes. ISBN 0-13-583873-8

2. A set of diskettes for 256K IBM PCs. This package is the same as above, except that the C compiler is not included due to the limited memory and RAM disk space. Everything else, including all the sources, are the same as the 640K version. ISBN 0-13-583881-9

3. A set of diskettes for the IBM PC/AT (512K required). This package is identical to the 640K PC package, except that the RAM disk is slightly smaller, and 1.2M diskettes are used, instead of 360K diskettes. ISBN 0-13-583865-7

4. A nine-track, industry standard 1600 bpi magnetic tape in UNIX "tar" format. This version contains all the sources, as well as the IBM PC simulator and some libraries and programs that make it possible to run the MINIX file system on a VAX or other minicomputer running UNIX. Ports to other systems are up to the user, but since the file system and test programs are entirely written in C, this should not be difficult. ISBN 0-13-583899-1.

The only pieces of MINIX software not included in the distributions above are the compiler sources. These were made using the Amsterdam Compiler Kit (see *Communications of the ACM*, Sept. 1983, pp. 654-660), which has also been used to make compilers for many other languages and machines. The compiler sources can be ordered from the following companies:

In North and South America: In Europe and elsewhere

UniPress Software   Transmediair Utrecht BV
2025 Lincoln Highway   Melkweg 3
Edison, NJ 08817   3721 RG Bilthoven
U.S.A.   Holland
Telephone: (201) 985-8000   Telephone: (30) 78 18 20

1

INTRODUCTION

Without its software, a computer is basically a useless lump of metal. With its software, a computer can store, process, and retrieve information, find spelling errors in manuscripts, play adventure, and engage in many other valuable activities to earn its keep. Computer software can be roughly divided into two kinds: the system programs, which manage the operation of the computer itself, and the application programs, which solve problems for their users. The most fundamental of all the system programs is the **operating system**, which controls all the computer's resources and provides the base upon which the application programs can be written.

A modern computer system consists of one or more processors, some main memory (often known as "core memory," even though magnetic cores have not been used in memories for over a decade), clocks, terminals, disks, network interfaces, and other input/output devices. All in all, a complex system. Writing programs that keep track of all these components and use them correctly, let alone optimally, is an extremely difficult job. If every programmer had to be concerned with how disk drives work, and with all the dozens of things that could go wrong when reading a disk block, it is unlikely that many programs could be written at all.

Many years ago it became abundantly clear that some way had to be found to shield programmers from the complexity of the hardware. The way that has gradually evolved is to put a layer of software on top of the bare hardware, to manage all parts of the system, and present the user with an interface or **virtual**

1

machine that is easier to understand and program. This layer of software is the operating system, and forms the subject of this book.

The situation is shown in Fig. 1-1. At the bottom is the hardware, which in many cases is itself composed of two or more layers. The lowest layer contains physical devices, consisting of integrated circuit chips, wires, power supplies, cathode ray tubes, and similar physical devices. How these are constructed and how they work is the province of the electrical engineer.

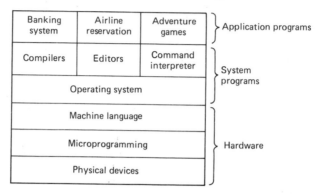

Fig. 1-1. A computer system consists of hardware, system programs and application programs.

Next comes a layer of primitive software that directly controls these devices and provides a cleaner interface to the next layer. This software, called the **microprogram,** is usually located in read-only memory. It is actually an interpreter, fetching the machine language instructions such as ADD, MOVE, and JUMP, and carrying them out as a series of little steps. To carry out an ADD instruction, for example, the microprogram must determine where the numbers to be added are located, fetch them, add them, and store the result somewhere. The set of instructions that the microprogram interprets defines the **machine language,** which is not really part of the hard machine at all, but computer manufacturers always describe it in their manuals as such, so many people think of it as being the real "machine." On some machines the microprogram is implemented in hardware, and is not really a distinct layer.

The machine language typically has between 50 and 300 instructions, mostly for moving data around the machine, doing arithmetic, and comparing values. In this layer, the input/output devices are controlled by loading values into special **device registers.** For example, a disk could be commanded to read by loading the values of the disk address, main memory address, byte count, and direction (READ or WRITE) into its registers. In practice, many more parameters are needed, and the status returned by the drive after an operation is highly complex. Furthermore, for many I/O devices, timing plays an important role in the programming.

A major function of the operating system is to hide all this complexity and give the programmer a more convenient set of instructions to work with. For example, READ BLOCK FROM FILE is conceptually simpler than having to worry about the details of moving disk heads, waiting for them to settle down, and so on.

On top of the operating system is the rest of the system software. Here we find the command interpreter (shell), compilers, editors and similar application-independent programs. It is important to realize that these programs are definitely not part of the operating system, even though they are typically supplied by the computer manufacturer. This is a crucial, but subtle, point. The operating system is that portion of the software that runs in **kernel mode** or **supervisor mode**. It is protected from user tampering by the hardware (ignoring for the moment some of the older microprocessors that do not have hardware protection at all). Compilers and editors run in **user mode**. If a user does not like a particular compiler, he† is free to write his own if he so chooses; he is not free to write his own disk interrupt handler, which is part of the operating system and protected by hardware against attempts by users to modify it.

Finally, above the system programs come the application programs. These programs are written by the users to solve their particular problems, such as commercial data processing, engineering calculations, or game playing.

1.1. WHAT IS AN OPERATING SYSTEM?

Most computer users have had some experience with an operating system, but it is difficult to pin down precisely what an operating system is. Part of the problem is that operating systems perform two basically unrelated functions, and depending on who is doing the talking, you hear mostly about one function or the other. Let us now look at both.

1.1.1. The Operating System as an Extended Machine

As mentioned earlier, the **architecture** (instruction set, memory organization, I/O and bus structure) of most computers at the machine language level is primitive and awkward to program, especially for input/output. To make this point more concrete, let us briefly look at how floppy disk I/O is done using the NEC PD765 controller chip, which is used on the IBM PC and many other personal computers. (Throughout this book we will use the terms "floppy disk" and "diskette" interchangeably.) The PD765 has 16 commands, each specified by loading between 1 and 9 bytes into a device register. These commands are for reading and writing data, moving the disk arm, and formatting tracks, as well as initializing, sensing, resetting, and recalibrating the controller and the drives.

The most basic commands are READ and WRITE, each of which requires 13

---

† "He" should be read as "he or she" throughout the book.

parameters, packed into 9 bytes. These parameters specify such items as the address of the disk block to be read, the number of sectors per track, the recording mode used on the physical medium, the intersector gap spacing, and what to do with a deleted-data-address-mark. If you do not understand this mumbo jumbo, do not worry, that is precisely the point—it is rather esoteric. When the operation is completed, the controller chip returns 23 status and error fields packed into 7 bytes. As if this were not enough, the floppy disk programmer must also be constantly aware of whether the motor is on or off. If the motor is off, it must be turned on (with a long start-up delay) before data can be read or written. The motor cannot be left on too long, however, or the floppy disk will wear out. The programmer is thus forced to deal with the trade-off between long start-up delays versus wearing out floppy disks (and losing the data on them).

Without going into the *real* details, it should be clear that the average programmer probably does not want to get too intimately involved with the programming of floppy disks (or Winchester disks, which are just as complex and quite different). Instead, what the programmer wants is a simple, high-level abstraction to deal with. In the case of disks, a typical abstraction would be that the disk contains a collection of named files. Each file can be opened for reading or writing, then read or written, and finally closed. Details such as whether or not recording should use modified frequency modulation and what the current state of the motor is should not appear in the abstraction presented to the user.

The program that hides the truth about the hardware from the programmer and presents a nice, simple view of named files that can be read and written is, of course, the operating system. Just as the operating system shields the programmer from the disk hardware and presents a simple file-oriented interface, it also conceals a lot of unpleasant business concerning interrupts, timers, memory management, and other low-level features. In each case, the abstraction presented to the user of the operating system is simpler and easier to use than the underlying hardware.

In this view, the function of the operating system is to present the user with the equivalent of an **extended machine** or **virtual machine** that is easier to program than the underlying hardware. How the operating system achieves this goal is a long story, which we will study in detail throughout this book.

1.1.2. The Operating System as a Resource Manager

The concept of the operating system as primarily providing its users with a convenient interface is a top-down view. An alternative, bottom-up, view holds that the operating system is there to manage all the pieces of a complex system. Modern computers consist of processors, memories, timers, disks, terminals, magnetic tape drives, network interfaces, laser printers, and a wide variety of other devices. In the alternative view, the job of the operating system is to provide for an orderly and controlled allocation of the processors, memories, and I/O devices among the various programs competing for them.

Imagine what would happen if three programs running on some computer all tried to print their output simultaneously on the same printer. The first few lines of printout might be from program 1, the next few from program 2, then some from program 3, and so forth. The result would be chaos. The operating system can bring order to the potential chaos by buffering all the output destined for the printer on the disk. When one program is finished, the operating system can then copy its output from the disk file where it has been stored to the printer, while at the same time the other program can continue generating more output, oblivious to the fact that the output is not really going to the printer (yet).

When a computer has multiple users, the need for managing and protecting the memory, I/O devices, and other resources is even more apparent. This need arises because it is frequently necessary for users to share expensive resources such as tape drives and phototypesetters. Economic issues aside, it is also often necessary for users who are working together to share information. In short, this view of the operating system holds that its primary task is to keep track of who is using which resource, to grant resource requests, to account for usage, and to mediate conflicting requests from different programs and users.

1.2. HISTORY OF OPERATING SYSTEMS

Operating systems have been evolving through the years. In the following sections we will briefly look at this development. Since operating systems have historically been closely tied to the architecture of the computers on which they run, we will look at successive generations of computers to see what their operating systems were like. This mapping of operating system generations to computer generations is admittedly crude, but it does provide some structure where there would otherwise be none.

The first true digital computer was designed by the English mathematician Charles Babbage (1792-1871). Although Babbage spent most of his life and fortune trying to build his "analytical engine," he never got it working properly because it was a purely mechanical design, and the technology of his day could not produce the wheels, gears, cogs and other mechanical parts to the high precision that he needed. Needless to say, the analytical engine did not have an operating system.

1.2.1. The First Generation (1945-1955): Vacuum Tubes and Plugboards

After Babbage's unsuccessful efforts, little progress was made in constructing digital computers until World War II. Around the mid-1940s, Howard Aiken at Harvard, John von Neumann at the Institute for Advanced Study in Princeton, J. Presper Eckert and William Mauchley at the University of Pennsylvania, and Konrad Zuse in Germany, among others, all succeeded in building calculating engines using vacuum tubes. These machines were enormous, filling up entire rooms with tens of thousands of vacuum tubes, but were much slower than even the cheapest home computer available today.

In these early days, a single group of people designed, built, programmed, operated, and maintained each machine. All programming was done in absolute machine language, often by wiring up plugboards to control the machine's basic functions. Programming languages were unknown (not even assembly language). Operating systems were unheard of. The usual mode of operation was for the programmer to sign up for a block of time on the signup sheet on the wall, then come down to the machine room, insert his or her plugboard into the computer, and spend the next few hours hoping that none of the 20,000 or so vacuum tubes would burn out during the run. Virtually all the problems were straightforward numerical calculations, such as grinding out tables of sines and cosines.

By the early 1950s, the routine had improved somewhat with the introduction of punched cards. It was now possible to write programs on cards and read them in, instead of using plugboards; otherwise the procedure was the same.

1.2.2. The Second Generation (1955-1965): Transistors and Batch Systems

The introduction of the transistor in the mid-1950s changed the picture radically. Computers became reliable enough that they could be manufactured and sold to paying customers with the expectation that they would continue to function long enough to get some useful work done. For the first time, there was a clear separation between designers, builders, operators, programmers, and maintenance personnel.

These machines were locked away in specially air conditioned computer rooms, with staffs of professional operators to run them. Only big corporations, or major government agencies or universities could afford the multimillion dollar price tag. To run a **job** (i.e., a program or set of programs), a programmer would first write the program on paper (in FORTRAN or assembly language), then punch it on cards. He would then bring the card deck down to the input room and hand it to one of the operators.

When the computer finished whatever job it was currently running, an operator would go over to the printer and tear off the output and carry it over to the output room, so that the programmer could collect it later. Then he would take one of the card decks that had been brought from the input room and read it in. If the FORTRAN compiler was needed, the operator would have to get it from a file cabinet and read it in. Much computer time was wasted while operators were walking around the machine room.

Given the high cost of the equipment, it is not surprising that people quickly looked for ways to reduce the wasted time. The solution generally adopted was the **batch system**. The idea behind it was to collect a tray full of jobs in the input room, and then read them onto a magnetic tape using a small, (relatively) inexpensive computer, such as the IBM 1401, which was very good at reading cards, copying tapes, and printing output, but not at all good at numerical calculations. Other, much more expensive machines, such as the IBM 7094, were used for the real computing. This situation is shown in Fig. 1-2.

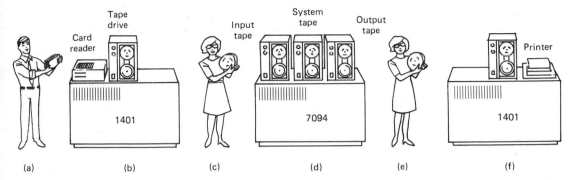

Fig. 1-2. An early batch system. (a) Programmers bring cards to 1401. (b) 1401 reads batch of jobs onto tape. (c) Operator carries input tape to 7094. (d) 7094 does computing. (e) Operator carries output tape to 1401. (f) 1401 prints output.

After about an hour of collecting a batch of jobs, the tape was rewound and brought into the machine room, where it was mounted on a tape drive. The operator then loaded a special program (the ancestor of today's operating system), which read the first job from tape and ran it. The output was written onto a second tape, instead of being printed. After each job finished, the operating system automatically read the next job from the tape and began running it. When the whole batch was done, the operator removed the input and output tapes, replaced the input tape with the next batch, and brought the output tape to a 1401 for printing **off line** (i.e., not connected to the main computer).

The structure of a typical input job is shown in Fig. 1-3. It started out with a $JOB card, specifying the maximum run time in minutes, the account number to be charged, and the programmer's name. Then came a $FORTRAN card, telling the operating system to load the FORTRAN compiler from the system tape. It was followed by the program to be compiled, and then a $LOAD card, directing the operating system to load the object program just compiled. (Compiled programs were often written on scratch tapes and had to be loaded explicitly.) Next came the $RUN card, telling the operating system to run the program with the data following it. Finally, the $END card marked the end of the job. These control cards, while primitive, were the forerunners of modern job control languages and command interpreters.

Large second generation computers were used mostly for scientific and engineering calculations, such as solving partial differential equations. They were largely programmed in FORTRAN and assembly language. Typical operating systems were FMS (the Fortran Monitor System) and IBSYS, IBM's operating system for the 7094.

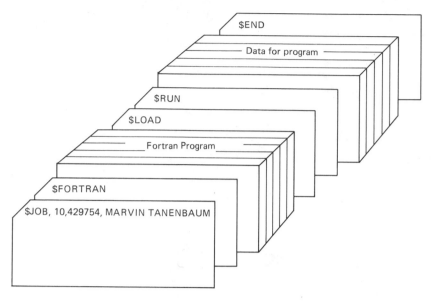

Fig. 1-3. Structure of a typical FMS job.

1.2.3. The Third Generation (1965-1980): ICs and Multiprogramming

By the early 1960s most computer manufacturers had two distinct, and totally incompatible, product lines. On the one hand there were the word-oriented, large-scale scientific computers, such as the 7094, which were used for numerical calculations in science and engineering. On the other hand, there were the character-oriented, commercial computers, such as the 1401, which were widely used for tape sorting and printing by banks and insurance companies.

Developing and maintaining two completely different product lines was an expensive proposition for the manufacturers. In addition, many new computer customers initially needed a small machine, but later outgrew it and wanted a bigger machine that would run all their old programs, but faster.

IBM attempted to solve both of these problems at a single stroke by introducing the System/360. The 360 was a series of software-compatible machines ranging from 1401-sized to much more powerful than the 7094. The machines differed only in price and performance (maximum memory, processor speed, number of I/O devices permitted, and so forth.). Since all the machines had the same architecture and instruction set, at least in theory, programs written for one machine could run on all the others. Furthermore, the 360 was designed to handle both scientific and commercial computing. Thus a single family of machines could satisfy the needs of all customers. In subsequent years, IBM has come out with compatible successors to the 360 line, using more modern technology, known as the 370, 4300, 3080, and 3090 series.

The 360 was the first major computer line to use (small-scale) integrated circuits (ICs), thus providing a major price/performance advantage over the second generation machines, which were built up from individual transistors. It was an immediate success, and the idea of a family of compatible computers was soon adopted by all the other major manufacturers. The descendants of these machines are still in use at large computer centers today.

The greatest strength of the "one family" idea was simultaneously its greatest weakness. The intention was that all software, including the operating system, had to work on all models. It had to run on small systems, which often just replaced 1401s for copying cards to tape, and on very large systems, which often replaced 7094s for doing weather forecasting and other heavy computing. It had to be good on systems with few peripherals and on systems with many peripherals. It had to work in commercial environments and in scientific environments. Above all, it had to be efficient for all of these different uses.

There was no way that IBM (or anybody else) could write a piece of software to meet all those conflicting requirements. The result was an enormous and extraordinarily complex operating system, probably two to three orders of magnitude larger than FMS. It consisted of millions of lines of assembly language written by thousands of programmers, and contained thousands upon thousands of bugs, which necessitated a continuous stream of new releases in an attempt to correct them. Each new release fixed some bugs and introduced new ones, so the number of bugs probably remained constant in time.

One of the designers of OS/360, Fred Brooks, subsequently wrote a witty and incisive book (Brooks, 1975) describing his experiences with OS/360. While it would be impossible to summarize the book here, suffice it to say that the cover shows a herd of prehistoric beasts stuck in a tar pit. The cover of Peterson and Silberschatz's book (1985) makes a similar point.

Despite its enormous size and problems, OS/360 and the similar third-generation operating systems produced by other computer manufacturers satisfied most of their customers reasonably well. They also popularized several key techniques absent in second generation operating systems. Probably the most important of these was **multiprogramming**. On the 7094, when the current job paused to wait for a tape or other I/O operation to complete, the CPU simply sat idle until the I/O finished. With heavily CPU-bound scientific calculations, I/O is infrequent, so this wasted time is not significant. With commercial data processing, the I/O wait time can often be 80 or 90 percent of the total time, so something had to be done about it.

The solution that evolved was to partition memory into several pieces, with a different job in each partition, as shown in Fig. 1-4. While one job was waiting for I/O to complete, another job could be using the CPU. If enough jobs could be held in main memory at once, the CPU could be kept busy nearly 100 percent of the time. Having multiple jobs in memory at once requires special hardware to protect each job against snooping and mischief by the other ones, but the 360 and other third generation systems were equipped with this hardware.

Another major feature present in third-generation operating systems was the

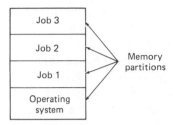

Fig. 1-4. A multiprogramming system with three jobs in memory.

ability to read jobs from cards onto the disk as soon as they were brought to the computer room. Then, whenever a running job finished, the operating system could load a new job from the disk into the now-empty partition and run it. This technique is called **spooling** (from Simultaneous Peripheral Operation On Line) and was also used for output. With spooling, the 1401s were no longer needed, and much carrying of tapes disappeared.

Although third-generation operating systems were well-suited for big scientific calculations and massive commercial data processing runs, they were still basically batch systems. Many programmers pined for the first generation days when they had the machine all to themselves for a few hours, so they could debug their programs quickly. With third generation systems, the time between submitting a job and getting back the output was often several hours, so a single misplaced comma could cause a compilation to fail, and the programmer to waste half a day.

This desire for quick response time paved the way for **time-sharing**, a variant of multiprogramming, in which each user has an on-line terminal. In a time-sharing system, if 20 users are logged in and 17 of them are thinking or talking or drinking coffee, the CPU can be allocated in turn to the three jobs that want service. Since people debugging programs usually issue short commands (e.g., compile a five-page program) rather than long ones (e.g., sort a million-record tape), the computer can provide fast, interactive service to a number of users and perhaps also work on big batch jobs in the background when the CPU is otherwise idle. Although the first serious time-sharing system (CTSS) was developed at MIT on a specially modified 7094 (Corbato et al., 1962), it did not really become popular until the necessary protection hardware became widespread during the third generation.

After the success of the CTSS system, MIT, Bell Labs, and General Electric (then a major computer manufacturer) decided to embark on the development of a "computer utility," a machine that would support hundreds of simultaneous time-sharing users. Their model was the electricity distribution system—when you need electric power, you just stick a plug in the wall, and within reason, as much power as you need will be there. The designers of this system, known as **MULTICS** (MULTiplexed Information and Computing Service), envisioned one huge machine providing computing power for everyone in Boston. The idea that machines as powerful as their GE-645 would be sold as personal computers for a few thousand dollars only 20 years later was pure science fiction at the time.

To make a long story short, MULTICS introduced many seminal ideas into the computer literature, but building it was a lot harder than anyone had expected. Bell Labs dropped out of the project, and General Electric quit the computer business altogether. Eventually MULTICS ran well enough to be used in a production environment at MIT and a few dozen sites elsewhere, but the concept of a computer utility fizzled out. Still, MULTICS had an enormous influence on subsequent systems. It is described in (Corbato et al., 1972; Corbato and Vyssotsky, 1965; Daley and Dennis, 1968; Organick, 1972; Saltzer, 1974).

Another major development during the third generation was the phenomenal growth of minicomputers, starting with the DEC PDP-1 in 1961. The PDP-1 had only 4K of 18-bit words, but at 120,000 dollars per machine (less than 5 percent of the price of a 7094), they sold like hotcakes. For certain kinds of nonnumerical work, it was almost as fast as the 7094, and gave birth to a whole new industry. It was quickly followed by a series of other PDPs (unlike IBM's family, all incompatible) culminating in the PDP-11.

One of the computer scientists at Bell Labs who had worked on the MULTICS project, Ken Thompson, subsequently found a small PDP-7 that no one was using and set out to write a stripped-down, one-user version of MULTICS. Brian Kernighan somewhat jokingly dubbed this system "UNICS" (UNiplexed Information and Computing Service), but the spelling was later changed to UNIX†. It was later moved to a small PDP-11/20, where it worked well enough to convince Bell Labs' management to invest in a larger PDP-11/45 to continue the work.

Another Bell Labs computer scientist, Dennis Ritchie, then teamed up with Thompson to rewrite the system in a high-level language called C, designed and implemented by Ritchie. Bell Labs licensed UNIX to universities almost for free, and within a few years hundreds of them were using it. It soon spread to the Interdata 7/32, VAX, Motorola 68000, and many other computers. UNIX has been moved ("ported") to more computers than any other operating system in history, and its use is still rapidly increasing.

1.2.4. The Fourth Generation (1980-1990): Personal Computers

With the development of LSI (Large Scale Integration) circuits, chips containing thousands of transistors on a square centimeter of silicon, the age of the personal computer dawned. In terms of architecture, personal computers were not that different from minicomputers of the PDP-11 class, but in terms of price they certainly were different. Where the minicomputer made it possible for a department in a company or university to have its own computer, the microprocessor chip made it possible for a single individual to have his or her own personal computer.

---

† UNIX is a trademark of AT&T Bell Laboratories.

The widespread availability of computing power, especially highly interactive computing power usually with excellent graphics, led to the growth of a major industry producing software for personal computers. Much of this software was **user-friendly**, meaning that it was intended for users who did not know anything about computers, and furthermore had absolutely no intention whatsoever of learning. This was certainly a major change from OS/360, whose job control language, JCL, was so arcane that entire books have been written about it (e.g., Cadow, 1970).

Two operating systems have dominated the personal computer scene: MS-DOS, written by Microsoft, Inc. for the IBM PC and other machines using the Intel 8088 CPU and its successors, and UNIX, which is dominant on the larger personal computers using the Motorola 68000 CPU family. It is perhaps ironic that the direct descendant of MULTICS, designed for a gigantic computer utility, has become so popular on personal computers, but mostly it shows how well thought out the basic ideas in MULTICS and UNIX were. Although the initial version of MS-DOS was relatively primitive, subsequent versions have included more and more features from UNIX, which is not entirely surprising given that Microsoft is a major UNIX supplier, using the trade name of XENIX†.

An interesting development that began taking place during the mid-1980s is the growth of networks of personal computers running **network operating systems** and **distributed operating systems**. In a network operating system, the users are aware of the existence of multiple computers, and can log in to remote machines and copy files from one machine to another. Each machine runs its own local operating system and has its own user (or users).

A distributed operating system, in contrast, is one that appears to its users as a traditional uniprocessor system, even though it is actually composed of multiple processors. In a true distributed system, users are not be aware of where their programs are being run or where their files are located; that should all be handled automatically and efficiently by the operating system.

Network operating systems are not fundamentally different from single-processor operating systems. They obviously need a network interface controller and some low-level software to drive it, as well as programs to achieve remote login and remote file access, but these additions do not change the essential structure of the operating system.

True distributed operating systems require more than just adding a little code to a uniprocessor operating system, because distributed and centralized systems differ in critical ways. Distributed systems, for example, often allow programs to run on several processors at the same time, thus requiring more complex processor scheduling algorithms in order to optimize the amount of parallelism achieved.

Communication delays within the network often mean that these (and other) algorithms must run with incomplete, outdated, or even incorrect information.

---

† XENIX is a trademark of Microsoft, Inc.

This situation is radically different from a single-processor system in which the operating system has complete information about the system state.

Fault-tolerance is another area in which distributed systems are different. It is common for a distributed system to be designed with the expectation that it will continue running, even if part of the hardware is currently broken. Needless to say, such an additional design requirement has enormous implications for the operating system. For a survey of current research about network and distributed operating systems, see the paper by Tanenbaum and van Renesse (1985).

1.2.5. History of MINIX

When UNIX was young (Version 6), the source code was widely available, under AT&T license, and frequently studied. John Lions, of the University of New South Wales in Australia, even wrote a little booklet describing its operation, line by line. This booklet was used (with permission of AT&T) as a text in many university operating system courses.

When AT&T released Version 7, it began to realize that UNIX was a valuable commercial product, so it issued Version 7 with a license that prohibited the source code from being studied in courses, in order to avoid endangering its status as a trade secret. Many universities complied by simply dropping the study of UNIX, and teaching only theory.

Unfortunately, teaching only theory leaves the student with a lopsided view of what an operating system is really like. The theoretical topics that are usually covered in great detail in courses and books on operating systems, such as scheduling algorithms, are in practice not really that important. Subjects that really are important, such as I/O and file systems, are generally neglected because there is little theory about them.

To remedy this situation, I decided to write a new operating system from scratch that would be compatible with UNIX from the user's point of view, but completely different on the inside. By not using even one line of AT&T code, this system avoids the licensing restrictions, so it can be used for class or individual study. In this manner, readers can dissect a real operating system to see what is inside, just as biology students dissect frogs. The name MINIX stands for mini-UNIX because it is small enough that even a nonguru can understand how it works.

In addition to the advantage of eliminating the legal problems, MINIX has another advantage over UNIX. It was written a decade after UNIX, and has been structured in a more modular way. The MINIX file system, for example, is not part of the operating system at all, but runs as a user program. Another difference is that UNIX was designed to be efficient; MINIX was designed to be readable (inasmuch as one can speak of any 12,649 line program as being readable). The MINIX code, for example, has over 3000 comments in it.

MINIX has been designed for compatibility with Version 7 (V7) UNIX. Version 7 was used as the model because of its simplicity and elegance. It is sometimes said that Version 7 was not only an improvement over all its predecessors, but also over all its successors.

Like UNIX, MINIX is written in the C programming language, and is intended to be easy to port to various computers. The initial implementation was for the IBM PC, because this computer is in widespread use. In keeping with the "Small is Beautiful" philosophy, MINIX does not even require a hard disk to run, thus bringing it within range of many students' budgets.

To the average user sitting at an IBM PC, running MINIX is similar to using any UNIX system. Most of the usual programs, such as *cat, grep, ls, make,* and the shell are present and perform the same functions as their UNIX counterparts. Like the operating system itself, all these utility programs have been completely rewritten from scratch by the author, his students, and some other dedicated people. Even the C compiler is completely new, being based on the Amsterdam Compiler Kit (Tanenbaum et al., 1983), rather than on the AT&T portable C compiler.

Throughout this book MINIX will be used as an example. Nearly all the comments about MINIX, however, except those about the actual code, also apply to UNIX. Many of them also apply to other systems as well. This should be kept in mind when reading the text.

1.3. OPERATING SYSTEM CONCEPTS

The interface between the operating system and the user programs is defined by the set of "extended instructions" that the operating system provides. These extended instructions are known as **system calls**. To really understand what operating systems do, we must examine these calls closely. The system calls vary from operating system to operating system (although the underlying concepts tend to be similar).

We are thus forced to make a choice between (1) vague generalities ("operating systems have system calls for reading files") and (2) some specific system ("MINIX has a READ system call with three parameters: one to specify the file, one to tell where the data are to be put, and one to tell how many bytes to read").

We have chosen the latter approach. It's more work that way, but it gives more insight into what operating systems really do. In Sec. 1-4 we will look closely at the system calls present in both UNIX and MINIX. For simplicity's sake, we will refer only to MINIX, but the corresponding UNIX V7 system calls are identical (the corresponding system calls for other versions of UNIX, such as System V, 4.3BSD, and XENIX are very similar, although each of these has some additional system calls that we will not discuss). Before we look at the actual system calls, however, it is worth taking a birds'-eye view of MINIX, to get a general feel for what an operating system is all about. This overview applies equally well to UNIX.

The MINIX system calls fall roughly in two broad categories: those dealing with processes and those dealing with the file system. We will now examine each of these in turn.

1.3.1. Processes

A key concept in MINIX, and in all operating systems, is the **process**. A process is basically a program in execution. It consists of the executable program, the program's data and stack, its program counter, stack pointer, and other registers, and all the other information needed to run the program.

We will come back to the process concept in much more detail in Chap. 2, but for the time being, the easiest way to get a good intuitive feel for a process is to think about time-sharing systems. Periodically, the operating system decides to stop running one process and start running another, for example, because the first one has had more than its share of CPU time in the past second.

When a process is temporarily suspended like this, it must later be restarted in exactly the same state it had when it was stopped. This means that all information about the process must be explicitly saved somewhere during the suspension. For example, if the process has several files open, the exact position in the files where the process was must be recorded somewhere, so that a subsequent READ given after the process is restarted will read the proper data. In many operating systems, all the information about each process, other than the contents of its own address space, is stored in an operating system table called the **process table**, which is an array (or linked list) of structures, one for each process currently in existence.

Thus, a (suspended) process consists of its address space, usually called the **core image** (in honor of the magnetic core memories used in days of yore), and its process table entry, which contains its registers, among other things.

The key process management system calls are those dealing with the creation and termination of processes. Consider a typical example. A process called the **command interpreter** or **shell** reads commands from a terminal. The user has just typed a command requesting that a program be compiled. The shell must now create a new process that will run the compiler. When that process has finished the compilation, it executes a system call to terminate itself.

If a process can create one or more other processes (referred to as **child processes**) and these processes in turn can create child processes, we quickly arrive at the process tree structure of Fig. 1-5.

Other process system calls are available to request more memory (or release unused memory), wait for a child process to terminate, and overlay its program with a different one.

Occasionally, there is a need to convey information to a running process that is not sitting around waiting for it. For example, a process that is communicating with another process on a different computer does so by sending messages over a network. To guard against the possibility that a message or its reply is

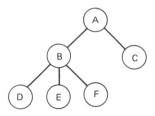

Fig. 1-5. A process tree. Process *A* created two child processes, *B* and *C*. Process *B* created three child processes, *D*, *E*, and *F*.

lost, the sender may request that its own operating system notify it after a specified number of seconds, so that it can retransmit the message if no acknowledgement has been received yet. After setting this timer, the program may continue doing other work.

When the specified number of seconds has elapsed, the operating system sends a **signal** to the process. The signal causes the process to temporarily suspend whatever it was doing, save its registers on the stack, and start running a special signal handling procedure, for example, to retransmit a presumably lost message. When the signal handler is done, the running process is restarted in the state it was just before the signal. Signals are the software analog of hardware interrupts, and can be generated by a variety of causes in addition to timers expiring. Many traps detected by hardware, such as executing an illegal instruction or using an invalid address, are also converted into signals to the guilty process.

Each person authorized to use MINIX is assigned a **uid** (user identification) by the system administrator. Every process started in MINIX has the uid of the person who started it. A child process has the same uid as its parent. One uid, called the **super-user**, has special power, and may violate many of the protection rules. In large installations, only the system administrator knows the password needed to become super-user, but many of the ordinary users (especially students) devote considerable effort to trying to find flaws in the system that allow them to become super-user without the password.

1.3.2. Files

The other broad category of system calls relates to the file system. As noted before, a major function of the operating system is to hide the peculiarities of the disks and other I/O devices, and present the programmer with a nice, clean abstract model of device-independent files. System calls are obviously needed to create files, remove files, read files, and write files. Before a file can be read, it must be opened, and after it has been read it should be closed, so calls are provided to do these things.

In order to provide a place to keep files, MINIX has the concept of a

directory as a way of grouping files together. A student, for example, might have one directory for each course he was taking (for the programs needed for that course), another directory for his electronic mail, and still another directory for his computer games. System calls are then needed to create and remove directories. Calls are also provided to put an existing file in a directory, and to remove a file from a directory. Directory entries may be either files or other directories. This model also gives rise to a hierarchy—the file system, as shown in Fig. 1-6.

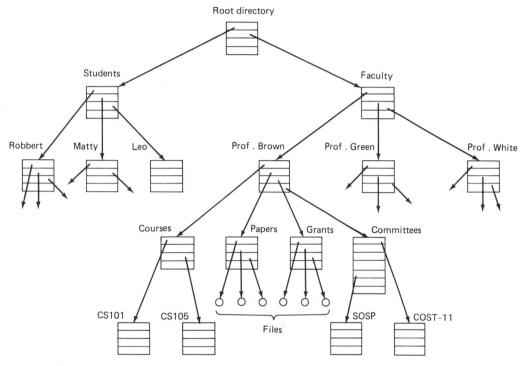

Fig. 1-6. A file system for a university department.

The process and file hierarchies both are organized as trees, but the similarity stops there. Process hierarchies usually are not very deep (more than three levels is unusual), whereas file hierarchies are commonly four, five, or even more levels deep. Process hierarchies are typically short-lived, generally a few minutes at most, whereas the directory hierarchy may exist for years. Ownership and protection also differ for processes and files. Typically, only a parent process may control or even access a child process, but mechanisms nearly always exist to allow files and directories to be read by a wider group than just the owner.

Every file within the directory hierarchy can be specified by giving its **path name** from the top of the directory hierarchy, the **root directory**. Such absolute path names consist of the list of directories that must be traversed from the root directory to get to the file, with slashes separating the components. In Fig. 1-6, the path for file *CS101* is */Faculty/Prof.Brown/Courses/CS101*. The leading slash indicates that the path is absolute, that is, starting at the root directory.

At every instant, each process has a current **working directory**, in which path names not beginning with a slash are looked for. In Fig. 1-6, if *Faculty/Prof.Brown* were the working directory, then use of the path name *Courses/CS101* would yield the same file as the absolute path name given above. Processes can change their working directory by issuing a system call specifying the new working directory.

Files and directories in MINIX are protected by assigning each one a 9-bit binary protection code. The protection code consists of three 3-bit fields, one for the owner, one for other members of the owner's group (users are divided into groups by the system administrator), and one for everyone else. Each field has a bit for read access, a bit for write access, and a bit for execute access. These 3 bits are known as the **rwx bits**. For example, the protection code *rwxr-x--x* means that the owner can read, write, or execute the file, other group members can read or execute (but not write) the file, and everyone else can execute (but not read or write) the file. For a directory, *x* indicates search permission. A dash means that the corresponding permission is absent.

Before a file can be read or written, it must be opened, at which time the permissions are checked. If the access is permitted, the system returns a small integer called a **file descriptor** to use in subsequent operations. If the access is prohibited, an error code is returned.

Another important concept in MINIX is the mounted file system. Nearly all microcomputers have one or more floppy disk drives into which floppy disks can be inserted and removed. To provide a clean way to deal with these removable media, MINIX allows the file system on a floppy disk to be attached to the main tree. Consider the situation of Fig. 1-7(a). Before the MOUNT call, the RAM disk (simulated disk in main memory) contains the primary, or **root file system**, and drive 0 contains a floppy disk containing another file system.

However, the file system on drive 0 cannot be used, because there is no way to specify path names on it. MINIX does not allow path names to be prefixed by a drive name or number; that would be precisely the kind of device dependence that operating systems ought to eliminate. Instead, the MOUNT system call allows the file system on drive 0 to be attached to the root file system wherever the program wants it to be. In Fig. 1-7(b) the file system on drive 0 has been mounted on directory *b*, thus allowing access to files */b/x* and */b/y*. If directory *b* had contained any files they would not be accessible while drive 0 was mounted, since */b* would refer to the root directory of drive 0. (Not being able to access these files is not as serious as it at first seems: file systems are nearly always mounted on empty directories.)

Another important concept in MINIX is the **special file**. Special files are provided in order to make I/O devices look like files. That way, they can be read and written using the same system calls as are used for reading and writing files. Two kinds of special files exist: **block special files** and **character special files**.

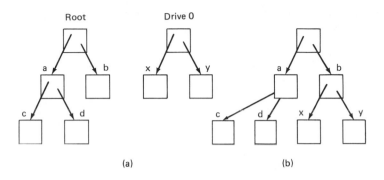

Fig. 1-7. (a) Before mounting, the files on drive 0 are not accessible. (b) After mounting, they are part of the file hierarchy.

Block special files are used to model devices that consist of a collection of randomly addressable blocks, such as disks. By opening a block special file and reading, say, block 4, a program can directly access the fourth block on the device, without regard to the structure of the file system contained on it. Programs that do system maintenance often need this facility. Access to special files is controlled by the same *rwx* bits used to protect all files, so the power to directly access I/O devices can be restricted to the system administrator, for example.

Character special files are used to model devices that consist of character streams, rather than fixed-size randomly addressable blocks. Terminals, line printers, and network interfaces are typical examples of character special devices. The normal way for a program to read and write on the user's terminal is to read and write the corresponding character special file. When a process is started up, file descriptor 0, called **standard input**, is normally arranged to refer to the terminal for the purpose of reading. File descriptor 1, called **standard output**, refers to the terminal for writing. File descriptor 2, called **standard error**, also refers to the terminal for output, but normally is used only for writing error messages.

All special files have a **major device number** and a **minor device number**. The major device number specifies the device class, such as floppy disk, hard disk, or terminal. The minor device number specifies which of the devices in the class is being addressed, for example, which floppy disk drive. All devices with the same major device number share the same device driver code within the operating system. The minor device number is passed as a parameter to the device driver to tell it which device to read or write. The device numbers can be seen by listing */dev*.

The last feature we will discuss in this overview is one that relates to both processes and files: pipes. A **pipe** is a sort of pseudo-file that can be used to connect two processes together, as shown in Fig. 1-8. When process *A* wants to send data to process *B*, it writes on the pipe as though it were an output file.

Process *B* can read the data by reading from the pipe as though it were an input file. Thus, communication between processes in MINIX looks very much like ordinary file reads and writes. Stronger yet, the only way a process can discover that the output file it is writing on is not really a file, but a pipe, is by making a special system call.

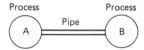

Fig. 1-8. Two processes connected by a pipe.

1.3.3. The Shell

The MINIX operating system is the code that carries out the system calls. Editors, compilers, assemblers, linkers, and command interpreters are definitely not part of the operating system, even though they are important and useful. At the risk of confusing things somewhat, in this section we will look briefly at the MINIX command interpreter, called the **shell**, which, although not part of the operating system, makes heavy use of many operating system features and thus serves as a good example of how the system calls can be used. It is also the primary interface between a user sitting at his terminal and the operating system.

When any user logs in, a shell is started up. The shell has the terminal as standard input and standard output. It starts out by typing the **prompt**, a character such as a dollar sign, which tells the user that the shell is waiting to accept a command. If the user now types

```
date
```

for example, the shell creates a child process and runs the *date* program as the child. While the child process is running, the shell waits for it to terminate. When the child finishes, the shell types the prompt again and tries to read the next input line.

The user can specify that standard output be redirected to a file by typing, for example,

```
date >file
```

Similarly, standard input can be redirected, as in

```
sort <file1 >file2
```

which invokes the sort program with input taken from *file1* and output sent to *file2*.

The output of one program can be used as the input for another program by connecting them with a pipe. Thus

```
cat file1 file2 file3 | sort >/dev/lp
```

invokes the *cat* program to concatenate three files and send the output to *sort* to arrange all the lines in alphabetical order. The output of *sort* is redirected to the file */dev/lp*, which is a typical name for the special character file for the line printer. (By convention, all the special files are kept in the directory */dev*.)

If a user puts an ampersand after a command, the shell does not wait for it to complete. Instead it just gives a prompt immediately. Consequently,

```
cat file1 file2 file3 | sort >/dev/lp &
```

starts up the sort as a background job, allowing the user to continue working normally while the sort is going on. The shell has a number of other interesting features that we do not have space to discuss here. See any of the suggested references on UNIX for more information about the shell.

1.4. SYSTEM CALLS

Armed with our general knowledge of how MINIX deals with processes and files, we can now begin to look at the system calls in detail. Again we emphasize that although we will constantly refer to MINIX here, the MINIX calls are identical to those of V7 UNIX, and almost identical to those in SYSTEM V, 4.3 BSD, XENIX and other versions of UNIX, although these systems also have additional system calls that are not discussed here. Furthermore, most other modern operating systems have system calls that perform the same functions as the MINIX calls, even if some of the details differ. Since the actual mechanics of issuing a system call are highly machine-dependent, and often must be expressed in assembly code, a procedure library is provided to make it possible to make system calls from C programs.

To make the system call mechanism clearer, let us take a quick look at READ. It has three parameters, the first one specifying the file, the second one specifying the buffer, and the third one specifying the number of bytes to read. A call to READ from a C program might look like this:

```
count = read(file, buffer, nbytes);
```

The system call (and the library procedure) return the number of bytes actually read in *count*. This value is normally the same as *nbytes*, but may be smaller, if, for example, end-of-file is encountered while reading.

If the system call cannot be carried out, either due to an invalid parameter or a disk error, *count* is set to −1, and the error number is put in a global variable, *errno*. Programs should always check the results of a system call to see if an error occurred.

MINIX has a total of 41 system calls, all of them identical to UNIX V7 calls in terms of name, function, and parameters. They are listed in Fig. 1-9, grouped for convenience in six categories. In the following sections we will briefly examine each call to see what it does. For more detail, see the UNIX manual or one of the books about UNIX that discusses the system calls. To a large extent, the services offered by these calls determine most of what the operating system has to do, since the resource management on personal computers is minimal (at least compared to big machines with many users).

```
Process Management
pid = fork( ) — create a child process identical to the parent
s = wait(&status) — wait for a child to terminate and get its exit status
s = execve(name,argv,envp) — replace a process' core image
exit(status) — terminate process execution and return exit status
size = brk(addr) — set the size of the data segment to "addr"
pid = getpid( ) — return the caller's process id

Signals
oldfunc = signal(sig,func) — arrange for some signal to be caught, ignored etc.
s = kill(pid, sig) — send a signal to a process
residual = alarm(seconds) — schedule a SIGALRM signal after a certain time
s = pause( ) — suspend the caller until the next signal

File Management
fd = creat(name,mode) — create a new file or truncate an existing file
fd = mknod(name,mode,addr) — create a regular, special, or directory i-node
fd = open(file,how — open a file for reading, writing or both
s = close(fd) — close an open file
n = read(fd,buffer,nbytes) — read data from a file into a buffer
n = write(fd,buffer,nbytes) — write data from a file into a buffer
pos = lseek(fd,offset,whence) — move the file pointer somewhere in the file
s = stat(name,&buf) — read and return a file's status from its i-node
s = fstat(fd,buf) — read and return a file's status from its i-node
fd = dup(fd1) — allocate another file descriptor for an open file
s = pipe(&fd[0]) — create a pipe
s = ioctl(fd,request,argp) — perform special operations on special files

Directory and File System Management
s = link(name1,name2) — create a new directory entry, name2 for file name1
s = unlink(name) — remove a directory entry
s = mount(special,name,rwflag) — mount a file system
s = unmount(special) — unmount a file system
s = sync( ) — flush all disk blocks cached in memory to the disk
s = chdir(dirname) — change the working directory
s = chroot(dirname) — change the root directory

Protection
s = chmod(name,mode) — change the protection bits associated with a file
uid = getuid( ) — get the caller's uid
gid = getgid( ) — get the caller's gid
s = setuid(uid) — set the caller's uid
s = setgid(gid) — set the caller's gid
s = chown(name,owner,group) — change a file's owner and group
oldmask = umask(complmode) — set a mask used to mask off protection bits

Time Management
seconds = time(&seconds) — get the elapsed time in seconds since Jan. 1, 1970
s = stime(tp) — set the elapsed time since Jan. 1, 1970
s = utime(file, timep) — set the "last access" time for the file
s = times(buffer) — get the user and system times used so far
```

Fig. 1-9. The MINIX system calls. The return code s is -1 if an error has occurred; *fd* is a file descriptor, n is a byte count. The other return codes are what the name suggests.

1.4.1. System Calls for Process Management

The first group of calls deals with process management. FORK is a good place to start the discussion. FORK is the only way to create a new process. It creates an exact duplicate of the original process, including all the file descriptors, registers—everything. After the FORK, the original process and the copy (the parent and child) go their separate ways. All the variables have identical values at the time of the FORK, but since the entire parent core image is copied to create the child, subsequent changes in one of them do not affect the other one. The FORK call returns a value, which is zero in the child, and equal to the child's process identifier or **pid** in the parent. Using the returned pid, the two processes can see which is the parent and which is the child.

In most cases, after a FORK, the child will need to execute different code from the parent. Consider the case of the shell. It reads a command from the terminal, forks off a child process, waits for the child to execute the command and then reads the next command when the child terminates. To wait for the child to finish, the parent executes a WAIT system call, which just waits until the child terminates (any child if more than one exists). WAIT has one parameter, the address of a variable that will be set to the child's exit status (normal or abnormal termination and exit value).

In the case of the shell, the child process must execute the command typed by the user. It does this by using the EXEC system call, which causes its entire core image to be replaced by the file named in its first parameter. A highly simplified shell illustrating the use of FORK, WAIT, and EXEC is shown in Fig. 1-10.

```
while (TRUE) {                              /* repeat forever */
     read_command(command, parameters);     /* read input from terminal */

     if (fork() != 0) {                      /* fork off child process */
            wait(&status);                   /* parent code */
     } else {
            execve(command, parameters, 0);  /* child  code */
     }
}
```

Fig. 1-10. A stripped-down shell. Throughout this book, *TRUE* is assumed to be defined as the constant 1, thus providing for an infinite loop.

In the most general case, EXEC has three parameters: the name of the file to be executed, a pointer to the argument array, and a pointer to the environment array. These will be described shortly. Various library routines, including *execl, execv, execle,* and *execve* are provided to allow the parameters to be omitted or specified in various ways. Throughout this book we will use the name EXEC to represent the system call invoked by all of these.

Let us consider the case of a command such as

```
cp file1 file2
```

used to copy *file1* to *file2*. After the shell has forked, the child locates and executes the file *cp* and passes it information about the files to be copied.

The main program of *cp* (and many other programs) contains the declaration

```
main(argc, argv, envp)
```

where *argc* is a count of the number of items on the command line, including the program name. For the example above, *argc* is 3.

The second parameter, *argv*, is a pointer to an array. Element *i* of that array is a pointer to the *i*-th string on the command line. In our example, *argv*[0] would point to the string "cp." (As an aside, the string pointed to contains *two* characters, a "c" and a "p," although, if you look closely at the previous sentence you will also see a period inside the quotes. The period ends the sentence, but the rules of English punctuation require most punctuation marks to be *inside* the quotes, even though this is totally illogical. Hopefully, this will not cause any confusion.) Similarly, *argv*[1] would point to the 5-character string "file1" and *argv*[2] would point to the 5-character string "file2."

The third parameter of *main*, *envp*, is a pointer to the environment, an array of strings containing assignments of the form *name = value* used to pass information such as the terminal type and home directory name to a program. In Fig. 1-10, no environment is passed to the child, so the third parameter of *execve* is a zero.

If EXEC seems complicated, do not despair; it is the most complex system call. All the rest are much simpler. As an example of a simple one, consider EXIT, which processes should use when they are finished executing. It has one parameter, the exit status (0 to 255), which is returned to the parent in the variable *status* of the WAIT system call. The low-order byte of *status* contains the termination status, with 0 being normal termination and the other values being various error conditions. The high-order byte contains the child's exit status (0 to 255). For example, if a parent process executes the statement

```
n = wait(&status);
```

it will be suspended until some child process terminates. If the child exits with, say, 4 as the parameter to *exit*, the parent will be awakened with *n* set to 0 (no error) and *status* set to 0x0400 (the C convention of prefixing hexadecimal constants with 0x will be used throughout this book).

Processes in MINIX have their memory divided up into three segments: the **text segment** (i.e., the program code), the **data segment**, and the **stack segment**. The data segment grows upward and the stack grows downward, as shown in Fig. 1-11. Between them is a gap of unused address space. The stack grows into the gap automatically, as needed, but expansion of the data segment is done explicitly by using the BRK system call. It has one parameter, giving the address where the data segment is to end. This address may be more than the current value (data segment is growing) or less than the current value (data segment is shrinking). The parameter must, of course, be less than the stack pointer or the data and stack segments would overlap, something that is forbidden. MINIX supports separate instruction and data spaces, so a program on the IBM PC, for example, can have 64K bytes of text and another 64K bytes for the data and stack segments combined, for a total of 128K bytes for text, data, and stack, total.

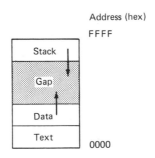

Fig. 1-11. Processes have three segments: text, data, and stack. In this example, all three are in one address space, but separate instruction and data space is also supported.

As a convenience to the programmer, a library routine *sbrk* is provided that also changes the size of the data segment, only its parameter is the number of bytes to add to the data segment (negative parameters make the data segment smaller). It works by keeping track of the current size of the data segment, which is the value returned by BRK, computing the new size, and making a call asking for that number of bytes.

The last process system call is also the simplest, GETPID. It just returns the caller's pid. Remember that in FORK, only the parent was given the child's pid. If the child wants to find out its own pid, it must use GETPID.

1.4.2. System Calls for Signaling

Certain situations exist in which processes need to handle software interrupts. For example, if a user accidently tells a text editor to print the entire contents of a very long file, and then realizes the error, some way is needed to interrupt the editor. In MINIX, the user can hit the DEL key on the keyboard, which sends a signal to the editor. The editor catches the signal and stops the print-out. Signals can also be used to report certain traps detected by the hardware, such as illegal instruction or floating point overflow.

When a signal is sent to a process that has not announced its willingness to accept that signal, the process is simply killed without further ado. To avoid this fate, a process can use the SIGNAL system call to announce that it is prepared to accept some signal type, and to provide the address of the signal handling procedure. After a SIGNAL call, if a signal of the relevant type (e.g., the DEL key) is generated, the state of the process is pushed onto its own stack, and then the signal handler is called. It may run for as long as it wants to and perform any system calls it wants to. In practice, though, signal handlers are usually fairly short. When the signal handling procedure is done, it just returns in the usual way. The run time system in the user's address space then restores the process' state from the stack and continues execution from the point where it was interrupted.

The signal types are shown in Fig. 1-12. The ones in parentheses are UNIX signals that are not supported by MINIX, mostly because they are not generated by the IBM PC hardware. They are easy to add, however, if the need arises in the future.

(1)	SIGHUP	Modem has detected broken phone connection
2	SIGINT	DEL key has been hit on keyboard
3*	SIGQUIT	Quit signal from keyboard
(4)*	SIGILL	Illegal instruction
(5)*	SIGTRAP	Trace trap
(6)*	SIGIOT	IOT instruction
(7)*	SIGEMT	EMT instruction
(8)*	SIGFPE	Floating point overflow/underflow
9	SIGKILL	Kill
(10)*	SIGBUS	Bus error
(11)*	SIGSEGV	Segmentation violation
(12)*	SIGSYS	Bad argument to system call
13	SIGPIPE	Write on pipe with no reader
14	SIGALRM	Alarm
15	SIGTERM	Software generated termination signal
16	unassigned	

Fig. 1-12. Signal types. The signals in parentheses are not supported by MINIX. The asterisks denote signals that cause core dumps if not caught or ignored.

After a signal has been caught, it is necessary to re-enable the signal catching with another SIGNAL call. If another signal of the same type arrives before the signal catching has been re-enabled, the default action is taken (i.e., the process is killed). If you try very hard, you may be able to hit DEL fast enough in succession to cause the shell to get a second signal before it has finished processing the first one, thus killing the shell (and logging yourself out).

Instead of providing a function to catch a signal, the program may also specify the constant SIG_IGN to have all subsequent signals of the specified type ignored, or SIG_DFL to restore the default action of killing the process when a signal occurs. As an example of how SIG_IGN is used, consider what happens when the shell forks off a background process as a result of

```
command &
```

It would be undesirable for a DEL signal from the keyboard to affect the background process, so after the FORK but before the EXEC, the shell does

```
signal(SIGINT, SIG_IGN);
```

and

```
signal(SIGQUIT, SIG_IGN);
```

to disable the DEL and quit signals. (The quit signal is generated by CTRL-\; it is the same as DEL except that if it is not caught or ignored, it makes a core dump of the process killed.) For foreground processes (no ampersand), these signals are not ignored.

Hitting the DEL key is not the only way to send a signal. The KILL system call allows a process to signal another process (provided they have the same uid—unrelated processes cannot signal each other). Getting back to the example of background processes used above, suppose a background process is started up, but later it is decided that the process should be terminated. SIGINT and SIGQUIT have been disabled, so something else is needed. The solution is to use the *kill* program, which uses the KILL system call to send a signal to any process. By sending signal 9 (SIGKILL), to a background process, that process can be killed. SIGKILL cannot be caught or ignored.

For many real-time applications, a process needs to be interrupted after a specific time interval to do something, such as to retransmit a potentially lost packet over an unreliable communication line. To handle this situation, the ALARM system call has been provided. The parameter specifies an interval, in seconds, after which a SIGALRM signal is sent to the process. A process may only have one alarm outstanding at any instant. If an ALARM call is made with a parameter of 10 seconds, and then 3 seconds later another ALARM call is made with a parameter of 20 seconds, only one signal will be generated, 20 seconds after the second call. The first signal is canceled by the second call to ALARM. If the parameter to ALARM is zero, any pending alarm signals are canceled. If an alarm signal is not caught, the default action is taken and the signaled process is killed. Technically, alarm signals may be ignored, but that is a pointless thing to do.

It sometimes occurs that a process has nothing to do until a signal arrives. For example, consider a computer aided instruction program that is testing reading speed and comprehension. It displays some text on the screen and then calls ALARM to signal it after 30 seconds. While the student is reading the text, the program has nothing to do. It could sit in a tight loop doing nothing, but that would waste CPU time that a background process or other user might need. A better solution is to use the PAUSE system call, which tells MINIX to suspend the process until the next signal arrives.

1.4.3. System Calls for File Management

Many system calls relate to files and the file system. In this section we will look at the system calls that operate on individual files; in the next one we will examine those that involve directories or the file system as a whole. To create a new file, the CREAT call is used (why the call is CREAT and not CREATE has been lost in the mists of time). Its parameters provide the name of the file and the protection mode. Thus

```
fd = creat("abc", 0751);
```

creates a file called *abc* with mode 0751 octal (in C, a leading zero means that a constant is in octal). The low-order 9 bits of 0751 specify the *rwx* bits for the owner (7 means read-write-execute permission), his group (5 means read-execute), and others (1 means execute only).

CREAT not only creates a new file, but also opens it for writing, regardless of the file's mode. The file descriptor returned, *fd*, can be used to write the file. If a CREAT is done on an existing file, that file is truncated to length 0, provided, of course, that the permissions are all right.

Special files are created using MKNOD rather than CREAT. A typical call is

```
fd = mknod("/dev/tty2", 020744, 0x0402);
```

which creates a file named */dev/tty2* (the usual name for terminal 2), and gives it mode 020744 octal (a character special file with protection bits *rwxr--r--*). The third parameter contains the major device (4) in the high-order byte and the minor device (2) in the low-order byte. The major device could have been anything, but a file named */dev/tty2* ought to be minor device 2. Calls to MKNOD fail unless the caller is the super-user.

To read or write an existing file, the file must first be opened using OPEN. This call specifies the file name to be opened, either as an absolute path name or relative to the working directory, and a code of 0, 1, or 2, meaning open for reading, writing, or both. The file descriptor returned can then be used for reading or writing. Afterward, the file can be closed by CLOSE, which makes the file descriptor available for reuse on a subsequent CREAT or OPEN.

The most heavily used calls are undoubtedly READ and WRITE. We saw READ earlier. WRITE has the same parameters.

Although most programs read and write files sequentially, for some applications programs need to be able to access any part of a file at random. Associated with each file is a pointer that indicates the current position in the file. When reading (writing) sequentially, it normally points to the next byte to be read (written). The LSEEK call changes the value of the position pointer, so that subsequent calls to READ or WRITE can begin anywhere in the file, or even beyond the end of it.

LSEEK has three parameters: the first one is the file descriptor for the file, the second one is a file position, and the third one tells whether the file position is relative to the beginning of the file, the current position, or the end of the file. The value returned by LSEEK is the absolute position in the file after the file pointer was changed.

For each file, MINIX keeps track of the file mode (regular file, special file, directory, and so on), size, time of last modification, and other information. Programs can ask to see this information via the STAT and FSTAT system calls. These differ only in that the former specifies the file by name, whereas the latter takes a file descriptor, making it useful for inherited files whose names are not known. Both calls provide as the second parameter a pointer to a structure

where the information is to be put. The structure is shown in Fig. 1-13. In
MINIX the three times are identical. Three of them are provided for compatibility
with UNIX, where they are different.

```
struct stat {
    short st_dev;                  /* device where i-node belongs */
    unsigned short st_ino;         /* i-node number */
    unsigned short st_mode;        /* mode word */
    short st_nlink;                /* number of links */
    short st_uid;                  /* user id */
    short st_gid;                  /* group id */
    short st_rdev;                 /* major/minor device for special files */
    long st_size;                  /* file size */
    long st_atime;                 /* same as st_mtime */
    long st_mtime;                 /* time of last modification */
    long st_ctime;                 /* same as st_mtime */
};
```

Fig. 1-13. The structure used to return information for the STAT and FSTAT system calls. Three times are present for UNIX compatibility.

When manipulating file descriptors, the DUP call is occasionally helpful.
Consider, for example, a program that needs to close standard output (file
descriptor 1), substitute another file as standard output, call a function that writes
some output onto standard output, and then restore the original situation. Just
closing file descriptor 1 and then opening a new file will make the new file standard output (assuming standard input, file descriptor 0, is in use), but it will be
impossible to restore the original situation later.

The solution is first to execute the statement

```
fd = dup(1);
```

which uses the DUP system call to allocate a new file descriptor, *fd*, and arrange
for it to correspond to the same file as standard output. Then standard output
can be closed and a new file opened and used. When it is time to restore the original situation, file descriptor 1 can be closed, and then

```
n = dup(fd)
```

executed to assign the lowest file descriptor, namely, 1, to the same file as *fd*.
Finally, *fd* can be closed and we are back where we started.

The DUP call has a variant that allows an arbitrary unassigned file descriptor
to be made to refer to a given open file. It is called by

```
dup2(fd, fd2);
```

where *fd* refers to an open file and *fd2* is the unassigned file descriptor that is to
be made to refer to the same file as *fd*. Thus if *fd* refers to standard input (file
descriptor 0) and *fd2* is 4, after the call, file descriptors 0 and 4 will both refer to
standard input.

Interprocess communication in MINIX uses pipes, as described earlier. When a user types

```
cat filel file2 | sort
```

the shell creates a pipe and arranges for standard output of the first process to write to the pipe, so standard input of the second process can read from it. The PIPE system call creates a pipe and returns two file descriptors, one for writing and one for reading. The call is

```
pipe(&fd[0]);
```

where *fd* is an array of two integers and *fd*[0] is the file descriptor for reading and *fd*[1] is the one for writing.

Figure 1-14 depicts a skeleton procedure that creates two processes, with the output of the first one piped into the second one. (A more realistic example would do error checking and handle arguments.) First a pipe is created, and then the procedure forks, with the parent eventually becoming the first process in the pipeline and the child process becoming the second one. Since the files to be executed, *process1* and *process2*, do not know that they are part of a pipeline, it is essential that the file descriptors be manipulated so that the first process' standard output be the pipe and the second one's standard input be the pipe. The parent first closes off the file descriptor for reading from the pipe. Then it closes standard output and does a DUP call that allows file descriptor 1 to write on the pipe. It is important to realize that DUP always returns the lowest available file descriptor, in this case, 1. Then the program closes the other pipe file descriptor.

After the EXEC call, the process started will have file descriptors 0 and 2 be unchanged, and file descriptor 1 for writing on the pipe. The child code is analogous. The parameter to *execl* is repeated because the first one is the file to be executed and the second one is the first parameter, which most programs expect to be the file name.

The last system call we will describe in this section, IOCTL, is applicable only to special character files, primarily terminals. It is used to change the characters used for correcting typing errors on the terminal, changing the terminal mode, and so forth. In **cooked mode**, the erase and kill characters work normally, CRTL-S and CRTL-Q can be used for stopping and starting terminal output, CTRL-D means end of file, DEL generates an interrupt signal, and CRTL-\ generates a quit signal to force a core dump.

In **raw mode**, all of these functions are disabled; every character is passed directly to the program with no special processing. Furthermore, in raw mode, a read from the terminal will give the program any characters that have been typed, even a partial line, rather than waiting for a complete line as in cooked mode.

Cbreak mode is in between. The erase and kill characters for editing are disabled, as is CRTL-D, but CRTL-S, CTRL-Q, DEL, and CTRL-\ are enabled.

```
#define STD_INPUT  0          /* file descriptor for standard input */
#define STD_OUTPUT 1          /* file descriptor for standard output */

pipeline(process1, process2)
char *process1, *process2;    /* pointers to program names */
{
  int fd[2];

  pipe(&fd[0]);               /* create a pipe */
  if (fork() != 0) {
        /* The parent process executes these statements. */
        close(fd[0]);         /* process 1 does not need to read from pipe */
        close(STD_OUTPUT);    /* prepare for new standard output */
        dup(fd[1]);           /* set standard output to fd[1] */
        close(fd[1]);         /* pipe not needed any more */
        execl(process1, process1, 0);
  } else {
        /* The child process executes these statements. */
        close(fd[1]);         /* process 2 does not need to write to pipe */
        close(STD_INPUT);     /* prepare for new standard input */
        dup(fd[0]);           /* set standard input to fd[0] */
        close(fd[0]);         /* pipe not needed any more */
        execl(process2, process2, 0);
  }
}
```

Fig. 1-14. A skeleton for setting up a two-process pipeline.

Like raw mode, partial lines can be returned to programs (if intraline editing is turned off, there is no need to wait until a whole line has been received—the user cannot change his mind and delete it, as he can in cooked mode).

IOCTL has three parameters, for example

```
ioctl(fd, TIOCSETP, &sgttyb);
```

The first parameter specifies a file, the second one specifies an operation, and the third one is the address of a structure containing various flags. MINIX supports the operation TIOCSETP for setting the terminal parameters to the values in the structure, and TIOCGETP for filling the structure with the current values. The structure is defined in the header file *sgtty.h*, as shown in Fig. 1-15.

Bits in *sg_flags* can be set to enter raw or cbreak mode. The XTABS bit should be turned on to have MINIX replace tabs on output with the proper number of spaces. It should be turned off only when using terminals that correctly interpret the tab character in hardware. CRMOD should normally be on to cause line feeds sent to the terminal to also produce carriage returns. Finally, ECHO should be turned on to have the terminal echo characters, except when passwords and other secrets are being typed in.

IOCTL also has another call with a data structure, *tchars* (analogous to *sgtty*)

```
/* Data structures for IOCTL calls TIOCGETP/TIOCSETP calls. */

struct sgttyb {
  char sg_ispeed;              /* input speed (not used at present) */
  char sg_ospeed;              /* output speed (not used at present) */
  char sg_erase;               /* erase character */
  char sg_kill;                /* kill character */
  int  sg_flags;               /* mode flags */
};

/* Fields in sg_flags. */
#define XTABS        0006000    /* set to cause tab expansion */
#define RAW          0000040    /* set to enable raw mode */
#define CRMOD        0000020    /* set to map lf to cr + lf */
#define ECHO         0000010    /* set to enable echoing of typed input */
#define CBREAK       0000002    /* set to enable cbreak mode */
#define COOKED       0000000    /* neither CBREAK nor RAW */

#define TIOCGETP (('t'<<8) | 8)
#define TIOCSETP (('t'<<8) | 9)
```

Fig. 1-15. The data structure used as the third parameter in IOCTL.

for changing the interrupt character, quit character, terminal start and stop characters, and terminal end-of-file character.

1.4.4. System Calls for Directory Management

In this section we will look at some system calls that relate more to directories or the file system as a whole, rather than just to one specific file as in the previous section. LINK is a good place to start. Although it only refers to one file, it does so under two path names. The purpose of LINK is to allow the same file to appear under two or more names, often in different directories. A typical use is to allow several members of the same programming team to share a common file, with each of them having the file appear in his own directory, possibly under different names. Sharing a file is not the same as giving every team member a private copy, because having a shared file means that changes that any member of the team makes are instantly visible to the other members—there is only one file. When copies are made of a file, subsequent changes made to one copy do not affect the other ones.

To see how LINK works, consider the situation of Fig. 1-16(a). Here two users, *ast* and *jim*, each having their own directories with some files. If *ast* now executes a program containing the system call

```
link("/usr/jim/memo", "/usr/ast/note");
```

the file *memo* in *jim*'s directory is now entered into *ast*'s directory under the name *note*. Thereafter, */usr/jim/memo* and */usr/ast/note* refer to the same file.

```
   /usr/ast         /usr/jim            /usr/ast         /usr/jim

 16  mail          31  bin           16  mail          31  bin
 81  games         70  memo          81  games         70  memo
 40  test          59  f.c           40  test          59  f.c
                   38  prog1         70  note          38  prog1



        (a)                                   (b)
```

Fig. 1-16. (a) Two directories before linking */usr/jim/memo* to ast's directory. (b) The same directories after linking.

Understanding how LINK works will probably make it clearer what it does. Every file in MINIX has a unique number, its i-number, that identifies it. A directory is simply a file containing a set of (i-number, ASCII name) pairs. In Fig. 1-16, *mail* has i-number 16, and so on. What LINK does is simply create a new directory entry with a (possibly new) name, using the i-number of an existing file. In Fig. 1-16(b), two entries have the same i-number (70), and thus refer to the same file. If either one is later removed, using the UNLINK system call, the other one remains. If both are removed, MINIX sees that no entries to the file exist (a field in the i-node keeps track of the number of directory entries pointing to the file), so the file is removed from the disk.

As we have mentioned earlier, the MOUNT system call allows two file systems to be merged into one. A common situation is to have the **root file system**, containing the binary (executable) versions of the common commands and other heavily used files, on the RAM disk. The user can then insert a floppy disk, for example, containing user programs, into drive 0.

By executing the MOUNT system call, the drive 0 file system can be attached to the root file system, as shown in Fig. 1-17. A typical statement in C to perform the mount is

```
mount("/dev/fd0", "/mnt", 0);
```

where the first parameter is the name of a block special file for drive 0 and the second parameter is the place in the tree where it is to be mounted.

After the MOUNT call, a file on drive 0 can be accessed by just using its path from the root directory or the working directory, without regard to which drive it is on. In fact, second, third and fourth drives can also be mounted anywhere in the tree. The MOUNT command makes it possible to integrate removable media into a single integrated file hierarchy, without having to worry about which device a file is on. Although this example involves floppy disks, hard disks or portions of hard disks (often called **partitions** or **minor devices**) can also be mounted this way. When a file system is no longer needed, it can be unmounted with the UMOUNT system call.

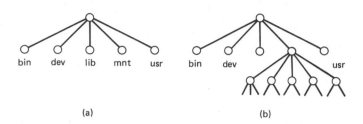

Fig. 1-17. (a) File system before the mount. (b) File system after the mount.

MINIX maintains a cache of recently used disks in main memory to avoid having to read them from the disk if they are used again quickly. If a block in the cache is modified (by a WRITE on a file) and the system crashes before the modified block is written out to disk, the file system will be damaged. To limit the potential damage, it is important to flush the cache periodically, so that the amount of data lost by a crash will be small. The system call SYNC tells MINIX to write out all the cache blocks that have been modified since being read in. When MINIX is started up, a program called *update* is started as a background process to do a SYNC every 30 seconds, to keep flushing the cache.

Two other calls that relate to directories are CHDIR and CHROOT. The former changes the working directory and the latter changes the root directory. After the call

```
chdir("/usr/ast/test");
```

an open on the
file *xyz* will open */usr/ast/test/xyz*. CHROOT works in an analogous way. Once a process has told the system to change its root directory, all absolute path names (path names beginning with a "/") will start at the new root. Only super-users may execute CHROOT, and even super-users do not do it very often.

1.4.5. System Calls for Protection

In MINIX every file has an 11-bit mode used for protection. Nine of these bits are the read-write-execute bits for the owner, group and others. The CHMOD system call makes it possible to change the mode of a file. For example, to make a file read-only by everyone except the owner, one could execute

```
chmod("file", 0644);
```

The other two protection bits, 02000 and 04000, are the SETGID (set-group-id) and SETUID (set-user-id) bits, respectively. When any user executes a program with the SETUID bit on, for the duration of that process the user's effective uid is changed to that of the file's owner. This feature is heavily used to allow users to execute programs that perform super-user only functions, such as creating directories. Creating a directory uses MKNOD, which is for the super-user only. By arranging for the *mkdir* program to be owned by the superuser and have mode 04755, ordinary users can be given the power to execute MKNOD but in a highly restricted way.

When a process executes a file that has the SETUID or SETGID bit on in its mode, it acquires an effective uid or gid different from its real uid or gid. It is sometimes important for a process to find out what its real and effective uid or gid is. The system calls GETUID and GETGID have been provided to supply this information. Each call returns both the real and effective uid or gid, so four library routines are needed to extract the proper information: *getuid*, *getgid*, *geteuid*, and *getegid*. The first two get the real uid/gid, and the last two the effective ones.

Ordinary users cannot change their uid, except by executing programs with the SETUID bit on, but the super-user has another possibility: the SETUID system call, which sets both the effective and real uids. SETGID sets both gids. The super-user can also change the owner of a file with the CHOWN system call. In short, the super-user has plenty of opportunity for violating all the protection rules, which explains why so many students devote so much of their time to trying to become super-user.

The last two system calls in this category can be executed by ordinary user processes. The first one, UMASK, sets an internal bit mask within the system, which is used to mask off mode bits when a file is created. After the call

```
umask(022)
```

the mode supplied by CREAT and MKNOD will have the 022 bits masked off before being used. Thus the call

```
creat("file", 0777);
```

will set the mode to 0755 rather than 0777. Since the bit mask is inherited by child processes, if the shell does a UMASK just after login, none of the user's processes in that session will accidently create files that other people can write on.

When a program owned by the root has the SETUID bit on, it can access any file, because its effective uid is the super-user. Frequently it is useful for the program to know if the person who called the program has permission to access a given file. If the program just tries the access, it will always succeed, and thus learn nothing.

What is needed is a way to see if the access is permitted for the real uid. The ACCESS system call provides a way to find out. The *mode* parameter is 4 to check for read access, 2 for write access, and 1 for execute access. Combinations are also allowed, for example, with *mode* equal to 6, the call returns 0 if both read and write access are allowed for the real uid; otherwise −1 is returned. With *mode* equal to 0, a check is made to see if the file exists and the directories leading up to it can be searched.

1.4.6. System Calls for Time Management

MINIX has four system calls that involve the time-of-day clock. TIME just returns the current time in seconds, with 0 corresponding to Jan. 1, 1970 at midnight (just as the day was starting, not ending). Of course the system clock must be set at some point in order to allow it to be read later, so STIME has been provided to let the clock be set (by the super-user). The third time call is UTIME, which allows the owner of a file (or the super-user) to change the time stored in a file's inode. Application of this system call is fairly limited, but a few programs need it, for example, *touch*, which sets the file's time to the current time. Finally, we have TIMES, which returns the accounting information to a process, so it can see how much CPU time it has used directly, and how much CPU time the system itself has expended on its behalf. The accumulated user and system times for its children are also returned.

1.5. OPERATING SYSTEM STRUCTURE

Now that we have seen what operating systems look like on the outside (i.e, the programmer's interface), it is time to take a look inside. In the following sections, we will examine four different structures that have been tried, in order to get some idea of the spectrum of possibilities.

1.5.1. Monolithic Systems

By far the most common organization, this approach might well be subtitled "The Big Mess." The structure is that there is no structure. The operating system is written as a collection of procedures, each of which can call any of the other ones whenever it needs to. When this technique is used, each procedure in the system has a well-defined interface in terms of parameters and results, and each one is free to call any other one, if the latter provides some useful computation that the former needs.

To construct the actual object program of the operating system when this approach is used, one compiles all the individual procedures, or files containing the procedures, and then binds them all together into a single object file with the linker. In terms of information hiding, there is essentially none—every procedure is visible to every other one (as opposed to a structure containing modules or packages, in which much of the information is local to a module, and only officially designated entry points can be called from outside the module).

Even in monolithic systems, however, it is possible to have at least a little structure. The services (system calls) provided by the operating system are requested by putting the parameters in well-defined places, such as in registers or on the stack, and then executing a special trap instruction known as a **kernel call** or **supervisor call**.

This instruction switches the machine from **user mode** to **kernel mode** (also known as **supervisor mode**), and transfers control to the operating system, shown as event (1) in Fig. 1-18. (Most CPUs have two modes: kernel mode, for the operating system, in which all instructions are allowed; and user mode, for user programs, in which I/O and certain other instructions are not allowed.)

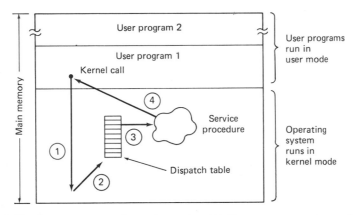

Fig. 1-18. How a system call can be made: (1) User program traps to the kernel. (2) Operating system determines service number required. (3) Operating system locates and calls service procedure. (4) Control is returned to user program.

The operating system then examines the parameters of the call to determine which system call is to be carried out, shown as (2) in Fig. 1-18. Next, the operating system indexes into a table that contains in slot k a pointer to the procedure that carries out system call k. This operation, shown as (3) in Fig. 1-18, identifies the service procedure, which is then called. Finally, the system call is finished and control is given back to the user program.

This organization suggests a basic structure for the operating system:

1. A main program that invokes the requested service procedure.

2. A set of service procedures that carry out the system calls.

3. A set of utility procedures that help the service procedures.

In this model, for each system call there is one service procedure that takes care of it. The utility procedures do things that are needed by several service procedures, such as fetching data from user programs. This division of the procedures into three layers is shown in Fig. 1-19.

1.5.2. Layered Systems

A generalization of the approach of Fig. 1-19 is to organize the operating system as a hierarchy of layers, each one constructed upon the one below it. The first system constructed in this way was the THE system built at the Technische

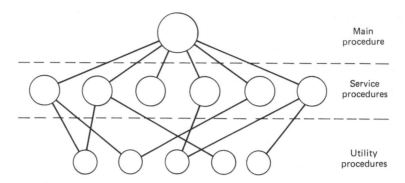

Fig. 1-19. A simple structuring model for a monolithic system.

Hogeschool Eindhoven in the Netherlands by E. W. Dijkstra (1968) and his students. The THE system was a simple batch system for a Dutch computer, the Electrologica X8, which had 32K of 27-bit words (bits were expensive in those days).

The system had 6 layers, as shown in Fig. 1-20. Layer 0 dealt with allocation of the processor, switching between processes when interrupts occurred or timers expired. Above layer 0, the system consisted of sequential processes, each of which could be programmed without having to worry about the fact that multiple processes were running on a single processor. In other words, layer 0 provided the basic multiprogramming of the CPU.

5	The operator
4	User programs
3	Input/output management
2	Operator-process communication
1	Memory and drum management
0	Processor allocation and multiprogramming

Fig. 1-20. Structure of the THE operating system.

Layer 1 did the memory management. It allocated space for processes in main memory and on a 512K word drum used for holding parts of processes (pages) for which there was no room in main memory. Above layer 1, processes did not have to worry about whether they were in memory or on the drum; the layer 1 software took care of making sure pages were brought into memory whenever they were needed.

Layer 2 handled communication between each process and the operator console. Above this layer each process effectively had its own operator console.

Layer 3 took care of managing the I/O devices and buffering the information streams to and from them. Above layer 3 each process could deal with abstract

I/O devices with nice properties, instead of real devices with many peculiarities.

Layer 4 was where the user programs were found. They did not have to worry about process, memory, console, or I/O management. The system operator process was located in layer 5.

A further generalization of the layering concept was present in the MULTICS system. Instead of layers, MULTICS was organized as a series of concentric rings, with the inner ones being more privileged than the outer ones. When a procedure in an outer ring wanted to call a procedure in an inner ring, it had to make the equivalent of a system call, that is, a TRAP instruction whose parameters were carefully checked for validity before allowing the call to proceed. Although the entire operating system was part of the address space of each user process in MULTICS, the hardware made it possible to designate individual procedures (memory segments, actually) as protected against reading, writing, or executing.

Whereas the THE layering scheme was really only a design aid, because all the parts of the system were ultimately linked together into a single object program, in MULTICS, the ring mechanism was very much present at run time and enforced by the hardware. The advantage of the ring mechanism is that it can easily be extended to structure user subsystems. For example, a professor could write a program to test and grade student programs and run this program in ring n, with the student programs running in ring $n + 1$ so that they could not change their grades.

1.5.3. Virtual Machines

The initial releases of OS/360 were strictly batch systems. Nevertheless, many 360 users wanted to have time-sharing, so various groups, both inside and outside IBM decided to write time-sharing systems for it. The official IBM time-sharing system, TSS/360, was delivered late, and when it finally arrived it was so big and slow that few sites converted over to it. It was eventually abandoned after its development had consumed some 50 million dollars (Graham, 1970). But a group at IBM's Scientific Center in Cambridge, MA, produced a radically different system that IBM eventually accepted as a product, and which is now widely used.

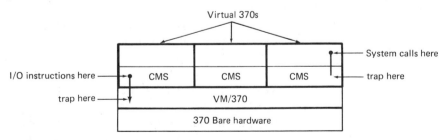

Fig. 1-21. The structure of VM/370 with CMS.

This system, originally called CP/CMS and now called VM/370 (Meyer and Seawright, 1970; Seawright and MacKinnon, 1979), was based on an astute observation: a time-sharing system provides (1) multiprogramming and (2) an extended machine with a more convenient interface than the bare hardware. The essence of VM/370 is to completely separate these two functions.

The heart of the system, known as the **virtual machine monitor**, runs on the bare hardware and does the multiprogramming, providing not one, but several virtual machines to the next layer up, as shown in Fig. 1-21. However, unlike all other operating systems, these virtual machines are not extended machines, with files and other nice features. Instead, they are *exact* copies of the bare hardware, including kernel/user mode, I/O, interrupts, and everything else the real machine has.

Because each virtual machine is identical to the true hardware, each one can run any operating system that will run directly on the hardware. In fact, different virtual machines can, and usually do, run different operating systems. Some run one of the descendants of OS/360 for batch processing, while other ones run a simple, single-user, interactive system called **CMS** (Conversational Monitor System) for time-sharing users.

When a CMS program executes a system call, the call is trapped to the operating system in its own virtual machine, not to VM/370, just as it would if it were running on a real machine instead of a virtual one. CMS then issues the normal hardware I/O instructions for reading its virtual disk or whatever is needed to carry out the call. These I/O instructions are trapped by VM/370, which then performs them as part of its simulation of the real hardware. By making a complete separation of the functions of multiprogramming and providing an extended machine, each of the pieces can be much simpler and more flexible.

1.5.4. Client-Server Model

VM/370 gains much in simplicity by moving a large part of the traditional operating system code (implementing the extended machine) into a higher layer, CMS. Nevertheless, VM/370 itself is still a complex program because simulating a number of virtual 370s is not *that* simple (especially if you want to do it efficiently).

A trend in modern operating systems is to take this idea of moving code up into higher layers even further, and remove as much as possible from the operating system, leaving a minimal **kernel**. The usual approach is to implement most of the operating system functions in user processes. To request a service, such as reading a block of a file, a user process (now known as the **client process**) sends the request to a **server process**, which then does the work and sends back the answer.

In this model, shown in Fig. 1-22, all the kernel does is handle the communication between clients and servers. By splitting the operating system up into parts, each of which only handles one facet of the system, such as file service,

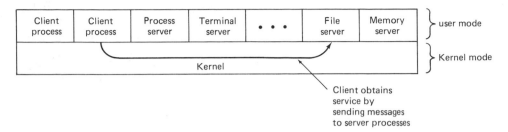

Fig. 1-22. The client-server model.

process service, terminal service, or memory service, each part becomes small and manageable. Furthermore, because all the servers run as user-mode processes, and not in kernel mode, they do not have direct access to the hardware. As a consequence, if a bug in the file server is triggered, the file service may crash, but this will not usually bring the whole machine down.

Another advantage of the client-server model is its adaptability to use in distributed systems (see Fig. 1-23). If a client communicates with a server by sending it messages, the client need not know whether the message is handled locally in its own machine, or whether it was sent across a network to a server on a remote machine. As far the client is concerned, the same thing happens in both cases: a request was sent and a reply came back.

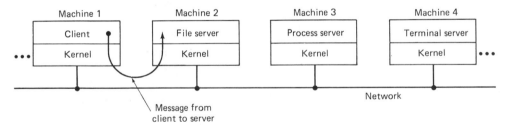

Fig. 1-23. The client-server model in a distributed system.

The picture painted above of a kernel that handles only the transport of messages from clients to servers and back is not completely realistic. Some operating system functions (such as loading commands into the physical I/O device registers) are difficult, if not impossible, to do from user-space programs. There are two ways of dealing with this problem. One way is to have some critical server processes (e.g., I/O device drivers) actually run in kernel mode, with complete access to all the hardware, but still communicate with other processes using the normal message mechanism.

The other way is to build a minimal amount of **mechanism** into the kernel, but leave the **policy** decisions up to servers in user space. For example, the kernel might recognize that a message sent to a certain special address means to take the contents of that message and load it into the I/O device registers for some disk, to start a disk read. In this example, the kernel would not even inspect the bytes in the message to see if they were valid or meaningful; it would just blindly copy them into the disk's device registers. (Obviously some scheme for limiting such messages to authorized processes only must be used.) The split between mechanism and policy is an important concept; it occurs again and again in operating systems in various contexts.

1.6. OUTLINE OF THE REST OF THIS BOOK

Operating systems typically have four major components: process management, I/O device management, memory management and file management. MINIX is also divided into these four parts. The next four chapters deal with these four topics, one topic per chapter. Chap. 6 is a list of suggested readings and a bibliography. The appendices provide an introduction to the C programming language, an introduction to the IBM PC, guides to using and maintaining MINIX, a complete listing of the MINIX source code, and a cross reference map.

The chapters on processes, I/O, memory management, and file systems have the same general structure. First the general principles of the subject are laid out. Then comes an overview of the corresponding area of MINIX (which also applies to UNIX). Finally, the MINIX implementation is discussed in detail.

The implementation section may be skimmed or skipped without loss of continuity by readers just interested in the principles of operating systems and not interested in the MINIX code. Readers who *are* interested in finding out how a real operating system (MINIX) works, and who are not familiar with C or the IBM PC, should read Appendices A and B before starting with Chap. 2.

Although the book does not contain a separate chapter on distributed operating systems, it contains material on distributed systems throughout. For example, the section on interprocess communication discusses message passing and remote procedure calls, and the chapter on file systems has sections on file servers and atomic transactions. More information about distributed operating systems can be found in Tanenbaum and van Renesse (1985).

1.7. SUMMARY

In this chapter we started out by looking at operating systems from two viewpoints: resource managers and extended machines. In the resource manager view, the operating system's job is to efficiently manage the different parts of the system. If the extended machine view, the job of the system is to provide the users with a virtual machine that is more convenient to use than the actual machine.

We then briefly glanced back at the history of computers and their operating systems, to see how we got where we are now. Then we took a close look at MINIX and its system calls, to see what an operating system really does. We saw a group of system calls relating to processes and another group relating to files. This information will be important later in the book when it is time to see how the system calls are implemented.

Finally, we examined different ways of structuring an operating system: as a monolithic system, as a hierarchy of layers, as a virtual machine system and as a client-server model.

PROBLEMS

1. What are the two main functions of an operating system?

2. What is multiprogramming?

3. What is spooling? Do you think that advanced personal computers will have spooling as a standard feature in the future?

4. On early computers, every byte of data read or written was directly handled by the CPU (i.e., there was no DMA—Direct Memory Access). What implications does this organization have for multiprogramming?

5. Why was time-sharing not widespread on second generation computers?

6. Which of the following instructions should be allowed only in kernel mode?
    (a) Disable all interrupts.
    (b) Read the time-of-day clock.
    (c) Set the time-of-day clock.
    (d) Change the memory map.

7. List some differences between personal computer operating systems and mainframe operating systems.

8. A MINIX file whose owner has uid = 12 and gid = 1 has mode *rwxr-x---*. Another user with uid = 6, gid = 1 tries to execute the file. What will happen?

9. In view of the fact that the mere existence of a super-user can lead to all kinds of security problems, why does such a concept exist?

10. The client-server model is popular in distributed systems. Can it also be used in a single-computer system?

11. Why is the process table needed in a time-sharing system? Is it also needed in personal computer systems in which only one process exists, that process taking over the entire machine until it is finished?

12. What is the essential difference between a block special file and a character special file?

13. If you hit DEL (sometimes called RUBOUT) often and fast enough, you may kill the shell. Explain.

14. In MINIX, if user 2 links to a file owned by user 1, then user 1 removes the file, what happens when user 2 tries to read the file?

15. Why is the CHROOT system call limited to the super-user? (Hint: think about protection problems.)

16. Why does MINIX have the program *update* running in the background all the time?

17. Write a program (or series of programs) to test all the MINIX system calls. For each call, try various sets of parameters, including some incorrect ones, to see if they are detected.

18. Write a shell that is similar to Fig. 1-10, but contains enough code that it actually works so you can test it. You might also add some features such as redirection of input and output, pipes, and background jobs.

2

PROCESSES

We are now about to embark on a detailed study of how operating systems in general and MINIX in particular are designed and constructed. The most central concept in any operating system is the *process*: an abstraction of a running program. Everything else hinges on this concept, and it is important that the operating system designer (and student) know what a process is as early as possible.

2.1. INTRODUCTION TO PROCESSES

All modern computers can do several things at the same time. While running a user program, a computer can also be reading from a disk and printing on a terminal or printer. In a multiprogramming system, the CPU also switches from program to program, running each for tens or hundreds of milliseconds. While, strictly speaking, at any instant of time, the CPU is running only one program, in the course of 1 second, it may work on several programs, thus giving the users the illusion of parallelism. Sometimes people speak of **pseudoparallelism** to mean this rapid switching back and forth of the CPU between programs, to contrast it with the true hardware parallelism of the CPU computing while one or more I/O devices are running. Keeping track of multiple, parallel activities is hard to do. Therefore, operating system designers over the years have evolved a model that makes parallelism easier to deal with. That model is the subject of this chapter.

2.1.1. The Process Model

In this model, all the runnable software on the computer, often including the operating system, is organized into a number of **sequential processes,** or just **processes** for short. A process is just an executing program, including the current values of the program counter, registers, and variables. Conceptually, each process has its own virtual CPU. In reality, of course, the real CPU switches back and forth from process to process, but to understand the system, it is much easier to think about a collection of processes running in (pseudo) parallel, than to try to keep track of how the CPU switches from program to program. This rapid switching back and forth is called **multiprogramming,** as we saw in the previous chapter. In Fig. 2-1(a) we see a computer multiprogramming four programs in memory.

In Fig. 2-1(b) we see how this is abstracted into four processes, each with its own flow of control (i.e., its own program counter), and each one running independent of the other ones. In Fig. 2-1(c) we see that viewed over a long enough time interval, all the processes have made progress, but at any given instant only one process is actually running.

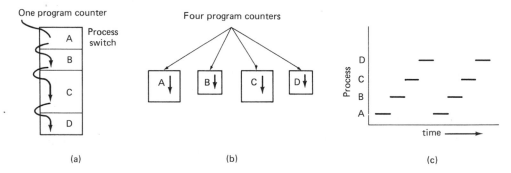

Fig. 2-1. (a) Multiprogramming of four programs. (b) Conceptual model of four independent, sequential processes. Only one program is active at any instant.

With the CPU switching back and forth among the processes, the rate at which a process performs its computation will not be uniform, and probably not even reproducible if the same processes are run again. Thus, processes must not be programmed with built-in assumptions about timing. Consider, for example, an I/O process that starts a magnetic tape in motion, executes an idle loop 1000 times to let the tape get up to speed, and then issues a command to read the first record. If the CPU decides to switch to another process during the idle loop, the tape process might not run again until after the first record was already past the read head. When a process has critical real-time requirements like this, that is, certain events absolutely must occur within a specified number of milliseconds, special measures must be taken to ensure that they do occur. Normally, however, most processes are not affected by the underlying multiprogramming of the CPU or the relative speeds of different processes.

The difference between a process and a program is subtle, but crucial. An analogy may help make this point clearer. Consider a culinary-minded computer scientist who is baking a birthday cake for his daughter. He has a birthday cake recipe and a kitchen well-stocked with the necessary input: flour, eggs, sugar, and so on. In this analogy, the recipe is the program (i.e., an algorithm expressed in some suitable notation), the computer scientist is the processor (CPU), and the cake ingredients are the input data. The process is the activity consisting of our baker reading the recipe, fetching the ingredients, and baking the cake.

Now imagine that the computer scientist's son comes running in crying, saying that he has been stung by a bee. The computer scientist records where he was in the recipe (the state of the current process is saved), gets out a first aid book, and begins following the directions in it. Here we see the processor being switched from one process (baking) to a higher priority process (administering medical care), each having a different program (recipe vs. first aid book). When the bee sting has been taken care of, the computer scientist goes back to his cake, continuing at the point where he left off.

The key idea here is that a process is an activity of some kind. It has a program, input, output, and a state. A single processor may be shared among several processes, with some scheduling algorithm being used to determine when to stop work on one process and service a different one.

Process Hierarchies

Operating systems that support the process concept must provide some way to create all the processes needed. In very simple systems, or in systems designed for running only a single application, it may be possible to have all the processes that will ever be needed be present when the system comes up. In most systems, however, some way is needed to create and destroy processes as needed during operation. In MINIX, processes are created by the FORK system call, which creates an identical copy of the calling process. The child process can also execute FORK, so it is possible to get a whole tree of processes. In other operating systems, system calls exist to create a process, load its memory, and start it running. Whatever the exact nature of the system call, processes need a way to create other processes. Note that each process has one parent but zero, one, two, or more children.

As a simple example of how process trees are used, let us look at how MINIX initializes itself when it is started. A special process, called *init*, is present on the boot diskette. When it starts running, it reads a file telling how many terminals there are. Then it forks off one new process per terminal. These processes wait for someone to log in. If a login is successful, the login process executes a shell to accept commands. These commands may start up more processes, and so forth. Thus, all the processes in the whole system belong to a single tree, with *init* at the root. (*Init* is not listed in the book; neither is the shell. The line had to be drawn somewhere.)

Process States

Although each process is an independent entity, with its own program counter and internal state, processes often need to interact with other processes. One process may generate some output that another process uses as input. In the shell command

```
cat chapter1 chapter2 chapter3 | grep tree
```

the first process, running *cat*, concatenates and outputs three files. The second process, running *grep*, selects all lines containing the word "tree." Depending on the relative speeds of the two processes (which depends on both the relative complexity of the programs and how much CPU time each one has had), it may happen that *grep* is ready to run, but there is no input waiting for it. It must then **block** until some input is available.

When a process blocks, it does so because logically it cannot continue, typically because it is waiting for input that is not yet available. It is also possible for a process that is conceptually ready and able to run to be stopped because the operating system has decided to allocate the CPU to another process for a while. These two conditions are completely different. In Fig. 2-2 we see a state diagram showing the three states a process may be in:

1. Running (actually using the CPU at that instant).

2. Blocked (unable to run until some external event happens).

3. Ready (runnable; temporarily stopped to let another process run).

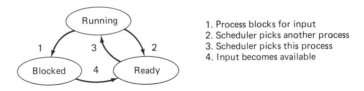

1. Process blocks for input
2. Scheduler picks another process
3. Scheduler picks this process
4. Input becomes available

Fig. 2-2. A process can be in *running, blocked* or *ready* (also called *runnable*) state.

Four transitions are possible among these three states, as shown. Transition 1 occurs when a process discovers that it cannot continue. In some systems the process must execute a system call, BLOCK, to get into blocked state. In other systems, including MINIX, when a process reads from a pipe or special file (e.g., a terminal) and there is no input available, the process is automatically blocked.

Transitions 2 and 3 are caused by the process scheduler, a part of the operating system, without the process even knowing about them. Transition 2 occurs when the scheduler decides that the running process has run long enough, and it is time to let another process have some CPU time. Transition 3 occurs when all the other processes have had their share and it is time for the first process to run again. The subject of scheduling, that is, deciding which process should run when and for how long, is an important one; we will look at it later in this chapter. Many algorithms have been devised to try to balance the competing demands of efficiency for the system as a whole and fairness to individual processes.

Transition 4 occurs when the external event for which a process was waiting (such as the arrival of some input) happens. If no other process is running at that instant, transition 3 will be triggered immediately, and the process will start running. Otherwise it may have to wait in *ready* state for a little while until the CPU is available.

Using the process model, it becomes much easier to think about what is going on inside the system. Some of the processes run programs that carry out commands typed in by a user. Other processes are part of the system and handle tasks such as carrying out requests for file services or managing the details of running a disk or a tape drive. When a disk interrupt occurs, the system makes a decision to stop running the current process and run the disk process, which was blocked waiting for that interrupt. Thus, instead of thinking about interrupts, we can think about user processes, disk processes, terminal processes, and so on, which block when they are waiting for something to happen. When the disk block has been read or the character typed, the process waiting for it is unblocked and is eligible to run again.

This view gives rise to the model shown in Fig. 2-3. Here the lowest level of the operating system is the scheduler, with a variety of processes on top of it. All the interrupt handling and details of actually starting and stopping processes are hidden away in the scheduler, which is actually quite small. The rest of the operating system is nicely structured in process form. The model of Fig. 2-3 is used in MINIX, with the understanding that "scheduler" really means not just process scheduling, but also interrupt handling and all the interprocess communication as well.

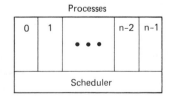

Fig. 2-3. The lowest layer of a process-structured operating system handles interrupts and does scheduling. The rest of the system consists of sequential processes.

2.1.2. Implementation of Processes

To implement the process model, the operating system maintains a table (an array of structures), called the **process table**, with one entry per process. This entry contains information about the process' state, its program counter, stack pointer, memory allocation, the status of its open files, its accounting and scheduling information, and everything else about the process that must be saved when the process is switched from *running* to *ready* state so that it can be restarted later as if it had never been stopped.

In MINIX the process management, memory management, and file management are each handled by separate modules within the system, so the process table is partitioned, with each module maintaining the fields that it needs. Figure 2-4 shows some of the more important fields.

Process management	Memory management	File management
Registers	Pointer to text segment	UMASK mask
Program counter	Pointer to data segment	Root directory
Program status word	Pointer to bss segment	Working directory
Stack pointer	Exit status	File descriptors
Process state	Signal status	Effective uid
Time when process started	Process id	Effective gid
CPU time used	Parent process	System call parameters
Children's CPU time	Process group	Various flag bits
Time of next alarm	Real uid	
Message queue pointers	Effective uid	
Pending signal bits	Real gid	
Process id	Effective gid	
Various flag bits	Bit maps for signals	
	Various flag bits	

Fig. 2-4. Some of the fields in the MINIX process table.

Now that we have looked at the process table, it is possible to explain a little more about how the illusion of multiple sequential processes is maintained on a machine with one CPU and many I/O devices. What follows is technically a description of how the "scheduler" of Fig. 2-3 works in MINIX but most modern operating systems work essentially the same way. Associated with each I/O device class (e.g., floppy disks, hard disks, timers, terminals) is a location near the bottom of memory called the **interrupt vector**. It contains the address of the interrupt service procedure. Suppose user process 3 is running when a disk interrupt occurs. The program counter, program status word, and possibly one or more registers are pushed onto the stack by the interrupt hardware. The computer then jumps to the address specified in the disk interrupt vector. That is all the hardware does. From here on, it is up to the software.

The interrupt service procedure starts out by saving all the registers in the process table entry for the current process. The current process number and a pointer to its entry are kept in global variables so they can be found quickly. Then the information deposited by the interrupt is removed from the stack, and the stack pointer is set to a temporary stack used by the process handler. Actions such as saving the registers and setting the stack pointer cannot even be expressed in C, so they are performed by a small assembly language routine. When this routine is finished, it calls a C procedure to do the rest of the work.

Interprocess communication in MINIX is via messages, so the next step is to build a message to be sent to the disk process, which will be blocked waiting for it. The message says that an interrupt occurred, to distinguish it from messages from user processes requesting disk blocks to be read and things like that. The state of the disk process is now changed from *blocked* to *ready* and the scheduler is called. In MINIX, different processes have different priorities, to give better service to I/O device handlers than to user processes. If the disk process is now the highest priority runnable process, it will be scheduled to run. If the process that was interrupted is just as important or more so, then it will be scheduled to run again, and the disk process will have to wait a little while.

Either way, the C procedure called by the assembly language interrupt code now returns, and the assembly language code loads up the registers and memory map for the now-current process and starts it running. The interrupt handling and scheduling are summarized in Fig. 2-5.

1. Hardware stacks program counter, etc.
2. Hardware loads new program counter from interrupt vector.
3. Assembly language procedure saves registers.
4. Assembly language procedure sets up new stack.
5. C procedure marks interrupt service process as ready.
6. Scheduler decides which process to run next.
7. C procedure returns to the assembly code.
8. Assembly language procedure starts up current process.

Fig. 2-5. Skeleton of what the lowest level of the operating system does when an interrupt occurs.

2.2. INTERPROCESS COMMUNICATION

Processes frequently need to communicate with other processes. When a user process wants to read from a file, it must tell the file process what it wants. Then the file process has to tell the disk process to read the required block. In a shell pipeline, the output of the first process must be passed to the second process. In short, there is a need for communication between processes, preferably in a well-structured way not using interrupts. In the following sections we will look at some of the pitfalls and issues related to this InterProcess Communication or **IPC**.

2.2.1. Race Conditions

In some operating systems, processes that are working together often share some common storage that each one can read and write. The shared storage may be in main memory or it may be a shared file; the location of the shared memory does not change the nature of the communication or the problems that arise. To see how interprocess communication works in practice, let us consider a simple but common example, a print spooler. When a process wants to print a file, it enters the file name in a special **spooler directory**. Another process, the **printer daemon**, periodically checks to see if there are any files to be printed, and if there are it prints them and then removes their names from the directory.

Imagine that our spooler directory has a large (potentially infinite) number of slots, numbered 0, 1, 2, ..., each one capable of holding a file name. Also imagine that there are two shared variables, *out*, which points to the next file to be printed, and *in*, which points to the next free slot in the directory. These two variables might well be kept on a two-word file available to all processes. At a certain instant, slots 0 to 3 are empty (the files have already been printed) and slots 4 to 6 are full (with the names of files queued for printing). More or less simultaneously, processes *A* and *B* decide they want to queue a file for printing. This situation is shown in Fig. 2-6.

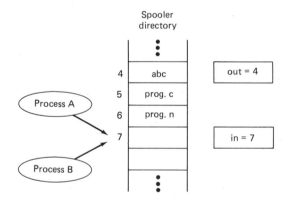

Fig. 2-6. Two processes want to access shared memory at the same time.

In jurisdictions where Murphy's law is applicable, the following might happen. Process *A* reads *in* and stores the value, 7, in a local variable called *next_free_slot*. Just then a clock interrupt occurs and the CPU decides that process *A* has run long enough, so it switches to process *B*. Process *B* also reads *in*, and also gets a 7, so it stores the name of its file in slot 7 and updates *in* to be an 8. Then it goes off and does other things.

Eventually process *A* runs again, starting from the place it left off. It looks at *next_free_slot*, finds a 7 there, and writes its file name in slot 7, erasing the name that process *B* just put there. Then it computes *next_free_slot* + 1, which is 8, and sets *in* to 8. The spooler directory is now internally consistent, so the printer daemon will not notice anything wrong, but process *B* will never get any output. Situations like this, where two or more processes are reading or writing some shared data and the final result depends on who runs precisely when, are called

race conditions. Debugging programs containing race conditions is no fun at all. The results of most test runs are usually fine, but once in a rare while something weird and unexplained happens.

2.2.2. Critical Sections

How do we avoid race conditions? The key to preventing trouble here and in many other situations involving shared memory, shared files, and shared everything else, is to find some way to prohibit more than one process from reading and writing the shared data at the same time. Put in other words, what we need is **mutual exclusion**—some way of making sure that if one process is using a shared variable or file, the other processes will be excluded from doing the same thing. The difficulty above occurred because process *B* started using one of the shared variables before process *A* was finished with it. The choice of appropriate primitive operations for achieving mutual exclusion is a major design issue in any operating system, and a subject that we will examine in great detail in the following sections.

The problem of avoiding race conditions can also be formulated in an abstract way. Part of the time, a process is busy doing internal computations and other things that do not lead to race conditions. However, sometimes a process may be accessing shared memory or files, or doing other critical things that can lead to races. That part of the program where the shared memory is accessed is called the **critical section**. If we could arrange matters such that no two processes were ever in their critical sections at the same time, we could avoid race conditions.

Although this requirement avoids race conditions, this is not sufficient for having parallel processes cooperate correctly and efficiently using shared data. We need four conditions to hold to have a good solution:

1. No two processes may be simultaneously inside their critical sections.

2. No assumptions are made about relative process speeds or number of CPUs.

3. No process stopped outside its critical section should block other processes.

4. No process should wait arbitrarily long to enter its critical section.

2.2.3. Mutual Exclusion with Busy Waiting

In this section we will examine various proposals for achieving mutual exclusion, so that while one process is busy updating shared memory in its critical region, no other process will enter *its* critical region and cause trouble.

Disabling Interrupts

The simplest solution is to have each process disable all interrupts just after entering its critical region and re-enable them just before leaving it. With interrupts disabled, no clock interrupts can occur. The CPU is only switched from process to process as a result of clock or other interrupts, after all, and with interrupts turned off the CPU will not be switched to another process. Thus, once a process has disabled interrupts, it can examine and update the shared memory without fear that any other process will intervene.

This approach is generally unattractive because it is unwise to give user processes the power to turn off interrupts. Suppose one of them did it, and never turned them on again? That would be the end of the system. Furthermore, if the computer has two or more CPUs, disabling interrupts affects only the CPU that executed the disable instruction. The other ones will continue to run normally and may well access the shared memory.

On the other hand, it is frequently convenient for the kernel itself to disable interrupts for a few instructions while it is updating variables or lists. If an interrupt occurred while the list of ready processes, for example, was in an inconsistent state, race conditions could occur. The conclusion is: disabling interrupts is sometimes a useful technique within the kernel, but is not appropriate as a general mutual exclusion mechanism for user processes.

Lock Variables

As a second attempt, let us look for a software solution. Consider having a single, shared, (lock) variable, initially 0. When a process wants to enter its critical region, it first tests the lock. If the lock is 0, the process sets it to 1 and enters the critical region. If the lock is already 1, the process just waits until it becomes 0. Thus, a 0 means that no process is in its critical region, and a 1 means that some process is in its critical region.

Unfortunately, this idea contains exactly the same fatal flaw that we saw in the spooler directory. Suppose one process reads the lock and sees that it is 0. Before it can set the lock to 1, another process is scheduled, runs, and sets the lock to 1. When the first process runs again, it will also set the lock to 1, and two processes will be in their critical regions at the same time.

Now you might think that we could get around this problem by first reading out the lock value, then checking it again just before storing into it, but that really does not help. The race now occurs if the second process modifies the lock just after the first process has finished its second check.

Strict Alternation

A third approach to the mutual exclusion problem is shown in Fig. 2-7. In this proposed solution, the integer variable *turn*, initially 0, keeps track of whose turn it is to enter the critical region and examine or update the shared memory. Initially, process 0 inspects turn, finds it to be 0, and enters its critical region. Process 1 also finds it to be 0, and therefore sits in a tight loop continually testing *turn* to see when it becomes 1. Continuously testing a variable waiting for some value to appear is called **busy waiting**. It should usually be avoided, since it wastes CPU time.

```
while (TRUE) {                        while (TRUE) {
   while (turn != 0) /* wait */ ;        while (turn != 1) /* wait */ ;
   critical_section();                   critical_section();
   turn = 1;                             turn = 0;
   noncritical_section();                noncritical_section();
}                                     }

          (a)                                   (b)
```

Fig. 2-7. A proposed solution to the critical section problem.

When process 0 leaves the critical section, it sets *turn* to 1, to allow process 1 to enter its critical section. Suppose process 1 finishes its critical section quickly, so both processes are in their noncritical sections, with *turn* set to 0. Now process 0 executes its whole loop quickly, coming back to its noncritical section with *turn* set to 1. At this point, process 0 finishes its noncritical section and goes back to the top of its loop. Unfortunately, it is not permitted to enter its critical section now, because *turn* is 1 and process 1 is busy with its noncritical section. Put in a different way, taking turns is not a good idea when one of the processes is much slower than the other.

This situation violates condition 3 set out above: process 0 is being blocked by a process not in its critical section. Going back to the spooler directory earlier, if we now associate the critical section with reading and writing the spooler directory, process 0 would not be allowed to print another file because process 1 was doing something else.

In fact, this solution requires that the two processes strictly alternate in entering their critical regions, for example, in spooling files. Neither one would be permitted to spool two in a row. While this algorithm does avoid all races, it is not really a serious candidate as a solution.

Peterson's Solution

By combining the idea of taking turns with the idea of lock variables and warning variables, the Dutch mathematician T. Dekker was the first one to devise a software solution to the mutual exclusion problem that does not require strict alternation. Unfortunately, his solution is quite complicated, so in practice it is never used. For a discussion of Dekker's algorithm, see Dijkstra (1965).

In 1981, Peterson discovered a much simpler way to achieve mutual exclusion. It is shown in Fig. 2-8.

```
#define FALSE    0
#define TRUE     1
#define N        2                  /* number of processes */

int turn;                           /* whose turn is it? */
int interested[N];                  /* all values initially 0 (FALSE) */

enter_region(process)
int process;                        /* process number: 0 or 1 */
{
  int other;                        /* number of the other process */

  other = 1 - process;             /* the opposite of process */
  interested[process] = TRUE;       /* show that you are interested */
  turn = process;                  /* set flag */
  while (turn == process && interested[other] == TRUE) /* null statement */ ;
}

leave_region(process)
int process;                        /* process leaving critical region */
{
  interested[process] = FALSE;  /* indicate departure from critical region */
}
```

Fig. 2-8. Peterson's solution for achieving mutual exclusion.

Before using the shared variables (i.e., before entering its critical region), each process calls *enter_region* with its own process number, 0 or 1, as parameter. This call will cause it to wait, if need be, until it is safe to enter. After it has finished with the shared variables, the process calls *leave_region* to indicate that it is done and to allow the other process to enter, if it so desires.

Let us see how this solution works. Initially neither process is in its critical region. Now process 0 calls *enter_region*. It indicates its interest by setting its array element, and sets *turn* to 0. Since process 1 is not interested, *enter_region* returns immediately. If process 1 now calls *enter_region*, it will hang there until *interested*[0] goes to *FALSE*, an event that only happens when process 0 calls *leave_region*.

Now consider the case that both processes call *enter_region* almost simultaneously. Both will store their process number in *turn*. Whichever store is done last is the one that has a lasting result; the first one is lost. Suppose process 1 stores last, so *turn* is 1. When both processes come to the while statement, process 0 executes it zero times, and enters its critical region. Process 1 loops and does not enter its critical region.

The TSL Instruction

Now let us look at a proposal that requires a little help from the hardware. Many computers, especially those designed with multiple processors in mind, have an instruction TEST AND SET LOCK (TSL) that works as follows. It reads the contents of the memory word into a register and then store a nonzero value at that memory address. The operations of reading the word and storing into it are guaranteed to be indivisible—no other processor can access the word until the instruction is finished. The CPU executing the TSL instruction locks the memory bus to prohibit other CPUs from accessing memory until it is done.

To use the TSL instruction, we will use a shared variable, *flag*, to coordinate access to shared memory. When *flag* is 0, any process may set it to 1 using the TSL instruction and then read or write the shared memory. When it is done, the process sets *flag* back to 0 using an ordinary MOVE instruction.

How can this instruction be used to prevent two processes from simultaneously entering their critical regions? The solution is given in Fig. 2-9. There a four-instruction subroutine in a fictitious (but typical) assembly language is shown. The first instruction copies the old value of *flag* to a register and then sets *flag* to 1. Then the old value is compared with 0. If it is nonzero, the lock was already set, so the program just goes back to the beginning and tests it again. Sooner or later it will become 0 (when the process currently in its critical section is done with its critical section), and the subroutine returns, with the lock set. Clearing the lock is simple. The program just stores a 0 in *flag*. No special instructions are needed.

```
enter_region:
        tsl register,flag      | copy flag to register and set flag to 1
        cmp register,#0        | was flag zero?
        jnz enter_region       | if it was non zero, lock was set, so loop
        ret                    | return to caller; critical region entered

leave_region:
        mov flag,#0            | store a 0 in flag
        ret                    | return to caller
```

Fig. 2-9. Setting and clearing locks using TSL.

One solution to the critical section problem is now straightforward. Before entering its critical section, a process calls *enter_region*, which does busy waiting until the lock is free, then it acquires the lock and returns. After the critical section the process calls *leave_region*. which stores a 0 in *flag*. As with all solutions based on critical regions, the processes must call *enter_region* and *leave_region* at the correct times for the method to work. If a process cheats, the mutual exclusion will fail.

2.2.4. Sleep and Wakeup

Both Peterson's solution and the solution using TSL are correct, but both have the defect of requiring busy waiting. In essence, what these solutions do is this: when a process wants to enter its critical section, it checks to see if the entry is allowed. If it is not, the process just sits in a tight loop waiting until it is.

Not only does this approach waste CPU time, but it can also have unexpected effects. Consider a computer with two processes, H, with high priority and L, with low priority. The scheduling rules are such that H is run whenever it is in ready state. At a certain moment, with L in its critical region, H becomes ready to run (e.g., an I/O operation completes). H now begins busy waiting, but since L is never scheduled while H is running, L never gets the chance to leave its critical region, so H loops forever.

Now let us look at some interprocess communication primitives that block instead of wasting CPU time when they are not allowed to enter their critical sections. One of the simplest is the pair SLEEP and WAKEUP. SLEEP is a system call that causes the caller to block, that is, be suspended until another process wakes it up. The WAKEUP call has one parameter, the process to be awakened. Alternatively, both SLEEP and WAKEUP each have one parameter, a memory address used to match up SLEEPs with WAKEUPs.

As an example of how these primitives are used, let us consider the **producer-consumer** problem (also known as the **bounded buffer** problem). Two processes share a common, fixed-size buffer. One of them, the producer, puts information into the buffer, and the other one, the consumer, takes it out.

Trouble arises when the producer wants to put a new item in the buffer, but it is already full. The solution is for the producer to go to sleep, to be awakened when the consumer has removed one or more items. Similarly, if the consumer wants to remove an item from the buffer and sees that the buffer is empty, it goes to sleep until the producer puts something in the buffer and wakes it up.

This approach sounds simple enough, but it leads to the same kinds of race conditions we saw earlier with the spooler directory. To keep track of the number of items in the buffer, we will need a variable, *count*. If the maximum number of items the buffer can hold is N, the producer's code will first test to see if *count* is N. If it is, the producer will go to sleep; if it is not, the producer will add an item and increment *count*.

The consumer's code is similar: first test *count* to see if it is 0. If it is, go to sleep; if it is nonzero, remove an item and decrement the counter. Each of the processes also tests to see if the other should be sleeping, and if so, wakes it up. The code for both producer and consumer is shown in Fig. 2-10.

To express system calls such as SLEEP and WAKEUP in C, we will show them as calls to library routines. They are not part of the standard C library, but presumably would be available on any system that actually had these system calls. The procedures *enter_item* and *remove_item*, which are not shown, handle the bookkeeping of putting items into and taking items out of the buffer.

```
#define N    100              /* number of slots in the buffer */
int count = 0;               /* number of items in the buffer */

producer()
{
  while (TRUE) {              /* repeat forever */
        produce_item();       /* generate next item */
        if (count == N) sleep();  /* if buffer is full, go to sleep */
        enter_item();         /* put item in buffer */
        count = count + 1;    /* increment count of items in buffer */
        if (count == 1) wakeup(consumer);     /* was buffer empty? */
  }
}


consumer()
{
  while (TRUE) {              /* repeat forever */
        if (count == 0) sleep();  /* if buffer is empty, got to sleep */
        remove_item();        /* take item out of buffer */
        count = count - 1;    /* decrement count of items in buffer */
        if (count == N-1) wakeup(producer);    /* was buffer full? */
        consume_item();       /* print item */
  }
}
```

Fig. 2-10. The producer-consumer problem with a fatal race condition.

Now let us get back to the race condition. It can occur because access to *count* is unconstrained. The following situation could possibly occur. The buffer is empty and the consumer has just read *count* to see if it is 0. At that instant, the scheduler decides to stop running the consumer temporarily and start running the producer. The producer enters an item in the buffer, increments *count*, and notices that it is now 1. Reasoning that *count* was just 0, and thus the consumer must be sleeping, the producer calls *wakeup* to wake the consumer up.

Unfortunately, the consumer is not yet logically asleep, so the wakeup signal is lost. When the consumer next runs, it will test the value of *count* it previously read, find it to be 0, and go to sleep. Sooner or later the producer will fill up the buffer and also go to sleep. Both will sleep forever.

The essence of the problem here is that a wakeup sent to a process that is not (yet) sleeping is lost. If it were not lost, everything would be all right. The obvious quick fix is to modify the rules to add a **wakeup waiting bit** to the picture. When a wakeup is sent to a process that is already awake, this bit is set. Later, when the process tries to go to sleep, if the wakeup waiting bit is on, it will be turned off, but the process will stay awake. The wakeup waiting bit is really a piggy bank for wakeup signals.

While the wakeup waiting bit saves the day in this simple example, it is easy to construct examples with three or more processes in which one wakeup waiting bit is insufficient. We could make another patch, and add a second wakeup waiting bit, or maybe 8 or 32 of them, but in principle the problem is still there.

2.2.5. Semaphores

This was the situation in 1965, when E. W. Dijkstra (1965) suggested using an integer variable to count the number of wakeups saved for future use. In his proposal, a new variable type, called a **semaphore**, was introduced. A semaphore could have the value 0, indicating that no wakeups were saved, or some positive value if one or more wakeups were pending.

Dijkstra proposed having two operations, DOWN and UP (generalizations of SLEEP and WAKEUP, respectively). The DOWN operation on a semaphore checks to see if the value is greater than 0. If so, it decrements the value (i.e., uses up one stored wakeup) and just continues. If the value is 0, the process is put to sleep. Checking the value, changing it, and possibly going to sleep is all done as a single, indivisible, **atomic action**. It is guaranteed that once a semaphore operation has started, no other process can access the semaphore until the operation has completed.

The UP operation increments the value of the semaphore addressed. If one or more processes were sleeping on that semaphore, unable to complete an earlier DOWN operation, one of them is chosen by the system at random, and is allowed to complete its DOWN. Thus, after an UP on a semaphore with processes sleeping on it, the semaphore will still be 0, but there will be one fewer process sleeping on it. The operation of incrementing the semaphore and waking up one process is also indivisible. No process ever blocks doing an UP, just as no process ever blocks doing a WAKEUP in the earlier model.

As an aside, in Dijkstra's original paper, he used the names P and V instead of DOWN and UP, respectively, but since these have no mnemonic significance to people who do not speak Dutch (and only marginal significance to those who do), we will use the terms DOWN and UP instead. These were first introduced in Algol 68.

Semaphores solve the lost-wakeup problem, as shown in Fig. 2-11. It is essential that they be implemented in an indivisible way. The normal way is to implement UP and DOWN as system calls, with the operating system briefly disabling all interrupts while it is testing the semaphore, updating it, and putting the process to sleep, if necessary. As all of these actions take only a few instructions, no harm is done in disabling interrupts. If multiple CPUs are being used, each semaphore should be protected by a lock variable, with the TSL instruction used to make sure that only one CPU at a time examines the semaphore. Be sure you understand that using TSL to prevent several CPUs from accessing the semaphore at the same time is quite different from busy waiting by the producer or consumer waiting for the other to empty or fill the buffer.

This solution uses three semaphores, one called *full* for counting the number

```
#define N 100                  /* number of slots in the buffer */
typedef int semaphore;         /* semaphores are a special kind of int */
semaphore mutex = 1;           /* controls access to critical region */
semaphore empty = N            /* counts empty buffer slots */
semaphore full = 0;            /* counts full buffer slots */

producer()
{
  int item;

  while (TRUE) {               /* TRUE is the constant 1 */
        produce_item(&item);   /* generate something to put in buffer */
        down(empty);           /* decrement empty count */
        down(mutex);           /* enter critical region */
        enter_item(item);      /* put new item in buffer */
        up(mutex);             /* leave critical region */
        up(full);              /* increment count of full slots */
  }
}


consumer()
{
  int item;

  while (TRUE) {               /* infinite loop */
        down(full);            /* decrement full count */
        down(mutex);           /* enter critical region */
        remove_item(&item);    /* take item from buffer */
        up(mutex);             /* leave critical region */
        up(empty);             /* increment count of empty slots */
        consume_item(item);    /* do something with the item */
  }
}
```

Fig. 2-11. The producer-consumer problem using semaphores.

of slots that are full, one called *empty* for counting the number of slots that are empty and one called *mutex* to make sure the producer and consumer do not access the buffer at the same time. *Full* is initially 0, *empty* is initially equal to the number of slots in the buffer, and *mutex* is initially 1. Semaphores that are initialized to 1 and used by two or more processes to ensure that only one of them can enter its critical region at the same time are called **binary semaphores**. If each process does a DOWN just before entering its critical region and an UP just after leaving it, mutual exclusion is guaranteed.

Now that we have a good interprocess communication primitive at our disposal, let us go back and look at the interrupt sequence of Fig. 2-5 again. In a system using semaphores, the natural way to hide interrupts is to have a semaphore, initially set to 0, associated with each I/O device. Just after starting an I/O device, the managing process does a DOWN on the associated semaphore, thus blocking immediately. When the interrupt comes in, the interrupt handler then does an UP on the associated semaphore, which makes the relevant process ready to run again. In this model, step 5 in Fig. 2-5 consists of doing an UP on the device's semaphore, so that in step 6 the scheduler will be able to run the device manager. Of course, if several processes are now ready, the scheduler may choose to run an even more important process next. We will look at how scheduling is done later in this chapter.

2.2.6. Event Counters

The solution to the producer-consumer problem using semaphores relied on mutual exclusion to avoid race conditions. It is also possible to program a solution without requiring mutual exclusion. In this section we will describe such a method. It uses a special kind of variable called an **event counter** (Reed and Kanodia, 1979).

Three operations are defined on an event counter E:

1. *Read(E)*: Return the current value of E.

2. *Advance(E)*: Atomically increment E by 1.

3. *Await(E, v)*: Wait until E has a value of v or more.

The producer-consumer problem does not use READ, but it is needed for other synchronization problems.

Notice that event counters only increase, never decrease. They always start at 0. Figure 2-12 shows the producer-consumer problem once more, this time using event counters.

Two event counters are used. The first one, *in*, counts the cumulative number of items that the producer has put into the buffer since the program started running. The other one, *out*, counts the cumulative number of items that the consumer has removed from the buffer so far. It is clear that *in* must be greater than or equal to *out*, but not by more than the size of the buffer.

When the producer has computed a new item, it checks to see if there is room in the buffer, using the AWAIT system call. Initially, *out* will be 0 and *sequence* $-N$ will be negative, so the producer does not block. If the producer manages to generate $N + 1$ items before the consumer has run at all, the AWAIT statement will wait until *out* becomes 1, something that will only happen after the consumer has removed one item.

The consumer's logic is even simpler. Before trying to remove the k-th item, it just waits until *in* has reached k, that is, until the producer has put k items into the buffer.

```
#define N      100          /* number of slots in the buffer */
typedef int event_counter;  /* event_counters are a special kind of int */
event_counter in;           /* counts items inserted into buffer */
event_counter out;          /* counts items removed from buffer */

producer()
{
  int item, sequence = 0;

  while (TRUE) {                   /* infinite loop */
       produce_item(&item);       /* generate something to put in buffer */
       sequence = sequence + 1;   /* count items produced so far */
       await(out, sequence - N);  /* wait until there is room in buffer */
       enter_item(item);          /* put item in slot (sequence-1) % N */
       advance(in);               /* let consumer know about another item */
  }
}


consumer()
{
  int item, sequence = 0;

  while (TRUE) {                   /* infinite loop */
       sequence = sequence + 1;   /* number of item to remove from buffer */
       await(in, sequence);       /* wait until required item is present */
       remove_item(&item);        /* take item from slot (sequence-1) % N */
       advance(out);              /* let producer know that item is gone */
       consume_item(item);        /* do something with the item */
  }
}
```

Fig. 2-12. The producer-consumer problem using event counters.

2.2.7. Monitors

With semaphores and event counters, interprocess communication looks easy, doesn't it? Forget it. Look closely at the order of the DOWNs before entering or removing items from the buffer in Fig. 2-11. Suppose the two DOWNs in the producer's code were reversed in order, so *mutex* was decremented before *empty* instead of after it. If the buffer were completely full, the producer would block, with *mutex* set to 0. Consequently, the next time the consumer tried to access the buffer, it would do a DOWN on *mutex*, now 0, and block too. Both processes would stay blocked forever and no more work would ever be done. This unfortunate situation is called a **deadlock**. We will study deadlocks in detail in Chap. 3.

This problem is pointed out to show how careful you must be when using semaphores. One subtle error and everything comes to a grinding halt. It is like programming in assembly language, only worse, because the errors are race conditions, deadlocks, and other forms of unpredictable and irreproducible behavior.

To make it easier to write correct programs, Hoare (1974) and Brinch Hansen (1975) proposed a higher level synchronization primitive called a **monitor**. Their proposals differed slightly, as described below. A monitor is a collection of procedures, variables, and data structures that are all grouped together in a special kind of module or package. Processes may call the procedures in a monitor whenever they want to, but they cannot directly access the monitor's internal data structures from procedures declared outside the monitor. Figure 2-13 illustrates a monitor written in an imaginary language, pidgin Pascal.

```
monitor example
    integer i;
    condition c;

    procedure producer(x);
    .
    .
    .
    end;

    procedure consumer(x);
    .
    .
    .
    end;
end monitor;
```

Fig. 2-13. A monitor.

Monitors have an important property that makes them useful for achieving mutual exclusion: only one process can be active in a monitor at any instant. Monitors are a programming language construct, so the compiler knows they are special and can handle calls to monitor procedures differently from other procedure calls. Typically, when a process calls a monitor procedure, the first few instructions of the procedure will check to see if any other process is currently active within the monitor. If so, the calling process will be suspended until the other process has left the monitor. If no other process is using the monitor, the calling process may enter.

It is up to the compiler to implement the mutual exclusion on monitor entries, but a common way is to use a binary semaphore. Because the compiler, not the programmer, is arranging for the mutual exclusion, it is much less likely that something will go wrong. In any event, the person writing the monitor does not have to be aware of how the compiler arranges for mutual exclusion. It is sufficient to know that by turning all the critical sections into monitor procedures, no two processes will ever execute their critical sections at the same time.

Although monitors provide an easy way to achieve mutual exclusion, as we have seen above, that is not enough. We also need a way for processes to block when they cannot proceed. In the producer-consumer problem, it is easy enough to put all the tests for buffer-full and buffer-empty in monitor procedures, but how should the producer block when it finds the buffer full?

The solution lies in the introduction of **condition variables**, along with two operations on them, WAIT and SIGNAL. When a monitor procedure discovers that it cannot continue (e.g., the producer finds the buffer full), it does a WAIT on some condition variable, say, *full*. This action causes the calling process to block. It also allows another process that had been previously prohibited from entering the monitor to enter now.

This other process, for example, the consumer, can wake up its sleeping partner by doing a SIGNAL on the condition variable that its partner is waiting on. To avoid having two active processes in the monitor at the same time, we need a rule telling what happens after a SIGNAL. Hoare proposed to let the newly awakened process run, suspending the other one. Brinch Hansen proposed finessing the problem by requiring that a process doing a SIGNAL *must* exit the monitor immediately. In other words, a SIGNAL statement may appear only as the final statement in a monitor procedure. We will use Brinch Hansen's proposal because it is conceptually simpler and is also easier to implement. If a SIGNAL is done on a condition variable on which several processes are waiting, only one of them, determined by the system scheduler, is revived.

A skeleton of the producer-consumer problem with monitors is given in Fig. 2-14 in pidgin Pascal.

You may be thinking that the operations WAIT and SIGNAL look similar to SLEEP and WAKEUP, which we saw earlier had fatal race conditions. They *are* very similar, but with one crucial difference: SLEEP and WAKEUP failed because while one process was trying to go to sleep, the other one was trying to wake it up. With monitors, that cannot happen. The automatic mutual exclusion on monitor procedures guarantees that if, say, the producer inside a monitor procedure discovers that the buffer is full, it will be able to complete the WAIT operation without having to worry about the possibility that the scheduler may switch to the consumer just before the WAIT completes. The consumer will not even be let into the monitor at all until the WAIT is finished and the producer has been marked as no longer runnable.

By making the mutual exclusion of critical regions automatic, monitors make parallel programming much less error-prone than with semaphores. Still, they too have some drawbacks. It is not for nothing that Fig. 2-14 is written in a strange kind of pidgin Pascal rather than in C, as are the other examples in this book. As we said earlier, monitors are a programming language concept. The compiler must recognize them and arrange for the mutual exclusion somehow. C, Pascal, and most other languages do not have monitors, so it is unreasonable to expect their compilers to enforce any mutual exclusion rules. In fact, how could the compiler even know which procedures were in monitors and which were not?

```
monitor ProducerConsumer
    condition full, empty;
    integer count;

    procedure enter;
    begin
        if count = N then wait(full);
        enter_item;
        count := count + 1;
        if count = 1 then signal(empty);
    end;

    procedure remove;
    begin
        if count = 0 then wait(empty);
        remove_item;
        count = count - 1;
        if count = N - 1 then signal(full);
    end

    count := 0;
end monitor;

procedure producer;
begin
    while true do
    begin
        produce_item;
        ProducerConsumer.enter;
    end
end;

procedure consumer;
begin
    while true do
    begin
        ProducerConsumer.remove;
        consume_item;
    end
end;
```

Fig. 2-14. The producer-consumer problem with monitors. The buffer has N slots.

These same languages do not have semaphores either, but adding semaphores is easy: all you need to do is add two short assembly language routines to the library to issue the UP and DOWN system calls. The compilers do not even have to know that they exist. Of course, the operating systems have to know about the semaphores, but at least if you have decided to write a semaphore-based operating system, you can write the user programs for it in C or Pascal or even BASIC if you are masochistic enough. With monitors, you need a language that has them built in. A few languages, such as Concurrent Euclid (Holt, 1983) have them, but they are rare.

Another problem with monitors, and also with semaphores, is that they were designed for solving the mutual exclusion problem on one or more CPUs that all have access to a common memory. By putting the semaphores (or event counters) in the shared memory and protecting them with TSL instructions, we can avoid races. When we go to a distributed system consisting of multiple CPUs, each with its own private memory, connected by a local area network, these primitives become inapplicable. The conclusion is that semaphores are too low level and monitors are not usable except in a few programming languages. Furthermore, none of the primitives provide for information exchange between machines. Something else is needed.

2.2.8. Message Passing

That something else is **message passing**. This method of interprocess communication uses two primitives SEND and RECEIVE, which, like semaphores and unlike monitors, are system calls rather than language constructs. As such, they can easily be put into library procedures, such as

```
send(destination, &message);
```

and

```
receive(source, &message);
```

The former sends a message to a given destination and the latter receives a message from a given source (or from *ANY*, if the receiver does not care). If no message is available, the receiver could block until one arrives.

Design Issues for Message Passing Systems

Message passing systems have many interesting problems and design issues that do not arise with semaphores or monitors, especially if the communicating processes are on different machines connected by a network. For example, messages can be lost by the network. To guard against lost messages, the sender and receiver can agree that as soon as a message has been received, the receiver will send back a special **acknowledgement** message. If the sender has not received the acknowledgement within a certain time interval, it retransmits the message.

Now consider what happens if the message itself is received correctly, but the acknowledgement is lost. The sender will retransmit the message, so the receiver will get it twice. It is essential that the receiver can distinguish a new message from the retransmission of an old one. Usually this problem is solved by putting consecutive sequence numbers in each original message. If the receiver gets a message bearing the same sequence number as the previous message, it knows that the message is a duplicate that can be ignored.

Message systems also have to deal with the question of how processes are named, so that the process specified in a SEND or RECEIVE call is unambiguous. Often a naming scheme of *process@machine* is used.

If the number of machines is very large, and there is no central authority that allocates machine names, it may happen that two organizations give their machine the same name. The problem of conflicts can be reduced considerably by grouping machines into **domains**, and then addressing processes as *process@machine.domain*. In this scheme there is no problem if two machines have the same name, provided that they are in different domains. The domain names must also be unique, of course.

Authentication is also an issue in message systems: how can the client tell that he is communicating with the real file server, and not with an imposter? How can the file server tell which client has requested a file? Encrypting the messages with akey known only to authorized users can often be helpful here.

At the other end of the spectrum, there are also design issues that are important when the sender and receiver are on the same machine. One of these is performance. Copying messages from one process to another is always slower than doing a semaphore operation or entering a monitor. Much work has gone into making message passing efficient. Cheriton (1984), for example, has suggested limiting message size to what will fit in the machine's registers, and then doing message passing using the registers.

Remote Procedure Call

Some message passing systems are structured with all message traffic taking the form of a request message from a client to a server, followed by a reply message from the server back to the client. From the client's point of view, sending a message to a server and then waiting for a reply looks very much like calling a procedure and then waiting for it to finish. In both cases, the caller provides some parameters, starts the operation, blocks until it completes, and then gets some result values.

Some distributed operating systems (e.g., Birrell and Nelson, 1984) exploit this similarity by having interprocess communication take the form of **remote procedure calls**. When a client process wants to read a block from a remote file, for example, it calls a procedure (called a **stub procedure**), *read* on its own machine using the normal procedure call instruction, as shown in Fig. 2-15. *Read* then sends a request message to the file server and waits for the reply.

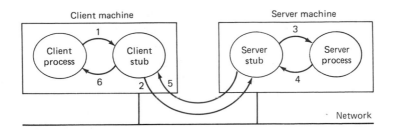

Fig. 2-15. Remote procedure call in six steps. (1) and (3) are ordinary procedure calls. (2) and (5) are messages. (4) and (6) are ordinary procedure returns.

On the server's machine, the message is accepted by the server stub procedure, which then calls the server using the standard procedure call instruction. When the server procedure has done the work, it returns to its caller, the stub, in the usual way. The server stub then sends a reply message back to the client stub. When the reply arrives, the client stub returns the results to the client procedure in the usual way.

The beauty of this scheme is that neither the client procedure nor the server procedure has to know that messages are being used. They just see ordinary procedure calls to local procedures. Only the stubs have to know about messages. The stubs are usually library procedures or are compiler generated.

Although the goal is to make remote procedure calls as much like local procedure calls as possible, it is a difficult goal to achieve. One problem is parameter passing. Passing parameters by value is not difficult, but passing them by reference is much harder. Furthermore, if the client and server machines have different representations for information, such as floating point numbers, much time may be wasted converting to and from a standard network format.

On some machines (e.g., 68000) the high-order byte of an integer has the lowest-numbered address and on other machines (e.g., 8088) it has the highest-numbered address. As a consequence, when an integer is sent from a 68000 to an 8088 a byte at a time, the integer will be byte-swapped when it arrives. This difference in architecture causes enormous problems and inefficiencies.

Another problem specific to remote procedure call is that of its failure semantics. Suppose the server crashes when executing a remote procedure call. What should be reported back to the client? It is not enough to merely report the crash, because the server may actually have finished the call just before crashing. If the client thinks the server crashed *before* executing the call, it will try again, which may not always be desirable.

As an example of this problem, consider an automated chocolate factory in which a remote procedure call is made to set a bit that causes a valve to open just long enough to fill a vat with chocolate. If the chocolate server crashes at approximately the time it was going to set the hardware bit, the client can never learn whether it crashed a microsecond *before* or *after* setting the bit. If the client repeats the call later, we may end up with a sticky brown floor. If the client does not repeat the call later, we may end up with an empty vat.

Depending on their implementations, remote procedure call systems can be divided into three categories based on their failure semantics. **At least once** systems guarantee that on a server crash the call will be executed one or more times (by simply timing out and repeating it until it is acknowledged). **At most once** systems guarantee that no call will ever be executed more than one time (no time out), but cannot guarantee that a call in progress during a crash will be executed at all. **Maybe** systems do not guarantee anything, but they are the easiest to implement.

The Producer-Consumer Problem with Message Passing

Now let us see how the producer-consumer problem can be solved with message passing and no shared memory. A solution is given in Fig. 2-16. We assume that all messages are the same size and that messages sent but not yet received are buffered automatically by the operating system. In this solution, a total of N messages is used, analogous to the N slots in a shared memory buffer. The consumer starts out by sending N empty messages to the producer. Whenever the producer has an item to give to the consumer, it takes an empty message and sends back a full one. In this way, the total number of messages in the system remains constant in time, so they can be stored in a given amount of memory.

If the producer works faster than the consumer, all the messages will end up full, waiting for the consumer; the producer will be blocked, waiting for an empty to come back. If the consumer works faster, then the reverse happens: all the messages will be empties waiting for the producer to fill them up; the consumer will be blocked, waiting for a full message.

Many variants are possible with message passing. For starters, let us look at how messages are addressed. One way is to assign each process a unique address and have messages be addressed to processes. An alternative way is to invent a new data structure, called a **mailbox**. A mailbox is a place to buffer a certain number of messages, typically specified when the mailbox is created. When mailboxes are used, the address parameters in the SEND and RECEIVE calls are mailboxes, not processes. When a process tries to send to a mailbox that is full, it is suspended until a message is removed from that mailbox.

For the producer-consumer problem, both the producer and consumer would create mailboxes large enough to hold N messages. The producer would send messages containing data to the consumer's mailbox, and the consumer would send empty messages to the producer's mailbox. When mailboxes are used, the buffering mechanism is clear: the destination mailbox holds messages that have been sent to the destination process but have not yet been accepted.

The other extreme from having mailboxes is to eliminate all buffering. When this approach is followed, if the SEND is done before the RECEIVE, the sending

```
#define N 100                       /* number of slots in the buffer */

producer()
{
  int item;
  message m;                        /* message buffer */

  while (TRUE) {
        produce_item(&item);        /* generate something to put in buffer */
        receive(consumer, &m);      /* wait for an empty to arrive */
        build_message(&m, item);    /* construct a message to send */
        send(consumer, &m);         /* send item to consumer */
  }
}

consumer()
{
  int item, i;
  message m;

  for (i = 0; i < N; i++) send(producer, &m);   /* send N empties */
  while (TRUE) {
        receive(producer, &m);      /* get message containing item */
        extract_item(&m, &item);         /* take item out of message */
        consume_item(item);         /* do something with the item */
        send(producer, &m);         /* send back empty reply */
  }
}
```

Fig. 2-16. The producer-consumer problem with N messages.

process is blocked until the RECEIVE happens, at which time the message can be copied directly from the sender to the receiver, with no intermediate buffering. Similarly, if the RECEIVE is done first, the receiver is blocked until a SEND happens. This strategy is often known as a **rendezvous**. It is easier to implement than a buffered message scheme but is less flexible since the sender and receiver are forced to run in lockstep.

The interprocess communication between user processes in MINIX (and UNIX) is via pipes, which are effectively mailboxes. The only real difference between a message system with mailboxes and the pipe mechanism is that pipes do not preserve message boundaries. In other words, if one process writes 10 messages of 100 bytes to a pipe and other process reads 1000 bytes from that pipe, the reader will get all 10 messages at once. With a true message system, each READ should return only one message. Of course, if the processes agree always to read and write fixed-size messages from the pipe, or to end each message with a special character (e.g., line feed), no problems arise. The processes that make up the MINIX operating system itself use a true message scheme with fixed size messages for communication among themselves.

2.2.9. Equivalence of Primitives

Reed and Kanodia (1979) described a different interprocess communication method called **sequencers**. Campbell and Habermann (1974) discussed a method called **path expressions**. Atkinson and Hewitt (1979) introduced **serializers**. While the list of different methods is not endless, it is certainly pretty long, with new ones being dreamed up all the time. Fortunately, space limitations prevent us from looking at all of them. Furthermore, many of the proposed schemes are similar to other ones.

In the previous sections we have studied four different interprocess communication primitives. Over the years, each one has accumulated supporters who maintain that their favorite way is the best way. The truth of the matter is that all these methods are essentially semantically equivalent (at least as far as single CPU systems are concerned). Using any of them, you can build the other ones.

We will now show the essential equivalence of semaphores, monitors, and messages. Not only is this interesting in its own right, but it also provides more insight and understanding about how the primitives work and how they can be implemented. Lack of space prevents us from dealing with event counters as well, but the general approach should be clear from the other examples.

Using Semaphores to Implement Monitors and Messages

Let us first see how we can build monitors and messages using semaphores. If the operating system provides semaphores as a basic feature, any compiler writer can easily implement monitors in his language as follows. Associated with each monitor is a binary semaphore, *mutex*, initially 1, to control entry to the monitor, and an additional semaphore, initially 0, per condition variable. When a monitor procedure is called, the first thing it does is a DOWN on its *mutex*. If the monitor is currently in use, the process will block. When leaving a monitor, a process does an UP on *mutex* to permit a waiting process to enter.

WAIT on a condition variable, *c*, is compiled into a sequence of three semaphore operations: UP *mutex*, then DOWN *c*, and finally DOWN *mutex*. The SIGNAL operation on a condition variable is translated into an UP on the corresponding semaphore.

To see why this mapping works, consider the producer-consumer problem again. The *mutex* semaphore guarantees that each process has exclusive access to the monitor for its critical section. Suppose the consumer starts first and discovers that there is no work for it in the buffer. It does a WAIT *empty*, which causes an UP on *mutex* and a DOWN on *empty*. The consumer goes to sleep, and the producer is allowed to enter as soon as it wants to. When the producer discovers that *count* (see Fig. 2-14) is 1, it will do SIGNAL *empty* to wake up the consumer. At this point both producer and consumer are active in the monitor, but since one of our rules of programming with monitors is that after doing SIGNAL a process must leave the monitor immediately, no harm is done.

Note that if the producer does its UP on *mutex* and leaves the monitor before the consumer has done its DOWN on *mutex*, it is possible that the producer could enter the monitor again before the consumer does its DOWN. Again, no harm is done, because the consumer cannot inspect or update any of the shared variables until after it has done the DOWN on *mutex*. If the producer is in the monitor at that moment, *mutex* will be 0 and the consumer will block until the producer leaves the monitor and does an UP on *mutex*.

Now let us look at how to implement message passing with semaphores. Associated with each process is a semaphore, initially 0, on which it will block when a SEND or RECEIVE must wait for completion. A shared buffer area will be used to hold mailboxes, each one containing an array of message slots. The slots in each mailbox are chained together in a linked list, so messages are delivered in the order received. Each mailbox has integer variables telling how many slots are full and how many are empty. Finally, each mailbox also contains the start of two queues, one queue for processes that are unable to send to the mailbox and one queue for processes that are unable to receive from the mailbox. These queues need to supply only the process numbers of the waiting processes so an UP can be done on the relevant semaphore. The whole shared buffer is protected by a binary semaphore, *mutex*, to make sure that only one process can inspect or update the shared data structures at once. It is shown in Fig. 2-17.

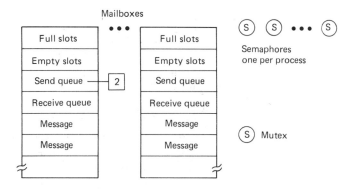

Fig. 2-17. The shared buffer for implementing message passing with semaphores.

When a SEND or RECEIVE is done on a mailbox containing at least one empty or full slot, respectively, the operation inserts or removes a message, updates the counters and links, and exits normally. The use of *mutex* at the start and end of the critical region ensures that only one process at a time can use the counters and pointers, in order to avoid race conditions.

When a RECEIVE is done on an empty mailbox, the process trying to receive a message first enters itself on the receive queue for the mailbox and then does an UP on *mutex* and a DOWN on its own semaphore, thus putting itself to sleep.

Later, when it is awakened, it will immediately do a DOWN on *mutex* just as in the case of using semaphores to construct monitors.

When a SEND is done, if room exists in the destination mailbox, the message is put there and the sender checks to see if the receiving queue for that mailbox has any waiting processes. If so, the first one is removed from the queue, and the sender does an UP on its semaphore. The sender then exits the critical region and the newly awakened receiver can continue. Their respective DOWN and UP on *mutex* cancel (in whatever order they occur) and no problems occur, provided that just as with monitors, a process that wakes up another process always does the WAKEUP as the very last thing before leaving the critical region.

When a SEND cannot complete due to a full mailbox, the sender first queues itself on the destination mailbox, then does an UP on *mutex* and a DOWN on its own semaphore. Later, when a receiver removes a message from the full mailbox and notices that someone is queued trying to send to that mailbox, the sender will be awakened.

Using Monitors to Implement Semaphores and Messages

Implementing semaphores and messages using monitors follows roughly the same pattern as what we have just described, but is simpler, because monitors are a higher level construct than semaphores. To implement semaphores, we need a counter and a linked list for each semaphore to be implemented, as well as a condition variable per process. When a DOWN is done, the caller checks (inside the monitor) to see if the counter for that semaphore is greater than zero. If it is, the counter is decremented and the caller simply exits the monitor. If the counter is zero, the caller adds its own process number to the linked list for that semaphore and does a WAIT on its condition variable.

When an UP is done on a semaphore, the calling process increments the counter (inside the monitor, of course) and then checks to see if the linked list for that semaphore has any entries. If the list has entries, the calling process removes one of them and does a SIGNAL on the condition variable for that process. Note that the calling process is not required to choose the first process on the linked list. In a more sophisticated implementation, each process could put its priority on the list along with its process number, so that the highest priority process would be awakened first.

Implementing messages using monitors is essentially the same as with semaphores, except that instead of a semaphore per process we have a condition variable per process. The mailbox structures are the same for both implementations.

Using Messages to Implement Semaphores and Monitors

If a message system is available, it is possible to implement semaphores and monitors using a little trick. The trick is to introduce a new process, the *synchronization process*. Let us first look at how this process can be used to implement semaphores. The synchronization process maintains a counter and a linked list of waiting processes for each semaphore. To do an UP or DOWN, a process calls the corresponding (library) procedure, *up* or *down*, which sends a message to the synchronization process specifying both the operation desired and the semaphore to be used. The library procedure then does a RECEIVE to get the reply from the synchronization process.

When the message arrives, the synchronization process checks the counter to see if the required operation can be completed. UPs can always complete, but DOWNs will block if the value of the semaphore is 0. If the operation is allowed, the synchronization process sends back an empty message, thus unblocking the caller. If, however, the operation is a DOWN and the semaphore is 0, the synchronization process enters the caller onto the queue and does not send a reply. The result is that the process doing the DOWN is blocked, just as it should be. Later, when an UP is done, the synchronization process picks one of the processes blocked on the semaphore, either in first-come-first-served order, priority order, or some other order, and sends it a reply. Race conditions are avoided here because the synchronization process handles only one request at a time.

Monitors can be implemented using messages using the same trick. We showed earlier how monitors can be implemented using semaphores. Now we have shown how semaphores can be implemented using messages. By combining the two, we get monitors from messages. One way to achieve this goal is to have the compiler implement the monitor procedures by calling the library procedures *up* and *down* for the *mutex* and per-process semaphores, as described at the beginning of this section. These procedures would then be implemented by sending messages to the synchronization process. Other implementations are also possible.

2.3. CLASSICAL IPC PROBLEMS

The operating systems literature is full of interesting problems that have been widely discussed and analyzed. In the following sections we will examine two of the better-known problems.

2.3.1. The Dining Philosophers Problem

In 1965, Dijkstra posed and solved a synchronization problem called the **dining philosophers problem**. Since that time, everyone inventing yet another synchronization primitive has tried to demonstrate how wonderful the new primitive is by showing how elegantly it solves the dining philosophers problem. The problem can be stated as follows. Five philosophers are seated around a circular table. Each philosopher has a plate of especially slippery spaghetti. The spaghetti is so slippery that a philosopher needs two forks to eat it. Between each plate is a fork. The table is shown in Fig. 2-18.

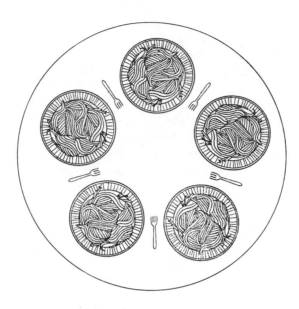

Fig. 2-18. Lunch time in the Philosophy Department.

The life of a philosopher consists of alternate periods of eating and thinking. (This is something of an abstraction, even for philosophers, but the other activities are irrelevant here.) When a philosopher gets hungry, she tries to acquire her left and right fork, one at a time, in either order. If successful in acquiring two forks, she eats for a while, then puts down the forks and continues to think. The key question is: can you write a program for each philosopher that does what it is supposed to do and never gets stuck? (It has been pointed out that the two-fork requirement is somewhat artificial; perhaps we should switch from Italian to Chinese food, substituting rice for spaghetti and chopsticks for forks.)

Figure 2-19 shows the obvious solution. The procedure *take_fork* waits until the specified fork is available and then seizes it. Unfortunately, the obvious solution is wrong. Suppose that all five philosophers take their left forks simultaneously. None will be able to take their right forks, and there will be a deadlock.

We could modify the program so that after taking the left fork, the program checks to see if the right fork is available. If it is not, the philosopher puts down the left one, waits for some time, and then repeats the whole process. This proposal too, fails, although for a different reason. With a little of bad luck, all the philosophers could start the algorithm simultaneously, picking up their left forks, seeing that their right forks were not available, putting down their left forks, waiting, picking up their left forks again simultaneously, and so on, forever. A situation like this, in which all the programs continue to run indefinitely but fail to make any progress is called **starvation**. (It is called starvation even when the problem does not occur in an Italian or a Chinese restaurant.)

```
#define N 5                      /* number of philosophers */

philosopher(i)
int i;                           /* philosopher number, 0-4 */
{
  while (TRUE) {
        think();                 /* philosopher is thinking */
        take_fork(i);            /* take left fork */
        take_fork((i+1) % N);    /* take right fork; % is modulo operator */
        eat();                   /* yum-yum, spaghetti */
        put_fork(i);             /* put left fork back on the table */
        put_fork((i+1) % N);     /* put right fork back on the table */
  }
}
```

Fig. 2-19. A nonsolution to the dining philosophers problem.

Now you might think, "If the philosophers would just wait a random time instead of the same time after failing to acquire the right-hand fork, the chance that everything would continue in lockstep for even an hour is very small." Of course this is true, but in some applications one would prefer a solution that always works and cannot fail due to an unlikely series of random numbers. (Think about safety control in a nuclear power plant.)

One improvement to Fig. 2-19 that has no deadlock and no starvation is to protect the five statements following the call to *think* by a binary semaphore. Before starting to acquire forks, a philosopher would do a DOWN on *mutex*. After replacing the forks, she would do an UP on *mutex*. From a theoretical viewpoint, this solution is adequate. From a practical one, it has a performance bug: only one philosopher can be eating at any instant. With five forks available, we should be able to allow two philosophers to eat at the same time.

The solution presented in Fig. 2-20 is correct and also allows the maximum parallelism for an arbitrary number of philosophers. It uses an array, *state*, to keep track of whether a philosopher is eating, thinking, or hungry (trying to acquire forks). A philosopher may move only into eating state if neither neighbor is eating. Philosopher *i*'s neighbors are defined by the macros *LEFT* and *RIGHT*. In other words, if *i* is 2, *LEFT* is 1 and *RIGHT* is 3.

The program uses an array of semaphores, one per philosopher, so hungry philosophers can block if the needed forks are busy. By now you should have enough background to understand this solution without any more help.

2.3.2. The Readers and Writers Problem

The dining philosophers problem is useful for modeling processes that are competing for exclusive access to a limited number of resources, such as tape drives or other I/O devices. Another famous problem is the readers and writers problem (Courtois et al., 1971), which models access to a data base. Imagine a

```
#define N              5        /* number of philosophers */
#define LEFT       (i-1)%N      /* number of i's left neighbor */
#define RIGHT      (i+1)%N      /* number of i's right neighbor */
#define THINKING       0        /* philosopher is thinking */
#define HUNGRY         1        /* philosopher is trying to get forks */
#define EATING         2        /* philosopher is eating */
typedef int semaphore;          /* semaphores are a special kind of int */
int state[N];                   /* array to keep track of everyone's state */
semaphore mutex = 1;            /* mutual exclusion for critical regions */
semaphore s[N];                 /* one semaphore per philosopher */

philosopher(i)
int i;                          /* philosopher number, 0 to N-1 */
{
  while (TRUE) {                /* repeat forever */
        think();               /* philosopher is thinking */
        take_forks(i);         /* acquire two forks or block */
        eat();                 /* yum-yum, spaghetti */
        put_forks(i);          /* put both forks back on table */
  }
}

take_forks(i)
int i;                          /* philosopher number, 0 to N-1 */
{
  down(mutex);                  /* enter critical region */
  state[i] = HUNGRY;            /* record fact that philosopher i is hungry */
  test(i);                      /* try to acquire 2 forks */
  up(mutex);                    /* exit critical region */
  down(s[i]);                   /* block if forks were not acquired */
}

put_forks(i)
int i;                          /* philosopher number, 0 to N-1 */
{
  down(mutex);                  /* enter critical region */
  state[i] = THINKING;          /* philosopher has finished eating */
  test(LEFT);                   /* see if left neighbor can now eat */
  test(RIGHT);                  /* see if right neighbor can now eat */
  up(mutex);                    /* exit critical region */
}

test(i)
int i;                          /* philosopher number, 0 to N-1 */
{
  if (state[i] == HUNGRY && state[LEFT] != EATING && state[RIGHT] != EATING) {
        state[i] = EATING;
        up(s[i]);
  }
}
```

Fig. 2-20. A solution to the dining philosophers problem.

big data base, such as an airline reservation system, with many competing processes wishing to read and write it. It is acceptable to have multiple processes reading the data base at the same time, but if one process is writing (i.e., changing) the data base, no other processes may have access to the data base, not even readers. The question is how do you program the readers and the writers? One solution of Courtois et al. is shown in Fig. 2-21.

```
typedef int semaphore;          /* use your imagination */
semaphore mutex = 1;            /* controls access to 'rc' */
semaphore db = 1;              /* controls access to the data base */
int rc = 0;                  /* # of processes reading or wanting to */

reader()
{
  while (TRUE) {              /* repeat forever */
        down(mutex);            /* get exclusive access to 'rc' */
        rc = rc + 1;            /* one reader more now */
        if (rc == 1) down(db);  /* if this is the first reader ... */
        up(mutex);             /* release exclusive access to 'rc' */
        read_data_base();       /* access the data */
        down(mutex);            /* get exclusive access to 'rc' */
        rc = rc - 1;            /* one reader fewer now */
        if (rc == 0) up(db);    /* if this is the last reader ... */
        up(mutex);             /* release exclusive access to 'rc' */
        use_data_read();        /* noncritical section */
  }
}


writer()
{
  while (TRUE) {              /* repeat forever */
        think_up_data();        /* noncritical section */
        down(db);             /* get exclusive access */
        write_data_base();      /* update the data */
        up(db);              /* release exclusive access */
  }
}
```

Fig. 2-21. A solution to the readers and writers problem.

In this solution, the first reader to get access to the data base does a DOWN on the semaphore *db*. Subsequent readers merely increment a counter, *rc*. As readers leave, they decrement the counter and the last one out does an UP on the semaphore, allowing a blocked writer, if there is one, to get in.

Implicit in this solution is that readers have priority over writers. If a writer appears while several readers are in the data base, the writer must wait. If new readers keep appearing, so that there is always at least one reader in the data base, the writer must keep waiting until no more readers are interested in the data base. Courtois et al. also presented a solution that gives priority to writers. For details, we refer you to their paper.

2.4. PROCESS SCHEDULING

In the examples of the previous sections, we have often had situations in which two or more processes (e.g., producer and consumer) were logically runnable. When more than one process is runnable, the operating system must decide which one to run first. That part of the operating system concerned with this decision is called the **scheduler**, and the algorithm it uses is called the **scheduling algorithm**. Back in the old days of batch systems with input in the form of card images on a magnetic tape, the scheduling algorithm was simple: just run the next job on the tape. With multi-user time-sharing systems, often combined with batch jobs in the background, the scheduling algorithm is more complex.

Before looking at specific scheduling algorithms, we should think about what the scheduler is trying to achieve. Various criteria come to mind as to what constitutes a good scheduling algorithm, among them:

1. Fairness: make sure each process gets its fair share of the CPU.

2. Efficiency: keep the CPU busy 100 percent of the time.

3. Response time: minimize response time for interactive users.

4. Turnaround: minimize the time batch users must wait for output.

5. Throughput: maximize the number of jobs processed per hour.

A little thought will show that some of these goals are contradictory. To minimize response time for interactive users, the scheduler should not run any batch jobs at all (except maybe between 3 A.M. and 6 A.M., when all the interactive users are snug in their beds). The batch users probably will not like this algorithm, however; it violates criterion 4. It can be shown (Kleinrock, 1975) that any scheduling algorithm that favors some class of jobs hurts another class of jobs. The amount of CPU time available is finite, after all. To give one user more you have to give another user less.

A complication that schedulers have to deal with is that every process is unique and unpredictable. Some spend a lot of time waiting for file I/O, while others would use the CPU for hours at a time if given the chance. When the scheduler starts running some process, it never knows for sure how long it will be until that process blocks, either for I/O, or on a semaphore, or for some other reason. To make sure that no process runs too long, nearly all computers have an electronic timer or clock built in, which causes an interrupt periodically. A frequency of 50 or 60 times a second (called 50 or 60 **Hertz** and abbreviated **Hz**) is common, but on many computers the operating system can set the timer frequency to anything it wants. At each clock interrupt, the operating system gets to run and decide whether the currently running process should be allowed to continue, or whether it has had enough CPU time for the moment and should be suspended to give another process the CPU.

The strategy of allowing processes that are logically runnable to be temporarily suspended is called **preemptive scheduling**, and is in contrast to the **run to completion** method of the early batch systems. As we have seen throughout this chapter, a process can be suspended at an arbitrary instant, without warning, so another process can be run. This leads to race conditions and necessitates semaphores, event counters, monitors, messages, or some other sophisticated method for preventing them. On the other hand, a policy of letting a process run as long as it wanted to would mean that somebody computing π to a billion places could deny service to all other users for weeks or months.

2.4.1. Round Robin Scheduling

Now let us look at some specific scheduling algorithms. One of the oldest, simplest, fairest, and most widely used algorithms is **round robin**. Each process is assigned a time interval, called its **quantum**, which it is allowed to run. If the process is still running at the end of the quantum, the CPU is preempted and given to another process. If the process has blocked or finished before the quantum has elapsed, the CPU switching is done when the process blocks, of course. Round robin is easy to implement. All the scheduler needs to do is maintain a list of runnable processes, as shown in Fig. 2-22(a). When the quantum runs out on a process, it is put on the end of the list, as shown in Fig. 2-22(b).

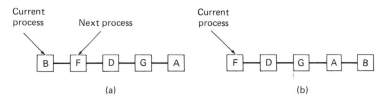

Fig. 2-22. Round robin scheduling. (a) The list of runnable processes. (b) The list of runnable processes after B's quantum runs out.

The only interesting issue with round robin is the length of the quantum. Switching from one process to another requires a certain amount of time for doing the administration—saving and loading registers and memory maps, updating various tables and lists, etc. Suppose this **process switch** or **context switch**, as it is sometimes called, takes 5 msec. Also suppose that the quantum is set at 20 msec. With these parameters, after doing 20 msec of useful work, the CPU will have to spend 5 msec on process switching. Twenty percent of the CPU time will be wasted on administrative overhead.

To improve the CPU efficiency, we could set the quantum to, say, 500 msec. Now the wasted time is less than 1 percent. But consider what happens if ten interactive users hit the carriage return key at roughly the same time. Ten processes will be put on the list of runnable processes. If the CPU is idle, the first one will start immediately, the second one may not start until about 1/2 sec later, and so on. The unlucky last one may have to wait 5 sec before getting a chance, assuming all the others use their full quanta. Most users will perceive a 5-sec response to a short command as terrible.

Conclusion: setting the quantum too short causes too many process switches and lowers the CPU efficiency, but setting it too long may cause poor response to short interactive requests. A quantum around 100 msec is often a reasonable compromise.

2.4.2. Priority Scheduling

Round robin scheduling makes the implicit assumption that all processes are equally important. Frequently, the people who own and operate computer centers have different ideas on that subject. At a university computer center, the pecking order may be deans first, then professors, secretaries, janitors, and finally students. The need to take external factors into account leads to **priority scheduling**. The basic idea is straightforward: each process is assigned a priority, and the runnable process with the highest priority is allowed to run.

To prevent high-priority processes from running indefinitely, the scheduler may decrease the priority of the currently running process at each clock tick (i.e., at each clock interrupt). If this action causes its priority to drop below that of the next highest process, a process switch occurs.

Priorities can be assigned to processes statically or dynamically. On a military computer, processes started by generals might begin at priority 100, processes started by colonels at 90, majors at 80, captains at 70, lieutenants at 60, and so on. Alternatively, at a commercial computer center, high-priority jobs might cost 100 dollars an hour, medium priority 75 dollars an hour, and low priority 50 dollars an hour. The UNIX system has a command, *nice*, which allows a user to voluntarily reduce the priority of his process, in order to be nice to the other users. Nobody ever uses it.

Priorities can also be assigned dynamically by the system to achieve certain system goals. For example, some processes are highly I/O bound and spend most of their time waiting for I/O to complete. Whenever such a process wants the CPU, it should be given the CPU immediately, to let it start its next I/O request, which can then proceed in parallel with another process actually computing. Making the I/O bound process wait a long time for the CPU will just mean having it around occupying memory for an unnecessarily long time. A simple algorithm for giving good service to I/O bound processes is to set the priority to $1/f$, where f is the fraction of the last quantum that a process used. A process that used only 2 msec of its 100 msec quantum would get priority 50, while a process that ran 50 msec before blocking would get priority 2, and a process that used the whole quantum would get priority 1.

It is often convenient to group processes into priority classes and use priority scheduling among the classes but round robin scheduling within each class. Figure 2-23 shows a system with four priority classes. The scheduling algorithm is as follows: as long as there are runnable processes in priority class 4, just run each one for one quantum, round robin fashion, and never bother with lower priority classes. If priority class 4 is empty, then run the class 3 processes round robin. If classes 4 and 3 are both empty, then run class 2 round robin, and so on. If priorities are not adjusted from time to time, lower priority classes may all starve to death.

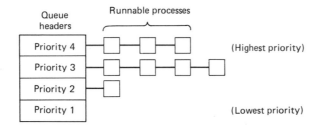

Fig. 2-23. A scheduling algorithm with four priority classes.

2.4.3. Multiple Queues

One of the earliest priority schedulers was in CTSS (Corbato et al., 1962). CTSS had the problem that process switching was very slow because the 7094 could hold only one process in memory. Each switch meant swapping the current process to disk and reading in a new one from disk. The CTSS designers quickly realized that it was more efficient to give CPU-bound processes a large quantum once in a while, rather than giving them small quanta frequently (to reduce swapping). On the other hand, giving all processes a large quantum would mean poor response time, as we have already seen. Their solution was to set up priority classes. Processes in the highest class were run for one quantum. Processes in the next highest class were run for two quanta. Processes in the next class were run for four quanta, and so on. Whenever a process used up all the quanta allocated to it, it was moved down one class.

As an example, consider a process that needed to compute continuously for 100 quanta. It would initially be given one quantum, then swapped out. Next time it would get two quanta before being swapped out. On succeeding runs it would get 4, 8, 16, 32, and 64 quanta, although it would have used only 37 of the final 64 quanta to complete its work. Only 7 swaps would be needed (including the initial load) instead of 100 with a pure round robin algorithm. Furthermore, as the process sank deeper and deeper into the priority queues, it would be run less and less frequently, saving the CPU for short, interactive processes.

The following policy was adopted to prevent a process that needed to run for a long time when it first started, but became interactive later, from being punished forever. Whenever a carriage return was typed at a terminal, the process belonging to that terminal was moved to the highest priority class, on the assumption that it was about to become interactive. One fine day some user with a heavily CPU-bound process discovered that just sitting at the terminal and typing carriage returns at random every few seconds did wonders for his response time. He told all his friends. Moral of the story: getting it right in practice is much harder than getting it right in principle.

Many other algorithms have been used for assigning processes to priority classes. For example, the influential XDS 940 system (Lampson, 1968), built at Berkeley, had four priority classes, called terminal, I/O, short quantum, and long quantum. When a process that was waiting for terminal input was finally awakened, it went into the highest priority class (terminal). When a process waiting for a disk block became ready, it went into the second class. When a process was still running when its quantum ran out, it was initially placed in the third class. However, if a process used up its quantum too many times in a row without blocking for terminal or other I/O, it was moved down to the bottom queue. Many other systems use something similar to favor interactive users.

2.4.4. Shortest Job First

Most of the above algorithms were designed for interactive systems. Now let us look at one that is especially appropriate for batch jobs for which the run times are known in advance. In an insurance company, for example, people can predict quite accurately how long it will take to run a batch of 1000 claims, since similar work is done every day. When several equally important jobs are sitting in the input queue waiting to be started, the scheduler should use **shortest job next**. Look at Fig. 2-24. Here we find four jobs A, B, C, and D, with run times of 8, 4, 4, and 4 minutes, respectively. By running them in that order, the turnaround time for A is 8 minutes, for B is 12 minutes, for C is 16 minutes, and for D is 20 minutes, for an average of 14 minutes.

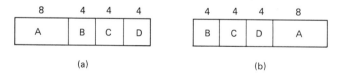

(a)   (b)

Fig. 2-24. An example of shortest job first scheduling.

Now let us consider running these four jobs using shortest job first, as shown in Fig. 2-24(b). The turnaround times are now 4, 8, 12, and 20 minutes, for an average of 11 minutes. Shortest job first is provably optimal. Consider the case of four jobs, with run times of a, b, c, and d, respectively. The first job finishes at time a, the second finishes at time $a + b$, and so on. The average run time is $(4a + 3b + 2c + d)/4$. It is clear that a contributes more to the average than the other times, so it should be the shortest job, with b next, then c and finally d as the longest as it affects only its own turnaround time. The same argument applies equally well to any number of jobs.

Because shortest job first always produces the minimum average response time, it would be nice if it could be used for interactive processes as well. To a certain extent, it can be. Interactive processes generally follow the pattern of wait for command, execute command, wait for command, execute command, and so on. If we regard the execution of each command as a separate "job," then we could minimize overall response time by running the shortest one first. The only problem is figuring out which of the currently runnable processes is the shortest one.

One approach is to make estimates based on past behavior and run the process with the shortest estimated running time. Suppose the estimated time per command for some terminal is T_0. Now suppose its next run is measured to be T_1. We could update our estimate by taking a weighted sum of these two numbers, that is, $aT_0 + (1 - a)T_1$. Through the choice of a we can decide to have the estimation process forget old runs quickly, or remember them for a long time. With $a = 1/2$, we get successive estimates of:

$$T_0, \quad T_0/2 + T_1/2, \quad T_0/4 + T_1/4 + T_2/2, \quad T_0/8 + T_1/8 + T_2/4 + T_3/2$$

Thus, after three new runs, the weight of T_0 in the new estimate has dropped to 1/8.

The technique of estimating the next value in a series by taking the weighted average of current measured value and the previous estimate is sometimes called **aging**. It is applicable to many situations where a prediction must be made based on previous values. Aging is especially easy to implement when $a = 1/2$. All that is needed is to add the new value to the current estimate and divide the sum by 2 (by shifting it right 1 bit).

It is worth pointing out that shortest job first is only optimal when all the jobs are available simultaneously. As a counterexample, consider five jobs, A through E, with run times of 2, 4, 1, 1, and 1, respectively. Their arrival times are 0, 0, 3, 3, and 3.

Initially, only A or B can be chosen, since the other three jobs have not arrived yet. Using shortest job first we will run the jobs in the order A, B, C, D, E, for an average wait of 4.6. However, running them in the order B, C, D, E, A has an average wait of 4.4.

2.4.5. Policy-Driven Scheduling

A completely different approach to scheduling is to make real promises to the user about performance and then live up to them. One promise that is realistic to make and easy to live up to is this: If there are n users logged in while you are working, you will receive about $1/n$ of the CPU power.

To make good on this promise, the system must keep track of how much

CPU time a user has had for all his processes since login, and also how long each user has been logged in. It then computes the amount of CPU each user is entitled to, namely the time since login divided by n. Since the amount of CPU time each user has actually had is also known, it is straightforward to compute the ratio of actual CPU had to CPU time entitled. A ratio of 0.5 means that a process has only had half of what it should have had, and a ratio of 2.0 means that a process has had twice as much as it was entitled to. The algorithm is then to run the process with the lowest ratio until its ratio has moved above its closest competitor.

A similar idea can be applied to real-time systems, in which there are absolute deadlines that must be met. Here one looks for the process in greatest danger of missing its deadline, and runs it first. A process that must finish in 10 seconds gets priority over one that must finish in 10 minutes.

2.4.6. Two-level Scheduling

Up until now we have more or less assumed that all runnable processes are in main memory. If insufficient main memory is available, some of the runnable processes will have to be kept on the disk. This situation has major implications for scheduling, since the process switching time to bring in and run a process from disk is one or two orders of magnitude more than switching to a process already in main memory.

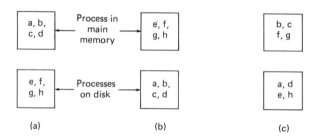

Fig. 2-25. A two-level scheduler must move processes between disk and memory, and also choose processes to run from among those in memory. Three different instants of time are represented by (a), (b), and (c) .

A more practical way of dealing with swapped out processes is to use a two-level scheduler. Some subset of the runnable processes is first loaded into main memory, as shown in Fig. 2-25(a). The scheduler then restricts itself to only choosing processes from this subset for a while. Periodically, a higher-level scheduler is invoked to remove processes that have been in memory long enough and to load processes that have been on disk too long. Once the change has been made, as in Fig. 2-25(b), the lower-level scheduler again restricts itself to only running processes that are actually in memory. Thus, the lower-level scheduler is concerned with making a choice among the runnable processes that are in memory at that moment, while the higher-level scheduler is concerned with shuttling processes back and forth between memory and disk.

Among the criteria that the higher-level scheduler could use to make its decisions are:

1. How long has it been since the process was swapped in or out?

2. How much CPU time has the process had recently?

3. How big is the process? (Small ones do not get in the way).

4. How high is the priority of the process?

Again here we could use round robin, priority scheduling, or various other methods.

2.5. OVERVIEW OF PROCESSES IN MINIX

Having completed our study of the principles of process management and interprocess communication, we can now take a look at how they are applied in MINIX. Unlike UNIX, whose kernel is a monolithic program not split up into modules, MINIX itself is a collection of processes that communicate with each other and with user processes using a single interprocess communication primitive—message passing. This design gives a more modular and flexible structure, making it easy, for example, to replace the entire file system by a completely different one.

2.5.1. The Internal Structure of MINIX

Let us begin our study of MINIX by taking a bird's-eye view of the system. MINIX is structured in four layers, with each layer performing a well-defined function. The four layers are illustrated in Fig. 2-26.

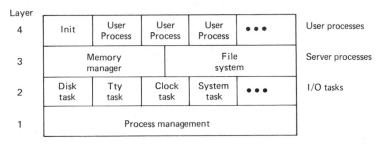

Fig. 2-26. MINIX is structured in four layers.

The bottom layer catches all interrupts and traps, and provides higher layers with a model of independent sequential processes that communicate using messages. The code in this layer has two major activities. The first is catching the traps and interrupts, saving and restoring registers, and the general nuts and bolts of actually making the process abstraction provided to the higher layers work. The second is handling the mechanics of messages; checking for legal destinations, locating send and receive buffers in physical memory, and copying bytes from sender to receiver. That part of the layer dealing with the lowest level of interrupt handling is written in assembly language. The rest of the layer and all of the higher layers, are written in C.

Layer 2 contains the I/O processes, one per device type. To distinguish them from ordinary user processes, we will call them **tasks**, but the differences between tasks and processes are minimal. In many systems the I/O tasks are called **device drivers**; we will use the terms "task" and "device driver" interchangeably. A task is needed for each device type, including disk, printer, terminal, and clock. If other I/O devices are present, a task is needed for each one of those too. One task, the system task, is a little different, since it does not correspond to any I/O device. We will discuss the tasks in the next chapter.

All the tasks in layer 2 and all the code in layer 1 are linked together into a single binary program called the **kernel**. On a machine with kernel mode and user mode, the kernel would run in kernel mode. Despite being linked together in the same object program, the tasks in layer 2 are all completely independent from one another, are scheduled independently, and communicate using messages. They are linked together into a single binary to make it easier to port MINIX to machines with two modes where only the kernel is allowed to do I/O.

Layer 3 contains two processes that provide useful services to the user processes. The **memory manager** (MM) carries out all the MINIX system calls that involve memory management, such as FORK, EXEC, and BRK. The **file system** (FS) carries out all the file system calls, such as READ, MOUNT, and CHDIR. As we noted at the start of Chap. 1, operating systems do two things: manage resources and provide an extended machine by implementing system calls. In MINIX the resource management is largely in the kernel (layers 1 and 2), and system call interpretation is in layer 3. The file system has been designed as a file "server" and can be moved to a remote machine with almost no changes. This also holds for the memory manager, although remote memory servers are not as useful as remote file servers.

Finally, layer 4 contains all the user processes—shells, editors, compilers, and user-written *a.out* programs.

2.5.2. Process Management in MINIX

Processes in MINIX follow the general process model given in this chapter. Processes can create subprocesses, which in turn can create more subprocesses, yielding a tree of processes. In fact, all the user processes in the whole system are part of a single tree with *init* (see Fig. 2-26) at the root.

To see how this situation comes about, we have to take a look at how MINIX is booted from floppy disk. When the computer is turned on, the hardware reads the first sector of the first track into memory and jumps to it. This sector contains a **bootstrap** program that loads the entire operating system (and the file system checker) into memory and starts it running. After the kernel, memory manager and file system have run and initialized themselves, control is passed to *init*.

Init starts out by reading the file */etc/ttys*, to see how many terminals are currently installed (in the standard distribution, just the console). It then forks off a child process for each terminal. Each of these children executes */bin/login* to wait until someone logs in.

After a successful login, */bin/login* executes the user's shell (specified in */etc/passwd*, normally */bin/sh*). The shell waits for commands to be typed and then forks off a new process for each command. In this way, the shells are the children of *init*, the user processes are the grandchildren, and all the processes in the system are part of a single tree.

The two principal system calls in MINIX for process management are FORK and EXEC. FORK, as we have seen, is the only way to create a new process. EXEC allows a process to execute a specified program. When a program is executed, it is allocated a portion of memory whose size is specified in the program file's header. It retains this memory allocation throughout its execution, although the distribution among data segment, stack segment, and unused can vary as the process runs.

All the information about a process is kept in the process table, which is divided up among the kernel, memory manager, and file system, with each one having those fields that it needs. When a new process comes into existence, by FORK, or an old process terminates, by EXIT or a signal, the memory manager first updates its part of the process table and then sends messages to the file system and kernel telling them to do likewise.

2.5.3. Interprocess Communication in MINIX

Interprocess communication within MINIX itself is by exchanging fixed-size messages. The size of the messages is determined by the size of a structure called *message*. On the 8088 it is 24 bytes, but if MINIX were moved to a CPU with 4-byte integers, the struct would become larger. Three primitives are provided for sending and receiving messages. They are called by the C library procedures

```
send(dest, &message);
```

to send a message to process *dest*,

```
receive(source, &message);
```

to receive a message from process *source* (or *ANY*), and

```
send_rec(src_dst, &message);
```

to send a message and wait for a reply from the same process. The reply overwrites the original message. Each process or task can send and receive messages from processes and tasks in its own layer, and from those in the layer directly below it. User processes may not communicate directly with the I/O tasks. The system enforces this restriction.

When a process (which also includes the tasks as a special case) sends a message to a process that is not currently waiting for a message, the sender blocks until the destination does a RECEIVE. In other words, MINIX uses the rendezvous method to avoid the problems of buffering sent, but not yet received, messages. Although less flexible than a scheme with buffering, it turns out to be adequate for this system, and much simpler because no buffer management is needed.

2.5.4. Process Scheduling in MINIX

The MINIX scheduler uses a multilevel queueing system with three levels, corresponding to layers 2, 3, and 4 in Fig. 2-26. Within each level, round robin is used. Tasks have the highest priority, the memory manager and file server are next, and user processes are last.

When picking a process to run, the scheduler checks to see if any tasks are ready. If one or more are ready, the one at the head of the queue is run. If no tasks are ready, a server (MM or FS) is chosen, if possible, otherwise a user is run. If no process is ready, the system sits in an idle loop waiting for the next interrupt.

At each clock tick, a check is made to see if the current process is a user process that has run more than 100 msec. If it is, the scheduler is called to see if another user process is waiting for the CPU. If one is found, the current process is moved to the end of its scheduling queue, and the process now at the head is run. Tasks, the memory manager, and the file system are never preempted, no matter how long they have been running.

2.6. IMPLEMENTATION OF PROCESSES IN MINIX

We are now moving closer to looking at the actual code, so a few words about the notation we will use to describe it are in order. The terms "procedure," "function," and "routine" will be used interchangeably. Variable names will be written in italics, as in *rw_flag*. When a variable or procedure name starts a sentence it will be capitalized, but the actual names all begin with lower case letters. System calls will be in small caps, for example, READ.

The book and the software, both of which are continuously evolving, did not "go to press" on the same day, so there may be minor discrepancies between the references to the code, the listing, and the disk or tape version. Such differences generally only affect a line or two, however.

2.6.1. Organization of the MINIX Source Code

Logically, the source code is organized as a single directory, *minix*, containing a few files and ten subdirectories:

1. *h* - header files used by the operating system

2. *kernel* - layers 1 and 2 (processes, messages, drivers)

3. *mm* - the code for the memory manager

4. *fs* - the code for the file system

5. *lib* - the library procedures (e.g., *open*, *read*)

6. *tools* - a collection of special programs needed to build MINIX

7. *commands* - the utility programs (e.g., *cat*, *cp*, *date*, *ls*, *pwd*)

8. *include* - header files used by the commands

9. *test* - programs to give MINIX a thorough testing

10. *doc* - documentation and manuals

The code for layers 1 and 2 is contained in the directory *kernel*. In this chapter we will study two key files, *mpx88.s* and *proc.c*, which handle the process management and message passing, respectively. In Chap. 3 we will look at the rest of the files in this directory, which are structured with one file per task. In this way, all the data and code for each I/O device are together in one place. In Chap. 4 we will look at the memory manager. In Chap. 5 we will study the file system.

When MINIX is compiled, all the source code files in *kernel*, *mm*, and *fs* are compiled to object files. Then all the object files in *kernel* are linked together to form a single executable program, *kernel*. The object files in *mm* are also linked together to form a single executable program, *mm*. The same holds for *fs*. A fourth executable program, *init*, is built in *tools*. The program *build* (also in *tools*) strips these four programs of their headers, pads each one out so that each is a multiple of 16 bytes, and concatenates them onto a new file. This new file is the binary of the operating system that is copied onto the boot diskette, and later loaded into memory and executed. Fig. 2-27 shows what memory looks like after the four concatenated programs are loaded into it.

It is important to realize that MINIX consists of four totally independent programs that communicate only by passing messages. A procedure called *panic* in *fs* does not conflict with a procedure called *panic* in *mm* because they ultimately are linked into different executable files. The only procedures that the four pieces of the operating system have in common are a few of the library routines

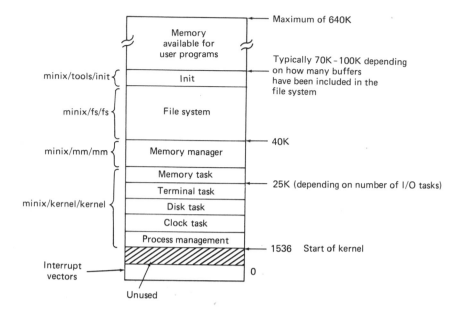

Fig. 2-27. Memory layout after MINIX has been loaded from the disk into memory. The four independently compiled and linked parts are clearly distinct. The sizes are approximate, depending on the configuration.

in *lib*. This modular structure makes it very easy to modify, say, the file system, without having these changes affect the memory manager. It also makes it straightforward to remove the file system altogether, and put it on a different machine as a remote file server, communicating with the user machines by sending messages over a network.

As an aside, throughout this book we will be referring frequently to specific procedures in the code. As an aid to finding procedures quickly, a cross reference listing of procedure names and macros is provided in Appendix F. We suggest that you color the edge of the first page of the appendix with a felt-tipped marking pen, so that it can be located quickly when the book is closed.

2.6.2. The Common Header Files

The directory *h* contains a collection of files defining constants, types, and macros used in more than one of the four pieces of MINIX. Let us take a brief look at these files, starting with *const.h* (line 0000). In this file we find a variety of constant definitions. Definitions that are used only in the kernel are included in the file *kernel/const.h*. Definitions that are used only in the file system are included in the file *fs/const.h*. The memory manager also has a file *mm/const.h* for its local definitions. Those definitions that are used in more than one of the directories are included in *h/const.h*.

A few of the definitions in *const.h* are especially noteworthy. *EXTERN* is defined as a macro expanding into *extern*. All global variables that are declared in header files and included in two or more files are declared *EXTERN*, as in

```
EXTERN int who;
```

If the variable were declared just as

```
int who;
```

and included in two or more files, some linkers would complain about a multiply defined variable. Furthermore, the C reference manual (Kernighan and Ritchie, 1978) explicitly forbids this construction.

To avoid this problem, it is necessary to have the declaration read

```
extern int who;
```

in all places but one. Using *EXTERN* prevents this problem by having it expand into *extern* everywhere except in the file *table.c* where it is redefined as the null string on lines 5129 and 5130. When the header files are included and expanded as part of the compilation of *table.c*, *extern* is not inserted anywhere (because *EXTERN* is now defined as the null string). Thus, storage for the global variables is actually reserved only in one place, in the object file *table.o*. The same trick is used in the file system and memory manager.

The file *table.c* is also used for the declaration of the array *task*, which contains the mapping between task numbers and the associated procedures. It has been put here because the trick used above to prevent multiple declarations does not work with variables that are initialized; that is, you may not say

```
extern int x = 3;
```

anywhere.

If you are new to C programming and do not quite understand what is going on here, fear not; the details are really not important. C allows something, include files, that almost no other language allows. This feature can cause problems for some linkers because it can lead to multiple declarations for included variables. The *EXTERN* business is simply a way to make MINIX more portable so it can be linked on machines whose linkers will not accept multiply defined variables.

PRIVATE is defined as a synonym for static. Procedures and data that are not referenced outside the file in which they are declared are always declared as *PRIVATE* to prevent their names from being visible outside the file in which they are declared. As a general rule, all variables and procedures should be declared with as local a scope as possible. *PUBLIC* is defined as the null string. Thus, the declaration

```
PUBLIC free_zone()
```

comes out of the C preprocessor as

```
free_zone()
```

which, according to the C scope rules, means that the name *free_zone* is exported from the file and can be used in other files. *PRIVATE* and *PUBLIC* are not necessary, but are attempts to undo the damage caused by the C scope rules (default is that names are exported outside the file; it should be just the reverse). The rest of *const.h* defines numerical constants used throughout the system.

Now let us examine the file *callnr.h* (line 0100). Processes execute the MINIX system calls by sending messages to the memory manager (MM for short) or the file system (FS for short). Each message contains the number of the system call desired. These numbers are defined in *callnr.h*.

The file *com.h* (line 0150) mostly contains common definitions used in messages from MM and FS to the I/O tasks. The task numbers are also defined. To distinguish them from process numbers, task numbers are negative. The header file also defines the message types (function codes) that can be sent to each task. For example, the clock task accepts codes *SET_ALARM* (to set a timer), *CLOCK_TICK* (when a clock interrupt has occurred), *GET_TIME* (request for the real time), and *SET_TIME* (to set the current time of day). The value *REAL_TIME* is the message type for the reply to the *GET_TIME* request.

The next file is *error.h* (line 0250). It contains the error messages that are returned to user programs in *errno* when a system call fails, as well as some internal errors, such as trying to send to a nonexistent task. They are negative to mark them as error codes. The values are made positive before being returned to user programs.

The file *sgtty.h* (line 0350) defines two structures used in the IOCTL system call, along with some constants also used in IOCTL.

The file *signal.h* (line 0400) defines the standard signal names. The file *stat.h* (line 0450) contains the structure returned by the STAT and FSTAT system calls. All three of *sgtty.h*, *signal.h*, and *stat.h* are used not only by the operating system itself, but also by some of the commands. They are duplicated in the directory *include*.

The last of the common header files is *type.h* (line 0500). It contains a number of key type definitions, along with related numerical values. It also contains the macros *MAX* and *MIN*, so we can say

```
z = MAX(x, y);
```

to assign the larger of x and y to z.

The most important definition in this file is *message* on lines 0554 to 0565. While we could have defined *message* to be an array of some number of bytes, it is better programming practice to have it be a structure containing union of the various message types that are possible. Six message formats, *mess_1* through *mess_6*, are defined. A message is a structure containing a field *m_source*, telling who sent the message, a field *m_type*, telling what the message type is (e.g., *GET_TIME* to the clock task) and the data fields. The six message types are shown in Fig. 2-28.

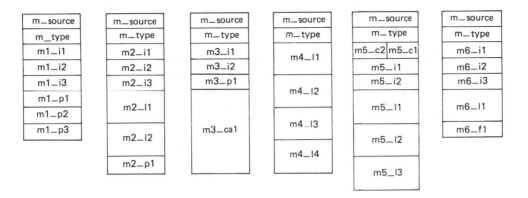

Fig. 2-28. The six messages types used in MINIX.

When it is necessary to send a message containing, say, three integers and three pointers (or three integers and two pointers), then the first format in Fig. 2-28 is the one to use. The same applies to the other formats. How does one assign a value to the first integer in the first format? Suppose the message is called *x*. Then *x.m_u* refers to the union portion of the message struct. To refer to the first of the six alternatives in the union, we use *x.m_u.m_m1*. Finally, to get at the first integer in this struct we say *x.m_u.m_m1.m1i1*. This is quite a mouthful, so somewhat shorter field names are defined as macros after the definition of *message* itself. Thus *x.m1_i1* can be used instead of *x.m_u.m_m1.m1i1*. The short names all have the form of the letter *m*, the format number, an underscore, one or two letters indicating whether the field is an integer, pointer, long, character, character array, or function, and a sequence number to distinguish multiple instances of the same type within a message.

2.6.3. Process Data Structures and Header Files

The ideas described above are straightforward, so let us dive in and see what the code looks like. Just as we have files *const.h* and *type.h* in the common header directory *minix/h*, we also have files *const.h* and *type.h* in *minix/kernel*. The file *const.h* (line 0650) contains a number of machine dependent values, that is, values that apply to the Intel 8088, but are likely to be different if MINIX is moved to a different machine. These values are enclosed between

```
#ifdef i8088
```

and

```
#endif
```

statements. (See lines 0652 to 0681).

When compiling MINIX the compiler is called with

```
cc -c -Di8088 file.c
```

to force the symbol i8088 to be defined, and the machine dependent code to be compiled. If MINIX is ported to, say, a Motorola 68000, the people doing the port will probably add sections of code bracketed by

```
#ifdef m68000
```

and

```
#endif
```

and call the compiler with

```
cc -c -Dm68000 file.c
```

to select out the 68000-dependent code. In this way, MINIX can deal with constants and code that are specific to one particular system. This construction does not especially enhance readability, so it should be used as little as possible.

A few of the definitions in *const.h* deserve special mention. The important interrupt vectors are defined here, as are some field values used for resetting the interrupt controller chip after each interrupt.

Each task within the kernel has its own stack, of size *TASK_STACK_BYTES*. While handling interrupts, a special stack of size *K_STACK_BYTES* is used.

The MINIX scheduler has *NQ* (3) priority queues, named *TASK_Q* (highest priority), *SERVER_Q* (middle priority), and *USER_Q* (lowest priority).

In the file *glo.h* (line 0700) we find the kernel's global variables. *Realtime* is the number of clock ticks since the system was booted. It is incremented 60 times a second by a crystal oscillator, independent of the line frequency. *Lost_ticks* is a counter that keeps track of how many clock ticks have been lost because the clock task was not waiting for a message when a clock interrupt occurred. The interrupt is just ignored and *lost_ticks* incremented so that the time of day can be corrected later.

Cur_proc is the number of the currently scheduled process. *Prev_proc* is the number of the previous process. It is needed for accounting purposes. *Sig_procs* counts the number of processes that have signals pending that have not yet been sent to the memory manager for processing.

When an interrupt occurs, a message is sent to the task associated with the interrupt. The message is built in the message buffer *int_mess*. Finally, we have the stacks. Each task has its own stack, in the array *t_stack*. During interrupt handling, the kernel uses a temporary stack, *k_stack*.

The final kernel header file, *proc.h* (line 0750), contains the process table. It contains storage for the process' registers, stack pointer, state, memory map, stack limit, process id, accounting, alarm time, and message information. When a process cannot complete a SEND because the destination is not waiting, the sender is put onto a queue pointed to by the destination's *p_callerq* field. That way, when the destination finally does a RECEIVE, it is easy to find all the processes wanting to send to it. The *p_sendlink* field is used to link the members of the queue together.

When a process does a RECEIVE and there is no message waiting for it, it blocks and the number of the process it wants to RECEIVE from is stored in *p_getfrom*. The address of the message buffer is stored in *p_messbuf*.

The last two fields are *p_nextready* and *p_pending*. The former is used to link processes together on the scheduler queues, and the latter is a bit map used to keep track of signals that have not yet been passed to the memory manager (because the memory manager is not waiting for a message).

The flag bits in *p_flags* define the state of each table entry. If any of the bits is set, the process cannot be run. If the slot is not in use, *P_SLOT_FREE* is set. After a FORK, *NO_MAP* is set to prevent the child process from running until its memory map has been set up. The other two flags indicate that the process is blocked trying to send or receive a message.

The macro *proc_addr* is provided because it is not possible to have negative subscripts in C. Logically, the array *proc* should go from $-NR\_TASKS$ to $+NR\_PROCS$. Unfortunately, it must start at 0, so *proc*[0] refers to the most negative task, and so forth. To make it easier to keep track of which slot goes with which process, we can write

```
rp = proc_addr(n);
```

to assign to *rp* the address of the process slot for process *n*, either positive or negative.

The variable *proc_ptr* points to the process table entry for the current process. When a system call or interrupt occurs, it tells where to store the registers and processor state. *Bill_ptr* points to the process being charged for the CPU. When a user process calls the file system, and the file system is running, *proc_ptr* will point to the file system process. However *bill_ptr* will point to the user making the call, since CPU time used by the file system is charged as system time to the caller.

The two arrays *rdy_head* and *rdy_tail* are used to maintain the scheduling queues. The first process on, say, the task queue is pointed to by *rdy_head[TASK_Q]*. Finally, *busy_map* and *task_mess* are used for handling interrupt messages to tasks that are busy when the message arrives and cannot accept them.

The file *type.h* (line 0800) contains only two type definitions, both machine dependent and both relating to interrupts. The struct *pc_psw* represents the three words, PSW (Program Status Word), CS (Code Segment register), and PC (Program Counter) pushed onto the stack by the interrupt hardware. The struct *sig_info* is the data structure pushed onto the stack of a user process when it catches a signal. It contains the same three words that the hardware pushes, and also the signal number.

2.6.4. System Initialization

Now it is time to start looking at the executable code. Let us begin at the beginning. When the PC is booted, the hardware reads the first sector of the floppy disk in drive 0 into memory and executes it. This **bootstrap** program loads the operating system and jumps to it. The operating system begins at the label *MINIX* in assembly code, sets up a few registers, and then calls *main* on line 0880 in *main.c*.

Main is responsible for initializing the system and then starting it up. It initializes the process table so that when the first tasks and processes are scheduled, their memory maps and registers will be set correctly. Part of the information for initialization comes from the array *sizes*, which contains the text and data sizes in clicks (a click is 16 bytes) for the kernel, memory manager, file system, and *init*. This information is patched into the system binary by a program called *build*, which concatenates the various system pieces to make the boot diskette. The first two elements of *sizes* are the kernel's text and data sizes; the next two are the memory manager's, and so on. If any of the four programs does not use separate I and D space, the text size is 0 and the text and data are lumped together as data.

Main also saves all the interrupt vectors, so if CRTL-ALT-DEL is ever typed, it will be possible to reboot the system with the vectors restored to their original situation.

The interrupt vectors are then changed to point to the MINIX interrupt handling routines. The vectors that are not used by MINIX are set to invoke the procedures *unexpected_int* (vectors below 16) or *trap* (vectors at or above 16). The unused vectors are sometimes trapped to by accident. The handling routines just print a message and then continue.

Part of the initialization done by *main* consists of calling *ready* (line 0915) to put all the tasks, the memory manager, and the file system onto their respective scheduling queues. When *main* exits, the task queued first (the one using slot 0 of the process table, i.e., the one with the most negative number) is run until it blocks trying to receive a message. Then the next task is run until it, too, blocks trying to receive a message. Eventually all the tasks are blocked, so the memory manager and file system can run, and also block. Finally *init* runs to fork off a login process for each terminal. These processes block until input is typed at some terminal, at which point the first user can log in and get the show on the road.

The procedure *panic* (line 1012) in the file *main.c* is called when the system has discovered a condition that makes it impossible to continue. Typical panic conditions are a critical disk block being unreadable, an inconsistent internal state being detected, or one part of the system calling another part with invalid parameters.

The last procedure in *main.c* is *set_vec* (line 1036). It takes care of the mechanics of setting interrupt vectors.

2.6.5. Interrupt Handling in MINIX

Running processes may be interrupted by clock interrupts, disk interrupts, terminal interrupts, or other interrupts. It is the job of the lowest layer of MINIX to hide these interrupts by turning them into messages. As far as the processes are concerned, when an I/O device completes an operation, it sends a message to some process, waking it up and making it runnable. Only a tiny part of the MINIX kernel actually sees hardware interrupts.

That code is in the file *mpx88.s*. Typical interrupt procedures are *tty_int* (line 1187), *lpr_int* (line 1196), *disk_int* (line 1203), and *clock_int* (line 1217). (The leading underscores present in the assembly code are due to the convention that all variable and procedure names generated by the C compiler begin with an underscore so that library procedures in assembly language not starting with an underscore will never conflict with user-chosen names.)

These procedures are structurally similar. Each begins by calling *save* to store all the registers (including the segment registers) in the process table slot belonging to the currently running process. The variable *proc_ptr* makes this slot easy to find. The actual code of *save* is a bit tricky because all the segment registers except CS have unknown values when the procedure starts. When it is finished, they all have been set to point to the start of the kernel.

Disk_int and *clock_int* build a message and call *interrupt* in file *proc.c* to take care of sending the message and calling the scheduler. Keyboard interrupts require more processing before *interrupt* is called, so *tty_int* calls a C procedure *keyboard* to do the initial processing and then call *interrupt* if necessary. Keyboard interrupts are generated both when a key is struck and when it is released. The processing needed when most keys are released is so simple that *keyboard* can do it directly, without the overhead of switching to the terminal task.

For clock interrupts, disk interrupts, and some keyboard and line printer interrupts, the next step in the interrupt processing is the procedure *interrupt* on line 1878. This procedure has two parameters passed to it by the assembly code: the task to send to and a pointer to the message. It starts off by reenabling the interrupt controller chip. This chip must be explicitly reenabled to allow subsequent interrupts after the interrupt processing is finished. Any interrupts that occur before processing is finished are kept pending by the interrupt controller chip. They are not lost.

After taking care of the interrupt controller, *interrupt* calls *mini_send* to actually send the message. If the send is successful (i.e., the task was waiting for a message), the corresponding bit in *busy_map* is turned off. If the send is unsuccessful, the corresponding bit in *busy_map* is turned on, to indicate that a message to that task is pending. The pointer to the message is stored in *task_mess*.

Either way, a check is now made (line 1909) to see if any tasks with pending messages are now ready to accept their messages. For example, if two keyboard interrupts happen in rapid succession, on the second one the terminal task may not yet be done with the first one, so a bit is set in *busy_map*. If the next interrupt is for the clock or disk, a check will be made to see if the terminal task is now ready to accept a message. If it is, the message is sent on line 1914.

This code is needed because the message system does not provide any buffering: you cannot send a message to someone unless he is waiting for it (rendezvous principle). For normal processes, the unsuccessful sender is just suspended for a while. With interrupts this strategy is impossible. In effect, the use of *busy_map* and *task_mess* forms a limited kind of buffering to avoid losing messages. For most devices, such as disks, it is technically impossible for the device to generate a second interrupt until the task has run and issued another command. For the clock, lost interrupts do not matter because they are counted on line 1897 and are compensated for later. Only the keyboard can give multiple unexpected interrupts, but the characters typed are recorded in a buffer before *interrupt* is called. The same message pointer is used for each keyboard interrupt, so lost keyboard interrupts do not result in lost characters. When the terminal task is finally called, it gets a message containing a pointer to the buffer where *keyboard* has safely stored all the characters.

When the message processing has been finished, a check is made on line 1921 to see if a higher priority process is now runnable. If so, *pick_proc* is called to schedule that process. Either way, when *interrupt* returns to its assembly code caller, *cur_proc* and *proc_ptr* will be set up for the process to be run.

The assembly language interrupt procedures all call *restart* to reload the current process' registers and start it running.

We make no claim that interrupt processing is easy to fully understand. It requires a little study. In fact, the whole concept of the process abstraction was invented precisely to hide all the messy details of interrupt handling in a very thin layer at the bottom of the system.

Now a quick word or two about *s_call* (line 1173). When a process wants to send or receive a message, it calls a little assembly language library procedure to put the source or destination number in AX, the message pointer in BX, and the SEND or RECEIVE code in CX, followed by a trap instruction. The trap is treated by the hardware the same as an interrupt, and is vectored to *s_call*. This procedure calls *save* and builds a message, just as the interrupt procedures do.

Instead of calling *interrupt*, *s_call* calls *sys_call* to do the work, starting by checking for invalid parameters, illegal calls and destinations, and so on. If everything is all right, it does the send on line 1957 or the receive on line 1963. If the operation can be done immediately, the status code *OK* is returned in *RET_REG* (AX) and control is returned to the assembly code to restart the caller. If the operation cannot complete, the process is blocked in *mini_send* or *mini_rec* and a new process is designated as the next one to run. When control passes back to the assembly code, the new process will be started. If no process is now runnable, the idle routine (line 1319) runs.

It is important to realize that the value of *cur_proc* may be different on exit from *sys_call* from what it was on entry. The same is true for *interrupt*. After *save* has run in the assembly code, all of the current process' state has been safely stored away, so *cur_proc* can be changed with no ill effects. In essence, after a trap or interrupt, the current process is stopped, and the operating system itself is run with its own stack. When the operating system is finished, it does not matter whether the next process is the same one as the previous one. The work to be done is identical: load the registers and start it off.

Study *mpx88.s* carefully. It is important. The only other comments we will make here concern *surprise* and *trp*. Programs can (but should not) execute the INT instruction to cause any interrupt. These are caught by *surprise* or *trp*, depending on the number of the vector.

2.6.6. The Kernel's Assembly Code Utilities

While we are on the subject of assembly code routines, let us briefly look at the file *klib88.s*. This file contains about a dozen utility routines that are in assembly code, either for efficiency or because they cannot be written in C at all. The first one is *phys_copy* (line 1387). It is called in C by

```
phys_copy(source_address, destination_address, bytes);
```

and copies a block of data from anywhere in physical memory to anywhere else. Both addresses are absolute, that is, address 0 really means the first interrupt vector, and all three parameters are longs.

Although *phys_copy* could have been used for copying messages, a faster, specialized procedure has been provided for that purpose (line 1490). It is called by

```
cp_mess(source, src_clicks, src_offset, dest_clicks, dest_offset);
```

where *source* is the sender's process number, which is copied into the *m_source* field of the receiver's buffer. Both the source and destination addresses are specified by giving a click number, typically the base of the segment containing the buffer, and an offset from that click. (A click is a multiple of 16 bytes on the IBM PC. Clicks are important because the PC hardware requires all segments to begin at a click.) This form of specifying the source and destination is more efficient than the 32-bit addresses used by *phys_copy*.

Values are output to I/O ports in C using the assembly language procedure *port_out* (line 1529). For example,

```
port_out(0x3F2, 0x1C);
```

writes the byte 0x1C to port 0x3F2 to set floppy disk motors on and off. Values are read from I/O ports by the analogous procedure, *port_in* (line 1547). The call

```
port_in(0x60, &code);
```

for example, reads the number of the key just struck on the keyboard and stores it in the variable *code*.

Occasionally it is necessary for a task to disable interrupts temporarily. It does this by calling *lock* (line 1567). When interrupts can be reenabled, the task can call either *unlock* (line 1578) to enable interrupts or *restore* (line 1587) to put them back the way they were before *lock* was called.

Build_sig (line 1612) is a highly specialized procedure that is used only to simulate an interrupt when sending a process a signal.

The next two procedures, *csv* (line 1638) and *cret* (line 1660), are highly compiler dependent and may have to be modified when any compiler other than the PC-IX compiler is used. Some compilers do not use them at all. When a procedure compiled by the PC-IX compiler (and many other compilers) starts running, the first thing it does is put the number of bytes of local variables in AX. Then it calls *csv* to save BP, SI, DI, and advance the stack by the number of bytes of locals. While doing this work, *csv* also checks to see if the stack has grown beyond the memory allocated for it. When a procedure wants to return, it calls *cret* to reset the stack pointer and restore the registers. The *csv* and *cret* routines provided in the compiler's library cannot be used because they check for stack overflow and make non-MINIX system calls to report them. The purpose of rewriting them is to get rid of the calls to *printf*.

The last two assembly code procedures shown are *get_chrome* (line 1673) and *vid_copy* (line 1701). The former makes a BIOS call to see whether the console screen is monochrome or color. It matters because they are programmed slightly differently. It returns 1 for color, 0 for monochrome. *Vid_copy* takes care of the actual mechanics of displaying text on the console. We will see how it is used in the next chapter. MINIX.

2.6.7. Interprocess Communication in MINIX

Processes (including tasks) in MINIX communicate by messages using the rendezvous principle. When a process does a SEND, the lowest layer of the kernel checks to see if the destination is waiting for a message from the sender (or from *ANY* sender). If so, the message is copied from the sender's buffer to the receiver's buffer, and both processes are marked as runnable. If the destination is not waiting for a message from the sender, the sender is marked as blocked and put onto a queue of processes waiting to send to the receiver.

When a process does a RECEIVE, the kernel checks to see if any process is queued trying to send to it. If so, the message is copied from the blocked sender to the receiver, and both are marked as runnable. If no process is queued trying to send to it, the receiver blocks until a message arrives.

The implementation of SEND and RECEIVE, as well as SENDREC, which is just a SEND to some process followed immediately by a RECEIVE from the same process, is handled in the file *proc.c*. Let us start with the implementation of SEND, which is done by *mini_send* (line 1971). It has three parameters: the caller, the process to be sent to, and a pointer to the buffer where the message is. It starts out by making sure that user processes cannot send messages to tasks. The parameter *caller,* supplied by the assembly code routine via *interrupt* or *sys_call,* is greater than or equal to *LOW_USER* if the caller is a user. For a hardware interrupt it is *HARDWARE* (-1). For a task it is less than -1.

After checking the destination address, *mini_send* checks to see if the message falls entirely within the user's data segment. If not, an error code is returned.

The key test in *mini_send* is on lines 2001 and 2002. Here a check is made to see if the destination is blocked on a RECEIVE, as shown by the *RECEIVING* bit in the *p_flags* field of its process table entry. If it is waiting, then the next question is: "Who is it waiting for?" If it is waiting for the sender, or for *ANY,* the code on lines 2004 to 2007 is executed to copy the message and ready the receiver (put it on the scheduling queues as runnable).

If, on the other hand, the receiver is not blocked, or is blocked but waiting for a message from someone else, the code on lines 2010 to 2023 is executed to block and queue the sender (except for sends done by interrupts). All processes wanting to send to a given destination are strung together on a linked list, with the destination's *p_callerq* field pointing to the process table entry of the process at the head of the queue. The example of Fig. 2-29(a) shows what happens when process 3 is unable to send to process 0. If process 4 is subsequently also unable to send to process 0, we get the situation of Fig. 2-29(b).

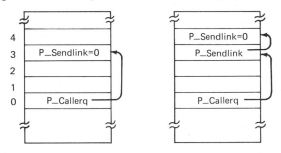

Fig. 2-29. Queueing of processes trying to send to process 0.

The RECEIVE call is carried out by *mini_rec.* The loop on line 2051 searches through all the processes queued waiting to send to the receiver to see if any are acceptable. If one is found, the message is copied from sender to receiver, then the sender is unblocked, made ready to run, and removed from the queue of processes trying to send to the receiver.

If no suitable sender is found, the source and buffer address are saved in its process table entry, and the receiver is marked as blocked on a RECEIVE call. The call to *unready* on line 2073 removes the receiver from the scheduler's queue of runnable processes.

The statement on line 2078 has to do with how kernel-generated signals (SIG-INT, SIGQUIT, and SIGALRM) are handled. When one of these occurs, a message is sent to the memory manager, if it is waiting for a message from *ANY.* If not, the signal is remembered in the kernel until the memory manager finally tries to receive from *ANY.* Then it is informed of pending signals.

2.6.8. Scheduling in MINIX

MINIX uses a multilevel scheduling algorithm that closely follows the structure shown in Fig. 2-26. In that figure we see I/O tasks in layer 2, server processes in layer 3, and user processes in layer 4. The scheduler maintains three queues of runnable processes, one for each layer, as shown in Fig. 2-30. The array *rdy_head* has one entry for each queue, with that entry pointing to the process at the head of the queue. Similarly, *rdy_tail* is an array whose entries point to the last process on each queue.

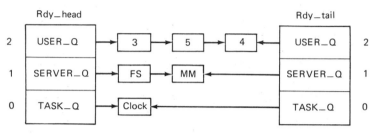

Fig. 2-30. The scheduler maintains three queues, one per priority level.

Whenever a blocked process is awakened, it is put on the end of its queue. The array *rdy_tail* makes adding a process at the end of a queue efficient. Whenever a running process becomes blocked, or a runnable process is killed by a signal, that process is removed from the scheduler's queues. Only runnable processes are queued.

Given the queue structures just described, the scheduling algorithm is simple: find the highest priority queue that is not empty and pick the process at the head of that queue. If all the queues are empty, the idle routine is run. In Fig. 2-30 *TASK_Q* has the highest priority. The queue is chosen in *pick_proc*, on lines 2092 to 2094. The process chosen to run next is not removed from its queue merely because it has been selected.

The procedures *ready* (line 2122) and *unready* (line 2153) are called to enter a runnable process on its queue and remove a no-longer runnable process from its queue, respectively. Any change to the queues that might affect the choice of which process to run next requires *pick_proc* to be called to set *cur_proc* again. Whenever the current process blocks on a SEND or a RECEIVE, *pick_proc* is called to reschedule the CPU. Also, after every interrupt, a check is made on line 1921 to see if a newly awakened task should now be scheduled. If a task was running at the time of the interrupt, then it continues to run after the interrupt processing is finished. All tasks are of equal priority, so the new one does not get preference over the old one.

Although most scheduling decisions are made when a process blocks or unblocks, there is one other situation in which scheduling is also done. When the clock task notices that the current user process has exceeded its quantum, it calls *sched* (line 2186) to move the process at the head of *USER_Q* to the end of that queue. This algorithm results in running the user processes in a straight round-robin fashion. The file system, memory manager, and I/O tasks are never put on the end of their queues because they have been running too long. They are trusted to work properly, and to block after having finished their work.

In summary, the scheduling algorithm maintains three priority queues, one for I/O tasks, one for the two server processes, and one for the user processes. The first process on the highest priority queue is always run next. If a user process uses up its quantum, it is put at the end of its queue, thus achieving a simple round-robin scheduling among the competing user processes.

2.7. SUMMARY

To hide the effects of interrupts, operating systems provide a conceptual model consisting of sequential processes running in parallel. Processes can communicate with each other using interprocess communication primitives, such as semaphores, monitors, or messages. These primitives are used to ensure that no two processes are ever in their critical sections at the same time. A process can be running, runnable, or blocked, and can change state when it or another process executes one of the interprocess communication primitives.

Interprocess communication primitives can be used to solve such problems as the producer-consumer, dining philosophers, and reader-writer problem. Even with these primitives, care has to be taken to avoid errors and deadlocks. Many scheduling algorithms are known, including round robin, priority scheduling, multilevel queues, and policy-driven schedulers.

MINIX supports the process concept, and provides messages for interprocess communication. Messages are not buffered, so a SEND succeeds only when the receiver is waiting for it. Similarly, a RECEIVE succeeds only when a message is already available. If either operation does not succeed, the caller is blocked.

When an interrupt occurs, the lowest level of the kernel creates and sends a message to the task associated with the interrupting device. The major steps needed to convert a disk interrupt to a message are listed below, with the numbers in parentheses telling where in the code it happens. (We assume the message succeeds and the disk task is scheduled to run next.)

1. The hardware jumps to the interrupt routine (line 1203).

2. The registers are saved in the process table (line 1249).

3. *Interrupt* is called to oversee sending the message (line 1878).

4. The actual copying is invoked in *mini_send* (line 2004).

5. The destination task is made runnable (line 2007).

6. The disk task is chosen to run next (lines 1921 and 1922).

7. The disk task's registers are loaded and it is started (line 1288).

The MINIX scheduling algorithm uses three priority queues, the highest one for tasks, the next one for the file system and memory manager, and the lowest one for user processes. User processes are run round robin for one quantum at a time. All the others are run until they block or are preempted by a higher priority process.

PROBLEMS

1. Suppose you were to design an advanced computer architecture that did process switching in hardware, instead of having interrupts. What information would the CPU need? Describe how the hardware process switching might work.

2. What is a race condition?

3. Does the busy waiting solution using the *turn* variable (Fig. 2-7) work when the two processes are running on two CPUs, sharing a common memory?

4. Consider a computer that does not have a TEST AND SET LOCK instruction, but does have an instruction to swap the contents of a register and a memory word in a single indivisible action. Can that be used to write a routine *enter_region* such as the one found in Fig. 2-9?

5. Give a sketch of how an operating system that can disable interrupts could implement semaphores.

6. Show how counting semaphores (i.e., semaphores that can hold an arbitrarily large value) can be implemented using only binary semaphores and ordinary machine instructions.

7. In Sec. 2.2.4, a situation with a high-priority process, H, and a low-priority process L was described, which led to H looping forever. Does the same problem occur if round robin scheduling is used instead of priority scheduling? Discuss.

8. Synchronization within monitors uses condition variables and two special operations, WAIT and SIGNAL. A more general form of synchronization would be to have a single primitive, WAITUNTIL that had an arbitrary Boolean predicate as parameter. Thus, one could say, for example,

   WAITUNTIL $x < 0$ or $y + z < n$

   The SIGNAL primitive would no longer be needed. This scheme is clearly more general than that of Hoare or Brinch Hansen, but it is not used. Why not? (Hint: think about the implementation.)

9. A fast food restaurant has four kinds of employees: (1) order takers, who take customer's orders; (2) cooks, who prepare the food; (3) packaging specialists, who stuff the food into bags; and (4) cashiers, who give the bags to customers and take their money. Each employee can be regarded as a communicating sequential process. What form of interprocess communication do they use? Relate this model to processes in MINIX.

10. Suppose we have a message-passing system using mailboxes. When sending to a full mailbox or trying to receive from an empty one, a process does not block. Instead, it gets an error code back. The process responds to the error code by just trying again, over and over, until it succeeds. Does this scheme lead to race conditions?

11. The implementation of monitors using semaphores did not use an explicit linked list of blocked processes, whereas the implementation of semaphores using monitors did. Explain. (Hint: think about the differences between semaphores and condition variables.)

12. In the solution to the dining philosophers problem (Fig. 2-20), why is the state variable set to *HUNGRY* in the procedure *take_forks*?

13. Consider the procedure *put_forks* in Fig. 2-20. Suppose the variable *state[i]* was set to *THINKING after* the two calls to *test*, rather than *before*. How would this change affect the solution for the case of 3 philosophers? For 100 philosophers?

14. The readers and writers problem can be formulated in several ways with regard to which category of process can be started when. Carefully describe three different variations of the problem, each one favoring (or not favoring) some category of processes. For each variation, specify what happens when a reader or a writer becomes ready to access the data base, and what happens when a process is finished using the data base.

15. The CDC 6600 computers could handle up to 10 I/O processes simultaneously using an interesting form of round robin scheduling called **processor sharing**. A process switch occurred after each instruction, so instruction 1 came from process 1, instruction 2 came from process 2, etc. The process switching was done by special hardware, and the overhead was zero. If a process needed T sec to complete in the absence of competition, how much time would it need if processor sharing was used with n processes?

16. Round robin schedulers normally maintain a list of all runnable processes, with each process occurring exactly once in the list. What would happen if a process occurred twice in the list? Can you think of any reason for allowing this?

17. Measurements of a certain system have shown that the average process runs for a time T before blocking on I/O. A process switch requires a time S, which is effectively wasted (overhead). For round robin scheduling with quantum Q, give a formula for the CPU efficiency for each of the following.
    - (a) $Q = \infty$
    - (b) $Q > T$
    - (c) $S < Q < T$
    - (d) $Q = S$
    - (e) Q nearly 0

18. Five batch jobs A through E, arrive at a computer center at almost the same time. They have estimated running times of 10, 6, 2, 4, and 8 minutes. Their (externally determined) priorities are 3, 5, 2, 1, and 4, respectively, with 5 being the highest

priority. For each of the following scheduling algorithms, determine the mean process turnaround time. Ignore process switching overhead.

(a) Round robin.
(b) Priority scheduling.
(c) First-come, first served (run in order 10, 6, 2, 4, 8).
(d) Shortest job first.

For (a), assume that the system is multiprogrammed, and that each job gets its fair share of the CPU. For (b) through (d) assume that only one job at a time runs, until it finishes. All jobs are completely CPU bound.

19. A process running on CTSS needs 30 quanta to complete. How many times must it be swapped in, including the very first time (before it has run at all)?

20. Five jobs are waiting to be run. Their expected run times are 9, 6, 3, 5, and X. In what order should they be run to minimize average response time? (Your answer will depend on X.)

21. The aging algorithm with $a = 1/2$ is being used to predict run times. The previous four runs, from oldest to most recent are 40, 20, 40, and 15 msec. What is the prediction of the next time?

22. Explain why two-level scheduling is commonly used.

23. During execution, MINIX maintains a variable *proc_ptr* that points to the process table entry for the current process. Why?

24. MINIX does not buffer messages. Explain how this design decision causes problems with clock and keyboard interrupts.

25. When a message is sent to a sleeping process in MINIX, the procedure *ready* is called to put that process on the proper scheduling queue. This procedure starts out by disabling interrupts. Explain.

26. The MINIX procedure *mini_rec* contains a loop. Explain what it is for.

27. Assume that you have an operating system that provides semaphores. Implement a message system. Write the procedures for sending and receiving messages.

28. A student majoring in anthropology and minoring in computer science has embarked on a research project to see if African baboons can be taught about deadlocks. He locates a deep canyon and fastens a rope across it, so the baboons can cross hand-over-hand. Several baboons can cross at the same time, provided that they are all going in the same direction. If eastward moving and westward moving baboons ever get onto the rope at the same time, a deadlock will result (the baboons will get stuck in the middle) because it is impossible for one baboon to climb over another one while suspended over the canyon. If a baboon wants to cross the canyon, he must check to see that no other baboon is currently crossing in the opposite direction. Write a program using semaphores that avoids deadlock. Do not worry about a series of eastward moving baboons holding up the westward moving baboons indefinitely.

29. Repeat the previous problem, but now avoid starvation. When a baboon that wants to cross to the east arrives at the rope and finds baboons crossing to the west, he waits until the rope is empty, but no more westward moving baboons are allowed to start until at least one baboon has crossed the other way.

30. Solve the dining philosophers problem using monitors instead of semaphores.

31. Add code to the MINIX kernel to keep track of the number of messages sent from process (or task) i to process (or task) j. Print this matrix when the F4 key is hit.

32. Modify the MINIX scheduler to keep track of how much CPU time each user process has had recently. When no task or server wants to run, pick the user process that has had the smallest share of the CPU.

3

INPUT/OUTPUT

One of the main functions of an operating system is to control all the computer's input/output devices. It must issue commands to the devices, catch interrupts, and handle errors. It should also provide an interface between the devices and the rest of the system that is simple and easy to use. To the extent possible, the interface should be the same for all devices (device independence). The I/O code represents a significant fraction of the total operating system. How the operating system manages I/O is the subject of this chapter.

An outline of the chapter is as follows. First we will look briefly at some of the principles of I/O hardware, and then we will look at I/O software in general. I/O software can be structured in layers, with each layer having a well-defined task to perform. We will look at these layers to see what they do and how they fit together.

After that comes a section on deadlocks. We will define deadlocks precisely, show how they are caused, give two models for analyzing them, and discuss some algorithms for preventing their occurrence.

Then we will take a bird's-eye view of I/O in MINIX. Following that introduction, we will look at four I/O devices in detail—the RAM disk, the floppy disk, the clock, and the terminal. For each device we will look at its hardware, software, and implementation in MINIX. Finally, the chapter closes with a short discussion of a little piece of MINIX that is located in the same layer as the I/O tasks, but is itself not an I/O task. It provides some services to the memory manager and file system, such as fetching blocks of data from a user process.

3.1. PRINCIPLES OF I/O HARDWARE

Different people look at I/O hardware in different ways. Electrical engineers look at it in terms of chips, wires, power supplies, motors and all the other physical components that make up the hardware. Programmers look at the interface presented to the software—the commands the hardware accepts, the functions it carries out, and the errors that can be reported back. In this book we are concerned with programming I/O devices, not designing, building, or maintaining them, so our interest will be restricted to how the hardware is programmed, not how it works inside. Nevertheless, the programming of many I/O devices is often intimately connected with their internal operation. In the next two sections we will provide a little general background on I/O hardware as it relates to programming.

3.1.1. I/O Devices

I/O devices can be roughly divided into two categories: **block devices** and **character devices**. A block device is one that stores information in fixed-size blocks, each one with its own address. Common block sizes range from 128 bytes to 1024 bytes. The essential property of a block device is that it is possible to read or write each block independently of all the other ones. In other words, at any instant, the program can read or write any of the blocks. Disks are block devices.

If you look closely, the boundary between devices that are block addressable and those that are not is not well defined. Everyone agrees that a disk is a block addressable device because no matter where the arm currently is, it is always possible to seek to another cylinder and then wait for the required block to rotate under the head. Now consider a magnetic tape containing blocks of 1K bytes. If the tape drive is given a command to read block N, it can always rewind the tape and go forward until it comes to block N. This operation is analogous to a disk doing a seek, except that it takes much longer. Also, it may or may not be possible to rewrite one block in the middle of a tape. Even if it were possible to use magnetic tapes as block devices, that is stretching the point somewhat: they are normally not used that way.

The other type of I/O device is the character device. A character device delivers or accepts a stream of characters, without regard to any block structure. It is not addressable and does not have any seek operation. Terminals, line printers, paper tapes, punched cards, network interfaces, mice (for pointing), rats (for psychology lab experiments), and most other devices that are not disk-like can be seen as character devices.

This classification scheme is not perfect. Some devices just do not fit in. Clocks, for example, are not block addressable. Nor do they generate or accept character streams. All they do is cause interrupts at well-defined intervals. Still, the model of block and character devices is general enough that it can be used as a basis for making some of the operating system software dealing with I/O device independent. The file system, for example, deals just with abstract block devices, and leaves the device-dependent part to lower-level software called **device drivers**.

3.1.2. Device Controllers

I/O units typically consists of a mechanical component and an electronic component. It is often possible to separate the two portions to provide a more modular and general design. The electronic component is called the **device controller** or **adapter**. On mini- and microcomputers, it often takes the form of a printed circuit card that can be inserted into the computer. The mechanical component is the device itself.

The controller card usually has a connector on it, into which a cable leading to the device itself can be plugged. Many controllers can handle two, four, or even eight identical devices. If the interface between the controller and device is a standard interface, either an official standard such as ANSI, IEEE or ISO, or a defacto one, then companies can make controllers or devices that fit that interface. Many companies, for example, make disk drives that match the IBM disk controller interface.

We mention this distinction between controller and device because the operating system nearly always deals with the controller, not the device. Nearly all microcomputers and minicomputers use the single bus model of Fig. 3-1 for communication between the CPU and the controllers. Large mainframes often use a different model, with multiple buses and specialized I/O computers called **I/O channels** taking some of the load off the main CPU.

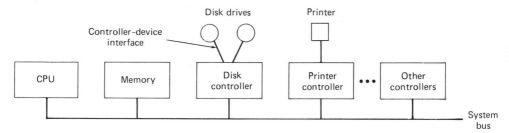

Fig. 3-1. A model for connecting the CPU, memory, controllers, and I/O devices.

The interface between the controller and the device is often a very low-level interface. A disk, for example, might be formatted with 8 sectors of 512 bytes per track. What actually comes off the drive, however, is a serial bit stream, starting with a **preamble**, then the 4096 bits in a sector, and finally a checksum or error-correcting code (ECC). The preamble is written when the disk is formatted, and contains the cylinder and sector number, the sector size, and similar data.

The controller's job is to convert the serial bit stream into a block of bytes and perform any error correction necessary. The block of bytes is typically first assembled, bit by bit, in a buffer inside the controller. After its checksum has been verified and the block declared to be error free, it can then be copied to main memory.

The controller for a CRT terminal also works as a bit serial device at an equally low level. It reads bytes containing the characters to be displayed from memory, and generates the signals used to modulate the CRT beam to cause it to write on the screen. The controller also generates the signals for making the CRT beam do a horizontal retrace after it has finished a scan line, as well as the signals for making it do a vertical retrace after the entire screen has been scanned. If it were not for the CRT controller, the operating system programmer would have to explicitly program the analog scanning of the tube. With the controller, the operating system initializes the controller with a few parameters, such as the number of characters per line and number of lines per screen, and lets the controller take care of actually driving the beam.

Each controller has a few registers that are used for communicating with the CPU. On some computers, these registers are part of the regular memory address space. On the PDP-11, for example, reserves addresses 0160000 to 0177777 for device registers. Other computers, including the IBM PC, use a special address space for I/O, with each controller allocated a certain portion of it. Figure 3-2 shows the I/O addresses and interrupt vectors allocated to some of the controllers on the IBM PC. The assignment of I/O addresses to devices is made by bus decoding logic associated with the controller. Some manufacturers of so-called IBM PC compatibles use different I/O addresses from what IBM uses. Programs that actually use I/O addresses (including MINIX) must be modified to run on these machines.

I/O Controller	I/O Addresses	Interrupt vector
Clock	040 – 043	8
Keyboard	060 – 063	9
Secondary RS232	2F8 – 2FF	11
Hard disk	320 – 32F	13
Printer	378 – 37F	15
Monochrome display	380 – 3BF	–
Color display	3D0 – 3DF	–
Floppy disk	3F0 – 3F7	14
Primary RS232	3F8 – 3FF	12

Fig. 3-2. Some examples of controllers, their I/O addresses and their interrupt vectors on the IBM PC.

The operating system performs I/O by writing commands into the controllers' registers. The IBM PC floppy disk controller, for example, accepts 15 different commands, such as READ, WRITE, SEEK, FORMAT, and RECALIBRATE. Many of the commands have parameters, which are also loaded into the controller's registers. When a command has been accepted, the CPU can leave the controller alone and go off to do other work. When the command has been completed, the controller causes an interrupt in order to allow the operating system to gain control of the CPU and test the results of the operation. The CPU gets the results and device status by reading one or more bytes of information from the controller's registers.

Direct Memory Access (DMA)

Many controllers, especially those for block devices, support **direct memory access** or **DMA**. To explain how DMA works, let us first look at how disk reads occur when DMA is not used. First the controller reads the block (one or more sectors) from the drive serially, bit by bit, until the entire block is in the controller's internal buffer. Next, it performs the checksum computation to verify that no read errors have occurred. The checksum can be computed only after the entire block has been read. Then the controller causes an interrupt. When the operating system starts running, it can read the disk block from the controller's buffer a byte or a word at a time by executing a loop, with each iteration reading one byte or word from a controller device register and storing it in memory.

Naturally, a programmed CPU loop to read the bytes one at a time from the controller wastes CPU time. DMA was invented to free the CPU from this low-level work. When it is used, the CPU gives the controller two items of information, in addition to the disk address of the block: the memory address where the block is to go, and the number of bytes to transfer, as shown in Fig. 3-3.

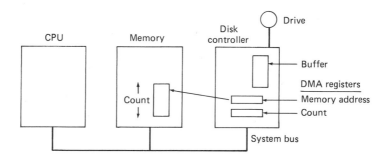

Fig. 3-3. A DMA transfer is done entirely by the controller.

After the controller has read the entire block from the device into its buffer and verified the checksum, it copies the first byte or word into the main memory at the address specified by the DMA memory address. Then it increments the DMA address and decrements the DMA count by the number of bytes just transferred. This process is repeated until the DMA count becomes zero, at which time the controller causes an interrupt. When the operating system starts up, it does not have to copy the block to memory: it is already there.

You may be wondering why the controller does not just store the bytes in main memory as soon as it gets them from the disk. In other words, why does it need an internal buffer? The reason is that once a disk transfer has started, the bits keep arriving from the disk at a constant rate, whether the controller is ready for them or not. If the controller tried to write data directly to memory, it would have to go over the system bus for each word transferred. If the bus were busy due to some other device using it, the controller would have to wait. If the next disk word arrived before the previous one had been stored, the controller would have to store it somewhere. If the bus were very busy, the controller might end up storing quite a few words and having a lot of administration to do as well. When the block is buffered internally, the bus is not needed until the DMA begins, so the design of the controller is much simpler because the DMA transfer to memory is not time critical. (Some controllers do, in fact, go directly to memory with only a small amount of internal buffering, but if the bus is very busy, a transfer may have to be terminated with an overrun error.)

The two-step buffering process described above has important implications for I/O performance. While the data are being transferred from the controller to the memory, either by the CPU or by the controller, the next sector will be passing under the disk head and the bits arriving in the controller. Simple controllers just cannot cope with doing input and output at the same time, so while a memory transfer is taking place, the sector passing under the disk head is lost.

As a result, the controller will be able to read only every other block. Reading a complete track will then require two full rotations, one for the even blocks and one for the odd blocks. If the time to transfer a block from the controller to memory over the bus is longer than the time to read a block from the disk, it may be necessary to read one block and then skip two (or more) blocks.

Skipping blocks to give the controller time to transfer data to memory is called **interleaving**. When the disk is formatted, the blocks are numbered to take account of the interleave factor. In Fig. 3-4(a) we see a disk with 8 blocks per track and no interleave. In Fig. 3-4(b) we see the same disk with single interleaving. In Fig. 3-4(c) double interleaving is shown.

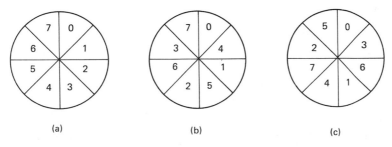

Fig. 3-4. (a) No interleaving. (b) Single interleaving. (c) Double interleaving.

The idea of numbering the blocks this way is to allow the operating system to read consecutively numbered blocks and still achieve the maximum speed the hardware is capable of. If the blocks were numbered as in Fig. 3-4(a) but the controller could read only alternate blocks, an operating system that allocated an 8-block file in consecutive disk blocks would require eight disk rotations to read blocks 0 through 7 in order. (Of course, if the operating system knew about the problem and allocated its blocks differently, it could solve the problem in software, but it is better to have the controller worry about the interleaving.)

3.2. PRINCIPLES OF I/O SOFTWARE

Let's turn away from the hardware and now look at how the I/O software is structured. The general goals of the I/O software are easy to state. The basic idea is to organize the software as a series of layers, with the lower ones concerned with hiding the peculiarities of the hardware from the upper ones, and the upper ones concerned with presenting a nice, clean, regular interface to the users. In the following sections we will look at these goals and how they are achieved.

3.2.1. Goals of the I/O Software

A key concept in the design of I/O software is **device independence**. It should be possible to write programs that can be used with files on a floppy disk or a hard disk, without having to modify the programs for each device type. In fact, it should be possible to move the program without even recompiling it. One should be able to type the command

```
sort <input >output
```

and have it work with input and output on floppy disk or on hard disk or even coming from, or going to, the terminal. It is up to the operating system to take care of the problems caused by the fact that these devices really are different and require very different device drivers.

Closely related to device independence is the goal of **uniform naming**. The name of a file or a device should simply be a string or an integer and not depend on the device in any way. In MINIX, floppy disks, hard disks and all other block devices can be mounted in the file system hierarchy in arbitrary places, so the user need not be aware of which name corresponds to which device. All files and devices are addressed the same way: by a path name.

Another important issue for I/O software is error handling. In general, errors should be handled as close to the hardware as possible. If the controller discovers a read error, it should try to correct the error itself if it can. If it cannot, then the device driver should handle it, perhaps by just trying to read the block again. Many errors are transient, such as read errors caused by specks of dust on the read head, and will go away if the operation is repeated. Only if the lower layers are not able to deal with the problem should the upper layers be told about it.

Still another key issue is synchronous (blocking) versus asynchronous (interrupt-driven) transfers. Most physical I/O is asynchronous—the CPU starts the transfer and goes off to do something else until the interrupt arrives. User programs are much easier to write if the I/O operations are blocking—after a READ command the program is automatically suspended until the data are available in the buffer. It is up to the operating system to make operations that are actually interrupt-driven look blocking to the user programs.

The final concept that we will deal with here is sharable versus dedicated devices. Some I/O devices, such as disks, can be used by many users at the same time. No problems are caused by multiple users having open files on the same disk at the same time. Other devices, such as printers, have to be dedicated to a single user until that user is finished. Having five users printing lines intermixed at random on the printer just would not work. Introducing dedicated devices also introduces a variety of problems, including deadlock. Again, the operating system must handle both shared and dedicated devices in a way that avoids problems.

These goals can be achieved in a comprehensible and efficient way by structuring the I/O software in four layers:

1. Interrupt handlers.

2. Device drivers.

3. Device-independent operating system software.

4. User level software.

These four layers are (not accidently) the same four layers that we saw in Fig. 2-26. In the following sections we will look at each one in turn, starting at the bottom. The emphasis in this chapter is on the device drivers (layer 2), but we will summarize the rest of the I/O software to show how the various pieces of the I/O system fit together.

3.2.2. Interrupt Handlers

Interrupts are an unpleasant fact of life. They should be hidden away, deep in the bowels of the system, so that as little of the system as possible knows about them. The way to hide them is to have a process, typically a device driver (an I/O task in MINIX terms), be blocked whenever an I/O command has been issued and an interrupt is expected.

When the interrupt happens, the interrupt procedure does whatever it has to in order to unblock the driver. In some systems it will do an UP on a semaphore. In others it will do a SIGNAL on a condition variable in a monitor. In still others, it will send a message to the blocked process. In all cases the net effect of the interrupt will be that a process that was previously blocked will now be able to run. Having studied the implementation of interrupt handling in detail in the previous chapter, let us now proceed with the device drivers themselves.

3.2.3. Device Drivers

All the device-dependent code goes in the device drivers. Each device driver handles one device type, or at most, one class of closely related devices. For example, it would probably be a good idea to have a single terminal driver, even if the system supported several different brands of terminal, all slightly different. On the other hand, a dumb, mechanical hardcopy terminal and an intelligent bit map graphics terminal with a mouse are so different that different drivers should be used.

Earlier in this chapter we looked at what device controllers do. We saw that each controller has one or more device registers used to give it commands. The device drivers issue these commands and check that they are carried out properly. Thus, the disk driver is the only part of the operating system that knows how many registers that disk controller has and what they are used for. It alone knows about sectors, tracks, cylinders, heads, arm motion, interleave factors, motor drives, head settling times, and all the other mechanics of making the disk work properly.

In general terms, the job of a device driver is to accept abstract requests from the device-independent software above it, and see to it that the request is carried out. A typical request is to read block n. If the driver is idle at the time a request comes in, it starts carrying out the request immediately. If, however, it is already busy with a request, it will normally enter the new request into a queue of pending requests to be dealt with as soon as possible.

The first step in actually carrying out an I/O request, say, for a disk, is to translate it from abstract to concrete terms. For a disk driver, this means figuring out where on the disk the requested block actually is, checking to see if the drive's motor is running, determining if the arm is positioned on the proper cylinder, and so on. In short, it must decide which controller operations are required and in what sequence.

Once it has determined which commands to issue to the controller, it starts issuing them by writing into the controller's device registers. Some controllers can handle only one command at a time. Other controllers are willing to accept a linked list of commands, which they then carry out by themselves without further help from the operating system.

After the command or commands have been issued, one of two situations will apply. In many cases the device driver must wait until the controller does some work for it, so it blocks itself until the interrupt comes in to unblock it. In other cases, however, the operation finishes without delay, so the driver need not block. As an example of the latter situation, scrolling the screen on some terminals (including the IBM PC) requires just writing a few bytes into the controller's registers. No mechanical motion is needed, so the entire operation can be completed in a few microseconds.

In the former case, the blocked driver will be awakened by the interrupt. In the latter case, it will never go to sleep. Either way, after the operation has been completed it must check for errors. If everything is all right, the driver may have data to pass to the device-independent software (e.g., a block just read). Finally it returns some status information for error reporting back to its caller. If any other requests are queued, one of them can now be selected and started. If nothing is queued, the driver blocks waiting for the next request.

3.2.4. Device-Independent I/O Software

Although some of the I/O software is device specific, a large fraction of it is device-independent. The exact boundary between the drivers and the device-independent software is system dependent, because some functions that could be done in a device-independent way may actually be done in the drivers, for efficiency or other reasons. The functions shown in Fig. 3-5 are typically done in the device-independent software. In MINIX, most of the device-independent software is part of the file system, in layer 3 (Fig. 2-26). Although we will study the file system in Chap. 5, we will take a quick look at the device-independent software here, to provide some perspective on I/O and show better where the drivers fit in.

Uniform interfacing for the device drivers
Device naming
Device protection
Providing a device–independent block size
Buffering
Storage allocation on block devices
Allocating and releasing dedicated devices
Error reporting

Fig. 3-5. Functions of the device-independent I/O software.

The basic function of the device-independent software is to perform the I/O functions that are common to all devices, and to provide a uniform interface to the user-level software.

A major issue in an operating system is how objects such as files and I/O devices are named. The device independent software takes care of mapping symbolic device names onto the proper driver. In MINIX a device name, such as /dev/tty0, uniquely specifies the inode for a special file, and this i-node contains the major device number, which is used to locate the appropriate driver. The i-node also contains the minor device number, which is passed as a parameter to the driver to specify the unit to be read or written.

Closely related to naming is protection. How does the system prevent users from accessing devices that they are not entitled to access? In most microcomputer systems, there is no protection at all. Any process can do anything it wants to. In most mainframe systems, access to I/O devices by user processes is completely forbidden. In MINIX, a more flexible scheme is used. The special files corresponding to I/O devices are protected by the usual *rwx* bits. The system administrator can then set the proper permissions for each device.

Different disks may have different sector sizes. It is up to the device-independent software to hide this fact and provide a uniform block size to higher layers, for example, by treating several sectors as a single logical block. In this way, the higher layers only deal with abstract devices that all use the same logical block size, independent of the physical sector size. Similarly, some character devices deliver their data one byte at a time (e.g., paper tape readers), while others deliver theirs in larger units (e.g., card readers). These differences must also be hidden.

Buffering is also an issue, both for block and character devices. For block devices, the hardware generally insists upon reading and writing entire blocks at once, but user processes are free to read and write in arbitrary units. If a user process writes half a block, the operating system will normally keep the data around internally until the rest of the data are written, at which time the block can go out to the disk. For character devices, users can write data to the system faster than it can be output, necessitating buffering. Keyboard input can also arrive before it is needed, also requiring buffering.

When a file is created and filled with data, new disk blocks have to be allocated to the file. To perform this allocation, the operating system needs a list or bit map of free blocks per disk, but the algorithm for locating a free block is device independent and can be done above the level of the driver.

Some devices, such as magnetic tape drives, can be used only by a single process at any given moment. It is up to the operating system to examine requests for device usage and accept or reject them, depending on whether the requested device is available or not. A simple way to handle these requests is to require processes to perform OPENs on the special files for devices directly. If the device is unavailable, the OPEN will fail. Closing such a dedicated device would then release it.

Error handling, by and large, is done by the drivers. Most errors are highly device-dependent, so only the driver knows what to do (e.g., retry, ignore it, panic). A typical error is caused by a disk block that has been damaged and cannot be read any more. After the driver has tried to read the block a certain number of times, it gives up and informs the device-independent software. How the error is treated from here on is device independent. If the error occurred while reading a user file, it may be sufficient to report the error back to the caller. However, if it occurred while reading a critical system data structure such as the block containing the bit map showing which blocks are free, the operating system may have no choice but to print an error message and terminate.

3.2.5. User-Space I/O Software

Although most of the I/O software is within the operating system, a small portion of it consists of libraries linked together with user programs, and even whole programs running outside the kernel. System calls, including the I/O system calls, are normally made by library procedures. When a C program contains the call

```
bytes_read = read(file_descriptor, buffer, bytes_wanted);
```

the library procedure *read* will be linked with the program and contained in the binary program present in memory at run time. The collection of all these library procedures is clearly part of the I/O system.

While these procedures do little more than put their parameters in the appropriate place for the system call, there are other I/O procedures that actually do real work. In particular, formatting of input and output is done by library procedures. One example from C is *printf*, which takes a format string and possibly some variables as input, builds an ASCII string, and then calls WRITE to output the string. An example of a similar procedure for input is *atoi* (Ascii TO Integer), which takes a string containing a decimal integer in ASCII and returns the binary value of that integer. The standard I/O library contains a number of procedures that involve I/O and all run as part of user programs.

Not all user-level I/O software consists of library procedures. Another important category is the spooling system. **Spooling** is a way of dealing with dedicated I/O devices in a multiprogramming system. Consider a typical spooled device: the line printer. Although it would be technically easy to let any user process open the character special file for the printer, suppose a process opened it and then did nothing for hours. No other process could print anything.

Instead what is done is to create a special process, called a **daemon**, and a special directory, called a **spooling directory**. To print a file, a process first generates the entire file to be printed and puts it in the spooling directory. It is up to the daemon, which is the only process having permission to use the printer's special file, to print the files in the directory. By protecting the special file against direct use by users, the problem of having someone keeping it open unnecessarily long is eliminated.

Spooling is not only used for printers. It is also used in other situations. For example, file transfer over a network often uses a network daemon. To send a file somewhere, a user puts it in a network spooling directory. Later on, the network daemon takes it out and transmits it. One particular use of spooled file transmission is the USENET network, which is primarily used as an electronic mail system. This network consists of thousands of machines around the world communicating by dial-up telephone lines and many computer networks. To send mail to someone on USENET, you call a program such as *send*, which accepts the letter to be sent and then deposits it in a spooling directory for transmission later. The entire mail system runs outside the operating system.

Figure 3-6 summarizes the I/O system, showing all the layers and the principal functions of each layer.

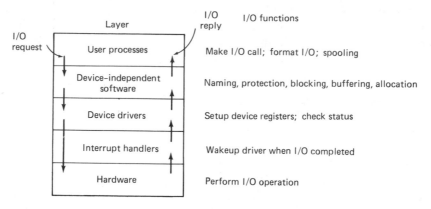

Fig. 3-6. Layers of the I/O system and the main functions of each layer.

3.3. DEADLOCKS

One problem with spooling is that the entire file to be output must be written to the disk before the output can be started. (What would happen if a daemon began printing a file before it had been fully generated and the process generating it stopped for a few hours before finishing its output?) Sometimes the output is so large that not enough disk space is available to hold it all. A program generating output for a magnetic tape might produce 50 megabytes of data. The only way to handle this situation is not to use spooling for the device, but to allow user processes to request, and be granted, exclusive access for as long as needed.

Unfortunately, allowing exclusive access to magnetic tape drives or any other kind of resource can lead to serious problems. Suppose a computer has one tape drive and one plotter, neither of them spooled. Process *A* requests the tape drive and process *B* requests the plotter. Both requests are granted. Now *A* requests the plotter (without giving up the tape drive) and *B* requests the tape drive (without giving up the plotter). Neither request can be granted, so both processes are put to sleep. They will remain asleep forever. This situation is called a **deadlock**.

Deadlocks can occur in many situations besides requesting dedicated I/O devices. In a data base system, a program may have to lock several records it is using, to avoid race conditions. If process *A* locks record *R1* and process *B* locks record *R2*, and then each process tries to lock the other one's record, we also have a deadlock.

Almost any situation in which processes can be granted exclusive access to devices, files, records, or other objects has the potential for deadlock. Thus the discussion of deadlocks could have gone in almost any chapter of this book. We put it here for pedagogical reasons: it is obvious that tape drives, plotters, and card punches can only be used by one process at a time. With records in a data base, for example, the need for exclusive access may be equally valid, but the reasoning is much more subtle.

In the following sections we will look at deadlocks more closely, see how they arise, and study some ways of preventing them. A great deal has been written about deadlocks. Two bibliographies on the subject have appeared in *Operating Systems Review* and should be consulted for references (Newton, 1979; Zobel 1983).

3.3.1. Resources

Deadlocks can occur when processes have been granted exclusive access to devices, files, and so forth. To make the discussion of deadlocks as general as possible, we will refer to the objects granted as **resources**. A resource can be a hardware device (e.g., a tape drive) or a piece of information (e.g., a locked record in a data base). A computer will normally have many different resources that can be acquired. For some resources, several identical instances may be available, such as three tape drives. When several copies of a resource are available, any one of them can be used to satisfy any request for the resource. In short, a resource is anything that can only be used by a single process at any instant of time.

The sequence of events required to use a resource is:

1. Request the resource.

2. Use the resource.

3. Release the resource.

If the resource is not available when it is requested, the requesting process is forced to wait. In some operating systems, the process is automatically blocked when a resource request fails, and awakened when it becomes available. In other systems, the request fails with an error code, and it is up to the calling process to wait a little while and try again.

The exact nature of requesting a resource is highly system dependent. In some systems, a REQUEST system call is provided to allow processes to ask for resources. In MINIX the only resources that the operating system (potentially) knows about are special files that only one process can have open at a time. These are opened by the usual OPEN call. If the file is already in use, an error code could be returned; what to do next would be up to the user.

3.3.2. Deadlock Modeling

Deadlock can be defined formally as follows. A set of processes is deadlocked if each process in the set is waiting for an event that only another process in the set can cause. Because all the processes are waiting, none of them will ever cause any of the events that could wake up any of the other members of the set, and all the processes continue to wait forever.

In most cases, the event that each process is waiting for is the release of some resource currently possessed by another member of the set. In other words, each member of the set of deadlocked processes is waiting for a resource that can be released only by a deadlocked process. None of the processes can run, none of them can release any resources, and none of them can be awakened. The number of processes and the number and kind of resources possessed and requested are unimportant.

Coffman et al. (1971) showed that four conditions must hold for there to be a deadlock:

1. Mutual exclusion condition. Each resource is either currently assigned to exactly one process or is available.

2. Hold and wait condition. Processes currently holding resources granted earlier can request new resources.

3. No preemption condition. Resources previously granted cannot be forcibly taken away from a process. They must be explicitly released by the process holding them.

4. Circular wait condition. There must be a circular chain of two or more processes, each of which is waiting for a resource held by the next member of the chain.

Holt (1972) showed how these four conditions can be modeled using directed graphs. The graphs have two kinds of nodes: processes, shown as circles, and resources, shown as squares. An arc from a resource node (square) to a process node (circle) means that the resource previously has been requested by, granted to, and is currently held by that process. In Fig. 3-7(a), resource R is currently assigned to process A.

An arc from a process to a resource means that the process is currently blocked waiting for that resource. In Fig. 3-7(b), process B is waiting for resource S. In Fig. 3-7(c) we see a deadlock: process C is waiting for resource T, which is currently held by process D. Process D is not about to release resource T because it is waiting for resource U, held by C. Both processes will wait forever. A cycle in the graph means that there is a deadlock involving the processes and resources in the cycle. In this example, the cycle is $C - T - D - U - C$.

Now let us look at an example of how resource graphs can be used. Imagine

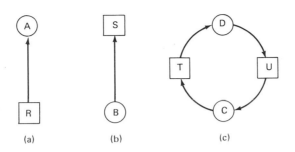

Fig. 3-7. Resource allocation graphs. (a) Holding a resource. (b) Requesting a resource. (c) Deadlock.

that we have three processes, *A*, *B*, and *C*, and three resources, *R*, *S*, and *T*. The requests and releases of the three processes are given in Fig. 3-8(a)-(c). The operating system is free to run any unblocked process at any instant, so it could decide to run *A* until *A* finished all its work, then run *B* to completion, and finally run *C*.

This ordering does not lead to any deadlocks (because there is no competition for resources) but it also has no parallelism at all. In addition to requesting and releasing resources, processes compute and do I/O. When the processes are run sequentially, there is no possibility that while one process is waiting for I/O, another can use the CPU. Thus running the processes strictly sequentially may not be optimal. On the other hand, if none of the processes do any I/O at all, shortest job first is better than round robin, so under some circumstances running all processes sequentially may be the best way.

Let us now suppose that the processes do both I/O and computing, so that round robin is a reasonable scheduling algorithm. The resource requests might occur in the order of Fig. 3-8(d). If these six requests are carried out in that order, the six resulting resources graphs are shown in Fig. 3-8(e)-(j). After request 4 has been made, *A* blocks waiting for *S,* as shown in Fig. 3-8(h). In the next two steps *B* and *C* also block, ultimately leading to a cycle and the deadlock of Fig. 3-8(j).

However, as we have already mentioned, the operating system is not required to run the processes in any special order. In particular, if granting a particular request might lead to deadlock, the operating system can simply suspend the process without granting the request (i.e., just not schedule the process) until it is safe. In Fig. 3-8, if the operating system knew about the impending deadlock, it could suspend *B* instead of granting it *S*. By running only *A* and *C*, we would get the requests and releases of Fig. 3-8(k) instead of Fig. 3-8(d). This sequence leads to the resource graphs of Fig. 3-8(l)-(q), which do not lead to deadlock.

After step (q), process *B* can be granted *S* because *A* is finished and *C* has everything it needs. Even if *B* should eventually block when requesting *T*, no deadlock can occur. *B* will just wait until *C* is finished.

Later in this chapter we will study a detailed algorithm for making allocation

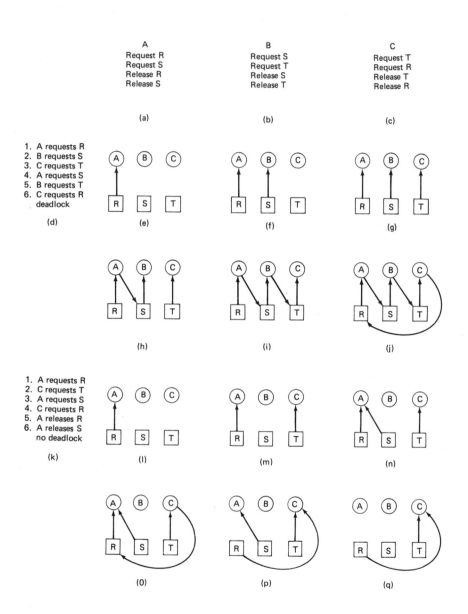

Fig. 3-8. An example of how deadlock occurs and how it can be avoided.

decisions that do not lead to deadlock. The point to understand now is that resource graphs are a tool that let us see if a given request/release sequence leads to deadlock. We just carry out the requests and releases step by step, and after every step check the graph to see if it contains any cycles. If so, we have a deadlock; if not, there is no deadlock. Resource graphs can also be generalized to handle multiple resources of the same type (Holt, 1972).

In general, four strategies are used for dealing with deadlocks.

1. Just ignore the problem altogether.

2. Detection and recovery.

3. Prevention, by negating one of the four necessary conditions.

4. Dynamic avoidance by careful resource allocation.

We will examine each of these methods in turn in the next four sections.

3.3.3. The Ostrich Algorithm

The simplest approach is the ostrich algorithm: stick your head in the sand and pretend there is no problem at all. Different people react to this strategy in different ways. Mathematicians find it totally unacceptable and say that deadlocks must be prevented at all costs. Engineers ask how often the problem is expected, how often the system crashes for other reasons, and how serious a deadlock is. If deadlocks occur on the average once every five years, but system crashes due to hardware failures, compiler errors, and operating system bugs occur once a month, most engineers would not be willing to pay a large penalty in performance or convenience to eliminate deadlocks.

To make this contrast more specific, UNIX (and MINIX) potentially suffer from deadlocks that are not even detected, let alone automatically broken. The total number of processes in the system is determined by the number of entries in the process table. Thus process table slots are finite resources. If a FORK fails because the table is full, a reasonable approach for the program doing the FORK is to wait a random time and try again.

Now suppose that a UNIX system has 100 process slots. Ten programs are running, each of which needs to create 12 (sub)processes. After each process has created 9 processes, the 9 original processes and the 90 new processes have exhausted the table. Each of the 10 original processes now sits in an endless loop forking and failing—a deadlock. The probability of this happening is minuscule, but it *could* happen. Should we abandon processes and the FORK call to eliminate the problem?

The maximum number of open files is similarly restricted by the size of the i-node table, so a similar problem occurs when it fills up. Swap space on the disk is another limited resource. In fact, almost every table in the operating system represents a finite resource. Should we abolish all of these because it might happen that a collection of n processes might each claim $1/n$ of the total, and then each try to claim another one?

The UNIX approach is just to ignore the problem on the assumption that most users would prefer an occasional deadlock to a rule restricting all users to one process, one open file, and one of everything. If deadlocks could be eliminated for free, there would not be much discussion. The problem is that the price is high, mostly in terms of putting inconvenient restrictions on processes, as we will see shortly. Thus we are faced with an unpleasant tradeoff between convenience and correctness, and a great deal of discussion about which is more important, and to whom.

3.3.4. Detection and Recovery

A second technique is detection and recovery. When this technique is used, the system does not do anything except monitor the requests and releases of resources. Every time a resource is requested or released, the resource graph is updated, and a check is made to see if any cycles exist. If a cycle exists, one of the processes in the cycle is killed. If this does not break the deadlock, another process is killed, and so on until the cycle is broken.

A somewhat cruder is method is to not even maintain the resource graph, but instead periodically check to see if there are any processes that have been continuously blocked for more than say, 1 hour. Such processes are then killed.

Detection and recovery is the strategy often used on large mainframe computers, especially batch systems in which killing a process and then restarting it later is usually acceptable. Care must be taken to restore any modified files to their original state, however.

3.3.5. Deadlock Prevention

The third deadlock strategy is to impose suitable restrictions on processes so that deadlocks are structurally impossible. The four conditions stated by Coffman et al. (1971) provide a clue to some possible solutions. If we can ensure that at least one of these conditions is never satisfied, then deadlocks will be impossible (Havender, 1968).

First let us attack the mutual exclusion condition. If no resource was ever assigned exclusively to a single process, we would never have deadlocks. However, it is equally clear that allowing two processes to write on the printer at the same time will lead to chaos. By spooling printer output, several processes can generate output at the same time. In this model, the only process that actually requests the physical printer is the printer daemon. Since the daemon never requests any other resources, we can eliminate deadlock for the printer.

Unfortunately, not all devices can be spooled (the process table does not lend itself well to being spooled). Furthermore, competition for disk space for spooling can itself lead to deadlock. What would happen if two processes each filled up half of the available spooling space with output and neither was finished? If the daemon was programmed to begin printing even before all the output was spooled, the printer might lie idle if an output process decided to wait several hours after the first burst of output. For this reason, daemons are normally programmed to print only after the complete output file is available. Neither process will ever finish, so we have a deadlock on the disk.

The second of the conditions stated by Coffman et al. looks more promising. If we can prevent processes that hold resources from waiting for more resources we can eliminate deadlocks. One way to achieve this goal is to require all processes to request all their resources before starting execution. If everything was available, the process would be allocated whatever it needed and could run to completion. If one or more resources were busy, nothing would be allocated and the process would just wait.

An immediate problem with this approach is that many processes do not know how many resources they will need until they have started running. Another problem is that resources will not be used optimally with this approach. Take, as an example, a process that reads data from an input tape, analyzes it for an hour, and then writes an output tape as well as plotting the results. If all resources must be requested in advance, the process will tie up the output tape drive and the plotter for an hour.

A slightly different way to break the hold-and-wait condition is to require a process requesting a resource to first temporarily release all the resources it currently holds. Only if the request is successful can it get the original resources back.

Attacking the third condition (no preemption) is even less promising than attacking the second one. If a process has been assigned the printer and is in the middle of printing its output, forcibly taking away the printer because a needed plotter is not available will lead to a mess.

Only one condition is left. The circular wait can be eliminated in several ways. One way is simply to have a rule saying that a process is entitled only to a single resource at any moment. If it needs a second one, it must release the first one. For a process that needs to copy a huge file from a tape to a printer, this restriction is unacceptable.

Another way to avoid the circular wait is to provide a global numbering of all the resources, as shown in Fig. 3-9(a). Now the rule is this: processes can request resources whenever they want to, but all requests must be made in numerical order. A process may request first a printer and then a tape drive, but it may not request first a plotter and then a printer.

With this rule, the resource allocation graph can never have cycles. Let us see why this is true for the case of two processes, in Fig. 3-9(b). We can get a deadlock only if A requests resource j and B requests resource i. Assuming i and j are distinct resources, they will have different numbers. If $i > j$ then A is not allowed to request j. If $i < j$ then B is not allowed to request i. Either way, deadlock is impossible.

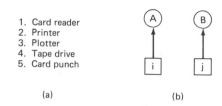

1. Card reader
2. Printer
3. Plotter
4. Tape drive
5. Card punch

(a)   (b)

Fig. 3-9. (a) Numerically ordered resources. (b) A resource graph.

With multiple processes the same logic holds. At every instant, one of the assigned resources will be highest. The process holding that resource will never ask for a resource already assigned. It will either finish, or at worst, request even higher numbered resources, all of which are available. Eventually it will finish and free its resources. At this point, some other process will hold the highest resource and can also finish. In short, there exists a scenario in which all processes finish, so no deadlock is present.

A minor variation of this algorithm is to drop the requirement that resources be acquired in strictly increasing sequence, and merely insist that no process request a resource lower than what it is already holding. If a process initially requests 9 and 10, and then releases both of them, it is effectively starting all over, so there is no reason to prohibit it from now requesting resource 1.

Although numerically ordering the resources eliminates the problem of deadlocks, it may be impossible to find an ordering that satisfies everyone. When the resources include process table slots, disk spooler space, locked data base records, and other abstract resources, the number of potential resources and different uses may be so large that no ordering could possibly work.

The various approaches to deadlock prevention are summarized in Fig. 3-10.

Condition	Approach
Mutual exclusion	Spool everything
Hold and wait	Request all resources initially
No preemption	Take resources away
Circular wait	Order resources numerically

Fig. 3-10. Summary of approaches to deadlock prevention.

3.3.6. Deadlock Avoidance

In Fig. 3-8 we saw that deadlock was avoided not by imposing arbitrary rules on processes, but by carefully analyzing each resource request to see if could be safely granted. The question arises: is there an algorithm that can always avoid deadlock by making the right choice all the time? The answer is a qualified yes—we can avoid deadlocks, but only if certain information is available in advance. In this section we examine ways to avoid deadlock by careful resource allocation.

The Banker's Algorithm for a Single Resource

A scheduling algorithm that can avoid deadlocks is due to Dijkstra (1965) and is known as the **banker's algorithm**. It is modeled on the way a small-town banker might deal with a group of customers to whom he has granted lines of credit. In Fig. 3-11(a) we see four customers, each of whom has been granted a certain number of credit units (e.g., 1 unit is 1K dollars). The banker knows that not all customers will need their maximum credit immediately, so he has only reserved 10 units rather than 22 to service them. (In this analogy, customers are processes, units are, say, tape drives, and the banker is the operating system.)

Name	Used	Maximum		Used	Maximum		Used	Maximum
Andy	0	6	Andy	1	6	Andy	1	6
Barbara	0	5	Barbara	1	5	Barbara	2	5
Marvin	0	4	Marvin	2	4	Marvin	2	4
Suzanne	0	7	Suzanne	4	7	Suzanne	4	7

Available: 10   Available: 2   Available: 1

(a)   (b)   (c)

Fig. 3-11. Three resource allocation states: (a) Safe. (b) Safe. (c) Unsafe.

The customers go about their respective businesses, making loan requests from time to time. At a certain moment, the situation is as shown in Fig. 3-11(b). A list of customers showing the money already loaned (tape drives already assigned) and the maximum credit available (maximum number of tape drives needed at once later) is called the **state** of the system with respect to resource allocation.

A state is said to be **safe** if it there exists a sequence of other states that leads to all the customers getting loans up to their credit limits (all the processes getting all their resources and terminating). The state of Fig. 3-11(b) is safe because with two units left, the banker can delay any requests except Marvin's, thus letting Marvin finish and release all four of his resources. With four units in hand, the banker can let either Suzanne or Barbara have the necessary units, and so on.

Consider what would happen if a request from Barbara for one more unit were granted in Fig. 3-11(b). We would have situation Fig. 3-11(c), which is unsafe. If all the customers suddenly asked for their maximum loans, the banker could not satisfy any of them, and we would have a deadlock. An unsafe state does not *have* to lead to deadlock, since a customer might not need the entire credit line available, but the banker cannot count on this behavior.

The banker's algorithm is thus to consider each request as it occurs, and see if granting it leads to a safe state. If it does, the request is granted, otherwise, it is postponed until later. To see if a state is safe, the banker checks to see if he has enough resources to satisfy the customer closest to his or her maximum. If so, those loans are assumed to be repaid, and the customer now closest to his or her limit is checked, and so on. If all loans can eventually be repaid, the state is safe and the initial request can be granted.

Resource Trajectories

The above algorithm was described in terms of a single resource class (e.g., only tape drives or only printers, but not some of each). In Fig. 3-12 we see a model for dealing with two processes and two resources, for example, a printer and a plotter. The horizontal axis represents the number of instructions executed by process A. The vertical axis represents the number of instructions executed by process B. At I_1 A requests a printer; at I_2 it needs a plotter. The printer and plotter are released at I_3 and I_4 respectively. Process B needs the plotter from I_5 to I_7 and the printer from I_6 to I_8.

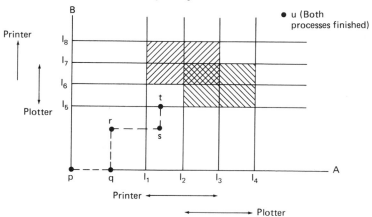

Fig. 3-12. Two process resource trajectories.

Every point in the diagram represents a joint state of the two processes. Initially, the state is at p, with neither process having executed any instructions. If the scheduler chooses to run A first, we get to the point q, in which A has executed some number of instructions, but B has executed none. At point q the trajectory becomes vertical, indicating that the scheduler has chosen to run B. With a single processor, all paths must be horizontal or vertical, never diagonal. Furthermore, motion is always to the north or east, never to the south or west (processes cannot run backwards).

When A crosses the I_1 line on the path from r to s, it requests and is granted the printer. When B reaches point t, it requests the plotter.

The regions that are shaded are especially interesting. The region with lines slanting from southwest to northeast represents both processes having the printer. The mutual exclusion rule makes it impossible to enter this region. Similarly, the region shaded the other way represents both processes having the plotter, and is equally impossible.

If the system ever enters the box bounded by I_1 and I_2 on the sides and I_5 and I_6 top and bottom, it will eventually deadlock when it gets to the intersection of I_2 and I_6. At this point, A is requesting the plotter and B is requesting the printer, and both are already assigned. The entire box is unsafe and must not be entered. At point t the only safe thing to do is run process A until it gets to I_4. Beyond that, any trajectory to u will do.

The Banker's Algorithm for Multiple Resources

This graphical model is difficult to apply to the general case of an arbitrary number of process and an arbitrary number of resource classes, each with multiple instances (e.g., two plotters, three tape drives). However, the banker's algorithm can be generalized to do the job. Figure 3-13 shows how it works.

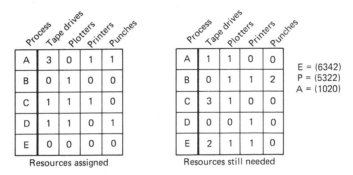

Fig. 3-13. The banker's algorithm with multiple resources.

In Fig. 3-13 we see two matrices. The one on the left shows how many of each resource is currently assigned to each of the five processes. The matrix on the right shows how many resources each process still needs in order to complete. As in the single resource case, processes must state their total resource needs before executing, so that the system can compute the right-hand matrix at each instant.

The three vectors at the right of the figure show the existing resources, E, the possessed resources, P, and the available resources, A, respectively. From E we see that the system has six tape drives, three plotters, four printers, and two punches. Of these, five tape drives, three plotters, two printers, and two punches are currently assigned. This fact can be seen by adding up the four resource columns in the left-hand matrix. The available resource vector is simply the difference between what the system has and what is currently in use.

The algorithm for checking to see if a state is safe can now be stated.

1. Look for a row, R, whose unmet resource needs are all smaller than A. If no such row exists, the system is deadlocked since no process can run to completion.

2. Assume the process of the row chosen requests all the resources it needs (which is guaranteed to be possible) and finishes. Mark that process as terminated and add all its resources to the A vector.

3. Repeat steps 1 and 2 until either all processes are marked terminated, in which case the initial state was safe, or until a deadlock occurs, in which case it was not.

If several processes are eligible to be chosen in step 1, it does not matter which one is selected: the pool of available resources either gets larger, or at worst, stays the same.

Now let us get back to the example of Fig. 3-13. The current state is safe. Suppose process B now requests a printer. This request can be granted because the resulting state is still safe (process D can finish, and then processes A or E, followed by the rest).

Now imagine that after giving B one of the two remaining printers, E wants the last printer. Granting that request would reduce the vector of available resources to (1 0 0 0), which leads to deadlock. Clearly E's request must be deferred for a while.

This algorithm was first published by Dijkstra in 1965. Since that time, nearly every book on operating systems has described it in detail. Innumerable papers have been written about various aspects of it. Unfortunately, few authors have had the audacity to point out that although in theory the algorithm is wonderful, in practice it is essentially useless because processes rarely know their maximum resource needs will be in advance. In addition, the number of processes is not fixed, but dynamically varying as new users log in and out. Furthermore, resources that were thought to be available can suddenly vanish (tape drives can break).

In summary, the schemes described earlier under the name "prevention" are overly restrictive, and the algorithm described here as "avoidance" requires information that is usually not available. If you can think of a general-purpose algorithm that does the job in practice as well as in theory, write it up and send it to your local computer science journal.

For specific applications, many excellent special-purpose algorithms are known. As an example, in many data base systems, an operation that occurs frequently is requesting locks on several records and then updating all the locked records. When multiple processes are running at the same time, there is a real danger of deadlock.

The approach often used is called **two-phase locking**. In the first phase, the process tries to lock all the records it needs, one at a time. If it succeeds, it performs its updates and releases the locks. If some record is already locked, it releases the locks it already has and just starts all over. In a certain sense, this approach is similar to requesting all the resources needed in advance, or at least before anything irreversible is done.

However, this strategy is not applicable in general. In real time systems and process control systems, for example, it is not acceptable to just terminate a process partway through because a resource is not available and start all over again. Neither is it acceptable to start over if the process has read or written messages to the network, updated files or anything else that cannot be safely repeated. The algorithm works only in those situations where the programmer has very carefully arranged things so that the program can be stopped at any point during the first phase and restarted. Many applications cannot be structured this way.

3.4. OVERVIEW OF I/O IN MINIX

MINIX I/O is structured as shown in Fig. 3-6. In the following sections we will look briefly at each of the layers, with the emphasis on the device drivers. Interrupt handling was covered in the previous chapter, and the device-independent I/O will be discussed when we come to the file system, in Chap. 5.

3.4.1. Interrupt Handlers in MINIX

Many of the device drivers start some I/O device and then block, waiting for a message to arrive. That message is generated by the interrupt handler, as we have seen. Other device drivers do not start any physical I/O (e.g., reading from RAM disk), and do not wait for a message from an I/O device. Since, as we have mentioned, the subject of interrupts has been gone over in great detail in the previous chapter, we will say no more about it here.

3.4.2. Device Drivers in MINIX

For each class of I/O device present in a MINIX system, a separate I/O task (device driver) is present. These drivers are full-fledged processes, each with its own state, registers, memory map, and so on. Device drivers communicate with each other (where necessary) and with the file system using the standard message passing mechanism used by all MINIX processes. Furthermore, each device driver is written as a single source file, such as *clock.c* or *floppy.c*. The only difference between device drivers and other processes is that the device drivers are linked together with the kernel, and thus all share a common address space.

This design is highly modular and moderately efficient. It is also one of the few places where MINIX differs from UNIX in an essential way. In MINIX a process reads a file by sending a message to the file system process. The file system, in turn, may send a message to the disk driver asking it to read the needed block. This sequence (slightly simplified from reality) is shown in Fig. 3-14(a). By making these interactions via the message mechanism, we force various parts of the system to interface in standard ways with other parts. Nevertheless, by putting all the device drivers in the kernel address space, they have easy access to the process table and other key data structures when needed.

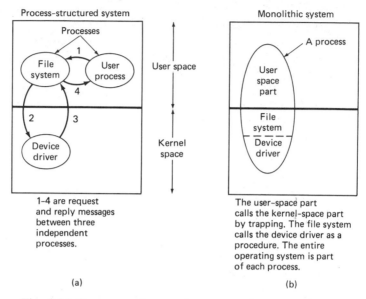

Fig. 3-14. Two ways of structuring user-system communication.

In UNIX all processes have two parts: a user-space part and a kernel-space part, as shown in Fig. 3-14(b). When a system call is made, the operating system switches from the user-space part to the kernel-space part in a somewhat magical way. This structure is a remnant of the MULTICS design, in which the switch was just an ordinary procedure call, rather than a trap followed by saving the state of the user-part, as it is in UNIX.

Device drivers in UNIX are simply kernel procedures that are called by the kernel-space part of the process. When a driver needs to wait for an interrupt, it calls a kernel procedure that puts it to sleep until some interrupt handler wakes it up. Note that it is the user process itself that is being put to sleep here, because the kernel and user parts are really different parts of the same process.

Among operating system designers, arguments about the merits of monolithic systems, as in UNIX, versus process-structured systems, as in MINIX, are endless. The MINIX approach is better structured (more modular), has cleaner interfaces between the pieces, and extends easily to distributed systems in which the various processes run on different computers. The UNIX approach is more efficient, because procedure calls are much faster than sending messages. MINIX was split into many processes because I believe that with increasingly powerful microcomputers available, cleaner software structure was worth making the system somewhat slower. Be warned that many operating systems designers do not share this belief.

The MINIX configuration described in this book contains drivers for RAM disk, floppy disk, clock, and terminal. (The MINIX software distribution contains additional drivers, such as printer and hard disk.) The request messages sent to these tasks contain a variety of fields used to hold the operation code (e.g., READ or WRITE) and its parameters.

For block devices, the fields of the request and reply messages are shown in Fig. 3-15. The fields for the character devices are basically similar but can vary slightly from task to task. Messages to the clock task, for example, contain times, and messages to the terminal task specify the characters to use for the intraline editing functions erase-character and kill-line.

REQUESTS

Field	Type	Meaning
m.m_type	int	Operation requested
m.DEVICE	int	Minor device to use
m.POSITION	long	Position on the minor device
m.PROC_NR	int	User process requesting the I/O
m.ADDRESS	char *	Address within PROC_NR
m.COUNT	int	Bytes to transfer

REPLIES

Field	Type	Meaning
m.m_type	int	Always TASK_REPLY
m.REP_PROC_NR	int	Same as PROC_NR in request
m.REP_STATUS	int	# Bytes transferred or error number

Fig. 3-15. Fields of the message m, sent to and by block device drivers.

The function of each task is to accept requests from other processes, normally the file system, and carry them out. All tasks have been written to get a message, carry it out, and send a reply. Among other things, this decision means that tasks are strictly sequential and do not contain any internal multiprogramming to keep them simple. When a hardware request has been issued, the task does a RECEIVE operation specifying that it is interested only in accepting interrupt messages, not new requests for work. Any new request messages are just kept waiting until the current work has been done (rendezvous principle).

The main program for each driver is structurally the same and is outlined in Fig. 3-16. When the system first comes up, each of the drivers is started up in turn to give them a chance to initialize internal tables and similar things. Then each one blocks by trying to get a message. When a message comes in, the identity of the caller is saved, and a procedure is called to carry out the work, with a different procedure invoked for each operation available. After the work has been finished, a reply is sent back to the caller, and the task then goes back to the top of the loop to wait for the next request.

```
message mess;                   /* message buffer */

io_task()
{
  int r, caller;

  initialize();                 /* only done once, during system init. */

  while (TRUE) {
        receive(ANY, &mess);    /* wait for a request for work */
        caller = mess.m_source; /* process from whom message came */

        switch(mess.m_type) {   /* handle each possible request type */
                case READ:      r = do_read();  break;
                case WRITE:     r = do_write(); break;
                case OTHER:     r = do_other(); break;
                default:        r = ERROR;
        }

        mess.m_type = TASK_REPLY;
        mess.REP_STATUS = r;    /* result code */
        send(caller, &mess);    /* send reply message back to caller */
  }
}
```

Fig. 3-16. Outline of the main procedure of an I/O task.

Each of the *do_xxx* procedures handles one of the operations of which the driver is capable. It returns a status code telling what happened. The status code, which is included in the reply message as the field *REP_STATUS*, is the count of bytes transferred (zero or positive) if all went well, or the error number (negative) if something went wrong. This count may differ from the number of bytes requested. On terminals, for example, at most one line is returned, even if the count requested is larger.

3.4.3. Device-Independent I/O Software in MINIX

The MINIX file system process contains all the device-independent I/O code. The I/O system is so closely related to the file system that they were merged into one process. The functions performed by the file system are those shown in Fig. 3-5, except for requesting and releasing dedicated devices, which do not exist in MINIX as it is presently configured, but which could easily be added to the relevant device drivers should the need arise in the future.

In addition to handling the interface with the drivers, buffering, block allocation and the like, the file system also handles protection and the management of i-nodes, directories, and mounted file systems. The file system will be covered in detail in Chap. 5.

3.4.4. User-level I/O Software in MINIX

The general model outlined earlier in this chapter also applies here. Library procedures are available for making system calls and for converting from binary to ASCII and ASCII to binary. The standard MINIX configuration does not contain any spooler daemons, but since they are just user processes, it is easy to add them as needed later.

3.4.5. Deadlock Handling in MINIX

True to its heritage, MINIX follows the same path as UNIX with respect to deadlocks: it just ignores the problem altogether. MINIX contains no dedicated I/O devices, although if someone wanted to hang an industry standard 9-track magnetic tape drive on an IBM PC, making the software for it would not pose any special problems. In short, the only place deadlocks can occur are with the implicit shared resources, such as process table slots, i-node table slots, and so on. None of the known deadlock algorithms can deal with resources like these that are not requested explicitly.

Actually, the above is not strictly true. A few places do exist where considerable care has been taken to avoid problems. The main one is the interaction between the file system and the memory manager. The memory manager sends messages to the file system to read the binary file (executable program) during an EXEC system call, as well as in other contexts. If the file system is not idle when the memory manager is trying to send to it, the memory manager will be blocked. If the file system should then try to send a message to the memory manager, it too would discover that the rendezvous fails, and would block, leading to a deadlock.

This problem has been avoided by constructing the system in such a way that the file system never sends *request* messages to the memory manager, just *replies*, with one minor exception. The one exception is that upon starting up, the file system reports its size to the memory manager, which is guaranteed to be waiting for it.

3.5. RAM DISKS

In the following sections we will get back to the device drivers, the main topic of this chapter, and study several of them in detail. The drivers to be covered are the RAM disk, floppy disk, clock, and terminal. Each of these is interesting for a different reason. The RAM disk is a good example to study because it has all the properties of block devices in general—except the actual I/O (because the "disk" is actually just a portion of memory). This simplicity makes it a good place to start. The floppy disk shows what a real disk driver looks like, warts and all. The clock is important because every system has one, and because it is completely different from all the other drivers. The terminal driver is important in its own right, and furthermore, is a good example of a character device driver.

Each of these sections describes the relevant hardware, the software principles behind the driver, an overview of the implementation, and the code itself. This structure makes the sections useful reading even for those readers who are not interested in the details of the code itself.

3.5.1. RAM Disk Hardware and Software

The idea behind a RAM disk is simple. A block device is a storage medium with two commands: write a block and read a block. Normally these blocks are stored on rotating memories, such as floppy disks or hard disks. A RAM disk is simpler. It just uses a preallocated portion of the main memory for storing the blocks. A RAM disk has the advantage of having instant access (no seek or rotational delay), making it suitable for storing programs or data that are frequently accessed.

In a system such as MINIX, which was designed to work even on computers with only one floppy disk, the RAM disk has another advantage. By putting the root device on the RAM disk, the one floppy disk can be mounted and unmounted at will, allowing for removable media. Putting the root device on the floppy disk would make it impossible to save files on floppies, since the root device (the only floppy) cannot be unmounted. In addition, having the root device on the RAM disk makes the system highly flexible: any combination of floppy disks or hard disks can be mounted on it.

As an aside, it is worth briefly pointing out a difference between systems that support mounted file systems and those that do not (e.g., MS-DOS). With mounted file systems, the root device is always present and in a fixed location, and removable file systems (i.e., disks) can be mounted in the file tree to form an integrated file system. Once everything has been mounted, the user need not worry at all about which device a file is on.

In contrast, with systems like MS-DOS, the user must specify the location of each file, either explicitly as in B:FILE or using certain defaults (current device, current directory, and so on). With only one or two floppy disks, this burden is manageable, but on a large computer system, with dozens of disks, having to keep track of devices all the time would be unbearable. Remember that UNIX runs on systems ranging from an IBM PC, through 68000s and VAXes to the Cray-2; MS-DOS runs only on very small systems.

Figure 3-17 shows the idea behind a RAM disk. The RAM disk is split up into n blocks, depending on how much memory has been allocated for it. Each block is the same size as the block size used on the real disks. When the driver receives a message to read or write a block, it just computes where in the RAM disk memory the requested block lies, and reads or writes from it, instead of from a floppy or hard disk. Normally the transfer will be done by calling an assembly language procedure that copies to or from the user program at the maximum speed of which the hardware is capable.

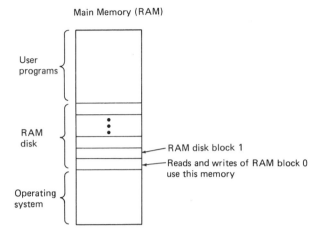

Fig. 3-17. A RAM disk.

A RAM disk driver may support several areas of memory used as RAM disk, each distinguished by a different minor device number. Usually these areas will be distinct, but in some situations it may be convenient to have them overlap, as we shall see in the next section.

3.5.2. Overview of the RAM Disk Driver in MINIX

The RAM disk driver is actually four closely related drivers in one. Each message to it specifies a minor device as follows:

0: /dev/ram   1: /dev/mem   2: /dev/kmem   3: /dev/null

The first special file listed above, */dev/ram*, is a true RAM disk. Neither its size nor its origin is built in to the driver. They are determined by the file system by booting the root file system when MINIX is booted. This strategy makes it possible to increase or reduce the amount of RAM disk present without having to recompile the operating system. All one needs to do is use a different root file system diskette.

The next two minor devices are used to read and write physical memory and kernel memory, respectively. When */dev/mem* is opened and read, it yields the contents of physical memory locations starting at absolute 0 (the interrupt vectors). Ordinary user programs will never do this, but a system program concerned with debugging the system might need this facility. Opening */dev/mem* and writing on it will change the interrupt vectors. Needless to say, this should only be done with the greatest of caution by an experienced user who knows exactly what he is doing.

The special file */dev/kmem* is like */dev/mem*, except that byte 0 of this file is byte 0 of the kernel's memory (physical address 0x600 or 1536 decimal in MINIX). It too is used mostly for debugging and very special programs. Note that the RAM disk areas covered by these two minor devices overlap. Opening /dev/mem and seeking to 1536 is the same as reading from /dev/kmem, except that the latter will continue to work even if in a subsequent version of MINIX the kernel is moved somewhere else in memory. Both of these special files are protected to prevent everyone except the super-user from using them. The last file in this group, /dev/null, is a special file that accepts data and throws them away. It is commonly used in shell commands when the program being called generates output that is not needed. For example,

```
a.out >/dev/null
```

runs the program *a.out*, but discards its output. The RAM disk driver effectively treats this minor device as having zero size, so no data are ever copied to or from it.

The overall structure of the RAM disk driver follows the model of Fig. 3-16. The main loop accepts messages and dispatches to either *do_mem* for reading and writing, or to *do_setup* for the special message telling the driver where the RAM disk is located. When MINIX is booted, the kernel runs, then the memory manager, and then the file system. One of the first things the file system does is to see how far up in memory the operating system extends. Then it reads the super block of the root file system to see how big it is (and thus how big the RAM disk must be to hold it). Once the file system knows where the operating system ends and how much memory the RAM disk needs, it sends the message to the RAM disk driver telling it the lower and upper limits of the RAM disk.

The code for handling /dev/ram, /dev/mem, and /dev/kmem is identical. The only difference among them is that each one corresponds to a different portion of memory, indicated by the arrays *ram_origin* and *ram_limit*, each indexed by minor device number.

3.5.3. Implementation of the RAM Disk Driver in MINIX

The implementation is straightforward and requires little comment. The main procedure, on line 2292, gets messages, dispatches to the appropriate procedure, and sends the replies. The procedure *do_mem* (line 2337) computes two key variables: *mem_phys*, the physical location in memory of the RAM disk block to be read or written, and *user_phys*, the physical location where the block is to go to or come from. Both of these absolute addresses are 32-bit quantities. The procedure *umap* (line 5021) computes the physical address corresponding to a given virtual address within a given process's address space. It is used throughout the kernel for this purpose.

Once *mem_phys* and *user_phys* have been computed, the only thing left to do is call *phys_copy*, the assembly code copy routine to move the block from RAM disk to the caller or vice versa. Normally, the only process to send messages to the RAM disk driver is the file system, which requests blocks to be copied to or from its buffer cache, not directly to user processes.

The procedure *do_setup* (line 2377) takes the parameters in the message and sets up the starting and ending points of the RAM disk, so they can be used in subsequent calls. The limits of the other minor devices are fixed and cannot be set.

3.6. DISKS

The RAM disk is a good introduction to disk drivers (because it is so simple), but real disks have a number of issues that we have not touched on yet. In the following sections we will first say a few words about disk hardware, and then take a look at disk drivers in general and the MINIX floppy disk driver in particular. We will not examine the hard disk driver because it is structurally similar, and besides, not every IBM PC has a hard disk.

3.6.1. Disk Hardware

All real disks are organized into cylinders, each one containing as many tracks as there are heads stacked vertically. The tracks are divided into sectors, with the number of sectors around the circumference typically being 8 to 32. All sectors contain the same number of bytes, although a little thought will make it clear that sectors close to the outer rim of the disk will be physically longer than those close to the hub. The extra space is not used.

A device feature that has important implications for the disk driver is the possibility of a controller doing seeks on two or more drives at the same time. These are known as **overlapped seeks**. While the controller and software are waiting for a seek to complete on one drive, the controller can initiate a seek on another drive. Many controllers can also read or write on one drive while seeking on one or more other drives, but none can read or write on two drives at the same time. (Reading or writing requires the controller to move bits on a microsecond time scale, so one transfer uses up most of its computing power.) The ability to perform two or more seeks at the same time can reduce the average access time considerably.

The parameters of the IBM PC floppy disks are shown in Fig. 3-18. These are the parameters of the standard double-sided, double-density diskettes as used by MINIX. Some other operating systems also support single-sided diskettes, 8 sectors per track, and other configurations. MINIX uses 1K blocks, so the blocks used by the software consist of two consecutive sectors, which are always read or written together as a unit.

Number of cylinders:	40	Seek time (adjacent cylinders)	6 msec
Tracks per cylinder:	2	Seek time (average case)	77 msec
Sectors per track:	9	Rotation time	200 msec
Sectors per diskette:	720	Motor start/stop time	250 msec
Bytes per sector:	512	Time to transfer 1 sector	22 msec
Bytes per diskette:	368640		

Fig. 3-18. Parameters of the IBM PC floppy disks.

3.6.2. Disk Software

In this section we will look at some of the issues related to disk drivers in general. The time to read or write a disk block is determined by three factors: the seek time (the time to move the arm to the proper cylinder), the rotational delay (the time for the proper sector to rotate under the head), and the actual transfer time. For most disks, the seek time dominates, so reducing the mean seek time can improve system performance substantially.

Disk Arm Scheduling Algorithms

If the disk driver accepts requests one at a time and carries them out in the order, that is, First-Come, First-Served (FCFS), little can be done to optimize seek time. However, another strategy is possible when the disk is heavily loaded. It is likely that while the arm is seeking on behalf of one request, other disk requests may be generated by other processes. Many disk drivers maintain a table, indexed by cylinder number, with all the pending requests for each cylinder chained together in a linked list headed by the table entries.

Given this kind of data structure, we can improve upon the First-Come, First-Served scheduling algorithm. To see how, consider a disk with 40 cylinders. A request comes in to read a block on cylinder 11. While the seek to cylinder 11 is in progress, new requests come in for cylinders 1, 36, 16, 34, 9, and 12, in that order. They are entered into the table of pending requests, with a separate linked for each cylinder. The requests are shown in Fig. 3-19.

When the current request (for cylinder 11) is finished, the disk driver has a choice of which request to handle next. Using FCFS, it would go next to cylinder 1, then to 36, and so on. This algorithm would require arm motions of 10, 35, 20, 18, 25, and 3, respectively, for a total of 111 cylinders.

Alternatively, it could always handle the closest request next, to minimize seek time. Given the requests of Fig. 3-19, the sequence is 12, 9, 16, 1, 34, and 36, as shown as the jagged line at the bottom of Fig. 3-19. With this sequence, the arm motions are 1, 3, 7, 15, 33, and 2, for a total of 61 cylinders. This algorithm, **shortest seek first** (SSF), cuts the total arm motion almost in half compared to FCFS.

Unfortunately, SSF has a problem. Suppose more requests keep coming in while the requests of Fig. 3-19 are being processed. For example, if, after going

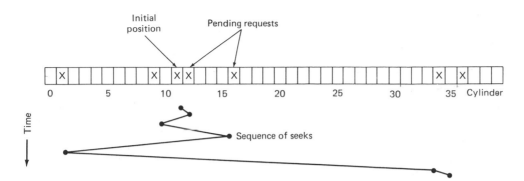

Fig. 3-19. Shortest seek first (SSF) disk scheduling algorithm.

to cylinder 15, a new request for cylinder 8 is present, that request will have priority over cylinder 1. If a request for cylinder 13 then comes in, the arm will next go to 13, instead of 1. With a heavily loaded disk, the arm will tend to stay in the middle of the disk most of the time, so requests at either extreme will have to wait until a statistical fluctuation in the load causes there to be no requests near the middle. Requests far from the middle may get poor service. The goals of minimal response time and fairness are in conflict here.

Tall buildings also have to deal with this tradeoff. The problem of scheduling an elevator in a tall building is similar to that of scheduling a disk arm. Requests come in continuously calling the elevator to floors (cylinders) at random. The microprocessor running the elevator could easily keep track of the sequence in which customers pushed the call button, and service them using FCFS. It could also use SSF.

However, most elevators use a different algorithm to reconcile the conflicting goals of efficiency and fairness. They keep moving in the same direction until there are no more outstanding requests in that direction, then they switch directions. This algorithm, known both in the disk world and the elevator world as the **elevator algorithm**, requires the software to maintain 1 bit: the current direction bit, *UP* or *DOWN*. When a request finishes, the disk or elevator driver checks the bit. If it is *UP*, the arm or cabin is moved to the next highest pending request, if any. If no requests are pending at higher positions, the direction bit is reversed. When the bit is set to *DOWN*, the move is to the next lowest requested position, if any.

Figure 3-20 shows the elevator algorithm using the same seven requests as Fig. 3-20, assuming the direction bit was initially *UP*. The order in which the cylinders are serviced is 12, 16, 34, 36, 9, and 1, which yields arm motions of 1, 4, 18, 2, 27, and 8, for a total of 60 cylinders. In this case the elevator algorithm is slightly better than SSF, although it is usually worse. One nice property that the elevator algorithm has is that given any collection of requests, the upper bound on the total motion is fixed: it is just twice the number of cylinders.

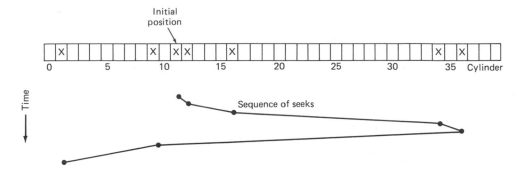

Fig. 3-20. The elevator algorithm for scheduling disk requests.

A slight modification of this algorithm that has a smaller variance in response times (Teory, 1972) is to always scan in the same direction. When the highest numbered cylinder with a pending request has been serviced, the arm goes to the lowest-numbered cylinder with a pending request and then continues moving in an upward direction. In effect, the lowest-numbered cylinder is thought of as being just above the highest-numbered cylinder.

Some disk controllers provide a way for the software to inspect the current sector number under the head. With one of these controllers, another optimization is possible. If two or more requests for the same cylinder are pending, the driver can issue a request for the sector that will pass under the head next. Note that when multiple tracks are present in a cylinder, consecutive requests can be for different tracks with no penalty. The controller can select any of its heads instantaneously, because head selection involves neither arm motion nor rotational delay.

When several drives are present a pending request table should be kept for each drive separately. Whenever any drive is idle, a seek should be issued to move its arm to the cylinder where it will be needed next (assuming the controller allows overlapped seeks). When the current transfer finishes, a check can be made to see if any drives are positioned on the correct cylinder. If one or more are, the next transfer can be started on a drive that is already on the right cylinder. If none of the arms is in the right place, the driver should issue a new seek on the drive that just completed a transfer, and wait until the next interrupt to see which arm gets to its destination first.

Error Handling

RAM disks do not have to worry about seek or rotational optimization: at any instant all blocks can be read or written without any physical motion. Another area in which RAM disks are considerably simpler than real disks is error handling. Real disks are subject to a wide variety of errors. Some of the more common ones are:

1. Programming error (e.g., request for nonexistent sector).

2. Transient checksum error (e.g., caused by dust on the head).

3. Permanent checksum error (e.g., disk block physically damaged).

4. Seek error (e.g., the arm sent to cylinder 6 but it went to 7).

5. Controller error (e.g., controller refuses to accept commands).

It is up to the disk driver to handle each of these as best it can.

Programming errors occur when the driver tells the controller to seek to a nonexistent cylinder, read from a nonexistent sector, use a nonexistent head, or transfer to or from nonexistent memory. Most controllers check the parameters given to them and complain if they are invalid. In theory, these errors should never occur, but what should the driver do if the controller indicates that one has happened? For a home-grown system, the best thing to do is stop and print a message like "Call the programmer" so the error can be tracked down and fixed. For a commercial software product in use at thousands of sites around the world, this approach is less attractive. Probably the only thing to do is terminate the current disk request with an error and hope it will not recur too often.

Transient checksum errors are caused by specks of dust in the air that get between the head and the disk surface. Most of the time they can be eliminated by just repeating the operation a few times. If the error persists, the block has to be marked as a **bad block** and avoided.

One way to avoid bad blocks is to write a very special program that takes a list of bad blocks as input, and carefully hand crafts a file containing all the bad blocks. Once this file has been made, the disk allocator will think these blocks are occupied and never allocate them. As long as no one ever tries to read the bad block file, no problems will occur.

Not reading the bad block file is easier said than done. Many disks are backed up by copying their contents a track at a time to a backup tape or disk drive. If this procedure is followed, the bad blocks will cause trouble. Backing up the disk one file at a time is slower, but will solve the problem, provided that the backup program knows the name of the bad block file and refrains from copying it.

Some "intelligent" controllers reserve a few tracks not normally available to user programs. When a disk drive is formatted, the controller determines which blocks are bad and automatically substitutes one of the spare tracks for the bad one. The table that maps bad tracks to spare tracks is kept in the controller's internal memory and on the disk. This substitution is transparent (invisible) to the driver, except that its carefully worked out elevator algorithm may perform poorly if the controller is secretly using cylinder 800 whenever cylinder 3 is requested.

Seek errors are caused by mechanical problems in the arm. The controller keeps track of the arm position internally. To perform a seek, it issues a series of pulses to the arm motor, one pulse per cylinder, to move the arm to the new cylinder. When the arm gets to its destination, the controller reads the actual cylinder number (written when the drive was formatted). If the arm is in the wrong place, a seek error has occurred.

Some controllers correct seek errors automatically, but others (including the IBM PC's) just set an error bit and leave the rest to the driver. The driver handles this error by issuing a RECALIBRATE command, to move the arm as far as out as it will go, and reset the controller's internal idea of the current cylinder to 0. Usually this solves the problem. If it does not, the drive must be repaired.

As we have seen, the controller is really a specialized little computer, complete with software, variables, buffers, and occasionally, bugs. Sometimes an unusual sequence of events such as an interrupt on one drive occurring simultaneously with a RECALIBRATE command for another drive will trigger a bug and cause the controller to go into a loop or lose track of what it was doing. Controller designers usually plan for the worst and provide a pin on the chip or board, which, when set high, forces the controller to forget whatever it was doing and reset itself. If all else fails, the disk driver can set a bit to invoke this signal and reset the controller. If that does not help, all the driver can do is print a message and give up.

Track-at-a-Time Caching

The time required to seek to a new cylinder is usually much more than the rotation or transfer time. In other words, once the driver has gone to the trouble of moving the arm somewhere, it hardly matters whether it reads one sector or a whole track. This effect is especially true if the controller provides rotational sensing, so the driver can see which sector is currently under the head and issue a request for the next sector, thereby making it possible to read a track in one rotation time. (Normally it takes half a rotation plus one sector time just to read a single sector, on the average.)

Some disk drivers take advantage of this property by maintaining a secret track-at-a-time cache, unknown to the device-independent software. If a sector that is in the cache is needed, no disk transfer is required. A disadvantage of track-at-a-time caching (in addition to the software complexity and buffer space needed) is that transfers from the cache to the calling program will have to be done by the CPU using a programmed loop, rather than letting the DMA hardware do the job.

Some controllers take this process a step further, and do track-at-a-time caching in their own internal memory, transparent to the driver, so that transfer between the controller and memory can use DMA. If the controller works this way, there is little point in having the disk driver do it as well. Note that both the controller and the driver are in a good position to read and write entire tracks in one command, but that the device-independent software cannot, because it regards a disk as a linear sequence of blocks, without regard to how they are divided up into tracks and cylinders.

3.6.3. Overview of the Floppy Disk Driver in MINIX

The floppy disk driver accepts and processes two messages: for reading a block and for writing a block. A block is of size *BLOCK_SIZE*, which is defined in *h/type.h*, and is 1024 bytes in the standard distribution, although it can be easily changed. The sector size on the disk is 512 bytes, so two consecutive sectors are always read or written together. The advantage of the larger block size is a reduction in the number of disk accesses required, and thus an improvement in performance. The price paid is that a file of only 1 character nevertheless ties up 1024 bytes of disk space.

The messages accepted by the floppy disk driver use the format of Fig. 3-15. These messages are normally sent by the file system, and request data to be transferred to or from buffers internal to the file system. The file system takes care of the transfer to or from the address space of the process making the system call. The reply messages also follow the form of Fig. 3-15, with the *REP_STATUS* field containing the number of bytes actually transferred or an error code if the request could not be carried out (e.g., disk error, invalid buffer address supplied).

The floppy disk driver does not use SSF or the elevator algorithm. It is strictly sequential, accepting a request and carrying it out before even accepting the next request (FCFS). The reason for using this simple strategy has to do with the environment for which MINIX was intended—a personal computer. On a personal computer, most of the time only one process is active; once in a while there are one or two background processes. Having five processes running at once is highly unusual. With only a small number of processes, the chance that a disk request will come in while another disk request is being carried out is slight, so the potential gain from reordering requests is small. This small gain is not enough to offset the considerable increase in software complexity required for queueing requests. A driver for a large time-sharing system would undoubtedly be written differently.

The main procedure of the floppy disk driver, *floppy_task*, is similar to that of the RAM disk driver and also that of Fig. 3-16. It accepts messages, calls procedures to do the work, and sends replies, all in an endless loop. The work that needs to be done for reading and writing is virtually identical, so both are handled by the same procedure, *do_rdwt*.

Figure 3-21 shows the relation between the major procedures within the driver. Under normal conditions (i.e., no errors), *do_rdwt* calls five other procedures, each of which does part of the work of a transfer. The first one, *dma_setup*, sets up the registers of the DMA chip so that on a read, after the controller has read the data into its internal buffer, the DMA chip will take care of requesting bus cycles to transfer the data to memory without bothering the CPU.

The next procedure, *start_motor*, checks to see if the motor is running. If it is, the procedure just returns. If it is off, the motor is turned on.

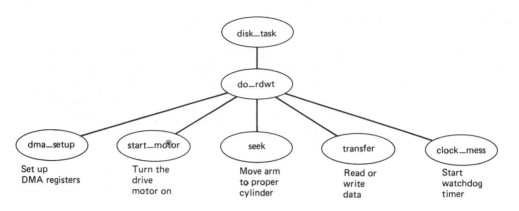

Fig. 3-21. The major procedures forming the floppy disk driver.

Seek checks to see if the drive happens to be positioned on the right cylinder already. If it is not, it commands the controller to seek, and then does a RECIEVE to wait for the interrupt message sent when the seek has been completed.

The actual command to read or write the disk is issued by *transfer*. It too, does a RECEIVE after issuing the command to wait for it to complete. When the command has completed, *transfer* inspects the controller's status registers to see if any errors occurred. If a checksum error occurred, the procedure returns an error code to *do_rdwt*, so the transfer can be tried again.

The final procedure in Fig. 3-21 sends a message to the clock task asking it to call a certain procedure (part of the disk driver) in 3 sec. This mechanism is needed for motor control. Floppy disks cannot be read or written unless their motors are on. Turning the motors on or off is slow. Leaving the motors on all the time causes the drive and diskette to wear out very quickly. The compromise chosen for MINIX is to leave a drive motor on for 3 sec after a drive is used. If the drive is used again within 3 sec, the timer is extended for another 3 sec. If the drive is not used in this interval, the motor is turned off.

Some subsidiary procedures used in the disk driver are listed below:

1. *stop_motor*- stop a drive motor.

2. *fdc_out*- issue a command to the controller.

3. *fdc_results*- extract the results of command from the controller.

4. *recalibrate*- recalibrate a drive after a seek error.

5. *reset*- reset the controller after a serious error.

6. *send_mess*- take care of actually sending a message.

3.6.4. Implementation of the Floppy Disk Driver in MINIX

The floppy disk driver is 13 pages long, despite the fact that conceptually it is hardly any more complicated than the RAM disk driver. It simply must manage a lot of detail. The first two pages contain a large number of definitions for constants. These could be removed to shorten the driver, but the resulting shorter driver would be much harder to understand than the present one.

The main data structure used in the floppy disk driver is *floppy* (line 2508), which is an array of structures, one per drive. Each structure holds information about the state of its drive and the command currently pending. It contains the disk address, memory address, controller status information and calibration state of the drive. On lines 2525 to 2530 we find the declarations for several variables global to the whole disk driver.

The main procedure is on line 2540. It is completely straightforward, basically the same as Fig. 3-16, with the addition of a little bit of error checking.

The procedure that controls the real work is *do_rdwt* on line 2576. It has one parameter, a pointer to the message just received. The first thing the procedure does (lines 2585 to 2587) is compute *fp*, the pointer to the *floppy* slot of the drive to be used. Then it dissects the message and converts the block number into cylinder, track, sector, and head positions, storing all the pieces in the *floppy* array. From this point on, *fp* is used to refer to the drive, since it now contains all the relevant information. The array *interleave* is provided to allow software interleave, if desired; at present this feature is not used.

The loop starting on line 2604 is used to allow the operation now stored in *fp* to be repeated if checksum errors occur. The code on lines 2610 to 2617 is not strictly necessary, but makes the driver more robust. If the standard double-density MINIX diskette should be run on a machine containing a quad-density drive, this code notices that many errors are occurring right at the start of operation. It then adjusts *steps_per_cyl* to have the controller issue more pulses to the arm when seeking, so that the arm takes larger steps, thus allowing the coarser double-density diskettes to be read and written anyway. In effect, the driver discovers empirically whether the drive is double- or quad-density, and adjusts its parameters accordingly.

On line 2620 a check is made to see if the flag *need_reset* is set. If it is, *reset* is called to reset the controller. If any of the procedures called by *do_rdwt* discover that the controller is no longer responding, they set *need_reset* so that next time through the loop it will be reset.

Now the DMA chip is set up with the user buffer address and count taken from the message and put in *floppy*. Next, the motor is started, if necessary, and the seek command issued, again, if necessary. If the seek fails, for example, due to a controller that is not responding, the current attempt is cut off on line 2631, and the whole process started again. The next time through the loop the controller will be reset by the call on line 2620, if that is needed.

The actual data transfer is initiated by the call on line 2633. If it succeeds, the loop is exited. The loop is also exited if a write fails because the diskette is write protected (retries will not help here).

The code following the loop (lines 2640 and 2641) sets the watchdog timer by sending a message to the clock task, asking it to call the procedure *stop_motor* in 3 sec to stop the motor. If the timer runs out, the variable *motor_goal* tells *stop_motor* what status to set the motors to.

The rest of the driver contains procedures that allow *do_rdwt* to function as described above. *Dma_setup* loads the memory address and count into the DMA chip. The only thing peculiar about it is the check to make sure that a DMA buffer does not cross a 64K boundary. That is, a 1K DMA buffer may begin at 64510, but not at 64514 because the latter extends just beyond the 64K boundary at 65536.

This annoying rule occurs because the IBM PC uses an old DMA chip, the Intel 8237A, which contains a 16-bit counter, whereas a counter of at least 20 bits is needed because DMA uses absolute addresses, not addresses relative to a segment register. The low-order 16 bits of the DMA address are loaded into the 8237A, and the high-order 4 bits are loaded into a 4-bit latch. When the 8237A goes from 0xFFFF to 0x0000 it does not generate a carry into the 4-bit latch, so the DMA address suddenly jumps down by 64K in memory. Unexpected hardware "features" like this can cause weeks of time spent looking for exceedingly obscure bugs (all the more so when, like this one, the technical reference manual says nary a word about them).

Start_motor (line 2703) manages the motors. It calls *lock* to disable interrupts temporarily while checking the motor status, and computes the new motor goal. The 2 low-order bits of *motor_goal* contain the drive being selected. The next 2 bits set the controller in normal (interrupt enabled) mode. The high-order 4 bits control the motors for the four drives the controller can handle, 1 meaning motor on and 0 meaning motor off.

If the motor is off, it is necessary to delay while it is starting up. This delay is achieved on line 2732 by sending the clock a message, requesting that it call the function *send_mess* after 250 msec. That function (line 3003) sends the message received on line 2733.

Stopping the motor works a little differently. When the timer runs out for killing the motor, the procedure *stop_motor* (line 2740) is called by the clock task. Instead of going to the trouble of sending a message to the disk task, it just outputs the desired motor status to the hardware directly.

The procedure *seek* (line 2757) first checks to see if the drive is uncalibrated, a condition that happens when a seek error occurs. If it is uncalibrated, it is first recalibrated. If the current cylinder is the one needed (line 2769), *seek* just returns immediately. Otherwise it issues a seek and waits for the interrupt message on line 2776. The test on line 2775 is needed because if the controller refused to accept the seek command, waiting for the interrupt would be fatal: it would never happen.

After the interrupt comes in, *seek* checks the status reported by calling *fdc_results* on line 2780 to ask the floppy disk controller (FDC) to report back what happened. Unfortunately, even the status reporting may fail, since asking for the status is itself a command that the controller may refuse to accept. If the status is reported back properly, but indicates that there was a seek error, then the drive must be recalibrated.

For someone used to ordinary application programs, it may appear that an inordinate amount of the code in the driver deals with balky controllers and drives that refuse to go where they are told to go. In truth, the controller and drives are fairly reliable, but not having all this checking would mean that every once in a while MINIX would just crash for no apparent reason. To spare the user from this unpleasantry, the driver must be on guard against all kinds of unlikely, but theoretically possible events. It is also worth mentioning that the IBM PC's floppy disk controller, the NEC PD765 (a single chip costing less than 10 dollars), is about as simple as they come. More sophisticated (and expensive) controllers do much more of the error handling themselves.

The procedure *transfer* actually issues the command to the controller to initiate the read or write. Issuing the command consists of successively outputting 9 bytes of information (lines 2805 to 2813). After the command has been issued, *transfer* waits for the interrupt message, gets the results, and checks for errors.

Getting the results from the controller is not just a matter of reading a register or two. It requires a complex negotiation protocol with the controller in *fdc_results* (line 2843). All kinds of things may go wrong and must be checked for. As if this were not enough, the timing of the negotiation protocol is also important.

Even outputting a byte to the controller is complicated and requires a whole procedure, *fdc_out* (line 2872). The problem is that the controller has a mind of its own. You cannot force it to accept a command. There has to a complex negotiation to determine whether it is in the mood or not. Recalibrating a drive and resetting the controller are handled by *recalibrate* (line 2903) and *reset* (line 2945), respectively.

The final two procedures in *floppy.c* take care of sending messages. *Clock_mess* (line 2986) sends a message to the clock task requesting a time out. *Send_mess* (line 3003) is called by the clock task itself when the motor has gotten up to speed. The message sent here is received on line 2733 to wake up the disk task.

All in all, the disk task is conceptually simple but full of detail, some of it inherent in running a real I/O device and some of it due to the fact that the PD765 is a very primitive controller. (On the other hand, a look *inside* the PD765 will quickly reveal how complex it is and how many things it does do by itself.) We will not study any more block devices in this book. Conceptually, they are all the same, differing only in the gory details, which, as we have seen, are plentiful.

3.7. CLOCKS

Clocks (also called **timers**) are essential to the operation of any time-sharing system for a variety of reasons. They maintain the time of day and prevent one process from monopolizing the CPU, among other things. The clock software generally takes the form of a device driver, even though a clock is neither a block device, like a disk, nor a character device, like a terminal. Our examination of clocks will follow the same pattern as in the previous sections: first a look at clock hardware and software in general, and then a closer look at how these ideas are applied in MINIX.

3.7.1. Clock Hardware

Two types of clocks are commonly used in computers, and both are quite different from the clocks and watches used by people. The simpler clocks are tied to the 110 or 220 volt power line, and cause an interrupt on every voltage cycle, at 50 or 60 Hz.

The other kind of clock is built out of three components: a crystal oscillator, a counter, and a holding register, as shown in Fig. 3-22. When a piece of quartz crystal is properly cut and mounted under tension, it can be made to generate a periodic signal of very high accuracy, typically in the range of 1 to 20 MHz, depending on the crystal chosen. This signal is fed into the counter to make it count down to zero. When the counter gets to zero, it causes a CPU interrupt.

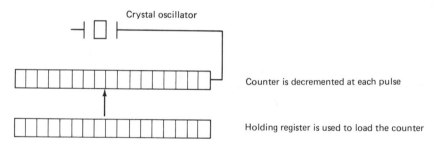

Fig. 3-22. A programmable clock.

Programmable clocks typically have several modes of operation. In **one-shot mode**, when the clock is started, it copies the value of the holding register into the counter, and then decrements the counter at each pulse from the crystal. When the counter gets to zero, it causes an interrupt and stops until it is explicitly started again by the software. In **square-wave mode**, after getting to zero and causing the interrupt, the holding register is automatically copied into the counter, and the whole process is repeated again indefinitely. These periodic interrupts are called **clock ticks**.

The advantage of the programmable clock is that its interrupt frequency can be controlled by software. If a 1 MHz crystal is used, then the counter will be pulsed every microsecond. With 16-bit registers, interrupts can be programmed to occur at rates from 1 microsec to 65.536 msec. Programmable clock chips usually contain two or three independently programmable clocks and have many other options as well (e.g., counting up instead of down, interrupts disabled, and more).

To implement a time-of-day clock, the software asks the user for the current time, which is then translated into the number of clock ticks since 12 A.M on Jan. 1, 1970, as UNIX and MINIX do, or since some other benchmark. At every clock tick, the real time is incremented by one count. To prevent the current time from being lost when the computer's power is turned off, some computers store the real time in a special register powered by a battery (battery backup).

3.7.2. Clock Software

All the clock hardware does is generate interrupts at known intervals. Everything else involving time must be done by the software, the clock driver. The exact duties of the clock driver vary among operating systems, but usually include most of the following:

1. Maintaining the time of day.

2. Preventing processes from running longer than they are allowed to.

3. Accounting for CPU usage.

4. Handling the ALARM system call made by user processes.

5. Providing watchdog timers for parts of the system itself.

6. Doing profiling, monitoring, and statistics gathering.

The first clock function, maintaining the time of day (also called the **real time**) is not difficult. It just requires incrementing a counter at each clock tick, as mentioned before. The only thing to watch out for is the number of bits in the time-of-day counter. With a clock rate of 60 Hz, a 32-bit counter will overflow in just over 2 years. Clearly the system cannot store the real time as the number of ticks since Jan. 1, 1970 in 32 bits.

Three approaches can be taken to solve this problem. The first way is to use a 64-bit counter, although doing so makes adding one to the counter a more expensive operation since it will have to be done many times a second. The second way is to maintain the time of day in seconds, rather than in ticks, using a subsidiary counter to count ticks until a whole second has been accumulated. Because 2^{32} seconds is more than 136 years, this method will work until well into the twenty-second century.

The third approach is to count in ticks, but do that relative to the time the system was booted, rather than relative to a fixed external moment. When the user types in the real time, the system boot time is calculated from the current time-of-day value and stored in memory in any convenient form. Later, when the time of day is requested, the stored time of day is added to the counter to get the current time of day. All three approaches are shown in Fig. 3-23.

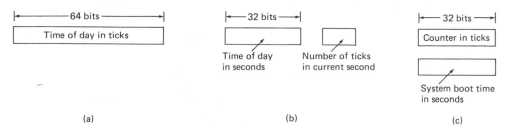

Fig. 3-23. Three ways to maintain the time of day.

The second clock function is preventing processes from running too long. Whenever a process is started, the scheduler should initialize a counter to the value of that process's quantum in clock ticks. At every clock interrupt, the clock driver decrements the quantum counter by 1. When it gets to zero, the clock driver calls the scheduler to set up another process.

The third clock function is doing CPU accounting. The most accurate way to do it is to start a second timer, distinct from the main system timer, whenever a process is started. When that process is stopped, the timer can be read out to tell how long the process has run. To do things right, the second timer should be saved when an interrupt occurs and restored afterward.

A less accurate, but much simpler, way to do accounting is to maintain a pointer to the process table entry for the currently running process in a global variable. At every clock tick, a field in the current process's entry is incremented. In this way, every clock tick is "charged" to the process running at the time of the tick. A minor problem with this strategy is that if many interrupts occur during a process's run, it will still be charged for a full tick, even though it did not get much work done. Properly accounting for the CPU during interrupts is too expensive and is never done.

In MINIX and many other systems, a process can request the operating system to give it a warning after a certain interval. The warning is usually a signal, interrupt, message, or something similar. One application requiring such warnings is networking, in which a packet not acknowledged within a certain time interval is retransmitted. Another application is computer aided instruction, where a student not providing a response within a certain time is told the answer.

If the clock driver had enough clocks, it could set a separate clock for each request. This not being the case, it must simulate multiple virtual clocks with a single physical clock. One way is to maintain a table in which the signal time for all pending timers is kept, as well as a variable giving the time of the next one. Whenever the time of day is updated, the driver checks to see if the closest signal has occurred. If it has, the table is searched for the next one to occur.

If many signals are expected, it is more efficient to simulate multiple clocks by chaining all the pending clock requests together, sorted on time, in a linked list, as shown in Fig. 3-24. Each entry on the list tells how many clock ticks following the previous one to wait before causing a signal. In this example, signals are pending for 4203, 4207, 4213, 4215, and 4216.

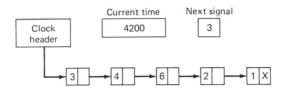

Fig. 3-24. Simulating multiple timers with a single clock.

In Fig. 3-24, the next interrupt occurs in 3 ticks. On each tick, *Next signal* is decremented. When it gets to 0, the signal corresponding to the first item on the list is caused, and that item is removed from the list. Then *Next signal* is reset to the value in the entry now at the head of the list, in this example, 4.

Note that during a clock interrupt, the clock driver has several things to do—increment the real time, decrement the quantum and check for 0, do CPU accounting, and decrement the alarm counter. However, each of these operations has been carefully arranged to be very fast because they have to be repeated many times a second.

Parts of the system also need to set timers. These are called **watchdog timers**. When studying the floppy disk driver we saw that after starting a drive motor the disk driver has to wait 250 msec before proceeding. Similarly, if no activity occurs on a drive for 3 sec after its last use, the motor has to be stopped. Some hardcopy terminals can print at 120 characters/sec (83 msec/character), but cannot return the print head to the left margin in 83 msec, so the terminal driver must delay after typing a carriage return.

The mechanism used by the clock driver to handle watchdog timers is the same as for user signals. The only difference is that when a timer goes off, instead of causing a signal, the clock driver calls a procedure supplied by the caller. The procedure is part of the caller's code, but since all the drivers are in the same address space, the clock driver can call it anyway. The called procedure can do whatever is necessary, even causing an interrupt, although within the kernel interrupts are often inconvenient and signals do not exist. That is why the watchdog mechanism is provided.

The last thing in our list is profiling. Some operating systems provide a mechanism by which a user program can have the system build up a histogram of its program counter, so it can see where it is spending its time. When profiling is a possibility, at every tick the driver checks to see if the current process is being profiled, and if so, computes the bin number (a range of addresses) corresponding to the current program counter. It then increments that bin by one. This mechanism can also be used to profile the system itself.

3.7.3. Overview of the Clock Driver in MINIX

The MINIX clock driver is contained in the file *clock.c*. It accepts these four message types, with the parameters shown:

1. SET_ALARM(process number, procedure to call, delay)

2. GET_TIME

3. SET_TIME(new time in seconds)

4. CLOCK_TICK

SET_ALARM allows a process to set a timer that goes off in a specified number of clock ticks. When a user process does an ALARM call, it sends a message to the memory manager, which then sends a message to the clock driver. When the alarm goes off, the clock driver sends a message back to the memory manager, which then takes care of making the signal happen.

SET_ALARM is also used by tasks that need to start a watchdog timer. When the timer goes off, the procedure provided is simply called. The clock driver has no knowledge of what the procedure does.

GET_TIME just returns the current real time as the number of seconds elapsed since Jan. 1, 1970 at 12:00 A.M.. *SET_TIME*, sets the real time. It can only be invoked by the super-user. Internal to the clock driver, the time is kept track of using the method of Fig. 3-23(c). When the time is set, the driver computes when the system was booted. It can make this computation because it has the current real time and it also knows how many ticks the system has been running. The system stores the real time of the boot in a variable. Later, when *GET_TIME* is called, it converts the current value of the tick counter to seconds and adds it to the stored boot time. This method is the same as that of Fig. 3-23(c).

CLOCK_TICK is the message sent to the driver when a clock interrupt occurs. It has no parameters. When the driver receives this message, it updates the real time, checks to see if it is time for the next signal or watchdog call, charges the current tick to some process, and checks to see if the quantum is up. MINIX does not currently support profiling.

The driver has a few global variables, but no major data structures. The variable *realtime* (line 0703) is a counter incremented at every clock tick. Together with the variable *boot_time* (line 3099) it allows the current time of day to be computed. *Next_alarm* records the time when the next signal or watchdog call may happen. The driver has to be careful here, because the process requesting the signal may exit or be killed before the signal happens. When it is time for the signal, a check is made to see if it is still needed. If it is not needed, it is not carried out. *Sched_ticks* keeps track of the number of ticks left until the scheduler is called. When it becomes zero, it is time to schedule a new process.

Each user process is allowed to have only one outstanding alarm timer.

Executing an ALARM call while a timer is still running cancels the first timer. Therefore, a convenient way to store the timers is to reserve one word in the process table entry for each process for its timer, if any. For tasks, the function to be called must also be stored somewhere, so an array, *watch_dog*, has been provided for this purpose.

The overall logic of the clock driver follows the same pattern as the disk drivers. The main program is an endless loop that gets messages, dispatches on the message type, and then sends a reply (except for *CLOCK_TICK*). Each message type is handled by a separate procedure, following our standard naming convention of naming all the procedures called from the main loop *do_xxx*, where *xxx* is different for each one, of course. As an aside, many linkers truncate procedure names to seven or eight characters, so the names *do_set_time* and *do_set_alarm* are potentially in conflict. The latter has been renamed *do_setalarm*. This problem occurs throughout MINIX, and is usually solved by mangling one of the names.

3.7.4. Implementation of the Clock Driver in MINIX

When MINIX starts up, all the drivers are called. Most of them just try to get a message and block. The clock driver does that too, but first it calls *init_clock* (line 3117) to initialize the programmable clock frequency to 60 Hz. Then it enters the main loop. The the main loop of the clock driver is essentially the same as the other drivers, so we will not comment on it further.

The procedure *do_setalarm* (line 3142) extracts the parameters from the message and stores the alarm time in the process table on line 3161. After setting the alarm, it scans the entire process table to find the next one.

Do_get_time (line 3175) is only two lines. It computes the current real time from the two variables *boot_time* (the system boot time in seconds) and *realtime* (the number of ticks since boot).

The procedure *do_set_time* (line 3187) is even simpler—just one line. It computes the boot time based on the given current real time and number of ticks since booting.

The procedure *do_clocktick* (line 3199) is more interesting. It first updates the real time. Remember that if a clock interrupt occurs and the clock task is not waiting for a message, the procedure *interrupt* adds one to *lost_ticks* and forgets the whole thing, knowing that another interrupt will occur soon. It is here that these lost ticks are compensated for.

Next a check is made to see if a signal or watchdog timer has gone off. If one has, all the alarm entries are inspected. Because lost ticks are compensated for all at once, several alarms may go off in one pass over the table. The procedure *cause_sig* checks to see if the memory manager is currently waiting for a message. If so, it sends a message telling about the alarm. If the memory manager is busy, a note is made to inform it at the first opportunity. For tasks, the watchdog procedure is just called directly on line 3228.

After taking care of the alarms, *accounting* is called to charge someone one clock tick.

Finally a check is made to see if it is time to call the scheduler. The variable *sched_ticks* is not reset whenever a new process is scheduled (because the file system and memory manager are allowed to run to completion). Instead it is just reset after every *SCHED_RATE* ticks. The comparison on line 3243 is to make sure that the current process has actually run at least one full scheduler tick before taking the CPU away from it.

Accounting in MINIX keeps track of both user time and system time. User time is charged against a process if it is running when the clock ticks. System time is charged if the file system or memory manager is running. The variable *bill_ptr* always points to the last user process scheduled (the two servers do not count), so the procedure *accounting* (line 3253) will know whom to charge.

3.8. TERMINALS

Every computer has one or more terminals used to communicate with it. Terminals come in an extremely large number of different forms. It is up to the terminal driver to hide all these differences, so that the device-independent part of the operating system and the user programs do not have to be rewritten for each kind of terminal. In the following sections we will follow our now-standard approach of first discussing terminal hardware and software in general, and then discussing the MINIX software.

3.8.1. Terminal Hardware

From the operating system's point of view, terminals can be divided into two broad categories based on how the operating system communicates with them. The first category consists of terminals that interface via the RS-232 standard; the second category consists of memory-mapped terminals. Each category can be further subdivided, as shown in Fig. 3-25.

RS-232 terminals are devices containing a keyboard and a display that communicate using a serial interface, one bit at a time. These terminals use a 25-pin connector, of which one pin is used for transmitting data, one pin is for receiving data, and one pin is ground. The other 22 pins are for various control functions, most of which are generally not used. To send a character to an RS-232 terminal, the computer must transmit it 1 bit at a time, prefixed by a start bit, and followed by 1 or 2 stop bits to delimit the character. Common transmission rates are 300, 1200, 2400, 4800, and 9600 bps.

Since both computers and terminals work internally with whole characters, but must communicate over a serial line a bit at a time, chips have been developed to do the character-to-serial and serial-to-character conversions. They

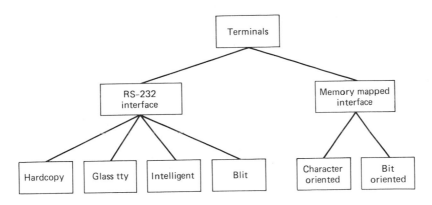

Fig. 3-25. Terminal types.

are called **UART**s (Universal Asynchronous Receiver Transmitters). UARTs are attached to the computer by plugging RS-232 interface cards into the bus as illustrated in Fig. 3-26.

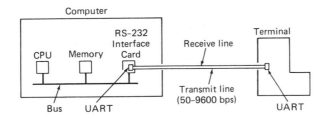

Fig. 3-26. An RS-232 terminal communicates with a computer over a communication line, one bit at a time. The computer and the terminal are completely independent.

To print a character, the terminal driver writes the character to the interface card, where it is buffered and then shifted out over the serial line one bit at a time by the UART. Even at 9600 bps, it takes just over 1 msec to send a character. As a result of this slow transmission rate, the driver will generally output a character to the RS-232 card and block, waiting for the interrupt generated by the interface when the character has been transmitted and the UART is able to accept another character. Some interface cards have a CPU and memory and can handle multiple lines, taking over much of the I/O load from the main CPU.

RS-232 terminals can be subdivided into several categories, as mentioned above. The simplest ones are hardcopy (printing) terminals. Characters typed on the keyboard are transmitted to the computer. Characters sent by the computer are typed on the paper. That's all there is.

Dumb CRT terminals work the same way, only with a screen instead of paper. These are often called "glass ttys" because they are functionally the same as hardcopy ttys. (The term "tty" is an abbreviation for Teletype†, an AT&T subsidiary that pioneered in the computer terminal business; "tty" has come to mean any terminal.)

Intelligent CRT terminals are in fact miniature computers. They have a CPU and memory, and contain complex programs, usually in EPROM or ROM. From the operating system's viewpoint, the main difference between a glass tty and an intelligent terminal is that the latter understands certain escape sequences. For example, by sending the ASCII ESC character (033), followed by various other characters, it may be possible to move the cursor to any position on the screen, insert text in the middle of the screen, and so forth.

The ultimate in intelligent terminals is a terminal that contains a CPU as powerful as the main computer, along with a megabyte or so of memory that can be downloaded from the computer to contain any program at all. The Blit (Pike et al., 1985) is an example of a terminal with a powerful microprocessor and a screen containing 800 by 1024 points, but still communicating with the computer over an RS-232 line. The advantage of the RS-232 interface is that every computer in the world has one. The disadvantage is that downloading the Blit is slow, even at 19.2 kbps.

Memory-Mapped Terminals

The other broad category of terminals named in Fig. 3-25 consists of memory-mapped terminals. These do not communicate with the computer over a serial line. They are an integral part of the computers themselves. Memory-mapped terminals are interfaced via a special memory called a **video RAM**, which forms part of the computer's address space and is addressed by the CPU the same way as the rest of memory (see Fig. 3-27).

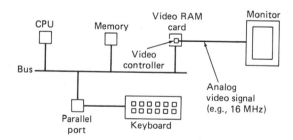

Fig. 3-27. Memory-mapped terminals write directly into video RAM.

Also on the video RAM card is a chip called a **video controller**. This chip pulls bytes out of the video RAM and generates the video signal used to drive the display (monitor). The monitor generates a beam of electrons that scans horizontally across the screen, painting lines on it. Typically the screen has 200 to

---

† Teletype is a Registered Trademark of Teletype Corp.

1200 lines from top to bottom, with 200 to 1200 points per line. These points are called **pixels**. The video controller signal modulates the electron beam, determining whether a given pixel will be light or dark. Color monitors have three beams, for red, green and blue, which are independently modulated.

A typical monochrome display might fit each character in a box 9 pixels wide by 14 pixels high (including the space between characters), and have 25 lines of 80 characters. The display would then have 350 scan lines of 720 pixels each. Each of these frames is redrawn 45 to 70 times a second. The video controller could be set up to fetch the first 80 characters from the video RAM, generate 14 scan lines, fetch another 80 characters from the video RAM, generate the following 14 scan lines, and so on. Since the first scan line contains parts of 80 characters, all 80 must be fetched into the video controller before starting the first scan line. The 9-by-14 bit patterns for the characters are kept in a ROM used by the video controller.

The IBM PC uses a character-mapped display for the console. In Fig. 3-28(a) we see a portion of the video RAM, which starts at address 0xB0000 for the monochrome display and 0xB8000 for the color display. Each character on the screen of Fig. 3-28(b) occupies two characters in the RAM. The low-order character is the ASCII code for the character to be displayed. The high-order character is the attribute byte, which is used to specify color, reverse video, blinking, and so on. The full screen of 25 by 80 characters requires 4000 bytes of video RAM.

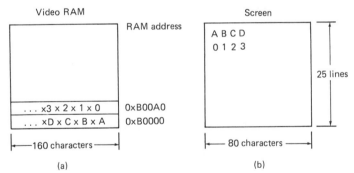

Fig. 3-28. (a) A video RAM image for the IBM monochrome display. (b) The corresponding screen. The *x*s are attribute bytes.

When a character is written into the video RAM by the CPU, it appears on the screen within one screen display time (1/50 sec for monochrome, 1/60 sec for color). The CPU can load a 4K precomputed screen image to the video RAM in 12 msec. At 9600 bps, writing 2000 characters to an RS-232 terminal takes 2083 msec, which is 174 times slower. Thus memory-mapped terminals allow for extremely fast interaction, which is why they are used.

Bit-map terminals use the same principle, except that every bit in the video RAM directly controls a single pixel on the screen. A screen of 800 by 1024 pixels requires 100K bytes of RAM (more for color), but provides complete flexibility in character fonts and sizes, allows multiple windows, and makes arbitrary graphics possible.

With a memory-mapped display, the keyboard is completely decoupled from the screen. It is usually interfaced via a parallel port, although keyboards with RS-232 interfaces also exist. On every keystroke the CPU is interrupted, and the keyboard driver extracts the character typed by reading an I/O port. On the IBM PC, interrupts are generated when every key is struck and also when it is released.

Furthermore, all that the keyboard hardware provides is the key number, not the ASCII code. When the A key is struck, the key code (30) is put in an I/O register. It is up to the driver to determine whether it is lower case, upper case, CTRL-A, ALT-A, CTRL-ALT-A, or some other combination. Since the driver can tell which keys have been struck but not yet released (e.g., shift), it has enough information to do the job. Although this keyboard interface puts the full burden on the software, it is extremely flexible. For example, user programs may be interested in whether a digit just typed came from the top row of keys or the numeric key pad on the side. In principle, the driver can provide this information.

3.8.2. Terminal Software

The keyboard and display are almost independent devices, so we will treat them separately here. (They are not quite independent, since typed characters must be displayed on the screen.) In MINIX the keyboard and screen drivers are part of the same task; in other systems they may be split into distinct drivers.

Input Software

The basic job of the keyboard driver is to collect input from the keyboard and pass it to user programs when they read from the terminal. Two possible philosophies can be adopted for the driver. In the first one, the driver's job is just to accept input and pass it upward unmodified. A program reading from the terminal gets a raw sequence of ASCII codes. (Giving user programs the key numbers is too primitive, as well as being highly machine dependent.)

This philosophy is well suited to the needs of sophisticated screen editors such as Emacs, which allow the user to bind an arbitrary action to any character or sequence of characters. It does, however, mean that if the user types *dste* instead of *date*, and then corrects the error by typing three backspaces and *ate*, followed by a line feed, the user program will be given all 11 ASCII codes typed.

Most programs do not want this much detail. They just want the corrected input, not the exact sequence of how it was produced. This observation leads to the second philosophy: the driver handles all the intraline editing, and just delivers corrected lines to the user programs. The first philosophy is character-oriented; the second one is line-oriented. They are sometimes referred to as **raw mode** and **cooked mode**, respectively. Some systems (including MINIX) provide both, with a system call available to select one or the other.

The first task of the keyboard driver is to collect characters. If every keystroke causes an interrupt, the driver can acquire the character during the interrupt. If interrupts are turned into messages by the low-level software, it is possible to put the newly acquired character in the message. Alternatively, it can be put in a small buffer in memory and the message used to tell the driver that something has arrived. The latter approach is actually safer if a message can be sent only to a waiting process and there is some chance that the keyboard driver might still be busy with the previous character.

Once the driver has received the character it must begin processing it. If the keyboard delivers key numbers rather than ASCII codes, then the driver must map the key numbers onto ASCII codes using some tables. It is worth noting that some IBM "compatibles" use nonstandard key numbering (e.g., Olivetti M24), so if the driver wants to support these machines, it must map different keyboards with different tables.

If the terminal is in cooked mode, characters must be stored until an entire line has been accumulated, because the user may subsequently decide to erase part of it. Even if the terminal is in raw mode, the program may not yet have requested input, so the characters must be buffered to allow type ahead. (System designers who do not allow users to type ahead ought to be tarred and feathered, or worse yet, be forced to use their own system.)

Two approaches to character buffering are common. In the first one, the driver contains a central pool of buffers, each buffer holding perhaps 10 characters. Associated with each terminal is a data structure, which contains, among other items, a pointer to the chain of buffers for input collected from that terminal. As more characters are typed, more buffers are acquired and hung on the chain. When the characters are passed to a user program, the buffers are removed and put back in the central pool.

The other approach is to do the buffering directly in the terminal data structure itself, with no central pool of buffers. Since it is common for users to type a command that will take a little while (say, a compilation), and then type a few lines ahead, to be safe the driver should allocate something like 200 characters per terminal. In a large-scale time-sharing system with 100 terminals, allocating 20K all the time for type ahead is clearly overkill, so a central buffer pool with space for perhaps 5K is probably enough. On the other hand, a dedicated buffer per terminal makes the driver simpler (no linked list management), and is to be preferred on personal computers with only one or two terminals. Figure 3-29 shows the difference between these two methods.

Although the keyboard and display are logically separate devices, many users have grown accustomed to seeing the characters they have just typed appear on the screen. Some terminals oblige by automatically displaying (in hardware)

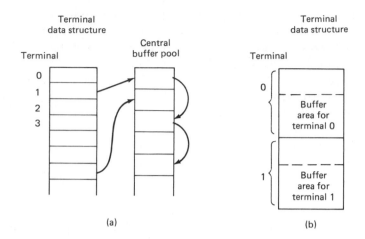

Fig. 3-29. (a) Central buffer pool. (b) Dedicated buffer for each terminal.

whatever has just been typed, which is not only a nuisance when passwords are being entered, but greatly limits the flexibility of sophisticated editors and other programs. Fortunately, most terminals display nothing when keys are typed. It is therefore up to the software to display the input. This process is called **echoing.**

Echoing is complicated by the fact that a program may be writing to the screen while the user is typing. At the very least, the keyboard driver will have to figure out where to put the new input without it being overwritten by program output.

Echoing also gets complicated when more than 80 characters are typed on a terminal with 80 character lines. Depending on the application, wrapping around to the next line may be appropriate. Some drivers just truncate lines to 80 characters.

Another problem is tab handling. Most terminals have a tab key, but few can handle tab on output. It is up to the driver to compute where the cursor is currently located, taking into account both output from programs and output from echoing, and compute the proper number of spaces to be echoed.

Now we come to the problem of device equivalence. Logically, at the end of a line of text one wants a carriage return, to move the cursor back to column 1, and a line feed, to advance to the next line. Requiring users to type both at the end of each line would not sell well (although some terminals have a key which generates both, with a 50 percent chance of doing so in the order that the software wants them). It is up to the driver to convert whatever comes in to the standard internal format used by the operating system.

If the standard form is just to store a line feed (the MINIX convention), then carriage returns should be turned into line feeds. If the internal format is to store both, then the driver should generate a line feed when it gets a carriage return and a carriage return when it gets a line feed. No matter what the internal convention, the terminal may require both a line feed and a carriage return to be echoed in order to get the screen updated properly. Since a large computer may well have a wide variety of different terminals connected to it, it is up to the keyboard driver to get all the different carriage return/line feed combinations converted to the internal system standard and arrange for all echoing to be done right.

A related problem is the timing of carriage return and line feeds. On some terminals, it takes longer to display a carriage return or line feed than a letter or number. If the microprocessor inside the terminal actually has to copy a large block of text to achieve scrolling, then line feeds may be slow. If a mechanical print head has to be returned to the left margin of the paper, carriage returns may be slow. In both cases it is up to the driver to insert **filler characters** (dummy null characters) into the output stream or just stop outputting long enough for the terminal to catch up. The amount of time to delay is often related to the terminal speed, for example, at 4800 bps or slower, no delays are needed, but at 9600 bps one filler character is required. Terminals with hardware tabs, especially hardcopy ones, may also require a delay after a tab.

When operating in cooked mode, a number of input characters have special meanings. Figure 3-30 shows these special characters for MINIX as an example. The **erase character** allows the user to rub out the character just typed. In MINIX it is the backspace (CTRL-H). It is not added to the character queue, but instead removes the previous character from the queue. It should be echoed as a sequence of three characters, backspace, space, and backspace, in order to remove the previous character from the screen. If the previous character was a tab, erasing it requires keeping track of where the cursor was prior to the tab. In most systems, backspacing will only erase characters on the current line. It will not erase a carriage return and back up into the previous line.

Character	Comment
Backspace	Back up and erase 1 character
@	Erase current line
\	Escape - accept next character literally
tab	Possibly expand to spaces on output
CTRL-S	Stop output
CTRL-Q	Start output
DEL	Interrupt process (SIGINT)
CTRL-\	Force core dump (SIGQUIT)
CTRL-D	End of file

Fig. 3-30. Characters that are handled specially in cooked mode.

When the user notices an error at the start of the line being typed in, it is often convenient to erase the entire line and start again. The **kill character** (in MINIX the @ sign) erases the entire line. It usually is echoed as itself plus a carriage return and line feed, so the user can begin typing at the left-hand margin again. (Some systems make the erased line vanish from the screen, but many users like to see the old line, so how to echo the kill character is a matter of taste.) As with the erase character, it is usually not possible to go further back than the current line. When a block of characters is killed, it may or may not be worth the trouble for the driver to return buffers to the pool, if one is used.

Sometimes the erase or kill characters must be entered as data. For example, the USENET mail system uses addresses of the form john@harvard. To make it possible to enter the local editing and other control characters, an escape character should be provided. In MINIX backslash is used. To enter an @ sign, one types \@. To enter a backslash, one types \\. After seeing a backslash, the driver sets a flag saying that the next character is exempt from special processing. The backslash itself is not entered in the character queue.

To allow users to stop a screen image from scrolling out of view, control codes are sometimes provided to freeze the screen and restart it later. In MINIX these are CTRL-S and CTRL-Q, respectively. They are not stored, but are used to set and clear a flag in the terminal data structure. Whenever output is attempted, the flag is inspected. If it is set, no output occurs. Whether echoing should also be suppressed along with program output is also a matter of the designer's taste and implementation convenience.

It is often necessary to kill a runaway program being debugged. The DEL, BREAK, or RUBOUT keys can be used for this purpose. In MINIX, DEL sends the SIGINT signal to all the processes started up from the terminal. Implementing DEL can be quite tricky. The hard part is getting the information from the driver to the part of the system that handles signals, which, after all, has not asked for this information. CRTL-\ is similar to DEL, except that it sends the SIGQUIT signal, which forces a core dump if not caught or ignored. When either of these keys is struck, the driver should echo a carriage return and line feed and discard all accumulated input to allow for a fresh start.

Another special character is CRTL-D, which in MINIX causes any pending read requests for the terminal to be satisfied with whatever is available in the buffer, even if the buffer is empty. Typing CRTL-D at the start of a line causes the program to get a read of 0 bytes, which is conventionally interpreted as end-of-file, and causes most programs to act the same way as they would upon seeing end-of-file on an input file.

Some terminal drivers allow much fancier intraline editing than we have sketched here. They have special control characters to erase a word, skip backward or forward characters or words, go to the beginning or end of the line being typed, and so forth. Adding all these functions to the terminal driver makes it much larger and, furthermore, is wasted when using fancy screen editors that work in raw mode anyway.

To allow programs to specify if they want raw mode or cooked mode input (and control other terminal parameters), MINIX provides a system call IOCTL called by

```
ioctl(file_descriptor, request, argp);
```

The variable *request* is used to specify whether the terminal parameters are to be read or changed, and which ones. The variable *argp* is a pointer to the *sgttyb* or *tchars* struct defined in *h/sgtty.h* (line 0350). It includes the erase and kill characters, which are user settable, and the terminal mode word, shown in Fig. 3-31. This particular choice of communication between program and driver was chosen for its UNIX compatibility, rather than for its inherent beauty.

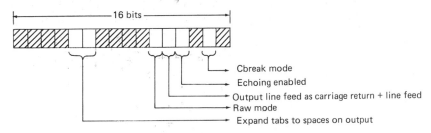

Fig. 3-31. The terminal mode word. The shaded bits are not used.

A few quick notes about the mode word are in order. Cbreak mode is a compromise between raw and cooked mode. Characters are passed to the program without waiting for a full line (as in raw mode), but DEL, CTRL-\, CTRL-S, and CTRL-Q are processed as in cooked mode. If neither raw mode nor cbreak mode is enabled, then cooked mode is the default. Echoing, carriage return generation and tab expansion can all be turned on or off independently.

Output Software

Output is simpler than input, but drivers for RS-232 terminals are radically different from drivers for memory-mapped terminals. The method that is commonly used for RS-232 terminals is to have output buffers associated with each terminal. The buffers can come from the same pool as the input buffers, or be dedicated, as with input. When programs write to the terminal, the output is first copied to the buffers. Similarly, output from echoing is also copied to the buffers. After all the output has been copied to the buffers (or the buffers are full), the first character is output, and the driver goes to sleep. When the interrupt comes in, the next character is output, and so on.

With memory-mapped terminals, a simpler scheme is possible. Characters to be printed are extracted one at a time from user space and put directly in the video RAM. With RS-232 terminals, each character to be output is just sent across the line to the terminal. With memory mapping, some characters require special treatment, among them, backspace, carriage return, line feed, and the bell (CTRL-G). A driver for a memory-mapped terminal must keep track in software of the current position in the video RAM, so that printable characters can be put there and the current position advanced. Backspace, carriage return, and line feed all require this position to be updated appropriately.

In particular, when a line feed is output on the bottom line of the screen, the screen must be scrolled. To see how scrolling works, look at Fig. 3-28. If the video controller always began reading the RAM at 0xB0000, the only way to scroll the screen would be to copy 24 × 160 characters from 0xB00A0 to 0xB0000, a time-consuming proposition.

Fortunately, the hardware usually provides some help here. Most video controllers contain a register that determines where in the video RAM to begin fetching bytes for the top line on the screen. By setting this register to point to 0xB00A0 instead of 0xB0000, the line that was previously number two will move to the top, and the whole screen will scroll up one line. The only other thing the driver must do is copy whatever is needed to the new bottom line. When the video controller gets to the top of the RAM, it just wraps around and continues fetching bytes starting at the lowest address.

Another issue that the driver must deal with on a memory mapped terminal is cursor positioning. Again, the hardware usually provides some assistance in the form of a register that tells where the cursor is to go. Finally, there is the problem of the bell. It is sounded by outputting a sine or square wave to the loudspeaker, a part of the computer quite separate from the video RAM.

It is worth noting that many of the issues faced by the terminal driver for a memory-mapped display (scrolling, bell, and so on) are also faced by the microprocessor inside an RS-232 terminal. From the viewpoint of the microprocessor, it is the main processor in a system with a memory-mapped display.

Screen editors and many other sophisticated programs need to be able to update the screen in more complex ways than just scrolling text onto the bottom of the display. To accommodate them, many terminal drivers support a variety of escape sequences. Some of the more common ones are:

1. Move cursor up, down, left, or right one position.

2. Move cursor to (x, y).

3. Insert character or line at cursor.

4. Delete character or line at cursor.

5. Scroll screen up or down n lines.

6. Clear screen from cursor to end of line or end of screen.

7. Enter reverse video, underlining, blinking, or normal mode.

8. Create, destroy, move, or otherwise manage windows.

When the driver sees the character that starts the escape sequences, it sets a flag and waits until the rest of the escape sequence comes in. When everything has arrived, the driver must carry it out in software. Inserting and deleting text requires moving blocks of characters around the video RAM. The hardware is of no help with anything except scrolling and displaying the cursor.

3.8.3. Overview of the Terminal Driver in MINIX

The terminal driver is far and away the largest source file in MINIX, being almost twice as long as the floppy disk driver, which is the second largest. The size of the terminal driver is partly explained by the observation that the driver handles both the keyboard and the display, each of which is a complicated device in its own right. Still, it comes as a surprise to most people to learn that terminal I/O requires thirty times as much code as the scheduler. (This feeling is reinforced by looking at the numerous books on operating systems that devote thirty times as much space to scheduling as to all I/O combined.)

The terminal driver accepts five messages:

1. Read characters from the terminal (from the file system on behalf of a user process).

2. Write characters to the terminal (from the file system on behalf of a user process).

3. Set terminal parameters for IOCTL (from the file system on behalf of a user process).

4. Character available (from the interrupt procedure).

5. Cancel previous read request (from the file system when a signal occurs).

(In the code a sixth message is mentioned, for signaling that output is completed; it is intended for future terminals whose output is interrupt driven. It is provided as an aid to future modifications of the driver.) The messages for reading and writing have the same format as shown in Fig. 3-15, except that no *POSITION* field is needed. With a disk, the program has to specify which block it wants to read. With a terminal, there is no choice: the program always gets the next character typed in. Terminals do not support seeks and random access.

The message sent to the driver when the IOCTL system call is made contains a function code (are the terminal parameters to be read or to be written?), the mode word shown in Fig. 3-31, and a long that may contain up to four characters. For one of the request types, *TIOCSETP*, only two of the characters are used: erase and kill. For another, *TIOCSETC*, all four characters are used: the SIGINT and SIGQUIT characters (DEL and CTRL-\), and the start and stop characters (CTRL-S and CTRL-Q). The message used to cancel requests specifies the terminal and process involved, and the message used for character arrival interrupts points to the input.

The terminal driver uses one main data structure, *tty_struct*, which is an array of structures, one per terminal. Even though the IBM PC generally has only one keyboard and display, the driver has been written to make it easy to add additional terminals, which is especially important if MINIX is ever ported to larger systems.

Tty_struct keeps track of both input and output. For input, it holds all characters that have been typed but not yet read by the program, requests to read characters that have not yet been typed, and the erase, kill, interrupt, quit, start, and stop characters. For output, it holds the parameters of write requests that are not yet finished, the current position on the screen and in the video ram, the current attribute byte for the display, and information about escape sequences currently being processed. It also holds various general variables, such as the terminal mode and the I/O port, if any, corresponding to the terminal.

Terminal Input

To better understand how the driver works, let us first look at how characters typed in on the terminal work their way through the system to the program that wants them.

When a user logs in (e.g., on terminal 0), a shell is created for him with */dev/tty0* as standard input, standard output, and standard error. The shell starts up by trying to read from standard input by calling the library procedure *read*. This procedure sends a message that contains the file descriptor, buffer address and count to the file system. This message is shown as (1) in Fig. 3-32. After sending the message, the shell blocks, waiting for the reply. (User processes execute only the SEND_REC primitive, which combines a SEND with a RECEIVE from the process sent to.)

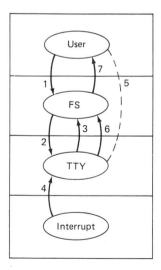

Fig. 3-32. Read request from terminal when no characters are pending. FS is the file system. TTY is the terminal task. Interrupt is the interrupt routine.

The file system gets the message and locates the i-node corresponding to the specified file descriptor. This i-node is for the character special file */dev/tty0*, and contains the major and minor device numbers for the terminal. The major device type for terminals in the standard distribution is 4; for terminal 0, the minor device number is 0.

The file system indexes into its device map, *dmap*, to find the number of the terminal task. Then it sends a message to the terminal task, shown as (2) in Fig. 3-32. Normally, the user will not have typed anything yet, so the terminal driver will be unable to satisfy the request. It sends a reply back immediately to unblock the file system and report that no characters are available, shown as (3). The file system records the fact that a process is waiting for terminal input in its tables, and then goes off to get the next request for work. The shell remains blocked, of course.

When a character is finally typed, it causes two interrupts, one when the key is depressed and one when it is released. This rule also applies to keys such as CTRL and SHIFT, which do not transmit any data by themselves, but still cause two interrupts per key hit. The interrupt routine in the assembly code file *mpx88.s* calls a C procedure, *keyboard* (line 4113) to extract the character from the keyboard hardware and put it in an array called *tty_driver_buf* along with the number of the line it came in on. *Keyboard* then calls *interrupt*, which, as we have seen in the previous chapter, sends a message to the terminal task (4) in the Fig. 3-32.

When enough characters have come in (meaning one character in raw or cbreak mode, or a line feed or CTRL-D in cooked mode), the terminal task calls the assembly language procedure *phys_copy* to copy the data to the address requested by the shell. This operation is not message passing and is shown by the dashed line in Fig. 3-32. Then the terminal driver sends a true message to the file system telling it that the work has been done (6). The file system reacts to this message by sending a message back to the shell to unblock it (7).

Note that the terminal driver copies the actual characters directly from its own address space to that of the shell. It does not first go through the file system. With block I/O, data do pass through the file system to allow it to maintain a buffer cache of the most recently used blocks. If a requested block happens to be in the cache, the request can be satisfied directly by the file system, without doing any disk I/O.

For terminal I/O, a cache makes no sense. Furthermore, a request from the file system to a disk driver can always be satisfied in at most a few hundred millisec, so there is no real harm in having the file system just wait. Terminal I/O may take hours to complete (it waits until something is typed in), so it is unacceptable to have the file system block that long.

Later on, it may happen that the user has typed ahead, and the characters are available before they have been requested. In that case, events 1, 2, 5, 6, and 7 all happen in quick succession after the read request; 3 and 4 do not occur.

When characters are typed in, they are put in the array *tty_driver_buf* as mentioned above. If the terminal task happens to be running at the time of the interrupt, no message can be sent to it because it is not waiting for one. Instead, a bit is set in the kernel variable *busy_map* in *interrupt*.

When the terminal task finally blocks, the bit is checked, and the message is sent then. If two or more terminal interrupts occur before the terminal driver finishes what it is doing, all the characters are stored in *tty_driver_buf*, and the bit in *busy_map* is repeatedly set. Ultimately, the terminal task gets one message; the rest are lost. But since all the characters are safely stored in *tty_driver_buf*, no typed input is lost.

The problem of what to do in an unbuffered message system (rendezvous principle) when an interrupt routine wants to send a message to a process that is busy is inherent in this kind of design. For most devices, such as disks, interrupts occur only in response to commands issued by the driver, so only one interrupt can be pending at any instant. The only devices that generate interrupts on their own are the clock and the terminal. The clock is handled by just counting lost interrupts, so they can be exactly compensated for later. The terminal is handled by having the interrupt routine accumulate the characters in a fixed buffer, so losing the second, third, and subsequent messages in a series is unimportant, as long as the first one is not lost. In MINIX the bit in *busy_map* guarantees that the first one is never lost.

In all fairness, this is not a part of the system that we are most proud of, but it does the job without too much additional software complexity and no loss in performance. The obvious alternative, to throw away the rendezvous principle and have the system buffer all messages sent to destinations not waiting for them, is much more complicated and also slower.

While it was not our primary purpose to air our dirty linen in public, real system designers are often faced with a tradeoff between using the general case, which is elegant all the time but slow, and using a simpler technique, which is usually fast but in one or two cases requires a trick to make it work properly. Experience is really the only guide to which approach is better under given circumstances. A considerable amount of experience on designing operating systems is summarized by Lampson (1984) and Brooks (1975).

When a message comes into the terminal task requesting characters, the main procedure, *tty_task* (line 3500) calls *do_read* (line 3784) to handle the request (see Fig. 3-33). *Do_read* stores the parameters of the call in *tty_struct*, just in case there are insufficient characters already buffered to satisfy the request now.

Then it calls *rd_chars* (line 3813) to check to see if enough input is available. If it is, the input is copied to the user. If no input is available, nothing is copied. In both cases, *rd_chars* returns a code to *do_read* reporting what happened, so that *do_read* can tell the file system.

When a character is typed, the interrupt procedure sends a message to the terminal driver telling it that one or more characters are now available in *tty_driver_buf*. Upon receiving this message, *tty_task* calls *do_charint* (line 3528) to loop on the characters accumulated in *tty_driver_buf* (almost always just one, but in theory, two or more are also possible) and call *in_char* (line 3581) for each character found (see Fig. 3-33).

Before doing any processing, *in_char* converts the key codes (scan codes)

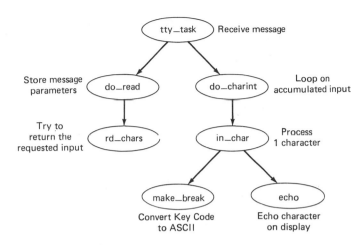

Fig. 3-33. Input handling in the terminal driver. The left branch of the tree is taken to process a request to read characters. The right branch is taken when a character-has-been-typed message is sent to the driver.

generated by the hardware into ASCII characters by calling *make_break* to look them up in the appropriate table. After that, *in_char* distinguishes between cooked mode, cbreak mode, and raw mode, and handles all the characters that need special processing. These are shown in Fig. 3-30. It also calls *echo* (line 3746) to have the characters displayed on the screen.

Terminal Output

Terminal output in MINIX is simpler than terminal input because the display is memory mapped. When a process wants to print something, it generally calls *printf* to format a line. *Printf* calls WRITE to send a message to the file system. The message contains a pointer to the characters to be printed (not the characters themselves). The file system then sends a message to the terminal driver, which fetches them and copies them to the video RAM.

When a message comes in to the terminal task to write on the screen, *do_write* (line 3905) is called to store the parameters in *tty_struct*. It then calls the output procedure for memory-mapped displays. (If RS-232 terminals are added later, a different procedure will be called for them.) This output procedure, called *console* (line 4178), consists mainly of a loop that fetches one byte directly from the user process and calls *out_char* (line 4217) to print it. Figure 3-34 shows the main procedures involved in output.

Logically, the bytes fetched from the user process could be written into the video RAM one per loop iteration. Unfortunately, writing into the video RAM while the 6845 is fetching characters from it interferes with the 6845's critical timing and may generate visual garbage all over the screen. Only during vertical retrace of the CRT beam is it always safe to write in the video RAM. Vertical

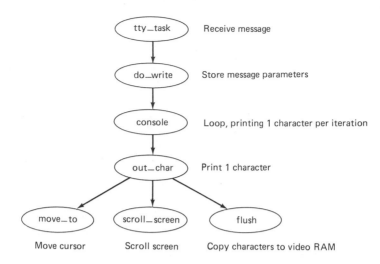

Fig. 3-34. Major procedures used on terminal output.

retrace periods occur 50 or 60 times a second, each one lasting a few msec. To deal with this problem, *out_char* accumulates characters in *tty_ram_queue* rather than writing them directly into the video RAM.

When this buffer fills up, or a character involving cursor motion has to be printed, *flush* (line 4326) is called to output the buffer to the screen. *Flush* calls the assembly language procedure *vid_copy* to wait until the vertical retrace bit comes on, and then it quickly copies the buffer to the screen.

Out_char also checks for characters that need special handling, such as the bell, line feed, carriage return, tab, backspace, some cursor motion keys, and the escape sequences. If one of these is found, it is processed directly.

The current cursor position is stored in *tty_struct* in the fields *tty_row* and *tty_column*. The coordinate (0, 0) is in the lower left-hand corner of the screen, even though the hardware fills the screen starting in the upper left-hand corner. Each video scan begins at the address given by *tty_org* and continues for $160 \times 25 = 4000$ bytes, wrapping around the video RAM, if necessary.

In other words, the 6845 chip pulls the word at offset *tty_org* from the video RAM, and displays the character in the upper left-hand corner using the attribute byte to control color, blinking, and so forth. Then it fetches the next word and displays the character at coordinate (1, 25). This process continues until it gets to (79, 0), at which time it begins again. Adding 160 to *tty_org* and then loading it into the 6845 causes the screen to scroll upward by one line.

The position of the cursor relative to the start of the video RAM can be derived from *tty_row* and *tty_column*, but it is faster to store it explicitly, which is done in the field *tty_vid*. When a character is to be printed, it is put into the video RAM at location *tty_vid*, which is then updated, as is *tty_column*. Figure 3-35 summarizes the fields of *tty_struct* that affect the current position and the display origin.

tty_row	Current row (0-24) with 0 at bottom
tty_column	Current column (0-79) with 0 at left
tty_vid	Offset into video RAM for cursor
tty_org	Position in video RAM where scan begins

Fig. 3-35. Fields of the tty structure that relate to the current screen position.

The characters that affect the cursor position (e.g., line feed, backspace) are handled by simply adjusting the values of *tty_row*, *tty_column*, and *tty_vid*. This work is done by *move_to* (line 4343). When a line feed is to be printed on the bottom line of the screen, *scroll_screen* (line 4304) is called to add 160 to *tty_org* and scroll the screen. It must also copy a row of blanks to the video RAM to ensure that the new line that suddenly appears at the bottom of the screen is empty.

The terminal driver supports a few escape sequences to allow screen editors and other interactive programs to update the screen in a flexible way. These escape sequences are all 3 bytes long and are shown in Fig. 3-36. By having ESC 32 32 correspond to moving to (0, 0), we have arranged that the parameters for cursor motion are printable characters. (When output to the screen, the escape sequences are not printed, but when they appear in programs they can be seen.)

Byte 1	Byte 2	Byte 3	
ESC	n1	n2	Move cursor to (n1–32, n2–32)
ESC	z	n1	Set attribute byte to n1
ESC	~	0	Clear screen from cursor to end
ESC	~	1	Scroll screen 1 line backward

Fig. 3-36. The escape sequences accepted by the terminal driver on output. ESC denotes the ASCII escape character (033).

3.8.4. Implementation of the Terminal Driver in MINIX

In this section we will inspect the actual code of the terminal driver in detail, first doing the input part and then doing the output part. The main loop of the driver (line 3508) is similar to that of the other drivers, except that the replies are sent by the procedures that are called here, rather than in *tty_task* itself.

Terminal Input

After our study of the other drivers, the only part of the terminal driver that is genuinely new is the way characters are processed as they are typed. When a key is struck or released, the CPU interrupts to line 1187, which saves the registers and calls the C procedure *keyboard* on line 4113. This procedure first plucks the key code (scan code) from the hardware and acknowledges this fact to the keyboard hardware. If the high-order bit of the key code is set, the key in question was released; otherwise, it was struck. Key releases, other than case shifts such as SHIFT, CTRL, and ALT, are just ignored and do not cause messages to be sent to the terminal task. This optimization reduces the message traffic within the system.

On lines 4144 to 4150 a check is made to see if the character is CTRL-S, which freezes the display. If it is, the *tty_inhibited* field is set to *STOPPED*, which causes the output loop in *console* (line 4196) to stop, if it is running.

On line 4145 a check is made to see if CTRL-ALT-DEL has been typed. If it has, the computer is rebooted. The code for *reboot* is in *klib88.s*. The rest of *keyboard* deals with storing the key code in the array *tty_driver_buf* and sending a message to the terminal task to have it process the stored characters.

When that message is received later, it is handled in *do_charint* (line 3528), which is mostly concerned with looping over the characters in *tty_driver_buf* and passing them to *in_char* one at a time. After each character is processed, a check is made to see if a previously incomplete read request can now be satisfied. In cooked mode this happens when a line feed is processed. In the other modes it happens on any character. If the read request can be completed now, *rd_chars* is called on line 3566 to copy the data to the user process.

The basic processing of each character typed in is done by *in_char* (line 3581). Early on it calls *make_break* (line 3695) to convert the key code received from the keyboard to an ASCII code by table lookup. Four tables are used, corresponding to lower and upper case for the IBM PC and for the Olivetti M24. The flag *olivetti* is set when the system is initialized, depending on which key code was typed in when the system asked for an equal sign.

Make_break keeps track of the state of five different case shifts in software. These shifts are SHIFT, CTRL, ALT, CAPS LOCK, and NUM LOCK. The entries above 0200 in the tables are used to indicate that the key code is for one of these shifts. Because the code output for each key is completely determined by software, we have been able to use a more flexible approach than most keyboard drivers. The basic idea is simple: each key outputs a unique code, so, for example, the software can distinguish between the "+" in the numeric pad and the "+" in the top row of keys, if it so desires. All the values between 1 and 255 are used.

Getting back to *in_char*, the tests on lines 3607 to 3653 check for the characters that are handled specially in cooked mode. The tests on lines 3655 to 3678 process those characters that are special in both cooked and cbreak mode. In raw mode, all of these characters are passed through to the user without any special processing. The actual queueing of characters is done at the end of *in_char*.

When a key is struck, neither the hardware nor the interrupt routine puts the character just typed on the display. It is up to the terminal driver to display it. The last thing *in_char* does before finishing up is call *echo* (line 3746) to print the character on the screen. All *echo* does is check to see if ECHO mode is enabled and the character is displayable. If so, it calls *out_char* to have it copied to *tty_ramqueue*, and then it calls *flush* to have that queue actually copied to the screen.

The procedure *chuck* (line 3761) is used for the erase and kill local editing characters to remove characters already typed from the input queue. We have now finished the story of how input characters are processed.

The procedure *do_read* (line 3784), as we have already seen, is concerned with handling read requests from user programs. It stores the message parameters in *tty_struct* because it may not be possible to satisfy the request now. When enough characters finally come in, the driver needs to have the information about the request so it can carry it out then.

The actual transfer of data from the driver to user space is done by *rd_chars*. It computes the physical address within user space where the data are to go, *user_phys*, by calling *umap*. It also computes the physical address of the input buffer, *tty_phys*. Given these two addresses, the two nested loops starting on line 3841 perform the actual copying, one buffer at a time. The inner loop fills up one buffer, a character at a time, and copies it to user space. The outer loop repeats this process, copying as many buffer loads as necessary to satisfy the request. When it is finished, *rd_chars* returns *cum*, which is the number of characters actually transferred. Note that a read from a terminal never returns more than one line, no matter how many characters are requested, so it is important to report how many characters have been put in the user's buffer.

The next procedure, *finish* (line 3884), is used to terminate output and reply to the file system. It is used for normal output termination, but also when a DEL or CTRL-\ is typed, to stop all output immediately and tell the file system that output has been completed.

Terminal Output

Having finished looking at how input works, let us look at output. The procedure *do_write* is called from *tty_task*, just as *do_read* is, and like *do_read*, does little more than store the message parameters in *tty_struct*. It also computes the physical address within user space of the data to be printed.

On line 3934 *do_write* calls a device-dependent procedure to perform the output. For terminal 0, this procedure is *console* (line 4178), but if RS-232 terminals are added later, it will call a different procedure for them. The device-dependent code is listed at the end of *tty.c*, starting at line 4050.

The heart of *console* is the loop on lines 4196 to 4201. Each iteration of that loop uses the assembly code procedure *get_byte* to fetch one byte from the user's output buffer into the local variable *c*. The byte is then output by calling *out_char*, specifying the terminal and the character. Finally, the pointer is advanced to the next character and the count of remaining bytes is decremented.

The output loop terminates either when the entire buffer has been printed, or when *tty_inhibited* comes on. Normally, this flag is off, but when CTRL-S is typed, the interrupt handler sets it (line 4147). This strategy has been chosen because once the driver starts doing output, it does not accept any more messages until it has finished its work. If the CTRL-S character were to be sent to the driver in a message, it would always have to wait until the current output was finished. With the implementation actually used, CTRL-S stops the output instantly. When CTRL-Q is typed, *console* is called (line 3676) to pick up where it left off.

Every character printed on the screen passes through *out_char*, including characters being echoed (line 3753). It contains a simple finite state machine to handle escape sequences, all of which are exactly three characters long, to keep things simple. The finite state machine, shown in Fig. 3-37, has three states, depending on whether the field *tty_esc_state* is 0, 1, or 2.

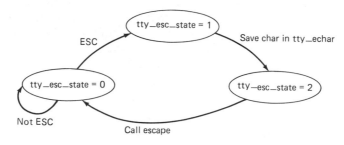

Fig. 3-37. Escape sequences are three characters long.

Normally, *tty_esc_state* is 0. When an ASCII ESC character (033) is output, the state switches to 1. After another character arrives, the character is saved in *tty_echar* and the state switches to 2. When the next character arrives, *escape* (line 4362) is called with both characters to handle it, and the state is reset to 0.

If the character being output is not part of an escape sequence, a check is made on line 4241 to see if it is a printable character or something special. The bell (CTRL-G) is handled by *beep* (line 4427), which generates a tone by directing one of the clock channels to the built-in loudspeaker. The characters involving cursor motion, such as carriage return, backspace, and line feed, all call *move_to* (line 4343) to update the current row, column, and position within the video RAM.

Printable characters are handled on lines 4291 to 4296. As discussed earlier, they are stored in the buffer *tty_ramqueue* along with their attribute byte so that the number of times the video RAM has to be accessed can be reduced. In this manner, each vertical retrace interval can be used to deposit perhaps tens of characters in the video RAM, instead of just a few.

Scroll_screen (line 4304) can scroll the screen one line in either direction, depending on *dir*. Scrolling is accomplished by adding or subtracting 160 bytes from *tty_org* and then updating the 6845. The 6845's registers that are used by MINIX are shown in Fig. 3-38.

Registers	Function
10 - 11	Cursor size
12 - 13	Start address for drawing screen
14 - 15	Cursor position

Fig. 3-38. Some of the 6845's registers.

Each register is 8 bits wide, but they work in pairs to form 16-bit registers. All of them address the video RAM in words, rather than bytes. For this reason, *tty_org* (which is in bytes) is shifted right to convert it to words on line 4319. The 6845 registers not shown in Fig. 3-38 control the sync pulses that determine the width, height, and offset of the displayable area on the screen. They are set by the ROM when the IBM PC is booted and not touched by MINIX.

Flush (line 4326) calls *vid_copy* to copy the accumulated characters from the queue to the screen. Then it moves the cursor and clears the queue.

Move_to (line 4343) updates the row, column, and video RAM position, and moves the cursor. It is called whenever the cursor is explicitly moved. Before doing its work it flushes the buffer, to prevent the queued characters from being eventually displayed in the wrong place.

Escape sequences are detected in *out_char* but processed by *escape* (line 4362). Each of the four possibilities of Fig. 3-36 is checked for and handled.

The 6845 registers shown in Fig. 3-38 are set by calls to *set_6845* (line 4403). A 16-bit value is output as two 8-bit values, to consecutive registers. A value is loaded into a register by first loading the register number into an I/O port, and then loading the value into another I/O port.

Ringing the bell for CTRL-G is done in *beep* (line 4427). It is accomplished by programming channel 2 of the timer chip. Interrupts are disabled on line 4438 because it sounds funny otherwise. The frequency and duration of the beep tone are completely programmable, and can be changed by modifying the constants *BEEP_FREQ* and *B_TIME*.

When MINIX starts up, each task is called to give it the opportunity to initialize itself. On line 3507, the terminal task calls *tty_init* (line 4453) to do the initialization. First it sets up the default mode and special characters, such as erase, kill, and interrupt. Then it sets some of the 6845 display parameters, which differ for color and monochrome displays.

The global variable *color* used on line 4474 is set in *main.c* by calling the assembly language procedure *get_chrome*, which makes a BIOS call to find out. The BIOS finds out by reading an I/O port connected to the DIP switches on the PC's motherboard. This call is the only place in MINIX that the BIOS is used.

The cursor shape is set on line 4487. As you can see, the IBM PC is extremely flexible: the meaning of each key, the sound of the bell, the shape of the cursor, and many other things are all programmable. The keyboard type is set on line 4495 by looking at the number corresponding to the equals sign typed to start MINIX. It is different on the IBM PC and Olivetti M24.

In a few places in the kernel, the procedure *printf* is called. The MINIX version of *printf* is part of the standard I/O library, which sends messages to the file system to print its strings. A simpler procedure is needed within the kernel, and is provided in the form of the procedure *printk*, which calls the kernel version of *putc* directly. All occurrences of the string "printf" are changed into "printk" by the macro on line 0696.

The final procedure in the driver is temporary and used only for helping to debug MINIX. At the start of *in_char*, a check is made to see if the key is a function key. If it is, *func_key* (line 4519) is called to provide some debug information on the screen. This feature has been included to help people who plan to modify MINIX. It can be removed when this assistance is no longer needed. The dump procedures are in the file *dmp.c*, which is not really a permanent part of MINIX and is not shown in this book.

3.9. THE SYSTEM TASK IN MINIX

One consequence of making the file system and memory manager user processes outside the kernel is that occasionally they have some piece of information that the kernel needs. This structure, however, forbids them from just writing it into a kernel table. For example, the FORK system call is handled by the memory manager. When a new process is created, the kernel must know about it, in order to schedule it. How can the memory manager tell the kernel?

The solution to this problem is to have a kernel task that communicates with the file system and memory manager via the standard message mechanism, and which also has access to all the kernel tables. This task, called the **system task**, is in layer 2 in Fig. 2-26, and functions like the other tasks we have studied in this chapter. The only difference is that it does not control any I/O device. Nevertheless, it makes more sense to study it here than in any other chapter.

The system task accepts nine kinds of messages, shown in Fig. 3-39. The main program of the system task, *sys_task* (line 4627), is structured the same way as the other tasks. It gets a message, dispatches to the appropriate service procedure, and then sends a reply. We will now look at each of these messages and its service procedure.

SYS_FORK is used by the memory manager to tell the kernel that a new process has come into existence. The kernel needs to know this in order to schedule it. The message contains the slot numbers within the process table corresponding to the parent and child. The memory manager and file system also have process tables, with entry *k* referring to the same process in all three. In this manner, the memory manager can specify just the parent and child slot numbers, and the kernel will know which processes are meant.

The procedure *do_fork* (line 4658) copies the parent's process table entry to the child's slot and zeros the accounting information. The check on line 4674 to see if the memory manager is feeding the kernel garbage is pure paranoia, but a

Message type	From	Meaning
SYS_FORK	MM	A process has forked
SYS_NEWMAP	MM	Install memory map for a new process
SYS_EXEC	MM	Set stack pointer after EXEC call
SYS_XIT	MM	A process has exited
SYS_GETSP	MM	MM wants a process' stack pointer
SYS_TIMES	FS	FS wants a process' execution times
SYS_ABORT	Both	Panic: MINIX is unable to continue
SYS_SIG	MM	Interrupt a process with a signal
SYS_COPY	Both	Copy data between processes

Fig. 3-39. The nine message types accepted by the system task.

little internal consistency checking does no harm. Similar checks are made in a number of other places in the system as well.

After a FORK, the memory manager allocates memory for the child. The kernel must know where the child is located in memory so it can set up the segment registers properly when running the child. The *SYS_NEWMAP* message allows the memory manager to give the kernel any process's memory map. This message can also be used after a BRK system call changes the map.

The message is handled by *do_newmap* (line 4698), which must first copy the new map from the memory manager's address space. The map is not contained in the message itself because it is too big. In theory, the memory manager could tell the kernel that the map is at address m, where m is an illegal address. The memory manager is not supposed to do this, but the kernel checks anyway. The 18-byte map is copied directly into the process table's *p_map* field. Information from it is also extracted and loaded into the *p_reg* fields that hold the segment registers.

When a process does an EXEC system call, the memory manager sets up a new stack for it containing the arguments and environment. It passes the resulting stack pointer to the kernel using *SYS_EXEC*, which is handled by *do_exec* (line 4746). In addition to setting the stack pointer, *do_exec* kills off the alarm timer, if any, by storing a zero on top of it. It is for this reason that the clock task always checks when a timer has run out to see if anybody is still interested.

The EXEC call causes a slight anomaly. The process invoking the call sends a message to the memory manager and blocks. With other system calls, the resulting reply unblocks it. With EXEC there is no reply, because the newly loaded core image is not expecting a reply. Therefore, *do_exec* unblocks the process itself on line 4762.

Processes can exit in MINIX either by doing an EXIT system call, which sends a message to the memory manager, or by being killed by a signal. In both cases, the memory manager tells the kernel by the *SYS_XIT* message. The work is done by *do_xit* (line 4771), which is more complicated than you might expect. Taking care of the accounting information is straightforward. The tricky part is that the process might have been queued trying to send or receive at the time it was killed. The code on lines 4796 to 4816 checks for this possibility, and if, found, carefully removes it from all the queues it is on.

In contrast to the previous message, which is slightly complicated, *SYS_GETSP* is completely trivial. It is used by the memory manager to find out the value of the current stack pointer for some process. This value is needed for the BRK and SBRK system calls to see if the data segment and stack segment have collided. The code is in *do_getsp* (line 4825).

Now we come to the only message type used exclusively by the file system, *SYS_TIMES*. It is needed to implement the TIMES system call, which returns the accounting times to the caller. All *do_times* (line 4844) does is put the requested times into the reply message.

It can happen that either the memory manager or the file system discovers an error that makes it impossible to continue operation. For example, if upon first starting up, the file system sees that the super block on the root device has been corrupted, it panics and sends a *SYS_ABORT* message to the kernel. All *do_abort* (line 4868) does is call *panic* to terminate MINIX immediately.

Most of the signal handling is done in the memory manager. It checks to see if the process to be signaled is enabled to catch or ignore the signal, if the sender of the signal is entitled to do so, and so on. The one thing the memory manager cannot do is actually cause the signal, that is, push the PSW, CS register, program counter, and signal number onto the stack of the signaled process. That work is done by sending the *SYS_SIG* message to the system task.

The message is handled by *do_sig* (line 4880). After extracting the parameters of the message, *do_sig* calls the assembly language procedure *build_sig* to construct an 8-byte array containing the interrupt information. The array, *sig_stuff*, is copied onto the stack of the signaled process by *phys_copy* on line 4910. The process's stack pointer is then decremented by the size of the block of information just copied.

The final message, *SYS_COPY*, is the most heavily used one. It is needed to allow the file system and memory manager to copy information to and from user processes.

When a user does a READ call, the file system checks its cache to see if it has the block needed. If not, it sends a message to the appropriate disk task to load it into the cache. Then the file system sends a message to the system task telling it to copy the block to the user process. In the worst case, six messages are needed to read a block; in the best case four messages are needed. Both cases are shown in Fig. 3-40. These messages are a significant source of overhead in MINIX, and are the price paid for the highly modular design.

As an aside, on the 8088, which has no protection, it would be easy enough to cheat and let the file system copy the data to the caller's address space, but this would violate the design principle. Anyone interested in improving the performance of MINIX should look carefully at this mechanism to see how much improper behavior one can tolerate for how much gain in performance. The

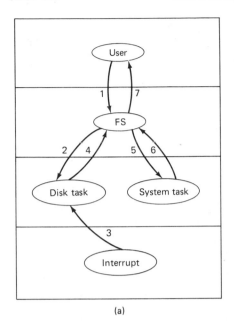

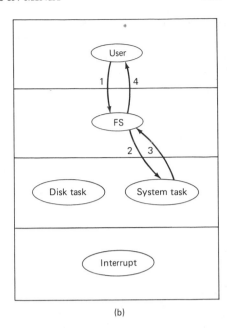

(a)   (b)

Fig. 3-40. (a) Worst case for reading a block requires six messages. (b) Best case for reading a block requires four messages.

implementation of this procedure is straightforward. It is done by *do_copy* (line 4922) and consists of little more than extracting the message parameters and calling *phys_copy*.

At the end of *system.c* are three utility procedures used in various places throughout the kernel. When a task needs to cause a signal (e.g., the clock task needs to cause a SIGALRM signal, or the terminal task needs to cause a SIGINT signal), it calls *cause_sig* (line 4960). This procedure sets a bit in the *p_pending* field of the process table entry for the process to be signaled, and then calls *inform* to tell the memory manager to handle the signal.

Inform (line 4987) checks to see if the memory manager is currently waiting for a message from *ANY*, that is, if it is idle and waiting for the next request to process. If it is idle, *inform* builds a message of type *KSIG* and sends it the message. The task calling *cause_sig* continues running as soon as the message has been copied into the memory manager's receive buffer. It does not wait for the memory manager to run.

When the signaling task finishes, the scheduler will be called. If the memory manager is the highest priority runnable process, it will run and process the signal.

The procedure *umap* (line 5021) is a generally useful procedure that maps a virtual address onto a physical address. Its parameters are a pointer to the process table entry for the process or task whose virtual address space is to be mapped, a flag specifying the text, data, or stack segment, the virtual address itself, and a byte count. The byte count is useful because *umap* checks to make sure that the entire buffer starting at the virtual address is within the process's address space. For this reason, it must know how big the buffer is. The byte count is not used for the mapping itself, just this check. All the tasks that copy data to or from user space compute the physical address of the buffer using *umap*.

3.10. SUMMARY

Input/Output is an often neglected, but important, topic. A substantial fraction of any operating system is concerned with I/O. We started out by looking at I/O hardware, and the relation of I/O devices to I/O controllers, which are what the software has to deal with. Then we looked at the four levels of I/O software: the interrupt routines, the device drivers, the device-independent I/O software, and the I/O libraries and spoolers that run in user space.

Next we studied the problem of deadlock and how it can be tackled. Deadlock occurs when a group of processes each have been granted exclusive access to some resources, and each one wants yet another resource that belongs to another process in the group. All of them are blocked and none will ever run again. Deadlock can be prevented by structuring the system so it can never occur, for example, by allowing a process to hold only one resource at any instant. It can also be avoided by examining each resource request to see if it leads to a situation in which deadlock is possible, and denying or delaying those that lead to trouble.

Device drivers in MINIX are implemented as processes embedded in the kernel. All of them are located in the same address space, but they are otherwise completely independent. We have looked at the RAM disk driver, floppy disk driver, clock driver, terminal driver, and system task, which is not a device driver but is structurally very similar to one. Each of these drivers has a main loop that gets requests and processes them, eventually sending back replies to report on what happened.

PROBLEMS

1. Imagine that advances in chip technology make it possible to put an entire controller, including all the bus access logic, on an inexpensive chip. How will that affect the model of Fig. 3-1?

2. If a disk controller writes the bytes it receives from the disk to memory as fast as it receives them, with no internal buffering, is interleaving conceivably useful? Discuss.

3. A disk is double interleaved, as in Fig. 3-3(c). It has eight sectors of 512 bytes per track, and a rotation rate of 300 Hz. How long does it take to read all the sectors

of a track in order, assuming the arm is already correctly positioned, and 1/2 rotation is needed to get sector 0 under the head? What is the data rate? Now repeat the problem for a noninterleaved disk with the same characteristics. How much does the data rate degrade due to interleaving?

4. The DM-11 terminal multiplexer, which was used on the PDP-11 many, many years ago, sampled each (half-duplex) terminal line at seven times the baud rate to see if the incoming bit was a 0 or a 1. Sampling the line took 5.7 microsec. How many 1200 baud lines could the DM-11 support?

5. A local network is used as follows. The user issues a system call to write to the network. The operating system then copies the data to a kernel buffer. Then it copies the data to the network controller board. When all the bytes are safely inside the controller, they are sent over the network at a rate of 10 megabits/sec. The receiving network controller stores each bit a microsecond after it is sent. When the last bit arrives, the destination CPU is interrupted, and the kernel copies the newly arrived packet to a kernel buffer to inspect it. Once it has figured out which user the packet is for, the kernel copies the data to the user space. If we assume that each interrupt and its associated processing takes 1 msec, that packets are 1024 bytes (ignore the headers), and that copying a byte takes 1 microsec, what is the maximum rate at which one process can pump data to another?

6. What is "device independence"?

7. In which of the four I/O software layers is each of the following done.

  (a) Computing the track, sector, and head for a disk read.
  (b) Maintaining a cache of recently used blocks.
  (c) Writing commands to the device registers.
  (d) Checking to see if the user is permitted to use the device.
  (e) Converting binary integers to ASCII for printing.

8. Why are output files for the printer normally spooled on disk before being printed?

9. Consider Fig. 3-8. Suppose that in step (o) C requested S instead of requesting R. Would this lead to deadlock? Suppose it requested both S and R?

10. All the trajectories in Fig. 3-12 are horizontal or vertical. Can you envision any circumstances in which diagonal trajectories were also possible?

11. Take a careful look at Fig. 3-11(b). If Suzånne asks for one more unit, does this lead to a safe state or an unsafe one? What if the request came from Marvin instead of Suzanne?

12. Suppose that process A in Fig. 3-13 requests the last tape drive. Does this action lead to a deadlock?

13. A computer has six tape drives, with n processes competing for them. Each process may need two drives. For which values of n is the system deadlock free?

14. Can a system be in a state that is neither deadlocked nor safe? If so, give an example. If not, prove that all states are either deadlocked or safe.

15. A distributed system using mailboxes has two IPC primitives, SEND and RECEIVE. The latter primitive specifies a process to receive from, and blocks if no message

from that process is available, even though messages may be waiting from other processes. There are no shared resources, but processes need to communicate frequently about other matters. Is deadlock possible? Discuss.

16. In an electronic funds transfer system, there are hundreds of identical processes that work as follows. Each process reads an input line specifying an amount of money, the account to be credited, and the account to be debited. Then it locks both accounts and transfers the money, releasing the locks when done. With many processes running in parallel, there is a very real danger that having locked account x it will be unable to lock y because y has been locked by a process now waiting for x. Devise a scheme that avoids deadlocks. Do not release an account record until you have completed the transactions. (In other words, solutions that lock one account and then release it immediately if the other is locked, are not allowed.)

17. The banker's algorithm is being run in a system with m resource classes and n processes. In the limit of large m and n, the number of operations that must be performed to check a state for safety is proportional to $m^a n^b$. What are the values of a and b?

18. Cinderella and the Prince are getting divorced. To divide their property, they have agreed on the following algorithm. Every morning, each one may send a letter to the other's lawyer requesting one item of property. Since it takes a day for letters to be delivered, they have agreed that if both discover that they have requested the same item on the same day, the next day they will send a letter canceling the request. Among their property is their dog, Woofer, Woofer's doghouse, their canary, Tweeter, and Tweeter's cage. The animals love their houses, so it has been agreed that any division of property separating an animal from its house is invalid, requiring the whole division to start over from scratch. Both Cinderella and the Prince desperately want Woofer. So they can go on (separate) vacations, each spouse has programmed a personal computer to handle the negotiation. When they come back from vacation, the computers are still negotiating. Why? Is deadlock possible? Is starvation possible? Discuss.

19. The message format of Fig. 3-15 is used for sending request messages to drivers for block devices. Which fields, if any, could be omitted for messages to character devices?

20. Disk requests come in to the disk driver for cylinders 10, 22, 20, 2, 40, 6, and 38, in that order. A seek takes 6 msec per cylinder moved. How much seek time is needed for

    (a) First-come, first served.
    (b) Closest cylinder next.
    (c) Elevator algorithm (initially moving upwards).

In all cases, the arm is initially at cylinder 20.

21. A personal computer salesman visiting a university in South-West Amsterdam remarked during his sales pitch that his company had devoted substantial effort to making their version of UNIX very fast. As an example, he noted that their disk driver used the elevator algorithm and also queued multiple requests within a cylinder in sector order. A student, Harry Hacker, was impressed and bought one.

He took it home and wrote a program to randomly read 10,000 blocks spread across the disk. To his amazement, the performance that he measured was identical to what would be expected from first-come, first-served. Was the salesman lying?

22. A UNIX process has two parts—the user part and the kernel part. Is the kernel part like a subroutine or a coroutine?

23. The clock interrupt handler on a certain computer requires 2 msec (including process switching overhead) per clock tick. The clock runs at 60 Hz. What fraction of the CPU is devoted to the clock?

24. Two examples of watchdog timers were given in the text: timing the start-up of the floppy disk motor and allowing for carriage return on hard copy terminals. Give a third example.

25. Why are RS232 terminals interrupt driven, but memory mapped terminals not interrupt driven?

26. Consider how a terminal works. The driver outputs one character and then blocks. When the character has been printed, an interrupt occurs and a message is sent to the blocked driver, which outputs the next character and then blocks again. If the time to pass a message, output a character, and block is 4 msec, does this method work well on 110 baud lines? How about 4800 baud lines?

27. A bit map terminal contains 1200 by 800 pixels. To scroll a window, the CPU (or controller) must move all the lines of text upwards by copying their bits from one part of the video RAM to another. If a particular window is 66 lines high by 80 characters wide (5280 characters, total), and a character's box is 8 pixels wide by 12 pixels high, how long does it take to scroll the whole window at a copying rate of 500 nsec per byte? If all lines are 80 characters long, what is the equivalent baud rate of the terminal? Putting a character on the screen takes 50 microsec. Now compute the baud rate for the same terminal in color, with 4 bits/pixel. (Putting a character on the screen now takes 200 microsec.)

28. Why do operating systems provide escape characters, such as \ in MINIX?

29. After receiving a DEL (SIGINT) character, the MINIX driver discards all output currently queued for that terminal. Why?

30. Many RS232 terminals have escape sequences for deleting the current line and moving all the lines below it up one line. How do you think this feature is implemented inside the terminal?

31. On the IBM PC's color display, writing to the video RAM at any time other than during the CRT beam's vertical retrace causes ugly spots to appear all over the screen. A screen image is 25 by 80 characters, each of which fits in a box 8 pixels by 8 pixels. Each row of 640 pixels is drawn on a single horizontal scan of the beam, which takes 63.6 microsec, including the horizontal retrace. The screen is redrawn 60 times a second, each of which requires a vertical retrace period to get the beam back to the top. What fraction of the time is the video RAM available for writing in?

32. Write an RS232 driver for MINIX.

33. Write a graphics driver for the IBM color display, or some other suitable bit map display. The driver should accept commands to set and clear individual pixels, move rectangles around the screen, and any other features you think are interesting. User programs interface to the driver by opening */dev/graphics* and writing commands to it.

34. Modify the MINIX floppy disk driver to do track-at-a-time caching.

35. Implement a floppy disk driver that works as a character, rather than a block device, to bypass the file system's buffer cache. In this way, users can read large chunks of data from the disk, which are DMA'ed directly to user space, greatly improving performance. This driver would primarily be of interest to programs that need to read the raw bits on the disk, without regard to the file system. File system checkers fall into this category.

36. Implement the UNIX PROFIL system call, which is missing from MINIX.

37. Modify the terminal driver so that in addition to a having a special key to erase the previous character, there is a key to erase the previous word.

4

MEMORY MANAGEMENT

Memory is an important resource that must be carefully managed. While the average home computer nowadays has ten times as much memory as the IBM 7094, the largest computer in the world in the early 1960s, programs are getting bigger just as fast as memories. To paraphrase Parkinson's law, "Programs expand to fill the memory available to hold them." In this chapter we will study how operating systems manage their memory.

The part of the operating system that manages memory is called the **memory manager**. Its job is to keep track of which parts of memory are in use and which parts are not in use, to allocate memory to processes when they need it and deallocate it when they are done, and to manage swapping between main memory and disk when main memory is not big enough to hold all the processes.

In this chapter we will investigate a number of different memory management schemes, ranging from very simple to highly sophisticated. We will start at the beginning and look first at the simplest possible memory management system, and then gradually progress to more and more elaborate ones.

4.1. MEMORY MANAGEMENT WITHOUT SWAPPING OR PAGING

Memory management systems can be divided into two classes: those that move processes back and forth between main memory and disk during execution (swapping and paging), and those that do not. The latter are simpler, so we will study them first. Later in the chapter we will examine swapping and paging. Throughout this chapter the reader should keep in mind that swapping and paging are largely artifacts caused by the lack of sufficient main memory to hold all the programs at once. As main memory gets cheaper, the arguments in favor of one kind of memory management scheme or another may become obsolete.

4.1.1. Monoprogramming without Swapping or Paging

The simplest possible memory management scheme is to have just one process in memory at a time, and to allow that process to use all of memory. The user loads the entire memory with a program from disk or tape, and it takes over the whole machine. Although this approach was common up until about 1960, it is not used any more, not even on inexpensive home computers, mostly because it implies that every process must contain within it a device driver for each I/O device it uses.

The usual technique used on simple microcomputers is shown in Fig. 4-1. The memory is divided up between the operating system and a single user process. The operating system may be at the bottom of memory in RAM (Random Access Memory), as shown in Fig. 4-1(a), or it may be in ROM (Read Only Memory) at the top of memory, as shown in Fig. 4-1(b), or the device drivers may be at the top of memory in a ROM and the rest of the operating system in RAM at the bottom of memory, as shown in Fig. 4-1(c). The IBM PC, for example, uses the model of Fig. 4-1(c), with the device driver ROM located in the highest 8K block of the 1M address space. The program in the ROM is called the **BIOS** (Basic Input Output System).

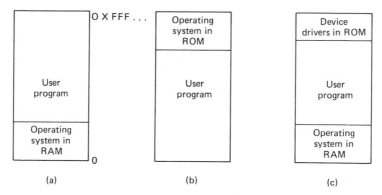

Fig. 4-1. Three ways of organizing memory with an operating system and one user process.

When the system is organized in this way, only one process at a time can be running. The user types a command on the terminal, and the operating system loads the requested program from disk into memory and executes it. When the process finishes, the operating system types a prompt character on the terminal and then waits for a command from the terminal to load another process, overwriting the first one.

4.1.2. Multiprogramming and Memory Usage

Although monoprogramming is sometimes used on small computers, on larger computers with multiple users it is rarely used. In Chap. 2 we already saw one reason for multiprogramming—to make it easier to program an application by splitting it up into two or more processes. Another motivation is that large computers often provide interactive service to several people simultaneously, which requires the ability to have more than one process in memory at once in order to get reasonable performance. Loading a process, running it for 100 msec, and then spending a few hundred milliseconds swapping it to disk is inefficient. But if the quantum is set too much above 100 msec, the response time will be poor.

Another reason for multiprogramming a computer (also applicable to batch systems), is that most processes spend a substantial fraction of their time waiting for disk I/O to complete. It is common for a process to sit in a loop reading data blocks from a disk file and then doing some computation on the contents of the blocks read. If it takes 40 msec to read a block, and the computation takes 10 msec, with monoprogramming the CPU will be idle waiting for the disk 80 percent of the time.

Modeling Multiprogramming

When multiprogramming is used, the CPU utilization can be improved. Crudely put, if the average process computes only 20 percent of the time it is sitting in memory, with five processes in memory at once, the CPU should be busy all the time. This model is unrealistically optimistic, however, since it assumes that all five processes will never be waiting for I/O at the same time.

A better model is to look at CPU usage from a probabilistic viewpoint. Suppose that a process spends a fraction p of its time in I/O wait state. With n processes in memory at once, the probability that all n processes are waiting for I/O (in which case the CPU will be idle) is p^n. The CPU utilization is then $1 - p^n$. Figure 4-2 shows the CPU utilization as a function of n, called the **degree of multiprogramming**.

From the figure it is clear that if processes spend 80 percent of their time waiting for I/O, at least 10 processes must be in memory at once to get the CPU waste below 10 percent. When you realize that an interactive process waiting for a user to type something at a terminal is in I/O wait state, it should be clear that I/O wait times of 80 percent and more are not unusual. But even in batch systems, processes doing a lot of disk or tape I/O will often have this percentage or more.

For the sake of complete accuracy, it should be pointed out that the

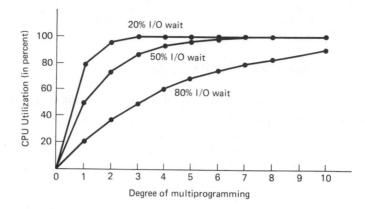

Fig. 4-2. CPU utilization as a function of the number of processes in memory.

probabilistic model just described is only an approximation. It implicitly assumes that all n processes are independent, meaning that it is quite acceptable for a system with five processes in memory to have three running and two waiting. But with a single CPU, we cannot have three processes running at once, so a process becoming ready while the CPU is busy will have to wait. Thus the processes are not independent. A more accurate model can be constructed using queueing theory, but the point we are making—multiprogramming lets processes use the CPU when it would be otherwise idle—is, of course, still valid, even if the true curves of Fig. 4-2 are slightly different.

Even though the model of Fig. 4-2 is simple-minded, it can still be used to make specific, although approximate, predictions about CPU performance. Suppose, for example, that a computer has 1M of memory, with the operating system taking up 200K and each user program also taking up 200K. With an 80 percent average I/O wait, we have a CPU utilization (ignoring operating system overhead) of about 60 percent. Adding another megabyte of memory allows the system to go from four-way multiprogramming to nine-way multiprogramming, thus raising the CPU utilization to 87 percent. In other words, the second megabyte will raise the throughput by 45 percent.

Adding a third megabyte would only increase CPU utilization from 87 percent to 96 percent, thus raising the throughput by only another 10 percent. Using this model the computer's owner might decide that a second megabyte was a good investment, but that a third megabyte was not.

Analysis of Multiprogramming System Performance

This model can also be used to analyze batch systems. Consider, for example, a computer center whose jobs average 80 percent I/O wait time. On a particular morning, four jobs are submitted as shown in Fig. 4-3(a). The first job, arriving at 10:00 A.M., requires 4 minutes of CPU time. With 80 percent I/O wait, the job uses only 12 seconds of CPU time for each minute it is sitting in memory, even if no other jobs are competing with it for the CPU. The other 48 seconds are spent waiting for I/O to complete. Thus the job will have to sit in memory for at least 20 minutes in order to get 4 minutes of CPU work done, even in the absence of competition for the CPU.

Job	Arrival time	CPU minutes needed
1	10:00	4
2	10:10	3
3	10:15	2
4	10:20	2

(a)

#Processes	1	2	3	4
CPU idle	.80	.64	.51	.41
CPU busy	.20	.36	.49	.59
CPU/process	.20	.18	.16	.15

(b)

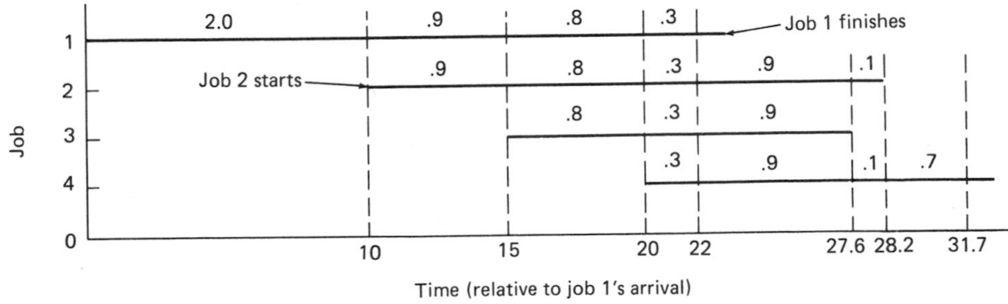

Job 1: 2.0   .9   .8   .3   — Job 1 finishes
Job 2: Job 2 starts —   .9   .8   .3   .9   .1
Job 3: .8   .3   .9
Job 4: .3   .9   .1   .7

Time markers: 10   15   20   22   27.6   28.2   31.7

Time (relative to job 1's arrival)

(c)

Fig. 4-3. (a) Arrival and work requirements of four jobs. (b) CPU utilization for 1 to 4 jobs with 80 percent I/O wait. (c) Sequence of events as jobs arrive and finish. The numbers above the horizontal lines show how much CPU time, in minutes, each job gets in each interval.

From 10:00 A.M. to 10:10 A.M., job 1 is all by itself in memory and gets 2 minutes of work done. When job 2 arrives at 10:10 A.M., the CPU utilization increases from 0.20 to 0.36, due to the higher degree of multiprogramming (see Fig. 4-2). However, with round robin scheduling, each job gets half of the CPU, so each job gets 0.18 minutes of CPU work done for each minute it is in memory. Notice that the addition of a second job cost the first job only 10 percent of its performance (from 0.20 to 0.18 minutes of CPU per minute of real time).

At 10:15 A.M. the third job arrives. At this point job 1 has received 2.9 minutes of CPU and job 2 has had 0.9 minutes of CPU. With three-way multiprogramming, each job gets 0.16 minutes of CPU time per minute of real time, as shown in Fig. 4-3(b). From 10:15 A.M. to 10:20 A.M. each of the three jobs gets 0.8 minutes of CPU time. At 10:20 A.M. a fourth job arrives. Fig. 4-3(c) shows the complete sequence of events.

4.1.3. Multiprogramming with Fixed Partitions

By now it should be clear that it is often useful to have more than one process in memory at once. The question is then: "How should memory be organized to achieve this goal?" The easiest way is simply to divide memory up into *n* (possibly unequal) partitions. This partitioning can, for example, be done manually by the operator when the system is started up.

When a job arrives, it can be put into the input queue for the smallest partition large enough to hold it. Since the partitions are fixed in this scheme, any space in a partition not used by a job is lost. In Fig. 4-4(a) we see how this system of fixed partitions and separate input queues looks.

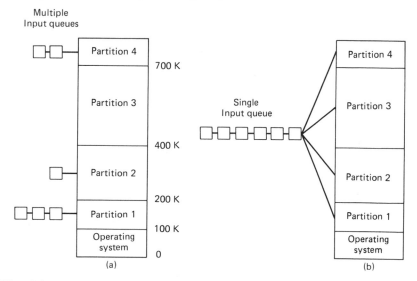

Fig. 4-4. (a) Fixed memory partitions with separate input queues for each partition. (b) Fixed memory partitions with a single input queue.

The disadvantage of sorting the incoming jobs into separate queues becomes apparent when the queue for a large partition is empty but the queue for a small partition is full, as is the case for partitions 1 and 3 in Fig. 4-4(a). An alternative organization is to maintain a single queue as in Fig. 4-4(b). Whenever a partition becomes free, the job closest to the front of the queue that fits in it could be loaded into the empty partition and run. Since it is undesirable to waste a large partition on a small job, a different strategy is to search the whole input queue whenever a partition becomes free and pick the largest job that fits. Note that the latter algorithm discriminates against small jobs as being unworthy of having a whole partition, whereas usually it is desirable to give the smallest jobs the best service, not the worst.

This system, with fixed partitions set up by the operator in the morning and not changed thereafter, was used by OS/360 on large IBM mainframes for many years. It was called **MFT** (Multiprogramming with a Fixed number of Tasks or OS/MFT). It is simple to understand and equally simple to implement: incoming jobs are queued until a suitable partition is available, at which time the job is loaded into that partition and run until it terminates.

Relocation and Protection

Multiprogramming introduces two essential problems that must be solved— relocation and protection. Look at Fig. 4-4. From the figure it is clear that different jobs will be run at different addresses. When a program is linked (i.e., the main program, user-written procedures, and library procedures are combined into a single address space), the linker must know at what address the program will begin in memory.

For example, suppose that the first instruction is a call to a procedure at relative address 100 within the binary file produced by the linker. If this program is loaded in partition 1, that instruction will jump to absolute address 100, which is inside the operating system. What is needed is a call to 100K + 100. If the program is loaded into partition 2, it must be carried out as a call to 200K + 100, and so on. This problem is known as the **relocation** problem.

One possible solution is to actually modify the instructions as the program is loaded into memory. Programs loaded into partition 1 have 100K added to each address, programs loaded into partition 2 have 200K added to addresses, and so forth. To perform relocation during loading like this, the linker must include in the binary program a list or bit map telling which program words are addresses to be relocated and which are opcodes, constants, or other items that must not be relocated. OS/MFT worked this way. Some microcomputers also work like this.

Relocation during loading does not solve the protection problem. A malicious program can always construct a new instruction and jump to it. Because programs in this system use absolute memory addresses rather than addresses relative to a register, there is no way to stop a program from building an instruction that reads or writes any word in memory. In multiuser systems, it is undesirable to let processes read and write memory belonging to other users.

The solution that IBM chose for protecting the 360 was to divide memory into blocks of 2K bytes and assign a 4-bit protection code to each block. The PSW contained a 4-bit key. The 360 hardware trapped any attempt by a running process to access memory whose protection code differed from the PSW key. Since only the operating system could change the protection codes and key, user processes were prevented from interfering with one another and with the operating system itself.

An alternative solution to both the relocation and protection problems is to equip the machine with two special hardware registers, called the **base** and **limit** registers. When a process is scheduled, the base register is loaded with the address of the start of its partition, and the limit register is loaded with the length of the partition. Every memory address generated automatically has the base register contents added to it before being sent to memory. Thus if the base register is 100K, a CALL 100 instruction is effectively turned into a CALL 100K + 100 instruction, without the instruction itself being modified. Addresses are also checked against the limit register to make sure that they do not attempt to address memory outside the current partition. The hardware protects the base and limit registers to prevent user programs from modifying them. The IBM PC uses a weaker version of this scheme—it has base registers (the segment registers), but no limit registers (see Appendix B).

An additional advantage of using a base register for relocation is that a program can be moved in memory after it has started execution. After it has been moved, all that needs to be done to make it ready to run is change the value of the base register. When the relocation is done by modifying the program as it is loaded, it cannot be moved without going through the entire modification process again.

4.2. SWAPPING

With a batch system, organizing memory into fixed partitions is simple and effective. As long as enough jobs can be kept in memory to keep the CPU busy all the time, there is no reason to use anything more complicated. With time-sharing, the situation is different: there are normally more users than there is memory to hold all their processes, so it is necessary to keep excess processes on disk. To run these processes, they must be brought into main memory, of course. Moving processes from main memory to disk and back is called **swapping**, and is the subject of the following sections.

4.2.1. Multiprogramming with Variable Partitions

In principle, a swapping system could be based on fixed partitions. Whenever a process blocked, it could be moved to the disk and another process brought into its partition from the disk. In practice, fixed partitions are unattractive when memory is scarce because too much of it is wasted by programs that are smaller than their partitions. A different memory management algorithm is used instead. It is known as **variable partitions**.

When variable partitions are used, the number and size of the processes in memory vary dynamically throughout the day. Figure 4-5 shows how variable partitions work. Initially only process A is in memory. Then processes B and C are created or swapped in from disk. In Fig. 4-5(d) A terminates or is swapped out to disk. Then D comes in and B goes out. Finally E comes in.

The main difference between the fixed partitions of Fig. 4-4 and the variable partitions of Fig. 4-5 is that the number, location, and size of the partitions vary dynamically in the latter as processes come and go, whereas they are fixed in the former. The flexibility of not being tied to a fixed number of partitions that may

Time ———→

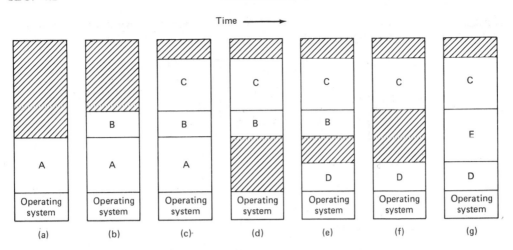

Fig. 4-5. Memory allocation changes as processes come into memory and leave it. The gray regions are unused memory.

be too large or too small improves memory utilization but it also complicates allocating and deallocating memory, as well as keeping track of it.

It is possible to combine all the holes into one big one by moving all the processes downward as far as possible. This technique is known as **memory compaction**. It is usually not done because it requires a lot of CPU time. For example, on a 1M micro that can copy 1 byte per microsec (1 megabyte/sec), it takes 1 sec to compact all of memory. It is, however, done on the large CDC Cyber mainframes because they have special hardware that can compact at a rate of 40 megabytes/sec.

A point that is worth making concerns how much memory should be allocated for a process when it is created or swapped in. If processes are created with a fixed size and never change it, then the allocation is simple: you allocate exactly what is needed, no more and no less.

If, however, processes' data segments can grow, for example, by dynamically allocating memory from a heap, as in many programming languages, a problem occurs whenever a process tries to grow. If a hole is adjacent to the process, it can be allocated and the process allowed to grow into the hole. On the other hand, if the process is adjacent to another process, the growing process will either have to be moved to a hole in memory large enough for it, or one or more processes will have to be swapped out to create a large enough hole. If a process cannot grow in memory and the swap area on the disk is full, the process will have to be killed.

If it is expected that most processes will grow as they run, it is probably a good idea to allocate a little extra memory whenever a process is swapped in or moved, to reduce the overhead associated with moving or swapping processes that no longer fit in their allocated memory. However, when swapping processes to disk, only the memory actually in use should be swapped; it is wasteful to swap the extra memory as well. In Fig. 4-6(a) we see a memory configuration in which space for growth has been allocated to two processes.

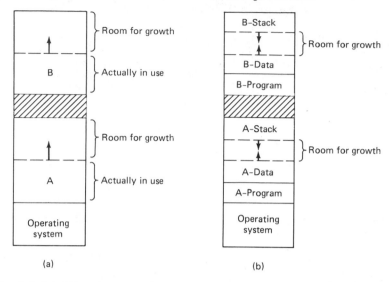

Fig. 4-6. (a) Allocating space for a growing data segment. (b) Allocating space for a growing stack and a growing data segment.

If processes can have two growing segments, for example, the data segment being used as a heap and the stack, an alternative arrangement suggests itself, namely that of Fig. 4-6(b). In this figure we see that each process has a stack at the top of its allocated memory growing downward, and a data segment just beyond the program text, growing upward. The memory between them can be used for either segment. If it runs out, either the process will have to be moved to a hole with enough space, swapped out of memory until a large enough hole can be created, or killed.

In general terms, there are three ways of keeping track of memory usage: bit maps, lists, and buddy systems. In the following sections we will look at each of these in turn.

4.2.2. Memory Management with Bit Maps

With a bit map, memory is divided up into allocation units, perhaps as small as a few words and perhaps as large as several kilobytes. Corresponding to each allocation unit is a bit in the bit map, which is 0 if the unit is free and 1 if it is occupied (or vice versa). Figure 4-7 shows part of memory and the corresponding bit map.

The size of the allocation unit is an important design issue. The smaller the allocation unit, the larger the bit map. However, even with an allocation unit as small as 4 bytes, 32 bits of memory will require only 1 bit of the map. A

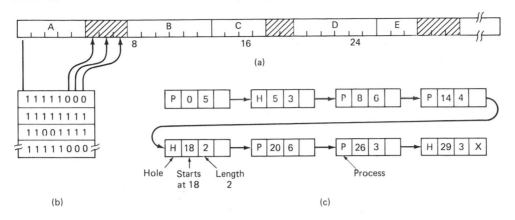

Fig. 4-7. (a) A part of memory with five processes and 3 holes. The tick marks show the memory allocation units. The shaded regions (0 in the bit map) are free. (b) The corresponding bit map. (c) The same information as a linked list.

memory of $32n$ bits will use n map bits, so the bit map will take up only 3 percent of memory. If the allocation unit is chosen large, the bit map will be small, but appreciable memory may be wasted in the last unit if the process size is not an exact multiple of the allocation unit.

A bit map provides a simple way to keep track of memory words in a fixed amount of memory because the size of the bit map depends only on the size of memory and the size of the allocation unit. The main problem with it is that when it has been decided to bring a k word process into memory, the memory manager must search the bit map to find a run of k consecutive 0 bits in the map. Searching a bit map for a run of a given length is a slow operation, so in practice, bit maps are not often used.

4.2.3. Memory Management with Linked Lists

Another way of keeping track of memory is maintaining a linked list of allocated and free memory segments, where a segment is either a process or a hole between two processes. The memory of Fig. 4-7(a) is represented in Fig. 4-7(c) as a linked list of segments. Each entry in the list specifies a hole (H) or process (P), the address at which it starts, the length, and a pointer to the next entry.

In this example, the segment list is kept sorted by address. Sorting this way has the advantage that when a process terminates or is swapped out, updating the list is straightforward. A terminating process normally has two neighbors (except when it is at the very top or bottom of memory). These may be either processes or holes, leading to the four combinations of Fig. 4-8. In Fig. 4-8(a) updating the list requires replacing a P by an H. In Fig. 4-8(b) and Fig. 4-8(c), two entries are coalesced into one, and the list becomes one entry shorter. In Fig. 4-8(d), three entries are merged and two items are removed from the list. Since the process table slot for the terminating process will normally point to the list entry for the process itself, it may be more convenient to have the list as a double-linked list, rather than the single-linked list of Fig. 4-7(c) This is done to find the previous entry and to see if a merge is possible.

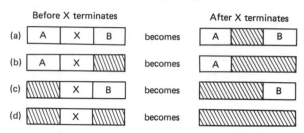

Fig. 4-8. Four neighbor combinations for the terminating process, X.

When the processes and holes are kept on a list sorted by address, several algorithms can be used to allocate memory for a newly created or swapped in process. We assume that the memory manager knows how much memory to allocate. The simplest algorithm is **first fit**. The memory manager scans along the list of segments until it finds a hole that is big enough. The hole is then broken up into two pieces, one for the process and one for the unused memory, except in the unlikely case of an exact fit. First fit is a fast algorithm because it searches as little as possible.

A minor variation of first fit is **next fit**. It works the same way as first fit, except that it keeps track of where it is when it finds a suitable hole. The next time it is called, it starts searching from where it left off, instead of always at the beginning, as first fit does. Simulations by Bays (1977) show that next fit gives slightly worse performance than first fit.

Another well-known algorithm is **best fit**. Best fit searches the entire list and takes the smallest hole that is adequate. Rather than breaking up a big hole that might be needed later, best fit tries to find a hole that is close to the actual size needed.

As an example of first fit and best fit, consider Fig. 4-7 again. If a block of size 2 is needed, first fit will allocate the hole at 5, but best fit will allocate the hole at 18.

Best fit is slower than first fit because it must search the entire list every time it is called. Somewhat surprisingly, it also results in more wasted memory than first fit or next fit because it tends to fill up memory with tiny, useless holes. First fit generates larger holes on the average.

To get around the problem of breaking up nearly exact matches into a process and a tiny hole, one could think about **worst fit**, that is, always take the largest available hole, so that the hole broken off will be big enough to be useful. Simulation has shown that worst fit is not a very good idea.

All four algorithms can be speeded up by maintaining separate lists for processes and holes. In this way, all of them devote their full energy to inspecting holes, not processes. The price paid for this speedup on allocation is the additional complexity and slowdown when deallocating memory, since a freed segment has to be removed from the process list and inserted into the hole list.

If distinct lists are maintained for processes and holes, the hole list may be kept sorted on size, to make best fit faster. When best fit searches a list of holes from smallest to largest, as soon as it finds a hole that fits, it knows that the hole is the smallest one that will do the job, hence the best fit. With a hole list sorted by size, first fit and best fit are equally fast, and next fit is pointless.

When the holes are kept on separate lists from the processes, a small optimization is possible. Instead of having a separate set of data structures for maintaining the hole list, as is done in Fig. 4-7(c), the holes themselves can be used. The first word of each hole could be the hole size, and the second word a pointer to the following entry. The nodes of the list of Fig. 4-7(c), which require three words and one bit (P/H), are no longer needed.

Yet another allocation algorithm is **quick fit**, which maintains separate lists for some of the more common sizes requested. For example, it might have a table with n entries, in which the first entry was a pointer to the head of a list of 4K holes, the second entry was a pointer to a list of 8K holes, the third entry a pointer to 12K holes, and so on. Holes of say, 21K, could either be put on the 20K list or on a special list of odd-sized holes. With quick fit, finding a hole of the required size is extremely fast, but it has the same disadvantage as all schemes that sort by hole size, namely, when a process terminates or is swapped out, finding its neighbors to see if a merge is possible is expensive. If merging is not done, memory will quickly fragment into a large number of small, useless holes.

If we drop our implicit assumption that nothing is known in advance about the probability distribution of requested sizes and process lifetimes, then various other algorithms become applicable. The work of Oldehoeft and Allan (1985), Stephenson (1983), and Beck (1982) describe some of the possibilities.

4.2.4. Memory Management with the Buddy System

We saw in the previous section that keeping all the holes on one or more lists sorted by hole size made allocation very fast, but deallocation slow because all the hole lists had to be searched to find the deallocated segment's neighbors. The buddy system (Knuth 1973; Knowlton 1965) is a memory management algorithm that takes advantage of the fact that computers use binary numbers for addressing in order to speed up the merging of adjacent holes when a process terminates or is swapped out.

It works like this. The memory manager maintains a list of free blocks of size 1, 2, 4, 8, 16, etc., bytes, up to the size of memory. With a 1M memory, for example, 21 such lists are needed, ranging from 1 byte to 1 megabyte. Initially, all of memory is free, and the 1M list has a single entry containing a single 1M hole. The other lists are empty. The initial memory configuration is shown in Fig. 4-9 in the top row.

	0	128 K	256 K	384 K	512 K	640 K	768 K	896 K	1 M	Holes
Initially										1
Request 70	A	128		256		512				3
Request 35	A	B	64	256		512				3
Request 80	A	B	64	C	128	512				3
Return A	128		B	64	C	128	512			4
Request 60	D	64	B	64	C	128	512			4
Return B	D	64	128		C	128	512			4
Return D	256				C	128	512			3
Return C	1024									1

Fig. 4-9. The buddy system. The horizontal axis represents memory addresses. The numbers are the sizes of unallocated blocks of memory in K. The letters represent allocated blocks of memory.

Now let us see how the buddy system works when a 70K process is swapped into an empty 1M memory. As the hole lists are only for powers of 2, 128K will be requested, that being the smallest power of 2 that is big enough. No 128K block is available, nor are blocks for 256K or 512K. Thus the 1M block is split into two 512K blocks, called **buddies**, one at memory address 0 and the other at memory address 512K. One of these, the one at 0, is then split into two 256K buddy blocks, one at 0 and one at 256K. The lower of these is then split into two 128K blocks, and the one at address 0 (marked *A* in Fig. 4-9) is allocated to the process.

Next, a 35K process is swapped in. This time we round 35K up to a power of 2 and discover that no 64K blocks are available, so we split the 128K block into two 64K buddies, one at 128K and one at 192K. The block at 128K is allocated to the process, marked as *B* in Fig. 4-9. The third request is for 80K.

Now let us see what happens when a block is returned. Imagine that 128K block *A* (of which only 70K is used) is freed at this point. It just goes on the free list for 128K blocks at this point. Now a 60K block is needed, so the newly returned 128K block is split and the buddy at 0 allocated to the new process as *D*. The buddy at 64K remains on the free list.

Now block *B* is returned. At this point we have three 64K blocks, at 64K, at 128K, and at 192K. The two 64K blocks at 128K and 192K are buddies, and can be merged to form a 128K block, as shown. The 64K block at 64K cannot be merged because its buddy is still allocated. When block *D* is returned, we can reconstruct the 256K block at address 0. Finally, when block *C* is returned, we return to the initial configuration of a single hole of 1M.

Buddy systems have an advantage over algorithms that sort blocks by size but not necessarily at addresses that are multiples of the block size. The advantage is that when a block of size 2^k bytes is freed, the memory manager has to search only the list of 2^k holes to see if a merge is possible. With other algorithms that allow memory blocks to be split in arbitrary ways, all the hole lists must be searched. The result is that the buddy system is fast.

Unfortunately, it is also extremely inefficient in terms of memory utilization. The problem comes from the fact that all requests must be rounded up to a power of 2. A 35K process must be allocated 64K. The extra 29K is just wasted. This form of overhead is known as **internal fragmentation** because the wasted memory is internal to the allocated segments. In Fig. 4-5 we have holes *between* the segments, but no wasted space *within* the segments. This form of waste is called **external fragmentation** or **checkerboarding**.

Various authors (e.g., Peterson and Norman, 1977; Kaufman, 1984) have modified the buddy system in various ways to try to get around some of its problems.

4.2.5. Allocation of Swap Space

The algorithms presented above are for keeping track of main memory so that when processes are swapped in, the system can find space for them. In some systems, when a process is in memory, no disk space is allocated to it. When it must be swapped out, space must be allocated in the disk swap area for it. On each swap, it may be placed somewhere else on disk. The algorithms for managing swap space are the same ones used for managing main memory.

In other systems, when a process is created, swap space is allocated for it on disk (using one of the algorithms we have studied). Whenever the process is swapped out, it is always swapped to its allocated space, rather than going to a different place each time. When the process exits, the swap space is deallocated.

The only difference is that disk space for a process must be allocated as an integral number of disk blocks. Therefore, a process of size 13.5K using a disk with 1K blocks will be rounded up to 14K before the free disk space data structures are searched.

4.2.6. Analysis of Swapping Systems

The free list and bit map algorithms lead to a form of external fragmentation that is easy to analyze. Imagine a simulation run to determine how much memory is wasted in holes at any instant. The simulator might start at 0, generating segment sizes at random, and marking them as process or hole, also at random. This simulation would lead to as many holes as processes. However, if adjacent holes were then merged, the number of holes would become smaller than the number of segments.

The ratio of holes to processes can be found by the following analysis (Knuth, 1973). Consider an average process in the middle of memory after the system has come to equilibrium. During its stay in memory, half of the operations on the segment just above it will be process allocations and half will be process deallocations. Thus, half the time it has another process as upper neighbor, and half the time it has a hole as upper neighbor. Averaged over time, there must be half as many holes as processes. In other words, if the mean number of processes in memory is n, the mean number of holes is $n/2$. This result is known as the **fifty percent rule**.

The fifty percent rule has its origin in a fundamental asymmetry between processes and holes. When two holes are adjacent in memory, they are merged into a single hole. Adjacent processes are not merged. This mechanism systematically reduces the number of holes.

Another useful result is the **unused memory rule**. Let f be the fraction of memory occupied by holes, s be the average size of the n processes, and ks be the average hole size for some $k > 0$. With a total memory of m bytes, the $n/2$ holes occupy $m - ns$ bytes. Algebraically,

$$(n/2) \times ks = m - ns$$

Solving this equation for m, we get

$$m = ns(1 + k/2)$$

The fraction of memory in holes is just the number of holes, $n/2$, times the average hole size, ks, divided by the total memory, m, or

$$f = \frac{nks/2}{m} = \frac{nks/2}{ns(1 + k/2)} = \frac{k}{k + 2}$$

As an example, if the average hole is 1/2 as large as the average process, $k = 1/2$, and 20 percent of the memory will be wasted in holes. If we reduce the average hole size to 1/4 of the average process size, for example, by using best fit instead of first fit, the wastage will drop to about 11 percent. As long as the average hole size is an appreciable fraction of the average process size, a substantial amount of memory will be wasted.

4.3. VIRTUAL MEMORY

Many years ago people were first confronted with programs that were too big to fit in the available memory. The solution usually adopted was to split the program into pieces, called **overlays**. Overlay 0 would start running first. When it was done, it would call another overlay. Some overlay systems were highly complex, allowing multiple overlays in memory at once. The overlays were kept on the disk and swapped in and out of memory by the operating system.

Although the actual work of swapping overlays in and out was done by the system, the work of splitting the program into pieces had to be done by the programmer. Spitting up large programs into small, modular pieces was time consuming and boring. It did not take long before someone thought of a way to turn the whole job over to the computer.

The method that was devised (Fotheringham, 1961) has come to be known as **virtual memory**. The basic idea behind virtual memory is that the combined size of the program, data, and stack may exceed the amount of physical memory available for it. The operating system keeps those parts of the program currently in use in main memory, and the rest on the disk. For example, a 1M program can run on a 256K machine by carefully choosing which 256K to keep in memory at each instant, with pieces of the program being swapped between disk and memory as needed.

Virtual memory can also work in a multiprogramming system. For example, eight 1M programs can each be allocated a 256K partition in a 2M memory, with each program operating as though it had its own, private 256K machine. In fact, virtual memory and multiprogramming fit together very well. While a program is waiting for part of itself to be swapped in, it is waiting for I/O and cannot run, so the CPU can be given to another process.

4.3.1. Paging

Most virtual memory systems use a technique called **paging**, which we will now describe. On any computer, there exists a set of memory addresses that programs can produce. When a program uses an instruction like MOVE REG,1000, it is moving the contents of memory address 1000 to REG (or vice versa, depending on the computer). Addresses can be generated using indexing, base registers, segment registers, and other ways.

These program-generated addresses are called **virtual addresses** and form the **virtual address space**. On computers without virtual memory, the virtual address is put directly onto the memory bus and causes the physical memory word with the same address to be read or written. When virtual memory is used, the virtual addresses do not go directly to the memory bus. Instead, they go to a **memory management unit** (MMU), a chip or collection of chips that maps the virtual addresses onto the physical memory addresses as illustrated in Fig. 4-10.

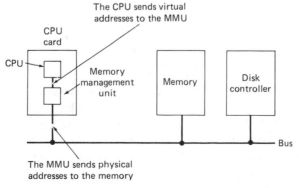

Fig. 4-10. The position and function of the MMU.

An example of how this mapping works is shown in Fig. 4-11. In this example, we have a computer that can generate 16-bit addresses, from 0 up to 64K. These are the virtual addresses. This computer, however, has only 32K of physical memory, so although 64K programs can be written, they cannot be loaded into memory in their entirety and run. A complete copy of a program's core image, up to 64K, must be present on the disk, however, so that pieces can be brought in by the system as needed.

The virtual address space is divided up into units called **pages**. The corresponding units in the physical memory are called **page frames**. The pages and page frames are always the same size. In this example they are 4K, but page sizes of 512 bytes, 1K, and 2K are also commonly used. With 64K of virtual address space and 32K of physical memory, we have 16 virtual pages and 8 page frames. Transfers between memory and disk are always in units of a page.

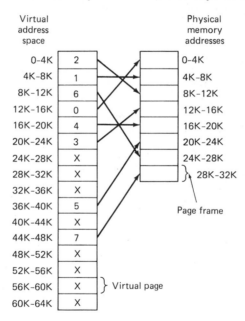

Fig. 4-11. The relation between virtual addresses and physical memory addresses is given by the page table.

When the program tries to access address 0, for example, using the instruction MOVE REG,0, the virtual address 0 is sent to the MMU. The MMU sees that this virtual address falls in page 0 (0 to 4095), which according to its mapping is page frame 2 (8192 to 12387). It thus transforms the address to 8192 and outputs address 8192 onto the bus. The memory board knows nothing at all about the MMU, and just sees a request for reading or writing address 8192, which it honors. Thus, the MMU has effectively mapped all virtual addresses between 0 and 4095 onto physical addresses 8192 to 12387.

Similarly, an instruction MOVE REG,8192 is effectively transformed into

MOVE REG,24576 because virtual address 8192 is in virtual page 2 and this page is mapped onto physical page frame 6 (physical addresses 24576 to 28671). As a third example, virtual address 21500 is 20 bytes from the start of virtual page 5 (virtual addresses 20480 to 24575) and maps onto physical address $12288 + 20 = 12308$.

By itself, this ability to map the 16 virtual pages onto any of the eight page frames by setting the MMU's map appropriately does not solve the problem that the virtual address space is larger than the physical memory. Since we have only eight physical page frames, only eight of the virtual pages in Fig. 4-11 are mapped onto physical memory. The others, shown as a cross in the figure, are not mapped. In the actual hardware, a present/absent bit in each entry keeps track of whether the page is mapped or not.

What happens if the program tries to use an unmapped page, for example, by using the instruction MOVE REG,32780, which is byte 12 within virtual page 8 (starting at 32768)? The MMU notices that the page is unmapped (indicated by a cross in the figure), and causes the CPU to trap to the operating system. This trap is called a **page fault**. The operating system picks a little-used page frame and writes its contents back to the disk. It then fetches the page just referenced into the page frame just freed, changes the map, and restarts the trapped instruction.

For example, if the operating system decided to evict page frame 1, it would load virtual page 8 at physical address 4K and make two changes to the MMU's map. First, it would mark virtual page 1's entry as unmapped, to trap any future accesses to virtual addresses between 4K and 8K. Then it would replace the cross in virtual page 8's entry with a 1, so that when the trapped instruction is re-executed, it will map virtual address 32780 onto physical address 4108.

Now let us look inside the MMU to see how it works and why we have chosen to use a page size that is a power of 2. In Fig. 4-12 we see an example of a virtual address, 8196 (0010000000000100 in binary), being mapped using the MMU map of Fig. 4-11. The incoming 16-bit virtual address is split up into a 4-bit page number and a 12-bit offset within the page. With 4 bits for the page number, we can represent 16 pages, and with 12 bits for the offset, we can address all 4096 bytes within a page.

The page number is used as an index into the page table, yielding the page frame corresponding to that virtual page. If the present/absent bit is 0, a trap is caused. If it is 1, the page frame number found in the page table is copied to the high-order 4 bits of the output register, along with the 12-bit offset, which is copied unmodified from the incoming virtual address. The output register is then put onto the memory bus as the physical memory address.

4.3.2. Segmentation

Paging provides a technique for implementing a large linear address space in a limited physical memory. For some applications, a two-dimensional address

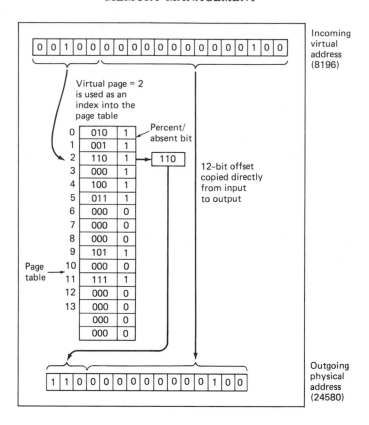

Fig. 4-12. The internal operation of the MMU with 16 4K pages.

space is more convenient. Ideally, each program should have a very large number of segments (e.g., 2^{32}), each consisting of a large number of bytes (e.g., also 2^{32}). The first, say, 64K segments could be reserved for procedures, data, stacks, and heaps, belonging to the running program. The remaining segments could each contain one file per segment, so that processes could directly address all their files, without having to open them and use special I/O primitives to read and write them. Each file could grow and shrink completely independently of the others in this arrangement, with each byte of memory addressed by a (segment, offset) pair.

The MULTICS system designers (Corbato and Vyssotsky 1965; Daley and Neumann 1965; Organick, 1972) attempted to build a segmented system of this type, with moderate success. MULTICS had only 36 bits of addressing, which eventually proved to be inadequate. No major system since that time has attempted anything quite so grand, although the idea of using a very large segmented memory to eliminate file I/O is still as attractive as ever.

In the MULTICS design, the idea was that each segment should support a logical entity, such as a file, procedure, or array. Thus, unlike paging, where the programmer is generally unaware of the page boundaries, with segmentation the programmer (or the compiler) made a definite attempt to put different objects in different segments. This strategy facilitated the sharing of objects among multiple processes

The idea of a segmented memory has survived to this date. In a much watered-down form, it is common in many 68000-based microcomputers. A typical implementation provides hardware support for up to 16 processes, each with 1024 2K or 4K pages. If we stick to 4K pages for this example, each process has a 4M virtual address space, consisting of 1024 pages of 4K each.

This scheme *could* be implemented by giving each process its own page table with 1024 page frame numbers, but it is generally not implemented that way. Instead, the MMU hardware contains a table with 16 sections, one for each of up to 16 processes. Each section has 64 segment descriptors, so the address space of each 4M process is divided up into 64 segments, each containing 16 pages. The segment and page tables are depicted in Fig. 4-13(a).

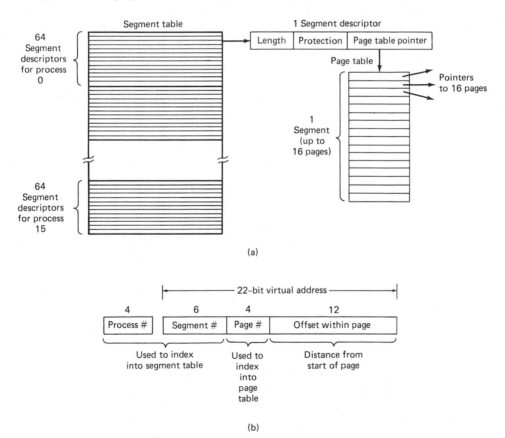

(a)

(b)

Fig. 4-13. (a) MMU used in many 68000-based microcomputer systems. (b) Virtual address for a 4M system.

Each of the segment descriptors contains the segment length (0 to 16 pages), protection bits telling whether the segment can be read or written, and a pointer to the page table itself. The page tables each contain up to 16 entries, with each entry pointing to a page frame in memory (actually, holding the page frame number).

When the operating system starts up a process, it loads a 4-bit process number into a special hardware register. Whenever that process references memory, the MMU translates the virtual address as follows. It takes the 4-bit process number and the 6 high-order bits of the 22-bit virtual address (needed to address 4M) and combines them into a 10-bit number used to index into the segment table and locate the relevant segment descriptor.

It then checks the protection bits in the segment descriptor to see if the access is allowed. If access is allowed, the MMU then checks the page number extracted from the virtual address against the segment length field in the segment descriptor, to see if the segment is long enough. If it is long enough, the page number is used as an index into the page table, whose address is provided in the segment descriptor. (All the page tables are kept in a special fast memory inside the MMU.) Once the page frame number is found, it is combined with the offset field of the virtual address to form the physical memory address, which is then put out onto the bus.

One of the key features of this MMU design is that when the operating system does a process switch, all it has to do is change the 4-bit process number register. It does not have to reload all the segment or page tables. Two or more processes can share a segment by just having their segment descriptors point to the same page table. Any changes made to the pages of that segment by any process are automatically visible to the other ones.

While the design of Fig. 4-13 provides each of 16 processes with only 64 segments of 64K each, the idea can easily be extended to larger address spaces at the price of requiring more table space within the MMU. Most of the table space is for the page tables. If we had four times as much page table memory inside the MMU and were content with 4 processes instead of 16, the MMU could support 64 1M segments per process.

While this address space is clearly not enough to hold all the files a single user owns, it is beginning to get closer to at least holding all the files that a given process needs while it is running. After all, not many programs need more than, say, 50 files, and most files are well below 1M.

It is worth pointing out that the segmentation scheme of Fig. 4-13 is not the only one possible. In the MULTICS system, for example, each process had a segment table stored in main memory. Each table entry pointed to a page table, also stored in main memory. The segment and page tables could be so large that they themselves were paged. Special hardware was present to avoid having to reference the segment and page tables for pages that were heavily used. This hardware stored the 16 most recently used (segment, page) entries in an associative memory for fast lookup.

4.4. PAGE REPLACEMENT ALGORITHMS

When a page fault occurs, the operating system has to choose a page to remove from memory to make room for the page that has to be brought in. If the page to be removed has been modified while in memory, it must be rewritten to the disk to bring the disk copy up to date. If, however, the page has not been changed (e.g., a page contains program text), the disk copy is already up to date, so no rewrite is needed. The page to be read in just overwrites the page being evicted.

While it would be possible to pick a random page to replace at each page fault, system performance is much better if a page that is not heavily used is chosen. If a heavily used paged is removed, it will probably have to be brought back in quickly, resulting in extra overhead. Much work has been done on the subject of page replacement algorithms, both theoretical and experimental. The bibliography by Smith (1978) lists over 300 papers on the subject. In the following sections we will describe some of the more interesting algorithms that have been found.

4.4.1. Optimal Page Replacement

The best possible page replacement algorithm is easy to describe but impossible to implement. The algorithm goes like this. At the moment that a page fault occurs, some set of pages is in memory. One of these pages will be referenced on the very next instruction (the page containing that instruction). Other pages may not be referenced until 10, 100, or perhaps 1000 instructions later. Each page can be labeled with the number of instructions that will be executed before that page is first referenced.

The optimal page algorithm simply says that the page with the highest label should be removed. If one page will not be used for 8 million instructions and another page will not be used for 6 million instructions, removing the former pushes the page fault that will fetch it back as far into the future as possible. Computers, like people, try to put off unpleasant events for as long as they can.

The only problem with this algorithm is that it is unrealizable. At the time of the page fault, the operating system has no way of knowing when each of the pages will be referenced next. (We saw a similar situation earlier with the shortest job first scheduling algorithm—how can the system tell which job is shortest?) Still, by running a program on a simulator and keeping track of all page references, it is possible to implement optimal page replacement on the *second* run by using the page reference information collected on the *first* run.

In this way it is possible to compare the performance of realizable algorithms with the best possible one. If an operating system achieves a performance of, say, only 1 percent worse than the optimal algorithm, effort spent in looking for a better algorithm will yield at most a 1 percent improvement.

4.4.2. Not-Recently-Used Page Replacement

In order to allow the operating system to collect useful statistics about which pages are being used and which ones are not, most computers with virtual memory have two bits associated with each page. One bit, the **R** or **referenced bit**, is set by the hardware on any read or write to the page. The other bit, the **M** or **Modified bit**, is set by the hardware when a page is written (i.e., a byte on it is stored into). It is important to realize that these bits must be updated on every memory reference, so it is essential that they be set by the hardware. Once a bit has been set to 1, it stays a 1 until the operating system resets it to 0 in software.

If the hardware does not have R and M bits, they can be simulated as follows. When a process is started up, all of its page table entries are marked as not in memory. As soon as any page is referenced, a page fault will occur. The operating system then sets the R bit (in its internal tables), changes the page table entry to point to the correct page, with mode READ ONLY, and restarts the instruction. If the page is subsequently written on, another page fault will occur, allowing the operating system to set the M bit and change the page's mode to READ/WRITE.

The R and M bits can be used to build a simple paging algorithm as follows. When a process is started up, both page bits for all its pages are set to 0 by the operating system. Periodically (e.g., on each clock interrupt), the R bit is cleared, to distinguish pages that have not been referenced recently from those that have been.

When a page fault occurs, the operating system inspects all the pages and divides them into four categories based on the current values of their R and M bits:

Class 0: not referenced, not modified.
Class 1: not referenced, modified.
Class 2: referenced, not modified.
Class 3: referenced, modified.

Although class 1 pages seem, at first glance, impossible, they occur when a class 3 page has its R bit cleared by a clock interrupt. Clock interrupts do not clear the M bit because this information is needed to know whether the page has to be rewritten to disk or not.

The **not recently used** or **NRU** algorithm removes a page at random from the lowest numbered nonempty class. Implicit in this algorithm is that it is better to remove a modified page that has not been referenced in at least one clock tick (typically 20 msec) than a clean page that is in heavy use. The main attraction of NRU is that it is easy to understand, efficient to implement, and gives a performance that, while certainly not optimal, is often adequate.

4.4.3. First-In, First-Out Page Replacement

Another low-overhead paging algorithm is **first-in, first-out** or **FIFO**. To illustrate how this works, consider a supermarket that has enough shelves to display exactly k different products. One day, some company introduces a new convenience food—instant, freeze-dried, organic yogurt that can be reconstituted in a microwave oven. It is an immediate success, so our finite supermarket has to get rid of one old product in order to stock it.

One possibility is to find the product that the supermarket has been stocking the longest (i.e., something it began selling 120 years ago), and get rid of it on the grounds that no one is interested any more. In effect, the supermarket maintains a linked list of all the products it currently sells in the order they were introduced. The new one goes on the back of the list, and the one at the front of the list is dropped.

As a page replacement algorithm, the same idea is applicable. The operating system maintains a list of all pages currently in memory, with the page at the head of the list the oldest one and the page at the tail the most recent arrival. On a page fault, the page at the head is removed and the new page added to the tail of the list. When applied to stores, FIFO might remove mustache wax, but it might also remove flour, salt, or butter. When applied to computers the same problem arises.

A simple modification to FIFO that avoids the problem of throwing out a heavily used page is to inspect the R and M bits of the oldest page. If the page belongs to class 0 (not referenced, not modified), it is evicted, otherwise, the next oldest page is inspected, and so forth. If no class 0 pages are present in memory, then the algorithm is repeated up to three more times looking for class 1, 2, and 3 pages.

Another variation on FIFO is **second chance**. The idea here is to first inspect the oldest page as a potential victim. If its R bit is 0, the page is replaced immediately. If the R bit is 1, the bit is cleared and the page is put onto the end of the list of pages, as though it had just arrived in memory. Then the search continues. What second chance is doing is looking for an old page that has not been referenced in the previous clock interval. If all the pages have been referenced, second chance degenerates into pure FIFO.

A minor technical variation of second chance is to keep all the pages on a circular list. Instead of putting pages at the end of the list to give them a second chance, the pointer to the "front" of the list is just advanced one page, giving the same effect. This variation is often called **clock**.

Intuitively it might seem that the more page frames the memory has, the fewer page faults a program will get. Belady et al. (1969) discovered a counter example, in which FIFO caused more page faults with four page frames than with three. This strange situation has become known as **Belady's anomaly**. It is illustrated in Fig. 4-14 for a program with five virtual pages, numbered from 0 to 4. The pages are referenced in the order

0 1 2 3 0 1 4 0 1 2 3 4

In Fig. 4-14(a) we see how with three page frames a total of nine page faults are caused. In Fig. 4-14(b) we get ten page faults with four page frames.

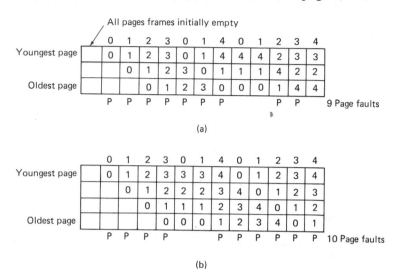

(a)

(b)

Fig. 4-14. Belady's anomaly. (a) FIFO with three page frames. (b) FIFO with four page frames. The P's show which page references cause page faults.

4.4.4. Least Recently Used Page Replacement

A good approximation to the optimal algorithm is based on the common observation that pages that have been heavily used in the last few instructions will probably be heavily used again in the next few. Conversely, pages that have not been used for a long time will probably remain unused for a long time. This observation suggests a realizable algorithm: when a page fault occurs, throw out the page that has been unused for the longest time. This strategy is called **least recently used** or **LRU** paging.

Although LRU is theoretically realizable, it is not cheap. To fully implement LRU, it is necessary to maintain a linked list of all pages in memory, with the most recently used page at the front and the least recently used page at the rear. The difficulty is that the list must be updated on every memory reference. Finding a page in the list, deleting it, and then moving it to the front is a very time consuming operation. Either (expensive) special hardware is needed, or we will have to find a cheaper approximation in software.

Searching and manipulating a linked list on every instruction is prohibitively slow, even in hardware. However, there are other ways to implement LRU with special hardware. Let us consider the simplest way first. This method requires equipping the hardware with a 64-bit counter, C, that is automatically incremented after each instruction. Furthermore, each page table entry must also have a field large enough to contain the counter. After each memory reference, the current value of C is stored in the page table entry for the page just referenced. When a page fault occurs, the operating system examines all the counters in the page table to find the lowest one. That page is the least recently used.

Now let us look at a second hardware LRU algorithm. For a machine with n page frames, the LRU hardware must maintain a matrix of $n \times n$ bits, initially all zero. Whenever page k is referenced, the hardware first sets all the bits of row k to 1, then sets all the bits of column k to 0. At any instant, the row whose binary value is lowest is the least recently used, the row whose value is next lowest is next least recently used, and so forth. The workings of this algorithm are given in Fig. 4-15 for four page frames and the page reference string

0 1 2 3 2 1 0 3 2 3

After page 0 is referenced we have the situation of Fig. 4-15(a), and so on.

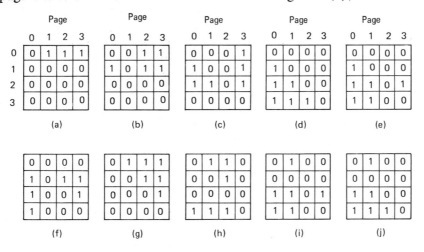

Fig. 4-15. LRU using a matrix.

4.4.5. Simulating LRU in Software

Although both of the previous algorithms are realizable, they are dependent on special hardware, and are of little use to the operating system designer who is making a system for a machine that does not have this hardware. Instead, a solution that can be implemented in software is needed. One possibility is called the **not frequently used** or **NFU** algorithm. It requires a software counter associated with each page, initially zero. At each clock interrupt, the operating system scans all the pages in memory. For each page, the R bit, which is 0 or 1, is added to the counter. In effect, the counters are an attempt to keep track of how often each page has been referenced. When a page fault occurs, the page with the lowest counter is chosen for replacement.

The main problem with NFU is that it never forgets anything. For example, in a multipass compiler, pages that were heavily used during pass 1 may still have a high count well into later passes. In fact, if pass 1 happens to have the longest execution time of all the passes, the pages containing the code for subsequent passes will always have lower counts than the pass 1 pages. Consequently, the operating system will remove useful pages instead of pages that are no longer in use.

Fortunately, a small modification to NFU makes it able to simulate LRU quite well. The modification has two parts. First, the counters are each shifted right 1 bit before the R bit is added in. Second, the R bit is added to the leftmost, rather than the rightmost bit.

Figure 4-16 illustrates how the modified algorithm, known as **aging**, works. Suppose that after the first clock tick the R bits for pages 0 to 5 have the values 1, 0, 1, 0, 1, and 1 respectively (page 0 is 1, page 1 is 0, page 2 is 1, etc.). In other words, between tick 0 and tick 1, pages 0, 1, and 4 were referenced, setting their R bits to 1, while the other ones remain 0. After the six corresponding counters have been shifted and the R bit inserted at the left, they have the values shown in Fig. 4-16(a). The four remaining columns show the six counters after the next four clock ticks.

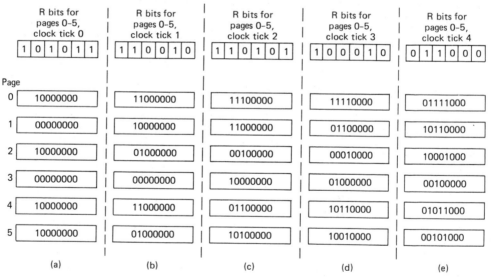

Fig. 4-16. The aging algorithm simulates LRU in software. Shown are six pages for five clock ticks. The five clock ticks are represented by (a) to (e).

When a page fault occurs, the page whose counter is the lowest is removed. It is clear that a page that has not been referenced for, say, four clock ticks will have four leading zeros in its counter, and thus will have a lower value than a counter that has not been referenced for three clock ticks.

This algorithm differs from LRU in two ways. Consider pages 3 and 5 in

Fig. 4-16(e). Neither has been referenced for two clock ticks; both were referenced in the tick prior to that. According to LRU, if a page must be replaced, we should choose one of these two. The trouble is, we do not know which of these two was referenced last in the interval between tick 1 and tick 2. By recording only one bit per time interval, we have lost the ability to distinguish references early in the clock interval from those occurring later. All we can do is remove page 3, because page 5 was also referenced two ticks earlier and page 3 was not.

The second difference between LRU and aging is that in aging the counters have a finite number of bits, 8 bits in this example. Suppose two pages each have a counter value of 0. All we can do is pick one of them at random. In reality, it may well be that one of the pages was last referenced 9 ticks ago and the other was last referenced 1000 ticks ago. We have no way of seeing that. In practice, however, 8 bits is generally enough if a clock tick is around 20 msec. If a page has not been referenced in 160 msec, it probably is not that important.

4.5. DESIGN ISSUES FOR PAGING SYSTEMS

In the previous sections we have explained how paging works and have given a few of the basic page replacement algorithms. But knowing the bare mechanics is not enough. To design a system, you have to know a lot more to make it work well. It is like the difference between knowing how to move the rook, knight, bishop, and other pieces in chess, and being a good player. In the follow sections, we will look at other issues that operating system designers must consider carefully in order to get good performance from a paging system.

4.5.1. The Working Set Model

In the purest form of paging, processes are started up with none of their pages in memory. As soon as the CPU tries to fetch the first instruction, it gets a page fault, causing the operating system to bring in the page containing the first instruction. Other page faults for global variables and the stack usually follow quickly. After a while, the process has most of the pages it needs and settles down to run with relatively few page faults. This strategy is called **demand paging** because pages are loaded only on demand, not in advance.

Of course, it is easy enough to write a test program that systematically reads all the pages in a large address space, causing so many page faults that there is not enough memory to hold them all. Fortunately, most processes do not work this way. They exhibit a **locality of reference**, meaning that during any phase of execution, the process references only a relatively small fraction of its pages. Each pass of a multipass compiler, for example, references only a fraction of all the pages, and a different fraction at that.

The set of pages that a process is currently using is called its **working set** (Denning, 1968a; Denning, 1980). If the entire working set is in memory, the process will run without causing many faults until it moves into another execution phase (e.g., the next pass of the compiler). If the available memory is too small to hold the entire working set, the process will cause many page faults and run very slowly since executing an instruction typically takes a microsecond and reading in a page from the disk typically takes tens of milliseconds. At a rate of one or two instructions per 30 milliseconds, it will take a long time to finish. A program causing page faults every few instructions is said to be **thrashing** (Denning, 1968b).

In a time-sharing system, processes are frequently moved to disk (i.e., all their pages are removed from memory) to let other processes have a turn at the CPU. The question arises of what to do when a process is brought back in again. Technically, nothing need be done. The process will just cause page faults until its working set has been loaded. The problem is that having 20, 50, or even 100 page faults every time a process is loaded is slow, and it also wastes considerable CPU time, since it takes the operating system a few milliseconds of CPU time to process a page fault.

Therefore, many paging systems try to keep track of each process' working set, and make sure that it is in memory before letting the process run. This approach is called the **working set model** (Denning, 1970). It is designed to greatly reduce the page fault rate. Loading the pages *before* letting processes run is also called **prepaging.**

The most important property of the working set is its size. If the total size of the working sets of all the processes "in memory" exceeds the available memory, thrashing will occur. Note that the whole concept of being "in memory" is pretty fuzzy in a paging system. What is usually meant is that the system normally has a set of processes that it regards as runnable, regardless of which pages are actually in memory. The scheduler restricts its choices to processes in this set.

From time to time, this set is changed, and if the working set model is being used, the pages comprising the working sets of the newly runnable processes will be brought into memory. It is up to the operating system to make sure that the sum of the working sets of the runnable processes fits in memory, if need be, by reducing the degree of multiprogramming (i.e., having fewer runnable processes).

To implement the working set model, it is necessary for the operating system to keep track of which pages are in the working set. One way to monitor this information is to use the aging algorithm discussed above. Any page containing a 1 bit among the high order n bits of the counter is considered to be a member of the working set. If a page has not been referenced in n consecutive clock ticks, it is dropped from the working set. The parameter n has to be determined experimentally for each system, but the system performance is usually not especially sensitive to the exact value.

4.5.2. Local versus Global Allocation Policies

In the preceding sections we have discussed several algorithms for choosing a page to replace when a fault occurs. A major issue associated with this choice (which we have carefully swept under the rug until now) is how memory should be allocated among the competing runnable processes.

Take a look at Fig. 4-17(a). In this figure, three processes, A, B, and C, make up the set of runnable processes. Suppose A gets a page fault. Should the page replacement algorithm try to find the least recently used page considering only the six pages currently allocated to A, or should it consider all the pages in memory? If it looks only at A's pages, the page with the lowest age value is $A5$, so we get the situation of Fig. 4-17(b).

	Age				
A0	10		A0		A0
A1	7		A1		A1
A2	5		A2		A2
A3	4		A3		A3
A4	6		A4		A4
A5	3		(A6)		A5
B0	9		B0		B0
B1	4		B1		B1
B2	6		B2		B2
B3	2		B3		(A6)
B4	5		B4		B4
B5	6		B5		B5
B6	12		B6		B6
C1	3		C1		C1
C2	5		C2		C2
C3	6		C3		C3
(a)			(b)		(c)

Fig. 4-17. Local versus global page replacement. (a) Original configuration. (b) Local page replacement. (c) Global page replacement.

On the other hand, if the page with the lowest age value is removed without regard to whose page it is, page $B3$ will be chosen and we will get the situation of Fig. 4-17(c). The algorithm of Fig. 4-17(b) is said to be a **local** page replacement algorithm, whereas Fig. 4-17(c) is said to be a **global** algorithm. Local algorithms correspond to assigning each process a fixed amount of memory. Global algorithms dynamically allocate page frames among the runnable processes.

In general, global algorithms work better, especially when the working set size can vary over the lifetime of a process. If a local algorithm is used and the working set grows, thrashing will result, even if there are plenty of free page frames. If the working set shrinks, local algorithms waste memory. If a global algorithm is used, the system must continually decide how many page frames to assign to each process. One way is to monitor the working set size as indicated by the aging bits, but this approach does not necessarily prevent thrashing. The working set may change size in microseconds, whereas the aging bits are a crude measure spread over a number of clock ticks.

A more direct way to control thrashing and allocate memory globally is to use the **page fault frequency** or **PFF** allocation algorithm. For a large class of page replacement algorithms, including LRU, it is known that the fault rate decreases as more pages are assigned. (Belady's anomaly occurred with FIFO, which does not have this property.) This property is illustrated in Fig. 4-18.

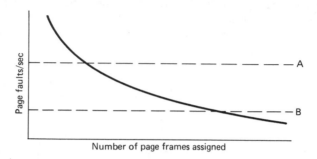

Fig. 4-18. Page fault rate as a function of the number of page frames assigned.

The dotted line marked A corresponds to a page fault rate that is unacceptably high, so the faulting process is given more page frames to reduce the fault rate. The dotted line marked B corresponds to a page fault rate so low that it can be concluded that the process has too much memory. In this case page frames are taken away from it. Thus, PFF tries to keep the paging rate within acceptable bounds. If it discovers that there are so many processes in memory that it is not possible to keep all of them below A, then some process is removed from memory, and its page frames are divided up among the remaining processes or put into a pool of available pages that can be used on subsequent page faults.

4.5.3. Page Size

The page size is often a parameter that can be chosen by the operating system designers. Even if the hardware has been designed with, for example, 512-byte pages, the operating system can easily regard pages 0 and 1, 2 and 3, 4 and 5, and so on, as 1K pages by always allocating two consecutive 512-byte page frames for them.

Determining the optimum page size requires balancing several competing factors. To start with, a randomly chosen text, data, or stack segment will not fill an integral number of pages. On the average, half of the final page will be empty. The extra space in that page is wasted (internal fragmentation). With n segments in memory and a page size of p bytes, $np/2$ bytes will be wasted on internal fragmentation. This reasoning argues for a small page size.

Another argument for a small page size becomes apparent if we think about a compiler consisting of 8 passes of 4K each. With a 32K page size, the program must be allocated 32K all the time. With a 16K page size, it needs only 16K. With a page size of 4K or smaller, it requires only 4K at any instant. In general, a large page size will cause more unused program to be in memory than a small page size.

On the other hand, small pages mean that programs will need many pages, hence a large page table. A 32K program needs only four 8K pages, but 64 512-byte pages. Transfers to and from the disk are generally a page at a time, with most of the time being for the seek and rotational delay, so that transferring a small page takes almost as much time as transferring a large page. It might take 64×15 msec to load 64 512-byte pages, but only 4×25 msec to load four 8K pages.

On some machines, the page table must be loaded into hardware registers every time the CPU switches from one process to another. On these machines having a small page size means that the time required to load the page registers gets longer as the page size gets smaller. Furthermore, the space occupied by the page table increases as the page size decreases.

This last point can be analyzed mathematically. Let the average process size be s bytes and the page size be p bytes. Furthermore, assume that each page entry requires e bytes. The approximate number of pages needed per process is then s/p, occupying se/p bytes of page table space. The wasted memory in the last page of the process due to internal fragmentation is $p/2$. Thus, the total overhead due to the page table and the internal fragmentation loss is give by

$$\text{overhead} = se/p + p/2$$

The first term (page table size) is large when the page size is small. The second term (internal fragmentation) is large when the page size is large. The optimum must lie somewhere in between. By taking the first derivative with respect to p and equating it to zero, we get the equation

$$-se/p^2 + 1/2 = 0$$

From this equation we find that the optimum page size (considering only memory wasted in fragmentation and page table size) to be given by

$$p = \sqrt{2se}$$

For $s = 64K$ and $e = 8$ bytes per page table entry, the optimum page size is 724 bytes. In practice 512 bytes or 1K would be used, depending on the other factors (e.g., disk speed). Most commercially available computers use page sizes of 512 bytes, 1K, 2K, or 4K.

4.5.4. Implementation Issues

Implementers of virtual memory systems have to make choices among the major theoretical algorithms such as second chance versus aging, local versus global page allocation, and demand paging versus prepaging. But they also have to be aware of a number of practical implementation issues as well. In this section we will take a look at a few of the more common problems and their solutions.

Instruction Backup

When a program references a page that is not in memory, the instruction causing the fault is stopped part way through and a trap to the operating system occurs. After the operating system has fetched the page needed, it must restart the instruction causing the trap. This is easier said than done.

For one thing, most instructions consist of several bytes. The Motorola 68000 instruction MOVE.L #6(A1),2(A0) is 6 bytes, for example (see Fig. 4-19). In order to restart the instruction, the operating system must determine where the first byte of the instruction is. The value of the program counter at the time of the trap depends on which operand faulted and how the CPU's microcode has been implemented.

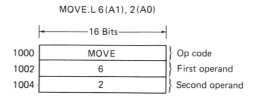

Fig. 4-19. An instruction causing a page fault

In Fig. 4-19, we have an instruction starting at address 1000 that makes three memory references: the instruction word, and two offsets for the operands. Depending on which of these three memory references caused the page fault, the program counter might be 1000, 1002, or 1004 at the time of the fault. It is frequently impossible for the operating system to determine unambiguously where the instruction began. If the program counter is 1002 at the time of the fault, the operating system has no way of telling whether the word in 1002 is a memory address associated with an instruction at 1000, or an instruction opcode.

Bad as this problem may be, it could have been worse. Instructions that use autoincrement mode can also fault. Depending on the details of the microcode, the increment may be done before the memory reference, in which case the operating system must decrement the register in software before restarting the instruction. Or, the autoincrement may be done after the memory reference, in which case it will not have been done at the time of the trap and must not be undone by the operating system. Autodecrement causes the same problem.

The precise details of whether autoincrements and autodecrements have or have not been done before the corresponding memory references may differ from instruction to instruction and from CPU model to CPU model. (In the DEC PDP-11 series, no two models worked the same way.) As a result, paging on the 68000 is not possible, at least not without enormous contortions on the part of the operating system.

Fortunately, on some machines the CPU designers provided a solution, usually in the form of a register into which the program counter is copied just before each instruction is executed. These machines generally also have a second register telling which registers have already been autoincremented or autodecremented, and by how much. Given this information, the operating system can unambiguously undo all the effects of the faulting instruction so it can be started all over again. The Motorola 68010, for example, contains these features; in fact, they are the principal difference between the 68000 and 68010, making paging possible on the latter and impossible on the former.

Locking Pages in Memory

Although we have not discussed I/O much in this chapter, the fact that a computer has virtual memory does not mean that I/O (especially terminal I/O) is absent. Virtual memory and I/O interact in subtle ways. Consider a process that has just issued a system call to read from some file or device into a buffer within its address space. While waiting for the I/O to complete, the process is suspended and another process is allowed to run. This other process gets a page fault.

If the paging algorithm is global, there is a small, but nonzero, chance that the page containing the I/O buffer will be chosen to be removed from memory. If an I/O device is currently in the process of doing a DMA transfer to that page, removing it will cause part of the data to be written in the buffer where it belongs, and part of the data to be written over the newly loaded page. One solution to this problem is to lock pages engaged in I/O in memory so that they will not be removed. Another solution is to do all I/O to kernel buffers and then copy the data to user pages later.

Shared Pages

Another implementation issue is sharing. In a large time-sharing system, it is common for several users to be running the same program (e.g., the editor, a compiler) at the same time. It is clearly more efficient to share the pages, to avoid having two copies of the same page in memory at the same time. One problem is that not all pages are shareable. In particular, pages that are read-only, such as program text, can be shared, but data pages cannot.

Even with this restriction, another problem occurs with shared pages. Suppose processes A and B are both running the editor and sharing its pages. If the scheduler decides to remove A from memory, evicting all its pages and filling the empty page frames with some other program will cause B to generate a large number of page faults to bring them back in again.

Similarly, when A terminates, it is essential to be able to discover that the pages are still in use so that their disk space will not be freed by accident. Searching all the page tables to see if a page is shared is too expensive, so special data structures are needed to keep track of shared pages.

4.6. OVERVIEW OF MEMORY MANAGEMENT IN MINIX

Memory management in MINIX is simple: neither paging nor swapping is used. The memory manager maintains a list of holes sorted in memory address order. When memory is needed, due either to a FORK or an EXEC system call, the hole list is searched using first fit for a piece that is big enough to hold the new process. Once a process has been placed in memory, it remains in exactly the same place until it terminates. It is never swapped out and also never moved to another place in memory. Nor does allocated area ever grow or shrink.

This strategy deserves some explanation. It derives from three factors: (1) the idea that MINIX is for personal computers, rather than for large time-sharing systems, (2) the desire to have MINIX work on the IBM PC, and (3) an attempt to make the system straightforward to implement on other small, personal computers in the future.

The first factor means that, on the average, the number of running processes will be small, so that typically enough memory will be available to hold all the processes with room left over. Swapping will generally not be needed. Since it adds considerable complexity to the system, not swapping makes the code much smaller. Furthermore, many personal computers do not have a hard disk, and a floppy disk is not exactly the ideal swapping device.

The desire to have MINIX run on the IBM PC also had substantial impact on the memory management design. The 8088's memory management architecture is very primitive. It does not support virtual memory in any form and does not even detect stack overflow, a defect that has major implications for the way processes are laid out in memory.

The portability issue argues for as simple a memory management scheme as possible. If MINIX used paging or segmentation, it would be difficult, if not impossible to port it to machines not having these features. By making a minimal number of assumptions about what the hardware can do, the number of machines to which MINIX can be ported is increased.

Another unusual aspect of MINIX is the way the memory management is implemented. It is not part of the kernel. Instead, it is handled by the memory manager process, which runs in user space and communicates with the kernel by the standard message mechanism. The position of the memory manager is shown in Fig. 4-20.

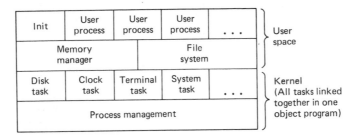

Fig. 4-20. The memory manager runs outside the kernel, in user space.

Moving the memory manager out of the kernel is an example of the separation of **policy** and **mechanism**. The decisions about which process will be placed where in memory (policy) are made by the memory manager. The actual setting of memory maps for processes (mechanism) is done by the system task within the kernel. This split makes it relatively easy to change the memory management policy (algorithms, etc.) without having to modify the lowest layers of the operating system.

Most of the memory manager code is devoted to handling the MINIX system calls that involve memory management, primarily FORK and EXEC, rather than just manipulating lists of processes and holes. In the next section we will look at the memory layout, and then in the ones following it we will take a bird's-eye view of how the memory management system calls are processed.

4.6.1. Memory Layout

Memory is allocated in MINIX on two occasions. First, when a process forks, an amount of memory equal in size to what the parent has is allocated for the child. Second, when a process changes its memory image via the EXEC system call, the old image is returned to the free list as a hole, and memory is allocated for the new one. Memory is released whenever a process terminates, either by exiting or by being killed by a signal.

Figure 4-21 shows both ways of allocating memory. In Fig. 4-21(a) we see two processes, A and B, in memory. If A forks, we get the situation of Fig. 4-21(b). If the child now executes the file C, the memory looks like Fig. 4-21(c).

Note that the old memory for the child is released before the new memory for C is allocated, so that C can use the child's memory. In this way, a series of FORK and EXEC pairs (such as the shell setting up a pipeline) results in all the processes being adjacent, with no holes between them, as would have been the case had the new memory been allocated before the old memory had been released.

When memory is allocated, either by the FORK or EXEC system calls, a

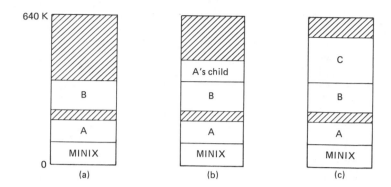

Fig. 4-21. Memory allocation. (a) Originally. (b) After a FORK. (c) After the child does an EXEC. The shaded regions are unused memory.

certain amount of it is taken for the new process. In the former case, the amount taken is identical to what the parent process has. In the latter case, the memory manager takes the amount specified in the header of the file executed. Once this allocation has been made, under no conditions is the process ever allocated any more total memory.

Figure 4-22 shows the internal memory layout used for a single MINIX process. For a program not using separate I and D space, the total amount of memory allocated is specified by a field in the header. If, for example, a program has 4K of text, 2K of data, and 1K of stack, and the header says to allocate 40K total, the gap of unused memory between the data segment and the stack segment will be 33K.

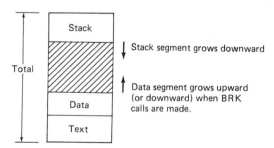

Fig. 4-22. Internal memory layout for a single process.

If the programmer knows that the total memory needed for the combined growth of the data and stack segments for the file *a.out* is at most 10K, he can give the command

```
chmem =10240 a.out
```

which changes the header field so that upon EXEC the memory manager allocates a space 10240 bytes more than the sum of the initial text and data segments. For the above example, a total of 16K would be allocated on all subsequent EXECs of the file. Of this amount, the topmost 1K would be used for the stack.

For a program using separate I and D space (indicated by a bit in the header that is set by the linker), the total field in the header applies to the data space only. A program with 4K of text, 2K of data, 1K of stack, and a total size of 64K would be allocated 68K (4K instruction space, 64K data space), leaving 61K for the data segment and stack to consume during execution. The boundary of the data segment can be moved only by the BRK system call. All BRK does is check to see if the new data segment bumps into the current stack pointer, and if not, note the change in some internal tables. No memory is allocated. If the new data segment bumps into the stack, the call fails.

This strategy has been chosen to make it possible to run MINIX on the IBM PC, which does not check for stack overflow in hardware. A user program can push as many words as it wants to on the stack without the operating system being aware of it. On computers with more sophisticated memory management hardware, the stack is allocated a certain amount of memory initially. If it attempts to grow beyond this amount, a trap to the operating system occurs, and the system allocates another piece of memory to the stack, if possible. This trap does not exist on the 8088, making it dangerous to have the stack adjacent to anything except a large chunk of unused memory, since the stack can grow quickly and without warning. MINIX has been designed so that if it is moved to a computer with better memory management, the better memory management can be used.

4.6.2. Message Handling

Like all the other components of MINIX, the memory manager is message driven. After the system has been initialized, the memory manager enters its main loop, which consists of waiting for a message, carrying out the request contained in the message, and sending a reply. Figure 4-23 gives the list of legal message types, their input parameters, and the value sent back in the reply message. FORK, EXIT, WAIT, BRK, and EXEC are clearly closely related to memory allocation and deallocation. The four signal calls, SIGNAL, KILL, ALARM, and PAUSE, also can affect what is in memory, because a signal that kills a process also causes its memory to be deallocated. The five GET/SET calls have nothing to do with memory management at all. They also have nothing to do with the file system. But they had to go either in the file system or the memory manager, since each system call is handled by one or the other. They were put here simply because the file system was large enough already.

The final two messages, KSIG and BRK2 are not system calls. KSIG is the message type used by the kernel to inform the memory manager of a signal originating in the kernel, such as SIGINT, SIGQUIT, or SIGALRM. BRK2 is used during system initialization to tell the memory manager how big the system is.

Although there is a library routine *sbrk*, there is no system call SBRK. The

Message type	Input parameters	Reply value
FORK	(none)	Child's pid
EXIT	Exit status	(No reply)
WAIT	(none)	Status code
BRK	New size	New size
EXEC	Pointer to initial stack	(No reply)
SIGNAL	Signal number and function	Old function
KILL	Process identifier and signal	0 if OK
ALARM	Number of seconds to wait	Residual time
PAUSE	(none)	0 if OK
GETPID	(none)	Pid
GETUID	(none)	Uid
GETGID	(none)	Gid
SETUID	New uid	0 if OK
SETGID	New gid	0 if OK
KSIG	Process slot and signals	(No reply)
BRK2	Init and total sizes	0 if OK

Fig. 4-23. The message types, input parameters, and reply values used for communicating with the memory manager.

library routine computes the amount of memory needed by adding the increment or decrement specified as parameter to the current size, and makes a BRK call to set the size. Similarly, there are no separate system calls for *geteuid* and *getegid*. The calls GETUID and GETGID return both the effective and real identifiers.

A key data structure used for message processing is the table *call_vector* declared in *table.c* (line 2400). It contains pointers to the procedures that handle the various message types. When a message comes in to the memory manager, the main loop extracts the message type and puts it in the global variable *mm_call*. This value is then used to index into *call_vector* to find the pointer to the procedure that handles the newly arrived message. That procedure is then called to execute the system call. The value that it returns is sent back to the caller in the reply message to report on the success or failure of the call. This mechanism is similar to that of Fig. 1-18, only in user space rather than in the kernel.

4.6.3. Memory Manager Data Structures and Algorithms

The memory manager has two key data structures: the process table and the hole table. We will now look at both of these in turn.

In Fig. 2-4 we saw that some of process table fields are needed for process management, others for memory management, and yet others for the file system. In MINIX, each of these three pieces of the operating system has its own process table, containing just those fields that it needs. The entries correspond exactly, to keep things simple. Thus, slot *k* of the memory manager's table refers to the same process as slot *k* of the file system's table. When a process is created or destroyed, all three parts update their tables to reflect the new situation, in order to keep them synchronized.

The memory manager's process table is called *mproc*. It contains all the fields related to a process' memory allocation, as well as some additional items. The most important field is the array *mp_seg*, which has three entries, for the text, data, and stack segments, respectively. Each entry is a structure containing the virtual address, physical address, and length of the segment, all measured in clicks rather than in bytes. All segments must start on a click boundary and occupy an integral number of clicks.

The method used for recording memory allocation is shown in Fig. 4-24. In this figure we have a process with 3K of text, 4K of data, a gap of 1K, and then a 2K stack, for a total memory allocation of 10K. In Fig. 4-24(b) we see what the virtual, physical, and length fields for each of the three segments are, assuming that the process does not have separate I and D space. In this model, the text segment is always empty, and the data segment contains both text and data. When a process references virtual address 0, either to jump to it or to read it (i.e., as instruction space or as data space), physical address 0x32000 (in decimal, 200K) will be used. This address is at click 0x3200.

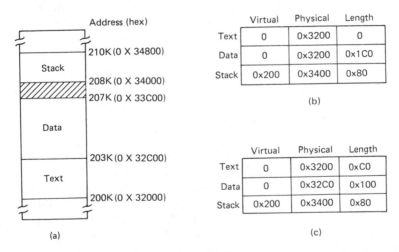

Fig. 4-24. (a) A process in memory. (b) Its memory representation for non-separate I and D space. (c) Its memory representation for separate I and D space.

Note that the virtual address at which the stack begins depends initially on the total amount of memory allocated to the process. If the *chmem* command were used to modify the file header to provide a larger dynamic allocation area (bigger gap between data and stack segments), the next time the file was executed, the stack would start at a higher virtual address. If the stack grows longer by one click, the stack entry *should* change from the triple (0x200, 0x3400, 0x80) to the triple (0x1FF, 0x33FF, 0x81).

Because the 8088 hardware does not have a stack limit trap, this change will not be made until the next BRK system call, at which point the operating system explicitly reads SP and recomputes the segment entries. On a machine with a stack trap, the stack segment's entry would be updated as soon as the stack outgrew its segment.

Fig. 4-24(c) shows the segment entries for the memory layout of Fig. 4-24(a) for separate I and D space. Here both the text and data segments are nonzero in length.

The *mp_seg* array shown in Fig. 4-24(b) or (c) is primarily used to map virtual addresses onto physical memory addresses. Given a virtual address and the space to which it belongs, it is a simple matter to see whether the virtual address is legal or not (i.e., falls inside a segment), and if legal, what the corresponding physical address is. The kernel procedure *umap* performs this mapping for the I/O tasks and for copying to and from user space, for example.

In addition to the segment information, *mproc* also holds the process id (pid) of the process itself and of its parent, the uids and gids (both real and effective), information about signals, and the exit status, if the process has already terminated but its parent has not yet done a WAIT for it.

The other major memory manager table is the hole table, *hole*, which lists every hole in memory in order of increasing memory address. The gaps between the data and stack segments are not considered holes since they have already been allocated. They are not contained in the free hole list. Each hole list entry has three fields: the base address of the hole, in clicks; the length of the hole, in clicks; and a pointer to the next entry on the list. The list is singly linked, so it is easy to find the next hole starting from any given hole, but to find the previous hole, you have to search the entire list from the beginning until you come to the given hole.

The reason for recording everything about segments and holes in clicks rather than bytes is simple: it is much more efficient. On the 8088, using byte addresses would require 20 bits per address, whereas recording addresses in clicks requires only 16 bits per address. Similar arguments hold for paging machines. A computer with a page size of 1K and 64M of memory needs only 16 bits to hold a page number, but 26 bits to hold a full memory address.

The principal operations on the hole list are allocating a piece of memory of a given size and returning an existing allocation. To allocate memory, the entire hole list is searched, starting at the hole with the lowest address, until a hole that is large enough is found (first fit). The segment is then allocated by reducing the hole by the amount needed for the segment, or in the rare case of an exact fit, removing the hole from the list. This scheme is fast and simple, but suffers from both internal fragmentation (up to 15 bytes may be wasted in the final click, since an integral number of clicks is always taken) and external fragmentation.

When a process terminates and is cleaned up, its memory is returned to the free list. If either or both of the memory's neighbors are holes, they are merged, so adjacent holes never occur. In this way, the number, location, and sizes of the holes vary continuously as the system runs. Whenever all user processes have terminated, all of available memory is once again in a single hole, ready for allocation.

4.6.4. The FORK, EXIT, and WAIT System Calls

When processes are created or destroyed, memory must be allocated or deallocated. Also, the process table must be updated, including the parts held by the kernel and the file system. It is the memory manager that coordinates all of this activity. Process creation is done by FORK, which is carried out as a series of steps, as shown in Fig. 4-25.

```
1. Check to see if process table is full.
2. Try to allocate memory for the child.
3. Copy the parent's image to the child's memory.
4. Find a free process slot and copy parent's slot to it.
5. Enter child's memory map in process table.
6. Choose a pid for the child.
7. Tell kernel and file system about child.
8. Report child's memory map to kernel.
9. Send reply messages to parent and child.
```

Fig. 4-25. The steps required to carry out the FORK system call.

It is difficult and inconvenient to stop a FORK call part way through, so the memory manager maintains a count at all times of the number of processes currently in existence in order to see easily if a process table slot is available. If the table is not full, an attempt is made to allocate memory for the child. If this step also succeeds, the FORK is guaranteed to work. The newly allocated memory is then filled in, a process slot is located and filled in, a pid is chosen, and the other parts of the system informed that a new process has been created.

A process fully terminates when two events happen: (1) the process itself has exited (or has been killed by a signal), and (2) its parent has executed a WAIT system call to find out what happened. A process that has exited or has been killed, but whose parent has not (yet) done a WAIT for it, enters a kind of suspended animation, sometimes known as **zombie state**. It is prevented from being scheduled and has its alarm timer turned off (if it was on), but it is not removed from the process table. Its memory is not freed, although it could have been. (Zombie state is unusual and rarely lasts long, and it was easier to program this way.) When the parent finally does the WAIT, the memory and process table slot are freed, and the file system and kernel are informed.

A problem arises if the parent of an exiting process is itself already dead. If no special action were taken, the exiting process would remain a zombie forever. Instead, the tables are changed to make it a child of the *init* process. When the system comes up, *init* reads the */etc/ttys* file to get a list of all terminals, and then forks off a login process to handle each one. It then spends most of its time waiting for processes to terminate. In this way, orphan zombies are cleaned up quickly.

4.6.5. The EXEC System Call

When a command is typed at the terminal, the shell forks off a new process, which then executes the command requested. It would have been possible to have a single system call to do both FORK and EXEC at once, but they were provided as two distinct calls for a very good reason: to make it easy to implement redirection. When the shell forks, the child process closes standard input and output if they are redirected, and then opens the redirected files. Then it executes the command, which inherits the redirected standard input and output.

EXEC is the most complex system call in MINIX. It must replace the current memory image with a new one, including setting up a new stack. It carries out its job in a series of steps, as shown in Fig. 4-26.

```
1. Check permissions — is the file executable?
2. Read the header to get the segment and total sizes.
3. Fetch the arguments and environment from the caller.
4. Release the old memory and allocate the new one.
5. Copy stack to new memory image.
6. Copy text and data segments to new memory image.
7. Check for and handle setuid, setgid bits.
8. Fix up process table entry.
9. Tell kernel that process is now runnable.
```

Fig. 4-26. The steps required to carry out the EXEC system call.

Each step consists, in turn, of yet smaller steps, some of which can fail. For example, there might be insufficient memory available. The order in which the tests are made has been carefully chosen to make sure the old memory image is not released until it is certain that the EXEC will succeed, to avoid the embarrassing situation of not being able to set up a new memory image, but not having the old one to go back to, either. Normally EXEC does not return, but if it fails, the calling process must get control again, with an error indication.

There are a few steps in Fig. 4-26 that deserve some more comment. First is the question of whether there is enough room or not. Checking to see if there is sufficient physical memory is done by searching the hole list *before* freeing the old memory—if the old memory were freed first and there was insufficient memory, it would be hard to get the old image back again.

However, this test is overly strict. It sometimes rejects EXEC calls that, in fact, could succeed. Suppose, for example, the process doing the EXEC call occupies 20K. Further suppose that there is a 30K hole available and that the new image requires 50K. By testing before releasing, we will discover that only 30K is available and reject the call. If we had released first, we might have succeeded, depending on whether or not the new 20K hole was adjacent to, and thus now merged with, the 30K hole. A more sophisticated implementation could handle this situation a little better.

A more subtle issue is whether the executable file fits in the *virtual* address space. The problem is that memory is allocated not in bytes, but in clicks (16 bytes on the 8088, 1 page on a virtual memory system). Each click must belong to a single segment, and may not be, for example, half data, half stack, because the entire memory administration is in clicks.

To see how this restriction can give trouble, note that the 64K address space of the 8088 can be divided into 4096 clicks. Suppose a separate I and D space program has 40,000 bytes of text, 32,770 bytes of data, and 32,760 bytes of stack. The data segment occupies 2049 clicks, of which the last one is only partially used; still, the whole click is part of the data segment. The stack segment is 2048 clicks. Together they exceed 4096 clicks, and thus cannot co-exist, even though the number of *bytes* needed fits in the virtual address space (barely). This problem exists on all machines whose click size is larger than 1 byte.

Another important issue is how the initial stack is set up. The library call normally used to invoke EXEC with arguments and an environment is

```
execve(name, argv, envp);
```

where *name* is a pointer to the name of the file to be executed, *argv* is a pointer to an array of pointers, each one pointing to an argument, and *envp* is a pointer to an array of pointers, each one pointing to an environment string.

It would be easy enough to implement EXEC by just putting the the three pointers in the message to the memory manager, and letting it fetch the file name and two arrays by itself. Then it would have to fetch each argument and each string one at a time. Doing it this way requires at least one message to the system task per argument or string and probably more, since the memory manager has no way of knowing how big each one is in advance.

To avoid the overhead of multiple messages to read all these pieces, a completely different strategy has been chosen. The *execve* library procedure builds the entire initial stack inside itself and passes its base address and size to the memory manager. Building the new stack within the user space is highly efficient, because references to the arguments and strings are just local memory references, not references to a different address space.

To make this mechanism clearer, let us consider an example. When a user types

```
ls -l f.c g.c
```

to the shell, the shell makes the call

```
execve("/bin/ls", argv, envp);
```

to the library procedure. The contents of the two pointer arrays are shown in Fig. 4-27(a). The procedure *execve*, within the shell's address space, now builds the initial stack, as shown in Fig. 4-27(b). This stack is eventually copied intact to the memory manager during the processing of the EXEC call.

When the stack is finally copied to the user process, it will not be put at

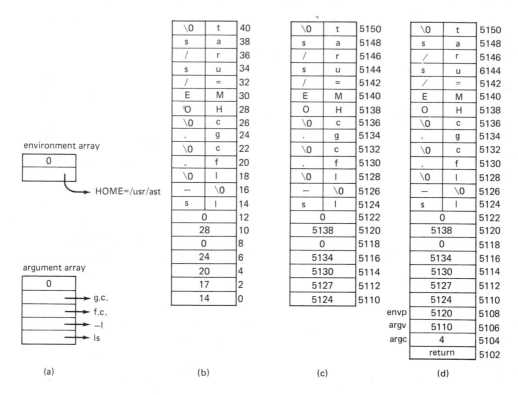

Fig. 4-27. (a) The arrays passed to *execve*. (b) The stack built by *execve*. (c) The stack after relocation by the memory manager. (d) The stack as it appears to *main* at the start of execution.

virtual address 0. Instead, it will be put at the end of the memory allocation, as determined by total memory size field in the executable file's header. As an example, let us arbitrarily assume that the stack begins at address 5110. It is up to the memory manager to relocate the pointers within the stack so that when deposited into the new address, the stack looks like Fig. 4-27(c).

When the EXEC call completes and the program starts running, the stack will indeed look exactly like Fig. 4-27(c), with the stack pointer having the value 5110. However, another problem is yet to be dealt with. The main program of the executed file is probably declared something like this:

```
main(argc, argv, envp);
```

As far as the C compiler is concerned, *main* is just another function. It does not know that *main* is special, so it compiles code to access the three parameters on the assumption that they will be passed according to the standard C calling convention, last parameter first. With one integer and two pointers, the three parameters are expected to occupy the three words just before the return address. Of course, the stack of Fig. 4-27(c) does not look like that at all.

The solution is that newly executed files do not begin with *main*. Instead, a small, assembly language routine called the C run-time, start-off procedure, is always linked in at text address 0 so it gets control first. Its job is to push three more words onto the stack and then to call *main* using the standard call instruction. This results in the stack of Fig. 4-27(d) at the time that *main* starts executing. Thus, *main* is tricked into thinking it was called in the usual way (actually, it is not really a trick; it *is* called that way).

If the programmer neglects to call *exit* at the end of *main*, control will pass back to the C run-time, start-off routine when main is finished. Again, the compiler just sees *main* as an ordinary procedure, and generates the usual code to return from it after the last statement. Thus *main* returns to its caller, the C run-time, start-off routine which then calls *exit* itself. The MINIX C run-time, start-off routine routine is called *crtso* and is located in the directory *lib* and its subdirectories, for various compilers.

4.6.6. The BRK System Call

The library procedures *brk* and *sbrk* are used to adjust the upper bound of the data segment. The former takes an absolute size and calls BRK. The latter takes a positive or negative increment to the current size, computes the new data segment size, and then calls BRK. There is no SBRK system call.

An interesting question is: "How does *sbrk* keep track of the current size, so it can compute the new size?" The answer is that a variable, *brksize*, always holds the current size so *sbrk* can find it. This variable is initialized to a compiler generated symbol giving the initial size of text plus data (nonseparate I and D) or just data (separate I and D). The name, and, in fact, very existence of such a symbol is compiler dependent.

Carrying out BRK is easy for the memory manager. All that must be done is to check to see that everything still fits in the address space, adjust the tables, and tell the kernel.

4.6.7. Signal Handling

Signals can be generated in two ways: by the KILL system call, and by the kernel. The kernel generated signals currently implemented are SIGINT, SIGQUIT, and SIGALRM, but if MINIX is ever ported to a machine that traps on illegal instructions, detects illegal addresses, or notices other hardware violations, the corresponding signals will also be generated by the kernel.

Whatever their origin, the memory manager processes all signals the same way. For each process to be signaled, a variety of checks are made to see if the signal is feasible. One process can signal another if both have the same uid, and were started from the same terminal. Furthermore, neither zombies nor processes that have explicitly called SIGNAL to ignore the signal can be signaled.

If all the conditions are met, the signal can be sent. If the signal is to be caught, a message is sent to the system task within the kernel, requesting that it push the 4 words of Fig. 4-28 onto the signaled process' stack. The exact layout of the words pushed is designed to be identical to what a hardware trap pushes (plus the signal number), so porting MINIX to a different system implies changing the layout of Fig. 4-28 accordingly.

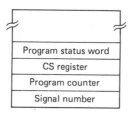

Program status word
CS register
Program counter
Signal number

Fig. 4-28. The four words pushed onto the stack of a signaled process on the 8088.

After the process has received the interrupt, a run time system routine, *catchsig*, is called. This routine first saves all the registers on the stack. Then it uses the signal number as an index into a local table to find the C function to be called. When the user executes a SIGNAL call, the pointer to the function to be called is stored in a local table; the memory manager is merely told which signal is being enabled. It is also given the address of *catchsig*, which it traps to on all signals. After *catchsig* has found the pointer to the signal handler, it calls the handler.

When the handler is done, it returns to *catchsig*, which restores the registers and does a RETURN FROM INTERRUPT instruction to resume processing at the point it was prior to the interrupt. Interrupts are completely invisible to the interrupted program.

If a signal is sent to a process that has not been enabled to handle it, the memory manager kills the process. If the parent is waiting for it, it is cleaned up and removed from the process table. If the parent is not waiting, it becomes a zombie. For certain signal numbers (e.g., SIGQUIT), the memory manager also writes a core dump of the process to the current directory.

It can easily happen that a signal is sent to a process that is currently blocked waiting for a READ on a terminal for which no input is available. If the process has not specified that the signal is to be caught, it is just killed in the usual way. If, however, the signal is caught, the issue arises of what to do after the signal interrupt has been processed. Should the process go back to waiting, or should it continue with the next statement?

What MINIX does is this: the system call is terminated in such a way as to return the error code EINTR, so the process can see that the call was broken off by a signal. Determining that a signaled process was blocked on a system call is not entirely trivial. The memory manager must ask the file system to check for it.

4.6.8. Other System Calls

The memory manager also handles a few more simple system calls: GETPID, GETUID, GETGID, SETUID, and SETGID. The first three calls just look up and return the requested information. GETUID returns both the real and effective uid. Depending on whether *getuid* or *geteuid* was called, one or the other is extracted from the message and returned to the user. The same holds for the gid. These five calls are the simplest MINIX system calls.

4.7. IMPLEMENTATION OF MEMORY MANAGEMENT IN MINIX

Armed with a general overview of how the memory manager works, let us now turn to the code itself. The memory manager is written entirely in C, is straightforward and contains a substantial amount of comment in the code itself, so our treatment of most parts need not be long or involved. We will first look briefly at the header files, then the main program, and finally the files for the various system call groups discussed previously.

4.7.1. The Header Files

The file *const.h* (line 5150) defines a few constants used by the memory manager. The conditional declaration of *MM_STACK_BYTES* is needed primarily for the array *mbuf* in *exec.c*. The array is used for several purposes and has to be large enough for all of them.

The memory manager's global variables are declared in *glo.h* (line 5200). The same trick used in the kernel with *EXTERN* is used here, namely, that *EXTERN* is normally a macro that expands to *extern*, except in the file *table.c*, where it becomes the null string so storage is actually reserved for them.

The first variable, *mp*, is a pointer to the *mproc* structure for the process whose system call is now being processed. The second variable, *dont_reply*, is initialized to *FALSE* when each new request arrives, but can be set to *TRUE* during the call if it is discovered that no reply message should be sent. No replies are sent for a successful EXEC, for example. The third variable, *procs_in_use*, keeps track of how many process slots are currently in use, making it easy to see if a FORK call is feasible.

The message buffers *mm_in* and *mm_out* are for the request and reply messages, respectively. *Who* is the index of the current process and is related to *mp* by

```
mp = &mproc[who];
```

When a message comes in, the system call number is extracted from it and put in *mm_call*.

The three variables *err_code*, *result2*, and *res_ptr* are used to hold values returned to the caller in the reply message. The most important one is *err_code*, which generally is set to *OK* if the call was completed without error.

The array *mm_stack* holds the memory manager's stack. The stack pointer is initialized to point to it in a tiny assembly code routine, called *head*, that is called before *main* starts. In a sense, *head* is analogous to *crtso*, which is not linked with the memory manager or file system, because they do not have arguments.

The file *mproc.h* (line 5250) contains the memory manager's version of the process table. Most of the fields are adequately described by their comments. The two bit maps, *mp_ignore* and *mp_catch*, each contain 16 bits, 1 bit per signal, with signal 1 being the rightmost bit. The *mp_flags* field is used to hold a miscellaneous collection of bits, as indicated at the end of the file.

Next comes *param.h* (line 5300), which contains macros for many of the system call parameters contained in the request message. It also contains three macros for fields in the reply message. If the statement

```
k = pid;
```

were to appear in any file in which *param.h* were included, the preprocessor would convert it to

```
k = mm_in.m_i1;
```

before feeding it to the compiler proper.

The final header file is *type.h* (line 5350). All it does is include the global type definition file. It is merely included for symmetry, since the kernel and file system have nonempty *type.h* files.

4.7.2. The Main Program

The memory manager is compiled and linked independently from the kernel and the file system. Consequently, it has its own main program, which is started up after the kernel has finished initializing itself. The main program is in *main.c* (line 5400). After doing its own initialization (line 5441), the memory manager enters its loop on line 5444. In this loop, it calls *get_work* to wait for an incoming request message, calls one of its *do_XXX* procedures via the *call_vector* table to carry out the request, and finally sends a reply, if needed. This structure should be familiar by now: it is the same used by the I/O tasks.

The procedures *get_work* (line 5471) and *reply* (line 5485) handle the actual receiving and sending, respectively. The remaining procedures in this file are all concerned with initializing the memory manager. They are not used after the system has started running.

4.7.3. Implementation of FORK, EXIT, and WAIT

The FORK, EXIT, and WAIT system calls are implemented by the procedures *do_fork*, *do_mm_exit*, and *do_wait* in the file *forkexit.c*. The procedure *do_fork* (line 5683) follows the steps shown in Fig. 4-25. Notice that it reserves the last few process table slots for the super-user. After computing how much memory the child needs, including the gap between the data and stack segments on the 8088, *mem_copy* is called to send a message to the system task to get the copying done.

Now a slot is found in the process table. The test involving *procs_in_use* earlier guarantees that one will exist. After the slot has been found, it is filled in, first by copying the parent's slot there, and afterward by updating the *mp_parent*, *mp_seg*, *mp_exitstatus*, and *mp_sigstatus* fields.

The next step is assigning a pid to the child. The variable *next_pid* keeps track of the next pid to be assigned. However, the following problem could conceivably occur. After assigning, say, pid 20 to a very long-lived process, 30,000 more processes might be created and destroyed, and *next_pid* might come back to 20 again. Assigning a pid that was still in use would be a disaster (suppose someone later tried to signal process 20), so we search the whole process table to make sure that the pid to be assigned is not already in use.

The calls to *sys_forked* and *tell_fs* inform the kernel and file system, respectively, that a new process has been created, so they can update their process tables. (All the procedures beginning with *sys_* are library routines that send a message to the system task in the kernel to request one of the services of Fig. 3-39.) Process creation and destruction are always initiated by the memory manager and then propagated to the kernel and file system when completed.

The reply message to the child is sent explicitly at the end of *do_fork*. The reply to the parent, containing the child's pid, is sent by the loop in *main*, as the normal reply to a request.

The next system call handled by the memory manager is EXIT. The procedure *do_mm_exit* (line 5767) accepts the call, but most of the work is done by *mm_exit*, a few lines further down. The reason for this division of labor is that *mm_exit* is also called to take care of processes terminated by a signal. The work is the same, but the parameters are different, so it is convenient to split things up this way.

The action taken by *mm_exit* depends on whether the parent is already waiting or not. If so, *cleanup* is called to release the memory and process table slot, and to get rid of the process entirely. If the parent is not waiting, the process becomes a zombie, indicated by the *HANGING* bit in the *mp_flags* word. Either way, if it has a running timer, the timer is killed. The call to the library procedure *sys_xit* sends a message to the system task telling it to mark the process as no longer runnable, so it will not be scheduled any more.

When the parent process does a WAIT, control comes to *do_wait* on line 5809. The loop in *do_wait* scans the entire process table to see if the process has any children at all, and if so, checks to see if any are zombies that can now be cleaned up. If a zombie is found (line 5828), it is cleaned up. The flag *dont_reply* is set because the reply to the parent is sent from inside *cleanup*, not from the loop in *main*.

If the process doing the WAIT has no children, it simply gets an error return (line 5842). If it has children, but none are zombies, then a bit is set on line 5838 to indicate that it is waiting, and the parent is suspended until a child terminates.

When a process has exited and its parent is waiting for it, in whichever order these events occur, the procedure *cleanup* (line 5849) is called to perform the last rites. The parent is awakened from its WAIT call and is given the pid of the terminated child, as well as its exit and signal status. The file system is told to mark the child's entry as free. (The kernel is told when the process terminates, as it must suspend scheduling immediately.) Then the child's memory is freed and the parent's and child's flags are updated.

The last step has to do with the problem discussed earlier of what happens to a process if its parent dies. To see if any existing process is a child of the process trying to exit, all the processes are inspected. If the test on line 5890 succeeds, the exiting process has children.

It is possible that a situation such as shown in Fig. 4-29(a) occurs. In this figure we see that process 12 is about to exit, and that its parent, 7, is waiting for it. *Cleanup* will be called to get rid of 12, so 52 and 53 are turned into children of *init*, as shown in Fig. 4-29(b). Now we have the situation that 53, which has already exited, is the child of a process doing a WAIT. Consequently, it can also be cleaned up. The code on lines 5893 to 5897 takes care of this. We see here one of the very few recursive calls in MINIX.

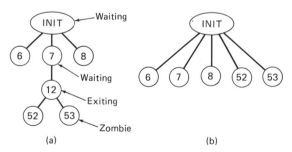

Fig. 4-29. (a) The situation as process 12 is about to exit. (b) The situation after it has exited.

4.7.4. Implementation of EXEC

The code for EXEC follows the outline of Fig. 4-26. It is contained in the procedure *do_exec* (line 5934). After making a few simple validity checks, the memory manager fetches the name of the file to be executed from the user space.

On line 5965 it sends a special message to the file system, to switch to the user's directory, so that the path just fetched will be interpreted relative to the user's, rather than to MM's, working directory.

If the file is present and executable, the memory manager reads the header to extract the segment sizes. Then it fetches the stack from user space (line 5981), allocates memory for the new image (line 5988), patches up the pointers [see the differences between Fig. 4-27(b) and (c)], and reads in the text and data segments (lines 6003 and 6004). Finally, it processes the setuid and setgid bits, updates the process table entry, and tells the kernel that it is finished, so that the process can be scheduled again.

Although the control of all the steps is in *do_exec*, many of the details are carried out by subsidiary procedures within *exec.c*. *Read_header*, for example, not only reads the header and returns the segment sizes, but also verifies that all the segments fit in the virtual address space.

Procedure *new_mem* checks to see if sufficient memory is available for the new memory image. If so, the old memory is released and the new memory acquired. If insufficient memory is available, the EXEC call fails. After the new memory is allocated, *new_mem* updates the memory map (in *mp_seg*) and reports it to the kernel by calling the library procedure *sys_newmap*.

The remainder of *new_map* is concerned with zeroing the bss segment, gap, and stack segment. (The bss segment is that part of the data segment that contains all the uninitialized global variables.) Many compilers generate explicit code to zero the bss segment, but doing it here allows MINIX to work even with compilers that do not explicitly zero the bss. The gap between data and stack segments is also zeroed, so that when the data segment is extended by BRK, the newly acquired memory will contain zeros.

The next procedure is *patch_ptr* (line 6183), which does the job of relocating the pointers of Fig. 4-27(b) to the form of Fig.4-27(c). The work is simple: Examine the stack to find all the pointers, and add the base address to each one.

The final procedure in *exec.c* is *load_seg* (line 6216), which is called twice per EXEC, once to load the text segment and once to load the data segment. Rather than just reading the file block by block and then copying the blocks to the user, a trick is used to allow the file system to load the entire segment directly to the user space. Loading is appreciably speeded up by this maneuver. In effect, the call is decoded by the file system in a slightly special way so that it appears to be a read of the entire segment by the user process itself. Only a few lines at the beginning of the file system's read routine know that some monkey business is going on here.

4.7.5. Implementation of BRK

As we have just seen, the memory model used by MINIX is quite simple. Each process is given a single contiguous allocation when it is created. It is never moved around in memory, it is never swapped out of memory, it never grows, and it never shrinks. All that can happen is that the data segment can eat away at the gap from the low end, and the stack can eat away at it from the high end. Under these circumstances, the implementation of the BRK call is especially easy. It consists of verifying that the new sizes are feasible, and then updating the tables to reflect them.

The top-level procedure is *do_brk* (line 6283), but most of the work is done in *adjust*. The latter checks to see if the stack and data segments have collided. If they have, the BRK call cannot be carried out, but the process is not killed immediately. It gets control back (with an error message), so it can print appropriate messages and shut down gracefully.

If *adjust* has to adjust the data segment, all it does is update the length field. If it also notices that the stack pointer, which is given to it as a parameter, has grown beyond the stack segment, both the origin and length are updated.

The procedure *size_ok* makes the test to see if the segment sizes fit within the address space, in clicks as well as in bytes. The last procedure in this file, *stack_fault*, is not used at present. If MINIX is ever ported to a machine that traps when the stack pointer moves outside the stack segment, then the memory manager will have to handle stack growth, analogous to data segment growth. This procedure will then be of use.

4.7.6. Implementation of Signal Handling

The four system calls relating to signals, SIGNAL, KILL, ALARM, and PAUSE, as well as the signals themselves, are processed in the file *signal.c*. Let us start with the SIGNAL call, since it is the easiest (line 6488). First the memory manager checks to see that the signal number is valid. If it is, the two bit maps, one for signals to be ignored and one for signals to be caught, are updated. Each bit map has 16 bits, one for each of signals 1 to 16, with signal 1 the right-most bit.

Next come two procedures, *do_kill* (line 6519) and *do_ksig* (line 6530), that are conceptually similar. Both are used to cause the memory manager to send a signal. *Do_kill* is called when a user process issues a KILL system call. *Do_ksig* is called when a message arrives from the kernel with one or more signals.

Although *do_ksig* has code to handle stack faults, the kernel does not generate them at present. This feature may be useful on other machines, however. Messages from the kernel may contain multiple signals, which are examined and processed one bit at a time by the loop on line 6564. Each signal bit set results in a call to *check_sig*, just as *do_kill*.

The procedure *check_sig* is where the memory manager checks to see if the signal can be sent. The call

```
kill(0, sig);
```

causes the indicated signal to be sent to all the processes in the caller's group (i.e., all the processes started from the same terminal). For this reason, *check_sig* contains a loop on line 6602 to scan through the process table to find all the processes to which a signal should be sent. The loop contains a large number of tests. Only if all of them are passed is the signal sent, by calling *sig_proc* on line 6627.

Now we come to *sig_proc* (line 6640), which actually does the signaling. The key test here is to distinguish processes that have been enabled to catch signals from those that have not. Those processes that want to catch signals but do not have enough stack space left for the interrupt information, are not signaled. If the signal is to be caught, the call to *sys_sig* on line 6663 sends a message to the system task requesting it to cause the signal.

If the signal is not to be caught (or cannot be caught due to lack of stack space), control passes to line 6668 to allow *mm_exit* to terminate the process as though it had exited, and then tries to dump core if that is appropriate for the signal class.

The third system call handled in *signal.c* is ALARM, which is controlled by *do_alarm* (line 6679). The work, done by *set_alarm* (line 6695), consists of sending a message to the clock task telling it to start the timer. When the timer runs out, the kernel announces the fact by sending the memory manager a message of type KSIG, which causes *do_ksig* to run, as discussed above. The complete sequence of events for a SIGALRM signal is shown in Fig. 4-30.

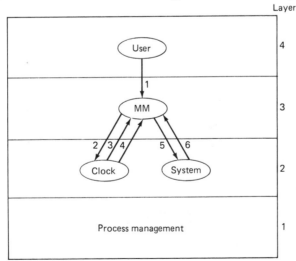

Fig. 4-30. Messages for an alarm. (1) User does ALARM. (2) MM sends request to clock task. (3) Clock task replies. (4) Signal arrives. (5) MM tells system task to copy interrupt block to user space. (6) Reply.

The final system call is PAUSE. All that is necessary for *do_pause* (line 6723) to do is set a bit and refrain from replying, thus keeping the caller blocked. The kernel need not even be informed, since the kernel knows that the caller is blocked.

The procedure *unpause* (line 6736) has to do with signals that are sent to processes suspended on READ, WRITE, PAUSE, and WAIT calls. The latter two can be checked directly, but the former two require asking the file system.

The final procedure in this file is *dump_core* (line 6774), which writes core dumps, block by block, to the disk.

4.7.7. Implementation of the Other System Calls

The file *getset.c* contains one procedure, *do_getset* (line 6867), which carries out the five remaining memory manager calls: GETPID, GETUID, GETGID, SETUID, and SETGID. They are all so simple that they are not worth an entire procedure each. The GETUID and GETGID calls both return the real and effective uid or gid.

Setting the uid or gid is slightly more complex than just reading it. A check has to be made to see if the caller is authorized to set the uid or gid. If the caller passes the test, the file system must be informed of the new uid or gid, since file protection depends on it.

4.7.8. Memory Manager Utilities

The remaining files contain utility routines and tables. The file *alloc.c* is where the system keeps track of which parts of memory are in use and which are free. It has four entry points:

alloc_mem	- request a block of memory of a given size.
free_mem	- return memory that is no longer needed.
max_hole	- compute the size of the largest available hole.
mem_init	- initialize the free list when the memory manager starts running.

As we have said before, *alloc_mem* (line 6987) just uses first fit on a list of holes sorted by memory address. If it finds a piece that is too big, it takes what it needs and leaves the rest on the free list, but reduced in size by the amount taken. If an entire hole is needed, *del_slot* (line 7072) is called to remove the entry from the free list.

Free_mem's job is to check if a newly released piece of memory can be merged with holes on either side. If it can, *merge* (line 7095) is called to join the holes and update the lists.

Max_hole (line 7131) scans the hole list and returns the largest item it finds. *Mem_init* (line 7153) builds the initial free list, consisting of all available memory in one big hole.

The next file is *utility.c*, which holds a few miscellaneous procedures used in various places in the memory manager. The procedure *allowed* (line 7224) checks to see if a given access is allowed to a file.

For example, *do_exec* needs to know if a file is executable. *Mem_copy* is the interface to the system task for copying data around in memory. It is used to copy the parent image to the child for FORK, and similar things.

The procedure *no_sys* (line 7298) should never be called. It is provided just in case a user ever calls the memory manager with a system call number that is invalid or is not handled by the memory manager.

Panic (line 7309) is called only when the memory manager has detected an error from which it cannot recover. It reports the error to the system task, which then brings MINIX to a screeching halt. It is not called lightly.

The two procedures in the file *putc.c* are also utilities, although of quite a different character from the previous ones. From time to time, calls to *printf* are inserted into the memory manager, mostly for debugging. Also, *panic* calls *printf*. The name *printf* is actually a macro defined as *printk*, so that calls to *printf* do not use the standard I/O library procedure that sends messages to the file system. *Printk* calls *putc* to communicate directly with the terminal task, something that is forbidden to ordinary users.

Our final file is *table.c*. It contains key statements on lines 2408 and 2409. Together, these redefine the macro *EXTERN* to be the null string, so that when all the include files are expanded during the compilation of *table.c*, the word *extern* will not be present, and storage will be allocated for all the variables.

The other major feature of *table.c* is the array *call_vector*. When a request message arrives, the system call number is extracted from it and used as an index into *call_vector* to locate the procedure that carries out that system call (see line 5458). System call numbers that are not valid calls all invoke *no_sys*, which just returns an error code.

4.8. SUMMARY

In this chapter we have examined memory management, both in general and in MINIX. We saw that the simplest systems do not swap at all. Once a program is loaded into memory, it remains there until it finishes. Some operating systems allow only one process at a time in memory, while others support multiprogramming.

The next step up is swapping. When swapping is used, the system can handle more processes than it has room for in memory. Processes for which there is no room are swapped out to the disk. Free space in memory and on disk can be kept track of with a bit map, a hole list, or the buddy system.

More advanced computers often have some form of virtual memory. In the simplest form, each process' address space is divided up into uniform sized blocks called pages, which can be placed into any available page frame in memory. Many page replacement algorithms are known, two of the better ones being second chance and aging. Sometimes segmentation and paging are combined to provide a two-dimensional virtual memory.

Memory management in MINIX is very simple. Memory is allocated when a process executes a FORK or EXEC system call. The memory so allocated is never increased or decreased as long as the process lives. Most of the work of the memory manager is concerned not with keeping track of free memory, which it does using a hole list and the first fit algorithm, but with carrying out the system calls relating to memory management.

PROBLEMS

1. Consider a swapping system in which memory consists of the following hole sizes in memory order: 10K, 4K, 20K, 18K, 7K, 9K, 12K, and 15K. Which hole is taken for successive segment requests of

   (a) 12K
   (b) 10K
   (c) 9K

   for first fit? Now repeat the question for best fit, worst fit, and next fit.

2. Using the model of Fig. 4-2, we can predict the increased throughput as a function of the degree of multiprogramming. Suppose that a computer has a 2M memory, of which the operating system takes 512K (one quarter of memory) and each user program also takes 512K. If all programs have 60 percent I/O wait, by what percentage will the throughput increase if another 1M is added?

3. Some swapping systems try to eliminate external fragmentation by compaction. Imagine that a computer with 1M user memory compacts once every second. If it takes 1/2 microsec to copy a byte, and the average hole is 0.4 as large as the average segment, what fraction of the total CPU time is used up on compaction?

4. A minicomputer uses the buddy system for memory management. Initially it has one block of 256K at address 0. After successive requests for 5K, 25K, 35K, and 20K come in, how many blocks are left and what are their sizes and addresses?

5. In a swapping system with variable partitions, the segments have the probability distribution $e^{s/10}/10$, where s is the segment size in kilobytes. The holes have the probability distribution $e^{h/5}/5$ where h is the hole size in kilobytes. What is the average fraction of wasted memory?

6. Using the page table of Fig. 4-11, give the physical address corresponding to each of the following virtual addresses:

   (a) 20
   (b) 4100
   (c) 8300

7. The Intel 8086 processor does not support virtual memory. Nevertheless, some companies have sold systems that contain an unmodified 8086 CPU and do paging. Make an educated guess as to how they did it. (Hint: think about the logical location of the MMU.)

8. Imagine that a computer uses a segmented MMU such as the one of Fig. 4-13, except that the process number is 3 bits and virtual address spaces are 8M with 4K pages and 32K segments. How many words are needed to hold all the page pointers? If the segment size is now changed to 64K, without changing any of the other parameters (i.e., fewer, but larger segments), how does that affect the number of page table pointers needed?

9. If an instruction takes 1 microsec and a page fault takes an additional n microsec, give a formula for the effective instruction time if page faults occur every k instructions on the average.

10. Below is the listing of a short assembly language program for a computer with 512-byte pages. The program is located at address 1020, and its stack pointer is at 8192 (the stack grows toward 0). Give the page reference string generated by this program. Each instruction occupies 4 bytes (1 word), and both instruction and data references count in the reference string.

    Load word 6144 into register 0
    Push register 0 onto the stack
    Call a procedure at 5120, stacking the return address
    Subtract the immediate constant 16 from the stack pointer
    Compare the actual parameter to the immediate constant 4
    Jump if equal to 5152

11. A computer whose processes have 1024 pages in their address spaces keeps its page tables in memory. The overhead required for reading a word from the page table is 500 nsec. To reduce this overhead, the computer has an associative memory, which holds 32 (virtual page, physical page frame) pairs, and can do a look up in 100 nsec. What hit rate is needed to reduce the mean overhead to 200 nsec?

12. A computer has four page frames. The time of loading, time of last access, and the R and M bits for each page are as shown below (the times are in clock ticks):

Page	Loaded	Last ref.	R	M
0	126	279	0	0
1	230	260	1	0
2	120	272	1	1
3	160	280	1	1

    (a) Which page will NRU replace?
    (b) Which page will FIFO replace?
    (c) Which page will LRU replace?
    (d) Which page will second chance replace?

13. If FIFO page replacement is used with four page frames and eight pages, how many page faults will occur with the reference string 0172327103 if the four frames are initially empty? Now repeat this problem for LRU.

14. A small computer has four page frames. At the first clock tick, the R bits are 0111 (page 0 is 0, the rest are 1). At subsequent clock ticks, the values are 1011, 1010, 1101, 0010, 1010, 1100, and 0001. If the aging algorithm is used with an 8-bit counter, give the values of the four counters after the last tick.

15. How long does it take to load a 64K program from a disk whose average seek time is 30 msec, whose rotation time is 20 msec, and whose tracks hold 32K

    (a) for a 2K page size?
    (b) for a 4K page size?

    The pages are spread randomly around the disk.

16. One of the first time-sharing machines, the PDP-1, had a memory of 4K 18-bit words. It held one process at a time in memory. When the scheduler decided to run another process, the process in memory was written to a paging drum, with 4K 18-bit words around the circumference of the drum. The drum could start writing (or reading) at any word, rather than only at word 0. Why do you suppose this drum was chosen?

17. A computer provides each process with 65536 bytes of address space divided into pages of 4096 bytes. A particular program has a text size of 32768 bytes, a data size of 16386 bytes, and a stack size of 15870 bytes. Will this program fit in the address space? If the page size were 512 bytes, would it fit? Remember that a page may not contain parts of two different segments.

18. It has been observed that the number of instructions executed between page faults is directly proportional to the number of page frames allocated to a program. If the available memory is doubled, the mean interval between page faults is also doubled. Suppose that a normal instruction takes 1 microsec, but if a page fault occurs, it takes 2001 microsec. If a program takes 60 sec to run, during which time it gets 15,000 page faults, how long would it take to run if twice as much memory were available?

19. Why does the MINIX memory management scheme make it necessary to have a program like *chmem*?

20. When a MINIX process makes the SIGNAL system call to cause some signal to be caught, the address of the function to be called is stored in a table within the process itself, rather than in the memory manager. Give an advantage of doing things in this way.

21. Modify MINIX to release a zombie's memory as soon as it enters the zombie state, rather than waiting until the parent waits for it.

22. In the current implementation of MINIX, when an EXEC system call is made, the memory manager checks to see if a hole large enough to contain the new memory image is currently available. If not, the call is rejected. A better algorithm would be to see if a sufficiently large hole would be available after the current memory image was released. Implement this algorithm.

23. When carrying out an EXEC system call, MINIX uses a trick to have the file system read in entire segments at once. Devise and implement a similar trick to allow core dumps to be written in a similar way.

24. Modify MINIX to do swapping.

5

FILE
SYSTEMS

The most visible part of any operating system is the file system. Most programs read or write at least one file, and users are always aware of the existence of files and their properties. For many people, the convenience and usability of the operating system is largely determined by the interface, structure, and reliability of the file system.

In this chapter we will look at the various ways a file system can appear to its users, how file systems are implemented, how files are protected against unauthorized usage, and finally, how the MINIX file system has been designed and implemented. We will also look at some design issues specific to distributed operating systems.

5.1. THE USER VIEW OF THE FILE SYSTEM

From the user's standpoint, the most important aspect of a file system is how it appears to him, that is, what constitutes a file, how files are named and protected, what operations are allowed on files, and so on. The details of whether linked lists or bit maps are used to keep track of free storage and how many sectors there are in a logical block are of less interest, although they are of great importance to the designers of the file system. In the following sections we will discuss a number of issues relating primarily to the user interface. Later on in the chapter we will look at how file systems are implemented.

5.1.1. File Basics

The best way to store information in a computer would be to provide each process with a large number of very large segments, for example, 2^{32} segments, each 2^{32} bytes long. When someone first began using a computer, he would be given a shell with standard segments in its address space (e.g., editors, compilers, and other utilities). As time went on, all the text typed in by the user, all the binaries of his programs, and all information acquired from third parties would accumulate in the shell's address space. Some of the segments would contain directories, to provide a hierarchical naming scheme for files (e.g., like UNIX).

This address space would be inherited by all processes, which could add more segments and then return the address space to the shell when finished. Accessing information would then just be a matter of reading and writing (virtual) memory.

In practice, this way of storing information is not yet feasible, although MULTICS made a serious attempt at it. For one thing, current address spaces are much too small and not all computers have virtual memory. For another, when a process crashes, its address space is normally lost, making address spaces ill-suited for long-term (e.g., months or years) storage. Still, as technology advances, the concept of holding all of a user's information within the address space of each of his processes will no doubt be reexamined from time to time.

While waiting for the millenium, most operating systems take a different approach to storing information. They allow users to define named objects called **files**, which can hold programs, data, or anything else the user wants. These files are not part of the address space of any process. Instead, the operating system provides special operations (i.e., system calls) to create and destroy them, read and write them, and manage them in other ways.

Figure 5-1 illustrates three common file organizations. The first way is a simple byte sequence. UNIX files are structured this way. The second way is a sequence of fixed-size records. Arbitrary records can be read or written, but records cannot be inserted or deleted in the middle of a file. CP/M works like this.

The third way is a tree of disk blocks, each block holding n keyed records. Records can be looked up by key, and new records can be inserted anywhere in the tree. If a record is added to a block that is full, the block is split into two blocks, both of which are then added to the tree in their correct alphabetical sequence. This method is used on many mainframes, where it is called **ISAM** (Indexed Sequential Access Method).

All operating systems aim at **device-independence**, that is, making access the same no matter where the file (or device) is. A program that reads an input file, sorts it, and writes the sorted output file should be able to work with files on floppy disk or hard disk, and should be able to write its output on a file, a terminal, or a printer without having special code to check for each of these cases.

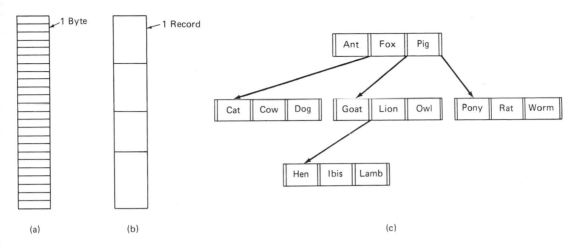

Fig. 5-1. Three kinds of files. (a) Byte sequence. (b) Record sequence. (c) Tree.

Some operating systems are better at device-independence than others. In UNIX, for example, a file system (e.g., a disk) can be mounted anywhere in the file tree, allowing any file to be accessed by its path name, without regard to which device it is on. In MS-DOS, on the other hand, the user must explicitly specify which device each file is on (except that one device is default and may be omitted). Thus if the default device is drive C:, to run a program located on drive A: with input and output files on drive B:, one would have to type:

```
A:program <B:input >B:output
```

Most operating systems have many distinct file types. UNIX, for example, has regular files, directories, and special files (block and character). Regular files contain user data. Directories contain the information needed to give files symbolic names (i.e., ASCII strings). Block and character special files are used to model disk devices and terminal-like devices, respectively, so that one can say, for example

```
cp abc /dev/tty
```

to copy a file, *abc*, to the terminal (character special file /dev/tty). Some versions of UNIX also support **named pipes**, which are pseudofiles that can be opened by two processes to set up an interprocess communication channel between them. As far as the user is concerned, the differences between these different file types are minimal (e.g., seeks on terminals are not allowed).

In most systems, regular files are further subdivided into different types based on their usage. The different types are distinguished by names that end with different **file extensions**. For example,

```
FILE.PAS   - Pascal source program
FILE.FTN   - FORTRAN source program
```

FILE.BAS   - BASIC source program
FILE.OBJ   - Object file (compiler output, not yet linked)
FILE.BIN   - Executable binary program
FILE.LIB   - Library of .OBJ files used by the linker
FILE.TXT   - Input text for the formatting program
FILE.DAT   - Data file

In some systems the extensions are simply a convention; the operating system itself does not use them for anything. In other systems, the operating system rigidly enforces rules relating to the naming. For example, it will not execute a file unless it ends in .BIN.

The TOPS-20 system goes so far as to examine the creation time of any file to be executed. Then it locates the source file and sees if the source has been modified since the binary was made. If it has, it automatically recompiles the source. In UNIX terms, the *make* program has been built into the shell. The extensions are mandatory so the operating system can tell which binary program was derived from which source.

Having strongly typed files like this causes problems whenever the user does anything that the system designers did not expect. Consider, as an example, a system in which program output files have type .DAT (data files). If a user writes a program that reads a .PAS file, transforms it (e.g., by converting it to a standard indentation layout), and then writes the transformed file as output, the output file will be of type .DAT. If the user tries to offer this to the Pascal compiler to compile it, the system will refuse because it has the wrong extension. Attempts to copy FILE.DAT to FILE.PAS will be rejected by the system as invalid (to protect the user against mistakes).

While this kind of "protection" may help novices, it drives experienced users up the wall since they have to devote considerable effort to circumventing the operating system's idea of what is reasonable and what is not.

The operations available on files differ slightly from operating system to operating system. Reading and writing bytes (or records) sequentially are always provided. **Random access** is commonly provided where that makes sense (on a regular file, but not on the special file for the line printer). In some operating systems random access is achieved by having the READ system call specify the number (or key) of the record to be read or written. In other systems (e.g., UNIX) a system call is provided to set the "current file position" anywhere within the file, so that subsequent READ or WRITE calls will operate at the new current position. Record-oriented files usually have operations to insert and delete records.

5.1.2. Directories

To keep track of files, the file system normally provides **directories**, which, in many systems, are themselves files. A directory typically contains a number of entries, one per file, as shown in Fig. 5-2. The simplest way is for the system to maintain a single directory containing all the files of all the users. If there are many users, and they choose the same file names (e.g., *mail* and *games*), conflicts and confusion will quickly make the system unworkable. This system model is used only by the most primitive microcomputer operating systems.

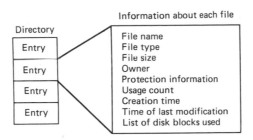

Fig. 5-2. A directory may have several entries, each describing one file. The entries may either contain information about the file, or point to other structures that do.

An improvement on the idea of having a single directory for all files is to have one directory per user [see Fig. 5-3(b)]. This design eliminates name conflicts among users, but is not very satisfactory for users with many files. It is quite common for users to want to group their files together in logical ways. A professor, for example, might have a collection of files that together form a book that he is writing for one course, a second collection of files containing student programs submitted for another course, a third group of files containing the code of an advanced compiler-writing system he is building, a fourth group of files containing grant proposals, as well as other files for incoming and outgoing mail, minutes of committee meetings, papers he is writing, games, and so on. Some way is needed to group these files together reasonably.

What is needed is a general hierarchy (i.e., a tree of directories). With this approach, each user can have as many directories as are needed so that files can be grouped together in natural ways. This approach is shown in Fig. 5-3(c).

When the file system is organized as a directory tree, some way is needed for specifying file names. Two different methods are commonly used. In the first method, each file is given an **absolute path name** consisting of the path from the root directory to the file. As an example, the path */usr/ast/mailbox* means that the root directory contains a subdirectory *usr*, which in turn contains a subdirectory *ast*, which contains the file *mailbox*. Absolute path names always start at the root directory and are unique.

The other kind of name is the **relative path name**. This is used in conjunction with the concept of the **working directory** (also called the **current directory**). A user can designate one directory as the current working directory, in which case all path names not beginning at the root directory are taken relative to the working directory. In UNIX, all path names beginning with a slash are absolute; all others are relative to the user's current working directory. If the current

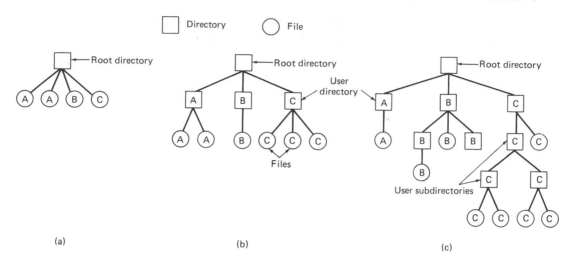

Fig. 5-3. Three file system designs. (a) Single directory shared by all users. (b) One directory per user. (c) Arbitrary tree per user. The letters indicate the directory or file's owner.

working directory is */usr/ast*, then the file whose absolute path is */usr/ast/mailbox* can be referenced simply as *mailbox*.

5.2. FILE SYSTEM DESIGN

Now it is time to turn from the user's view of the file system to the designer's view. Users are concerned with how files are named, what operations are allowed on them, what the directory tree looks like and similar interface issues. Designers are interested in how disk space is managed, how files are stored, and how to make everything work efficiently and reliably. In the following sections we will examine a number of key design areas to see what the issues and tradeoffs are.

5.2.1. Disk Space Management

Files are normally stored on disk, so management of disk space is a major concern to file system designers. Two general strategies are possible for storing an *n* byte file: *n* consecutive bytes of disk space are allocated, or the file is split up into a number of (not necessarily) contiguous blocks. The same tradeoff is present in memory management systems between pure segmentation and paging.

Storing a file as a contiguous sequence of bytes has the obvious problem that if a file grows, which is a very common occurrence, it will probably have to be moved on the disk. The same problem holds for segments in memory, except that moving a segment in memory is a relatively fast operation compared to moving a file from one disk position to another. For this reason, nearly all file systems chop files up into fixed-size blocks that need not be adjacent.

Once it has been decided to store files in fixed-size blocks, the question arises of how big the block should be. Given the way disks are organized, the sector, the track and the cylinder are obvious candidates for the unit of allocation. In a paging system, the page size is also a major contender.

Having a large allocation unit, such as a cylinder, means that every file, even a 1 byte file, ties up an entire cylinder. Studies (Mullender and Tanenbaum, 1984) have shown that the median file size in UNIX environments is about 1K, so allocating a 32K cylinder for each file would waste 31/32 or 97 percent of the total disk space. On the other hand, using a small allocation unit means that each file will consist of many blocks. Reading each block normally requires a seek and a rotational delay, so reading a file consisting of many small blocks will be slow.

As an example, consider a disk with 32768 bytes per track, a rotation time of 16.67 msec, and an average seek time of 30 msec. The time in milliseconds to read a random block of k bytes is then the sum of the seek, rotational delay, and transfer times:

$$30 + 8.3 + (k/32768) \times 16.67$$

The solid curve of Fig. 5-4 shows the data rate for such a disk as a function of block size. If we make the gross assumption that all files are 1K (the measured median size), the dashed curve of Fig. 5-4 gives the disk space efficiency. The bad news is that good space utilization (block size < 2K) means low data rates and vice versa. Time efficiency and space efficiency are inherently in conflict.

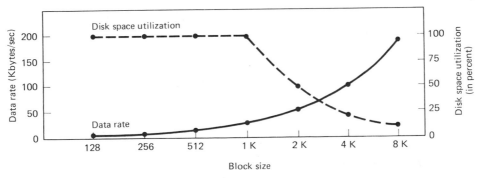

Fig. 5-4. The solid curve (left-hand scale) gives the data rate of a disk. The dashed curve (right-hand scale) gives the disk space efficiency. All files are 1K.

The usual compromise is to choose a block size of 512, 1K or 2K bytes. If a 1K block size is chosen on a disk with a 512-byte sector size, then the file system will always read or write two consecutive sectors, and treat them as a single, indivisible unit.

Once a block size has been chosen, the next issue is how to keep track of free blocks. Two methods are widely used, as shown in Fig. 5-5. The first one consists of using a linked list of disk blocks, with each block holding as many free disk block numbers as will fit. With a 1K block and a 16-bit disk block number, each block on the free list holds the numbers of 512 free blocks. A 20M disk needs a free list of maximum 40 blocks to hold all 20,000 disk block numbers.

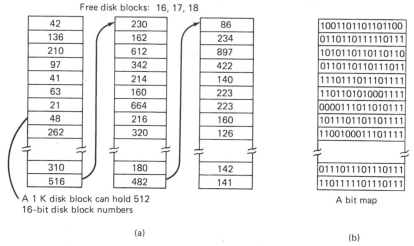

Fig. 5-5. (a) Holding the free list on a linked list. (b) A bit map.

The other free space management technique is the bit map. A disk with n blocks requires a bit map with n bits. Free blocks are represented by 1s in the map; allocated blocks by 0s (or vice versa). A 20M disk requires 20,000 bits for the map, which is only 3 blocks. It is not surprising that the bit map requires less space, since it uses 1 bit per block, versus 16 bits in the linked list model. Only if the disk is nearly full will the linked list require fewer blocks than the bit map.

If there is enough main memory to hold the bit map, that method is generally preferable. If, however, only 1 block of memory can be spared for keeping track of free disk blocks, and the disk is nearly full, then the linked list may be better. With only 1 block of the bit map in memory, it may turn out that no free blocks can be found on it, causing disk accesses to read the rest of the bit map. When a fresh block of the linked list is loaded into memory, 512 disk blocks can be allocated before having to go to the disk to fetch the next block from the list.

5.2.2. File Storage

If a file consists of a sequence of blocks, the file system must have some way of keeping track of the blocks of each file. The most obvious way—storing the blocks consecutively—is generally not feasible because files can grow. In fact, it was just this problem that led us to split files up into blocks in the first place.

A method that is feasible is to store the blocks of a file as a linked list. Each

1024-byte disk block contains 1022 bytes of data and a 2-byte pointer to the next block on the chain. This method has two disadvantages, however. First, the number of data bytes in a block is no longer a power of two, which is frequently a nuisance. Second, and more serious, random access is expensive to implement. If a program seeks to byte 32768 of a file and then starts reading, the operating system has to search its way through 32768/1022 or 33 blocks to find the data needed. Having to read 33 disk blocks to do the seek is inefficient.

Still, the idea of representing a file as a linked list can be salvaged if we keep the pointers in memory. Figure 5-6 shows the allocation scheme used by MS-DOS. In this example, we have three files, *A*, with blocks 6, 8, 4, and 2; *B* with blocks 5, 9, and 12; and *C*, with blocks 10, 3, and 13.

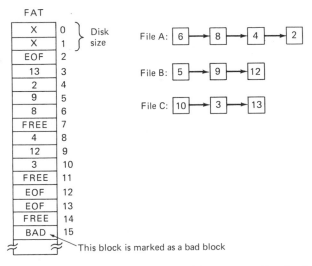

Fig. 5-6. The linked list allocation scheme used by MS-DOS. Entries 0 and 1 are used for specifying the disk size. The codes EOF and FREE are used for End Of File and Free entries, respectively.

Associated with each disk is a table called the **file allocation table** (FAT). It has one entry for each disk block. The directory entry for each file gives the block number of the first block of the file. That slot in the FAT contains the block number of the next block. File *A* begins at block 6, so FAT entry 6 contains the number of the next block of file *A*, which is 8. FAT entry 8 contains the next block number, 4. Entry 4 points to entry 2, and entry 2 is marked as End of File.

This scheme was originally designed for 320K floppy disks using a 1K block size (standard for MS-DOS). Block numbers are 12 bits, so a 320-entry FAT requires 480 bytes, which fits conveniently in one 512-byte sector. When IBM decided to format the floppy disks as 360K, starting with DOS 2.0, the FAT grew to 540 bytes, which no longer fit in one sector and necessitated changing the disk layout to accommodate the larger (2-sector) FAT. When hard disks with more than 4096 blocks were introduced, the 12-bit block number became inadequate, and the FAT had to be changed again. A little foresight would have come in handy.

It is also clear that with large disks, this scheme becomes increasingly unattractive. Suppose we have a 64M disk containing 64K 1K-disk blocks (a 70M disk would require disk block numbers larger than 16 bits and more troubles). The FAT will have 64K 2-byte entries and will occupy 128K. Keeping all of this in memory all the time uses up quite a bit of memory. However, keeping it on disk means that doing a seek to position 32K in a file might require as little as 1 or as many as 33 disk reads to follow the chain.

The essence of the problem with the FAT is that pointers for all the files on the whole disk are mixed up at random in the same table. This means that the whole FAT is potentially needed, even if only one file is open. A better method would be to keep the block lists for different files in different places. This is what UNIX does.

Associated with each file in UNIX is a little table (on disk) called an **i-node**, as shown in Fig. 5-7. It contains accounting and protection information, which we will come back to later. For the moment the key items are the 10 disk block numbers and the 3 indirect block numbers. For files up to 10 blocks long, all the disk addresses are kept right in the i-node, making them easy to find.

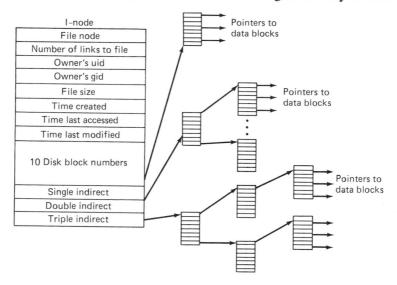

Fig. 5-7. Structure of an i-node.

When a file grows beyond 10 disk blocks, a free disk block is acquired and the single indirect pointer is set to point to it. This block is used to contain disk block pointers. With a 1K disk block and 32-bit disk addresses, the single indirect block can hold 256 disk addresses. This scheme suffices for files up to 266 blocks (10 in the i-node, 256 in the single indirect block).

Above 266 blocks, the double indirect pointer is used to point to a disk block of up to 256 pointers. Only these pointers do not point to data blocks. They point to 256 single indirect blocks. The double indirect block is sufficient for files up to $266 + 256^2 = 65,802$ blocks. For files longer than about 64M, the triple indirect pointer is used to point to a block containing pointers to 256 double indirect blocks.

Files longer than 16 gigabytes cannot be handled. Of course, by going to a 2K disk block, each pointer block holds 512 pointers instead of 256, and the maximum file size becomes 128 gigabytes. The size of the FAT for a 128 gigabyte disk is unpleasant to contemplate. The strength of the UNIX scheme is that the indirect blocks are used only when they are needed. For files under 10K, no indirect blocks at all are needed. Note that for even the longest files, at most three disk references are needed to locate the disk address for any byte in the file (excluding the disk reference to get the i-node, which is fetched when the file is opened and kept in memory until it is closed).

The MINIX storage scheme is the same as that of UNIX, except that only seven disk block numbers are kept in the i-node, and there is no triple indirect block. With 2-byte disk addresses and 1K blocks, files of to 262M can be handled, which is usually enough for personal computers.

5.2.3. Directory Structure

Before a file can be read, it must be opened. When a file is opened, the operating system uses the path name supplied by the user to locate the disk blocks, so that it can read and write the file later. Mapping path names onto i-nodes (or the equivalent) brings us to the subject of how directory systems are organized. These vary from quite simple to reasonably sophisticated.

Let us start with a particular simple directory system, that of CP/M (Golden and Pechura, 1986), illustrated in Fig. 5-8. In this system, there is only one directory, so all the file system has to do to look up a file name is search the one and only directory. When it finds the entry, it also has the disk block numbers, since they are stored right in the directory entry. If the file uses more disk blocks than fit in one entry, the file is allocated additional directory entries.

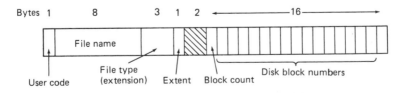

Fig. 5-8. A directory that contains the disk block numbers for each file.

The fields in Fig. 5-8 have the following meanings. The *user code* field keeps track of which user owns the file. During a search, only those entries belonging to the currently logged-in user are checked. The next two fields give the name and extension of the file. The *extent* field is needed because a file larger than 16 blocks occupies multiple directory entries. This field is used to tell which entry comes first, second, and so on. The *block count* field tells how many of the 16 potential disk block entries are in use. The final 16 fields contain the disk block numbers themselves. The last block may not be full, so the system has no way to determine the exact size of a file down to the last byte (i.e., it keeps track of file sizes in blocks, not bytes).

Now let us consider some examples of systems with hierarchical directory trees. Fig. 5-9 shows an MS-DOS directory entry. It is 32 bytes long and contains the file name and the first block number, among other items. The first block number can be used as an index into the FAT, to find the second block number, and so on. In this way all the blocks can be found for a given file. Except for the root directory, which is fixed size (112 entries for a 360K floppy disk), MS-DOS directories are files and may contain an arbitrary number of entries.

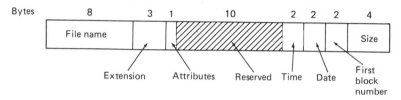

Fig. 5-9. The MS-DOS directory entry.

The directory structure used in UNIX and MINIX is extremely simple, as shown in Fig. 5-10. Each entry contains just a file name and its i-node number. All the information about the type, size, times, ownership, and disk blocks is contained in the i-node (see Fig. 5-7). All directories in UNIX are files, and may contain arbitrarily many of these 16-byte entries.

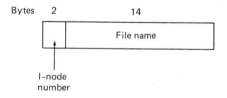

Fig. 5-10. A UNIX directory entry.

When a file is opened, the file system must take the file name supplied and locate its disk blocks. Let us consider how the path name */usr/ast/mbox* is looked up. We will use UNIX as an example, but the algorithm is basically the same for all hierarchical directory systems. First the file system locates the root directory. In UNIX its i-node is located at a fixed place on the disk.

Then it looks up the first component of the path, *usr*, in the root directory to find the i-node of the file /usr. From this i-node, the system locates the directory for /usr and looks up the next component, ast, in it. When it has found the entry for ast, it has the i-node for the directory /usr/ast. From this i-node it can find the directory itself and look up mbox. The i-node for this file is then read into memory and kept there until the file is closed. The lookup process is illustrated in Fig. 5-11.

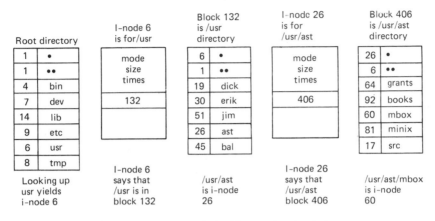

Fig. 5-11. The steps in looking up /usr/ast/mbox.

Relative path names are looked up the same way as absolute ones, only starting from the working directory instead of starting from the root directory. Every directory has entries for . and .. which are put there when the directory is created. The entry . has the i-node number for the current directory, and the entry for .. has the i-node number for the parent directory. Thus, a procedure looking up ../dick/prog.c simply looks up .. in the working directory, finds the i-node number for the parent directory, and searches that directory for dick. No special mechanism is needed to handle these names. As far as the directory system is concerned, they are just ordinary ASCII strings.

5.2.4. Shared Files

When several users are working together on a project, they often need to share files. As a result, it is often convenient for a shared file to appear simultaneously in different directories belonging to different users. Figure 5-12 shows the file system of Fig 5-3(c) again, only with one of C's files now present in one of B's directories as well. The connection between B's directory and the shared file is called a **link**. The file system itself is now a **directed acyclic graph**, or **DAG**, rather than a tree.

Sharing files is convenient, but it also introduces some problems. To start with, if directories really do contain disk addresses, as in CP/M, then a copy of the disk addresses will have to be made in B's directory when the file is linked.

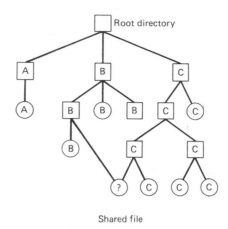

Fig. 5-12. File system containing a shared file.

If either *B* or *C* subsequently appends to the file, the new blocks will be listed only in the directory of the user doing the append. The changes will not be visible to the other user, thus defeating the purpose of sharing.

This problem can be solved in two ways. In the first solution, disk blocks are not listed in directories, but in a little data structure associated with the file itself. The directories would then point just to the little data structure. This is the approach used in UNIX (where the little data structure is the i-node).

In the second solution, *B* links to one of *C*'s files by having the system create a new file, of type LINK, and entering that file in *B's* directory. The new file contains just the path name of the file linked to. When *B* reads from the linked file, the operating system sees that the file being read from is of type LINK, looks up the name of the file linked to, and reads that file. This approach is called **symbolic linking**.

Each of these methods has its drawbacks. In the first method, at the moment that *B* links to the shared file, the i-node records the file's owner as *C*. Creating a link does not change the ownership (see Fig. 5-13), but it does increase the link count in the i-node, so the system knows how many directory entries currently point to the file.

If *C* subsequently tries to remove the file, the system is faced with a problem. If it removes the file and clears the i-node, *B* will have a directory entry pointing to an invalid i-node. If the i-node is later reassigned to another file, *B*'s link will point to the wrong file. The system can see from the count in the i-node that the file is still in use, but there is no way for it to find all the directory entries for the file, in order to erase them. Pointers to the directories cannot be stored in the i-node because there can be an unlimited number of directories.

The only thing to do is remove *C*'s directory entry, but leave the i-node intact, with count set to 1, as shown in Fig. 5-13(c). We now have a situation in

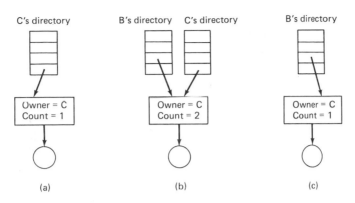

Fig. 5-13. (a) Situation prior to linking. (b) After the link is created. (c) After the original owner removes the file.

which B is the only user having a directory entry for a file owned by C. If the system does accounting or has quotas, C will continue to be billed for the file until B decides to remove it, at which time the count goes to 0 and the file is deleted.

With symbolic links this problem does not arise because only the true owner has a pointer to the i-node. Users who have linked to the file just have path names, not i-node pointers. When the *owner* removes the file, it is destroyed. Subsequent attempts to use the file via a symbolic link will fail when the system is unable to locate the file. Removing a symbolic link does not affect the file at all.

The problem with symbolic links is the extra overhead required. The file containing the path must be read, then the path must be parsed and followed, component by component, until the i-node is reached. All of this activity may require a considerable number of extra disk accesses. Furthermore, an extra i-node is needed for each symbolic link, as is an extra disk block to store the path, although if the path name is short, the system could store it in the i-node itself, as an optimization. Symbolic links have the advantage that they can be used to link to files on machines anywhere in the world, by simply providing the network address of the machine where the file resides in addition to its path on that machine.

There is also another problem introduced by links, symbolic or otherwise. When links are allowed, files can have two or more paths. Programs that start at a given directory and find all the files in that directory and its subdirectories will locate a linked file multiple times. For example, a program that dumps all the files in a directory and its subdirectories onto a tape may make multiple copies of a linked file. Furthermore, if the tape is then read into another machine, unless the dump program is clever, the linked file will be copied twice onto the disk, instead of being linked.

5.2.5. File System Reliability

Destruction of a file system is often a far greater disaster than destruction of a computer. If a computer is destroyed by fire, lightning surges, or a cup of coffee poured onto the keyboard, it is annoying and will cost money, but generally a replacement can be purchased with a minimum of fuss. Inexpensive personal computers can even be replaced within a few hours by just going to the dealer (except at universities where issuing a purchase order takes three committees, five signatures, and 90 days).

If a computer's file system is irrevocably lost, whether due to hardware, software, or rats gnawing on the floppy disks, restoring all the information will be difficult, time consuming, and in many cases, impossible. For the people whose programs, documents, customer files, tax records, data bases, marketing plans, or other data are gone forever, the consequences can be catastrophic. While the file system cannot offer any protection against physical destruction of the equipment and media, it can help protect the information. In this section we will look at some of the issues involved in safeguarding the file system.

Disks often have bad blocks, as we pointed out in Chap. 3. Floppy disks are generally perfect when they leave the factory, but they can develop bad blocks during use. Winchester disks frequently have bad blocks right from the start: it is just too expensive to manufacture them completely free of all defects. In fact, most hard disk manufacturers supply with each drive a list of the bad blocks their tests have discovered.

Two solutions to the bad block problem are used, one hardware and one software. The hardware solution is to dedicate a sector on the disk to the bad block list. When the controller is first initialized, it reads the bad block list and picks a spare block (or track) to replace the defective ones, recording the mapping in the bad block list. Henceforth, all requests for the bad block will use the spare.

The software solution requires the user or file system to carefully construct a file containing all the bad blocks. This technique removes them from the free list, so they will never occur in data files. As long as the bad block file is never read or written, no problems will arise. Care has to be taken during disk backups to avoid reading this file.

Backups

Even with a clever strategy for dealing with bad blocks, it is important to back up the files frequently. After all, automatically switching to a spare track after a crucial data block has been ruined is somewhat akin to locking the barn door after the prize race horse has escaped.

File systems on floppy disk can be backed up by just copying the entire floppy disk to a blank one. File systems on small Winchester disks can be backed up by dumping the entire disk to magnetic tape, either industry standard

9-track tape (which holds about 50M per reel), or streamer tape (which comes in many sizes).

For large Winchesters (e.g., 500M), backing up the entire drive on tape is awkward and time consuming. One strategy that is easy to implement but wastes half the storage is to provide each computer with two drives instead of one. Both drives are divided into two halves: data and backup. Each night the data portion of drive 0 is copied to the backup portion of drive 1, and vice versa, as shown in Fig. 5-14. In this way, even if one drive is completely ruined, no information is lost.

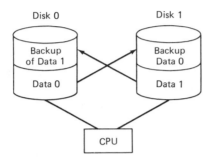

Fig. 5-14. Backing up each drive on the other one wastes half the storage.

An alternative to dumping the entire file system every day is to make **incremental dumps**. The simplest form of incremental dumping is to make a complete dump periodically, say weekly or monthly, and to make a daily dump of only those files that have been modified since the last full dump. A better scheme is to dump only those files that have changed since they were last dumped.

To implement this method, a list of the dump times for each file must be kept on disk. The dump program then checks each file on the disk. If it has been modified since it was last dumped, it is dumped again and its time-of-last-dump is changed to the current time. If done on a monthly cycle, this method requires 31 daily dump tapes, one per day, plus enough tapes to hold a full dump, made once a month. Other more complex schemes that use fewer tapes are also in use.

File System Consistency

Another area where reliability is an issue is file system consistency. Many file systems read blocks, modify them, and write them out later. If the system crashes before all the modified blocks have been written out, the file system can be left in an inconsistent state. This problem is especially critical if some of the blocks that have not been written out are i-node blocks, directory blocks, or blocks containing the free list.

To deal with the problem of inconsistent file systems, most computers have a utility program that checks file system consistency. It can be run whenever the system is booted, particularly after a crash. The following description tells how such a utility works in UNIX and MINIX, but most other systems have something similar. These file system checkers verify each file system (disk) independently of the other ones.

Two kinds of consistency checks can be made: blocks and files. To check for block consistency, the program builds a table with two counters per block, both initially 0. The first counter keeps track of how many times the block is present in a file; the second records how often it is present in the free list (or bit map of free blocks).

The program then reads all the i-nodes. Starting from an i-node, it is possible to build a list of all the block numbers used in the corresponding file. As each block number is read, its counter in the first table is incremented. The program then examines the free list or bit map, to find all the blocks that are not in use. Each occurrence of a block in the free list results in its counter in the second table being incremented.

If the file system is consistent, each block will have a 1 either in the first table or in the second table, as illustrated in Fig. 5-15(a). However, as a result of a crash, the tables might look like Fig. 5-15(b), in which block 2 does not occur in either table. It will be reported as being a **missing block**. While missing blocks do no real harm, they do waste space and thus reduce the capacity of the disk. The solution to missing blocks is straightforward: the file system checker just adds them to the free list.

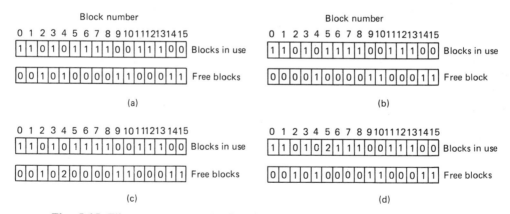

Fig. 5-15. File system states. (a) Consistent. (b) Missing block. (c) Duplicate block in free list. (d) Duplicate data block.

Another situation that might occur is that of Fig. 5-15(c). Here we see a block, number 4, that occurs twice in the free list. (Duplicates can occur only if the free list is really a list; with a bit map it is impossible.) The solution here is also simple: rebuild the free list.

The worst thing that can happen is that the same data block is present in two or more files, as shown in Fig. 5-15(d) with block 5. If either of these files is removed, block 5 will be put on the free list, leading to a situation in which the same block is both in use and free at the same time. If both files are removed, the block will be put onto the free list twice.

The appropriate action for the file system checker to take is to allocate a free block, copy the contents of block 5 into it, and insert the copy into one of the files. In this way, the information content of the files is unchanged (although almost assuredly garbled), but the file system structure is at least made consistent. The error should be reported, to allow the user to inspect the damage.

In addition to checking to see that each block is properly accounted for, the file system checker also checks the directory system. It too, uses two tables of counters, but these are per file, rather than per block. It starts at the root directory and recursively descends the tree, inspecting each directory in the file system. For every file in every directory, it increments the counter for that file's i-node (see Fig. 5-10 for the layout of a directory entry).

When it is all done, it has a list, indexed by i-node number, telling how many directories point to that i-node. It then compares these numbers with the link counts stored in the i-nodes themselves. In a consistent file system, both counts will agree. However, two kinds of errors can occur: the link count in the i-node can be too high or it can be too low.

If the link count is higher than the number of directory entries, then even if all the files are removed from the directories, the count will still be nonzero and the i-node will not be removed. This error is not serious, but it wastes space on the disk with files that are not in any directory. It should be fixed by setting the link count in the i-node to the correct value.

The other error is potentially catastrophic. If two directory entries are linked to a file, but the i-node says that there is only one, when either directory entry is removed, the i-node count will go to zero. When an i-node count goes to zero, the file system marks it as unused and releases all of its blocks. This action will result in one of the directories now pointing to an unused i-node, whose blocks may soon be assigned to other files. Again, the solution is just to force the link count in the i-node to the actual number of directory entries.

These two operations, checking blocks and checking directories, are often integrated for efficiency reasons (i.e., only one pass over the i-nodes is required). Other heuristic checks are also possible. For example, directories have a definite format, with i-node numbers and ASCII names. If an i-node number is larger than the number of i-nodes on the disk, the directory has been damaged.

Furthermore, each i-node has a mode, some of which are legal but strange, such as 0007, which allows the owner and his group no access at all, but allows outsiders to read, write, and execute the file. It might be useful to at least report files that give outsiders more rights than the owner. Directories with more than, say, 1000 entries are also suspicious. Files located in user directories, but which are owned by the super-user and have the SETUID bit on, are potential security problems. With a little effort, one can put together a fairly long list of legal, but peculiar, situations that might be worth reporting.

The previous paragraphs have discussed the problem of protecting the user against crashes. Some file systems also worry about protecting the user against himself. If the user intends to type

```
rm *.o
```

to remove all the files ending with *.o* (compiler generated object files), but accidently types

```
rm * .o
```

(note the space after the asterisk), *rm* will remove all the files in the current directory and then complain that it cannot find *.o*. In MS-DOS and some other systems, when a file is removed, all that happens is that a bit is set in the directory or i-node marking the file as removed. No disk blocks are returned to the free list until they are actually needed. Thus, if the user discovers the error immediately, it is possible to run a special utility program that "unremoves" (i.e., restores) the removed files.

5.2.6. File System Performance

Access to disk is much slower than access to memory. Reading a memory word typically takes a few hundred nanoseconds at most. Reading a disk block takes tens of milliseconds, a factor of 10,000 slower. As a result of this difference in access time, many file systems have been designed to reduce the number of disk accesses needed.

The most common technique used to reduce disk accesses is the **block cache** or **buffer cache**. (Cache is pronounced "cash," and is derived from the French *cacher*, meaning to hide.) In this context, a cache is a collection of blocks that logically belong on the disk, but are being kept in memory for performance reasons.

Various algorithms can be used to manage the cache, but a common one is to check all read requests to see if the needed block is in the cache. If it is, the read request can be satisfied without a disk access. If the block is not in the cache, it is first read into the cache, and then copied to wherever it is needed. Subsequent requests for the same block can be satisfied from the cache.

When a block has to be loaded into a full cache, some block has to be removed and rewritten to the disk if it has been modified since being brought in. This situation is very much like paging, and all the usual paging algorithms described in Chap. 4, such as FIFO, second chance, and LRU are applicable. One pleasant difference between paging and caching is that cache references are relatively infrequent, so that it is feasible to keep all the blocks in exact LRU order with linked lists.

Unfortunately, there is a catch. Now that we have a situation in which exact LRU is possible, it turns out that LRU is undesirable. The problem has to do with the crashes and file system consistency discussed in the previous section. If a critical block, such as an i-node block, is read into the cache and modified, but not rewritten to the disk, a crash will leave the file system in an inconsistent state. If the i-node block is put at the end of the LRU chain, it may be quite a while before it reaches the front and is rewritten to the disk.

Furthermore, some blocks, such as double indirect blocks, are rarely referenced two times within a short interval. These considerations lead to a modified LRU scheme, taking two factors into account:

1. Is the block likely to be needed again soon?

2. Is the block essential to the consistency of the file system?

For both questions, blocks can be divided into categories such as i-node blocks, indirect blocks, directory blocks, full data blocks, and partly-full data blocks. Blocks that will probably not be needed again soon go on the front, rather than the rear of the LRU list, so their buffers will be reused quickly. Blocks that might be needed again soon, such as a partly full block that is being written, go on the end of the list, so they will stay around for a long time.

The second question is independent of the first one. If the block is essential to the file system consistency (basically, everything except data blocks), and it has been modified, it should be written to disk immediately, regardless of which end of the LRU list it is put on. By writing critical blocks quickly, we greatly reduce the probability that a crash will wreck the file system.

Even with this measure to keep the file system integrity intact, it is undesirable to keep data blocks in the cache too long before writing them out. Consider the plight of someone who is using a personal computer to write a book. Even if our writer periodically tells the editor to write the file being edited to the disk, there is a good chance that everything will still be in the cache and nothing on the disk. If the system crashes, the file system structure will not be corrupted, but a whole day's work will be lost.

This situation need not happen very often before we have a fairly unhappy user. Systems take two approaches to dealing with it. The UNIX way is to have a system call, SYNC, which forces all the modified blocks out onto the disk immediately. When the system is started up, a program, usually called *update*, is started up in the background to sit in an endless loop issuing SYNC calls, sleeping for 30 sec between calls. As a result, no more than 30 seconds of work is lost due to a crash.

The MS-DOS way is to write every modified block to disk as soon as it has been written. Caches in which all modified blocks are written back to the disk immediately are called **write-through caches**. They require much more disk I/O than nonwrite-through caches. The difference between these two approaches can be seen when a program writes a 1K block full, one character at a time. UNIX will collect all the characters in the cache, and write the block out once every 30 seconds, or whenever the block is removed from the cache. MS-DOS will make a disk access for every character written. Of course most programs do internal buffering, so they normally write not a character, but a line or a larger unit on each WRITE system call.

A consequence of this difference in caching strategy is that just removing a (floppy) disk from a UNIX system without doing a SYNC will almost always result in lost data, and frequently in a corrupted file system as well. With MS-DOS, no problem arises. These differing strategies were chosen because UNIX was developed in an environment in which all disks were hard disks and not removable, whereas MS-DOS started out in the floppy disk world. As hard disks become the norm, even on small microcomputers, the UNIX approach, with its better efficiency, will definitely be the way to go.

Caching is not the only way to increase the performance of a file system. Another important technique is to reduce the amount of disk arm motion by putting blocks that are likely to be accessed in sequence close to each other, preferably in the same cylinder. When an output file is written, the file system has to allocate the blocks one at a time, as they are needed. If the free blocks are recorded in a bit map, and the whole bit map is in main memory, it is easy enough to choose a free block as close as possible to the previous block. With a free list, part of which is on disk, it is much harder to allocate blocks close together.

However, even with a free list, some block clustering can be done. The trick is to keep track of disk storage not in blocks, but in groups of consecutive blocks. If a track consists of 64 sectors of 512 bytes, the system could use 1K blocks (2 sectors), but allocate disk storage in units of 2 blocks (4 sectors). This is not the same as having a 2K disk block, since the cache would still use 1K blocks and disk transfers would still be 1K but reading a file sequentially on an otherwise idle system would reduce the number of seeks by a factor of two, considerably improving performance.

A variation on the same theme is to take account of rotational positioning. When allocating blocks, the system attempts to place consecutive blocks in a file in the same cylinder, but interleaved for maximum throughput. Thus, if a disk has a rotation time of 16.67 msec and it takes about 4 msec for a user process to request and get a disk block, each block should be placed at least a quarter of the way around from its predecessor.

Another performance bottleneck in systems that use i-nodes or anything equivalent to i-nodes is that reading even a short file requires two disk accesses: one for the i-node and one for the block. The usual i-node placement is shown in Fig. 5-16(a). Here all the i-nodes are near the beginning of the disk, so the average distance between an i-node and its blocks will be about half the number of cylinders, requiring long seeks.

One easy performance improvement is to put the i-nodes in the middle of the disk, rather than at the start, thus reducing the average seek between the i-node and the first block by a factor of two. Another idea, shown in Fig. 5-16(b), is to divide the disk into cylinder groups, each with its own i-nodes, blocks, and free list (McKusick et al., 1984). When creating a new file, any i-node can be

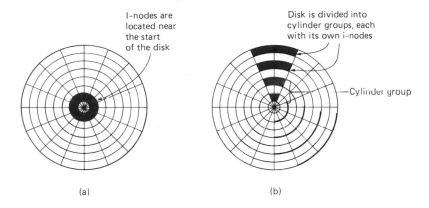

Fig. 5-16. (a) I-nodes placed at the start of the disk. (b) Disk divided into cylinder groups, each with its own blocks and i-nodes.

chosen, but having done this, an attempt is made to find a block in the same cylinder group as the i-node. If none is available, then a block in a cylinder group close by is used.

5.3. FILE SERVERS

Distributed systems often have machines that offer file service to other machines. They are called **file servers** (Birrell and Needham, 1980; Fridrich and Older, 1981; Svobodova, 1984; Swinehart et al. 1979). One popular way of keeping the cost of a distributed system low is to provide users with diskless workstations, and have them access files by sending READ and WRITE requests over the network to a common file server.

In principle, such a network file server could have an interface identical to UNIX or MS-DOS or any other popular file system. In practice, the people building these things are researchers who are generally interested in trying out new ideas. The result is that many file servers have features not present in traditional file systems. In the following sections we will look at some of these.

5.3.1. Interface Level

File servers can present an interface to their users (clients) at any one of three levels. The simplest one is **remote disk**. In this model, each user is allocated a **virtual disk**, which is just a private portion of the file server's disk. The user can then use the virtual disk the same way he would use a local disk. The file server provides commands: READ BLOCK and WRITE BLOCK, just as a local disk does. In effect, the network is being used to simulate a disk controller. All the file system code runs in the user machines, just as it does with local disks.

The next step up in complexity is to have the file server support files but not directories. Commands are present to create and delete files, read, write, and seek on files, and perform other file-specific operations. When a user creates a file, the file server generally returns an identifier that can be used for subsequent operations on the file. The identifier, might, for example, be a long random number, to make it difficult for unauthorized users to guess. It is up to the user to maintain directories that map ASCII names onto the file server's identifiers. These identifiers are then analogous to the i-node numbers stored in UNIX directories.

One problem with this scheme is that if a user creates a file on a file server and then crashes before recording the identifier in a directory, the file is "lost." It will continue to exist forever, but no one will ever be able to access it because its identifier is no longer known. The only way out of this situation is to have the file server provide a command by which a user can request a complete list of all his files.

The third kind of interface is to have the file server offer a complete file system, possibly UNIX, but often something more sophisticated. When this approach is taken, commands are present not only to manipulate files, but also to create and delete directories, change working directories, make and delete links to existing files, and similar operations. When a remote file server offers a complete directory service, it is sometimes possible for user workstations to mount a remote file system on the workstation's file tree. Thereafter, a remote file can be accessed merely by giving its absolute path from the local root, or by giving its relative path from the current working directory (which may be on the remote disk). The fact that it is remote is no longer visible.

5.3.2. Atomic Update

In a certain sense, improved technology has led to file systems that are *less* reliable than they used to be. Consider the way many companies kept track of their inventory in the early days of computing, before disks were invented. The company typically had a master tape containing a complete list of its products and how many of each were in stock. A backup copy of the tape was generally kept too, in case the original became unreadable due to dust, moisture, or damage by the tape drive.

Once a day the master tape was mounted on drive 1, a tape containing the day's sales was mounted on drive 2, and a blank tape was mounted on drive 3. Then an update program ran, reading the master and sales tapes, and producing a new master tape (which was immediately copied, for backup purposes). If this program crashed part way through, all three tapes were rewound, and the whole process started again.

This system had the attractive property that an update run either ran successfully to completion, producing a new master tape, or it failed, leaving the original file intact. Furthermore, if the master tape was ever damaged, for whatever reason, a backup was always available.

When disks were introduced, it was natural to have the master tape become a file of records on disk. Updating the master tape was replaced by reading and updating records in this file. The only problem was, if an update run crashed part way through, it was not possible to bring the system back up and rerun the update program, since an unknown number of records had already been updated. Data base systems have been dealing with this problem for years, but now with the advent of self-contained file servers, we are starting to see file systems that also address it.

The property that the three-tape system had, but the update-in-place disk system lacked, is often called **atomic update** or **failure atomicity**. What it means is that an update to a record, block or file either happens completely, or does not happen at all, leaving the system in its original state. If the atomic update fails, changing nothing, the update program can just be run again. What must be avoided at all costs is an update that changes part of the data, but not all of it, leaving the file in an unknown, partially updated state.

Another useful property that the tape system had was **fault tolerance**. A bad spot on the master tape was not fatal; the backup was always available. In theory, file systems could also maintain two copies of all files, but in practice few of them do.

File servers that offer fault-tolerant, atomic update usually implement a logical disk drive as two physical drives, as illustrated in Fig. 5-17. When information is written to logical block n, the server first writes it to physical block n on drive 1. Then it reads it back to make sure that it has been written correctly. If everything is all right, the server then writes the same information to physical block n on drive 2, and verifies it as well.

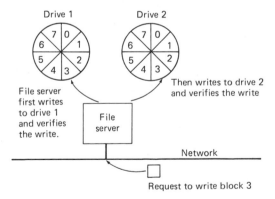

Fig. 5-17. Stable storage can be implemented using two disk drives containing the same information.

This technique is known as **stable storage** (Lampson and Sturgis, 1979) and has some interesting properties. First, consider what happens if a bad block spontaneously appears on either drive. Periodically, at night for example, the file server reads both disks looking for bad blocks, that is, blocks with checksum errors. If it finds one, it overwrites the bad block with the copy from the other drive, thus recovering from the error. (If the block has been physically damaged, the server can use a spare track kept in reserve for such emergencies.) If we assume that the probability of two corresponding blocks spontaneously going bad on the same day is negligible, stable storage will never lose data, in spite of occasional disk errors.

Now let us consider the effect of file server crashes. If a crash occurs while writing on either drive, the block being written will have a checksum error. Since this can always be detected, the good block can be used to overwrite the bad block. If the server crashes while writing on drive 1, the system will be restored to its original state. If it crashes while writing on drive 2, the system will be restored to its updated state. Either way, a write to stable storage either happens or it does not happen, but it never leaves the system in an ambiguous intermediate state.

An idea somewhat related to atomic update is that of **multiversion files.** When a file server supports multiversion files, a file is never modified after it has been created. Instead, changes are recorded by requesting a temporary copy of the file, modifying the copy, and then making the changes permanent by freezing the temporary copy in an atomic update. Thus, a file consists of a time-ordered sequence of immutable versions. Requests to read a file always read the latest version, unless an earlier version has been explicitly requested.

5.3.3. Concurrency Control

In a traditional file system (e.g., UNIX), if two users are updating a file at the same time, the READ and WRITE commands will be carried out in the order received. Consider what happens in a banking system if two customers each deposit money to the same account at the same time. The account initially contains 500 dollars, and the customers want to deposit 200 and 300 dollars, respectively. The following sequence of actions might occur.

1. Customer 1's program reads the balance and sees that it is 500.

2. Customer 2's program reads the balance and also sees that it is 500.

3. Customer 1's program updates the balance to be 500 + 200 = 700.

4. Customer 2's program updates the balance to be 500 + 300 = 800.

The final result is 800. If customer 1 had been a little bit slower, the final balance would have been 700. In any event, because the two updates are interleaved, the final result is wrong. What is needed is a way to ensure that first one customer runs his program and then the other, in either order, but not interleaved as above.

The property of having simultaneous updates yield a result that is equivalent to having the updates run sequentially in some order is called **serializability.** Techniques to achieve serializability are called **concurrency control algorithms**. Like atomic updates, they are widely used in data base systems, but are now beginning to appear in file servers as well.

Many file servers offer some form of **locking** to their clients as a concurrency control technique. When a file is locked by one client, all attempts to use or lock the file by other clients are rejected by the server. Locks can be used to achieve concurrency control as follows. Before starting an update run, the client first locks all the files that will be needed. If some file is already locked (by another client), all the files just locked are unlocked, and the run fails with no changes made. Once all the locks have been acquired, the files are read and written, and the locks are released.

One difficult problem with locking is what to do if a client requests a lock on a file and then crashes. To prevent the file from remaining locked, some servers start a timer whenever a lock is set. If the timer runs out before the lock is released, the server assumes that the client has crashed and unlocks the file. This strategy causes obvious problems if the client is alive and well, but just slow.

Concurrency control closely resembles the mutual exclusion problem we studied in detail in Chap. 2 but it differs in a subtle way. In Chap. 2 we approached the problem from the program side, establishing critical regions and making sure no two critical regions were active at once. With locking, we are approaching it from the data side, directly protecting each file, without regard to which piece of program text is executing. When there are potentially many programs that might access some file, it makes more sense to put the controls on the file, rather than on the programs.

The implementation is also different, because keeping a semaphore around for each file in the file system for the (unlikely) event that someone might want to lock it is too expensive. Instead, a table of locked files is kept in memory. The problems of crashes, timeouts, and other factors are also different.

5.3.4. Transactions

Automatic locking is often combined with atomic update in a form known as a **transaction**. Transactions have the property of either running successfully to completion, or failing and leaving the system state unchanged. To run a transaction, the client process sends a BEGIN TRANSACTION message to the file server. It can then read and write one or more files, as needed. When it is done, the process sends an END TRANSACTION message to the file server, to cause all the changes to be **committed**, that is, made permanent, in a single atomic update. If the commit is not possible, the transaction fails and nothing is changed. Until the END TRANSACTION message is received, none of the writes will be visible to other processes using any of the files. They see just the original, unmodified files.

If two or more processes are simultaneously performing transactions, it is up to the file server to give each one the illusion that it is the only one busy at that instant. In other words, the file server must automatically make all the transactions serializable. How the file server efficiently implements serializability and atomic update on multiple files is a subject of much research. Below we will just give a brief sketch of one simple approach.

When a process starts a transaction, the file server creates a **transaction record** on stable storage to keep track of its status. Because it is on stable storage, it will survive both server and disk crashes. When the process reads a file for the first time, the file server locks the file to prevent other processes from accessing it. If the lock cannot be acquired, the transaction fails and no changes are made.

When the process tries to write a block on a file for the first time, the file is locked and a copy of the file is made. The write (and all subsequent writes to that file) are made to the copy, not the original.

When the END TRANSACTION command is executed, the server will have a collection of newly created files that have to replace the old files, which still have not been modified. It then builds an **intentions list**, listing all the files that have to be updated, and for each one it notes where the new file is to be found. The intentions list goes in the transaction record on stable storage, so that even if the server crashes, when it comes back up it will know what to do. Then it sets a bit to inhibit all other operations until the transaction is finished and marked as committed.

Next, it returns all the blocks in the files to be overwritten, and replaces them with the new files by atomically updating their i-nodes. At this point, the transaction has completed and all the locks can be released. These steps are summarized in Fig. 5-18.

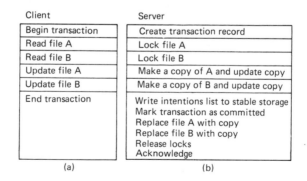

Client	Server
Begin transaction	Create transaction record
Read file A	Lock file A
Read file B	Lock file B
Update file A	Make a copy of A and update copy
Update file B	Make a copy of B and update copy
End transaction	Write intentions list to stable storage Mark transaction as committed Replace file A with copy Replace file B with copy Release locks Acknowledge

(a)   (b)

Fig. 5-18. (a) The steps performed by a client during a transaction. (b) The action taken by the server for each step.

Other, more efficient algorithms are known. For a discussion of some of them, see the paper by Svobodova (1984), and the references it contains.

5.3.5. Replicated Files

Another useful feature provided by some file servers is **replication**. Instead of keeping just one copy of each file, the server keeps n copies. If one of the copies should be accidentally destroyed, the data will not be lost forever. If a standard directory is implemented as a list of (ASCII name, i-node number) pairs, then replication can be achieved by changing the directory to contain an ASCII string and n i-node numbers, for the n copies of the file, as shown in Fig. 5-19. For a discussion of replicated files, see, for example, Pu et al. (1986).

ASCII name	I-node
file 1	17
file 2	22
file 3	12
file 4	84

(a)

ASCII name	I-nodes		
file 1	17	19	40
file 2	22	72	91
file 3	12	30	29
file 4	84	15	66

(b)

Fig. 5-19. (a) An ordinary directory. (b) A directory with replicated files.

When one copy of a file has been modified, it is up to the file server to handle the replication. Two strategies are possible. The first one is to locate the duplicates listed in the directory and send the blocks that have been changed to each of them, so they can be brought up to date. The other strategy is to abandon the now-obsolete duplicates, create new copies of the modified file, and enter these in the directory.

When the duplicates are all kept on different file servers, some of which are isolated due to network failures at the time the replication is to occur, the divergent copies must be reconciled when the network comes back up. If the replicated file happens to be a directory, and all the copies are independently modified while the network is down, when the network is restored to service, the file servers will be confronted with multiple, inconsistent copies of the directory, and somehow have to make them consistent again. For a more thorough discussion of this problem and some solutions, see Popek et al. (1981), Walker et al. (1983), and Weinstein et al. (1985).

5.4. SECURITY

File systems often contain information that is highly valuable to their users. Protecting this information against unauthorized usage is therefore a major concern of all file systems. In the following sections we will look at a variety of issues concerned with security and protection.

5.4.1. The Security Environment

The terms "security" and "protection" are often used interchangeably. Nevertheless, it is frequently useful to make a distinction between the general problems involved in making sure that files are not read or modified by unauthorized persons, which include technical, managerial, legal, and political issues on the one hand, and the specific operating system mechanisms used to provide security, on the other. To avoid confusion, we will use the term **security** to refer to the overall problem, and the term **protection mechanisms** to refer to the specific operating system mechanisms used to safeguard information in the computer. The boundary between them is not well defined, however. First we will look at security; later on in the chapter we will look at protection.

Security has many facets. Two of the more important ones are data loss and intruders. Some of the common causes of data loss are:

1. Acts of God: fires, floods, earthquakes, wars, riots, rats gnawing cards, tapes, or floppy disks.

2. Hardware or software errors: CPU malfunctions, unreadable disks or tapes, telecommunication errors, program bugs.

3. Human errors: incorrect data entry, wrong tape or disk mounted, wrong program run, lost disk or tape.

Most of these can be dealt with by maintaining adequate backups, preferably far away from the original data.

A more interesting problem is what to do about intruders. These come in two varieties. Passive intruders just want to read files they are not authorized to read. Active intruders are more malicious; they want to make unauthorized changes to data. When designing a system to be secure against intruders, it is important to keep in mind the kind of intruder one is trying to protect against. Some common categories are:

1. Casual prying by nontechnical users. Many people have terminals to time-sharing systems on their desks, and human nature being what it is, some of them will read other people's electronic mail and other files if no barriers are placed in the way. Most UNIX systems, for example, have the default that all files are publicly readable.

2. Snooping by insiders. Students, system programmers, operators, and other technical personnel often consider it to be a personal challenge to break the security of the local computer system. They often are highly skilled and are willing to devote a substantial amount of time to the effort.

3. Determined attempt to make money. Some bank programmers have attempted to break into a banking system to steal from the bank. Schemes have varied from changing the software to truncate rather than round interest, keeping the fraction of a cent for themselves, to siphoning off accounts not used in years, to blackmail ("Pay me or I will destroy all the bank's records.").

4. Commercial or military espionage. Espionage refers to a serious and well-funded attempt by a competitor or a foreign country to steal programs, trade secrets, patents, technology, circuit designs, marketing plans, and so forth. Often this attempt will involve wiretapping or even erecting antennas directed at the computer to pick up its electromagnetic radiation.

It should be clear that trying to keep the KGB from stealing military secrets is quite a different matter from trying to keep students from inserting a funny message-of-the-day into the system. The amount of effort that one puts into security and protection clearly depend on who the enemy is thought to be.

Another aspect of the security problem is **privacy**: protecting individuals from misuse of information about them. This quickly gets into many legal and moral issues. Should the government compile dossiers on everyone in order to catch X-cheaters, where X is "welfare" or "tax," depending on your politics? Should the police be able to look up anything on anyone in order to stop organized crime? Do employers and insurance companies have rights? What happens when these rights conflict with individual rights? All of these issues are extremely important, but are beyond the scope of this book (see the references in Chap. 6 for some suggested readings, however).

5.4.2. Famous Security Flaws

Just as the transportation industry has the *Titanic* and the *Hindenburg*, computer security experts have a few things they would rather forget about. In this section we will look at some interesting security problems that have occurred in four different operating systems: UNIX, MULTICS, TENEX, and OS/360.

The UNIX utility *lpr*, which prints a file on the line printer, has an option to remove the file after it has been printed. In early versions of UNIX it was possible for anyone to use *lpr* to print, and then have the system remove, the password file.

Another way to break into UNIX was to link a file called *core* in the working directory to the password file. The intruder then forced a core dump of a SETUID program, which the system wrote on the *core* file, that is, on top of the password file. In this way, a user could replace the password file with one containing a few strings of his own choosing (e.g., command arguments).

Yet another subtle flaw in UNIX involved the command

```
mkdir foo
```

Mkdir, which is a SETUID program owned by the root, first created the i-node for the directory *foo* with the system call MKNOD, and then changed the owner of *foo* from its effective uid (i.e., root) to its real uid (the user's uid). When the system was slow, it was sometimes possible for the user to quickly remove the directory i-node and make a link to the password file under the name *foo* after the MKNOD but before the CHOWN. When *mkdir* did the CHOWN it made the user the owner of the password file. By putting the necessary commands in a shell script, they could be tried over and over until the trick worked.

The MULTICS security problem had to do with the fact that the system designers always perceived MULTICS as a time-sharing system, with batch facilities thrown in as an afterthought to pacify some old batch diehards. The time-sharing security was excellent; the batch security was nonexistent. It was possible for anyone to submit a batch job that read a deck of cards into an arbitrary user's directory.

To steal someone's files, all one had to do was get a copy of the editor source code, modify it to steal files (but still work perfectly as an editor), and read it into the victim's *bin* directory. The next time the victim called the editor, he got the intruder's version, which edited fine, but stole all his files as well. The idea of modifying a normal program to do nasty things in addition to its usual function and arranging for the victim to use the modified version is now known as the **Trojan horse attack**.

The TENEX operating system used to be very popular on the DEC-10 computers. It is no longer used much, but it will live on forever in the annals of computer security due to the following design error. TENEX supported paging. To allow users to monitor the behavior of their programs, it was possible to instruct the system to call a user function on each page fault.

TENEX also used passwords to protect files. To access a file, a program had to present the proper password. The operating system checked passwords one character at a time, stopping as soon as it saw that the password was wrong. To break into TENEX an intruder would carefully position a password as shown in Fig. 5-20(a), with the first character at the end of one page, and the rest at the start of the next page.

The next step was to make sure that the second page was not in memory, for example, by referencing so many other pages that the second page would surely be evicted to make room for them. Now the program tried to open the victim's file, using the carefully aligned password. If the first character of the real password was anything but *A*, the system would stop checking at the first character and report back with ILLEGAL PASSWORD. If, however, the real password did begin with *A*, the system continued reading, and got a page fault, about which the intruder was informed.

If the password did not begin with *A*, the intruder changed the password to that of Fig. 5-20(b) and repeated the whole process to see if it began with *B*. It

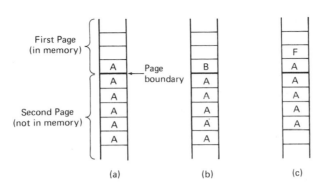

Fig. 5-20. The TENEX password problem.

took at most 128 tries to go through the whole ASCII character set, and thus determine the first character.

Suppose the first character was an F. The memory layout of Fig. 5-20(c) allowed the intruder to test strings of the form FA, FB, and so on. Using this approach it took at most $128n$ tries to guess an n character ASCII password, instead of 128^n.

Our last flaw concerns OS/360. The description that follows is slightly simplified, but preserves the essence of the flaw. In this system it was possible to start up a tape read and then continue computing while the tape drive was transferring data to the user space. The trick here was to carefully start up a tape read, and then do a system call that required a user data structure, for example, a file to read and its password.

The operating system first verified that the password was indeed the correct one for the given file. Then it went back and read the file name again for the actual access (it could have saved the name internally, but it did not). Unfortunately, just before the system went to fetch the file name the second time, the file name was overwritten by the tape drive. The system then read the new file, for which no password had been presented. Getting the timing right took some practice, but it was not that hard. Besides, if there is one thing that computers are good at, it is repeating the same operation over and over *ad nauseam*.

5.4.3. Generic Security Attacks

The flaws described above have been fixed but the average operating system still leaks like a sieve. The usual way to test a system's security is to hire a group of experts, known as **tiger teams** or **penetration teams**, to see if they can break in. Hebbard et al. (1980) tried the same thing with graduate students. In the course of the years, these penetration teams have discovered a number of areas in which systems are likely to be weak. Below we have listed some of the more common attacks that are often successful. When designing a system, be sure it can withstand attacks like these.

1. Request memory pages, disk space, or tapes and just read them. Many systems do not erase them before allocating them, and they may be full of interesting information written by the previous owner.

2. Try illegal system calls, or legal system calls with illegal parameters, or even legal system calls with legal but unreasonable parameters. Many systems can easily be confused.

3. Start logging in and then hit DEL, RUBOUT or BREAK halfway through the login sequence. In some systems, the password checking program will be killed and the login considered successful.

4. Try modifying complex operating system structures kept in user space. In many systems, to open a file, the program builds a large data structure containing the file name and many other parameters and passes it to the system. As the file is read and written, the system sometimes updates the structure itself. Changing these fields can wreak havoc with the security.

5. Spoof the user by writing a program that types "login:" on the screen and go away. Many users will walk up to the terminal and willingly tell it their login name and password, which the program carefully records for its evil master.

6. Look for manuals that say "Do not do X". Try as many variations of X as possible.

7. Convince a system programmer to change the system to skip certain vital security checks for any user with your login name. This attack is known as a **trapdoor**.

8. All else failing, the penetrator might find the computer center director's secretary and trick or bribe her. The secretary probably has easy access to all kinds of wonderful information, and is usually poorly paid. Do not underestimate the problems caused by personnel.

These and other attacks are discussed by Linde (1975 NCC).

5.4.4. Design Principles for Security

Saltzer and Schroeder (1975) have identified several general principles that can be used as a guide to designing secure systems. A brief summary of their ideas (based on experience with MULTICS) is given below.

First, the system design should be public. Assuming that the intruder will not know how the system works serves only to delude the designers.

Second, the default should be no access. Errors in which legitimate access is refused will be reported much faster than errors in which unauthorized access is allowed.

Third, check for current authority. The system should not check for permission, determine that access is permitted, and then squirrel away this information for subsequent use. Many systems check for permission when a file is opened, and not afterward. This means that a user who opens a file, and keeps it open for weeks, will continue to have access, even if the owner has long since changed the file protection.

Fourth, give each process the least privilege possible. If an editor has only the authority to access the file to be edited (specified when the editor is invoked), editors with Trojan horses will not be able to do much damage. This principle implies a fine-grained protection scheme. We will discuss such schemes later in this chapter.

Fifth, the protection mechanism should be simple, uniform, and built in to the lowest layers of the system. Trying to retrofit security to an existing insecure system is nearly impossible. Security, like correctness, is not an add-on feature.

Sixth, the scheme chosen must be psychologically acceptable. If users feel that protecting their files is too much work, they just will not do it. Nevertheless, they will complain loudly if something goes wrong. Replies of the form "It is your own fault" will generally not be well received.

5.4.5. User Authentication

Many protection schemes are based on the assumption that the system knows the identity of each user. The problem of identifying users when they log in is called **user authentication**. Most authentication methods are based on identifying something the user knows, something the user has, or something the user is.

Passwords

The most widely used form of authentication is to require the user to type a password. Password protection is easy to understand and easy to implement. In UNIX it works like this. The login program asks the user to type his name and password. The password is immediately encrypted. The login program then reads the password file, which is a series of ASCII lines, one per user, until it finds the line containing the user's login name. If the (encrypted) password contained in this line matches the encrypted password just computed, the login is permitted, otherwise it is refused.

Password authentication is easy to defeat. One frequently reads about groups of high school, or even junior high school school students who, with the aid of their trusty home computers, have just broken into some top secret system owned by a giant corporation or government agency. Virtually all the time the break-in consists of guessing a user name and password combination.

Morris and Thompson (1979) made a study of passwords on UNIX systems. They compiled a list of likely passwords: first names, last names, street names, city names, words from a moderate-sized dictionary (also words spelled backward), valid license plate numbers, and short strings of random characters.

They then encrypted each of these using the known password encryption algorithm, and checked to see if any of the encrypted passwords matched entries in their list. Over 86 percent of all passwords turned up in their list.

If all passwords consisted of 7 characters chosen at random from the 95 printable ASCII characters, the search space becomes 95^7, which is about 7×10^{13}. At 1000 encryptions per second, it would take 2000 years to build the list to check the password file against. Furthermore, the list would fill 20 million magnetic tapes. Even requiring passwords to contain at least one lowercase character, one uppercase character, and one special character, and be at least seven characters long would be a big improvement on user-chosen passwords.

Even if it is considered politically impossible to require users to pick reasonable passwords, Morris and Thompson have described a technique that renders their own attack (encrypting a large number of passwords in advance) almost useless. Their idea is to associate an n-bit random number with each password. The random number is changed whenever the password is changed. The random number is stored in the password file in unencrypted form, so that everyone can read it. Instead of just storing the encrypted password in the password file, the password and the random number are first concatenated and then encrypted together. This encrypted result is stored in the password file.

Now consider the implications for an intruder who wants to build up a list of likely passwords, encrypt them, and save the results in a sorted file, f, so that any encrypted password can be looked up easily. If an intruder suspects that *Marilyn* might be a password, it is no longer sufficient just to encrypt *Marilyn* and put the result in f. He has to encrypt 2^n strings, such as *Marilyn0000*, *Marilyn0001*, *Marilyn0002*, and so forth and enter all of them in f. This technique increases the size of f by 2^n. UNIX uses this method with $n = 12$.

Although this method offers protection against intruders who try to precompute a large list of encrypted passwords, it does little to protect a user *David* whose password is also *David*. One way to encourage people to pick better passwords is to have the computer offer advice. Some computers have a program that generates random easy-to-pronounce nonsense words, such as *fotally*, *garbungy*, or *bipitty* that can be used as passwords (preferably with some upper case and special characters thrown in).

Other computers require users to change their passwords regularly, to limit the damage done if a password leaks out. The most extreme form of this approach is the **one time password**. When one-time passwords are used, the user gets a book containing a list of passwords. Each login uses the next password in the list. If an intruder ever discovers a password, it will not do him any good, since next time a different password must be used. It is suggested that the user try to avoid losing the password book.

It goes almost without saying that while a password is being typed in, the computer should not display the typed characters, to keep them from prying eyes near the terminal. What is less obvious is that passwords should never be stored in the computer in unencrypted form, and that not even the computer center management should have unencrypted copies. Keeping unencrypted passwords anywhere is looking for trouble.

A variation on the password idea is to have each new user provide a long list of questions and answers that are then stored in the computer in encrypted form. The questions should be chosen so that the user does not need to write them down. Typical questions are:

1. Who is Marjolein's sister?

2. On what street was your elementary school?

3. What did Mrs. Woroboff teach?

At login, the computer asks one of them at random and checks to see if the answer is correct.

Another variation is **challenge-response**. When this is used, the user picks an algorithm when signing up as a user, for example x^2. When the user logs in, the computer types an argument, say 7, in which case the user types 49. The algorithm can be different in the morning and afternoon, on different days of the week, from different terminals, and so on.

Physical Identification

A completely different approach to authorization is to check to see if the user has some item, normally a plastic card with a magnetic stripe on it. The card is inserted into the terminal, which then checks to see whose card it is. This method can be combined with a password, so a user can only log in if he (1) has the card and (2) knows the password. Automated cash-dispensing machines usually work this way.

Yet another approach is to measure physical characteristics that are hard to forge. For example, a fingerprint or a voiceprint reader in the terminal could verify the user's identity. (It makes the search go faster if the user tells the computer who he is, rather than making the computer compare the given fingerprint to the entire data base.) Direct visual recognition is not yet feasible, but may be one day.

Another technique is signature analysis. The user signs his name with a special pen connected to the terminal, and the computer compares it to a known specimen stored on line. Even better is not to compare the signature, but compare the pen motions made while writing it. A good forger may be able to copy the signature, but will not have a clue as to the exact order in which the strokes were made.

Finger length analysis is surprisingly practical. When this is used, each terminal has a device like the one of Fig. 5-21. The user inserts his hand into it, and the length of all his fingers is measured and checked against the data base.

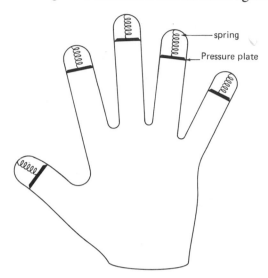

Fig. 5-21. A device for measuring finger length.

We could go on and on with more examples, but two more will help make an important point. Cats and other animals mark off their territory by urinating around its perimeter. Apparently cats can identify each other this way. Suppose someone comes up with a tiny device capable of doing an instant urinalysis, thereby providing a foolproof identification. Each terminal could be equipped with one of these devices, along with a discrete sign reading: "For login, please deposit sample here." This might be an absolutely unbreakable system, but it would probably have a fairly serious user acceptance problem.

The same could be said of a system consisting of a thumbtack and a small spectrograph. The user would be requested to press his thumb against the thumbtack, thus extracting a drop of blood for spectrographic analysis. The point is that any authentication scheme must be psychologically acceptable to the user community. Finger-length measurements probably will not cause any problem, but even something as nonintrusive as storing fingerprints on line may be unacceptable to many people.

Countermeasures

Computer installations that are really serious about security, something that frequently happens the day after an intruder has broken in and done major damage, often take steps to make unauthorized entry much harder. For example, each user could be allowed to log in only from a specific terminal, and only during certain days of the week and hours of the day.

Dialup telephone lines could be made to work as follows. Anyone can dial up and log in, but after a successful login, the system immediately breaks the connection and calls the user back at an agreed upon number. This measure means than an intruder cannot just try breaking in from any phone line; only the user's (home) phone will do. In any event, with or without call back, the system should take at least 10 seconds to check any password typed in on a dialup line, and should increase this time after several consecutive unsuccessful login attempts, in order to reduce the rate at which intruders can try. After three failed login attempts, the line should be disconnected for 10 minutes and security personnel notified.

All logins should be recorded. When a user logs in, the system should report the time and terminal of the previous login, so he can detect possible break ins.

The next step up is laying baited traps to catch intruders. A simple scheme is to have one special login name with an easy password (e.g., login name: guest, password: guest). Whenever anyone logs in using this name, the system security specialists are immediately notified. Other traps can be easy-to-find bugs in the operating system and similar things, designed for the purpose of catching intruders in the act.

5.5. PROTECTION MECHANISMS

In the previous sections we have looked at many potential problems, some of them technical and some of them not. In the following sections we will concentrate on some of the detailed technical ways that are used in operating systems to protect files and other things. All of these techniques make a clear distinction between policy (whose data are to be protected from whom) and mechanism (how the system enforces the policy). The separation of policy and mechanism is discussed in (Levin et al., 1975). Our emphasis will be on the mechanism, not the policy.

5.5.1. Protection Domains

A computer system contains many **objects** that need to be protected. These objects can be hardware, such as CPUs, memory segments, terminals, disk drives, or printers, or they can be software, such as processes, files, data bases, or semaphores.

Each object has a unique name by which it is referenced, and a set of operations that can be carried out on it. READ and WRITE are operations appropriate to a file; UP and DOWN make sense on a semaphore. Objects are the operating system equivalent of what in programming languages are called **abstract data types**.

It is obvious that a way is needed to prohibit processes from accessing objects that they are not authorized to access. Furthermore, this mechanism must also make it possible to restrict processes to a subset of the legal operations when that is needed. For example, process *A* may be entitled to read, but not write, file *F*.

To provide a way to discuss different protection mechanisms, it is convenient to introduce the concept of a domain. A **domain** is a set of (object, rights) pairs. Each pair specifies an object and some subset of the operations that can be performed on it. A **right** in this context means permission to perform one of the operations.

Figure 5-22 depicts three domains, showing the objects in each domain and the rights [Read, Write, eXecute] available on each object. Note that *Printer1* is in two domains at the same time. Although not shown in this example, it is possible for the same object to be in multiple domains, with *different* rights in each domain.

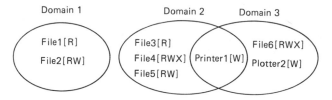

Fig. 5-22. Three protection domains.

At every instant of time, each process runs in some protection domain. In other words, there is some collection of objects it can access, and for each object it has some set of rights. Processes can also switch from domain to domain during execution. The rules for domain switching are highly system dependent.

To make the idea of a protection domain more concrete, let us look at UNIX. In UNIX, the domain of a process is defined by its uid and gid. Given any (uid, gid) combination, it is possible to make a complete list of all objects (files, including I/O devices represented by special files) that can be accessed, and whether they can be accessed for reading, writing, or executing. Two processes with the same (uid, gid) combination will have access to exactly the same set of objects. Processes with different (uid, gid) values will have access to a different set of files, although there will be considerable overlap in most cases.

Furthermore, each process in UNIX has two halves: the user part and the kernel part. When the process does a system call, it switches from the user part to the kernel part (see Fig. 3-14). The kernel part has access to a different set of objects from the user part. For example, the kernel can access all the pages in physical memory, the entire disk, and all the other protected resources. Thus, a system call causes a domain switch.

When a process does an EXEC on a file with the SETUID or SETGID bit on, it acquires a new effective uid or gid. With a different (uid, gid) combination, it has a different set of files and operations available. Running a program with SETUID or SETGID is also a domain switch.

The division of a UNIX process into a kernel part and a user part is a remnant

of a much more powerful domain switching mechanism that was used in MUL-
TICS. In that system, the hardware supported not two domains (kernel and user)
per process, but up to 64. A MULTICS process could consist of a collection of
procedures, each one running in some domain, which were called **rings**
(Schroeder and Saltzer, 1972). Procedures could also be linked dynamically to a
running process during execution.

Figure 5-23 shows four rings. The innermost ring, the operating system kernel, had the most power. Moving outward from the kernel, the rings became
successively less powerful. Ring 1, for example, might contain the code for
functions that in UNIX are handled by SETUID programs owned by the root,
such as *mkdir*. Ring 2 might contain the grading program used to evaluate student programs, and ring 3 might contain the student programs.

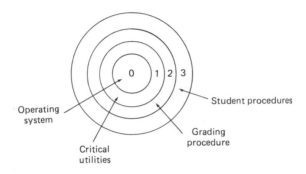

Fig. 5-23. A process in MULTICS occupying four rings. Each ring is a separate
protection domain.

When a procedure in one ring called a procedure in another ring, a trap
occurred, giving the system the opportunity to change the protection domain of
the process. Thus, a MULTICS process could operate in as many as 64 different
domains during its lifetime. (Actually, the situation was more complicated than
we have sketched above; procedures could live in multiple consecutive rings, and
parameter passing between rings was carefully controlled.) For a detailed
description of MULTICS, see Organick (1972).

An important question is how the system keeps track of which object belongs
to which domain. Conceptually, at least, one can envision a large matrix, with
the rows being the domains and the columns being the objects. Each box lists
the rights, if any, that the domain contains for the object. The matrix for
Fig. 5-22 is shown in Fig. 5-24. Given this matrix and the current domain
number, the system can always tell if an attempt to access a given object in a
particular way from a specified domain is allowed.

Domain switching itself, as in MULTICS, can be easily included in the matrix
model by realizing that a domain is itself an object, with the operation ENTER.
Figure 5-25 shows the matrix of Fig. 5-24 again, only now with the three
domains as objects themselves. Processes in domain 1 can switch to domain 2,

Object

Domain	File1	File2	File3	File4	File5	File6	Printer1	Plotter2
1	Read	Read Write						
2			Read	Read Write Execute	Read Write		Write	
3						Read Write Execute	Write	Write

Fig. 5-24. A protection matrix.

but once there, they cannot go back. This situation models executing a SETUID program in UNIX. No other domain switches are permitted in this example.

Object

Domain	File1	File2	File3	File4	File5	File6	Printer1	Plotter2	Domain1	Domain2	Domain 3
1	Read	Read Write								Enter	
2			Read	Read Write Execute	Read Write		Write				
3						Read Write Execute	Write	Write			

Fig. 5-25. A protection matrix with domains as objects.

5.5.2. Access Control Lists

In practice, actually storing the matrix of Fig. 5-25 is rarely done because it is large and sparse. Most domains have no access at all to most objects, so storing a big, empty matrix is a waste of disk space. Two methods that are practical, however, are storing the matrix by rows or by columns, and then storing only the nonempty elements. The two approaches are surprisingly different. In this section we will look at storing it by column; in the next one we will study storing it by row.

The first technique consists of associating with each object an (ordered) list containing all the domains that may access the object, and how. This list is called the **access control list** or **ACL**. If it were to be implemented in UNIX, the easiest way would be to put the ACL for each file in a separate disk block, and include the block number in the file's i-node. As only the nonempty entries of the matrix are stored, the total storage required for all the ACLs combined is much less than what would be needed for the whole matrix.

As an example of how ACLs work, let us continue to imagine that they were used in UNIX, where a domain is specified by a (uid, gid) pair. Actually, ACLs were used in UNIX's predecessor, MULTICS, more or less in the way we will describe, so the example is not so hypothetical.

Let us now assume that we have four users (i.e., uids) Jan, Els, Jelle, and Maaike, who belong to groups system, staff, student, and student, respectively. Suppose some files have the following ACLs:

File0: (Jan, *, RWX)
File1: (Jan, system, RWX)
File2: (Jan, *, RW-), (Els, staff, R-), (Maaike, *, R--)
File3: (*, student, R--)
File4: (Jelle, *, ---), (*, student, R--)

Each ACL entry, in parentheses, specifies a uid, a gid, and the allowed accesses (Read, Write, eXecute). An asterisk means all uids or gids. *File0* can be read, written, or executed by any process with uid = Jan, and any gid. *File1* can be accessed only by processes with uid = Jan and gid = system. A process with uid = Jan and gid = staff can access *File0* but not *File1*. *File2* can be read or written by processes with uid = Jan and any gid, by processes with uid = Els and gid = staff, or by processes with uid = Maaike and any gid. *File3* can be read by any student. *File4* is especially interesting. It says that anyone with uid = Jelle, in any group, has no access at all, but all other students can read it. By using ACL's it is possible to prohibit specific uids or gids from accessing an object, while allowing everyone else in the same class.

So much for what UNIX does not do. Now let us look at what it *does* do. It provides three bits, *rwx*, per file for the owner, the owner's group, and others. This scheme is just the ACL again, but compressed to 9 bits. It is a list associated with the object saying who may access it and how. While the 9-bit UNIX scheme is clearly less general than a full-blown ACL system, in practice it is adequate, and its implementation is much simpler and cheaper.

The owner of an object can change its ACL at any time, thus making it easy to prohibit accesses that were previously allowed. The only problem is that changing the ACL will probably not affect any users who are currently using the object (e.g., have the file open).

5.5.3. Capabilities

The other way of slicing up the matrix of Fig. 5-25 is by rows. When this method is used, associated with each process is a list of objects that may be accessed, along with an indication of which operations are permitted on each, in other words, its domain. This list is called a **capability list**, and the individual items on it are called **capabilities** (Dennis and Van Horn, 1966; Fabry, 1974).

A typical capability list is shown in Fig. 5-26. Each capability has a *type* field, which tells what kind of an object it is, a *rights* field, which is a bit map indicating which of the legal operations on this type of object are permitted, and an *object* field, which is a pointer to the object itself (e.g., its i-node number). Capability lists are themselves objects, and may be pointed to from other capability lists, thus facilitating sharing of subdomains. Capabilities are often referred to by their position in the capability list. A process might say: "Read 1K from the file pointed to by capability 2." This form of addressing is similar to using file descriptors in UNIX.

	Type	Rights	Object
0	File	R — —	Pointer to File3
1	File	RWX	Pointer to File4
2	File	RW—	Pointer to File5
3	Printer	—W—	Pointer to Printer1

Fig. 5-26. The capability list for domain 2 in Fig. 5-24.

It is fairly obvious that capability lists, or **C-lists** as they are often called, must be protected from user tampering. Three methods have been proposed to protect them. The first way requires a **tagged architecture**, a hardware design in which each memory word has an extra (or tag) bit that tells whether the word contains a capability or not. The tag bit is not used by arithmetic, comparison, or similar ordinary instructions, and it can be modified only by programs running in kernel mode (i.e., the operating system).

The second way is to keep the C-list inside the operating system, and just have processes refer to capabilities by their slot number, as mentioned above. Hydra (Wulf, 1974) worked this way. The third way is to keep the C-list in user space, but encrypt each capability with a secret key unknown to the user. This approach is particularly suited to distributed systems, and is used by Amoeba (Tanenbaum et al., 1986).

In addition to the specific object-dependent rights, such as read and execute, capabilities usually have **generic rights** which are applicable to all objects. Examples of generic rights are

1. Copy capability: create a new capability for the same object.

2. Copy object: create a duplicate object with a new capability.

3. Remove capability: delete entry from C-list; object unaffected.

4. Destroy object: permanently remove object and capability.

Many capability systems are organized as a collection of modules, with **type manager modules** for each type of object. Requests to perform operations on a file are sent to the file manager, whereas requests to do something with a mailbox go to the mailbox manager. These requests are accompanied by the relevant capability. A problem arises here, because the type manager module is just an ordinary program, after all. The owner of a file capability can perform only some of the operations on the file, but cannot get at its internal representation (e.g., its i-node). It is essential that the type manager module be able to do more with the capability than an ordinary process.

This problem was solved in Hydra by a technique called **rights amplification,** in which type managers were given a rights template that gave them more rights to an object than the capability itself allowed. Other capability systems that have strong typing of objects also need something like this.

A last remark worth making about capability systems is that revoking access to an object is quite difficult. It is hard for the system to find all the outstanding capabilities for any object to take them back, since they may be stored in C-lists all over the disk. One approach is to have each capability point to an indirect object, rather than to the object itself. By having the indirect object point to the real object, the system can always break that connection, thus invalidating the capabilities. (When a capability to the indirect object is later presented to the system, the user will discover that the indirect object is now pointing to a null object.)

Another way to achieve revocation is the scheme used in Amoeba. Each object contains a long random number, which is also present in the capability. When a capability is presented for use, the two are compared. Only if they agree is the operation allowed. The owner of an object can request that the random number in the object be changed, thus invalidating existing capabilities. Neither of these schemes allows selective revocation, that is, taking back, say, John's permission, but nobody else's.

5.5.4. Protection Models

Protection matrices, such as that of Fig. 5-24, are not static. They frequently change as new objects are created, old objects are destroyed, and owners decide to increase or restrict the set of users for their objects. A considerable amount of attention has been paid to modeling protection systems in which the protection matrix is constantly changing. In the remainder of this section, we will touch briefly upon some of this work.

Harrison et al. (1976) identified six primitive operations on the protection matrix that can be used as a base to model any protection system. These operations are: CREATE OBJECT, DELETE OBJECT, CREATE DOMAIN, DELETE DOMAIN, INSERT RIGHT, and REMOVE RIGHT. The two latter primitives insert and remove rights from specific matrix elements, such as granting domain 1 permission to read *File6*.

These six primitives can be combined into **protection commands**. It is these protection commands that user programs can execute to change the matrix. They may not execute the primitives directly. For example, the system might have a command to create a new file, which would test to see if the file already existed, and if not, create a new object and give the owner all rights to it. There might also be a command to allow the owner to grant permission to read the file to everyone in the system, in effect, inserting the "read" right in the new file's entry in every domain.

At any instant, the matrix determines what a process in any domain can do, not what it is authorized to do. The matrix is what is enforced by the system; authorization has to do with management policy. As an example of this distinction, let us consider the simple system of Fig. 5-27 in which domains correspond to users (similar to the UNIX model). In Fig. 5-27(a) we see the intended protection policy: *Henry* can read and write *mailbox7*, *Robert* can read and write *secret*, and all three users can read and execute *compiler*.

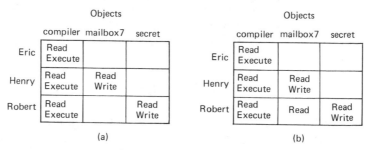

Fig. 5-27. (a) An authorized state. (b) An unauthorized state.

Now imagine that *Robert* is very clever and has found a way to issue commands to have the matrix changed to Fig. 5-27(b). He has now gained access to *mailbox7*, something he is not authorized to have. If he tries to read it, the operating system will carry out his request because it does not know that the state of Fig. 5-27(b) is unauthorized.

It should now be clear that the set of all possible matrices can be partitioned into two disjoint sets: the set of all authorized states and the set of all unauthorized states. A question around which much theoretical research has revolved is this: "Given an initial authorized state and a set of commands, can it be proven that the system can never reach an unauthorized state?"

In effect, we are asking if the available mechanism (the protection commands) is adequate to enforce some protection policy. As a simple example of a policy, consider the security scheme used by the military. Each object is unclassified, confidential, secret, or top secret. Each domain (and thus each process) also belongs to one of these four security levels. The security policy has two rules:

1. No process may read any object whose level is higher than its own, but it may freely read objects at a lower level or at its own level. A secret process may read confidential objects, but not top secret ones.

2. No process may write information into any object whose level is lower than its own. A secret process may write in a top secret file but not in a confidential one.

In military terms, if we assume that privates operate at confidential level, lieutenants at secret level, and generals at top secret level, then a lieutenant may look at a private's papers, but not at a general's. Similarly, a lieutenant may tell a general anything he knows, but he may not tell a private anything, because privates cannot be trusted.

Given this policy, some initial state of the matrix (including some way of telling which object is at which level), and the set of commands for modifying the matrix, what we would like is a way to prove that the system is secure. Such a proof turns out quite difficult to acquire; many general purpose systems are not theoretically secure. For more information about this subject see Landwehr (1981) and Denning (1982).

5.5.5. Covert Channels

In the previous section we saw how it is possible to make formal models for protection systems. In this section we will see how futile it is to make such models. In particular, we will show that even in a system that has been rigorously proven to be absolutely secure, leaking information between processes that in theory cannot communicate at all is relatively straightforward. These ideas are due to Lampson (1973).

Lampson's model involves three processes, and is primarily applicable to large time-sharing systems. The first process is the client, which wants some work performed by the second one, the server. The client and the server do not entirely trust each other. For example, the server's job is to help clients with filling out their tax forms. The clients are worried that the server will secretly record their financial data, for example, maintaining a secret list of who earns how much, and then selling the list. The server is worried that the clients will try to steal the valuable tax program.

The third process is the collaborator, which is conspiring with the server to indeed steal the client's confidential data. The collaborator and server are typically owned by the same person. These three processes are shown in Fig. 5-28. The object of this exercise is to design a system in which it is impossible for the server to leak to the collaborator the information that it has legitimately received from the client. Lampson called this the **confinement problem**.

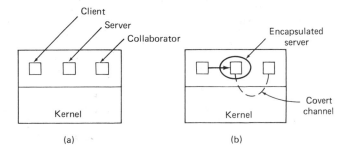

Fig. 5-28. (a) The client, server and collaborator processes. (b) The encapsulated server can still leak to the collaborator via covert channels.

From the system designer's point of view, the goal is to encapsulate or confine the server in such a way that it cannot pass information to the collaborator. Using a protection matrix scheme we can easily guarantee that the server cannot communicate with the collaborator by writing into a file to which the collaborator has read access. We can probably also ensure that the server cannot communicate with the collaborator by using the system's interprocess communication mechanism.

Unfortunately, more subtle communication channels may be available. For example, the server can try to communicate a binary bit stream as follows. To send a 1 bit, it computes as hard as it can for a fixed interval of time. To send a 0 bit, it goes to sleep for the same length of time.

The collaborator can try to detect the bit stream by carefully monitoring its response time. In general, it will get better response when the server is sending a 0 than when the server is sending a 1. This communication channel is known as a **covert channel**, and is illustrated in Fig. 5-28(b).

Of course the covert channel is a noisy channel, containing a lot of extraneous information, but information can be reliably sent over a noisy channel by using an error-correcting code (e.g., a Hamming code, or even something more sophisticated). The use of an error-correcting code reduces the already low bandwidth of the covert channel even more, but it still may be enough to leak substantial information. It is fairly obvious that no protection model based on a matrix of objects and domains is going to prevent this kind of leakage.

Modulating the CPU usage is not the only covert channel. The paging rate can also be modulated (many page faults for a 1, no page faults for a 0). In fact, almost any way of degrading system performance in a clocked way is a candidate. If the system provides a way of locking files, then the server can lock some file to indicate a 1, and unlock it to indicate a 0. It may be possible to detect the status of a lock even on a file that you cannot access.

Acquiring and releasing dedicated resources (tape drives, plotters, etc.) can also be used for signaling. The server acquires the resource to send a 1 and releases it to send a 0. In UNIX, the server could create a file to indicate a 1 and remove it to indicate a 0; the collaborator could use the ACCESS system call to see if the file exists. This call works even though the collaborator has no permission to use the file. Unfortunately, many other covert channels exist.

Lampson also mentions a way of leaking information to the (human) owner of the server process. Presumably the server process will be entitled to tell its owner how much work it did on behalf of the client, so the client can be billed. If the actual computing bill is, say, 100 dollars and the client's income is 53K dollars, the server could report the bill as 100.53 to its owner.

Just finding all the covert channels, let alone blocking them, is extremely difficult. In practice, there is little that can be done about them. Introducing a process that causes page faults at random, or otherwise spends its time degrading system performance in order to reduce the bandwidth of the covert channels is not an attractive proposition.

5.6. OVERVIEW OF THE MINIX FILE SYSTEM

Like all file systems, the MINIX file system must deal with all the issues we have just studied. It must allocate and deallocate space for files, keep track of disk blocks and free space, provide some way to protect files against unauthorized usage, an so on. In the remainder of this chapter we will look closely at MINIX to see how it accomplishes these goals.

In the first part of this chapter, we have repeatedly referred to UNIX rather that to MINIX for the sake of generality, although the external interface of the two is virtually identical. Now we will concentrate on the internal design of MINIX. For information about the UNIX internals, see Thompson (1978) and Bach (1986). The MINIX file system is just a big C program that runs in user space (see Fig. 4-20). To read and write files, user processes send messages to the file system telling what they want done. The file system does the work and then sends back a reply. The file system is, in fact, a network file server that happens to be running on the same machine as the caller.

This design has some important implications. For one thing, the file system can be modified, experimented with, and tested almost completely independently of the rest of MINIX. For another, it is very easy to move the whole file system to any computer that has a C compiler, compile it there, and use it as a free-standing UNIX-like remote file server. The only changes that need to be made are in the area of how messages are sent and received, which differs from system to system.

In the following sections, we will present an overview of many of the key areas of the file system design. Specifically, we will look at messages, the file system layout, i-nodes, the block cache, the bit maps, directories and path names, the process table, and special files (plus pipes). After studying all of these topics, we will show a simple example of how the pieces fit together by tracing what happens when a user process executes the READ system call.

5.6.1. Messages

The file system accepts 29 types of messages requesting work. All but two are for MINIX system calls. The two exceptions are for messages generated by other parts of MINIX. All the messages, their parameters, and results are shown in Fig. 5-29. The file system also gets messages from the memory manager telling about work that the latter has done on behalf of a few other system calls, such as FORK and EXIT. These are not listed in the figure since they are primarily handled by the memory manager.

The structure of the file system is basically the same as that of the memory manager and all the I/O tasks. It has a main loop that waits for a message to arrive. When a message arrives, its type is extracted and used as an index into a table containing pointers to the procedures within the file system that handle all the types. Then the appropriate procedure is called, it does its work and returns

Message type	Input parameters	Reply value
ACCESS	File name, access mode	status
CHDIR	Name of new working directory	status
CHMOD	File name, new mode	status
CHOWN	File name, new owner, new group	status
CHROOT	Name of new root directory	status
CLOSE	File descriptor of file to close	status
CREAT	Name of file to be created, mode	File descriptor
DUP	File descriptor (for DUP2, two of them)	New file descr
FSTAT	Name of file whose status is wanted, buffer	status
IOCTL	File descriptor, function code, argument	status
LINK	Name of file to link to, name of link	status
LSEEK	File descriptor, offset, whence	New position
MKNOD	Name of dir or special file, mode, address	status
MOUNT	Special file, where to mount it, ro-flag	status
OPEN	Name of file to open, read/write flag	File descriptor
PIPE	(none)	File descriptor
READ	File descriptor, buffer, how many bytes	# bytes read
STAT	File name, status buffer	status
STIME	Pointer to current time	status
SYNC	(none)	Always OK
TIME	Pointer to place where current time goes	Real time
TIMES	Pointer to buffer for process and child times	status
UMASK	Complement of mode mask	Always OK
UMOUNT	Name of special file to unmount	status
UNLINK	Name of file to unlink	status
UTIME	File name, file times	Always OK
WRITE	File descriptor, buffer, how many bytes	# bytes written
REVIVE	Process to revive	(no reply)
UNPAUSE	Process to check	(see text)

Fig. 5-29. The principal message types accepted by the file system. File name parameters are always pointers to the name. The code *status* as reply value means OK or ERROR.

a status value. The file system then sends a reply back to the caller and goes back to the top of the loop to wait for the next message.

5.6.2. File System Layout

A MINIX file system is a logical, self-contained entity with i-nodes, directories, and data blocks. It can be stored on any block device, such as a floppy disk or a (portion of a) hard disk. In all cases, the layout of the file system has the same structure. Figure 5-30 shows this layout for a 360K floppy disk with 127 i-nodes and a 1K block size. Larger file systems, or those with more or fewer i-nodes or a different block size, will have the same six components in the same order, but their relative sizes may be different.

Each file system begins with a **boot block**. When the computer is turned on, the hardware reads the boot block into memory and jumps to it. Not every disk drive can be used as a boot device, but to keep the structure uniform, every

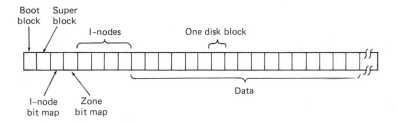

Fig. 5-30. Disk layout for a typical 360K floppy disk, with 127 i-nodes and a 1K block size (i.e., two consecutive 512-byte sectors are treated as a single block).

device has a boot block. Once the system has been booted, the boot block is not used any more.

The **super-block** contains information describing the layout of the file system. It is illustrated in Fig. 5-31.

The main function of the super-block is to tell the file system how big the various pieces of Fig. 5-30 are. Given the block size and the number of i-nodes, it is easy to calculate the size of the i-node bit map and the number of blocks of i-nodes. For example, for a 1K block, each block of the bit map has 1K bytes (8K bits), and thus can keep track of the status of up to 8191 i-nodes (i-node 0 always contains zeros and is effectively unused). For 10,000 i-nodes, two bit map blocks are needed. Since i-nodes are 32 bytes, a 1K block holds up to 32 i-nodes. With 127 usable i-nodes, 4 disk blocks are needed to contain them all.

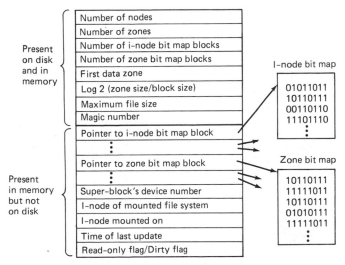

Fig. 5-31. The MINIX super-block.

We will explain the difference between zones and blocks in detail later, but for the time being it is sufficient to say that disk storage can be allocated in units (zones) of 1, 2, 4, 8, or in general 2^n blocks. The zone bit map keeps track of free storage in zones, not blocks. For the standard 360K floppy disk MINIX distribution, the zone and block sizes are the same (1K), so for a first approximation a zone is the same as a block on these devices. Until we come to the details of storage allocation later in the chapter, it is adequate to think "block" whenever you see "zone."

Note that the number of blocks per zone is not stored in the super-block, as it is never needed. All that is needed is the base 2 logarithm of the zone to block ratio, which is used as the shift count to convert zones to blocks and vice versa. For example, with 8 blocks per zone, $\log_2 8 = 3$, so to find the zone containing block 128 we shift 128 right 3 bits to get zone 16. Zone 0 is the boot block, but the zone bit map includes only the data zones.

The information in the super-block is redundant because sometimes it is needed in one form and sometimes in another. With 1K devoted to the super-block, it makes sense to compute this information in all the forms it is needed, rather than having to recompute it frequently during execution. The zone number of the first data zone on the disk, for example, can be calculated from the block size, zone size, number of i-nodes, and number of zones, but it is faster just to keep it in the super-block. The rest of the super-block is wasted anyhow, so using up another word of it costs nothing.

When MINIX is booted, the super-block for the root device is read into a table in memory. Similarly, as other file systems are mounted, their super-blocks are also brought into memory. The super-block table holds a few fields not present on the disk, such as the device from which it came, a field telling whether it has been mounted read-only or not, and a field that is set whenever the memory version is modified.

Before a disk can be used as a MINIX file system, it must be given the structure of Fig. 5-30. The utility program *mkfs* has been provided to build file systems. This program can be called either by a command like

```
mkfs /dev/fd1 360
```

to build an empty 360 block file system on the floppy disk in drive 1, or it can be given a prototype file listing directories and files to include in the new file system. Attempts to mount a file system not in MINIX format, such as an MS-DOS diskette will be rejected by the MOUNT system call, which checks the super-block for the magic number and other things.

5.6.3. Bit Maps

MINIX keeps tracks of which i-nodes and zones are free by using two bit maps (see Fig. 5-31). When the system is booted, the super-block and bit maps for the root device are loaded into memory. As mentioned, the super-block table in memory holds some fields not present on the disk. One of these fields is an array whose k-th entry is a pointer to the k-th i-node bit map block (in memory).

When a file is removed, it is then a simple matter to calculate which block of the bit map contains the bit for the i-node being freed, and to find it via pointer array. Once the block is found, the bit corresponding to the freed i-node is set to 1. A similar set of pointers is used for the zone bit map.

When a file is created, the file system searches through the bit map blocks, one at a time, until it finds a free i-node. This i-node is then allocated for the new file. If every i-node slot on the disk is full, the search routine returns a 0, which is why i-node 0 is not used. (When *mkfs* creates a new file system, it zeros i-node 0 and sets the lowest bit in the bit map to 1, so the file system will never attempt to allocate it.)

With this background, we can now explain the difference between zones and blocks. The idea behind zones is to help ensure that disk blocks that belong to the same file are located on the same cylinder, to improve performance when the file is read sequentially. The approach chosen is to make it possible to allocate several blocks at a time. If, for example, the block size is 1K and the zone size is 4K, the zone bit map keeps track of zones, not blocks. A 20M disk has 5K zones of 4K, hence 5K bits in its zone map.

Most of the file system works with blocks. Disk transfers are always a block at a time, and the buffer cache also works with individual blocks. Only a few parts of the system that keep track of physical disk addresses (e.g., the zone bit map and the i-nodes) know about zones.

Another reason for having zones has to do with the desire to keep disk addresses to 16 bits, primarily to be able to store lots of them in the indirect blocks. However, with a 16-bit zone number and a 1K zone, only 65K zones can be addressed, limiting disks to 65M. As disks get larger, it is easy to switch to 2K or 4K zones, without changing the block size. Most files are smaller than 1K, so increasing the block size means wasting disk bandwidth reading and writing mostly empty blocks, and wastes precious main memory storing them in the buffer cache. Of course, a larger zone size means more wasted disk space, but since large zones are needed only with large disks, the problem of disk space efficiency is not so acute.

Zones also introduce an unexpected problem, best illustrated by a simple example, again with 4K zones and 1K blocks. Suppose a file is of length 1K, meaning that 1 zone has been allocated for it. The blocks between 1K and 4K contain garbage (residue from the previous owner), but no harm is done because the file size is clearly marked in the i-node as 1K. Reads beyond the end of a file always return a count of 0 and no data.

Now someone seeks to address 32768 and writes 1 byte. The file size is now changed to 32769. Subsequent seeks to 1K followed by attempts to read the data will now be able to read the previous contents of the block, which is a serious security breach.

The solution is to check for this situation when a write is done beyond the end of a file, and explicitly zero all the not-yet-allocated blocks in the zone that was previously the last one. Although this situation rarely occurs, the code has to deal with it, making the system slightly more complex. In retrospect, it is not clear whether having zones is worth the extra trouble. In the standard distribution of MINIX the zone size and block size are both set to 1K, so the problem does not arise.

5.6.4. I-nodes

The layout of the MINIX i-node is given in Fig. 5-32. It differs from the UNIX i-node in several ways. First, shorter disk pointers are used (2 bytes vs. 3 bytes). Second, fewer pointers are stored (9 vs. 13). Third, MINIX only records one time, whereas UNIX records three of them. Finally, the *links* and *gid* fields have been reduced to 1 byte in MINIX. These changes reduce the size from 64 bytes to 32 bytes, to reduce the disk and memory space needed to store i-nodes.

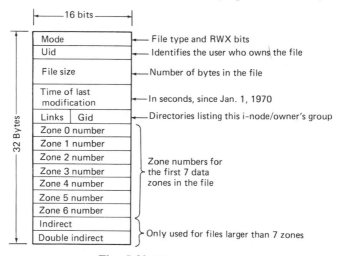

Fig. 5-32. The MINIX i-node.

When a file is opened, its i-node is located and brought into the *inode* table in memory, where it remains until the file is closed. The *inode* table has a few additional fields not present on the disk, such as the i-node's device and number, so the file system knows where to rewrite it if it is modified while in memory. It also has a counter per i-node. If the same file is opened more than once, only one copy of the i-node is kept in memory, but the counter is incremented each time the file is opened and decremented each time it is closed. Only when the counter goes to zero is the i-node removed from the table (and rewritten to the disk, if it has been modified).

The main function of a file's i-node is to tell where the data blocks are. The first seven zone numbers are given right in the i-node itself. For the standard distribution, with zones and blocks both 1K, files up to 7K do not need indirect blocks. Beyond 7K, indirect zones are needed, using the scheme of Fig. 5-7, except that only single and double are present. With 1K blocks and zones and

16-bit zone numbers, a single indirect block holds 512 entries, representing half a megabyte of storage. A double indirect block points to 512 single indirect blocks, giving up to 256 megabytes. (Actually this limit is not reachable, because with 16-bit zone numbers and 1K zones, we can address only 64K zones, which is 64 megabytes; for a larger disk we would have to go to a 2K zone.)

The i-node also holds the mode information, which tells what kind of a file it is (regular, directory, block special, character special, or pipe), and gives the protection and SETUID and SETGID bits. The *link* field in the i-node records how many directory entries point to the i-node, so the file system knows when to release the file's storage. This field should not be confused with the counter (present only in the *inode* table in memory, not on the disk) that tells how many times the file is currently open.

5.6.5. The Block Cache

MINIX uses a block cache to improve its performance. The cache is implemented as an array of buffers, each consisting of a header containing pointers, counters, and flags, and a body with room for one disk block. All the blocks are chained together in a double-linked list, from most recently used (MRU) to least recently used (LRU) as shown in Fig. 5-33.

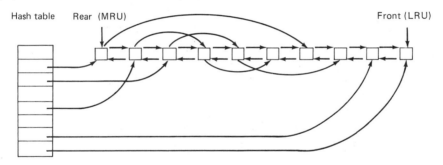

Fig. 5-33. The linked lists used by the block cache.

In addition, to be able to quickly determine if a given block is in the cache or not, a hash table is used. All the blocks that have hash code k are linked together on a single-linked list pointed to by entry k in the hash table. At present, the hash function just extracts the low-order n bits from the block number, so blocks from different devices appear on the same hash chain.

When the file system needs a block, it calls a procedure, *get_block*, which computes the hash code for that block and searches the appropriate list. If the block is found, a counter in the block's header is incremented to show that the block is in use, and a pointer to it is returned. If the block is not found, the LRU list is searched to find a block to evict from the cache. If the block at the front (the least recently used block) has count 0, it is chosen, otherwise the next block is inspected, and so on. It is important to check the counter because some blocks, such as the bit maps, must never be evicted while they are still in use, no matter how infrequently they are used.

Once a block has been chosen for eviction, another flag in its header is checked to see if the block has been modified since being read in. If so, it is rewritten to the disk. At this point the block needed is read in by sending a message to the disk task. The file system is suspended until the block arrives, at which time it continues and a pointer to the block is returned to the caller.

When the procedure that requested the block has done its job, it calls another procedure, *put_block*, to free the block. One of the parameters to *put_block* tells what class of block (e.g., i-nodes, directory, data) is being freed. Depending on the class, two key decisions are made:

1. Whether to put the block on the front or rear of the LRU list.

2. Whether to write the block (if modified) to disk immediately or not.

Blocks that are not likely to be needed again soon, such as double indirect blocks, go on the front of the list so they will be claimed the next time a free buffer is needed. Blocks that are likely to be needed again soon go on the rear of the list in true LRU fashion.

When a directoryto check the counter because some blocks, such ahas been modified, it is written to disk immediately, to reduce has been modified, it is written to disk immediately, to reduce the chance of corrupting the file system in the event of a crash. An ordinary data block that has been modified is not rewritten until either one of two events occurs: (1) it reaches the front of the LRU chain and is evicted, or (2) a SYNC system call is executed.

Note that the header flag indicating that a block has been modified is set by the procedure within the file system that requested and used the block. The procedures *get_block* and *put_block* are concerned just with manipulating all the linked lists. They have no idea which file system procedure wants which block or why.

5.6.6. Directories and Paths

Another important subsystem within the file system is the management of directories and path names. Many system calls, such as OPEN, have a file name as a parameter. What is really needed is the i-node for that file, so it is up to the file system to look up the file in the directory tree and locate its i-node.

A MINIX directory consists of a file containing 16-byte entries. The first 2 bytes form a 16-bit i-node number, and the remaining 14 bytes are the file name. To look up the path /user/ast/mbox the system first looks up user in the root directory, then it looks up ast in /user, and finally it looks up mbox in /user/ast. The actual lookup proceeds one path component at a time, as illustrated in Fig. 5-11.

As an aside, the standard MINIX configuration uses /usr for floppy disk 0 (system files) and /user for floppy disk 1 (user files). Most UNIX systems have the whole file tree under /usr. In the following examples, we will use /user/ast as an example of a typical user directory.

The only complication is what happens when a mounted file system is encountered. To see how that works, we must look at how mounting is done. When the user types the command

```
/etc/mount /dev/fd1 /user
```

on the terminal, the file system contained on floppy disk 1 is mounted on top of /user in the root file system. The file systems before and after mounting are shown in Fig. 5-34.

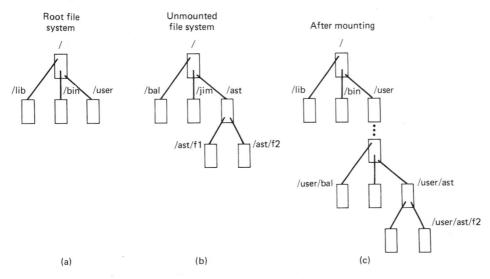

Fig. 5-34. (a) Root file system. (b) An unmounted file system. (c) The result of mounting the file system of (b) on /user.

The key to the whole mount business is a flag set in the i-node of /user after a successful mount. This flag indicates that the i-node is mounted on. The MOUNT call also loads the super-block for the newly mounted file system into the *super_block* table and sets two pointers in it. Furthermore, it puts the root i-node of the mounted file system in the *inode* table.

In Fig. 5-31 we see that super-blocks in memory contain two fields related to mounted file systems. The first of these, the *i-node-of-the-mounted-file-system*, is set to point to the root i-node of the newly mounted file system. The second, the *i-node-mounted-on*, is set to point to the i-node mounted on, in this case, the i-node for /user. These two pointers serve to connect the mounted file system to the root, and, represent the "glue" that holds the mounted file system to the root [shown as the dots in Fig. 5-34(c)].

When a path such as /user/ast/f2 is being looked up, the file system will see a flag in the i-node for /user and realize that it must continue searching at the root i-node of the file system mounted on /user. The question is: "How does it find this root i-node?"

The answer is straightforward. The system searches all the super-blocks in memory until it finds the one whose *i-node mounted on* field points to /user. This must be the super-block for the file system mounted on /user. Once it has the super-block, it is easy to follow the other pointer to find the root i-node for the mounted file system. Now the file system can continue searching. In this example, it looks for *ast* in the root directory of floppy disk 1.

5.6.7. File Descriptors

Once a file has been opened, a file descriptor is returned to the user process for use in subsequent READ and WRITE calls. In this section we will look at how file descriptors are managed within the file system.

Like the kernel and the memory manager, the file system maintains part of the process table within its address space. Three of its fields are of particular interest. The first two are pointers to the i-nodes for the root directory and the working directory. Path searches, such as that of Fig. 5-11, always begin at one or the other, depending on whether the path is absolute or relative. These pointers are changed by the CHROOT and CHDIR system calls to point to the new root or new working directory, respectively.

The third interesting field in the process table is an array indexed by file descriptor number. It is used to locate the proper file when a file descriptor is presented. At first glance, it might seem sufficient to have the k-th entry in this array just point to the i-node for the file belonging to file descriptor k. After all, the i-node is fetched into memory when the file is opened and kept there until it is closed, so it is sure to be available.

Unfortunately, this simple plan fails because files can be shared in subtle ways in MINIX (as well as in UNIX). The trouble arises because associated with each file is a 32-bit number that indicates the next byte to be read or written. It is this number, called the **file position**, that is changed by the LSEEK system call. The problem can be stated easily: "Where should the file pointer be stored?"

The first possibility is to put it in the i-node. Unfortunately, if two or more processes have the same file open at once, they must all have their own file pointers, since it would hardly do to have an LSEEK by one process affect the next read of a different process. Conclusion: the file position cannot go in the i-node.

What about putting it in the process table? Why not have a second array, paralleling the file descriptor array, giving the current position of each file? This idea does not work either, but the reasoning is more subtle. Basically, the trouble comes from the semantics of the FORK system call. When a process forks, both the parent and the child are required to share a single pointer giving the current position of each open file.

To understand the problem better, consider the case of a shell script whose output has been redirected to a file. When the shell forks off the first program, its file position for standard output is 0. This position is then inherited by the child, which writes, say, 1K of output. When the child terminates, the shared file position must now be 1K.

Now the shell reads some more of the shell script and forks off another child. It is essential that the second child inherit a file position of 1K from the shell, so it will begin writing at the place where the first program left off. If the shell did not share the file position with its children, the second program would overwrite the output from the first one, instead of appending to it.

As a result, it is not possible to put the file position in the process table. It really must be shared. The solution used in MINIX is to introduce a new, shared table, *filp*, which contains all the file positions. Its use is illustrated in Fig. 5-35. By having the file position truly shared, the semantics of FORK can be implemented correctly, and shell scripts work properly.

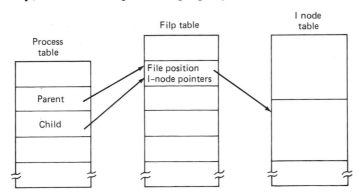

Fig. 5-35. How file positions are shared between a parent and a child.

Although the only thing that the *filp* table really must contain is the shared file position, it is convenient to put the i-node pointer there as well. In this way, all that the file descriptor array in the process table contains is a pointer to a *filp* entry. The *filp* entry also contains a count of the number of processes using it, so the file system can tell when the last process using the entry has terminated, in order to reclaim the slot.

5.6.8. Pipes and Special Files

Pipes and special files differ from ordinary files in an important way. When a process tries to read or write from a disk file, it is certain that the operation will complete within a few hundred milliseconds at most. In the worst case, two or three disk accesses might be needed. When reading from a pipe, the situation is different: if the pipe is empty, the reader will have to wait until some other process puts data in the pipe, which might take hours. Similarly, when reading from a terminal, a process will have to wait until somebody types something.

As a consequence, the file system's normal rule of handling a request until it is finished does not work. It is necessary to suspend these requests and restart them later. When a process tries to read or write from a pipe, the file system can check the state of the pipe immediately to see if the operation can be completed. If it can be, it is, but if it cannot be, the file system records the parameters of the system call in the process table, so it can restart the process when the time comes.

Note that the file system need not take any action to have the caller suspended. All it has to do is refrain from sending a reply, leaving the caller blocked waiting for the reply. Thus, after suspending a process, the file system goes back to its main loop to wait for the next system call. As soon as another process modifies the pipe's state so that the suspended process can complete, the file system sets a flag so that next time through the main loop it extracts the suspended process' parameters from the process table and executes the call.

The situation with terminals and other character special files is slightly different. The i-node for each special file contains two numbers, the major device and the minor device. The major device number indicates the device class (e.g., RAM disk, floppy disk, hard disk, terminal). It is used as an index into a file system table that maps it onto the number of the corresponding task (i.e., I/O driver). In effect, the major device determines which I/O driver to call. The minor device number is passed to the driver as a parameter. It specifies which device is to be used, for example, terminal 2 or drive 1.

When a process reads from a special file, the file system extracts the major and minor device numbers from the file's i-node, and uses the major device number as an index in a file system table to map it onto the corresponding task number. Once it has the task number, the file system sends the task a message, including as parameters the minor device, the operation to be performed, the caller's process number and buffer address, and the number of bytes to be transferred. The format is the same as in Fig. 3-15, except that *POSITION* is not used.

If the driver is able to carry out the work immediately (e.g., a line of input has already been typed on the terminal), it copies the data from its own internal buffers to the user and sends the file system a reply message saying that the work is done. The file system then sends a reply message to the user, and the call is finished. Note that the driver does not copy the data to the file system. Data from block devices go through the block cache, but data from character special files do not.

On the other hand, if the driver is not able to carry out the work, it records the message parameters in its internal tables, and immediately sends a reply to the file system saying that the call could not be completed. At this point, the file system is in the same situation as having discovered that someone is trying to read from an empty pipe. It records the fact that the process is suspended, and waits for the next message.

When the driver has acquired enough data to complete the call, it transfers it to the buffer of the still-blocked user, and then sends the file system a message reporting what it has done. All the file system has to do is send a reply message to the user to unblock it and report the number of bytes transferred.

5.6.9. An Example: The READ System Call

As we shall see shortly, most of the code of the file system is devoted to carrying out system calls. Therefore, it is appropriate that we conclude this overview with a brief sketch of how the most important call, READ, works.

When a user program executes the statement

```
n = read(fd, buffer, nbytes);
```

to read an ordinary file, the library procedure *read* is called with three parameters. It builds a message containing these parameters, along with the code for READ as the message type, sends the message to the file system, and blocks waiting for the reply. When the message arrives, the file system uses the message type as an index into its tables to call the procedure that handles reading.

This procedure extracts the file descriptor from the message, and uses it to locate the *filp* entry and then the i-node for the file to be read (see Fig. 5-35). The request is then broken up into pieces such that each piece fits within a block. For example, if the current file position is 600 and 1K bytes have been requested, the request is split into two parts, for 600 to 1023, and for 1024 to 1623 (assuming 1K blocks).

For each of these pieces in turn, a check is made to see if the relevant block is in the cache. If it is not, the file system picks the least recently used buffer not currently in use and claims it, sending a message to the disk task to rewrite it if it is dirty. Then the disk task is asked to fetch the block to be read.

Once the block is in the cache, the file system sends a message to the system task asking it to copy the data to the appropriate place in the user's buffer (i.e., bytes 600 to 1023 to the start of the buffer, and bytes 1024 to 1623 to offset 424 within the buffer). After the copy has been done, the file system sends a reply message to the user specifying how many bytes have been copied.

When the reply comes back to the user, the library function *read* extracts the reply code and returns it as the function value to the caller.

5.7. IMPLEMENTATION OF THE MINIX FILE SYSTEM

The MINIX file system is relatively large (more than 100 pages of C) but quite straightforward. Requests to carry out system calls come in, are carried out, and replies are sent. In the following sections we will go through it a file at a time, pointing out the highlights. The code itself contains many comments to aid the reader.

5.7.1. The Header Files

Like the kernel and memory manager, the file system has some header files that define various data structures and tables. Let us begin our study of the file system with them.

The file *const.h* (line 7500) defines some constants, such as table sizes and flags, that are used throughout the file system. Some of them, such as *NR_BUFS* and *NR_BUF_HASH*, can be changed to tune the system's performance. Others, such as *BOOT_BLOCK* and *SUPER_BLOCK*, do not affect the performance.

The next file, *buf.h* (line 7550), defines the block cache. The array *buf* holds all the buffers, each of which contains a block, *b*, and a header full of pointers, flags, and counters. The data part is declared as a union of 5 types (line 7565) because sometimes it is convenient to refer to the block as a character array, sometimes as a directory, and so on.

The proper way to refer to the data part of buffer 3 as a character array is *buf[3].b.b__data* because *buf[3].b* refers to the union as a whole, from which the *b__data* field is selected. Although this syntax is correct, it is a little cumbersome, so on line 7588 we define a macro *b_data*, which allows us to write *buf[3].b_data* instead. Note that *b__data* (the field of the union) contains two underscores, whereas *b_data* (the macro) contains just one, to distinguish them. Macros for other ways of accessing the block are contained in lines 7588 to 7592.

Another interesting aspect of this file is the use of *EXTERN* for all the arrays and variables. When this file is included in code files, *EXTERN* has the value *extern*, as defined on line 0000. However, in the file *table.c*, it is defined as the null string, to cause storage to be allocated. The rules of C (Kernighan and Ritchie, 1978, p. 206) clearly specify that global variables must be declared as *extern* in all files except one, although some compilers and many programmers do not understand this point. We saw the same issue in the kernel and memory manager.

The macros at the end of the file (lines 7601 to 7610) define different block types. When a block is returned to the buffer cache after use, one of these values is supplied to tell the cache manager whether to put the block on the front or rear of the LRU list, and whether to write it to disk immediately or not.

The file *dev.h* (line 7650) provides the definition of the *dmap* table. The table itself is declared in *table.c* with initial values, so that version cannot be included in several files. This is why *dev.h* is needed. The table provides the mapping between the major device number and the corresponding task.

The file *file.h* (line 7700) contains the intermediate table used to hold the current file position and i-node pointer (see Fig. 5-35). It also tells whether the file was opened for reading, writing, or both, and how many file descriptors are currently pointing to the entry.

The file system's part of the process table is contained in *fproc.h* (line 7750). It holds the mode mask, pointers to the i-nodes for the current root directory and working directory, the file descriptor array, uid, gid, and terminal number. The remaining fields are used to store the parameters of system calls that are suspended part way through, such as reading from an empty pipe. The fields *fp_suspended* and *fp_revived* actually require only single bits, but nearly all compilers generate better code for characters than bit fields.

Next comes the file with the global variables, *glo.h*. The message buffers for the incoming and reply messages are also here, as is the file system's stack. When the file system starts up for the first time after MINIX is booted, a tiny assembly code procedure sets the stack pointer to the top of *fstack*.

Now we come to the i-node table in *inode.h* (line 7850). As we have said several times, when a file is opened, its i-node is read into memory and kept there until the file is closed. These i-nodes are kept in this table. Most of the fields should be self-explanatory at this point. However, *i_seek* deserves some comment. As an optimization, when the file system notices that a file is being read sequentially, it tries to read blocks into the cache even before they are asked for. For randomly accessed files there is no read ahead. When an LSEEK call is made, the field *i_seek* is set to inhibit read ahead.

The file *param.h* (line 7900) is analogous to the file of the same name in the memory manager. It defines names for message fields containing parameters, so the code can refer to, for example, *buffer*, instead of *m.m1_p1*, which selects one of the fields of the message buffer *m*.

In *super.h* (line 7950), we have the declaration of the super-block table. When the system is booted, the super-block for the root device is loaded here. As file systems are mounted, their super-blocks go here as well.

Finally, we come to the type declarations, in *type.h* (line 8000). Two types are defined, the directory entry and the disk i-node.

5.7.2. Table Management

Associated with each of the main tables—blocks, i-nodes, super-blocks, and so forth—is a file that contains procedures that manage the table. These procedures are heavily used by the rest of the file system, and form the principal interface between tables and the file system. For this reason, it is appropriate to begin our study of the file system code with them.

Block Management

The block cache is managed by the procedures in the file *cache.c*. This file contains five procedures, which are listed in Fig. 5-36. The first one, *get_block* (line 8079), is the standard way the file system acquires data blocks. When a file system procedure needs to read a user data block, a directory block, a super-block, or any other kind of block, it calls *get_block*, specifying the device and block number desired.

get—block	Fetch a block for reading or writing
put—block	Return a block previously requested with get—block
alloc—zone	Allocate a new zone (to make a file longer)
free—zone	Release a zone (when a file is removed)
rw—block	Transfer a block between disk and cache
invalidate	Purge all the cache blocks for some device

Fig. 5-36. Procedures used for block management.

When *get_block* is called, it first looks in the block cache to see if the requested block is present. If so, it returns a pointer to it. Otherwise, it has to read the block in. The blocks in the cache are linked together on *NR_BUF_HASH* (32) linked lists. All the blocks on each list have block numbers that end with the same string of 5 bits, that is 00000, 00001, ..., or 11111.

The statement on line 8099 sets *bp* to point to the start of the list on which the requested block would be, if it were in the cache. The loop on line 8101 searches this list to see if the block can be found. If so, the pointer to it is returned to the caller on line 8106.

If the block is not on the list, it is not in the cache, so the least recently used block that is not currently in use is taken. Bit maps and similar blocks that are still in use are never chosen for eviction. The buffer chosen is removed from its hash chain, since it is about to acquire a new block number and hence belongs on a different hash chain. If it is dirty, it is rewritten to the disk on line 8139.

As soon as the buffer is available, the new parameters are filled in and the block is read in from the disk, with one exception. If the file system needs a block just to rewrite all of it, it is wasteful to first read the old version in. In this case, the disk read is omitted (line 8149). When the new block has been read in, *get_block* returns to its caller with a pointer to it.

Suppose that the file system needs a directory block temporarily, to look up a file name. It calls *get_block* to acquire the directory block. When it has looked up its file name, it calls *put_block* (line 8157) to return the block to the cache, thus making the buffer available in case it is needed later for a different block.

The procedure *put_block* takes care of putting the newly returned block on the LRU list, and in some cases, rewriting it to the disk. First (lines 8179 to 8189), it removes the block from its current position on the LRU list. Next it puts it on the front or rear of the LRU list, depending on *block_type*, a flag provided by the caller telling what kind of a block it is. Blocks that are not likely to be needed again soon are put on the front, where they will be reused quickly. Blocks that may be needed again soon go on the rear, so they will stay around for a while.

After the block has been repositioned on the LRU list, another check is made (lines 0057 and 8225) to see if the block should be rewritten to disk immediately. I-nodes, directory blocks, and other blocks that are essential for the correct functioning of the file system itself fall into this category and are rewritten on the spot.

As a file grows, from time to time a new zone must be allocated to hold the new data. The procedure *alloc_zone* (line 8235) takes care of allocating new zones. It does this by causing the zone bit map to be searched for a free zone. An attempt is made to find a zone close to zone 0 of the current file, in order to keep the zones of a file together. The mapping between bit number in the bit map and zone number is handled on line 8268, with bit 1 corresponding to the first data zone.

When a file is removed, its zones must be returned to the bit map. *Free_zone* (line 8275) is responsible for returning these zones. All it does is call *free_bit*, passing the zone map and the bit number as parameters. *Free_bit* is also used to return free i-nodes, but then with the i-node map as the first parameter, of course.

Managing the cache requires reading and writing blocks. To provide a simple interface to the disk, the procedure *rw_block* (line 8295) has been provided. It reads or writes a single block. Similar procedures *rw_inode* and *rw_super* exist to read and write i-nodes and super-blocks as well.

The last procedure in the file is *invalidate* (line 8326). It is called when a disk is unmounted, for example, to remove from the cache all the blocks belonging to the file system just unmounted. If this were not done, then when the device were reused (with a different floppy disk), the file system might find the old blocks instead of the new ones.

I-node Management

The block cache is not the only table that needs support procedures. The i-node table does too. Many of the procedures are similar in function to the block management procedures. They are listed in Fig. 5-37.

get_inode	Fetch an i-node into memory
put_inode	Return an i-node that is no longer needed
alloc_inode	Allocate a new i-node (for a new file)
wipe_inode	Clear some fields in an i-node
free_inode	Release an i-node (when a file is removed)
rw_inode	Transfer an i-node between memory and disk
dup_inode	Indicate that someone else is using an i-node

Fig. 5-37. Procedures used for i-node management.

The procedure *get_inode* (line 8379) is analogous to *get_block*. When any part of the file system needs an i-node, it calls *get_inode* to acquire it. *Get_inode* first searches the *inode* table to see if the i-node is already present. If so, it increments the usage counter and returns a pointer to it. This search is contained on lines 0057 to 8406. If the i-node is not present in memory, the i-node is loaded by calling *rw_inode*.

When the procedure that needed the i-node is finished with it, the i-node is returned by calling the procedure *put_inode* (line 8421), which decrements the usage count *i_count*. If the count is then zero, the file is no longer in use, and the i-node can be removed from the table. If it is dirty, it is rewritten to disk.

If the *i_link* field is zero, no directory entry is pointing to the file, so all its zones can be freed. Note that the usage count going to zero and the number of links going to zero are quite different events, with different causes and different consequences.

When a new file is created, an i-node must be allocated for it. This work is done by *alloc_inode* (line 8446). Unlike zones, where an attempt is made to keep the zones of a file close together, any i-node will do.

After the i-node has been acquired, *get_inode* is called to fetch the i-node into the table in memory. Then its fields are initialized, partly in-line (lines 8482 to 8486) and partly using *wipe_inode* (line 8503). This split has been made because *wipe_inode* is also needed elsewhere in the file system to clear certain i-node fields (but not all of them).

When a file is removed, its i-node is freed by calling *free_inode* (line 8525). All that happens here is that the corresponding bit in the i-node bit map is set to 1.

The procedure *rw_inode* (line 8543) is analogous to *rw_block*. Its job is to fetch an i-node from the disk. It does its work by carrying out the following steps:

1. Calculate which block contains the required i-node.

2. Read in the block by calling *get_block*.

3. Extract the i-node and copy it to the *inode* table .

4. Return the block by calling *put_block*.

The procedure *dup_inode* (line 8579) just increments the usage count of the i-node.

Super-block Management

The file *super.c* contains procedures that manage the super-block and the bit maps. There are seven procedures in this file, listed in Fig. 5-38.

Load_bit_maps (line 8631) is called when the root device is loaded, or when a new file system is mounted. It reads in all the bit map blocks, and sets up the super-block to point to them. The arrays *s_imap* and *s_zmap* in the super-block point to the i-node bit map blocks and zone bit map blocks, respectively.

When a file system is unmounted, its bit maps are copied back to disk by *unload_bit_maps* (line 8669).

load_bit_maps	Fetch the bit maps for some file system
unload_bit_maps	Return the bit maps after a file system is unmounted
alloc_bit	Allocate a bit from the zone or i-node map
free_bit	Free a bit in the zone or i-node map
get_super	Search the super-block table for a device
scale_factor	Look up the zone-to-block conversion factor
rw_super	Transfer a super-block between memory and disk

Fig. 5-38. Procedures used to manage the super-block and bit maps.

When an i-node or zone is needed, *alloc_inode* or *alloc_zone* is called, as we have seen above. Both of these call *alloc_bit* (line 8689) to actually search the relevant bit map. The search involves three nested loops, as follows:

1. The outer one loops on all the blocks of a bit map.

2. The middle one loops on all the words of a block.

3. The inner one loops on all the bits of a word.

The middle loop works by seeing if the current word is equal to the one's complement of zero, that is, a complete word full of 1s. If so, it has no free i-nodes or zones, so the next word is tried. When a word with a different value is found, it must have at least one 0 bit in it, so the inner loop is entered to find the free (i.e., 0) bit. If all the blocks have been tried without success, there are no free i-nodes or zones, so the code *NO_BIT* (0) is returned.

Freeing a bit is simpler than allocating one, because no search is needed. *Free_bit* (line 8747) calculates which bit map block contains the bit to free, and sets the proper bit to 1. The block itself is always in memory, and can be found by following the *s_imap* or *s_zmap* pointers in the super-block.

The next procedure *get_super* (line 8771), is used to search the super-block table for a specific device. For example, when a file system is to be mounted, it is necessary to check that it is not already mounted. This check can be performed by asking *get_super* to find the file system's device. If it does not find the device, then the file system is not mounted.

The conversion between block and zone is done by shifting block numbers left or zone numbers right. The amount to shift depends on the number of blocks per zone, which can be different for each file system. The procedure *scale_factor* (line 8810) does the lookup.

Finally, we have *rw_super* (line 8824), which is analogous to *rw_block* and *rw_inode*, as we have mentioned. It is called to read and write super-blocks.

File Descriptor Management

MINIX contains special procedures to manage file descriptors and the *filp* table (see Fig. 5-35). They are contained in the file *filedes.c*. When a file is created or opened, a free file descriptor and a free *filp* slot are needed. The procedure *get_fd* (line 8871) is used to find them. They are not marked as in use, however, because many checks must first be made before it is known for sure that the CREAT or OPEN will succeed.

Get_filp (line 8916) is used to see if a file descriptor is in range, and if so, returns its *filp* pointer.

The last procedure in this file is *find_filp* (line 8930). It is needed to find out when a process is writing on a broken pipe (i.e., a pipe not open for reading by any other process). It locates potential readers by a brute force search of the *filp* table.

5.7.3. The Main Program

The main loop of the file system is contained in file *main.c*, starting at line 8992. Structurally, it is very similar to the main loop of the memory manager and the I/O tasks. The call to *get_work* waits for the next request message to arrive (unless a process previously suspended on a pipe or terminal can now be handled). It also sets a global variable, *who*, to the caller's process table slot number and another global variable, *fs_call*, to the number of the system call to be carried out.

Once back in the main loop, three flags are set: *fp* points to the caller's process table slot, *super_user* tells whether the caller is the super-user or not, and *dont_reply* is initialized to *FALSE*. Then comes the main attraction—the call to the procedure that carries out the system call. The procedure to call is selected by using *fs_call* as an index into the array of procedure pointers, *call_vector*.

When control comes back to the main loop, if *dont_reply* has been set, the reply is inhibited (e.g., a process has blocked trying to read from an empty pipe). Otherwise a reply is sent. The final statement in the main loop has been designed to detect that a file is being read sequentially, and to load the next block into the cache before it is actually requested, to improve performance.

The procedure *get_work* (line 9016) checks to see if any previously blocked procedures have now been revived. If so, these have priority over new messages. Only if there is no internal work to do does the file system call the kernel to get a message, on line 9042.

After a system call has been completed, successfully or otherwise, a reply is sent back to the caller by *reply* (line 9053). In principle, *send* should never fail, but the kernel returns a status code, so we might as well check it.

Before the file system starts running, it initializes itself by calling *fs_init* (line 9069). This procedure builds the linked lists used by the block cache, deleting any buffers that happen to lie across a 64K boundary (because the IBM PC's DMA chip cannot cross 64K boundaries). It then loads the RAM disk from the boot diskette, initializes the super-block table, and reads in the super-block and root i-node for the root device. If everything appears to be in good shape, the i-node and zone bit maps are loaded. Finally, some tests are made on the constants, to see if they make sense.

When a boot diskette is created, a bit-for-bit copy of the RAM disk image is included on it after the MINIX binary. The procedure *load_ram* copies this image, block by block, to the RAM disk, after first doing some housekeeping (including telling the RAM disk driver where the RAM disk will go and how big it is).

The Dispatch Table

The file *table.c* (line 9300) contains the pointer array used in the main loop for determining which procedure handles which system call number. We saw a similar table inside the memory manager.

Something new, however, is the table *dmap* on line 9416. This table has one row for each major device, starting at zero. When a device is opened, closed, read, or written, it is this table that provides the name of the procedure to call to handle the operation. All of these procedures are located in the file system's address space. Many of these procedures do nothing, but some call a task to actually request I/O. The task number corresponding to each major device is also provided by the table.

Whenever a new major device is added to MINIX, a line must be appended to this table telling what action, if any, is to be taken when the device is opened, closed, read, or written. As a simple example, if a tape drive is added to MINIX, when its special file is opened, the procedure in the table could check to see if the tape is already in use.

5.7.4. Operations on Individual Files

In this section we will look at the system calls that operate on files (as opposed to, say, directories). We will start with how files are created, opened, and closed, and then see how they are read and written.

Creating, Opening, and Closing Files

The file *open.c* contains the code for five system calls: CREAT, MKNOD, OPEN, CLOSE, and LSEEK. We will examine each of these in turn. Creating a file involves three steps:

1. Allocating and initializing an i-node for the new file.

2. Entering the new file in the proper directory.

3. Setting up and returning a file descriptor for the new file.

The procedure that handles CREAT is *do_creat* (line 9479). As in the memory manager, the convention is used in the file system that system call XXX is performed by procedure *do_xxx*.

Do_creat starts out by fetching the name of the new file, and making sure that free file descriptor and *filp* table slots are available. The new i-node is actually created by the procedure *new_node*, which is called on line 9496. If the i-node cannot be created, *new_node* sets the global variable *err_code*.

The specific actions carried out by *do_creat* depend on whether the file already exists. If the file does not exist, lines 9504 to 9521 are skipped, the table slots claimed, and the file descriptor returned.

If the file does exist, then the file system must test to see what kind of a file it is, what its mode is, and so on. Doing a CREAT on an ordinary file causes it to be truncated to length zero; doing it on a special file that is writable causes it to be opened for writing; doing it on a directory is always rejected.

The code of *do_creat*, as well as many other file system procedures, contains a substantial amount of code that checks for various errors and illegal combinations. While not glamorous, this code is essential to having an error-free, robust file system. If everything is in order, the file descriptor and *filp* slot located at the beginning are now marked as allocated and the file descriptor is returned. They were not marked as allocated in the beginning in order to make it easier to exit part way through if that had been needed.

The MKNOD call is handled by *do_mknod* (line 9541). This procedure is similar to *do_creat*, except that it justs creates the i-node and makes a directory entry for it. If the i-node already exists, the call terminates with an error. The case-by-case analysis we saw in *do_creat* is not needed here.

The allocation of the i-node and the entering of the path name into the file system are done by *new_node* (line 9557). The statement on line 9575 parses the path name (i.e., looks it up component by component) as far as the final directory; the call to *advance* three lines later tries to see if the final component can be opened.

For example, on the call

```
fd = creat(
```

last_dir tries to load the i-node for */user/ast* into the tables and return a pointer to it. If the file does not exist, we will need this i-node shortly in order to add *foobar* to the directory. All the other system calls that add or delete files also use *last_dir* to first open the final directory in the path.

If *new_node* discovers that the file does not exist, it calls *alloc_inode* on line 9581 to allocate and load a new i-node, returning a pointer to it. If no free i-nodes are left, *new_node* fails, and returns *NIL_INODE*.

If an i-node can be allocated, we continue at line 9591, filling in some of the fields, writing it back to the disk, and entering the file name in the final directory (on line 9596). Again we see that the file system must constantly check for errors, and upon encountering one, carefully release all the resources, such as i-nodes and blocks that it is holding. If we were prepared to just let MINIX panic when we ran out of, say, i-nodes, rather than undoing all the effects of the current call, and returning an error code to the caller, the file system would be appreciably simpler.

The next procedure is *do_open* (line 9622). After making a variety of checks, it calls *eat_path* to parse the file name and fetch the i-node into memory. Once the i-node is available, the mode can be checked to see if the file may be opened. The call to *forbidden* on line 9645 does the *rwx* bit checking. Directories and special files are handled afterward. Finally, the file descriptor is returned as the function value.

Closing a file is even easier than opening one. The work is done by *do_close* (line 9680). Pipes and special files need some attention, but for regular files, all that needs to be done is to decrement the *filp* counter and check to see if it is zero, in which case the i-node is returned with *put_inode*.

Note that returning an i-node means that its counter in the *inode* table is decremented, so it can be removed from the table eventually. This operation has nothing to do with freeing the i-node (i.e., setting a bit in the bit map saying that it is available). The i-node is only freed when the file has been removed from all directories.

The final procedure in this file is *do_lseek* (line 9721). When a seek is done, this procedure is called to set the file position to a new value.

Reading a File

Once a file has been opened, it can be read or written. First we will discuss reading, then writing. They differ in a number of ways, but have enough similarities that both *do_read* (line 9784) and *do_write* (line 10125) call a common procedure *read_write* (line 9794), to do most of the work.

The code on lines 9811 to 9818 is used by the memory manager to have the file system load entire segments in user space for it. Normal calls are processed starting on line 9821, where some validity checks are made (e.g., reading on a file opened only for writing) and some variables are initialized. Reads from character special files do not go through the block cache, so they are filtered out on line 9836.

The tests on lines 9844 to 9854 apply only to writes, and have to do with files that may get bigger than the device can hold, or writes that will create a hole in the file by writing *beyond* the end-of-file. As we discussed in the MINIX overview, the presence of multiple blocks per zone causes problems that must be dealt with explicitly. Pipes are also special and are checked for.

The heart of the read mechanism, at least for ordinary files, is the loop starting on line 9861. This loop breaks the request up into chunks, each of which fits in a single disk block. A chunk begins at the current position and extends until one of the following conditions is met:

1. All the bytes have been read.

2. A block boundary is encountered.

3. The end-of-file is hit.

These rules mean that a chunk never requires two disk blocks to satisfy it. Figure 5-39 shows three examples of how the chunk size is determined. The actual calculation is done on lines 9862 to 9871.

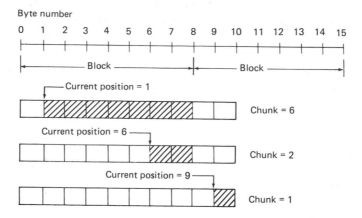

Fig. 5-39. Three examples of how the first chunk size is determined for a 10-byte file. The block size is 8 bytes, and the number of bytes requested is 6. The chunk is shown shaded.

The actual reading of the chunk is done by *rw_chunk* (line 9874). When control comes back, various counters and pointers are incremented, and the next iteration begins. When the loop terminates, the file position and other variables may be updated (e.g., pipe pointers).

Finally, if read ahead is called for, the i-node to read from and the position to read from are stored in global variables, so that after the reply message is sent to the user, the file system can start working on getting the next block. In many cases the file system will block, waiting for the next disk block, during which time the user process will be able to work on the data it already has.

The procedure *rw_chunk* (line 9919) is concerned with taking an i-node and a file position, converting them into a physical disk block number, and requesting the transfer of that block (or a portion of it) to the user space. The mapping of the relative file position to the physical disk address is done by *read_map*, which understands about i-nodes and indirect blocks. For an ordinary file, the variables *b* and *dev* on lines 9944 and 9945 contain the physical block number and device number, respectively. The call to *get_block* on line 9964 is where the cache handler is asked to find the block, reading it in if need be.

Once we have a pointer to the block, the call to *rw_user* on line 9972 takes care of transferring the required portion of it to the user space. The block is then released by *put_block*, so that it can be evicted from the cache later, when the time comes. (After being acquired by *get_block*, the counter in the block's header will show that it is in use, so it will be exempt from eviction; *put_block* decrements the counter.)

Read_map (line 9984) converts a logical file position to the physical block number by inspecting the i-node. For blocks close enough to the beginning of the file that they fall within one of the first seven zones (the ones right in the i-node), a simple calculation is sufficient to determine which zone is needed, and then which block. For blocks further into the file, one or more indirect blocks may have to be read.

The procedure *rw_user* (line 10042) just formats a message for the system task and sends it. The actual copying is done by the kernel. The file system could hardly do the copying; it does not even know where the user is located in memory. This extra overhead is the price that must be paid for the highly modular design.

Finally, *read_ahead* (line 10082) converts the logical position to a physical block number, calls *get_block* to make sure the block is in the cache, and then returns the block immediately. It cannot do anything with the block, after all. It just wants to improve the chance that the block is around if it should be used soon.

Note that *read_ahead* is called only from the main loop in *main*. It is not called as part of the processing of the READ system call. It is important to realize that the call to *readahead* is performed *after* the reply is sent, so that the user will be able to continue running even if the file system has to wait for a disk block while reading ahead. Figure 5-40 shows the relations between some of the major procedures involved in reading a file.

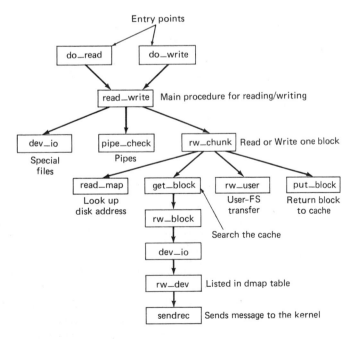

Fig. 5-40. Some of the procedures involved in reading a file.

Writing a File

Writing a file is similar to reading one, except that writing requires allocating new disk blocks. One difference is *write_map* (line 10135), which is analogous to *read_map*, only instead of looking up physical block numbers in the i-node and its indirect blocks, it enters new ones there (to be precise, it enters zone numbers, not block numbers).

The code of *write_map* is somewhat long and detailed because it must deal with several cases. If the zone to be inserted is close to the beginning of the file, it is just inserted into the i-node on (line 10160).

The worst case is when the file is at the maximum size that can be handled by a single-indirect block, so a double-indirect block must be allocated. Next, a single-indirect block must be allocated and its address put into the double-indirect block. If the double-indirect block is successfully allocated, but the single-indirect block cannot be allocated (i.e., disk full), then the double one must be carefully released so as not to corrupt the bit map.

Again, if we could just toss in the sponge and panic at this point, the code would be much simpler. However, from the user's point of view it is much nicer that running out of disk space just returns an error from WRITE, rather than crashing the computer with a corrupted file system.

The next procedure in *write.c* is *clear_zone*, which takes care of the problem of erasing blocks that are suddenly in the middle of a file, when a seek is done beyond the end of file, followed by a write of some data. Fortunately, this situation does not occur very often.

New_block (line 10265) is called by *rw_chunk* on line 9955 whenever a new block is needed. Figure 5-41 shows six successive stages of the growth of a sequential file. The block size is 1K and the zone size is 2K in this example.

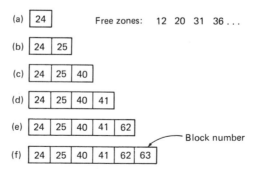

Fig. 5-41. (a) - (f) The successive allocation of 1K blocks. The zone size is 2K.

The first time *new_block* is called, it allocates zone 12 (blocks 24 and 25). The next time it uses block 25, which has already been allocated but is not yet in use. On the third call, zone 20 (blocks 40 and 41) is allocated, and so on. *Zero_block* (line 10318) clears a block, erasing its previous contents.

Pipes

Pipes are similar to ordinary files in many respects. In this section we will focus on the differences. First of all, they are created differently, by the PIPE call, rather than the CREAT call. The PIPE call is handled by *do_pipe* (line 10384) in file *pipe.c*. All *do_pipe* really does is allocate an i-node for the pipe, and return two file descriptors for it.

Reading and writing a pipe is slightly different from reading and writing a file, because a pipe has a finite capacity. An attempt to write to a pipe that is already full will cause the writer to be suspended. Similarly, reading from an empty pipe will suspend the reader. In effect, a pipe has two pointers, the current position (used by readers) and the size (used by writers), to determine where data comes from or goes to.

The various checks to see if an operation on a pipe is possible are carried out by *pipe_check* (line 10433). In addition to the above tests, which may lead to the caller being suspended, *pipe_check* calls *release* to see if a process previously suspended due to no data or too much data can now be revived. These revivals are done on line 10457 and line 10478, for sleeping writers and readers, respectively. Writing on a broken pipe (no readers) is also detected here.

The act of suspending a process is done by *suspend* (line 10488). All it does is save the parameters of the call in the process table, and set the flag *dont_reply* to *TRUE*, to inhibit the file system's reply message.

The procedure *release* (line 10510) is called to check to see if a process that was suspended on a pipe can now be allowed to continue. If it finds one, it calls *revive* to set a flag so that the main loop will notice it later.

The last procedure in *pipe.c* is *do_unpause* (line 10572). When the memory manager is trying to signal a process, it must find out if that process is hanging on a pipe or special file (in which case it must be awakened with an *EINTR* error). Since the memory manager knows nothing about pipes or special files, it sends a message to the file system to ask. That message is processed by *do_unpause*, which revives the process, if it is blocked.

5.7.5. Directories and Paths

We have now finished looking at how files are read and written. Our next task is to see how path names and directories are handled.

Converting a Path to an I-node

Many system calls (e.g., OPEN, UNLINK, and MOUNT) have path names (i.e., file names) as a parameter. Most of these calls must fetch the i-node for the named file before they can start working on the call itself. How a path name is converted to an i-node is a subject we will now look at in detail. We already saw the general outline in Fig. 5-11.

The parsing of path names is done in the file *path.c*. The first procedure, *eat_path* (line 10675), accepts a pointer to a path name, parses it, arranges for its i-node to be loaded into memory, and returns a pointer to the i-node. It does its work by calling *last_dir* to get the i-node to the final directory, and then calling *advance* to get the final component of the path. If the search fails, for example, because one of the directories along the path does not exist, or exists but is protected against being searched, *NIL_INODE* is returned instead of a pointer to the i-node.

Pathnames may be absolute or relative, and may have arbitrarily many components, separated by slashes. These issues are dealt with by *last_dir* (line 10703). It begins (line 10722) by examining the first character of the path name to see if it is an absolute path or a relative one. For absolute paths, *rip* is set to point to the root i-node; for relative ones, it is set to point to the i-node for the current working directory.

At this point, *last_dir* has the path name and a pointer to the i-node of the directory to look up the first component in. It enters a loop on line 10726 now, parsing the path name, component by component. When it gets to the end, it returns a pointer to the final directory.

Get_name (line 10749) is a utility procedure that extracts components from strings. More interesting is *advance* (line 10792), which takes as parameters a directory pointer and a string, and looks up the string in the directory. If it finds the string, *advance* returns a pointer to its i-node. The details of transferring across mounted file systems are handled here.

Although *advance* controls the string lookup, the actual comparison of the string against the directory entries is done in *search_dir*, which is the only place in the file system where directory files are actually examined. It contains two nested loops, one to loop over the blocks in a directory, and one to loop over the entries in a block. The procedure *search_dir* is also used to enter and delete names from directories. Figure 5-42 gives the relations between some of the major procedures used in looking up path names.

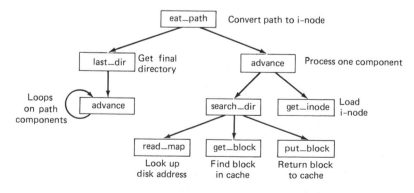

Fig. 5-42. Some of the procedures used in looking up path names.

Mounting File Systems

Two system calls that affect the file system as a whole are MOUNT and UMOUNT. They allow independent file systems on different minor devices to be "glued" together to form a single naming tree. Mounting, as we saw in Fig. 5-31, is effectively achieved by reading in the root i-node and super-block of the file system to be mounted, and setting two pointers in its super-block. One of them points to the i-node mounted on, and the other points to the root i-node of the mounted file system.

The setting of these pointers is done in the file *mount.c* by *do_mount* on lines 11116 and 11117. The two pages of code that precede setting the pointers are almost entirely concerned with checking for all the errors that can occur while mounting a file system, among them:

1. The special file given is not a block device.

2. The special file is a block device, but is already mounted.

3. The file system to be mounted has a rotten magic number.

4. The file system to be mounted is invalid (e.g., no i-nodes).

5. The file to be mounted on does not exist or is a special file.

6. There is no room for the mounted file system's bit maps.

7. There is no room for the mounted file system's super-block.

8. There is no room for the mounted file system's root i-node.

Perhaps it seems inappropriate to keep harping on this point, but the reality of any practical operating system is that a substantial fraction of the code is devoted to doing minor chores that are not intellectually very exciting, but are crucial to making a system usable. If a user attempts to mount the wrong floppy disk by accident, say, once a month, and this leads to a crash and a corrupted file system, the user will perceive the system as being unreliable and blame the designer, not himself.

Thomas Edison once made a remark that is relevant here. He said that "genius" is one percent inspiration and 99 percent perspiration. The difference between a good system and a mediocre one is not the brilliance of the former's scheduling algorithm, but its attention to getting all the details right.

Unmounting a file system is easier than mounting one—there are fewer things that can go wrong. The only real issue is making sure that no process has any open files or working directories on the file system to be removed. This check is straightforward: just scan the whole i-node table to see if any i-nodes in memory belong to the file system to be removed (other than the root i-node). If so, the UMOUNT call fails.

The last procedure in *mount.c* is *name_to_dev* (line 11180), which takes a special file, gets its i-node, and extracts its major and minor device numbers. These are stored in the i-node itself, in the place where the first zone would normally go. This slot is available because special files do not have zones.

Linking and Unlinking Files

The next file is *link.c*, which deals with linking and unlinking files. The procedure *do_link* (line 11275) is very much like *do_mount* in that nearly all of the code is concerned with error checking. Some of the possible errors that can occur in the call

```
link(file_name, link_name);
```

are

1. *File_name* does not exist or cannot be accessed.

2. *File_name* already has the maximum number of links.

3. *File_name* is a directory (only super-user can link to it).

4. *Link_name* already exists.

5. *File_name* and *link_name* are on different devices.

If no errors are present, a new directory entry is made with the string *link_name* and the i-node number of *file_name*. The actual entry is made by *searchdir*, called from *do_link* on line 11324.

Files are removed by unlinking them. The work is done by *do_unlink* (line 11342). Again, a variety of checks are made first. If no errors are found, the directory entry is cleared and the link count in the i-node is reduced by one.

If the link count is now zero, all the zones are freed by *truncate* (line 11388). This procedure works by simply stepping through the i-node a zone at a time, freeing all the zones it finds.

5.7.6. Other System Calls

The last group of system calls is a mixed bag of things involving status, directories, protection, time, and other services.

Changing Directories and File Status

The file *stadir.c* contains the code for four system calls: CHDIR, CHROOT, STAT, and FSTAT. In *last_dir*, on line 10722, we saw how path searches start out by looking at the first character of the path, to see if it is a slash or not. Depending on the result, a pointer is then set to the working directory or the root directory.

Changing from one working directory (or root directory) to another is just a matter of changing these two pointers within the caller's process table. These changes are made by *do_chdir* (line 11475) and *do_chroot* (line 11500). Both of them do the necessary checking, and then call *change* (line 11515) to open the new directory to replace the old one.

The code on lines 11483 to 11490 is not executed on CHDIR calls made by user processes. It is specifically for calls made by the memory manager, to change to a user's directory for the purpose of handling EXEC calls. When a user tries to execute a file, say, *a.out* in his working directory, it is easier for the memory manager to change to that directory than to try to figure out where it is.

The remaining two system calls handled in this file, STAT and FSTAT, are basically the same, except for how the file is specified. The former gives a path name, whereas the latter provides the file descriptor of an open file. The top-level procedures, *do_stat* and *do_fstat*, both call *stat_inode* to do the work. Before calling *stat_inode*, *do_stat* opens the file to get its i-node. In this way, both *do_stat* and *do_fstat* pass an i-node pointer to *stat_inode*.

All *stat_inode* does is extract information from the i-node and copy it into a buffer. The buffer must be explicitly copied to user space by *rw_user* on line 11624 because it is too large to fit in a message.

Protection

The MINIX protection mechanism uses the *rwx* bits. Three sets of bits are present for each file: for the owner, for his group, and for others. The bits are set by the CHMOD system call, which is carried out by *do_chmod* (line 11677). After making a series of validity checks, the mode is changed on line 11704.

The CHOWN system call is similar to CHMOD in that both of them change an internal i-node field in some file. The implementation is also similar although *do_chown* (line 11715) is available only to the super-user.

The UMASK system call allows the user to set a mask (stored in the process table), which then masks out bits in subsequent CREAT system calls. The complete implementation would be only one statement, line 11752, except that the call must return the old mask value as its result. This additional burden triples the number of lines of code required (lines 11751 to 11753).

The ACCESS system call makes it possible for a process to find out if it can access a file in a specified way (e.g., for reading). It is implemented by *do_access* (line 11760), which fetches the file's i-node and calls the internal procedure, *forbidden* (line 11782), to see if the access is forbidden. *Forbidden* checks the uid and gid, as well as the information in the i-node. Depending on what it finds, it selects one of the three *rwx* groups and checks to see if the access is permitted or forbidden.

Read_only line 11782(is a little internal procedure that tells whether the file system on which its i-node parameter is located is mounted read-only or read-write. It is needed to prevent writes on file systems mounted read-only.

Time

MINIX has several system calls that involve time: UTIME, TIME, STIME, and TIMES. They are summarized in Fig. 5-43. They are handled by the file system for no good reason. They just had to go somewhere.

UTIME	Set a file's "time of last modification"
TIME	Get the current real time in seconds
STIME	Set the real time clock
TIMES	Get the process accounting times

Fig. 5-43. The four system calls involving time.

Associated with each file is a 32-bit number that records the time when the file was last modified. This time is kept in the i-node. With the UTIME system call, this time can be set by the owner of the file or the super-user. The procedure *do_utime* (line 11877) performs the system call by fetching the i-node and storing the user-specified time in it.

The real time is not maintained by the file system. It is maintained by the clock task within the kernel. Consequently, the only way to get or set the real time is to send a message to the clock task. This is, in fact, what *do_time* and *do_stime* both do. The real time is in seconds, since Jan 1, 1970.

The accounting information is also maintained by the kernel. At each clock tick it charges one tick to some process. This information can be retrieved by sending a message to the system task, which is what *do_tims* (line 11937) does. The procedure is not named *do_times* because most C compilers add an underscore to the front of all external symbols, and most linkers truncate symbols to eight characters, thus making *do_time* indistinguishable from *do_times*.

Leftovers

The file *misc.c* contains procedures for a few system calls that do not fit in anywhere else. The DUP system call duplicates a file descriptor. In other words, it creates a new file descriptor that points to the same file as its argument.

The call has a variant that is slightly different. It is invoked by the call

dup2(fd, fd2);

in which *fd* is a file descriptor referring to an open file, and *fd2* is an integer that has no file assigned to it yet. The call makes *fd2* a valid file descriptor for the same file as *fd*.

The two system calls share the same message type. They are distinguished by the 0100 bit, which is set in *fd* for DUP2. Both versions of the call are handled by *do_dup* (line 11981). The work to be done is straightforward, consisting of manipulating file descriptors and *filp* entries.

The next system call is SYNC, which copies all blocks, i-nodes, and super-blocks that have been modified since being loaded back to the disk. The call is processed by *do_sync* (line 12018). It simply searches through all the tables looking for dirty entries.

The system calls FORK, EXIT, and SET are really memory manager calls, but the results have to be posted here as well. When a process forks, it is essential that the kernel, memory manager, and file system all know about it. These "system calls" do not come from user processes, but from the memory manager. Their job consists of recording the relevant information.

The last nonsystem call is handled by *do_revive* (line 12149). It is called when a task that was previously unable to complete work that the file system had requested, such as providing input data for a user process, has now completed the work. The file system now revives the process and sends it the reply message.

5.7.7. The I/O Device Interface

I/O in MINIX is done by sending messages to the tasks within the kernel. The file system's interface with these tasks is contained in the file *device.c*, which also contains procedures that do special things for special files. As a starter, when a special file is opened, the procedure *dev_open* (line 12233) is called, just in case some special processing is needed. This procedure extracts the major and minor device numbers for the special file, and uses the major device number as an index into the *dmap* table in file *table.c* to call a procedure within the file system for special processing (line 12240). Normally this entry is *no_call*, which does nothing, but other procedures can be entered into *dmap* as needed.

Closing a device is similar, with the work being done by *dev_close* (line 12248) in this case.

When actual device I/O is needed, *dev_io* (line 12261) is called. It builds a standard message (see Fig. 3-15) and sends it to the specified task. It is called from *read_write* to handle character special files, and from *rw_block* for block special files. While *dev_io* is waiting for a reply from the task, the file system waits. It has no internal multiprogramming. Usually these waits are quite short though (a few hundred milliseconds at worst).

One system call is handled in *device.c*, IOCTL. That call has been put here because it is closely tied to the task interface. When an IOCTL is done, *do_ioctl* is called to build a message and send it to the proper task.

Find_dev (line 12328) is a little helper procedure that extracts the major and minor device numbers from a full device number. The final three procedures in *device.c* are not mentioned explicitly in the file system. All three are procedures that are called indirectly, via *dmap*. Reads and writes use either *rw_dev* or *rw_dev2* (see Fig. 5-41 for the call hierarchy). When a null routine is needed, *no_call* is used.

5.7.8. General Utilities

The file system contains a few general purpose utility procedures that are used in various places. They are collected together in the file *utility.c*. The first procedure is *clock_time*. It sends messages to the clock task to find out what the current real time is. The next one is *cmp_string*. It compares two strings to see if they are the same. Then comes *copy*. It copies a block of data from one part of the file system's address space to another.

The procedure *fetch_name* is needed because many system calls have a file name as parameter. If the file name is short, it is included in the message from the user to the file system. If it is long, a pointer to the name in user space is put in the message. *Fetch_name* checks for both cases, and either way, gets the name.

No_sys is the error handler that is called when the file system receives a system call that is not one of its calls. Finally, *panic* prints a message and tells the kernel to throw in the towel when something catastrophic happens.

The last file is *putc.c*. It contains two procedures, both of which have to do with printing messages. The standard library procedures cannot be used, because they send messages to the file system. These procedures send messages directly to the terminal task.

5.8. SUMMARY

When seen from the outside, a file system is a collection of files and directories, plus operations on them. Files can be read and written, directories can be created and destroyed, and files can be moved from directory to directory. Most modern file systems support a hierarchical directory system, in which directories may have subdirectories *ad infinitum*.

When seen from the inside, a file system looks quite different. The file system designers have to be concerned with how storage is allocated, and how the system keeps track of which block goes with which file. We have also seen how different systems have different directory structures. File system reliability and performance are also important issues.

We looked at some of the ways network file servers have been constructed in recent years. Atomic updates and transactions are often key features of these systems.

Security and protection are of vital concern to both the system users and designers. We discussed some security flaws in older systems, and generic problems that many systems have. We also looked at authentication, with and without passwords, access control lists, and capabilities.

Finally, we studied the MINIX file system in detail. It is large, but not very complicated. It accepts requests for work from user processes, indexes into a table of procedure pointers, and calls that procedure to carry out the requested system call. Due to its modular structure and position outside the kernel, it can be removed from MINIX and used as a free-standing network file server with only minor modifications.

PROBLEMS

1. An operating system only supports a single directory, but allows that directory to have arbitrarily many files with arbitrarily long file names. Can something approximating a hierarchical file system be simulated? How?

2. Give 5 different path names for the file /etc/passwd. (Hint: think about the directory entries "." and "..".)

3. Free disk space can be kept track of using a free list or a bit map. Disk addresses require D bits. For a disk with B blocks, F of which are free, state the condition under which the free list uses less space than the bit map. For D having the value 16 bits, express your answer as a percentage of the disk space that must be free.

4. An MS-DOS computer uses a FAT to keep track of disk blocks. Compare its performance to UNIX with respect to doing random seeks on long files, if

   (a) The FAT is always on disk.
   (b) The FAT is always in memory.

5. How many disk references are needed to open the path games/zapper in UNIX?

6. The link count in the UNIX i-node is redundant. All it does it tell how many directory entries point to the i-node, something that can equally well be seen by looking at the directories. Why is this field used?

7. A UNIX file system uses 1024-byte blocks and 16-bit disk addresses. The i-node holds 8 disk addresses for data blocks, one single-indirect block address, and one double-indirect block address. What is the maximum file size? Think carefully.

8. In UNIX, files can be shared by having two directories point to the same i-node. MS-DOS does not have i-nodes. Could files be linked in two directories at the same time in MS-DOS? If so, how could it be implemented?

9. A file system checker has built up its counters as shown in Fig. 5-15. They are:

   In use: 1 0 1 0 0 1 0 1 1 0 1 0 0 1 0
   Free: 0 0 0 1 1 1 0 0 0 1 0 1 1 0 1
   Are there any errors? If so, are they serious? Why?

10. It has been suggested that the first part of each UNIX file be kept in the same disk block as its i-node. What good would this do?

11. The performance of a file system depends critically upon the cache hit rate (fraction of blocks found in the cache). If it takes 1 msec to satisfy a request from the cache, but 40 msec to satisfy a request if a disk read is needed, give a formula for the mean time required to satisfy a request if the hit rate is h. Plot this function for values of h from 0 to 1.0.

12. A floppy disk has 40 cylinders. A seek takes 6 msec per cylinder moved. If no attempt is made to put the blocks of a file close to each other, two blocks that are logically consecutive (i.e., follow one another in the file) will be about 13 cylinders apart, on the average. If, however, the operating system makes an attempt to cluster related blocks, the mean interblock distance can be reduced to 2 cylinders (for example). How long does it take to read a 100 block file in both cases, if the rotational latency is 100 msec and the transfer time is 25 msec per block?

13. Would compacting disk storage periodically be of any conceivable value? Why or why not?

14. A UNIX program creates a file and immediately seeks to byte 20 million. It then writes one byte. How many disk blocks does the file now occupy (including indirect blocks).

15. For a file system offering remote disk service, state whether each of the following is done in the client machine or the server machine.

    (a) Checking file permissions to see if the user may access the file.
    (b) Handling seek errors on the disk.
    (c) Looking up path names.

16. How could TENEX be modified not to have the password problem described in the text?

17. After getting your degree, you apply for a job as director of a large university computer center that has just put its ancient operating system out to pasture and switched over to UNIX. You get the job. Fifteen minutes after starting work, your assistant bursts into your office screaming: "Some students have discovered the algorithm we use for encrypting passwords and posted it on the bulletin board." What should you do?

18. The MOUNT system call in UNIX is restricted to the super-user. Why?

19. The Morris-Thompson protection scheme with the n-bit random numbers was designed to make it difficult for an intruder to discover a large number of passwords by encrypting common strings in advance. Does the scheme also offer protection against a student user who is trying to guess the super-user password on his machine?

20. A computer science department has a large collection of UNIX machines on its local network. Users on any machine can issue a command of the form

    `machine4 who`

    and have it executed on *machine4*, without having the user login on the remote machine. This feature is implemented by having the user's kernel send the command and his uid to the remote machine. Is this scheme secure if the kernels are all trustworthy (e.g., large time-shared minicomputers with protection hardware)? What if some of the machines are students' personal computers, with no protection hardware?

21. When a file is removed, its blocks are generally put back on the free list, but they are not erased. Do you think it would be a good idea to have the operating system

erase each block before releasing it? Consider both security and performance factors in your answer, and explain the effect of each.

22. Three different protection mechanisms that we have discussed are capabilities, access control lists, and the UNIX *rwx* bits. For each of the following protection problems, tell which of these mechanisms can be used.

    (a) Rick wants his files readable by everyone except Jennifer.
    (b) Helen and Anna want to share some secret files.
    (c) Cathy wants some of her files to be public.

    For UNIX, assume that groups are categories such as faculty, students, secretaries, and so on.

23. Consider the following protection mechanism. Each object and each process is assigned a number. A process can only access an object if the object has a higher number than the process. Which of the scheme discussed in the text does this resemble? In what essential way does it differ from the scheme in the text?

24. Can the Trojan Horse attack work in a system protected by capabilities?

25. Two computer science students, Carolyn and Elinor, are having a discussion about i-nodes in MINIX, Carolyn maintains that memories have gotten so large and so cheap that when a file is opened, it is simpler and faster just to fetch a new copy of the i-node into the i-node table, rather than search the entire table to see if it is already there. Elinor disagrees. Who is right?

26. Is it possible for an i-node in memory to have *i_count* equal to 1 but *i_link* equal to 0? How?

27. A MINIX file system for a 360K floppy disk has 360 1K disk blocks. It also has 63 i-nodes. How many blocks are available for directories and data?

28. If the i-node bit map in MINIX is completely garbled by a crash, is there any way to recover the contents of the file system, or is it lost forever? Explain.

29. Now repeat the previous problem, only this time assume it is the zone map that has been garbled.

30. Opening and reading a block special file is implemented almost the same way as opening and reading an ordinary file. Describe the differences between the two.

31. Why does the block cache use the hash table? Could it function without this table?

32. Find as many security flaws as you can in MINIX. Caution: do not try this exercise at your local computer center. They do not have much of a sense of humor there.

33. Write a printer spooling daemon for MINIX.

34. Implement named pipes in MINIX. A named pipe can be implemented as a special file with major device number 255. When one process opens it to read and another process opens it to write, it behaves the same way as a pipe created by the PIPE system call.

35. MINIX does not have any way to lock files. Implement a new system call, LOCK, that takes a file descriptor and locks the corresponding file. If the file is already

locked, the system call fails. Users can open locked files, but they cannot lock them again until they have been unlocked. Also implement an UNLOCK system call.

36. Implement symbolic links in MINIX. You may limit the path length to something that conveniently fits in an i-node. There is a spare bit in the mode (01000 bit) that can be used to indicate that a file is a symbolic link. Add a new system call to allow symbolic links to be made.

37. Implement a system of disk space quotas by having a file /etc/quota tell how much space each user is entitled to have, and how much the user currently has. Every time a zone is allocated on behalf of a user, update the current usage and check to see if the user is over quota. Users who are over quota do not get any more space. Make the design efficient.

6

READING LIST AND BIBLIOGRAPHY

In the previous five chapters we have touched upon a variety of topics. This chapter is intended as an aid to readers interested in pursuing their study of operating systems further. Section 6.1 is a list of suggested readings. Section 6.2 is an alphabetical bibliography of all books and articles cited in this book.

In addition to the references given below, the *Proceedings of the n-th ACM Symposium on Operating Systems Principles* (ACM) held every other year and the *Proceedings of the n-th International Conference on Distributed Computing Systems* (IEEE) held every year are good places to look for recent papers on operating systems. Furthermore, *ACM Transactions on Computer Systems* and *Operating Systems Review* are two journals that often have interesting articles on operating systems. Brumfield (1986) has published a useful guide to the operating systems literature. Useful bibliographies have been assembled by Metzner (1982), Newton (1979), Smith (1978, 1981), and Zobel (1983).

6.1. SUGGESTIONS FOR FURTHER READING

6.1.1. Introduction and General Works

Bach, *The Design of the UNIX Operating System*
  A detailed description of the internal structure and algorithms used by System

5.2. It covers the kernel, the buffer cache, files, processes, and memory management, among other topics.

Blair et al., "A Critique of UNIX"

A discussion of areas in which UNIX is weak, including file management, process creation, process scheduling, and resource management. A useful antidote to the numerous papers and books that describe UNIX as the greatest invention since sliced bread.

Brooks, *The Mythical Man-Month: Essays on Software Engineering*

A witty, amusing, and informative book on how *not* to write an operating system by someone who learned the hard way. Full of good advice.

Comer, *Operating System Design. The Xinu Approach*

A book about the Xinu operating system, which runs on the LSI-11 computer. It contains a detailed exposition of the code, including a complete listing in C.

Deitel, *An Introduction to Operating Systems*

The first part of this book contains standard material, but the last five chapters contain detailed case studies of UNIX, VMS, CP/M, MVS, and VM/370.

Finkel, *An Operating Systems Vade Mecum*

A general text on operating systems. It is practically-oriented, up-to-date, well-written and covers many of the topics treated in this book, making it a good place to look for a different perspective on the same subject.

Holt, *Concurrent Euclid, The UNIX System, and TUNIS*

TUNIS, like MINIX, is a rewrite of UNIX. This book describes the TUNIS system, but does not contain the source code. TUNIS is written not in C, but in Concurrent Euclid, and much of the book is devoted to explaining the various features of this language.

Lampson, "Hints for Computer System Design"

Butler Lampson, one of the world's leading designers of innovative operating systems, has collected many hints, suggestions, and guidelines from his years of experience and put them together in this entertaining and informative article. Like Brooks' book, this is required reading for every aspiring system designer.

Peterson and Silberschatz, *Operating System Concepts. 2nd Ed.*

Another text on operating systems. It covers many of the same topics as this book, and is a good general reference.

Quarterman et al., "4.2 BSD and 4.3 BSD as Examples of the UNIX System"
A survey of the structure, internal organization and algorithms used by Berkeley UNIX including processes, scheduling, paging, I/O, communications and networking.

Ritchie and Thompson, "The UNIX Time-Sharing System"
This is the original paper on UNIX by its designers. All the key ideas are here. It is as well worth reading now as when it was first published.

Tanenbaum and van Renesse, "Distributed Operating Systems"
A survey article about distributed operating systems. It focuses on those aspects of distributed operating systems that differ from single-processor systems, and thus complements the material in this book. Four existing distributed systems are examined in detail.

6.1.2. Processes

Andrews and Schneider, "Concepts and Notations for Concurrent Progr."
A tutorial and survey of processes and interprocess communication, including busy waiting, semaphores, monitors, message passing, and other techniques. The article also shows how these concepts are embedded in various programming languages.

Ben-Ari, *Principles of Concurrent Programming*
This little book is entirely devoted to the problems of interprocess communication. There are chapters on mutual exclusion, semaphores, monitors, and the dining philosophers problem, among others.

Birrell and Nelson, "Implementing Remote Procedure Calls"
Remote procedure calls are commonly used in distributed systems for interprocess communication. This paper describes the implementation of a particularly elegant remote procedure call system developed at Xerox PARC.

Kerridge and Simpson, "Communicating Parallel Processes"
A discussion of what is wrong with the standard interprocess communication primitives, and a proposal for a new language in which parallelism can be more easily expressed.

Lampson and Redell, "Experience with Processes and Monitors in Mesa"
When monitors are used in real systems, problems arise that do not come up in textbook examples. This paper describes some of these problems and their solutions.

Peterson and Silberschatz, *Operating Systems Concepts. 2nd Ed.*
Chapters 9 and 10 are devoted to processes and interprocess communication, including semaphores, monitors, and other techniques.

6.1.3. Input/Output

Calingaert, *Operating Systems Elements*
Chapter 5 on device management discusses such issues as: allocation, buffering, blocking and error recovery.

Coffman et al., "System Deadlocks"
A short introduction to deadlocks, what causes them, and how they can be prevented or detected.

Finkel, *An Operating Systems Vade Mecum*
Chapter 5 discusses I/O hardware and device drivers, particularly for terminals and disks.

Grosshans, *File Systems Design and Implementation*
Chapters 2-8 cover a variety of design issues for I/O systems, primarily for disks and magnetic tapes.

Holt, "Some Deadlock Properties of Computer Systems"
A discussion of deadlocks. Holt introduces a directed graph model that can be used to analyze some deadlock situations.

IEEE, *Computer Magazine*, July 1985
This special issue on mass storage has five papers on advanced disk systems, including optical disks.

Isloor and Marsland, "The Deadlock Problem: An Overview"
A tutorial on deadlocks, with special emphasis on data base systems. A variety of models and algorithms are covered.

Pike et al., "Hardware/Software Tradeoffs for Bitmap Graphics on the Blit"
A description of how the Blit terminal works. The authors argue that special hardware assistance for bitmap graphics is not necessary. Everything should be done in software.

6.1.4. Memory Management

Denning, "Virtual Memory"
A classic paper on many aspects of virtual memory. Denning was one of the pioneers in this field, and was the inventor of the working set concept.

Denning, "Working Sets Past and Present"
A good overview of numerous memory management and paging algorithms. A comprehensive bibliography is included.

Doran, "Virtual Memory"
A tutorial on virtual memory, covering both concepts and implementation. The Burroughs B6700 and GE 645 are used as examples.

Knuth, *The Art of Computer Programming*
First fit, best fit, buddy systems, and other memory management algorithms are discussed and compared in this book.

Peterson and Silberschatz, *Operating System Concepts. 2nd Ed.*
Chapters 5 and 6 deal with memory management, including swapping, paging, and segmentation. A variety of paging algorithms are mentioned.

6.1.5. File Systems

Anyanwu and Marshall, "A Crash Resistant UNIX File System"
A description of how the concept of stable storage can be integrated into an operating system. The conceptual background, implementation, and performance of the resulting system are discussed.

Denning, *Cryptography and Data Security*
A thorough treatment of the problems of protection, cryptography, and security in operating systems and data base systems. Many models and algorithms are discussed.

Denning and Denning, "Data Security"
A survey of security and protection issues, ranging from capabilities and cryptography at one end, to information flows and inference controls at the other.

Grampp and Morris, "UNIX Operating System Security"
A practical guide to making your UNIX system more secure. It covers passwords, file system security, the SETUID bit, Trojan horses, networking, encryption, and people problems.

Grosshans, *File Systems Design and Implementation*
The latter part of this book deals with file system design and access methods. It is oriented towards the kinds of file systems found on large mainframes, which are quite different from the ones covered in this book.

IEEE, *Proc. of the 1986 IEEE Symposium on Security and Privacy*
A collection of 24 papers on various aspects of security and privacy, including models as well as policies and applications such as operating systems, networks, cryptography, and data bases.

Kochan and Wood, *UNIX System Security*
An entire book telling how to run a secure UNIX shop. It deals with user security, system security, and network security.

McKusick et al., "A Fast File System for UNIX"
The UNIX file system was completely reimplemented for 4.2 BSD. This paper describes the design of the new file system, with emphasis on performance aspects.

Lampson, "Atomic Transactions"
A good introduction to the concept of atomic transactions, showing how they can be built up from simple primitives.

Linden, "Oper. System Structures to Support Security and Reliable Software"
A survey of protection mechanisms, with an emphasis on domains, capabilities, and typed objects.

Popek and Walker, *The LOCUS Distributed Systems Architecture*
Chapter 3 describes the operation of the LOCUS file system, which is physically distributed, replicated, but still compatible with that of UNIX.

Svobodova, "File Servers for Network-Based Distributed Systems"
A survey of file servers used in distributed systems. The emphasis is on file servers that provide atomic actions and transactions.

6.2. ALPHABETICAL BIBLIOGRAPHY

ANDREWS, G.R., and SCHNEIDER, F.B.: "Concepts and Notations for Concurrent Programming," *Computing Surveys*, vol. 15, pp. 3-43, March 1983.

ANYANWU, J.A., and MARSHALL, L.F.: "A Crash Resistant UNIX File System," *Software—Practice and Experience*, vol. 16, pp. 107-118, Feb. 1986.

ATKINSON, R., and HEWITT, C.: "Synchronization and Proof Techniques for Serializers," *IEEE Trans. on Software Eng.*, vol. SE-5, pp. 10-23, Jan. 1979.

BAYS, C.: "A Comparison of Next-Fit, First-Fit, and Best-Fit," *Commun. of the ACM*, vol. 20, pp. 191-192, March 1977.

BECK, L.L.: "A Dynamic Storage Allocation Technique Based on Memory Residence Time," *Commun. of the ACM*, vol. 25, pp. 714-724, Oct. 1982.

BELADY, L.A., NELSON, R.A., and SHEDLER, G.S.: "An Anomaly in Space-Time Characteristics of Certain Programs Running in a Paging Machine," *Commun. of the ACM*, vol. 12, pp. 349-353, June 1969.

BELL TELEPHONE LABORATORIES, INC.: *UNIX Programmer's Manual, Vol. 1.* New York: Holt, Rinehart, and Winston, 1983.

BEN-ARI, M: *Principles of Concurrent Programming*, Englewood Cliffs, N.J.: Prentice-Hall International, 1982.

BENSOUSSAN, A., CLINGEN, C.T., and DALEY, R.C.: "The MULTICS Virtual Memory: Concepts and Design," *Commun. of the ACM*, vol. 15, pp. 308-318, May 1972.

BIRRELL, A.D., and NEEDHAM, R.M.: "A Universal File Server," *IEEE Trans. on Software Eng.*, vol. SE-6, pp. 450-453, Sept. 1980.

BIRRELL, A.D., and NELSON, B.J.: "Implementing Remote Procedure Calls," *ACM Trans. on Computer Systems*, vol. 2, pp. 39-59, Feb. 1984.

BLAIR, G.S., MALONE, J.R., and MARIANI, J.A.: "A Critique of UNIX," *Software— Practice and Experience*, vol. 15, pp. 1125-1139, Dec. 1985.

BOLON, C.: *Mastering C*, Berkeley, CA: Sybex, 1986.

BOURNE, S.R.: *The UNIX System*, Reading, Mass: Addison-Wesley, 1982.

BRINCH HANSEN, P.: "The Programming Language Concurrent Pascal," *IEEE Trans. on Software Eng.*, vol. SE-1, pp. 199-207, June 1975.

BROOKS, F. P., Jr.: *The Mythical Man-Month: Essays on Software Engineering*, Reading, Mass: Addison-Wesley, 1975.

BROWN, P.: *Starting with UNIX*, Reading, Mass.: Addison-Wesley, 1984.

BRUMFIELD, J.A.: "A Guide to Operating Systems Literature," *Operating Systems Review*, vol. 20, pp. 38-42, April 1986.

CADOW, H.: *OS/360 Job Control Language*, Englewood Cliffs, N.J.: Prentice-Hall, 1970.

CALINGAERT, P.: *Operating System Elements*, Englewood Cliffs, N.J.: Prentice-Hall, 1982.

CAMPBELL, R.H., and HABERMANN, A.N.: "The Specification of Process Synchronization by Path Expressions," in *Operating Systems*, Kaiser, C. (ed.), Berlin: Springer-Verlag, 1974.

CHERITON, D.R.: "An Experiment Using Registers for Fast Message-Based Interprocess Communication," *Operating Systems Review*, vol. 18, pp. 12-20, Oct. 1984.

CHRISTIAN, K.: *The UNIX Operating System*, New York: John Wiley, 1983.

COFFMAN, E.G., ELPHICK, M.J., and SHOSHANI, A.: "System Deadlocks," *Computing Surveys*, vol. 3, pp. 67-78, June 1971.

COMER, D.: *Operating System Design. The Xinu Approach*, Englewood Cliffs, N.J.: Prentice-Hall, 1984.

CORBATO, F.J., MERWIN-DAGGETT, M., and DALEY, R.C: "An Experimental Time-Sharing System," *Proc. AFIPS Fall Joint Computer Conf.*, pp. 335-344, 1962.

CORBATO, F.J., SALTZER, J.H., and CLINGEN, C.T.: "MULTICS—The First Seven Years," *Proc. AFIPS Spring Joint Computer Conf.*, pp. 571-583, 1972.

CORBATO, F.J., and VYSSOTSKY, V.A.: "Introduction and Overview of the MULTICS System," *Proc. AFIPS Fall Joint Computer Conf.*, pp. 185-196, 1965.

COURTOIS, P.J., HEYMANS, F., and PARNAS, D.L.: "Concurrent Control with Readers and Writers," *Commun. of the ACM*, vol. 10, pp. 667-668, Oct. 1971.

DALEY, R.C., and NEUMANN, P.G.: "A General Purpose File System for Secondary Storage," *Proc. AFIPS Fall Joint Computer Conf.*, pp. 213-229, 1965.

DEITEL, H.M.: *An Introduction to Operating Systems*, Reading, Mass.: Addison-Wesley, 1983.

DENNING, D: *Cryptography and Data Security*, Reading, Mass: Addison-Wesley, 1982.

DENNING, P.J.: "The Working Set Model for Program Behavior," *Commun. of the ACM*, vol. 11, pp. 323-333, 1968a.

DENNING, P.J.: "Thrashing: Its Causes and Prevention," *Proc. AFIPS National Computer Conf.*, pp. 915-922, 1968b.

DENNING, P.J.: "Virtual Memory," *Computing Surveys*, vol. 2, pp. 153-189, Sept. 1970.

DENNING, P.J.: "Working Sets Past and Present," *IEEE Trans. on Software Eng.*, vol. SE-6, pp. 64-84, Jan. 1980.

DALEY, R.C., and DENNIS, J.B.: "Virtual Memory, Process, and Sharing in MULTICS," *Commun. of the ACM*, vol. 11, pp. 306-312, May 1968.

DALEY, R.C., and NEUMANN, P.G.: "A General Purpose File System for Secondary Storage," *Proc. AFIPS Fall Joint Computer Conf.*, pp. 213-229, 1965.

DENNIS, J.B., and VAN HORN, E.C.: "Programming Semantics for Multiprogrammed Computations," *Commun. of the ACM*, vol. 9, pp. 143-155, March 1966.

DIJKSTRA, E.W.: "Co-operating Sequential Processes," in *Programming Languages*, Genuys, F. (ed.), London: Academic Press, 1965.

DIJKSTRA, E.W.: "The Structure of THE Multiprogramming System," *Commun. of the ACM*, vol. 11, pp. 341-346, May 1968.

DORAN, R.W.: "Virtual Memory" *Computer*, vol. 9, pp. 27-37, Oct. 1976.

FABRY, R.S.: "Capability-Based Addressing," *Commun. of the ACM*, vol. 17, pp. 403-412, July 1974.

FELDMAN, S.I.: "Make—A Computer Program for Maintaining Programs," *Software—Practice and Experience*, vol. 9, pp. 255-266, April 1979.

FINKEL, R.A.: *An Operating Systems Vade Mecum*, Englewood Cliffs, N.J.: Prentice-Hall, 1986.

FOTHERINGHAM, J.: "Dynamic Storage Allocation in the Atlas Computer Including an Automatic Use of a Backing Store," *Commun. of the ACM*, vol. 4, pp. 435-436, Oct. 1961.

FOXLEY, E.: *UNIX for Super-Users*, Reading, Mass.: Addison-Wesley, 1985.

FRIDRICH, M., and OLDER, W.: "The Felix File Server," *Proc. of the Eighth Symposium on Operating Systems Principles*, ACM, pp. 37-46, 1981.

GEHANI, N.: *Advanced C: Food for the Educated Palate*, Rockville, Md.: Computer Science Press, 1985.

GOLDEN, D., and PECHURA, M.: "The Structure of Microcomputer File Systems," *Commun. of the ACM*, vol. 29, pp. 222-230, March 1986.

GRAHAM, R.: "Use of High-Level Languages for System Programming," Project MAC Report TM-13, M.I.T., Sept. 1970.

GRAMPP, F.T., and MORRIS, R.H.: "UNIX Operating System Security," *AT&T Bell Laboratories Technical Journal*, vol. 63, pp. 1649-1672, Oct. 1984.

GROSSHANS, D.: *File Systems Design and Implementation*, Englewood Cliffs, N.J.: Prentice-Hall, 1986.

HANCOCK, L., and KRIEGER, M.: *The C Primer. 2nd Ed.*, New York: McGraw-Hill, 1986.

HARBISON, S., and STEELE, G., Jr.: *C: A Reference Manual*, Englewood Cliffs, N.J.: Prentice-Hall, 1984.

HARRISON, M.A., RUZZO, W.L., and ULLMAN, J.D.: "Protection in Operating Systems," *Commun. of the ACM*, vol. 19, pp. 461-471, Aug. 1976.

HAVENDER, J.W.: "Avoiding Deadlock in Multitasking Systems," *IBM Systems Journal*, vol. 7, pp. 74-84, 1968.

HEBBARD, B. et al.: "A Penetration Analysis of the Michigan Terminal System," *Operating Systems Review*, vol. 14, pp. 7-20, Jan. 1980.

HOARE, C.A.R.: "Monitors, An Operating System Structuring Concept," *Commun. of the ACM*, vol. 17, pp. 549-557, Oct. 1974; Erratum in *Commun. of the ACM*, vol. 18, p. 95, Feb. 1975.

HOLT, R.C: "Some Deadlock Properties of Computer Systems," *Computing Surveys*, vol. 4, pp. 179-196, Sept. 1972.

HOLT, R.C: *Concurrent Euclid, The UNIX System, and TUNIS*, Reading, Mass: Addison-Wesley, 1983.

IEEE: *Proc. of the 1986 IEEE Symposium on Security and Privacy*, IEEE, 1986.

ISLOOR, S.S., and MARSLAND, T.A.: "The Deadlock Problem: An Overview," *Computer*, vol. 13, pp. 58-78, Sept. 1980.

KAUFMAN, A.: "Tailored-List and Recombination-Delaying Buddy Systems," *ACM Trans. on Programming Languages and Systems*, vol. 6, pp. 118-125, Jan. 1984.

KERNIGHAN, B.W., and MASHEY, J.R.: "The UNIX Programming Environment," *IEEE Computer*, vol. 14, pp. 12-24, April 1981.

KERNIGHAN, B.W., and PIKE, R. *The UNIX Programming Environment*, Englewood Cliffs, N.J.: Prentice-Hall, 1984.

KERNIGHAN, B.W., and RITCHIE, D.M.: *The C Programming Language*, Englewood Cliffs, N.J.: Prentice-Hall, 1978.

KERRIDGE, J., and SIMPSON, D.: "Communicating Parallel Processes," *Software— Practice and Experience*, vol. 16, pp. 63-86, Jan. 1986.

KLEINROCK, L.: *Queueing Systems. Vol. 2. Computer Applications*, New York: John Wiley, 1975.

KNOWLTON, K.C.: "A Fast Storage Allocator," *Commun. of the ACM*, vol. 8, pp. 623-625, Oct. 1965.

KNUTH, D.E.: *The Art of Computer Programming, Volume 1: Fundamental Algorithms. 2nd ed.*, Reading, Mass.: Addison-Wesley, 1973.

KOCHAN, S.G., and WOOD, P.H.: *UNIX System Security*, Hasbrouck Heights, N.J.: Hayden, 1985.

LINDEN, T.A.: "Operating System Structures to Support Security and Reliable Software" *Computing Surveys*, vol. 8, pp. 409-445, Dec. 1976.

LAMPSON, B.W.: "A Scheduling Philosophy for Multiprogramming Systems," *Commun. of the ACM*, vol. 11, pp. 347-360, May 1968.

LAMPSON, B.W.: "A Note on the Confinement Problem," *Commun. of the ACM*, vol. 10, pp. 613-615, Oct. 1973.

LAMPSON, B.W.: "Atomic Transactions," in *Distributed Systems—Architecture and Implementation*, Lampson, B.W. (ed.), Springer-Verlag, pp. 246-264, 1981.

LAMPSON, B.W.: "Hints for Computer System Design," *IEEE Software*, vol. 1, pp. 11-28, Jan. 1984.

LAMPSON, B.W., and REDELL, D.D.: "Exprience with Processes and Monitors in Mesa," *Commun. of the ACM*, vol. 23, pp. 105-117, Feb. 1980.

LAMPSON, B.W., and STURGIS, H.E.: "Crash Recovery in a Distributed Data Storage System," Xerox PARC Report, April 1979.

LANDWEHR, C.E.: "Formal Models of Computer Security," *Computing Surveys*, vol. 13, pp. 247-278, Sept. 1981.

LEVIN, R., COHEN, E.S., CORWIN, W.M., POLLACK, F.J., and WULF, W.A.: "Policy/Mechanism Separation in Hydra," *Proc. of the Fifth Symposium on Operating System Principles*, ACM, pp. 132-140, 1975.

LINDE, R.R.: "Operating System Penetration," *Proc. AFIPS National Computer Conf.*, pp. 361-368, 1975.

LOMUTO, A.N., and LOMUTO, N.: *A UNIX Primer*, Englewood Cliffs, N.J.: Prentice-Hall, 1983.

McGILTON, H., and MORGAN, R.: *Introducing the UNIX System*, New York: McGraw-Hill, 1983.

McKUSICK, M.J., JOY, W.N., LEFFLER, S.J., and FABRY, R.S.: "A Fast File System for UNIX," *ACM Trans. on Computer Systems*, vol. 2, pp. 181-197, Aug. 1984.

METZNER, J.R.: "Structuring Operating Systems Literature for the Graduate Course," *Operating Systems Review*, vol. 16, pp. 10-25, Oct. 1982.

MORRIS, R., and THOMPSON, K.: "Password Security: A Case History," *Commun. of the ACM*, vol. 22, pp. 594-597, Nov. 1979.

MULLENDER, S.J., and TANENBAUM, A.S.: "Immediate Files," *Software—Practice and Experience*, vol. 14, pp. 365-368, April 1984.

NEWTON, G.: "Deadlock Prevention, Detection, and Resolution: An Annotated Bibliography," *Operating Systems Review*, vol. 13, pp. 33-44, April 1979.

OLDEHOEFT, R.R., and ALLAN, S.J.: "Adaptive Exact-Fit Storage Management," *Commun. of the ACM*, vol. 28, pp. 506-511, May 1985.

ORGANICK, E.I.: *The Multics System*, Cambridge, Mass: M.I.T. Press, 1972.

PASTERNACK, I.: *Exploring the UNIX Environment*, New York: Bantam Books, 1985.

PETERSON, G.L.: "Myths about the Mutual Exclusion Problem," *Information Processing Letters*, vol. 12, pp. 115-116, June 1981.

PETERSON, J.L., and NORMAN, T.A.: "Buddy Systems," *Commun. of the ACM*, vol. 20, pp. 421-431, June 1977.

PETERSON, J.L., and SILBERSCHATZ, A.: *Operating System Concepts. 2nd Ed.* Reading, Mass.: Addison-Wesley, 1985.

PIKE, R., LOCANTHI, B., and REISER, J.: "Hardware/Software Tradeoffs for Bitmap Graphics on the Blit," *Software—Practice and Experience*, vol. 15, pp. 131-152, Feb. 1985.

POOLE, P.C., and POOLE, N.: *Using UNIX by Example*, Reading, Mass: Addison-Wesley, 1986.

POPEK, G., and WALKER, B.: *The LOCUS Distributed System Architecture*, Cambridge, Mass.: MIT Press, 1985.

POPEK, G., WALKER, B., CHOW, J., EDWARDS, D., KLINE, C., RUDISIN, G., and THIEL, G.: "LOCUS A Network Transparent, High Reliability Distributed System," *Proc. Eighth Symp. Operating Syst. Prin.*, ACM, pp. 160-168, 1981.

PU, C., NOE, J.D., and PROUDFOOT, A: "Regeneration of Replicated Objects: A Technique and its Eden Implementation," *Proc. Second Int'l Conf. on Data Eng.*, pp. 175-187, Feb 1986.

QUARTERMAN, J.S., SILBERSCHATZ, A., and PETERSON, J.L.: "4.2BSD and 4.3BSD as Examples of the UNIX System," *Computing Surveys*, vol. 17, Dec. 1985.

REED, D.P., and KANODIA, R.K.: "Synchronization with Eventcounts and Sequencers," *Commun. of the ACM*, vol. 23, pp. 115-123, Feb. 1979.

RITCHIE, D.M., and THOMPSON, K.: "The UNIX Time-Sharing System," *Commun. of the ACM*, vol. 17, pp. 365-375, July 1974.

ROCHKIND, M.J.: *Advanced UNIX Programming*, Englewood Cliffs, N.J.: Prentice-Hall, 1985.

SALTZER, J.H.: "Protection and Control of Information Sharing in MULTICS," *Commun. of the ACM*, vol. 17, pp. 388-402, July 1974.

SALTZER, J.H., and SCHROEDER, M.D.: "The Protection of Information in Computer Systems," *Proc. IEEE*, vol. 63, pp. 1278-1308, Sept. 1975.

SCHROEDER, M.D., and SALTZER, J.H.: "A Hardware Architecture for Implementing Protection Rings," *Commun. of the ACM*, vol. 15, pp. 157-170, March 1972.

SEAWRIGHT, L.H., and MACKINNON, R.A.: "VM/370—A Study of Multiplicity and Usefulness," *IBM Systems Journal*, vol. 18, pp. 4-17, 1979.

SMITH, A.J.: "Bibliography on Paging and Related Topics," *Operating Systems Review*, vol. 12, pp. 39-56, Oct. 1978.

SMITH, A.J.: "Bibliography on File and I/O System Optimization and Related Topics," *Operating Systems Review*, vol. 15, pp. 39-54, Oct. 1981.

STEPHENSON, C.J.: "Fast Fits: A New Method for Dynamic Storage Allocation," *Proc. Ninth Symposium on Operating Systems Principles*, ACM, pp. 30-32, 1983.

SVOBODOVA, L.: "File Servers for Network-Based Distributed Systems," *Computing Surveys*, vol. 16, pp. 353-398, Dec. 1984.

SWINEHART, D., MCDANIEL, G., and BOGGS, D.R.: "WFS: A Simple Shared File System for a Distributed Environment," *Proc. Seventh Symposium on Operating System Principles*, ACM, pp. 9-17, 1979.

TANENBAUM, A.S., MULLENDER, S.J., and VAN RENESSE, R.: "Using Sparse Capabilities in a Distributed Operating System," *Proc. Sixth Int'l Conf. on Distributed Computer Systems*, IEEE, pp. 558-563, 1986.

TANENBAUM, A.S., and VAN RENESSE, R.: "Distributed Operating Systems," *Computing Surveys*, vol. 17, Dec. 1985.

TANENBAUM, A.S., VAN STAVEREN, H., KEIZER, E.G., and STEVENSON, J.W.: "A Practical Tool Kit for Making Portable Compilers," *Commun. of the ACM*, vol. 26, pp. 654-660, Sept. 1983.

TEORY, T.J.: "Properties of Disk Scheduling Policies in Multiprogrammed Computer Systems," *Proc. AFIPS Fall Joint Computer Conf.*, pp. 1-11, 1972.

THOMPSON, K.: "Unix Implementation," *Bell System Technical Journal*, vol. 57, pp. 1931-1946, July-Aug. 1978.

WALKER, A.N.: *The UNIX Environment*, New York: John Wiley, 1984.

WALKER, B., POPEK, G., ENGLISH, R., KLINE, C., and THIEL, G.: "The LOCUS Distributed Operating System," *Proc. Ninth Symp. Operating Syst. Prin.*, ACM, pp. 49-70, 1983.

WEINSTEIN, M.J., PAGE, T.W., Jr., LIVESEY, B.K., and POPEK, G.J.: "Transactions and Synchronization in a Distributed Operating System," *Proc. Tenth Symp. Oper. Syst. Prin.*, pp. 115-125, Dec. 1985.

WULF, W.A., COHEN, E.S., CORWIN, W.M., JONES, A.K., LEVIN, R., PIERSON, C., and POLLACK, F.J.: "HYDRA: The Kernel of a Multiprocessor Operating System," *Commun. of the ACM*, vol. 17, pp. 337-345, June 1974.

ZOBEL, D.: "The Deadlock Problem: A Classifying Bibliography," *Operating Systems Review*, vol. 17, pp. 6-16, Oct. 1983.

A

INTRODUCTION TO C

C was invented by Dennis Ritchie of AT&T Bell Laboratories to provide a high-level language in which UNIX could be programmed. It is now widely used for many other applications as well. C is especially popular with systems programmers because it allows programs to be expressed simply and concisely. The definitive work describing C is *The C Programming Language* by Kernighan and Ritchie (1978). Bolon (1986), Gehani (1984), Hancock and Krieger (1986), Harbison and Steele (1984), and numerous others have also written books about C.

In this appendix we will attempt to provide enough of an introduction to C that someone who is familiar with high-level languages such as Pascal, PL/I, or Modula 2 will be able to understand most of the MINIX code given in this book. Features of C not used in MINIX are not discussed here. Numerous subtle points are omitted. The emphasis is on reading C, not writing it.

A.1. FUNDAMENTALS OF C

A C program is made up of a collection of procedures (often called functions, even when they do not return values). These procedures contain declarations, statements, and other elements that together tell the computer to do something. Figure A-1 shows a little procedure that declares three integer variables and assigns them all values. The procedure's name is *main*. It has no formal parameters, as indicated by the absence of any identifiers between the parentheses. Its body is enclosed between braces (curly brackets). This example shows that C has variables, and that these variables must be declared before being used. C also has statements, in this example, assignment statements. All statements must be terminated by semicolons (unlike Pascal, which uses semicolons between statements, not after them). Comments are started by the /* symbol and ended by the */ symbol, and may extend over multiple lines.

```
main()                          /* this is a comment */
{
  int i, j, k;                  /* declaration of 3 integer variables */

  i = 10;                       /* set i to 10 (decimal) */
  j = i + 015;                  /* set j to i + 15 (octal) */
  k = j * j + 0xFF;             /* set k to j * j + 0xFF (hexadecimal) */
}
```

Fig. A-1. An example of a procedure in C.

The procedure contains three constants. The constant 10 in the first assignment is an ordinary decimal constant. The constant 015 is an octal constant (equal to 13 decimal). Octal constants always begin with a leading zero. The constant 0xFF is a hexadecimal constant (equal to 255 decimal). Hexadecimal constants always begin with 0x. All three radices are commonly used in C.

A.2. BASIC DATA TYPES

C has two principal data types: integer and character, written int and char, respectively. There is no Boolean data type. Instead, integers are used, with 0 meaning false and everything else meaning true. C also has floating point types, but MINIX does not use them.

The type int may be qualified with the "adjectives" short, long, or unsigned, which determine the (compiler dependent) range of values. Most 8088 compilers use 16-bit integers for int and short int and 32-bit integers for long int. Unsigned integers on the 8088 range from 0 to 65535, rather than −32768 to +32767 as ordinary integers do. Characters are 8 bits.

The qualifier register is also allowed for both int and char and is a hint to the compiler that the variable being declared might be worth putting in a register instead of in memory, to make the program run faster. Some declarations are shown in Fig. A-2.

Conversion between types is allowed. For example, the statement

```
flag_pole = i;
```

is allowed even though *i* is an integer and *flag_pole* is a long. In many cases when converting between types it is necessary or useful to force one type to

```
int i;                    /* one integer */
short int z1, z2;         /* two short integers */
char c;                   /* one character */
unsigned short int k;     /* one unsigned short integer */
long flag_pole;           /* the 'int' may be omitted */
register int r;           /* a register variable */
```

Fig. A-2. Some declarations.

another. This can be done by putting the target type in parentheses in front of the expression to be converted, as in

```
p( (long) i);
```

to convert the integer *i* to a long before passing it as a parameter to a procedure *p*, which expects a long.

One thing to watch out for when converting between types is **sign extension**. When converting a character to an integer, some compilers treat characters as being signed, that is, from -128 to $+127$, whereas others treat them as being unsigned, that is, from 0 to 255. In MINIX one frequently sees statements like

```
i = c & 0377
```

which converts *c* (a character) to an integer and then performs a Boolean AND (the ampersand) with the octal constant 0377. The result is that the upper 8 bits are set to zero, effectively forcing *c* to be treated as an unsigned 8-bit quantity, in the range 0 to 255.

A.3. CONSTRUCTED TYPES

In this section we will look at four ways of building up more complex data types: arrays, structures, unions, and pointers. An **array** is a collection of items of the same type. All arrays in C start with element 0. The declaration

```
int a[10];
```

declares an array, *a*, with 10 integers, referred to as *a*[0] through *a*[9] . Two, three, and higher dimensional arrays exist, but they are not used in MINIX.

A **structure** is a collection of variables, usually of different types. A structure in C is similar to a record in Pascal. The declaration

```
struct {int i; char c;} s;
```

declares *s* to be a structure containing two **members**, an integer *i*, and a character *c*. To assign the member *i* the value 6, one would write

```
s.i = 6;
```

where the dot operator indicates that a member is being selected from a structure.

A **union** is also a collection of members, except that at any one moment, it can only hold one of them. The declaration

```
union {int i; char c;} u;
```

means that *u* can either hold an integer or a character, but not both. The compiler must allocate enough space for a union to hold the largest member. Unions are only used in two places in MINIX (for the definition of a message as a union of several different structures, and for the definition of a disk block as a union of a data block, an i-node block, a directory block, etc.).

Pointers are used to hold machine addresses in C. They are very heavily used. An asterisk is used to indicate a pointer in declarations. The declaration

```
int i, *pi, a[10], *b[10], **ppi;
```

declares an integer *i*, a pointer to an integer *pi*, an array with 10 elements *a*, an array of 10 pointers to integers *b*, and a pointer to a pointer to an integer *ppi*. The exact syntax rules for complex declarations combining arrays, pointers, and other types is somewhat complex. Fortunately, MINIX only uses simple declarations.

Figure A-3 shows a declaration of an array *z*, of structures, each of which has three members, an integer *i,* a pointer to a character, *cp*, and a character, *c*. Arrays of structures are common in MINIX. The name *table* is defined as the type of the structure, allowing struct table to be used in declarations to mean this structure. For example,

```
register struct table *p;
```

declares *p* to be a pointer to a structure of type *table*, and suggests that it be kept in a register. During program execution, *p* might point, for example, to *z*[4] or to any of the other elements of *z*, all 20 of which are structures of type *table*.

```
struct table {          /* each structure is of type table */
  int i;                /* an integer */
  char *cp, c;          /* a pointer to a character and a character */
} z[20];                /* this is an array of 20 structures */
```

Fig. A-3. An array of structures.

To make *p* point to *z*[4] , we would write

```
p = &z[4];
```

where the ampersand as a unary (monadic) operator means "take the address of what follows." To copy to the integer variable *n* the value of the member *i* of the structure pointed to by *p* we would write

```
n = p->i;
```

Note that the arrow is used to access a member of a structure via a pointer. If we were to use z itself, we would use the dot operator:

```
n = z[4].i;
```

The difference is that $z[4]$ is a structure, and the dot operator selects members from structures. With pointers, we are not selecting a member directly. The pointer must first be followed to find the structure; only then can a member be selected.

It is sometimes convenient to give a name to a constructed type. For example,

```
typedef unsigned short int unshort;
```

defines *unshort* as an unsigned short integer. It can be used as though it were a basic type. For example,

```
unshort u1, *u2, u3[5];
```

declares an unsigned short integer, a pointer to an unsigned short integer, and an array of unsigned short integers.

A.4. STATEMENTS

Procedures in C contain declarations and statements. We have already seen the declarations, so now we will look at the statements. The assignment, if, and while statements are essentially the same as in other languages. Figure A-4 shows some examples of them. The only points worth making are that braces are used for grouping compound statements, and the while statement has two forms, the second of which is similar to Pascal's **repeat** statement.

C also has a for statement, but this is unlike the for statement in any other language. It has the general form

```
for (initializer; condition; expression) statement;
```

The meaning of the statement is

```
initializer;
while (condition) {
      statement;
      expression;
}
```

As an example, consider the statement

```
for (i = 0; i < n; i = i + 1) a[i] = 0;
```

```
if (x < 0) k = 3;              /* a simple if statement */

if (x > y) {                   /* a compound if statement */
     j = 2;
     k = j + 1;
}

if (x + 2 < y) {               /* an if-else statement */
     j = 2;
     k = j - 1;
} else {
     m = 0;
}

while (n > 0) {                /* a while statement */
     k = k + k;
     n = n - 1;
}

do {                           /* another kind of while statement */
     k = k + k;
     n = n - 1;
} while ( n > 0);
```

Fig. A-4. Some if and while statements in C.

This statement sets the first *n* elements of *a* to zero. It starts out by initializing *i* to zero (outside the loop). Then it iterates as long as $i < n$, executing the assignment and incrementing *i*. The statement can, of course, be a compound statement enclosed by braces, rather than just a simple assignment, as is shown here.

C has a construction that is similar to Pascal's **case** statement. It is called a switch statement. Figure A-5 shows an example. Depending on the value of the expression following the keyword switch, one clause or another is chosen. If the expression does not match any of the cases, the default clause is selected. If the expression does not match any case and no default is present, control just continues with the next statement following the switch.

One thing to note is that after one of the cases has been executed, control just continues with the next one, unless a break statement is present. In practice, the break is virtually always needed.

The break statement is also valid inside for and while loops, and when executed causes control to exit the loop. If the break statement is located in the innermost of a series of nested loops, only one level is exited.

A related statement is the continue statement, which does not exit the loop, but causes the current iteration to be terminated and the next iteration to start immediately. In effect, it is a jump back to the top of the loop.

C has procedures, which may be called with or without parameters.

```
    switch (k) {
        case 10:
            i = 6;
            break;                    /* do not continue with case 20 */

        case 20:
            j = 2;
            k = 4;
            break;

        default:
            j = 5;
    }
```

Fig. A-5. An example of a switch statement.

According to Kernighan and Ritchie (p. 121) it is not permitted to pass arrays, structures, or procedures as parameters, although pointers to all of these are allowed. Book or no book, many C compilers allow structures as parameters.

The name of an array, when written without a subscript, is taken to mean a pointer to the array, making it easy to pass an array pointer. Thus if *a* is the name of an array of any type, it can be passed to a procedure *g* by writing

```
g(a);
```

This rule holds only for arrays, not structures.

Procedures can return values by executing the return statement. This statement may provide an expression to be returned as the value of the procedure, but the caller may safely ignore it. If a procedure returns a value, the type of the value is written before the procedure name, as shown in Fig. A-6. As with parameters, procedures may not return arrays, structures, or procedures, but may return pointers to them. This rule is designed to make the implementation efficient—all parameters and results always fit in a single machine word. Compilers that allow structures as parameters usually allow them as return values as well.

```
int sum(i, j)                    /* this procedure returns an integer */
int i,j;                         /* formal parameters declared before { */
{
   return(i + j);                /* add the parameters and return the sum */
}
```

Fig. A-6. An example of a simple procedure that returns a value.

C does not have any built-in input/output statements. I/O is done by calling library procedures, the most common of which is illustrated below:

```
printf("x = %d   y = %o   z = %x\n", x , y, z);
```

The first parameter is a string of characters between quotation marks (it is actually a character array). Any character that is not a percent is just printed as is. When a percent is encountered, the next parameter is printed, with the letter following the percent telling how to print it:

d - print as a decimal integer
o - print as an octal integer
u - print as unsigned decimal integer
x - print as a hexadecimal integer
s - print as a string
c - print as a single character

The letters *D*, *O*, and *X* are also allowed, for printing decimal, octal, and hexadecimal longs.

A.5. EXPRESSIONS

Expressions are constructed by combining operands and operators. The arithmetic operators, such as $+$ and $-$, and the relational operators, such as $<$ and $>$ are similar to their counterparts in other languages. The % operator is used for modulo. It is worth noting that the equality operator is $==$ and the not equals operator is $!=$. To see if a and b are equal, one can write

```
if (a == b) statement;
```

C also allows assignments and operators to be combined, so

```
a += 4;
```

means the same as

```
a = a + 4;
```

The other operators may also be combined this way.

Operators are provided for manipulating the bits of a word. Both shifts and bitwise Boolean operations are allowed. The left and right shift operators are $<<$ and $>>$ respectively. The bitwise Boolean operators $\&$, $|$, and $\hat{}$ are AND, INCLUSIVE OR, and EXCLUSIVE OR, respectively. If i has the value 035 (octal), then the expression i & 06 has the value 04 (octal). As another example, if i is 7, then

```
j = (i << 3) | 014;
```

assigns 074 to j.

Another important group of operators is the unary operators, all of which take only one operand. As a unary operator, the ampersand takes the address of a variable. Thus &i has the value of the machine location at which *i* is located. If *p* is a pointer to an integer and *i* is an integer, the statement

```
p = &i;
```

computes the address of *i* and stores it in the variable *p*.

The opposite of taking the address of something (e.g., to put it in a pointer) is taking a pointer as input and computing the value of the thing pointed to. If we have just assigned the address of *i* to *p*, then *p has the same value as *i*. In other words, as a unary operator, the asterisk is followed by a pointer (or an expression yielding a pointer), and yields the value of the item pointed to. If *i* has the value 6, then the statement

```
j = *p;
```

will assign 6 to *j*.

The ! operator returns 0 if its operand is nonzero and 1 if its operator is 0. It is primarily used in if statements, for example

```
if (!x) k = 8;
```

checks the value of *x*. If *x* is zero (false), *k* is assigned the value 8. In effect, the ! operator negates the condition following it, just as the **not** operator does in Pascal.

The operator is the bitwise complement operator. Each 0 in its operand becomes a 1 and each 1 becomes a 0. In fact, this is the one's complement of the operand.

The sizeof operator tells how big its operand is, in bytes. If applied to an array of 20 integers, *a*, on a machine with 2-byte integers, for example, sizeofa will have the value 40. When applied to a structure, it tells how big the structure is.

The last group of operators are the increment and decrement operators. The statement

```
p++;
```

means increment *p*. How much it is incremented by depends on its type. Integers or characters are incremented by 1, but pointers are incremented by the size of the object pointed to. Thus if *a* is an array of structures, and *p* a pointer to one of these structures, and we write

```
p = &a[3];
```

to make *p* point to one of the structures in the array, then after we increment *p* it will point to *a*[4] no matter how big the structures are. The statement

```
p--;
```

is analogous, except that it decrements instead of incrementing.

In the assignment

```
n = k++;
```

where both variables are integers, the original value of *k* is assigned to *n* and then the increment happens. In the assignment

```
n = ++k;
```

first k is incremented, *then* its new value is stored in *n*. Thus the ++ (or --) operator can be written either before or after its operand, with different meanings.

One last operator is the ? operator, which selects one of two alternatives separated by a colon. For example,

```
i = (x < y ? 6 : k + 1);
```

compares *x* to *y*. If *x* is less than *y*, then *i* gets the value 6; otherwise, it gets the value *k* + 1. The parentheses are optional.

A.6. PROGRAM STRUCTURE

A C program consists of one or more files containing procedures and declarations. These files can be separately compiled, yielding separate object files, which are then linked together (by the linker) to form the executable program. Unlike Pascal, procedure declarations may not be nested, so they all appear at the "top level" in the file.

It is permitted to declare variables outside procedures, for example, at the beginning of a file before the first procedure declaration. These variables are global, and can be used in any procedure in the whole program, unless the keyword static precedes the declaration, in which case it is not permitted to use the variables in another file. The same rules apply to procedures. Variables declared inside a procedure are local to the procedure in which they are declared.

A procedure may access an integer variable, *v*, declared in a file other than its own (provided that the variable is not static), by saying

```
extern int v;
```

The extern declaration merely serves to tell the compiler what type the variable has; no storage is allocated by extern declarations. Each global variable must be declared exactly once without the attribute extern, in order to allocate storage for it.

Variables may be initialized, as in

```
int size = 100;
```

Arrays and structures may also be initialized. Global variables that are not explicitly initialized get the default value of zero.

A.7. THE C PREPROCESSOR

Before a source file is even given to the C compiler, it is automatically run through a program called the **preprocessor**. The preprocessor output, not the original program, is what is fed into the compiler. The preprocessor carries out three major transformations on the file before giving it to the compiler:

1. File inclusion.

2. Macro definition and expansion.

3. Conditional compilation.

Preprocessor directives all begin with a number sign (#) in column 1.
When a directive of the form

```
#include "file.h"
```

is encountered by the preprocessor, it bodily includes the file, line by line, in the program given to the compiler. When the directive is written as

```
#include <file.h>
```

the directory /usr/include rather than the working directory is searched for the file. It is common practice in C to group declarations used by several files in a **header file** (usually with suffix .h), and include them where they are needed.
The preprocessor also allows macro definitions. For example,

```
#define BLOCK_SIZE 1024
```

defines a macro *BLOCK_SIZE* and gives it the value 1024. From that point on, every occurrence of the 10-character string "BLOCK_SIZE" in the file will be replaced by the 4-character string "1024" before the compiler sees the file. All that is happening here is that one character string is being replaced by another one. By convention, macro names are written in upper case. Macros may have parameters, but in practice few of them do.
The third preprocessor feature is conditional compilation. There are several places in MINIX where the code is special for the 8088, and should not be included when compiling for a different CPU. These sections look something like this:

```
#ifdef i8088
   statements for the 8088 only
#endif
```

If the symbol *i8088* is defined at the time the statements between the two preprocessor directives are included in the preprocessor output; otherwise they are omitted. By calling the compiler with the command

```
cc -c -Di8088 prog.c
```

or by including in the program the statement

```
#define i8088
```

we force the symbol *i8088* to be defined, hence all the 8088 dependent code to be included. As MINIX evolves, it may acquire special code for 68000s and other processors, which would also be handled like this. As an example of what the preprocessor does, consider the program of Fig. A-7(a) It includes one file, *prog.h*, whose contents are as follows:

```
int x;
#define MAX_ELEMENTS 100
```

Imagine that the compiler has been called with the command

```
cc -c -Di8088 file.c
```

After the file has been run through the preprocessor, the output is as shown in Fig. A-7(b). It is this output, not the original file, that is given as input to the C compiler.

```
#include "prog.h"                          main();
                                           {
main()                                       int a[100];
{
  int a[MAX_ELEMENTS];                       x = 4;
                                             a[x] = 6;
  x = 4;
  a[x] = 6;                                  printf("8088.   a[x]=%d\n",a[x]);
                                           }
#ifdef i8088
  printf("8088.   a[x]=%d\n", a[x]);
#endif

#ifdef m68000
  printf("68000. x=%d\n", x);
#endif
}
              (a)                                         (b)
```

Fig. A-7. (a) Contents of *file.c*. (b) The preprocessor output.

Notice that the preprocessor has done its job and removed all the lines starting with the # sign. If the compiler had been called with

```
cc -c -Dm68000 file.c
```

the other print statement would have been included. If it had been called with

```
cc -c file.c
```

neither print statement would have been included. (We will leave it up to the reader to speculate about what would have happened if the compiler had been called with both –D flags.)

A.8. IDIOMS

In this section we will look at a few constructions that are characteristic of C, but are not common in other programming languages. As a starter, consider the loop

```
while (n--) *p++ = *q++;
```

The variables p and q are typically character pointers, and n is a counter. What the loop does is copy an n-character string from the place pointed to by q to the place pointed to by p. On each iteration of the loop, the counter is decremented, until it gets to 0, and each of the pointers is incremented, so they successively point to higher numbered memory locations.

Another common construction is

```
for (i = 0; i < N; i++) a[i] = 0;
```

which sets the first N elements of a to 0. An alternative way of writing this loop is

```
for (p = &a[0]; p < &a[N]; p++) *p = 0;
```

In this formulation, the integer pointer, p, is initialized to point to the zeroth element of the array. The loop continues as long as p has not reached the address of $a[N]$, which is the first element that is too far. On each iteration, a different element is set to 0. The pointer construction is much more efficient than the array construction, and is therefore commonly used.

Assignments may appear in unexpected places. For example,

```
if (a = f(x)) statement;
```

first calls the function f, then assigns the result of the function call to a, and finally tests a to see if it is true (nonzero) or false (zero). If a is nonzero, the statement is executed. The statement

```
if (a = b) statement;
```

is similar, in that it assigns b to a and then tests a to see if it is nonzero. It is totally different from

```
if (a == b) statement;
```

which compares two variables and executes the statement if they are equal.

INTRODUCTION TO THE IBM PC

Unlike, say, a program in artificial intelligence that does medical diagnoses and knows nothing whatsoever about the hardware on which it is running, an operating system must know a great deal about its hardware. To handle error recovery on a disk, the operating system needs a fairly detailed knowledge of how the disk works, what kinds of errors it can make, and how the errors can be handled.

Despite this need for detailed, low-level information, operating systems can be made fairly portable by constructing them in a modular way, with, say, all the code and data structures for disk handling in one module, all the code and data structures for terminal handling in another module, and so on. MINIX has been carefully constructed this way so the addition or removal of some I/O device affects only a limited portion of the system, usually one module. Nevertheless, to write, or even understand, each of these modules, one must have some knowledge of the relevant hardware. In the following sections, we will look at the hardware and architecture of the IBM PC in a general way, to provide the necessary background information.

B.1. The Intel 8088 CPU

The heart of the IBM PC is the 8088 CPU, made by the Intel Corp. From the programmer's point of view, the 8088 is a 16-bit CPU, in that the registers are all 16 bits wide and most instructions operate on 16 bit words. Intel also makes several other compatible CPU chips, such as the 8086, 80186, 80286, and 80386, which differ from the 8088 in speed, price, and other ways that will not concern us here.

The 8088 has an address space of 1 megabyte, with each byte having a unique address, from 0 to $2^{20} - 1$. Words may begin at any address, although for compatibility with other CPUs it is good practice to have a word occupy an even byte and the following odd byte, as shown in Fig. B-1. If the byte at address 0 contains the value 0x05 and the byte at address 1 contains 0x77, the word at address 0 contains 0x7705. (0x followed by a number is the C convention for writing hexadecimal numbers; numbers beginning with a 0 but no x are octal, as in 0777.) The Intel byte numbering scheme is different from the one IBM uses on its large machines and the one that Motorola uses, so be careful to avoid confusion.

Byte 3	Byte 2	—— Word at 2
Byte 1	Byte 0	—— Word at 0

Fig. B-1. Bytes and words on the 8088.

The 8088 has 12 registers, all different. They fall into three groups of four registers each (see Fig. B-2). The first group, AX, BX, CX, and DX are primarily used for arithmetic but also have other purposes. Each of these is 16 bits wide, and is divided into a high part and low part, each of 8 bits. The high-order part of AX is called AH; the low-order part is called AL. Moving a byte to, AH, for example, does not affect the byte in AL, although it does affect the value of AX, of course. Multiplication of two 16-bit values yields a 32-bit value, stored in DX-AX, which for the purposes of multiplication and division are regarded as a single 32-bit register, with DX being the high-order half. Similarly, 32-bit dividends for division also use the DX-AX pair. CX is also used for holding shift and repetition counts.

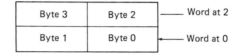

Fig. B-2. The 8088 has 12 registers, all different.

The second group of registers contains four 16-bit pointers. These registers are not divided into upper and lower halves. SI and DI are used by the hardware for certain string and block movement and comparison instructions. Since these instructions are relatively rare, many compilers use SI and DI for register variables, saving and restoring them when required. BP is a general pointer register. Many compilers use it to point to the base of the current stack frame. SP is the hardware stack pointer.

The third group consists of the four 16-bit segment registers. It is easier to think of them as 20-bit registers, of which the low-order 4 bits are always 0, so only 16 bits need to be stored. The segment registers are relocation registers and are needed because programs may be located anywhere in the 8088's 1 megabyte address space, but instruction addresses are only 16 bits. Look at program 1 in Fig. B-3. Suppose the instruction at the start of program 1 needed to jump to address 1K relative to the start of the program. Since program 1 has been loaded at address 100K, just beyond the operating system, the address to jump to is 101K. With only 16 bit addresses, there is no way to express the concept JUMP 101K.

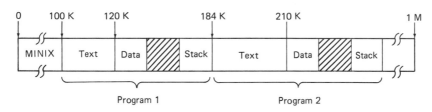

Fig. B-3. 8088 memory layout. Each program has instructions (text), data, and a stack. The area between the data and stack is unused, and can be used when either the stack grows downward or the data grows upward.

The solution Intel chose is to make all memory references relative to some segment register. Each one has its low-order four bits permanently set to 0, so only 16 bits are actually stored. CS points to the start of the code segment (program text). When program 1 is running, CS is 100K, and since all program addresses are interpreted by the 8088 chip as relative to CS, then JUMP 1K indeed jumps to 101K, as it should.

The DS register relocates references to data. When a program does MOV AX,25000, the 8088 moves the word at DS + 25000 to AX. Most programs set DS to CS, so the program has a simple address space from 0 to 64K, which maps onto the physical addresses CS to CS + 64K. Large programs can have DS set to the start of the data segment, thus allowing 64K of program and an additional 64K of data.

This feature is called **separate I(nstruction) and D(ata) space** and is supported by MINIX. If program 1 in Fig. B-3 were using separate I and D space (DS = 120K), then to fetch the first data word into AX it would say MOV AX,0. On the other hand, if separate I and D space were not being used, DS would be 100K and the first data word would be fetched by MOV AX,20480

(1K = 1024, so 20K = 20480). It is normally up to the compiler and linker to get the addresses right.

In theory, the SS register can be used for relocating the stack. For somewhat complex technical reasons, in practice it is always set equal to DS, so the data segment and stack are part of the same 64K address space. Normally the stack pointer is initially set to 65534, so the stack grows downward toward the data segment. The data segment may grow upward, toward the stack. If they collide, the program is terminated.

The final segment register, ES, is the Extra Segment register. Programs can set it to any value, to make an occasional reference to any word in the full 1 megabyte address space. Any memory reference instruction can be prefixed by a special code to tell the 8088 to use ES instead of DS for the next memory reference.

Because each of the segment registers contains four implicit 0s in the low-order bits, each segment effectively must begin at an address that is a multiple of 16 bytes. A group of 16 bytes beginning at an address that is a multiple of 16 is called a **click**. The click is the basic unit used for memory allocation. We will hear a lot about clicks when we study memory management in MINIX.

The 8088 CPU actually contains one more register, which Intel calls the **flags** and everybody else calls the **program status word**, or **PSW**. It contains the condition code bits (set on compare instructions), a bit telling whether interrupts are enabled or disabled, and a few other bits. On machines with a kernel mode and a user mode, a bit in the PSW tells which mode is current. The 8088 has only one mode (in essence, kernel mode). We are treating the PSW differently from the other 12 registers since it works quite differently from the other registers. Its main function occurs in interrupt processing, something we will deal with later.

Most 8088 instructions have a 1-byte opcode followed by a byte specifying the addressing modes and registers. The addressing modes are not as regular as they are on, say, a PDP-11, VAX, or 68000, so we will not look at them in detail. The most important addressing modes are register, register indirect, direct addressing, and indexed addressing. Direct addressing (in the range of 0 to 64K) is used to access global variables whose address is known at compile time. Indexed addressing is used to access variables local to some procedure.

Figure B-4 illustrates the normal layout of the address space of a running program. At a certain instant, some procedure is executing and the memory looks like Fig. B-4(a). Now suppose that the running procedure executed the call

```
startup(a,b);
```

The compiler will have generated instructions to first push *b* onto the stack and then push *a* onto the stack. The C calling convention is that the last parameter is always pushed first, and the first parameter is always pushed last. This convention is used because C allows a variable number of parameters (think about *printf*) and this way the called procedure can always find the first parameter in a known place.

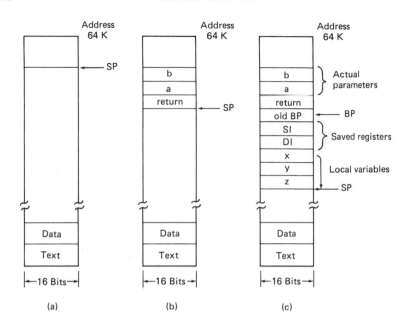

Fig. B-4. The effect of procedure calls on a program's stack.

After the parameters have been pushed, the calling procedure executes a CALL instruction to stack the return address and jump to the called procedure. At this point we have the picture of Fig. B-4(b). The called procedure now starts running. It usually first stacks BP and then sets BP to point to the old BP value on the stack. Then it stacks any registers that might be used for register variables (SI and DI in this example). Finally it decrements SP by the number of bytes the called procedure needs for local variables (6 in this example).

Since procedures must start out by stacking the old BP, setting the new BP, saving registers, and decrementing the stack pointer, many compilers put the number of bytes of locals in AX and call an internal procedure (usually called *csv*) to do the work. Using a procedure saves space but wastes a little time compared to doing the same steps in inline code. While the called procedure is executing, the stack is as shown in Fig. B-4(c).

The important thing to see here is how memory is addressed. Global variables are accessed by direct addressing because the compiler knows their position within the address space at compile time. If the compiler puts n at 3000, to load it into AX the compiler might generate MOV AX,3000.

Actual parameters, such as a and b in Fig. B-4(c) are addressed using indexed addressing with BP as the index register and positive offsets. To fetch a into AX, the instruction MOV AX,4(BP) would be used. This instruction adds the contents of BP and the constant 4, storing the result in an internal CPU register not visible to the programmer. This address is then used to locate the word to load into AX.

Local variables are also accessed using indexed addressing but with negative offsets. The local variable x would be fetched using MOV AX,-6(BP). In all cases, the address computed by adding the contents of BP to a constant is relative to DS (which is always equal to SS in MINIX). In case you are wondering why compilers do not just index off SP for both locals and parameters, thus saving the trouble of managing BP, there is a simple answer: the 8088 does not have an indexed addressing mode that uses SP.

When the called procedure is finished, it sets SP to BP, pops the old BP into BP, and then executes a RET instruction. Many C compilers use a little subroutine, usually called *cret*, to do these things. The return instruction pops the return address from the stack and puts it in the program counter, thus returning the calling procedure. The caller then adds a constant to SP to remove the parameters from the stack. This gets the caller back to the state it was in just prior to the call. Notice that calling a procedure is considerably more complex than just a single CALL instruction, and involves work by both the calling and called procedure.

The 8088 has a large number of instructions. A few examples of the more important ones are given in Fig. B-5. An important point to realize here is that although all 8088s have exactly the same instruction set, not all assemblers for the 8088 use the same syntax to describe those instructions. One assembler may expect MOV AX,#X to move the address of the variable X to AX, and another may expect MOV AX,OFFSET X, or maybe even something more ridiculous. The examples of assembly code in this book all use the notation of the PC-IX assembler, which is probably the simplest of all the assemblers and the easiest to understand. Furthermore, the MINIX assembler accepts the same input notation as the PC-IX assembler. Besides, in a book about a UNIX-like system, it seems appropriate to use the UNIX notation. (PC-IX is IBM's version of UNIX for the PC-XT.)

add ax, var	— add the contents of a memory word var to register ax
and bx,6(bp)	— Boolean AND bx with memory word located at 6(bp)
call _ panic	— call procedure panic
cli	— disable interrupts (clear interrupt flag)
cmp ax,#6	— compare ax to the constant 6 and set condition codes
dec −4(bp)	— subtract 1 from memory word whose address is given by −4(bp)
in	— load register al with a byte from the I/O port named in dx
inc si	— add 1 to register si
iret	— return from interrupt, popping PC, CS, PSW
je label	— jump to label if previous compare was "equal"
jl label	— jump if previous compare was "less" (jg, jne, etc. also exist)
loop label	— subtract 1 from cx; if it is now nonzero, jump to label
mov ax,var	— move the contents of the memory word var to ax
movb ah, varb	— move the contents of the memory byte varb to ah
out 0x20	— output contents of register al to I/O port 0x20
pop var	— pop one word from the stack and put it in var
push bx	— push the bx register onto the stack
rep	— repeat following instruction until cx is 0
ret	— return from procedure call (pop return address and jump there)
sti	— enable interrupts (set interrupt flag)

Fig. B-5. Some 8088 instructions.

B.2. The IBM PC System Architecture

The IBM PC consists of more than just the 8088 CPU. It also contains memory, a keyboard, display, diskette (floppy disk) drive, and a variety of other peripherals. The CPU communicates with these components over a set of 62 parallel wires known as the **system bus**. Some of the bus wires are used for addresses, some for data, and some for control.

The CPU gives commands to the I/O devices by executing the OUT instruction, which outputs a byte (or, rarely, a word) to the device's **controller** (adapter). The controller contains the electronics that convert the digital commands from the CPU into analog control signals to cause the I/O device to move. Each controller has a set of I/O addresses assigned to it. The diskette controller, for example, has I/O addresses 0x3F0 to 0x3F7, and the color display has I/O addresses 0x3D0 to 0x3DF. These I/O addresses belong to a distinct I/O address space, and are unrelated to ordinary memory addresses. There is no memory-mapped I/O.

As a simple example, when the CPU outputs a byte to 0x3F2, the byte is loaded into a register on the diskette controller card. The low-order 2 bits select one of the four possible drives. The next bit resets the controller if it is 0. The next bit enables diskette interrupts if it is 1. The high-order 4 bits turn the four drive motors on (1) or off (0). By giving a series of commands like this, the CPU can issue instructions to the I/O devices, read their status, and so on.

When an I/O device has finished its command, it can signal the CPU by sending an interrupt signal over the bus. The interrupt signal causes the CPU to push three words onto the current stack: first the PSW, then CS, and finally PC, as shown in Fig. B-6. Next, the interrupt bit in the PSW is turned off, to disable further interrupts. Finally, a new PC and CS are loaded from an address in the first 1K of memory. The PSW is not loaded, except that the interrupt enable bit is turned off. The address used depends on the controller that caused the interrupt; each controller has its own, unique address. The 4 bytes containing the new PC and CS are called the controller's **interrupt vector**.

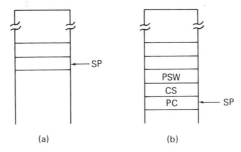

Fig. B-6. (a) Stack before an interrupt. (b) Stack after an interrupt.

Loading PC and CS effectively forces the CPU to jump to an address somewhere in the 1 megabyte address space. Since each controller has its own interrupt vector, each one has its own jump address. This address contains the interrupt service procedure for that controller. What happens next is up to the software.

As we have mentioned several times, the 8088 has an address space of 1 megabyte. IBM has chosen to allocate the lowest 640K to ordinary RAM for programs and data. The upper 360K is used for various ROMS (BASIC interpreters and the like) and for special RAMs. At address 0xFE000 is a special ROM called the **BIOS** (Basic Input Output System). It contains a collection of procedures for reading and writing disk blocks, writing characters on the screen, and other I/O.

Unfortunately, none of these procedures is interrupt driven. They all wait for the I/O to complete before returning control to the user. Thus, if one program is waiting for input from the keyboard, the entire system, including all the background processes, comes to a screeching halt. In a time-sharing system like MINIX, stopping the entire system because one program needs input is intolerable. Consequently, MINIX makes no use of the BIOS. It does all of its own I/O right down at the controller level. All versions of UNIX for the IBM PC, including IBM's own PC-IX also work this way.

MINIX USERS' GUIDE

This appendix tells you how to run MINIX. If you are an experienced UNIX user, there will be relatively little new here. Using MINIX is very similar to using UNIX. If you are not familiar with UNIX at all, it is suggested that you first read the papers by Ritchie and Thompson (1974) or Kernighan and Mashey (1981), and then at least glance through one of the many books on UNIX now available. A few of them are: Bourne (1982), Brown (1984), Christian (1983), Foxley (1985), Kernighan and Pike (1984). Lomuto and Lomuto (1983), McGilton and Morgan (1983), Pasternack (1985), Poole and Poole (1986), Rochkind (1985), and Walker (1984). For a detailed description of Version 7 UNIX (as opposed to the various other versions), the best place to look is the official Bell Labs *UNIX Programmer's Manual*, published as a book by Holt, Rinehart, and Winston (1983).

This appendix is intended to provide enough information to get you started, and to point out some of the differences between MINIX and UNIX. To begin with, MINIX was designed with the idea of being similar to Version 7 UNIX, the last version of UNIX produced by Ken Thompson, Dennis Ritchie, and the other members of the Computing Science Research Center at Bell Labs. Subsequent versions from AT&T, Berkeley, and other sources have tended to acquire many features, just as ships acquire many barnacles when they have been in the water too long. Features grafted onto UNIX after the release of Version 7 are not present in MINIX. Small is beautiful. The best way to tell if some feature is present in MINIX is to try it.

C.1. HOW TO START MINIX

The first step in running MINIX is to acquire an IBM PC, XT, AT, or true compatible. The latter point deserves some explanation. Many manufacturers have brought out machines that are similar to the IBM PC in some ways, but different in other ways. MINIX will not run on all these machines. Like all versions of UNIX for the IBM PC, MINIX does not use the BIOS (because the BIOS is not interrupt-driven, making it totally unsuitable for time-sharing). Instead, it programs all the I/O chips directly. Therefore it will only run on machines using the same I/O chips as the IBM PC.

MINIX comes in several versions, for different memory sizes. Be sure that the version you have is appropriate for your machine. The smallest configuration on which MINIX will run is 256K RAM and one 360K floppy drive, but not all programs will run on this configuration. A system with 640K RAM and two floppy disk drives is better. For information about running MINIX with a hard disk, see /*doc* in the software distribution.

Before running MINIX for the first time, make a backup of all the floppy disks, to prevent disaster if one of them should be subsequently damaged. They are not copy protected.

To boot MINIX, proceed as follows.

1. Turn off the PC and then insert the boot diskette in drive 0. You can also type CRTL-ALT-DEL to boot a running PC, but sometimes the PC is in a peculiar state and the boot message fails to appear or appears in a peculiar way. It does not matter that you cannot see it. Wait 15 seconds and then proceed with step 3. Alternatively, just turn off the PC and start again.

2. You should get a message like: "Booting MINIX 1.0" as soon as the power-on self-tests have finished.

3. About 15 seconds after the above message, you will get a menu on the screen offering you several options. Remove the boot diskette from drive 0, insert the root file system in its place, and hit the = (equal sign) key.

4. MINIX will now erase the screen and display a line at the top telling how much memory the machine has, how large the operating system (including all its tables and buffers) is, how large the RAM disk is, and how much memory is available for user programs (the first number minus the next two). Check to see that the available memory is at least positive. MINIX will not run with negative memory. To do anything useful, however, at least 100K is needed.

5. Now the root file system will be copied from drive 0 to the RAM disk. The MINIX root device is always on the RAM disk, no matter how many disks of what kind are being used.

6. When the RAM disk has been loaded, the system initialization file, */etc/rc*, is executed. It asks you to remove the root file system and then insert the */usr* file system in drive 0 and type a carriage return. Do so.

7. After */usr* has been mounted, you will next be requested to enter the date (and time). Enter a 12-digit number in the form MMDDYYhhmmss, followed by a carriage return. For example, 3:35 p.m. on July 4, 1976 was 070476153500.

8. You will now get the message

    ```
    login:
    ```

    on the screen. Type

    ```
    ast
    ```

    and wait for the system to ask for your password. Then type

    ```
    Wachtwoord
    ```

    being careful to type the first letter in upper case. Lower and upper case letters are always distinct in MINIX.

9. If you have successfully logged in, the shell will display a prompt (dollar sign) on the screen. Try typing

    ```
    ls -l
    ```

    to see what is in your directory. Then type

    ```
    ls -l /bin
    ```

    to see what is in the */bin* directory on the root device. After that, try

    ```
    ls -l /usr/bin
    ```

    to see what is on the drive 0 diskette. To stop the display from scrolling out of view, type CTRL-S; to restart it, type CTRL-Q. (Note that CTRL-S means depress the "control" key on the keyboard and then hit the *S* key while "control" is still depressed.)

10. If you have two drives, you can mount the */user* diskette by inserting it into drive 1 and typing

    ```
    /etc/mount /dev/fd1 /user
    ```

    Use *ls* to inspect it. The shell script */user/test/run* runs some tests to see if MINIX is working properly. To use it, first back up the diskette as described in Section C.2.4. Then remove all the source code and documentation (to create more free space) and type

    ```
    cd /user/test; run
    ```

The tests take a number of minutes. After they have been completed, you can remove the entire *test* directory, leaving only */user/bin*. The rest of the diskette space is for your own files.

11. You can now edit files, compile programs, or do many other things. The reference manuals given later in this chapter give a brief description of the programs available. On the standard */usr* diskette, there is very little free space. If you have only one 360K drive, it will be probably be necessary to delete some files to create more space.

12. When you are finished working, and want to log out, type CTRL-D. The

```
login:
```

message will appear, and you or another user can log in again.

13. When you want to shut the computer down, make sure all processes have finished, if need be, by killing them with *kill*. Then type sync or just log out. When the disk light goes out, you can turn the computer power off. Never turn the system off without first running *sync* or logging out (which does an implied *sync*). Failure to obey this rule will generally result in a garbled file system and lost data.

C.2. HOW TO USE MINIX

In the following sections we will look at some aspects of MINIX that will be of interest to many users. These include the standard file system, mounted file systems, working with disks, printing files, and so on.

C.2.1. Introduction

As a general rule, most aspects of MINIX work the same way as they do in UNIX. When you log in, you get a shell, which is functionally similar to the standard V7 shell (Bourne shell). Most programs are called the same way as in UNIX, have the same flags, and perform the same functions as their UNIX counterparts.

The MINIX shell, for example, recognizes redirection of standard input and standard output, pipes, magic characters in file names, semicolons to separate multiple commands on a line, and the ampersand, to indicate a background process. The (default) keyboard editing conventions are also similar to UNIX: the backspace key (CTRL-H) is used to correct typing errors, the @ symbol is used to erase the current input line, CTRL-S is used to stop the screen from scrolling out of view, CTRL-Q is used to start the screen moving again, and CTRL-D is used to indicate end-of-file from the keyboard. These key bindings can be changed using the IOCTL system call and *stty* program, the same way as they can be changed in UNIX.

One major difference between MINIX and UNIX is the editor. The standard UNIX editor, *ed*, was designed with slow, mechanical, hardcopy terminals in mind. More modern editors, such as *vi* and *emacs* were designed for computers with megabytes of memory and large disks. The MINIX editor, *mined*, was designed and implemented especially for MINIX. It is a small, fast, and easy to learn full-screen editor. Its commands are described later in this chapter.

C.2.2. A Tour Through the MINIX File System

The MINIX file tree is organized the same way as the standard UNIX file tree. The root directory (which is always located on the RAM disk, in memory) contains the following subdirectories:

/bin - contains the most important binary (executable) programs
/dev - contains the special files for the I/O devices
/etc - contains various files and programs for system administration
/lib - contains some programs called by other programs
/tmp - used to hold temporary files
/user - the user file system is mounted here
/usr - the system disk is mounted here

Let us briefly examine these directories one at a time. In */bin* we find the most heavily used programs such as *cat*, *cp*, and *ls* as well as some programs such as *login* and *sh* needed to bring the system up. Because access to the RAM disk is much faster than to the rotating disks, */bin* should be used to hold programs that are frequently used. In principle, MINIX will run with only the root file system (i.e., no disks at all), but the amount of space available for user files will be extremely limited.

The directory */dev* contains the special files for the I/O devices, including:

/dev/ram - the RAM disk
/dev/mem - absolute memory
/dev/kmem - kernel memory
/dev/null - null device (data written to it are discarded)
/dev/fd0 - floppy disk drive 0
/dev/fd1 - floppy disk drive 1
/dev/hd0 - hard disk minor device 0
/dev/hd1 - hard disk minor device 1
/dev/lp - line printer
/dev/tty - current terminal
/dev/tty0 - terminal 0 (console)

When */dev/ram* is opened and read, for example, by the command

```
od -x /dev/ram
```

the contents of the RAM disk are read out, byte by byte, starting at byte 0. Similarly, reading */dev/mem* reads out absolute memory, starting at address 0 (the interrupt vectors). The file */dev/kmem* is similar to */dev/mem*, except that it starts at the address in memory where the kernel is located (0x600). The next file, */dev/null*, is the null device. It is used as a place for redirecting program output that is not needed. Data copied to */dev/null* are lost forever.

The next two files are for floppy disk drives 0 and 1, respectively. Reading or writing from one of these files reads or writes on the corresponding floppy disk, without regard to the structure of the file system on it. They are normally only used for operations such as copying complete floppy disks, block by block or creating fresh file systems.

The character special file */dev/lp* is for the line printer. It is write only. Bytes written to this file are sent to the line printer without modification (to make it possible to send escape sequences to graphics printers). Users normally print files by using the *lpr* program, rather than copying files directly to */dev/lp*. The latter method takes care of converting line feed to carriage return plus line feed, expanding tabs to spaces, etc., whereas the former method does not.

The final group of special files is for the terminal. Both */dev/tty* and */dev/tty0* refer to the terminal (console). In a system with only one terminal, there is no difference, but MINIX has been designed to make it easy to expand to multiple terminals, in which case */dev/tty1*, */dev/tty2*, etc. should be added for the new terminals. When more than one terminal is present, a specific terminal can be read or written by using one of the special files of the form */dev/ttyn*. In contrast, */dev/tty* always accesses the terminal associated with the process making the system call. In this way, a process can refer to its terminal without having to know the terminal number.

Another important directory is */etc*. This directory contains files and programs used for mounting and unmounting file systems, making new file systems, and other forms of system management. We will look at them later.

The directory */lib* holds two pieces of the C compiler that are not normally directly called by users: the C preprocessor, *cpp*, and the front end, *cem*.

The */tmp* directory is used by many programs for temporary files. By putting this directory on the RAM disk, these programs are speeded up.

The directories */user* and */usr* are empty. They should be used for mounting the user disk and system disk, respectively. When the standard */usr* file system is mounted, the directory */usr/bin* is where most of the executable binary programs are kept, and */usr/lib* is where the rest of the C compiler and its libraries are stored.

C.2.3. Mounted File Systems

When MINIX is started up, the only device present is the root device (on the RAM disk). After the files and directories that belong on the root device are copied there from the root file system diskette, MINIX prints a message asking the user to remove the diskette. It then executes the shell script /etc/rc as the final step in bringing up the system.

The file /etc/rc first prints a message asking the user to put the /usr diskette in drive 0. Then it pauses to allow the diskette to be inserted and the date entered. The shell script now executes the command

```
/etc/mount /dev/fd0 /usr
```

to mount the system disk on /usr. From this point on, all the files in /usr, including the binary programs in /usr/bin, are available.

On PCs with two floppy disk drives, the user should insert a user file system diskette (or any other file system diskette) in drive 1 and type:

```
/etc/mount /dev/fd1 /user
```

Users planning to mount the same diskette in drive 1 whenever the system is brought up can modify /etc/rc to perform the mount on drive 1 analogously to the mount on drive 0. Note, however, that changes made to /etc/rc on the RAM disk will be lost when the system is next booted unless they are also made to the root file system diskette, which can be mounted and modified, just like any other diskette.

If it is desired to remove the diskette in drive 1 during operation, first type the command:

```
/etc/umount /dev/fd1
```

and wait until it types "ok" before removing the diskette. (Note that the program is called *umount*, just as it is in UNIX, not *unmount*.)

If you remove a diskette while it is still mounted, the system may hang, but it can be brought back to life by simply re-inserting the same diskette. If you remove a diskette while it is still mounted and insert another in its place, the contents of both file systems will be seriously damaged and information may be irretrievably lost (see below about repairing damaged file systems). During normal MINIX operation, the diskettes are mounted when the system is booted, and not touched thereafter. Experienced MS-DOS users who are used to constantly switching diskettes without telling the operating system should post discrete KEEP OFF signs on their drives as a reminder.

Although it is permitted to *insert* a non-MINIX diskette in a drive (e.g., to read an MS-DOS diskette), only MINIX file system diskettes can be *mounted*. Attempts to mount a diskette not containing a MINIX file system will be detected and rejected.

C.2.4. Helpful Hints

In this section we will point out several aspects of MINIX that will frequently be useful. As a starter, it is wise to back up floppy disks periodically. To make a backup, first format a floppy disk with 9 sectors/track. MINIX does not have a format program, but the MS-DOS 2.0 and subsequent format programs can be used. Formatting a floppy disk writes timing information, sector preambles, and similar information on it. The MS-DOS formatter also puts an MS-DOS file system on the floppy disk, but that will be erased when the backup is made. The important thing is getting the timing and preambles onto the disk.

Next, unmount the file systems in drives 0 and 1. It is possible to back up a mounted file system, but only if no background processes are running. To be doubly safe, give a *sync* command. Insert the newly formatted diskette in drive 1, and then type

```
cp /dev/fd0 /dev/fd1
```

to copy information from drive 0 to drive 1. When the drive lights go out, the floppy disks can be removed.

Files can be printed using the *lpr* program. It can be given an explicit list of files, as in

```
lpr file1 file2 file3 &
```

If no arguments are supplied, *lpr* prints its standard input, for example

```
pr file1 file2 file3 | lpr &
```

Note that *lpr* is not a spooling daemon. It sits in a loop copying files to */dev/lp*. For this reason, it should be started off in the background with the ampersand, so the user can continue working while printing is going on. Only one *lpr* at a time may be running.

Disk space is always in short supply on floppy disk systems. To find out how much space and how many i-nodes are left on drive 0, type

```
df /dev/fd0
```

Similar commands can be used for other devices, including */dev/ram*.

When you log in, the shell checks to see if there is a file *.profile* in your home directory. If it finds one, it executes the file as a shell script. This file is commonly used to set shell variables, *stty* parameters, and so on. See */usr/ast/.profile* as a simple example.

It is possible to copy files from an MS-DOS disk to MINIX or vice versa. See the description of *dosread* and *doswrite* for details.

The ASCII codes produced by the IBM PC keyboard are determined by software, not hardware. A mapping has been chosen to try to produce a unique value for each key, so programs can see the difference between, for example, the + in the top row and the + in the numeric keypad. The codes 1 through 255 are used. To see which code a given key produces, use *od −b*, and then type the key or keys followed by a return and a CTRL-D.

The IBM PC does not have any protection hardware. As a result, if a program's stack overruns the area available for it, it will overwrite the data segment. This usually results in a system crash. When a program crashes unexpectedly or acts strange, it is probably worthwhile to find out how much memory is allocated for it (the "memory" column in the output of *size*). If this is less than 64K, it can be increased using *chmem*. When working with unreliable programs, doing *syncs* frequently is advisable.

The 640K version of MINIX can be used on 512K machines, although there are some limitations and problems to watch out for. The main problem is the small amount of memory available for user programs. It will be difficult to run several programs at once. When using the C compiler, it will be necessary to use the –F flag to avoid having the preprocessor and front end run at the same time, connected by a pipe. Running them separately means that enough disk space must be available for the intermediate file. If a program cannot be executed due to its size, *chmem* can sometimes be used to reduce the stack size, to allow it to run with less memory. If the stack is made too small, however, the program may go berserk or crash the system due to stack overrun. Unfortunately the hardware does not detect stack overrun.

The problems with memory allocation are due to a large chunk of memory being taken up by the operating system, its buffers, and the RAM disk, plus the fact that multiple programs can be running at once. This, plus the lack of hardware protection, requires that a more economical approach be taken to memory use than the standard MS-DOS method of just giving each program the whole machine to itself. In practice, once the sizes have been set right for a given configuration, they need not to fiddled with any more.

Even on 640K machines, it sometimes happens that a program (or a compiler pass) cannot be executed due to lack of memory for it. When this happens, the shell prints a message of the form *program: cannot execute*. The solution is to run fewer programs at once, or reduce the program's size with *chmem*. The amount of stack space assigned to the shell, *make*, etc. in the standard distribution may not be optimal for all applications. Change it if problems arise. To see how much is currently assigned, type

```
size /bin/* /usr/bin/* | mined
```

Several of the utility programs, including the C compiler, create their temporary files in */tmp*, on the RAM disk. If the RAM disk fills up, a message will be printed on the terminal. The first thing to do is check */tmp* to see if there is any debris left over from previous commands, and if so, remove it. If that does not solve the problem, temporarily removing some of the larger files from */bin* or */lib* will usually be enough. These files can be restored later by mounting the root file system on any drive and copying the needed files from it.

MINIX, like UNIX, will not break off a system call part way through just because the DEL key has been struck. When the system call in question happens to be an EXEC, which is loading a long program from a slow floppy disk, it can take a few seconds before the shell prompt appears. Be patient. Hitting DEL again makes things worse, rather than better.

Although it is really intended as a debugging aid, rather than a permanent part of the system, the F1 and F2 function keys cause dumps of some of the internal tables to be printed on the screen. F1 gives a dump like the UNIX *ps* command, which is not present in MINIX. Frequently, the system appears to be stopped, but it is actually thinking its little head off and using the RAM disk, which, unlike the other disks, is not accompanied by whirring and clicking noises and flashing lights. The nervous user can press F1 to see the internal process table to verify that progress is still being made. The F1 and F2 keys are intercepted directly by the keyboard driver, so they always work, no matter what the computer is doing. The values in the columns *user* and *sys* are the number of clock ticks charged to each process. By hitting F1 twice, a few seconds apart, it is possible to see where the CPU time is going.

Additional documentation can be found in the */doc* directory on the */user* disk.

C.3. HOW TO BEHAVE LIKE A SUPER-USER

Your days as an ordinary user are over. You will now have to learn how to be a system administrator as well. In fact, within a minute you will learn how to become a super-user. Fortunately, being a super-user is not difficult. However, super-users have more power than ordinary users. They can violate nearly all of the system's protection rules. Although there is no Hippocratic Oath for super-users (yet), tradition requires them to exercise their great power with care and responsibility. Super-users get a special prompt (#), to remind them of their awesome power.

To become super-user, login as *root* using the password *Geheim*. (Notice the capital *G*). Alternatively, use the *su* program with the same password. Hackers will no doubt enjoy trying to become super-user the hard way—by logging in as *ast* and hunting for loopholes in the system that allow one to become super-user without using the super-user password. In fact, I am prepared to offer a *rijksdaalder* to the first person reporting each successful new method.

C.3.1. Making New File Systems

One of the things that super-users do is make new file systems. Two ways are provided. First, when MINIX is booted, the initial menu offers several options. To run the system, type = (equal sign). Another possibility is making an empty file system. This option is exercised by typing the letter *m* instead of =. This file system can be subsequently mounted and files copied to it.

It is often convenient to make a file system during normal MINIX operation. This is possible using the program *mkfs* (make file system). To make an empty 360 block file system on drive 1, type

```
mkfs /dev/fd1 360
```

When the program finishes, the file system will be ready to mount. On a system with only one disk drive, *mkfs* will first have to be copied to */bin*, the */dev/fd0* file system unmounted, a blank diskette inserted into drive 0 and then the file system made using */dev/fd0* as the second argument to *mkfs*.

It is also possible to make a file system that is initialized with files and directories. A command for doing this is

```
mkfs /dev/fd1 proto
```

where *proto* is a prototype file. The description of *mkfs* later in this chapter gives an example of a prototype file.

C.3.2. File System Checking

File systems can be damaged by system crashes, by accidently removing a mounted file system, by forgetting to run *sync* before shutting the system down and in other ways. Repairing a file system by hand is a tricky business (see the discussion in Chap. 5), so a program has been provided to automate the job.

When MINIX is booted, one of the choices on the initial menu is to check a file system. To use this option, first insert the file system to be checked in drive 0, and then type *f*. The file system checker, *fsck*, then reads the i-nodes, bit maps, and directories to see if the file system is consistent. If it is, *fsck* prints some statistics and then redisplays the menu. At this point another file system can be checked, or MINIX can be started (after first inserting the root file system diskette in drive 0).

If *fsck* finds a problem, it will display a message. Before making changes to the file system, it always asks permission. In general, if you type *y* (followed by a carriage return), *fsck* will do its best to repair the system. It will always yield a correct file system, but if the file system has been badly damaged, files may be lost.

C.3.3. The /etc Directory

The */etc* directory contains several files that super-users should know about. One of these is the password file, */etc/passwd*. You can enter new users by editing this file and adding a line for each new user. The entry for a user named *kermit* might be

```
kermit::15:1:Kermit the Frog:/user/kermit:/bin/sh
```

The entry contains seven fields, separated by colons. These fields contain the login name, password (initially null), uid, gid, name, home directory, and shell for the new user. When a new user is entered, the corresponding home directory must also be created, using *mkdir*, and its owner set correctly, using *chown*. Each user must have a unique uid, but the numerical values are unimportant. It is probably adequate to put all ordinary users in group 3, unless there really are distinct groups of users. When the new user logs in for the first time, he should choose a password and enter it using *passwd*.

Another important file is */etc/rc*. Each time the system is booted, this file is run as a shell script just before the login: message is printed. It can be used to mount file systems, request the date, erase temporary files, and anything else that needs to be done before starting the system. It also forks off *update*, which runs in the background and issues a SYNC system call every 30 seconds to flush the buffer cache.

If you have two drives, it may be convenient to modify */etc/rc* to mount */dev/fd1* on */user* during system boot. If you do this, you can also change */etc/passwd* to put your home directory on */user* instead of */usr*.

The file */etc/ttys* contains one line for each terminal in the system. During startup, *init* reads this file and forks off a login process for each terminal. When the console is the only terminal, *ttys* contains only 1 line.

Also contained in */etc* are the programs *mount*, and *umount* for mounting and unmounting file systems, respectively.

When any of the files on the RAM disk, such as */etc/passwd*, are modified, the changes will be lost when the system is shut down unless the modified files are explicitly copied back to the root file system. This can be done by mounting the root file system diskette and then copying the files with *cp*.

C.3.4. Modifying File Systems

As distributed, MINIX comes with three file system diskettes: the root file system, */usr*, and */user*. When the system is booted, the root file system diskette is copied to the RAM disk, and not used thereafter. One implication of this design is that changes made to the RAM disk during system operation will be lost when the system is shut down. To modify the root file system, it should be mounted, for example, by putting it in drive 1 and typing

```
/etc/mount /dev/fd1 /user
```

Programs can then be copied to or from it, files can be removed, and so on. When the modification is done, it must be unmounted and removed from the drive.

More generally, the contents of the three file systems can be reorganized by mounting and copying. Programs that are heavily used should be put on the root file system, but at least 50K should be left unused for */tmp*. Once a root file system diskette has been made, its size cannot be changed, but a new one can always be made using *mkfs*, as discussed in Appendix D.

One simple way to build a new */usr* or */user* file system is to make an empty file system using the "m" option of the initial menu, or *mkfs*, mount this file system, and then copy files to it from one or more other file systems, possibly mounting and unmounting several of them during the process.

For systems containing only one floppy disk drive, a careful choice has to be made about which programs will be on the root file system and which will be on /usr since together they are too small to hold all the programs.

One way to build a file system is to start with an empty file system. Programs that are currently on the root device that are to go on the new file system are copied to it. Then, /lib and /bin, are emptied, except for rm and cp, to make more space on the root device. Next, the file system being built is unmounted, and another one mounted in its place. Useful programs from it are copied to the now-empty root device. Then the file system being built is remounted, and files copied to it from the root device. This process may have to be repeated several times, depending on how many files are being copied and from where.

C.3.5. Miscellaneous Notes

A number of MINIX programs can only be executed by the super-user. These include: *mkfs*, *chown*, and *mknod*. Other programs, such as *mkdir*, can be executed by any user, but are owned by the root and have the SETUID bit on, so that when they are executed, the effective uid is that of the super-user, even though the real uid is not.

In general, if a program, *prog*, needs to run as the super-user but is to be made generally available to all users, it can be made into a SETUID program owned by the root by the command line:

```
chown root prog;   chmod 4755 prog
```

Needless to say, only the super-user can execute these commands.

C.4. MINIX COMMANDS

In this section the MINIX commands (programs) that are supplied with the system are summarized. Books on UNIX should be consulted for more detail, especially (Bell Telephone Laboratories, 1983). Most MINIX commands have the same flags and arguments as their UNIX counterparts. A few of the programs listed below are on the /user diskette, and will not be available unless that diskette is mounted.

In the notation used, square brackets denote optional quantities and the ellipsis (...) is used to indicate that the previous item may be present 1 or more times. In the **Syntax** lines, words and flags printed in **boldface** type must be entered exactly as shown. Words and symbols printed in lightface type are arguments, and must be replaced by file names, numeric arguments, and so forth. In the examples, all the information following a number sign (#) is comment.

Command: ar – archiver
Syntax: **ar [–adprtvx]** archive file ...
Flags: **–a** Append files to the archive
                   –d Delete files from the archive
                   –p Print the files on standard output
                   –r Replace files (append when not present)
                   –t List archive's table of contents
                   –v Verbose mode (give more information)
                   –x Extract files from the archive
Examples: ar –r clib *.c   # Replace all the C files
                ar –d lib.a file.s   # Remove *file.s* from the archive

Ar maintains archives and libraries. An archive can be created with the **–r** flag by listing a nonexistent archive name. Members of the archive can be replaced, deleted, printed, or extracted.

Command: asld – assembler-loader
Syntax: **asld [–d] [–s] [–o** name**]** file ...
Flags: **–L** A listing is produced on standard output
                   –T Used to specify a directory for the temporary file
                   –o Output goes to file named by next argument
                   –s A symbol table is produced on standard output
Examples: asld –s file.s   # Assemble *file.s and* list symbols
                asld –o output file.s   # Assemble *file.s*, put binary on *output*
                asld –T. file1.s file2.s   # Use current directory for temporary file

Asld is the MINIX assembler and loader combined. It accepts a language similar to that accepted by the PC-IX assembler. Symbols are made up of letters, digits and underscores. The machine instructions and addressing modes are the same as those used by PC-IX, except that modes using multiple registers are written like this example: *mov ax,(bx_si)*. Constant operands are denoted by a number sign. Local labels are permitted in the usual UNIX style: the instruction *jmp 1f* jumps forward to the closest label *1:*

The pseudoinstructions accepted by the assembler are listed below:

.align n   Align to a multiple of *n* bytes
.ascii str   Assemble a string
.asciz str   Assemble a zero-terminated string
.bss   What follows goes in the bss segment
.byte n   Assemble one or more bytes
.data   What follows goes in the data segment
.define sym   Export *sym* from the file
.errnz n   Force error if *n* is nonzero
.even   Align to an even address
.extern sym   Declare *sym* external

.globl sym	Same as **extern**
.long n	Assemble *n* as a long
.org adr	Set address within current segment
.short n	Assemble *n* as a short
.space n	Skip *n* bytes
.text	What follows goes in the text segment
.word n	Assemble *n* as a word
.zerow n	Assemble *n* words of zeros

In the above pseudoinstructions, *adr* is an expression yielding a machine address, *n* is a numeric expression, *str* is a quoted string, and *sym* is a symbol. The library */usr/lib/libc.a* is a packed archive of assembly code. To see some examples of it, extract some files from the archive with *ar* and then use the filter *libupack* to convert them to readable ASCII.

MINIX does not use *.o* files. Compiler output is packed assembly language, as are the modules in an archive. This scheme requires reassembling archive modules all the time, but it saves precious diskette space. Unfortunately, the strategy also makes assembling and linking slow.

It is not possible at present to have the assembler (hence the C compiler) produce separate I & D program, even though the operating system supports such programs compiled with other compilers.

Command: basename – strip off file prefixes and suffixes
Syntax: basename file [suffix]
Flags: (none)
Examples: basename /user/ast/file   # Strips path to yield *file*
                basename /user/file.c .c   # Strips path and *.c* to yield *file*

The initial directory names (if any) are removed yielding the name of the file itself. If a second argument is present, it is interpreted as a suffix and is also stripped, if present. This program is primarily used in shell scripts.

Command: cat – concatenate files and write them to standard output
Syntax: cat [–u] file ...
Flags: –u Unbuffered output
Examples: cat file   # Display file on the terminal
                cat file1 file2 | lpr   # Concatenate 2 files and print result

Cat concatenates its input files and copies the result to standard output. If no input file is named, or – is encountered as a file name, standard input is used. Output is buffered in 512 byte blocks unless the **–u** flag is given.

Command: **cc – C compiler**
Syntax: **cc [option] ... file ...**
Flags: **–D** The flag **–D**x=y defines a macro x with value y
                  –F Use a file instead of a pipe for preprocessor output
                  –I **–I***dir* searches *dir* for include files
                  –LIB Produce a library module
                  –R Complain about all non Kernighan & Ritchie code
                  –S Produce an assembly code file, then stop
                  –T The flag **–T***dir* tells *cem* to use *dir* for temporary files
                  –U Undefine a macro
                  –c Compile only. Do not link. (Same as **–S**)
                  –o Put output on file named by next arg
                  –v Verbose. Print pass names
                  –w Suppress warning messages

Examples: cc –c file.c   # Compile *file.c*
                cc –Di8088 file.c   # Treat the symbol *i8088* as defined
                cc –c —LIB file.c   # Make a module for the library
                cc –R –o out file.c   # Check for K & R; output to *out*

This is the C compiler. It has five passes, as follows:

Program	Input	Output	Operation performed
/lib/cpp	prog.c	prog.i	C preprocessor: #include, #define, #ifdef
/lib/cem	prog.i	prog.k	Parsing and semantic analysis
/usr/lib/opt	prog.k	prog.m	Optimization of the intermediate code
/usr/lib/cg	prog.m	prog.s	Code generation
/usr/lib/asld	prog.s	a.out	Assembly and linking

The main program, *cc*, forks appropriately to call the passes, transmitting flags and arguments. The **–v** flag causes the passes to be listed as they are called.

The **–c** or **–S** flags stop compilation when *cg* has produced an assembly code file (in packed format) because the current assembler-loader expects that (see under File Formats later in this appendix). The libraries are also archives of packed assembly code files, except that defined symbols must be declared by *.define* statements at the beginning. To make modules for inclusion in the library, use the **–c** and **–LIB** options. There is no way to get *.o* files; the packed assembly language files are used as a substitute. They can be unpacked with the filter *libupack*.

The **–R** flag gives warnings about all constructions not permitted by official Kernighan and Ritchie C. The average garden-variety C program that has been flawlessly acceptedly by most C compilers contains surprisingly many illegal constructions. Try it.

The compiler normally keeps *cpp* and *cem* in memory at the same time, transferring the output of *cpp* to *cem* using a pipe. However, if there is insufficient memory available to hold both at once, the **–F** flag can be given to cause these two passes to be run strictly sequentially, with the preprocessor output being stored on a file in */tmp* (unless **–T** is used). When available memory is very limited (e.g., a 512K machine), it may be necessary to run *chmem* to reduce the sizes of the compiler passes that do not fit, typically *cem*.

The other passes, especially *asld*, can create large temporary files in */tmp*. To compile very large programs, first type

```
cc -c *.c
```

to get *.s* files. Then remove */lib/cpp* and */lib/cem* and possibly other files from the RAM disk to make more space for */tmp*. Finally, type

```
cc *.s
```

which results in

```
asld /usr/lib/crtso.s *.s /usr/lib/libc.a /usr/lib/end.s
```

to produce the *a.out* file. The files removed from the RAM disk can be restored by mounting the root file system and copying them from there, or the system can be shut down and rebooted.

If the compiler (or, in fact, almost any program) begins acting strange, it is almost always due to its running out of space, either stack space or scratch file space. The relevant pass can be given more stack space using *chmem*. More space for scratch files can be obtained by removing other files on the device.

The compiler is derived from the ACK system (Tanenbaum et al., 1983), not from the AT&T portable C compiler. It has been shoehorned onto the PC with some loss of performance.

Command: chmem – change memory allocation
Syntax: chmem [+] [–] [=] amount file ...
Flags: (none)
Examples: chmem =50000 a.out   # Give *a.out* 50K of stack space
             chmem –4000 a.out   # Reduce the stack space by 4000 bytes
             chmem +1000 file1 file2 # Increase each stack by 1000 bytes

When a program is loaded into memory, it is allocated enough memory for the text and data+bss segments, plus an area for the stack. Data segment growth using *malloc*, *brk*, or *sbrk* eats up stack space from the low end. The amount of stack space to allocate is derived from a field in the executable program's file header. If the combined stack and data segment growth exceeds the stack space allocated, the program will be terminated.

It is therefore important to set the amount of stack space carefully. If too little is provided, the program may crash. If too much is provided, memory will be wasted, and fewer programs will be able to fit in memory and run simultaneously. MINIX does not swap, so that when memory is full, subsequent attempts to fork will fail. The compiler sets the stack space to the largest possible value (64K – text – data). For many programs, this value is far too large.

Nonrecursive programs that do not call *brk*, *sbrk*, or *malloc*, and do not have any local arrays usually do not need more than 1K of stack space.

The *chmem* command changes the value of the header field that determines the stack allocation, and thus indirectly the total memory required to run the program. The = option sets the stack size to a specific value; the + and – options increment and decrement the current value by the indicated amount. The old and new stack sizes are printed.

Command: chmod – change file mode
Syntax: **chmod** mode file ...
Flags: **(none)**
Examples: chmod 754 file   # Owner: rwx; Group r–x; Others r--
                      chmod 4755 file1 file2   # Turn on SETUID bit

The permission bits for each file are set to *mode* (octal). The 04000 bit is the SETUID bit. The 02000 bit is the SETGID bit. The low-order 9 bits are the *rwx* bits for the owner, group, and others.

Command: chown – change owner
Syntax: **chown** user file ...
Flags: **(none)**
Example: chown ast file1 file2   # Make *ast* the owner of the files

The owner field of the named files is changed to *user* (i.e., login name specified). Only the super-user may execute this command.

Command: clr – clear the screen
Syntax: **clr**
Flags: **(none)**
Example: clr   # Clear the screen

The screen is cleared to blanks.

Command: cmp – compare two files
Syntax: **cmp –ls** file1 file2
Flags: **–l** Loud mode. Print bytes that differ (in octal)
                      –s Silent mode. Print nothing, just return exit status
Examples: cmp file1 file2   # Tell whether the files are the same
                      cmp –l file1 file2   # Print all corresponding bytes that differ

Two files are compared. If they are identical, exit status 0 is returned. If they differ, exit status 1 is returned. If the files cannot be opened, exit status 2 is returned. If *file1* is - , standard input is compared to *file2*.

Command: comm – print lines common to two sorted files
Syntax: **comm [– [123]]** file1 file2
Flags: **–1** Suppress column 1 (lines only in *file1*)
              –2 Suppress column 2 (lines only in *file2*)
              –3 Suppress column 3 (lines in both files)
Examples: comm file1 file2   # Print all three columns
              comm –12 file1 file2   # Print only lines common to both files

Two sorted files are read and compared. A three column listing is produced. Files only in *file1* are in column 1; files only in *file2* are in column 2; files common to both files are in column 3. The file name – means standard input.

Command: cp – copy file
Syntax: **cp** file1 file2
              cp file ... directory
Flags: **(none)**
Examples: cp oldfile newfile   # Copy *oldfile* to *newfile*
              cp file1 file2 /user/ast   # Copy two files to a directory

Cp copies one file to another, or copies one or more files to a directory. A file cannot be copied to itself.

Command: date – print or set the date and time
Syntax: **date [[MMDDYY]hhmm[ss]]**
Flags: **–q** Read the date from standard input
Examples: date# Print the date and time
              date 0221881610   # Set date to Feb 21, 1988 at 4:10 p.m.

Without an argument, *date* prints the current date and time. With an argument, it sets the date and time. *MMDDYY* refers to the month, day, and year; *hhmmss* refers to the hour, minute and second. Each of the six fields must be two digits.

Command: dd – disk dumper
Syntax: **dd [option = value] ...**
Flags: **(none)**

Examples: dd if=/dev/fd0 of=/dev/fd1   # Copy disk 0 to disk 1
                dd if=x of=y bs=1w skip=4   # Copy *x* to *y*, skipping 4 words
                dd if=x of=y count=3   # Copy three 512–byte blocks

This command is intended for copying partial files. The block size, skip count, and number of blocks to copy can be specified. The options are:

if = file	- Input file (default is standard input)
of = file	- Output file (default is standard output)
ibs = n	- Input block size (default 512 bytes)
obs = n	- Output block size (default is 512 bytes)
bs = n	- Block size; sets *ibs* and *obs* (default is 512 bytes)
skip = n	- Skip *n* input blocks before reading
seek = n	- Skip *n* output blocks before writing
count = n	- Copy only *n* input blocks
conv = lcase	- Convert upper case letters to lower case
conv = ucase	- Convert lower case letters to upper case
conv = swab	- Swap every pair of bytes
conv = noerror	- Ignore errors and just keep going

Where sizes are expected, they are in bytes. However, the letters **w**, **b**, or **k** may be appended to the number to indicate words (2 bytes), blocks (512 bytes), or K (1024 bytes), respectively. When *dd* is finished, it reports the number of full and partial blocks read and written.

Command: df – report on free disk space and i-nodes
Syntax: **df** special ...
Flags: **(none)**
Examples: df /dev/ram   # Report on free RAM disk space
                df /dev/fd0 /dev/fd1 # Report on floppy disk space

The amount of disk space and number of i-nodes, both free and used is reported.

Command: dosdir – list an MS-DOS diskette directory
Syntax: **dosdir [–lr]** drive
Flags: **–l** Long listing
                –r Recursively descend and print subdirectories
Examples: dosdir 1 –l   # List root directory on drive 1
                dosdir 0 –r x/y   # Recursively list directory *x/y*

Dosdir reads standard IBM PC diskettes in MS-DOS format and lists their contents on standard output. Directory names should contain slashes to separate components, even though MS-DOS uses backslashes. The names *dosdir*, *dosread*, and *doswrite* are all links to the same program. The program sees which function to perform by seeing how it was called.

Command: dosread – read a file from an MS-DOS diskette
Syntax: **dosread**
Flags: **–a** ASCII file
Examples: dosread 1 g/adv >adv   # Read file *g/adv* from drive 1
              dosread 0 –a prog.c >x   # Read ASCII file *prog.c* from drive 0

    Dosread reads one file from an MS-DOS diskette and writes it on standard output. The file name should use slash, not backslash as a separator. ASCII files have the final CTRL-Z stripped, and carriage return plus line feed is mapped to line feed only, the usual MINIX convention.

Command: doswrite – write a file onto an MS-DOS diskette
Syntax: **doswrite [–a]** drive **file**
Flags: **–a** ASCII file
Examples: doswrite 1 x/y <z   # Write file *z* to disk as *x/y*
              doswrite 0 –a f   # Copy standard input to MS-DOS file *f*

    Doswrite writes its standard input to an MS-DOS diskette. The diskette must be formatted and have an MS-DOS file system already in place, including all the directories leading up to the file.

Command: echo – print the arguments
Syntax: **echo [–n]** argument ...
Flags: **–n** No line feed is output when done
Examples: echo Start Phase 1   # "Start Phase 1" is printed
              echo –n Hello   # "Hello"

    Echo writes its arguments to standard output. They are separated by blanks and terminated with a line feed unless **–n** is present. This command is used mostly in shell scripts.

Command: getlf – wait until a line has been typed
Syntax: **getlf**
Flags: **(none)**
Example: getlf   # Wait for a line

    In shell scripts it is sometimes necessary to pause to give the user a chance to perform some action, such as inserting a diskette. This command simply waits until a carriage return has been typed, at which time it terminates. It is used in */etc/rc*.

Command: grep – search a file for lines containing a given pattern
Syntax: **grep [–ensv] pattern [file] ...**
Flags: **–e** –e *pattern* is the same as *pattern*
                 –n Print line numbers
                 –s Status only, no printed output
                 –v Select lines that do not match
Examples: grep mouse file   # Find lines in *file* containing *mouse*
               grep [0–9] file   # Print lines containing a digit

    Grep searches one or more files (by default, standard input) and selects out all the lines that match the pattern. All the regular expressions accepted by *mined* are allowed. In addition, + can be used instead of * to mean 1 or more occurrences, ? can be used to mean 0 or 1 occurrences, and | can be used between two regular expressions to mean either one of them. Parentheses can be used for grouping. If a match is found, exit status 0 is returned. If no match is found, exit status 1 is returned. If an error is detected, exit status 2 is returned.

Command: gres – grep and substitute
Syntax: **gres [–g] pattern string [file] ...**
Flags: **–g** Only change the first occurrence per line
Examples: gres bug insect   # Replace *bug* with *insect*
               gres "^[A–Z]+$" CAPS   # Replace capital-only lines with *CAPS*

    Gres is a poor man's *sed*. It looks for the same patterns as *grep*, and replaces each one by the given string.

Command: head – print the first few lines of a file
Syntax: **head [–n] [file] ...**
Flags: *–n* How many lines to print
Examples: head –6   # Print first 6 lines of standard input
               head –1 file1 file2   # Print first line of two files

    The first few lines of one or more files are printed. The default count is 10 lines. The default file is standard input.

Command: kill – send a signal to a process
Syntax: **kill [–signal] process**
Flags: **(none)**
Examples: kill 35   # Send signal 15 to process 35
               kill –9 40   # Send signal 9 to process 40
               kill –2 0   # Send signal 2 to whole process group

A signal is sent to a given process. By default signal 15 (SIGTERM) is sent. Process 0 means all the processes in the sender's process group.

Command: libpack – pack an ASCII assembly code file
Syntax: **libpack**
Flags: **(none)**
Example: libpack <x.s >y.s   # Pack *x.s*
This program is a filter that reads an ASCII assembly code file from standard input and writes the corresponding packed file on standard output. The compiler libraries are archives of packed assembly code files.

Command: libupack – convert a packed assembly code file to ASCII
Syntax: **libupack**
Flags: **(none)**
Example: libupack <y.s >x.s   # Unpack *y.s*
This program is a filter that reads a packed assembly code file from standard input and writes the corresponding ASCII file on standard output.

Command: ln – create a link to a file
Syntax: **ln** file [name]
Flags: **(none)**
Examples: ln file newname   # Make *newname* a synonym for *file*
          ln /usr/games/chess   # Create a link called *chess*
A directory entry is created for *name*. The entry points to *file*. Henceforth, *name* and *file* can be used interchangeably. If *name* is not supplied, the last component of *file* is used as the link name.

Command: lpr – copy a file to the line printer
Syntax: **lpr** [file] ...
Flags: **(none)**
Examples: lpr file &   # Print *file* on the line printer
          pr file | lpr &   # Print standard input (*pr*'s output)
Each argument is interpreted as a file to be printed. *Lpr* copies each file to */dev/lp*, without spooling. It inserts carriage returns and expands tabs. Only one *lpr* at a time may be running.

Command: ls – list the contents of a directory
Syntax: ls [–adfgilrst] name ...
Flags: **–a** All entries are listed, even . and ..
               –d Do not list contents of directories
               –f List argument as unsorted directory
               –g Group id given instead of user id
               –i I-node number printed in first column
               –l Long listing: mode, links, owner, size and time
               –r Reverse the sort order
               –s Give size in blocks (including indirect blocks)
               –t Sort by time, latest first
Examples: ls –l   # List files in working directory
               ls –lis   # List with i-nodes and sizes

For each file argument, list it. For each directory argument, list its contents, unless **–d** is present. When no argument is present, the working directory is listed.

Command: make – a program for maintaining large programs
Syntax: make [–f file] [–ikns] [option] ... [target]
Flags: **–f** Use *file* as the makefile
               –i Ignore status returned by commands
               –k Kill branch on error
               –n Report, but do not execute
               –s Silent mode
Examples: make kernel   # Make *kernel* up to date
               make –n –f file   # Tell what needs to be done

Make is a program that is normally used for developing large programs consisting of multiple files. It keeps track of which object files depend on which source and header files. When called, it does the minimum amount of recompilation to bring the target file up to date.

The file dependencies are expected in *makefile* or *Makefile*, unless another file is specified with **–f**. *Make* has some default rules built in, for example, it knows how to make *.s* files from *.c* files. Here is a sample *makefile*.

```
d=/user/ast                       # d is a macro
program: head.s tail.s            # program depends on these
         cc –o program head.s tail.s # tells how to make program
         echo Program done.       # announce completion
head.s:  $d/def.h head.c          # head.s depends on these
tail.s:  $d/var.h tail.c          # tail.s depends on these
```

A complete description of *make* would require too much space here. For more information, see Feldman (1979). Many books on UNIX also discuss *make*.

Command: mined – MINIX editor
Syntax: **mined** [file]
Flags: **(none)**
Examples: mined /user/ast/book.3   # Edit an existing file
            mined   # Call editor to create a new file
            ls –l | mined   # Use *mined* as a pager to inspect listing

Mined (pronounced min-ed) is a simple full-screen editor. When editing a file, it holds the file in memory, thus speeding up editing, but limiting the editor to files of up to about 43K. Larger files must first be cut into pieces by *split*. Lines may be arbitrarily long. Output from a command may be piped into *mined* so it can be viewed without scrolling off the screen.

At any instant, a window of 24 lines is visible on the screen. The current position in the file is shown by the cursor. Ordinary characters typed in are inserted at the cursor. Control characters and keys on the numeric keypad (at the right-hand side of the keyboard) are used to move the cursor and perform other functions.

Commands exist to move forward and backward a word, and delete words. A word in this context is a sequence of characters delimited on both ends by white space (space, tab, line feed, start of file, or end of file). The commands for deleting characters and words also work on line feeds, making it possible to join two consecutive lines by deleting the line feed between them.

The editor maintains one save buffer (not displayed). Commands are present to move text from the file to the buffer, from the buffer to the file, and to write the buffer onto a new file. If the edited text cannot be written out due to a full disk, it may still be possible to copy the whole text to the save buffer and then write it to a different file on a different disk with CTRL-Q. It may also be possible to escape from the editor with CTRL-S and remove some files.

Some of the commands prompt for arguments (file names, search patterns, etc.). All commands that might result in loss of the file being edited prompt to ask for confirmation.

A key (command or ordinary character) can be repeated *n* times by typing *ESC n key* where *ESC* is the "escape" key.

Forward and backward searching requires a regular expression as the search pattern. Regular expressions follow the same rules as in the UNIX editor, *ed*:

1. Any displayable character matches itself.

2. . (period) matches any character except line feed.

3. ˆ (circumflex) matches the start of the line.

4. $ (dollar sign) matches the end of the line.

5. \c matches the character *c* (including period, circumflex, etc).

6. [string] matches any of the characters in the string.

7. [ˆstring] matches any of the characters except those in the string.

8. [x–y] matches any characters between *x* and *y* (e.g., [a–z]).

9. Pattern* matches any number of occurrences of *pattern*.

Some examples of regular expressions are:

The boy   matches the string "The boy"
^$ matches any empty line.
^A.*\.$ matches any line starting with an *A*, ending with a period.
^[A–Z]*$ matches any line containing only capital letters (or empty).
[A–Z0–9]   matches any line containing either a capital letter or a digit.

Control characters cannot be entered into a file simply by typing them because all of them are editor commands. To enter a control character, depress the ALT key, and then while holding it down, hit the ESC key. Release both ALT and ESC and type the control character. Control characters are displayed in reverse video.

The *mined* commands are as follows.

CURSOR MOTION

arrows   Move the cursor in the indicated direction
CTRL-A   Move cursor to start of current line
CTRL-Z   Move cursor to end of current line
CTRL-^   Move cursor to top of screen
CTRL-_   Move cursor to end of screen
CTRL-F   Move cursor forward to start of next word
CTRL-B   Move cursor backward to start of previous word

SCREEN MOTION

Home key   Move to first character of the file
End key   Move to last character of the file
PgUp key   Scroll window up 23 lines (closer to start of the file)
PgDn key   Scroll window down 23 lines (closer to end of the file)
CTRL-U   Scroll window up 1 line
CTRL-D   Scroll window down 1 line

MODIFYING TEXT

Del key   Delete the character under the cursor
Backspace   Delete the character to left of the cursor
CTRL-N   Delete the next word
CTRL-P   Delete the previous word
CTRL-T   Delete tail of line (all characters from cursor to end of line)
CTRL-O   Open up the line (insert line feed and back up)
CTRL-G   Get and insert a file at the cursor position

BUFFER OPERATIONS

CTRL-@	Set mark at current position for use with CTRL-C and CTRL-K
CTRL-C	Copy the text between the mark and the cursor into the buffer
CTRL-K	Delete text between mark and cursor; also copy it to the buffer
CTRL-Y	Yank contents of the buffer out and insert it at the cursor
CTRL-Q	Write the contents of the buffer onto a file

MISCELLANEOUS

numeric +	Search forward (prompts for regular expression)
numeric —	Search backward (prompts for regular expression)
numeric 5	Display the file status
CTRL-[	Go to specific line
CTRL-R	Global replace *pattern* with *string* (from cursor to end)
CTRL-L	Line replace *pattern* with *string*
CTRL-W	Write the edited file back to the disk
CTRL-X	Exit the editor
CTRL-S	Fork off a shell (use CTRL-D to get back to the editor)
CTRL-	Abort whatever the editor was doing and wait for command
CTRL-E	Erase screen and redraw it
CTRL-V	Visit (edit) a new file

Command: mkdir – make a directory
Syntax: **mkdir** directory ...
Flags: **(none)**
Examples: mkdir dir   # Create *dir* in the current directory
            mkdir /user/ast/dir   # Create the specified directory

The specified directory or directories are created. The entries . and .. are inserted into the new directory.

Command: mkfs – make a file system
Syntax: **mkfs** special prototype
Flags: –L Make a listing on standard output
Examples: mkfs /dev/fd1 proto   # Make a file system on */dev/fd1*
            mkfs /dev/fd1 360   # Make empty 360 block file system

Mkfs builds a file system and copies specified files to it. The prototype file tells which directories and files to copy to it. If the prototype file cannot be opened, and its name is just a string of digits, an empty file system will be made with the specified number of blocks. A sample prototype file follows. The text following the # sign is comment. In the real prototype file, comments are not allowed.

```
boot                                 # boot block file (ignored)
360 63                               # blocks and i-nodes
d--755 1 1                           # root directory
  bin d--755 2 1                     # bin dir: mode (755), uid (2), gid (1)
      sh    ---755 2 1 /user/ast/shell   # shell has mode rwxr-xr-x
      mv   -u-755 2 1 /user/ast/mv    # u = SETUID bit
      login -ug755 2 1 /user/ast/login # SETUID and SETGID
  $                                  # end of /bin
  dev d--755 2 1                     # special files: tty (char), fd0 (block)
      tty   c--777 2 1 4 0           # uid=2, gid=1, major=4, minor=0
      fd0   b--644 2 1 2 0 360       # uid, gid, major, minor, blocks
  $                                  # end of /dev
  user d--755 12 1                   # user dir: mode (755), uid (12), gid (1)
      ast   d--755 12 1              # /user/ast
      $                              # /user/ast is empty
  $                                  # end of /user
$                                    # end of root directory
```

The first entry on each line (except the first 3 and the $ lines, which terminate directories) is the name the file or directory will get on the new file system. Next comes its mode, with the first character being –dbc for regular files, directories, block special files and character special files, respectively. The next two characters are used to specify the SETUID and SETGID bits, as shown above. The last three characters of the mode are the *rwx* protection bits.

Following the mode are the uid and gid. For special files, the major and minor devices are needed. The size in blocks must also be specified for block special files (the MINIX block size is 1K; this can only be changed by changing *BLOCK_SIZE* and then recompiling the operating system).

Command: mknod – create a special file
Syntax: **mknod** file **[b] [c]** major minor
Flags: **(none)**
Example: mknod /dev/plotter c 7 0 # Create special file for a plotter
   Mknod creates a special file named *file*, with the indicated major and minor device numbers. The second argument specifies a block or character file.

Command: mount – mount a file system
Syntax: **/etc/mount** special file **[–r]**
Flags: **–r** File system is mounted read-only
Example: /etc/mount /dev/fd1 /user# Mount floppy disk 1 on */user*

The file system contained on the special file is mounted on *file*. In the example above, the root directory of the file system in drive 1 can be accessed as */user* after the mount. When the file system is no longer needed, it must be unmounted before being removed from the drive.

Command: mv – move or rename a file
Syntax: **mv file1 file2**
                 mv file ... directory
Flags: **(none)**
Examples: mv oldname newname   # Move *oldname* to *newname*
                 mv file1 file2 /user/ast   # Move two files to */user/ast*

Mv moves one or more files from one place in the file system to another. If the old path and new path are on the same device, it is done by linking and unlinking, otherwise by copying.

Command: od – octal dump
Syntax: **od [–bcdhox] [file] [[+] offset [.][b]]**
Flags: **–b** Dump bytes in octal
                 –c Dump bytes as ASCII characters
                 –d Dump words in decimal
                 –h Print addresses in hex (default is octal)
                 –o Dump words in octal (default)
                 –x Dump words in hex
Examples: od –ox file   # Dump *file* in octal and hex
                 od –d file +1000   # Dump *file* starting at byte 01000
                 od –c file +10.b   # Dump *file* starting at block 10

Od dumps a file in one or more formats. If *file* is missing, standard input is dumped. The *offset* argument tells *od* to skip a certain number of bytes or blocks before starting. The offset is in octal bytes, unless it is followed by a "." for decimal or **b** for blocks or both.

Command: passwd – change a login password
Syntax: **passwd [name]**
Flags: **(none)**
Examples: passwd   # Change current user's password
                 passwd ast   # Change ast's password (super-user only)

Passwd is used to change your password. It prompts for the old and new passwords. It asks for the new password twice, to reduce the effect of a typing error. Do not forget to copy the modified password file back to the root file system diskette, or the changes will be lost when the system is rebooted.

Command: pr – print a file
Syntax: **pr** [option] ... [–columns] [+page] [file] ...
Flags: **–h** Take next argument as page header
                 –l Sets page length in lines
                 –n Number the output lines
                 –t Do not print page header or trailer
                 –w Sets line length in characters
Examples: pr –w72 –l60 file   # Use 72 character line, 60 line page
                 pr –3 file   # List *file* three columns to a page
                 pr +4 file   # Start printing with page 4

    Pr formats one or more files for printing. If no files are specified, standard input is printed. Options are provided for setting the width and height of the page, the number of columns to use (default 1), and the page to start with, among others.

Command: pwd – print working directory
Syntax: **pwd**
Flags: **(none)**
Example: pwd   # Print the name of the working directory
    The full path name of the current working directory is printed.

Command: rev – reverse the characters on each line of a file
Syntax: **rev** [file] ...
Flags: **(none)**
Example: rev file   # Reverse each line
    Each file is copied to standard output with all the characters of each line reversed, last one first and first one last.

Command: rm – remove a file
Syntax: **rm** [–fir] name ...
Flags: **–f** Forced remove: no questions asked
                 –i Interactive remove: ask before removing
                 –r Remove directories too

Examples: rm file   # Remove *file*

                 rm –i *.c   # Remove .c files, asking about each

    Rm removes one or more files. If a file has no write permission, *rm* asks for permission (type "y" or "n") unless **–f** is specified. If the file is a directory, it will be recursively descended and removed if and only if the **–r** flag is present.

Command: rmdir – remove a directory

Syntax: **rmdir** directory ...

Flags: **(none)**

Examples: rmdir /user/ast/foobar   # Remove directory *foobar*

                 rmdir /user/ast/f*   # Remove 0 or more directories

    The specified directories are removed. Ordinary files are not removed.

Command: roff – text formatter

Syntax: **roff** [**–hs**] [+n] [–n] file ...

Flags: **–h** Expand tabs to spaces in output

            –s Stop before each page; continue on DEL

            +n Start printing with page *n*

            n   Stop after page *n*

Examples: roff file   # Run off *file*

                 roff +5 file   # Run off *file* starting at page 5

    Roff is a text formatter. Its input consists of the text to be output, intermixed with formatting commands. A formatting command is a line containing the control character followed by a two character command name, and possibly one or arguments. The control character is initially "." (dot). The formatted output is produced on standard output.

    The formatting commands are listed below, with *n* being a number, *c* being a character, and *t* being a title. A + before *n* means it may be signed, indicating a positive or negative change from the current value. Initial values for *n*, where relevant, are given in parentheses.

    .ad   Adjust right margin.

    .ar   Arabic page numbers.

    .br   Line break. Subsequent text will begin on a new line.

    .bl n   Insert *n* blank lines.

    .bp +n   Begin new page and number it *n*. No *n* means +1.

    .cc c   Control character is set to *c*.

    .ce n   Center the next *n* input lines.

    .de zz   Define a macro called *zz*. A line with ".." ends definition.

    .ds   Double space the output. Same as **.ls 2**.

    .ef t   Even page footer title is set to *t*.

    .eh t   Even page header title is set to *t*.

    .fi   Begin filling output lines as full as possible.

.fo t	Footer titles (even and odd) are set to *t*.
.hc c	The character *c* (e.g., %) tells *roff* where hyphens are permitted.
.he t	Header titles (even and odd) are set to *t*.
.hx	Header titles are suppressed.
.hy n	Hyphenation is done if *n* is 1, suppressed if it is 0. Default is 1.
.ig	Ignore input lines until a line beginning with ".." is found.
.in n	Indent *n* spaces from the left margin; force line break.
.ix n	Same as *.in* but continue filling output on current line.
.li n	Literal text on next *n* lines. Copy to output unmodified.
.ll +n	Line length (including indent) is set to *n* (65).
.ls +n	Line spacing: *n* (1) is 1 for single spacing, 2 for double, etc.
.m1 n	Insert *n* (2) blank lines between top of page and header.
.m2 n	Insert *n* (2) blank lines between header and start of text.
.m3 n	Insert *n* (1) blank lines between end of text and footer.
.m4 n	Insert *n* (3) blank lines between footer and end of page.
.na	No adjustment of the right margin.
.ne n	Need *n* lines. If fewer are left, go to next page.
.nn +n	The next *n* output lines are not numbered.
.n1	Number output lines in left margin starting at 1.
.n2 n	Number output lines starting at *n*. If 0, stop numbering.
.ni +n	Indent line numbers by *n* (0) spaces.
.nf	No more filling of lines.
.nx f	Switch input to file *f*.
.of t	Odd page footer title is set to *t*.
.oh t	Odd page header title is set to *t*.
.pa +n	Page adjust by *n* (1). Same as .bp
.pl +n	Paper length is *n* (66) lines.
.po +n	Page offset. Each line is started with *n* (0) spaces.
.ro	Page numbers are printed in Roman numerals.
.sk n	Skip *n* pages (i.e., make them blank), starting with next one.
.sp n	Insert *n* blank lines, except at top of page.
.ss	Single spacing. Equivalent to .ls 1.
.ta	Set tab stops, e.g., .ta 9 17 25 33 41 49 57 65 73 (default).
.tc c	Tabs are expanded into *c*. Default is space.
.ti n	Indent next line *n* spaces; then go back to previous indent.
.tr ab	Translate *a* into *b* on output.
.ul n	Underline the letters and numbers in the next *n* lines.

Command: **sh – shell**
Syntax: **sh [file]**
Flags: **(none)**
Example: sh < script   # Run a shell script

Sh is the shell. It permits redirection of input and output, pipes, magic characters, background processes, shell scripts and most of the other features of the V7 (Bourne) shell. A few of the more common commands are listed below:

```
date                    # Regular command
sort <file              # Redirect input
sort <file1 >file2      # Redirect input and output
cc file.c 2>error       # Redirect  standard error
a.out >f 2>&1           # Combine standard output and standard error
sort <file1 >>file2     # Append output to file2
sort <file1 >file2 &    # Background job
(ls –l; a.out) &        # Run two background commands sequentially
sort <file | wc         # Two-process pipeline
sort <f | uniq | wc     # Three-process pipeline
ls –l *.c               # List all files ending in .c
ls –l [a-c]*            # List all files beginning with a, b, or c
ls –l ?                 # List all one-character file names
ls \?                   # List the file whose name is question mark
ls '???'                # List the file whose name is three question marks
v=/usr/ast              # Set shell variable v
ls –l $v                # Use shell variable v
PS1='Hi! '              # Change the primary prompt to Hi!
PS2='More: '            # Change the secondary prompt to More:
ls –l $HOME             # List the home directory
echo $PATH              # Echo the search path
if ... then ... else ... fi    # If statement
for ... do ... done     # Iterate over argument list
while ... do ... done   # Repeat while condition holds
case ... esac           # Select clause based on condition
echo $?                 # Echo exit status of previous command
echo $$                 # Echo shell's pid
echo $#                 # Echo number of parameters (shell script)
echo $2                 # Echo second parameter (shell script)
echo $*                 # Echo all parameters (shell script)
```

Command: shar – shell archiver
Syntax: **shar** file ...
Flags: **(none)**
Examples: shar *.c >s   # Collect C programs in shell archive
                sh <s   # Extract files from a shell archive

The named files are collected together into a shell archive written onto standard output. The individual files can be extracted by redirecting the shell archive into the shell. The advantage of *shar* over *ar* is that *shar* archives can be read on

almost any UNIX system, whereas numerous, incompatible versions of *ar* are in
widespread use. Extracting the files from a shell archive requires that *gres* is
accessible. In the distribution, *gres* is in */user/bin* rather than */usr/bin*.

Command: **size – print text, data, and bss size of a program**
Syntax: **size** [file] ...
Flags: **(none)**
Example: size file   # Print the size of *file*
    The text, data, bss, and total sizes for each argument are printed. If no argu-
ments are present, *a.out* is assumed. The amount of memory available for combined stack and data segment growth is printed in the column "stack." This is the
value manipulated by the *chmem* command. The total amount of memory allocated to the program when it is loaded is listed under "memory." This value is
just the sum of the other four columns.

Command: **sleep – suspend execution for a given number of seconds**
Syntax: **sleep** seconds
Flags: **(none)**
Example: sleep 10   # Suspend execution for 10 sec.
    The caller is suspended for the indicated number of seconds. This command
is typically used in shell scripts.

Command: **sort – sort a file of ASCII lines**
Syntax: **sort** [**-bcdfimnru**] [**-t**x] [**-o** name] [**+**pos1] [**-**pos2] file ...
Flags: **-b** Skip leading blanks when making comparisons
            -c Check to see if a file is sorted
            -d Dictionary order: ignore punctuation
            -f Fold upper case onto lower case
            -i Ignore nonASCII characters
            -m Merge presorted files
            -n Numeric sort order
            -o Next argument is output file
            -r Reverse the sort order
            -t Following character is field separator
            -u Unique mode (delete duplicate lines)
Examples: sort -nr file   # Sort keys numerically, reversed
            sort +2 -4 file   # Sort using fields 2 and 3 as key
            sort +2 -t: -o out   # Field separator is *:*
            sort +.3 -.6   # Characters 3 through 5 form the key

Sort sorts one or more files. If no files are specified, standard input is sorted. Output is written on standard output, unless –o is specified. The options +*pos1* –*pos2* use only fields *pos1* up to but not including *pos2* as the sort key, where a field is a string a characters delimited by spaces and tabs, unless a different field delimiter is specified with –t. Both *pos1* and *pos2* have the form *m.n* where *m* tells the number of fields and *n* tells the number of characters. Either *m* or *n* may be omitted.

Command: **split – split a large file into several smaller files**
Syntax: split [–n] [file [prefix]]
Flags: –n Number of lines per piece (default: 1000)
Examples: split –200 file   # Split *file* into pieces of 200 lines each
                split file z   # Split *file* into *zaa, zab*, etc.
      Split reads *file* and writes it out in *n*-line pieces. By default, the pieces are called *xaa*, *xab*, etc. The optional second argument can be used to provide an alternative prefix for the output file names.

Command: **stty – set terminal parameters**
Syntax: stty [option ...]
Flags: **(none)**
Examples: stty –echo   # Suppress echoing of input
                stty erase #   # Set the erase character to #
      When given no arguments, *stty* prints the current terminal parameters. It can also be used to set the parameters, as follows:

cbreak	- Enter *cbreak* mode; erase and kill disabled
echo	- Echo input on the terminal
nl	- Accept only line feed to end lines
raw	- Enter *raw* mode; no input processing at all
tabs	- Output tabs (do not expand to spaces)
erase c	- Set erase character (initially backspace)
int c	- Set interrupt (SIGINT) character (initially DEL)
kill c	- Set kill line character (initially @)
quit c	- Set quit (SIGQUIT) character (initially CTRL-\)
default	- Set options back to original values

The first five options may be prefixed by – as in –**tabs** to turn the option off. The next four options each have a single character parameter separated by a space from the option. The **default** option sets the mode and the four settable characters back to the values they had when the system was booted. It is useful when a rogue program has messed them up.

Command: su – temporarily log in as super-user or another user
Syntax: su [name]
Flags: (none)
Examples: su   # Become super-user
                su ast   # Become *ast*

Su can be used to temporarily login as another user. It prompts for the super-user password. If the correct password is entered, *su* creates a shell with the desired uid. If no name is specified, *root* is assumed. To exit the temporary shell, type CTRL-D.

Command: sum – compute the checksum and block count of a file
Syntax: sum file
Flags: (none)
Examples: sum /user/ast/xyz   # Checksum */user/ast/xyz*

Sum computes the checksum of one or more files. It is most often used to see if a file copied from another machine has been correctly received. This program works best when both machines use the same checksum algorithm.

Command: sync – flush the cache to disk
Syntax: sync
Flags: (none)
Example: sync   # Write out all modified cache blocks

MINIX maintains a cache of recently used disk blocks. The *sync* command writes any modified cache blocks back to the disk. This is essential before stopping the system, and should be done before running any *a.out* program that might crash the system.

Command: tail – print the last few lines of a file
Syntax: tail [–n] [file] ...
Flags: –*n* How many lines to print
Examples: tail –6   # Print last 6 lines of standard input
                tail –1 file1 file2   # Print last line of two files

The last few lines of one or more files are printed. The default count is 10 lines. The default file is standard input.

Command: tar – tape archiver
Syntax: **tar [cxtv]** tarfile file ...
Flags: **–c** Create a new archive
              –t Print a table listing the archive's contents
              –v Verbose mode-tell what is going on as it happens
              –x The named files are extracted from the archive
Examples: tar c /dev/fd1 file1 file2 # Create a two-file archive
              tar xv /dev/fd1 file1 file2 # Extract two files from the archive

Tar is an archiver in the style of the standard tape archiver, except that it does not use tape. It's primary advantage over *ar* is that the *tar* format is somewhat more standardized than the *ar* format, making it theoretically possible to transport MINIX files to another computer, but do not bet on it. If the target machine runs MS-DOS, try *doswrite*.

Command: tee – divert standard input to a file
Syntax: **tee [–ai]** file ...
Flags: **–a** Append to the files, rather than overwriting
              –i Ignore interrupts
Examples: cat file1 file2 | tee x   # Save and display two files
              pr file | tee x | lpr   # Save the output of *pr* on *x*

Tee copies standard input to standard output. It also makes copies on all the files listed as arguments.

Command: time – report how long a command takes
Syntax: **time** command
Flags: **(none)**
Examples: time a.out   # Report how long *a.out* takes
              time ls –l *.c   # Report how long the command takes

The command is executed and the real time, user time, and system time (in seconds) are printed.

Command: touch – update a file's time of last modification
Syntax: **touch [–c]** file ...
Flags: **–c** Do not create the file
Example: touch *.h   # Make the *.h* files look recent

The time of last modification is set to the current time. This command is mostly used to trick *make* into thinking that a file is more recent than it really is. If the file being touched does not exist, it is created, unless the **–c** flag is present.

Command: **tr – translate character codes**
Syntax: **tr [–cds] [string1] [string2]**
Flags: **–c** Complement the set of characters in *string1*
–d Delete all characters specified in *string1*
–s Squeeze all runs of characters in *string1* to one character
Examples: tr "[a–z]" "[A–Z]" <x >y # Convert upper case to lower case
tr –d "0123456789" <f1 >f2 # Delete all digits from *f1*

Tr performs simple character translation. When no flag is specified, each character in *string1* is mapped onto the corresponding character in *string2*.

Command: **true – exit with the value true**
Syntax: **true**
Flags: **(none)**
Example: while true # List the directory until DEL is hit
do ls –l
done

This command returns the value *true*. It is used for shell programming.

Command: **umount – unmount a mounted file system**
Syntax: **/etc/umount special**
Flags: **(none)**
Example: /etc/umount /dev/fd1 # Unmount floppy disk 1

A mounted file system is unmounted after the cache has been flushed to disk. A floppy disk should never be removed while it is mounted. If this happens, and is discovered before another floppy disk is inserted, the original one can be replaced without harm. Attempts to unmount a file system holding working directories or open files will be rejected with a "device busy" message.

Command: **uniq – delete consecutive identical lines in a file**
Syntax: **uniq [–cdu] [+n] [–n] [input [output]]**
Flags: **–c** Give count of identical lines in the input
–d Only duplicate lines are written to output
–u Only unique lines are written to output
Examples: uniq +2 file # Ignore first 2 fields when comparing
uniq –d inf outf # Write duplicate lines to *outf*

Uniq examines a file for consecutive lines that are identical. All but duplicate entries are deleted, and the file is written to output. The +*n* option skips the first *n* fields, where a field is defined as a run of characters separated by white space. The –*n* option skips the first *n* spaces. Fields are skipped first.

Command: update – periodically write the buffer cache to disk
Syntax: /etc/update
Flags: (none)
Example: /etc/update &   # Start a process that flushes the cache
    When the system is booted, *update* is started up in the background from */etc/rc* to issue a SYNC system call every 30 sec.

Command: wc – count characters, words, and lines in a file
Syntax: wc [–clw] file ...
Flags: –c Print character count
              –l Print line count
              –w Print word count
Examples: wc file1 file2   # Print all three counts for both files
            wc –l file   # Print line count only
    Wc reads each argument and computes the number of characters, words and lines it contains. A word is delimited by white space (space, tab, or line feed). If no flags are present, all three counts are printed.

C.5. LIBRARIES

    The MINIX distribution contains a substantial number of library procedures, including the system call library, stdio, and many others. The procedures are contained in the archive */usr/lib/libc.a*.
    The archive contains several kinds of procedures, among them procedures called by the compiler that are not normally explicitly called by user programs. For example, when the compiler has to generate code to do multiplication or division on longs, it does not generate in-line code. It calls library procedures instead.
    The archive also calls user-callable procedures. The ones corresponding to the system calls have the same parameters as their UNIX counterparts, as do the *stdio* procedures for the most part. However, there are a few minor exceptions to this rule.
    For one thing, to keep them small, many of the standard MINIX programs do not use *stdio*. To avoid having the *stdio* package loaded with these (and all) programs, the C run-time start-off routine, *crtso*, (which is loaded with all C programs), does not flush *stdio*'s internal buffers when the main program returns to it after completion. User programs that use *stdio* should therefore make the call

```
_cleanup();
```

before exiting or returning from the main program. (Note the underscore, which is part of the name.)

Another minor difference between MINIX *stdio* and UNIX *stdio* is how buffering of *stdout* is done. The MINIX version collects all the characters generated by each call to *printf* (or *fprintf*) and makes one WRITE system call per *printf*.

For noninteractive programs such as *ls* it is more efficient not to flush the buffer per *printf*, but to wait until it fills up. To disable the flushing of *stdout* on each *printf*, put the statement

```
setbuf(stdout, buffer);
```

at the beginning of the program, where *buffer* is an array of characters of size *BUFSIZ* (defined in *stdio.h*). When the program exits, it is then essential to make the call

```
fflush(stdout);
```

to flush the final bytes, or alternatively, to call *_cleanup* to flush all the buffers if more than one output file has been used.

The header file *stdio.h* is located in */usr/include*, along with several other common header files.

The version of *printf* provided lacks some of the more exotic options of V7. One clear difference however, is that V7 accepts both %D and %ld for printing longs. MINIX only accepts the former. Similarly, MINIX only accepts %O and %X for printing longs in octal and hex.

The other library procedures, such as *abs*, *malloc*, and *strcmp*, have the same parameters as the corresponding V7 procedures, and they perform the same function. Space limitations make it impossible to provide detailed documentation here about them. To see which procedures are available, type

```
ar tv /usr/lib/libc.a | mined
```

C.6. FILE FORMATS

In this section we will describe the format of several important files: executable files, archives, and library modules.

C.6.1. Executable File Format (a.out files)

An executable file consists of three parts: a header, the program text and the initialized data. The uninitialized data (the so-called bss segment) is not present in the executable file.

Two memory models are supported by the operating system. The small model has up to 64K memory total, for text, data, and stack. The separate I and D space model has 64K for the text and an additional 64K for data plus stack.

There is no space between the header and text or between the text and data, except that for a separate I and D program, the text size must be a multiple of 16 bytes, the last 0 to 15 of which may be padding. The normal header is 32 bytes and is the same as that of PC-IX. It consists of eight longs as follows:

0: 0x04100301L (small model), or 0x04200301L (separate I and D)
1: 0x00000020L (32-byte header), or 0x00000030L (48-byte header)
2: size of text segment in bytes
3: size of initialized data in bytes
4: size of bss in bytes
5: 0x00000000L
6: total memory allocated to program
7: 0x00000000L

An alternative 48-byte header is also acceptable, and consists of the standard header followed by 16 bytes that are ignored. The longs are stored with the low-order byte first, so the first byte of the file is 0x01 and the next one is 0x03.

One of the fields in the header is the total amount of space that the program will be allocated when it is executed. It is equal to the sum of the text, data, bss, and dynamic allocation. (For separate I and D programs, it is the sum of the data, bss, and dynamic allocation only). The dynamic allocation is the total amount of memory reserved for the stack plus growth of the data segment. The dynamic allocation can be changed with the *chmem* command, which just updates long 6 in the header.

C.6.2. Archive Format

The archive format consists of a sequence of (header, file) pairs, with the magic number 0177545 prepended to the beginning of the file. Each file header consists of 26 bytes as follows (sizes in parentheses):

name	(14)	- File name
time	(4)	- Time of last modification
uid	(1)	- Used id (truncated to 1 byte)
gid	(1)	- Group id
mode	(2)	- File mode (protection bits)
size	(4)	- File length

If a file has an odd number of bytes, a zero byte is added at the end so that each header begins at an even address. The zero byte is not included in the size field. The two longs in the header are stored with the high-order word first, in order to be V7 compatible.

C.6.3. Library Format

The MINIX library format consists of an archive of compact assembly code files. Each file in the archive normally contains just one procedure, although in a few cases two or three closely related procedures are in the same file. Each symbol that is to be visible outside the file must be declared in a *.define* statement. All the *.define* statements must occur at the start of the file, with no other statements before them. These statements are generated only when the C compiler is called with the **–LIB** flag.

Compact assembly code can be generated from ordinary ASCII assembly code by using the filter *libpack*. Compact assembly code can be turned back into ASCII by using the filter *libupack*. If a file is packed and then unpacked, the result will not be identical to the original because comments and excess white space are removed during the packing and cannot be restored. The resulting file will assemble into exactly the same binary file, however.

The packing algorithm relies on the fact that input to the assembler is a sequence of bytes, but only codes 0 to 127 (the ASCII character set) are used. What *libpack* does is recognize commonly occurring strings, and replace them with codes 128 to 255. For example, code 128 is *push ax*, code 129 is *ret*, code 130 is *mov bp,sp*, and so on. The exact list of strings mapped can be found by looking at the source of *libpack* or *libupack*. In theory, any file can be compacted, but if none of the approximately 120 built in strings occur in the file, the output will be identical to the input.

The advantage of this scheme over, say, a Huffman code is that an archive may contain some packed files and some unpacked files. They need not be distinguished in any way. *Asld* has been programmed to expand code 128 into *push ax* whenever it occurs, and so forth. If only ASCII codes appear in the input, no expansion occurs and no harm is done.

MINIX IMPLEMENTERS' GUIDE

This appendix is intended for those readers who wish to modify MINIX or its utilities. In the following pages we will tell what the various files do and how the pieces are put together to form the whole.

One major problem is that some readers will undoubtedly want to use MINIX itself as the development system, others will want to use MS-DOS, and yet others will want to use one of the many UNIX systems available for the IBM PC (or even for other computers). Unfortunately, these systems all differ slightly, which gives rise to problems.

As a simple example, no two C compilers accept exactly the same dialect of C, and no two of them produce the same *a.out* file format. Furthermore, each assembler for the 8088 has its own input syntax and pseudoinstructions. Consequently this appendix is not a cookbook *(Joy of MINIX)*. All we can do is try to provide enough background information to enable the aspiring implementer to tackle any problems that arise.

MINIX was developed on an IBM PC-XT using PC-IX. If that system is used as the development system, few problems will be encountered. If a 640K PC with two 360K drives is available, MINIX itself can be used as the development system. With a little bit of work, other systems can also be used. MS-DOS is not needed, except for formatting new diskettes.

Before modifying MINIX it is strongly recommended that you gain experience using it. Try running the programs in Appendix C, especially *cp*, *df*, *mkdir*, *mkfs*, *mount*, *rm*, and *umount*, all of which will be heavily used during implementation. Try to recompile the original system in your own environment, to see how that is done. Only then is it sensible to begin modifying MINIX. It is probably easiest to work as root when modifying the system.

D.1. INTRODUCTION

A running MINIX system consists of three or four diskettes: the boot diskette, the root file system, the /usr file system (normally mounted on drive 0), and optionally the /user file system (mounted on drive 1, if available). All of these pieces are independent. You can construct one or more new file systems to use with the original operating system, which is on the boot diskette, or you can build a new operating system to use with the original file systems. You can also modify some, but not all, of the file systems. Each one is self contained.

The boot diskette contains the executable image of the operating system, as well as the file system checker, *fsck*. When the PC is booted from it, the operating system is loaded into memory at address 1536 and *fsck* is loaded just after it, typically at an address of about 85K.

Control is initially passed to *fsck*, which displays the menu and waits for a command. If the command specifies that a file system is to be checked or an empty file system is to be built, *fsck* performs the work and then displays the menu again. If the command is an equal sign, *fsck* jumps to address 1536 to start MINIX. The memory occupied by *fsck* will shortly be overwritten by the root file system on the RAM disk.

The boot diskette is built by a program called *build*, which concatenates six programs in a special way, removing headers, padding pieces out to multiples of 16 bytes, and making certain patches to the resulting file. The six programs are: (1) the boot block, (2) the kernel, (3) the memory manager, (4) the file system, (5) the system initializer, and (6) the file system checker. Each of these programs is compiled and linked independently of the others. It is thus possible to change the file system, for example, without having to touch the kernel at all, not even to relink it. We will discuss how each of these programs is made and how *build* works later in this appendix.

File systems, including the root file system, /usr, and /user, can be made using *mkfs*. It is also possible to make an empty file system using the *fsck* menu, mount the file system, and then copy files to it. Existing file systems can be modified by mounting them, and then copying files to them or removing files from them.

The only difference between a file system intended as the root file system and one intended as /usr or /user is the size. When a file system is created, either by *mkfs* or by *fsck*, the number of blocks and i-nodes is written into its super-block and cannot be changed. A file system intended for /usr or /user will normally use 360 blocks, but one intended as the root file system will usually be smaller, to avoid tying up so much memory for RAM disk. The RAM disk size is determined dynamically when the system is booted by simply reading the root file system's super-block to see how big it is. (Throughout this appendix it will be assumed that both the block size and zone size are 1K, and little distinction will be made between blocks and zones.)

The MINIX sources contain nine directories with code and header files, and one directory, *doc*, containing some documentation. The code and header directories are as follows:

kernel   - process, message, and I/O device handling
mm   - the memory manager
fs   - the file system
h   - the headers used by the operating system
lib   - the library routines
tools   - miscellaneous tools and utilities
commands   - the commands (e.g., *cp, grep, ls*)
test   - programs for testing MINIX
include   - the headers used by the commands

We will look at each of these directories in detail as we need them. Some of the directories contain subdirectories containing assembly code or other files specific to one compiler or operating system.

Setting Up

Before trying to carry out the instructions contained in this appendix, you should read it all the way through to get a reasonable grasp of what you have to do and why. In fact, it is a good idea to run *build* to make a new boot diskette using the binaries supplied (see Section D.5) before trying to recompile any of the parts of the operating system.

It will be tacitly assumed throughout this appendix that the development is being done on a PC with two 360K diskettes. For PC/ATs with a single 1.2M diskette, the procedure is slightly different, as noted in a few places. Furthermore, all references to diskette sizes of 360 blocks should be replaced by 1200 blocks for 1.2M diskettes.

MINIX is a large program. Unless you are a professional software developer, it is likely to be an order of magnitude larger than any program you have ever written. Many of the complications involved in recompiling it occur because the sources do not fit on a single diskette. This fact permeates every facet of the implementer's work.

To start with, you will need a large number of blank diskettes to hold the sources, intermediate files, executable programs, and new file systems. These diskettes should be standard IBM-compatible, double-sided, double-density, 360K diskettes. Before starting, format at least 10 diskettes with the format program of MS-DOS 2.0 or a later version. Format more diskettes as you need them. All diskettes must be formatted before being used.

The MINIX sources as distributed contain 9 directories with programs in them. As mentioned above, they are called *kernel, mm, fs, h, lib, tools, commands, test*, and *include*. To rebuild the operating system, you will need the first five; to rebuild the file systems you will need the last six. The directories *h, lib*, and *tools* are needed for both.

Before starting work, you should copy the information from the source diskettes to the newly formatted blank diskettes in a special way. The originals can then be put away for safe keeping. For each source diskette, make as many copies of it as there are directories on it. For example, for a diskette containing directories *a, b, c*, make three copies of it. This can be done by inserting the source diskette in drive 0 and the blank diskette in drive 1 (unmounted), and typing

```
cp /dev/fd0 /dev/fd1
```

Now remove directories *b* and *c* from the first copy, directories *a* and *c* from the second copy, and directories *a* and *b* from the third copy. The result will be that each directory will be on a diskette all by itself. Finally, copy the *h* directory and all its files to the *kernel, mm*, and *fs* diskettes. The *h* directory should be at the top level, not a subdirectory of *kernel* etc. because files are included as *../h/const.h* and so on.

On a system with only 1 drive, first put an empty MINIX file system on each blank diskette using *mkfs*. Then remove everything from the root file system except *cp*, mount a source diskette, and copy as much of it as possible to the RAM disk. The *df* program can be put in */bin* to keep track of available space. Then unmount the source diskette and mount the new (empty) diskette in its place, copying the files from the root device to it. Repeat several times until everything has been copied.

When doing the development on a single drive PC/AT, it will also be necessary to create directories *bin* and *lib* on each source diskette, and copy all the files from */usr/bin* and */usr/lib* to each one. That way, no matter which source diskette is mounted on */usr* at any instant, all the binaries and libraries will be available.

Some directories contain subdirectories called *MINIX, PCIX*, and *C86*. These directories contain assembly language files, makefiles, etc. that differ from system to system. If you are going to use MINIX as the development system, move all the files in the *MINIX* directory into the directory one level above it. For example, *kernel/MINIX/makefile* becomes *kernel/makefile*.

Similarly, if you are going to use PC-IX (or some other version of UNIX such as XENIX), use the files from *PCIX*. If you plan to use MS-DOS, use the *C86* directory. Although these files are specifically for the Computer Innovations C86 compiler, they are a better starting point for other MS-DOS compilers than the MINIX or PC-IX files. If you are using a system other than MINIX, PC-IX or MS-DOS with the C86 compiler, you will probably have to make minor changes to some of these files.

Once you have made a choice of subdirectory and moved its files one level up, remove all the subdirectories because every block of space will be needed later.

We now encounter the first obstacle thrown up by the large size of MINIX. The *commands* directory is too large to fit on a single diskette. Logically, it is a single directory, but when using floppy disks it will be necessary to split it up onto multiple diskettes, each one having a single directory, *commands*, at the top level, and holding some of the programs. Do not fill the diskettes completely full; at least 100K should be left unused on each one. The choice of which commands go on which diskette is unimportant.

A few programs need files from the *include* directory that are not contained in */usr/lib/include*. These are contained on one of the source diskettes. Other programs need files from *h*. These should be copied to the relevant diskette when their absence is noted by the compiler.

Implementers with a hard disk should create a directory *minix* on the hard disk and then create and load the nine subdirectories. As with the floppy disk systems, for each directory with subdirectories, one of them should be chosen and its contents placed in the directory. None of the subdirectories should be created on the hard disk.

The *tools* directory contains two or three programs that may be needed during the development process: *dos2out*, *build*, and *mkfs*. The first one, *dos2out*, converts MS-DOS *.EXE* files to MINIX format. It is only needed when MS-DOS is being used as the development system. The second one, *build*, puts together the compiled and linked pieces of MINIX to form the boot diskette. The third one, *mkfs*, builds MINIX file systems. To build a MINIX file system, you must use *this* version of *mkfs*. Accept no substitutes. Although *mkfs* is needed in both *commands* and in *tools*, its source is only included in the distribution once, so you have to get it into both directories by copying it.

Compile these programs to run on your development system, and use as directed. If your development system is MINIX or PC-IX, you will not need *dos2out*. If it is MS-DOS, compile these three programs with the flag *–DDOS*, for example,

```
cc -c -DDOS mkfs.c
```

After all these steps have been carried out, the original diskette distribution should be put away and all subsequent work done with the directory-per-diskette copies.

D.2. THE LIBRARY

The operating system and many of the commands use library procedures. These procedures must be linked in when the binary (i.e., executable) program is made. To speed up linking, they are precompiled, and kept in a library from which the linker extracts them. The following sections deal with how the library is built and maintained.

If you are using MINIX as the development system, it is not necessary to build the library. A complete, properly ordered MINIX library is already present as the archive */usr/lib/libc.a*. Just use it.

D.2.1. Internal Compiler Procedures

The necessary library procedures can be divided into two disjoint categories: user-callable procedures and internal compiler procedures. The user-callable procedures include the system call library procedures such as *open*, *read*, and *fork*, the standard I/O library procedures, such as *fopen*, *getc*, and *printf*, and miscellaneous procedures, such as *atoi*, *isatty*, and *strcmp*. The sources for all these procedures are provided in the distribution. They merely need to be compiled and put in the library.

The other category is much harder to deal with. Nearly all C compilers use library procedures as part of the generated code. For example, many C compilers do not compile in-line code for multiplication and division on longs. Instead they call the library routines *lmul* and *ldiv*. Similarly, the first or second instruction of each compiled C procedure is often a call to *csv*, which saves the registers and reserves storage for the local variables on the stack.

These internal procedures are written for use with one specific compiler. The version of *lmul* provided in the library that comes with compiler *X* is almost guaranteed not to work with compiler *Y* due to different calling conventions, assumptions about which registers it may and may not destroy, and so on. For this reason, none of the sources for the internal procedures are provided in the distribution. You have to use those that come with your compiler.

However, using the library that comes with your compiler can lead to serious problems. That library not only contains the small internal procedures, such as *lmul*, which are basically harmless, but it also contains the system call procedures such as *read*, which make foreign operating system calls. For example, if you were to compile and link one of the MINIX utilities with an MS-DOS compiler, the binary program produced might contain MS-DOS system calls, which would not work when the program ran on MINIX.

Thus we are faced with a situation in which the user-callable procedures must be derived from the supplied sources, but the internal procedures must be those that go with the particular compiler being used. The solution is to first compile the MINIX library sources and put them in the MINIX library. Then the necessary internal compiler procedures are extracted from the library supplied with the compiler and added to the MINIX library. When a MINIX program is linked, only the MINIX library is specified, thus preventing accidental use of a procedure that might make a foreign system call.

One problem with this approach is that in order to extract the compiler's internal procedures from the library, you must know which ones they are. For the PC-IX and C86 compilers, the necessary procedures are listed below. For other compilers, the only way to find out is to initially assume that none are needed, and try compiling some programs. If the compiler generates calls to internal procedures, these will be flagged by the linker as undefined external symbols. The necessary procedures can then be extracted from the compiler's library, inspected to make sure they contain no system calls, and added to the MINIX library. This process may have to be iterated several times before all of them have been pinpointed. To speed up the process, write a test program that does addition, subtraction, multiplication, division, and modulo on short integers, unsigned integers, and long integers, and try compiling and linking it.

This is an important point, so we will repeat it. Never link a MINIX program with any library other than the MINIX library, and never put any procedure in the MINIX library unless you are sure that it makes no system calls. Accidentally linking into a MINIX program a procedure that makes an MS-DOS, PC-IX, XENIX, or other foreign system call will lead to sure disaster. (Modifying MINIX so that it can handle not only all its own system calls, but also those of MS-DOS, PC-IX, and XENIX as well is left as an exercise for the reader who has a spare decade to kill.)

The directory /usr/lib contains three assembly language files, crtso.s, end.s, and head.s. The first one, crtso.s, is the C run-time start-off procedure. It must be the first procedure in any binary program. When a program gets control after an EXEC system call, execution always begins at address 0, which must be the start of crtso. This little routine puts argc, argv, and envp on the stack properly, and calls _main.

It also defines some compiler-dependent labels needed to mark the start of the text, data, and bss segments. The file end.s defines the labels needed at the end of these segments. When cc is called with the argument file.s, the command that is actually executed is

```
asld /usr/lib/crtso.s file.s /usr/lib/libc.a /usr/lib/end.s
```

The file head.s is analogous to crtso.s, but is only used for linking the memory manager, the file system, and init, because they are started off directly by the kernel, not by an EXEC system call.

D.2.2. Ordering the Procedures in the Library

Another issue that arises when building the library is the ordering of the procedures in it. Some linkers do not care about the order, but others do. Most linkers are one pass, which means that as the linker examines each procedure in the library, it makes the decision to extract it or not based on the information it has at that instant.

To see what consequences this strategy has for library ordering, consider a program that calls getc to get the next input character. The procedure getc calls read. If read happens to be placed before getc in the library, when the linker processes *read* while scanning the library, it will not extract it because it is not used in the user's program. When the linker comes to *getc*, it will extract it and see that *getc* calls *read*. As it continues to scan the library, the linker will keep an eye out for *read*, but it will never find it and will eventually terminate the link with a message saying that *read* is an undefined symbol.

The obvious solution is to order all library procedures in such a way that if X calls Y, then X is located before Y in the library. It is easy to dream up situations where such an ordering is impossible, for example, X calls Y, Y calls Z, and Z calls X. Fortunately, in practice such situations rarely occur. On UNIX systems, the *lorder* command can be used to order the modules in a library.

Another factor to be taken into account when ordering the library is performance. Some linkers stop scanning a library when they have found all the procedures that they need. This observation leads to the goal of placing the most commonly used procedures as early as possible in the library.

D.2.3. Assembly Language Procedures

Although nearly all of the MINIX library is written in C, a handful of procedures had to be written in assembly language. Some of these procedures are not located in the directory *lib* itself, but in one of its subdirectories. If you have followed the instructions given above, you will have already copied the files from one of the subdirectories into *lib*.

Another point concerning the assembly code is the peculiar property that some C compilers have of not handling long names the same way as their own assemblers. When confronted with the name *catchsig*, for example, virtually all C compilers will prepend an underscore and then truncate the result to eight characters, yielding _catchsi as the external symbol. When the name _catchsig is used in an assembly routine, most assemblers will also truncate it to eight characters, yielding the same name, but a few of them do not truncate it, resulting in an undefined symbol _catchsig used by the assembly language file but defined nowhere. If you discover undefined symbols of this kind, the solution is to edit the assembly code files and truncate all symbols to eight characters by hand.

At least one compiler does not prepend the underscore, but attaches it *after* the name. In the above example, the external symbol would be *catchsig_*. Again, the assembly code files must then be manually edited to make the names agree with what the C compiler generates.

D.2.4. Step-by-Step Instructions

The library sources are contained in the archive *libsrc.a* rather than as separate files (to save space on the distribution diskette). Extract them and delete the archive by typing:

```
ar x libsrc.a; rm libsrc.a
```

Compile all the C files and assemble all the assembly code files in *lib*, but do not link them. If the work is being done on UNIX, the shell script *run* can be used. If the work is being done on MINIX, nothing needs to be done. The library */usr/lib/libc.a* on the */usr* diskette is complete and ready for use.

At this point you will have over 100 object files. The next step is to augment this collection by extracting the necessary internal compiler routines from the compiler's own library. Below is a list of files that probably need to be extracted for the PC-IX and C86 compilers:

PC-IX   - *ldiv.o, lmul.o, lrem.o, aldiv.o, almul.o, alrem.o, divsub.o*

C86   - *zldivmod, ziswitch, zfloatpp, zlrsshift, zllshift, zlmul, zlrushift*
         zsswitch, zentry

If the MINIX C compiler is being used, no procedures need to be extracted since everything that is needed is already in the library.

The procedures *csv* and *cret* need special care. Some compilers use them for procedure entry and exit, and others do not. If your compiler uses them, be sure to check to see that they do not make system calls. Some versions of *csv* check for stack overflow, and call *write* to report the problem. If this is the case, you will have to program new versions that do not do the checking. In most cases these procedures are only a few instructions. An example is given in the file *csv.s*, which can be used with PC-IX.

Once all the object files have been assembled, the order must be determined based on who calls whom. The command

```
ar t /usr/lib/libc.a >listing
```

gives the order of the MINIX library, which is a good starting point for other compilers. With UNIX the library, */usr/lib/libc.a*, is built using the archiver, *ar*.

One last note. Most compilers produce *.o* files as the final compilation step. The MINIX C compiler produces only *.s* (assembly code) files, which are then put in the library. The MINIX assembler-loader expects *.s* files rather than *o* files. When using the MINIX compiler, for example, to recompile library procedures that have been modified, the **–LIB** and **–c** flags are required in order to get the proper *.define* pseudoinstructions into the output files.

D.3. MAKING NEW FILE SYSTEMS

MINIX uses several file systems: the root file system, */usr*, and possibly */user*. All of these are constructed the same way. The following sections describe how to make new file systems for MINIX.

D.3.1. Concepts

There are no hard and fast rules about which programs should go on the root file system diskette and which should go elsewhere, except that *login* and *sh* must go in */bin* because *init* expects them there. In general, programs that are heavily used should be put in the root file system, because the root file system goes on the RAM disk. At least 50K should be left free so temporary files can be created in */tmp*.

An important issue is how large to make the root file system. The larger it is, the less room there is in memory for user programs. For 640K computers, a 240K RAM disk is reasonable. The only difference between the distributions for 256K and 640K PC's is the size of the root file system and its consequences, such as the impossibility of having all the utilities online with only 256K.

The general strategy for making new file systems is to first compile and link all the programs that are to go on the new file system. If need be, the executable files will have to be converted to MINIX format. Then the *mkfs* program is run to build a new file system, usually on a diskette, but possibly as a hard disk file.

MINIX supports two memory models: small model and separate instruction and data space model. In the former, a maximum of 64K is allowed for the entire program. In the latter, a maximum of 64K is allowed for the program text, and an additional 64K is allowed for the data and stack combined. No other models are supported, to encourage programmers to write small, modular programs. The current assembler-loader does not generate separate I and D space programs, but when large programs are set up with separate I and D space by another compiler (e.g., on PC-IX), the operating system can handle them.

Any C compiler can be used to compile the commands, but it is essential that they be linked only with the MINIX library, as discussed in the previous section. Accidentally linking in a library procedure that makes a foreign system call will almost certainly lead to an unexpected kernel trap.

When MINIX executes a program, it loads the program into memory and then transfers control to address 0. Address 0 must contain the C run-time start-off procedure, *crtso*. This procedure arranges for *argc*, *argv*, and *envp* to be pushed onto the stack using the standard C calling sequence so that *main* can access them. Because *crtso* is the first procedure that the linker sees, it must contain directives to define the various segments used. These differ from compiler to compiler so several versions are provided.

All executable programs must be in MINIX format, as described in Appendix C. If an MS-DOS compiler is used, the resulting *.EXE* file will not be in MINIX format and thus cannot be executed by MINIX. A program, *dos2out* is provided in the *tools* directory to read a *.EXE* file and write a new file in MINIX format.

This conversion is not entirely trivial. The header format used for *.EXE* files does not include the text size, which MINIX needs. In order to force this information into the *.EXE* header, the *crtso* file used for MS-DOS (C68 compiler) forces the symbol *DGROUP* to be relocatable, thus getting its origin into the header. Since *DGROUP* is at the start of the data, its value is the size of the text. The utility *dos2out* expects *DGROUP* to be the only relocatable symbol.

It is normal in the UNIX world for C compilers to gather all the uninitialized variables, structures, and arrays together into the bss part of the data segment, following the initialized data. This scheme results in an executable program file whose size is equal to the sum of the sizes of the header, text, and initialized data. For example, a program with 3K text, 1K initialized data, and an uninitialized 50K array will have an executable file of about 4K. The bss area is set to zero by MINIX when the program is executed.

Unfortunately, some MS-DOS compilers do not distinguish between initialized and uninitialized data. They treat all variables as initialized data. If the above program were compiled with one of these compilers, the executable program would occupy about 54K of space on the disk, rather than 4K. Use of such a compiler will greatly limit the number of programs that can be kept in */bin* and */usr/bin*. If your compiler has this property, you are advised to replace it with one that does not.

The general strategy for making a new file system is to first compile all the commands that are to be put on it. These may well be spread over several diskettes. When all the compilations have been completed, and all the files converted to MINIX format, if need be, the resulting executable MINIX files should be gathered together in a single directory, conventionally *commands/bin*. On a system without a hard disk, a new diskette should be formatted and the directory *commands/bin* made on it. Then all the executable files should be copied there. A directory *tools* should also be put on the diskette, and loaded with *mkfs* and the prototype file.

A file system is made by running *mkfs*. If you are working on PC-IX, MS-DOS, or some other system, be sure to run the MINIX version of *mkfs* compiled for that system, not the version compiled for MINIX, and certainly not the *mkfs* that came with the development system. *Mkfs* takes a prototype file as described in Appendix C, and builds the new file system. The new file system is normally generated on a diskette, but when using a hard disk, it can also be written onto a file, and copied to a diskette later.

The above process should be repeated for each file system to be made. Once all the file systems have been constructed, MINIX can be run, and several file systems merged by copying the files. This last step may be required in order to make a file system that is full down to the last block because a diskette containing executable programs and *mkfs* cannot hold a full 360K worth of programs—*mkfs* also takes up some space.

D.3.2. Step-by-Step Instructions

The first step is to make the library, as described in D.2. Next, the programs to be compiled should be gathered together in the directory *commands*. On a system without a hard disk, the programs will have to be spread over several diskettes in order to leave enough room on each for the *h* and *include* directories, as well as space for the compiler and linker temporary files.

When using MINIX as the development system, a program can be compiled by typing

```
cc -I/usr/lib/include prog.c
```

(assuming the include files are located in */usr/lib/include*, where they normally are). The proper run-time start-off routine and libraries are automatically used.

When using PC-IX or another UNIX system for building the file system, the procedure is slightly different, in order to use the MINIX run-time start-off routine and the MINIX library instead of the native one. Compile, but do not link each program in *commands*, by typing

```
cc -c -O prog.c
```

To link *commands/prog.o* from inside the *commands* directory and put the resulting executable file on *bin/prog*, type

```
ld -s -o bin/prog ../lib/crtso.o prog.o ../lib/libc.a ../lib/end.o
```

The **–s** flag strips off the symbol table to make the binary file smaller. Alternatively, the flag can be omitted and *strip* used to get rid of the symbol table. An **–i** flag may be used to specify separate I and D space.

On PC-IX, *chmem* can now be used to reduce the dynamic allocation size. For many nonrecursive programs that have no local arrays and do not use the BRK system call, directly or indirectly, 1K is adequate for the stack. The command

```
chmem =1024 bin/prog
```

sets it to 1K. Using *chmem* does not affect the amount of disk space occupied by the program, but does change the amount of memory occupied when the program is executed. Smaller programs mean that more background processes can be running simultaneously. If a program crashes or acts strange, try giving it more stack space with *chmem*.

With MS-DOS, the exact command used to compile the program depends on the compiler being used. After compilation, linking can be typically performed by the command

```
link ..\lib\crtso.obj+prog.obj,prog,listing,..\lib\lib.a
```

After the *.EXE* file has been built, it must be converted to MINIX form by the command

```
dos2out -d prog
```

which reads *PROG.EXE* and writes the output on *PROG.OUT*. The flag **–d**, which is optional, specifies that *PROG.EXE* is to be deleted after *PROG.OUT* has been made.

The subdirectories in *commands* contain the files *makefile* and *make.bat* for use with *make* and MS-DOS, respectively. To compile and link *prog.c* on UNIX or MINIX, the call to make is

```
make f=prog
```

The macro *f* used in *makefile* is assumed to contain the name of the program, without the *.c* suffix. Unlike the *make* version, the MS-DOS batch file can handle several compilations on a single call, for example

```
make prog1 prog2 prog3
```

When all the programs that will go on the new file system have been compiled and linked, they should be gathered together in a single directory, for example, *commands/bin*. On a system with only floppy disks, this directory will normally be on a fresh diskette, not the ones containing the sources. An executable version of the program *mkfs* should also be present.

The directory must also contain the prototype file, as described in Appendix C under the listing for *mkfs*. This file tells how big the new file system is to be (e.g., 360 blocks for PC diskettes), and how many i-nodes it is to have. Since 32 i-nodes fit in a 1K block, and i-node 0 is not used but occupies space, the number of i-nodes should be one less than a multiple of 32. Typical values are 63, 95, or 127. Examples of prototype files can be found in the distribution as *tools/proto.ram* (root file system), *tools/proto.usr* (*/usr*), and *tools/proto.user* (*/user*).

The final step in making a file system is straightforward: just type

```
mkfs -L special proto >logfile
```

where *special* is a special file, such as */dev/fd0* and *proto* is the prototype file. The **–L** flag causes a description of the new file system to be produced on standard output.

After the file system has been made, but before it is put into production, it is a good idea to run MINIX and use *chmem* to reduce the dynamic allocation area of programs, if this step has not already been taken prior to making the file system.

Not all compilers produce equally good code. Before replacing all the binary programs that come with MINIX, determine whether your compiler produces smaller or larger code by compiling a few programs. If your compiler produces smaller code, it may be worthwhile to recompile all programs to replace the originals. However, if your compiler produces larger code, only recompile programs that you have modified.

D.4. RECOMPILING MINIX

Recompiling the operating system itself is not technically difficult, but its relatively large size requires some care when using a system having only two 360K floppy disks and no hard disk. Before modifying the system, it is strongly recommended that you try recompiling the system as distributed, to learn how to do it. Using a floppy disk based MINIX system, it takes two to three hours to compile and build the entire operating system from scratch.

The bootable image is composed of six parts: the kernel, memory manager, file system, initializer, boot block, and file system checker. You need only recompile those parts you have modified. The binaries of the other parts are already present in *tools*, and can be used as is. The instructions below tell how to recompile all the parts. Normally only some of them will have to be recompiled.

D.4.1. Concepts

The operating system is contained in three directories: *kernel*, *mm*, and *fs*. In addition, the directory *h* contains header files used by all three of these. The directory *kernel* contains the lowest two layers of the system, which do interrupt handling, process management, message passing, and I/O. All the files in this directory are linked into a single executable, binary program, *kernel*.

Although nearly all of the kernel is written in C, two assembly language files are also needed. They are *mpx88.s*, which contains the interrupt handlers (i.e., process multiplexing) and *klib88.s*, which holds several small library routines used only in the kernel.

As mentioned earlier, some compilers truncate long names different from their own assemblers, so if your linker complains about undefined symbols, it may be necessary to edit *mpx88.s* and *klib88.s* to truncate all the long names by hand.

If you are using an assembler that does not accept any of the assembly language versions provided, pick the closest one and modify it as need be. Most of the pseudoinstructions are present in all assemblers, sometimes with a different name however. The only one that may not be available everywhere is *.ASCIZ*, which generates a string terminated by a zero byte. In this case, the zero byte should be made explicit in the argument.

D.4.2. Step-by-Step Instructions

By now you should already have moved *mpx88.s* and *klib88.s* from one of the subdirectories to *kernel* and removed the subdirectories. When using a system with only 360K floppy disks, remove all other directories except *kernel* and *h* from the diskette, to provide room for the object files and compiler temporary files.

Now compile or assemble each of the files. On a PC with two diskette drives, the standard */usr* file system should be in drive 0 and the kernel diskette should be in drive 1 (mounted on */user*). When using MINIX as the development system, the easiest way is just to type

```
make
```

Alternatively the compilations can be done "by hand" by typing

```
cc -c -Di8088 -w *.c
```

The **-w** flag suppresses some irrelevant warning messages that occur because the source code is a compromise between what various compilers expect. This route is somewhat faster because the presence of *make* itself in memory means that there is not enough space left for both *cpp* and *cem* simultaneously. Consequently, the *makefile* uses the **-F** and **-T.** flags to direct the preprocessor output to disk instead of piping it into *cem*.

With MS-DOS, the *make.bat* file can also be used, but it should be checked first to see if it is appropriate for the configuration and compiler being used.

If the compilations have been done "by hand," link all the object files into a single executable binary program by just typing

```
make
```

For this step, the library described in Sec. D.2 will be needed, but the source files will not be. The assembler-linker, *asld*, is smaller than *cem*, so there is no shortage of memory here. However, it produces a large temporary file, so the *makefile* removes */lib/cem* to make room for it. It can be restored later by mounting the root file system and copying the file from it to */lib*.

If the development system is MS-DOS, the kernel binary must now be converted to MINIX format by running *dos2out*, which can be found in the *tools* directory of the distribution. The executable kernel file should be named simply *kernel*.

In a similar manner, compile and link the memory manager. It has no assembly code files, just C files. If */lib/cem* has been removed, restore it manually before starting. Then mount the diskette with the *mm* directory on */user*. Copy the *h* directory there if it is not already present and use the *makefile* or *make.bat* file to compile and link the memory manager. Alternatively, do it by hand with the command

```
cc -c -Di8088 -w *.c
```

Again, link and convert the final output to MINIX format, if necessary, and call it *mm*.

Repeat the above process for the file system. Then compile, link, and convert *tools/init*, putting the result on the file *init*. At this point you will have four independently compiled and linked files: *kernel*, *mm*, *fs*, and *init*. Ultimately, these four files will form the operating system.

However, before the boot diskette can be built, two more programs, *fsck* and *bootblok* must be prepared. Both are located in *tools*. *Fsck* has two files, a C file, *fsck.c*, and an assembly language file, *fsck1.s*. *Bootblok* is entirely contained in the assembly code file *bootblok.s*. (The MS-DOS versions of the assembly language files have extension *.asm* rather than *.s*).

To compile *fsck.c*, you need the include files *h/const.h*, *h/type.h*, *fs/const.h*, and *fs/type.h*. Furthermore, *fsck.c* is the largest single file in MINIX, and its compilation strains the system the space resources to the utmost. Be sure that */lib/cem* has enough stack space (about 51K) and that there are no unnecessary files anywhere taking up precious disk blocks. The command

```
cc -c -T. fsck.c
```

compiles *fsck.c* using the current directory for the (large) intermediate files. Link *fsck* with the command

```
asld -T. fsck1.s fsck.s /usr/lib/libc.a /usr/lib/end.s
```

Alternatively, just type

```
make fsck
```

Normally it will not be necessary to reassemble *bootblok* since changes to the operating system rarely require changes to the boot block. However, if the boot block must be changed, after assembling and linking it remove the header, for example, using *dd*, so that the first byte of the file is the first instruction. See *tools/makefile* for the command sequence.

D.5. BUILDING THE BOOT DISKETTE

In this section we will describe how the six independently compiled and linked programs, *bootblok*, *kernel*, *mm*, *fs*, *init*, and *fsck* are forged together to make the boot diskette. The first time you try making a new operating system, use the six binaries provided in *tools*, rather than making new ones.

D.5.1. Concepts

The boot diskette contains the six programs mentioned above, in the order given. The boot block occupies the first 512 bytes on the disk. When the computer is turned on, the ROM gets control and tries to read the boot block from drive 0 into memory at address 0x7C00. If this read succeeds, the ROM jumps to address 0x7C00 to start the boot program.

The MINIX boot program first copies itself to an address just below 192K, to get itself out of the way. Then it calls the BIOS repeatedly to load 16 cylinders full of data into memory starting at address 0x600 (1536). This data is the core image of the operating system, followed directly by *fsck*. When the loading is finished, the boot program jumps to the start of *fsck*, which then displays the initial menu. If the user types an equal sign, *fsck* jumps to 1536 to start MINIX.

The boot diskette is generated by *tools/build*. It takes the six programs listed above and concatenates them in a special way. The first 512 bytes of the boot diskette come from *bootblok*. If need be, some zero bytes are added to pad *bootblok* out to 512. *Bootblok* does not have a header, and neither does the boot diskette because when the ROM loads the boot block to address 0x7C00, it expects the first byte to be the start of the first instruction.

At position 512, the boot diskette contains the kernel, again without a header. Byte 512 of the boot diskette will be placed at memory address 1536 by the boot program, and will be executed as the first MINIX instruction when *fsck* terminates. After the kernel comes *mm*, *fs*, *init*, and *fsck*, each padded out to a multiple of 16 bytes so that the next one begins at a click boundary.

Each of the programs may be compiled either with or without separate I and D space. The two models are different, but *build* explicitly checks to see which model each program uses and handles it. In short, what *build* does is read six files, stripping the headers off the last five of them, and concatenate them onto the output, rounding the first one up to 512 bytes and the rest up to a multiple of 16 bytes.

After having completed the concatenation of the six files, *build* makes three patches to the output.

1. The last 4 words of the boot block are set to the number of cylinders to load, and the DS, PC, and CS values to use for running *fsck*. The boot program needs this information so that it can jump to *fsck* after it has finished loading. Without this information, the boot program would not know where to jump.

2. *Build* loads the first 8 words of the kernel's data segment with the CS and DS segment register values for *kernel*, *mm*, *fs*, and *init*. Without this information, the kernel could not run these programs when the time came: it would not know where they were. It also sets word 4 of the kernel's text segment to the DS value needed to run the kernel.

3. The origin and size of *init* are inserted at address 4 of the file system's data space. The file system needs this information to know where to put the RAM disk, which begins just after the end of *init*, exactly overwriting the start of *fsck*.

D.5.2. Step-by-Step Instructions

First, compile, link, and if need be, convert to MINIX format *bootblok*, *kernel*, *mm*, *fs*, *init*, and *fsck* as described above, or better yet, use the ones provided where possible. The file *bootblok* provided in the distribution has already been stripped of its header and is ready to use. If for any reason you need to reassemble it, do not forget to strip off the header, as is done in *makefile*.

If you have not already done so, compile *build* to run on the development system (see *makefile* and *make.bat*). If you are using a computer without a hard disk, collect the six parts of the operating system and *build* in *tools* in drive 1.

Next unmount */usr* and insert a blank diskette in drive 0. This will be the boot diskette. Now type

```
build bootblok kernel mm fs init fsck /dev/fd0
```

On a hard disk system, the command given from *tools* will probably be

```
build bootblok ../kernel/kernel ../mm/mm ../fs/fs init fsck /dev/fd0
```

When *build* finishes running, the boot diskette will be ready in drive 0 and a printout of the sizes will appear on standard output.

Alternatively, you can just type

```
make image
```

to produce a bootable operating system on */dev/fd0*. At the time you give the command, you need */usr* in drive 0 so *make* itself can be loaded. Just before *build*, is called */dev/fd0*, is unmounted and you are asked to insert a blank (formatted) diskette in drive 0, and pauses until you hit the return key.

If you wish to use *make*, you will have to create dummy files *fsck.s* and *init.s* to prevent *make* from trying to reconstruct *fsck* and *init*. Before running it for real, give the command

```
make -n image
```

to see what *make* intends to do. If need be, use *touch* to trick *make* into doing what *you* want, rather than what *it* wants.

D.6. TESTING MINIX

After having built a new version of MINIX, it is a good idea to test it. To aid in this testing, a collection of test programs have been provided on the */user* diskette. To use the test programs, bring up the system, except that when it asks you to insert */usr* in drive 0, insert */user* instead. Now change to */user/test* and list the files there. You should find a shell script called *run*, and a series of executable files called *test0*, *test1*, and so on, as well as a few other files used by the test programs. You can run any of the tests individually, or type

```
run
```

to run them all. If any errors are encountered, they will be reported. You will have to refer to the source code to see what each error means. The tests are quite comprehensive, and take more than 10 minutes to finish.

D.7. INSTALLING NEW DEVICE DRIVERS

Once you have successfully reached this point, you will now be able to modify MINIX. In general, if a modification only affects, say, the file system, you will not have to recompile the memory manager or kernel. If a modification affects any of the files in *h*, you should recompile the entire system, just to be safe.

One common modification is adding new I/O devices and drivers. To add a new I/O device to MINIX, it is necessary to write a driver for it. The new driver should use the same message interface as the existing ones. The driver should be put in the directory *kernel* and *makefile* or *make.bat* updated, if they are used. In addition, the entry point of the new task must be added to the list contained in the array *task* in *kernel/table.c*. If *dmp.c* is still in use, an entry also has to be made for it in *nayme*.

Two changes are also required in the *h* directory. In *h/const.h*, the constant *NR_TASKS* has to be increased by 1, and the new task has to be given a name in *h/com.h*.

A new special file will have to be created for the driver. This can be done by adding a line to the directory */dev* in *tools/proto.ram*.

To tell the file system which task is handling the new special file, a line has to be added to the array *dmap* in *fs/table.c*.

D.8. TROUBLESHOOTING

If you modify the system, there is always the possibility that you will introduce an error. In this section, we will discuss some of the more common problems and how to track them down.

To start with, if something is acting strange, turn the computer off and reboot from scratch. This gets everything into a known state. Rebooting with CTRL-ALT-DEL may leave the system in a peculiar state, which may be the cause of the trouble.

If the message

```
Booting MINIX 1.0
```

does not appear on the screen after the power-on self-tests have completed, something is wrong with the boot block. The boot block prints this message by calling the BIOS. Make a dump of the first block of the boot diskette and examine it by hand to see if it contains the proper program.

If the above message appears, but the initial menu does not, it is likely that *fsck* is not being started, since the first thing *fsck* does is print the menu. Check the last 6 bytes of the boot block to see if the segment and offset put there by *build* correspond to the address at which *fsck* is located (right after *init*).

If the menu appears, but the system does not respond to the equal sign,

MINIX is probably being started, but crashing during initialization. One possible cause is the introduction of print statements into the kernel. However, it is not permitted to display anything until after the terminal task has run to initialize itself. Be careful about where you put the print statements.

If the screen has been cleared and the message giving the sizes has appeared, the kernel has initialized itself, the memory manager has run and blocked waiting for a message, and the file system has started running. This message is printed as soon as the file system has read the super-block of the root file system.

If the system appears to hang before or after reading the root file system, some help can be obtained by hitting the F1 or F2 function keys (unless the dump routines have been removed). By hitting F1 twice a few seconds apart and noting the times in the display, it may be possible to see which processes are running. If, for example, *init* is unable to fork, for whatever reason, or cannot open */etc/ttys*, or cannot execute */bin/sh* or */bin/login*, the system will hang, but process 2 (*init*) may continue to use CPU cycles. If the F1 display shows that process 2 is constantly running, it is a good bet that *init* is unable to make a system call or open a file that is essential. The problem can usually be localized by putting statements in the main loops of the file system and memory manager to print a line describing each incoming message and each outgoing reply. Recompile and test the system using the new output as a guide.

E

MINIX
SOURCE CODE
LISTING

```
0000    /* Copyright (C) 1987 by Prentice-Hall, Inc.  Permission is hereby granted to
0001     * private individuals and educational institutions to modify and
0002     * redistribute the binary and source programs of this system to other
0003     * private individuals and educational institutions for educational and
0004     * research purposes.  For corporate or commercial use, permission from
0005     * Prentice-Hall is required.  In general, such permission will be granted,
0006     * subject to a few conditions.
0007     */
0008
0009    #define EXTERN       extern    /* used in *.h files */
0010    #define PRIVATE      static    /* PRIVATE x limits the scope of x */
0011    #define PUBLIC                 /* PUBLIC is the opposite of PRIVATE */
0012    #define FORWARD                /* some compilers require this to be 'static' */
0013
0014    #define TRUE         1         /* used for turning integers into Booleans */
0015    #define FALSE        0         /* used for turning integers into Booleans */
0016
0017    #define HZ           60        /* clock freq (software settable on IBM-PC) */
0018    #define BLOCK_SIZE   1024      /* # bytes in a disk block */
0019    #define SUPER_USER   (uid) 0   /* uid of superuser */
0020
0021    #define MAJOR        8         /* major device = (dev>>MAJOR) & 0377 */
0022    #define MINOR        0         /* minor device = (dev>>MINOR) & 0377 */
0023
0024    #define NR_TASKS     8         /* number of tasks in the transfer vector */
0025    #define NR_PROCS     16        /* number of slots in proc table */
0026    #define NR_SEGS      3         /* # segments per process */
0027    #define T            0         /* proc[i].mem_map[T] is for text */
0028    #define D            1         /* proc[i].mem_map[D] is for data */
0029    #define S            2         /* proc[i].mem_map[S] is for stack */
0030
0031    #define MAX_P_LONG   2147483647 /* maximum positive long, i.e. 2**31 - 1 */
0032
0033    /* Memory is allocated in clicks. */
0034    #define CLICK_SIZE   0020      /* unit in which memory is allocated */
0035    #define CLICK_SHIFT  4         /* log2 of CLICK_SIZE */
0036
0037    /* Process numbers of some important processes */
0038    #define MM_PROC_NR   0         /* process number of memory manager */
0039    #define FS_PROC_NR   1         /* process number of file system */
0040    #define INIT_PROC_NR 2         /* init -- the process that goes multiuser */
0041    #define LOW_USER     2         /* first user not part of operating system */
0042
0043    /* Miscellaneous */
0044    #define BYTE         0377      /* mask for 8 bits */
0045    #define TO_USER      0         /* flag telling to copy from fs to user */
0046    #define FROM_USER    1         /* flag telling to copy from user to fs */
0047    #define READING      0         /* copy data to user */
0048    #define WRITING      1         /* copy data from user */
0049    #define ABS          -999      /* this process means absolute memory */
```

```
0050
0051    #define WORD_SIZE          2                  /* number of bytes per word */
0052
0053    #define NIL_PTR    (char *) 0      /* generally useful expression */
0054
0055    #define NO_NUM           0x8000 /* used as numerical argument to panic() */
0056    #define MAX_PATH            128 /* max length of path names */
0057    #define SIG_PUSH_BYTES        8 /* how many bytes pushed by signal */
0058    #define MAX_ISTACK_BYTES   1024 /* maximum initial stack size for EXEC */
0059
0060    /* Device numbers of root (RAM) and boot (fd0) devices. */
0061    #define ROOT_DEV (dev_nr)   256 /* major-minor device number of root dev */
0062    #define BOOT_DEV (dev_nr)   512 /* major-minor device number of boot diskette */
0063
0064    /* Flag bits for i_mode in the inode. */
0065    #define I_TYPE           0170000 /* this field gives inode type */
0066    #define I_REGULAR        0100000 /* regular file, not dir or special */
0067    #define I_BLOCK_SPECIAL  0060000 /* block special file */
0068    #define I_DIRECTORY      0040000 /* file is a directory */
0069    #define I_CHAR_SPECIAL   0020000 /* character special file */
0070    #define I_SET_UID_BIT    0004000 /* set effective uid on exec */
0071    #define I_SET_GID_BIT    0002000 /* set effective gid on exec */
0072    #define ALL_MODES        0006777 /* all bits for user, group and others */
0073    #define RWX_MODES        0000777 /* mode bits for RWX only */
0074    #define R_BIT            0000004 /* Rwx protection bit */
0075    #define W_BIT            0000002 /* rWx protection bit */
0076    #define X_BIT            0000001 /* rwX protection bit */
0077    #define I_NOT_ALLOC      0000000 /* this inode is free */
```

```
0100    #define NCALLS          69      /* number of system calls allowed */
0101
0102    #define EXIT            1
0103    #define FORK            2
0104    #define READ            3
0105    #define WRITE           4
0106    #define OPEN            5
0107    #define CLOSE           6
0108    #define WAIT            7
0109    #define CREAT           8
0110    #define LINK            9
0111    #define UNLINK          10
0112    #define CHDIR           12
0113    #define TIME            13
0114    #define MKNOD           14
0115    #define CHMOD           15
0116    #define CHOWN           16
0117    #define BRK             17
0118    #define STAT            18
0119    #define LSEEK           19
0120    #define GETPID          20
0121    #define MOUNT           21
0122    #define UMOUNT          22
0123    #define SETUID          23
0124    #define GETUID          24
0125    #define STIME           25
0126    #define ALARM           27
0127    #define FSTAT           28
0128    #define PAUSE           29
0129    #define UTIME           30
0130    #define ACCESS          33
0131    #define SYNC            36
0132    #define KILL            37
0133    #define DUP             41
0134    #define PIPE            42
0135    #define TIMES           43
0136    #define SETGID          46
0137    #define GETGID          47
0138    #define SIGNAL          48
0139    #define IOCTL           54
0140    #define EXEC            59
0141    #define UMASK           60
0142    #define CHROOT          61
0143
0144    /* The following are not system calls, but are processed like them. */
0145    #define KSIG            64      /* kernel detected a signal */
0146    #define UNPAUSE         65      /* to MM or FS: check for EINTR */
0147    #define BRK2            66      /* to MM: used to say how big FS & INIT are */
0148    #define REVIVE          67      /* to FS: revive a sleeping process */
0149    #define TASK_REPLY      68      /* to FS: reply code from tty task */
```

```
0150   /* System calls. */
0151   #define SEND            1       /* function code for sending messages */
0152   #define RECEIVE         2       /* function code for receiving messages */
0153   #define BOTH            3       /* function code for SEND + RECEIVE */
0154   #define ANY   (NR_PROCS+100)    /* receive(ANY, buf) accepts from any source */
0155
0156   /* Task numbers, function codes and reply codes. */
0157   #define HARDWARE       -1       /* used as source on interrupt generated msgs */
0158
0159   #define SYSTASK        -2       /* internal functions */
0160   #       define SYS_XIT   1      /* fcn code for sys_xit(parent, proc) */
0161   #       define SYS_GETSP 2      /* fcn code for sys_sp(proc, &new_sp) */
0162   #       define SYS_SIG   3      /* fcn code for sys_sig(proc, sig) */
0163   #       define SYS_FORKED 4     /* fcn code for sys_forked(parent, child) */
0164   #       define SYS_NEWMAP 5     /* fcn code for sys_newmap(procno, map_ptr) */
0165   #       define SYS_COPY  6      /* fcn code for sys_copy(ptr) */
0166   #       define SYS_EXEC  7      /* fcn code for sys_exec(procno, new_sp) */
0167   #       define SYS_TIMES 8      /* fcn code for sys_times(procno, bufptr) */
0168   #       define SYS_ABORT 9      /* fcn code for sys_abort() */
0169
0170   #define CLOCK          -3       /* clock class */
0171   #       define SET_ALARM 1      /* fcn code to CLOCK, set up alarm */
0172   #       define CLOCK_TICK 2     /* fcn code for clock tick */
0173   #       define GET_TIME  3      /* fcn code to CLOCK, get real time */
0174   #       define SET_TIME  4      /* fcn code to CLOCK, set real time */
0175   #       define REAL_TIME 1      /* reply from CLOCK: here is real time */
0176
0177   #define MEM            -4       /* /dev/ram, /dev/(k)mem and /dev/null class */
0178   #       define RAM_DEV   0      /* minor device for /dev/ram */
0179   #       define MEM_DEV   1      /* minor device for /dev/mem */
0180   #       define KMEM_DEV  2      /* minor device for /dev/kmem */
0181   #       define NULL_DEV  3      /* minor device for /dev/null */
0182
0183   #define FLOPPY         -5       /* floppy disk class */
0184   #define WINCHESTER     -6       /* winchester (hard) disk class */
0185   #       define DISKINT   1      /* fcn code for disk interupt */
0186   #       define DISK_READ 3      /* fcn code to DISK (must equal TTY_READ) */
0187   #       define DISK_WRITE 4     /* fcn code to DISK (must equal TTY_WRITE) */
0188   #       define DISK_IOCTL 5     /* fcn code for setting up RAM disk */
0189
0190   #define TTY            -7       /* terminal I/O class */
0191   #define PRINTER        -8       /* printer  I/O class */
0192   #       define TTY_CHAR_INT 1   /* fcn code for tty input interrupt */
0193   #       define TTY_O_DONE 2     /* fcn code for tty output done */
0194   #       define TTY_READ  3      /* fcn code for reading from tty */
0195   #       define TTY_WRITE 4      /* fcn code for writing to tty */
0196   #       define TTY_IOCTL 5      /* fcn code for ioctl */
0197   #       define SUSPEND  -998    /* used in interrupts when tty has no data */
0198
0199   /* Names of message fields for messages to CLOCK task. */
```

```
0200   #define DELTA_TICKS     m6_l1    /* alarm interval in clock ticks */
0201   #define FUNC_TO_CALL    m6_f1    /* pointer to function to call */
0202   #define NEW_TIME        m6_l1    /* value to set clock to (SET_TIME) */
0203   #define CLOCK_PROC_NR   m6_i1    /* which proc (or task) wants the alarm? */
0204   #define SECONDS_LEFT    m6_l1    /* how many seconds were remaining */
0205
0206   /* Names of message fields used for messages to block and character tasks. */
0207   #define DEVICE          m2_i1    /* major-minor device */
0208   #define PROC_NR         m2_i2    /* which (proc) wants I/O? */
0209   #define COUNT           m2_i3    /* how many bytes to transfer */
0210   #define POSITION        m2_l1    /* file offset */
0211   #define ADDRESS         m2_p1    /* core buffer address */
0212
0213   /* Names of message fields for messages to TTY task. */
0214   #define TTY_LINE        m2_i1    /* message parameter: terminal line */
0215   #define TTY_REQUEST     m2_i3    /* message parameter: ioctl request code */
0216   #define TTY_SPEK        m2_l1    /* message parameter: ioctl speed, erasing */
0217   #define TTY_FLAGS       m2_l2    /* message parameter: ioctl tty mode */
0218
0219   /* Names of messages fields used in reply messages from tasks. */
0220   #define REP_PROC_NR     m2_i1    /* # of proc on whose behalf I/O was done */
0221   #define REP_STATUS      m2_i2    /* bytes transferred or error number */
0222
0223   /* Names of fields for copy message to SYSTASK. */
0224   #define SRC_SPACE       m5_c1    /* T or D space (stack is also D) */
0225   #define SRC_PROC_NR     m5_i1    /* process to copy from */
0226   #define SRC_BUFFER      m5_l1    /* virtual address where data come from */
0227   #define DST_SPACE       m5_c2    /* T or D space (stack is also D) */
0228   #define DST_PROC_NR     m5_i2    /* process to copy to */
0229   #define DST_BUFFER      m5_l2    /* virtual address where data go to */
0230   #define COPY_BYTES      m5_l3    /* number of bytes to copy */
0231
0232   /* Field names for accounting, SYSTASK and miscellaneous. */
0233   #define USER_TIME       m4_l1    /* user time consumed by process */
0234   #define SYSTEM_TIME     m4_l2    /* system time consumed by process */
0235   #define CHILD_UTIME     m4_l3    /* user time consumed by process' children */
0236   #define CHILD_STIME     m4_l4    /* system time consumed by proces children */
0237
0238   #define PROC1           m1_i1    /* indicates a process */
0239   #define PROC2           m1_i2    /* indicates a process */
0240   #define PID             m1_i3    /* process id passed from MM to kernel */
0241   #define STACK_PTR       m1_p1    /* used for stack ptr in sys_exec, sys_getsp */
0242   #define PR              m6_i1    /* process number for sys_sig */
0243   #define SIGNUM          m6_i2    /* signal number for sys_sig */
0244   #define FUNC            m6_f1    /* function pointer for sys_sig */
0245   #define MEM_PTR         m1_p1    /* tells where memory map is for sys_newmap */
0246   #define CANCEL          0        /* general request to force a task to cancel */
0247   #define SIG_MAP         m1_i2    /* used by kernel for passing signal bit map */
```

```
0250    /* Error codes.  They are negative since a few system calls, such as READ, can
0251     * either return a positive number indicating success, or an error code.
0252     */
0253
0254    #define NERROR          34
0255    #define OK               0
0256    #define ERROR           -1
0257    #define EPERM           -1
0258    #define ENOENT          -2
0259    #define ESRCH           -3
0260    #define EINTR           -4
0261    #define EIO             -5
0262    #define ENXIO           -6
0263    #define E2BIG           -7
0264    #define ENOEXEC         -8
0265    #define EBADF           -9
0266    #define ECHILD         -10
0267    #define EAGAIN         -11
0268    #define ENOMEM         -12
0269    #define EACCES         -13
0270    #define EFAULT         -14
0271    #define ENOTBLK        -15
0272    #define EBUSY          -16
0273    #define EEXIST         -17
0274    #define EXDEV          -18
0275    #define ENODEV         -19
0276    #define ENOTDIR        -20
0277    #define EISDIR         -21
0278    #define EINVAL         -22
0279    #define ENFILE         -23
0280    #define EMFILE         -24
0281    #define ENOTTY         -25
0282    #define ETXTBSY         26
0283    #define EFBIG          -27
0284    #define ENOSPC         -28
0285    #define ESPIPE         -29
0286    #define EROFS          -30
0287    #define EMLINK         -31
0288    #define EPIPE          -32
0289    #define EDOM           -33
0290    #define ERANGE         -34
0291
0292    #define E_LOCKED      -101
0293    #define E_BAD_CALL    -102
0294    #define E_LONG_STRING -103
0295
0296    /* The following error codes are generated by the kernel itself. */
0297    #define E_BAD_DEST      -1      /* destination address illegal */
0298    #define E_BAD_SRC       -2      /* source address illegal */
0299    #define E_TRY_AGAIN     -3      /* can't send-- tables full */
```

```
0300   #define E_OVERRUN        -4    /* interrupt for task that is not waiting */
0301   #define E_BAD_BUF        -5    /* message buf outside caller's addr space */
0302   #define E_TASK           -6    /* can't send to task */
0303   #define E_NO_MESSAGE     -7    /* RECEIVE failed: no message present */
0304   #define E_NO_PERM        -8    /* ordinary users can't send to tasks */
0305   #define E_BAD_FCN        -9    /* only valid fcns are SEND, RECEIVE, BOTH */
0306   #define E_BAD_ADDR      -10    /* bad address given to utility routine */
0307   #define E_BAD_PROC      -11    /* bad proc number given to utility */
```

```
0350    /* Data structures for IOCTL. */
0351
0352    struct sgttyb {
0353      char sg_ispeed;                   /* input speed (not used at present) */
0354      char sg_ospeed;                   /* output speed (not used at present) */
0355      char sg_erase;                    /* erase character */
0356      char sg_kill;                     /* kill character */
0357      int  sg_flags;                    /* mode flags */
0358    };
0359
0360    struct tchars {
0361      char t_intrc;                     /* character that generates SIGINT */
0362      char t_quitc;                     /* character that generates SIGQUIT */
0363      char t_startc;                    /* start output (initially CTRL-Q) */
0364      char t_stopc;                     /* stop output  (initially CTRL-S) */
0365      char t_eofc;                      /* end-of-file  (initially CTRL-D) */
0366      char t_brkc;                      /* input delimiter (like nl) */
0367    };
0368
0369    /* Fields in t_flags. */
0370    #define XTABS        0006000        /* set to cause tab expansion */
0371    #define RAW          0000040        /* set to enable raw mode */
0372    #define CRMOD        0000020        /* set to map lf to cr + lf */
0373    #define ECHO         0000010        /* set to enable echoing of typed input */
0374    #define CBREAK       0000002        /* set to enable cbreak mode */
0375    #define COOKED       0000000        /* neither CBREAK nor RAW */
0376
0377    #define TIOCGETP (('t'<<8) | 8)
0378    #define TIOCSETP (('t'<<8) | 9)
0379    #define TIOCGETC (('t'<<8) | 18)
0380    #define TIOCSETC (('t'<<8) | 17)
```

```
0400    #define NR_SIGS          16    /* number of signals used */
0401
0402    #define SIGHUP            1    /* hangup */
0403    #define SIGINT            2    /* interrupt (DEL) */
0404    #define SIGQUIT           3    /* quit (ASCII FS) */
0405    #define SIGILL            4    /* illegal instruction (not reset when caught)*/
0406    #define SIGTRAP           5    /* trace trap (not reset when caught) */
0407    #define SIGIOT            6    /* IOT instruction */
0408    #define SIGEMT            7    /* EMT instruction */
0409    #define SIGFPE            8    /* floating point exception */
0410    #define SIGKILL           9    /* kill (cannot be caught or ignored) */
0411    #define SIGBUS           10    /* bus error */
0412    #define SIGSEGV          11    /* segmentation violation */
0413    #define SIGSYS           12    /* bad argument to system call */
0414    #define SIGPIPE          13    /* write on a pipe with no one to read it */
0415    #define SIGALRM          14    /* alarm clock */
0416    #define SIGTERM          15    /* software termination signal from kill */
0417
0418    #define STACK_FAULT      16    /* used by kernel to signal stack fault */
0419
0420    int     (*signal())();
0421    #define SIG_DFL (int (*)())0
0422    #define SIG_IGN (int (*)())1
```

```
0450     struct stat {
0451         short int st_dev;
0452         unsigned short st_ino;
0453         unsigned short st_mode;
0454         short int st_nlink;
0455         short int st_uid;
0456         short int st_gid;
0457         short int st_rdev;
0458         long st_size;
0459         long st_atime;
0460         long st_mtime;
0461         long st_ctime;
0462     };
0463
0464     /* Some common definitions. */
0465     #define S_IFMT  0170000           /* type of file */
0466     #define S_IFDIR 0040000           /* directory */
0467     #define S_IFCHR 0020000           /* character special */
0468     #define S_IFBLK 0060000           /* block special */
0469     #define S_IFREG 0100000           /* regular */
0470     #define S_ISUID   04000           /* set user id on execution */
0471     #define S_ISGID   02000           /* set group id on execution */
0472     #define S_ISVTX   01000           /* save swapped text even after use */
0473     #define S_IREAD   00400           /* read permission, owner */
0474     #define S_IWRITE  00200           /* write permission, owner */
0475     #define S_IEXEC   00100           /* execute/search permission, owner */
```

```
0500    /* Macros */
0501    #define MAX(a,b)        (a > b ? a : b)
0502    #define MIN(a,b)        (a < b ? a : b)
0503
0504    /* Type definitions */
0505    typedef unsigned short unshort; /* must be 16-bit unsigned */
0506    typedef unshort block_nr;       /* block number */
0507    #define NO_BLOCK (block_nr) 0   /* indicates the absence of a block number */
0508    #define MAX_BLOCK_NR (block_nr) 0177777
0509
0510    typedef unshort inode_nr;       /* inode number */
0511    #define NO_ENTRY (inode_nr) 0   /* indicates the absence of a dir entry */
0512    #define MAX_INODE_NR (inode_nr) 0177777
0513
0514    typedef unshort zone_nr;        /* zone number */
0515    #define NO_ZONE    (zone_nr) 0  /* indicates the absence of a zone number */
0516    #define HIGHEST_ZONE (zone_nr) 0177777
0517
0518    typedef unshort bit_nr;         /* if inode_nr & zone_nr both unshort,
0519                                       then also unshort, else long */
0520
0521    typedef long zone_type;         /* zone size */
0522    typedef unshort mask_bits;      /* mode bits */
0523    typedef unshort dev_nr;         /* major | minor device number */
0524    #define NO_DEV    (dev_nr) ~0   /* indicates absence of a device number */
0525
0526    typedef char links;             /* number of links to an inode */
0527    #define MAX_LINKS       0177
0528
0529    typedef long real_time;         /* real time in seconds since Jan 1, 1980 */
0530    typedef long file_pos;          /* position in, or length of, a file */
0531    #define MAX_FILE_POS 017777777777L
0532    typedef short int uid;          /* user id */
0533    typedef char gid;               /* group id */
0534
0535    typedef unsigned vir_bytes;     /* virtual addresses and lengths in bytes */
0536    typedef unsigned vir_clicks;    /* virtual addresses and lengths in clicks */
0537    typedef long phys_bytes;        /* physical addresses and lengths in bytes */
0538    typedef unsigned phys_clicks;   /* physical addresses and lengths in clicks */
0539    typedef int signed_clicks;      /* same length as phys_clicks, but signed */
0540
0541    /* Types relating to messages. */
0542    #define M1              1
0543    #define M3              3
0544    #define M4              4
0545    #define M3_STRING       14
0546
0547    typedef struct {int mli1, mli2, mli3; char *mlp1, *mlp2, *mlp3;} mess_1;
0548    typedef struct {int m2i1, m2i2, m2i3; long m2l1, m2l2; char *m2p1;} mess_2;
0549    typedef struct {int m3i1, m3i2; char *m3p1; char m3ca1[M3_STRING];} mess_3;
```

```
0550    typedef struct {long m4l1, m4l2, m4l3, m4l4;} mess_4;
0551    typedef struct {char m5c1, m5c2; int m5i1, m5i2; long m5l1, m5l2, m5l3;} mess_5;
0552    typedef struct {int m6i1, m6i2, m6i3; long m6l1; int (*m6f1)();} mess_6;
0553
0554    typedef struct {
0555      int m_source;                     /* who sent the message */
0556      int m_type;                       /* what kind of message is it */
0557      union {
0558            mess_1 m_m1;
0559            mess_2 m_m2;
0560            mess_3 m_m3;
0561            mess_4 m_m4;
0562            mess_5 m_m5;
0563            mess_6 m_m6;
0564      } m_u;
0565    } message;
0566
0567    #define MESS_SIZE (sizeof(message))
0568    #define NIL_MESS (message *) 0
0569
0570    /* The following defines provide names for useful members. */
0571    #define m1_i1    m_u.m_m1.m1i1
0572    #define m1_i2    m_u.m_m1.m1i2
0573    #define m1_i3    m_u.m_m1.m1i3
0574    #define m1_p1    m_u.m_m1.m1p1
0575    #define m1_p2    m_u.m_m1.m1p2
0576    #define m1_p3    m_u.m_m1.m1p3
0577
0578    #define m2_i1    m_u.m_m2.m2i1
0579    #define m2_i2    m_u.m_m2.m2i2
0580    #define m2_i3    m_u.m_m2.m2i3
0581    #define m2_l1    m_u.m_m2.m2l1
0582    #define m2_l2    m_u.m_m2.m2l2
0583    #define m2_p1    m_u.m_m2.m2p1
0584
0585    #define m3_i1    m_u.m_m3.m3i1
0586    #define m3_i2    m_u.m_m3.m3i2
0587    #define m3_p1    m_u.m_m3.m3p1
0588    #define m3_ca1   m_u.m_m3.m3ca1
0589
0590
0591    #define m4_l1    m_u.m_m4.m4l1
0592    #define m4_l2    m_u.m_m4.m4l2
0593    #define m4_l3    m_u.m_m4.m4l3
0594    #define m4_l4    m_u.m_m4.m4l4
0595
0596    #define m5_c1    m_u.m_m5.m5c1
0597    #define m5_c2    m_u.m_m5.m5c2
0598    #define m5_i1    m_u.m_m5.m5i1
0599    #define m5_i2    m_u.m_m5.m5i2
```

```
0600   #define m5_l1   m_u.m_m5.m5l1
0601   #define m5_l2   m_u.m_m5.m5l2
0602   #define m5_l3   m_u.m_m5.m5l3
0603
0604   #define m6_i1   m_u.m_m6.m6i1
0605   #define m6_i2   m_u.m_m6.m6i2
0606   #define m6_i3   m_u.m_m6.m6i3
0607   #define m6_l1   m_u.m_m6.m6l1
0608   #define m6_f1   m_u.m_m6.m6f1
0609
0610   struct mem_map {
0611     vir_clicks mem_vir;            /* virtual address */
0612     phys_clicks mem_phys;          /* physical address */
0613     vir_clicks mem_len;            /* length */
0614   };
0615
0616   struct copy_info {               /* used by sys_copy(src, dst, bytes) */
0617           int cp_src_proc;
0618           int cp_src_space;
0619           vir_bytes cp_src_vir;
0620           int cp_dst_proc;
0621           int cp_dst_space;
0622           vir_bytes cp_dst_vir;
0623           vir_bytes cp_bytes;
0624   };
```

```
0650    /* General constants used by the kernel. */
0651
0652    #ifdef i8088
0653    /* p_reg contains: ax, bx, cx, dx, si, di, bp, es, ds, cs, ss in that order. */
0654    #define NR_REGS            11    /* number of general regs in each proc slot */
0655    #define INIT_PSW       0x0200    /* initial psw */
0656    #define INIT_SP (int*)0x0010    /* initial sp: 3 words pushed by kernel */
0657
0658    /* The following values are used in the assembly code.  Do not change the
0659     * values of 'ES_REG', 'DS_REG', 'CS_REG', or 'SS_REG' without making the
0660     * corresponding changes in the assembly code.
0661     */
0662    #define ES_REG              7    /* proc[i].p_reg[ESREG] is saved es */
0663    #define DS_REG              8    /* proc[i].p_reg[DSREG] is saved ds */
0664    #define CS_REG              9    /* proc[i].p_reg[CSREG] is saved cs */
0665    #define SS_REG             10    /* proc[i].p_reg[SSREG] is saved ss */
0666
0667    #define VECTOR_BYTES      260    /* bytes of interrupt vectors to save */
0668    #define MEM_BYTES     655360L    /* memory size for /dev/mem */
0669
0670    /* Interrupt vectors */
0671    #define CLOCK_VECTOR        8    /* clock interrupt vector */
0672    #define KEYBOARD_VECTOR     9    /* keyboard interrupt vector */
0673    #define FLOPPY_VECTOR      14    /* floppy disk interrupt vector */
0674    #define PRINTER_VECTOR     15    /* line printer interrupt vector */
0675    #define SYS_VECTOR         32    /* system calls are made with int SYSVEC */
0676
0677    /* The 8259A interrupt controller has to be re-enabled after each interrupt. */
0678    #define INT_CTL         0x20    /* I/O port for interrupt controller */
0679    #define INT_CTLMASK     0x21    /* setting bits in this port disables ints */
0680    #define ENABLE          0x20    /* code used to re-enable after an interrupt */
0681    #endif
0682
0683    #define TASK_STACK_BYTES 256    /* how many bytes for each task stack */
0684    #define K_STACK_BYTES    256    /* how many bytes for the kernel stack */
0685
0686    #define RET_REG             0    /* system call return codes go in this reg */
0687    #define IDLE             -999    /* 'cur_proc' = IDLE means nobody is running */
0688
0689    /* The following items pertain to the 3 scheduling queues. */
0690    #define NQ                  3    /* # of scheduling queues */
0691    #define TASK_Q              0    /* ready tasks are scheduled via queue 0 */
0692    #define SERVER_Q            1    /* ready servers are scheduled via queue 1 */
0693    #define USER_Q              2    /* ready users are scheduled via queue 2 */
0694
0695    #define printf         printk    /* the kernel really uses printk, not printf */
```

```
0700    /* Global variables used in the kernel. */
0701
0702    /* Clocks and timers */
0703    EXTERN real_time realtime;        /* real time clock */
0704    EXTERN int lost_ticks;            /* incremented when clock int can't send mess*/
0705
0706    /* Processes, signals, and messages. */
0707    EXTERN int cur_proc;              /* current process */
0708    EXTERN int prev_proc;             /* previous process */
0709    EXTERN sig_procs;                 /* number of procs with p_pending != 0 */
0710    EXTERN message int_mess;          /* interrupt routines build message here */
0711
0712    /* The kernel and task stacks. */
0713    EXTERN struct t_stack {
0714      int stk[TASK_STACK_BYTES/sizeof(int)];
0715    } t_stack[NR_TASKS - 1];          /* task stacks; task = -1 never really runs */
0716
0717    EXTERN char k_stack[K_STACK_BYTES];    /* The kernel stack. */
```

```
0750        /* Here is the declaration of the process table.  Three assembly code routines
0751         * reference fields in it.  They are restart(), save(), and csv().  When
0752         * changing 'proc', be sure to change the field offsets built into the code.
0753         * It contains the process' registers, memory map, accounting, and message
0754         * send/receive information.
0755         */
0756
0757        EXTERN struct proc {
0758          int p_reg[NR_REGS];            /* process' registers */
0759          int *p_sp;                     /* stack pointer */
0760          struct pc_psw p_pcpsw;                 /* pc and psw as pushed by interrupt */
0761          int p_flags;                   /* P_SLOT_FREE, SENDING, RECEIVING, etc. */
0762          struct mem_map p_map[NR_SEGS];/* memory map */
0763          int *p_splimit;                /* lowest legal stack value */
0764          int p_pid;                     /* process id passed in from MM */
0765
0766          real_time user_time;           /* user time in ticks */
0767          real_time sys_time;            /* sys time in ticks */
0768          real_time child_utime;         /* cumulative user time of children */
0769          real_time child_stime;         /* cumulative sys time of children */
0770          real_time p_alarm;             /* time of next alarm in ticks, or 0 */
0771
0772          struct proc *p_callerq;        /* head of list of procs wishing to send */
0773          struct proc *p_sendlink;       /* link to next proc wishing to send */
0774          message *p_messbuf;            /* pointer to message buffer */
0775          int p_getfrom;                 /* from whom does process want to receive? */
0776
0777          struct proc *p_nextready;      /* pointer to next ready process */
0778          int p_pending;                 /* bit map for pending signals 1-16 */
0779        } proc[NR_TASKS+NR_PROCS];
0780
0781        /* Bits for p_flags in proc[].  A process is runnable iff p_flags == 0 */
0782        #define P_SLOT_FREE      001    /* set when slot is not in use */
0783        #define NO_MAP           002    /* keeps unmapped forked child from running */
0784        #define SENDING          004    /* set when process blocked trying to send */
0785        #define RECEIVING        010    /* set when process blocked trying to recv */
0786
0787        #define proc_addr(n) &proc[NR_TASKS + n]
0788        #define NIL_PROC (struct proc *) 0
0789
0790        EXTERN struct proc *proc_ptr;   /* &proc[cur_proc] */
0791        EXTERN struct proc *bill_ptr;   /* ptr to process to bill for clock ticks */
0792        EXTERN struct proc *rdy_head[NQ];       /* pointers to ready list headers */
0793        EXTERN struct proc *rdy_tail[NQ];       /* pointers to ready list tails */
0794
0795        EXTERN unsigned busy_map;               /* bit map of busy tasks */
0796        EXTERN message *task_mess[NR_TASKS+1]; /* ptrs to messages for busy tasks */
```

```
0800    /* The 'pc_psw' struct is machine dependent.  It must contain the information
0801     * pushed onto the stack by an interrupt, in the same format as the hardware
0802     * creates and expects.  It is used for storing the interrupt status after a
0803     * trap or interrupt, as well as for causing interrupts for signals.
0804     */
0805
0806
0807    #ifdef i8088
0808    struct pc_psw {
0809      int (*pc)();                      /* storage for program counter */
0810      phys_clicks cs;                   /* code segment register */
0811      unsigned psw;                     /* program status word */
0812    };
0813
0814    /* This struct is used to build data structure pushed by kernel upon signal. */
0815    struct sig_info {
0816      int signo;                        /* sig number at end of stack */
0817      struct pc_psw sigpcpsw;
0818    };
0819    #endif
```

```
0850    /* This file contains the main program of MINIX.  The routine main()
0851     * initializes the system and starts the ball rolling by setting up the proc
0852     * table, interrupt vectors, and scheduling each task to run to initialize
0853     * itself.
0854     *
0855     * The entries into this file are:
0856     *   main:                MINIX main program
0857     *   unexpected_int:      called when an interrupt to an unused vector < 16 occurs
0858     *   trap:                called when an unexpected trap to a vector >= 16 occurs
0859     *   panic:               abort MINIX due to a fatal error
0860     */

0861
0862    #include "../h/const.h"
0863    #include "../h/type.h"
0864    #include "../h/callnr.h"
0865    #include "../h/com.h"
0866    #include "../h/error.h"
0867    #include "const.h"
0868    #include "type.h"
0869    #include "glo.h"
0870    #include "proc.h"
0871
0872    #define SAFETY            8      /* margin of safety for stack overflow (ints)*/
0873    #define VERY_BIG      39328      /* must be bigger than kernel size (clicks) */
0874    #define BASE           1536      /* address where MINIX starts in memory */
0875    #define SIZES             8      /* sizes array has 8 entries */
0876
0877    /*===========================================================================*
0878     *                                 main                                       *
0879     *===========================================================================*/
0880    PUBLIC main()
0881    {
0882    /* Start the ball rolling. */
0883
0884      register struct proc *rp;
0885      register int t;
0886      vir_clicks size;
0887      phys_clicks base_click, mm_base, previous_base;
0888      phys_bytes phys_b;
0889      extern unsigned sizes[8];      /* table filled in by build */
0890      extern int color, vec_table[], get_chrome(), (*task[])();
0891      extern int s_call(), disk_int(), tty_int(), clock_int(), disk_int();
0892      extern int lpr_int(), surprise(), trp();
0893      extern phys_bytes umap();
0894
0895      /* Set up proc table entry for user processes.  Be very careful about
0896       * sp, since the 3 words prior to it will be clobbered when the kernel pushes
0897       * pc, cs, and psw onto the USER's stack when starting the user the first
0898       * time.  This means that with initial sp = 0x10, user programs must leave
0899       * the words at 0x000A, 0x000C, and 0x000E free.
```

```
0900        */
0901
0902        lock();                         /* we can't handle interrupts yet */
0903        base_click = BASE >> CLICK_SHIFT;
0904        size = sizes[0] + sizes[1];   /* kernel text + data size in clicks */
0905        mm_base = base_click + size;  /* place where MM starts (in clicks) */
0906
0907        for (rp = &proc[0]; rp <= &proc[NR_TASKS+LOW_USER]; rp++) {
0908            for (t=0; t< NR_REGS; t++) rp->p_reg[t] = 0100*t;          /* DEBUG */
0909            t = rp - proc - NR_TASKS;          /* task number */
0910            rp->p_sp = (rp < &proc[NR_TASKS] ? t_stack[NR_TASKS+t+1].stk : INIT_SP);
0911            rp->p_splimit = rp->p_sp;
0912            if (rp->p_splimit != INIT_SP)
0913                    rp->p_splimit -= (TASK_STACK_BYTES - SAFETY)/sizeof(int);
0914            rp->p_pcpsw.pc = task[t + NR_TASKS];
0915            if (rp->p_pcpsw.pc != 0 || t >= 0) ready(rp);
0916            rp->p_pcpsw.psw = INIT_PSW;
0917            rp->p_flags = 0;
0918
0919            /* Set up memory map for tasks and MM, FS, INIT. */
0920            if (t < 0) {
0921                    /* I/O tasks. */
0922                    rp->p_map[T].mem_len  = VERY_BIG;
0923                    rp->p_map[T].mem_phys = base_click;
0924                    rp->p_map[D].mem_len  = VERY_BIG;
0925                    rp->p_map[D].mem_phys = base_click + sizes[0];
0926                    rp->p_map[S].mem_len  = VERY_BIG;
0927                    rp->p_map[S].mem_phys = base_click + sizes[0] + sizes[1];
0928                    rp->p_map[S].mem_vir = sizes[0] + sizes[1];
0929            } else {
0930                    /* MM, FS, and INIT. */
0931                    previous_base = proc[NR_TASKS + t - 1].p_map[S].mem_phys;
0932                    rp->p_map[T].mem_len  = sizes[2*t + 2];
0933                    rp->p_map[T].mem_phys = (t == 0 ? mm_base : previous_base);
0934                    rp->p_map[D].mem_len  = sizes[2*t + 3];
0935                    rp->p_map[D].mem_phys = rp->p_map[T].mem_phys + sizes[2*t + 2];
0936                    rp->p_map[S].mem_vir  = sizes[2*t + 3];
0937                    rp->p_map[S].mem_phys = rp->p_map[D].mem_phys + sizes[2*t + 3];
0938            }
0939
0940 #ifdef i8088
0941            rp->p_reg[CS_REG] = rp->p_map[T].mem_phys;
0942            rp->p_reg[DS_REG] = rp->p_map[D].mem_phys;
0943            rp->p_reg[SS_REG] = rp->p_map[D].mem_phys;
0944            rp->p_reg[ES_REG] = rp->p_map[D].mem_phys;
0945 #endif
0946      }
0947
0948      proc[NR_TASKS+(HARDWARE)].p_sp = (int *) k_stack;
0949      proc[NR_TASKS+(HARDWARE)].p_sp += K_STACK_BYTES/2;
```

```
0950        proc[NR_TASKS+(HARDWARE)].p_splimit = (int *) k_stack;
0951        proc[NR_TASKS+(HARDWARE)].p_splimit += SAFETY/2;
0952
0953        for (rp = proc_addr(LOW_USER+1); rp < proc_addr(NR_PROCS); rp++)
0954                rp->p_flags = P_SLOT_FREE;
0955
0956        /* Determine if display is color or monochrome. */
0957        color = get_chrome();           /* 0 = mono, 1 = color */
0958
0959        /* Save the old interrupt vectors. */
0960        phys_b = umap(proc_addr(HARDWARE), D, (vir_bytes) vec_table, VECTOR_BYTES);
0961        phys_copy(0L, phys_b, (long) VECTOR_BYTES);   /* save all the vectors */
0962
0963        /* Set up the new interrupt vectors. */
0964        for (t = 0; t < 16; t++) set_vec(t, surprise, base_click);
0965        for (t = 16; t < 256; t++) set_vec(t, trp, base_click);
0966        set_vec(SYS_VECTOR, s_call, base_click);
0967        set_vec(CLOCK_VECTOR, clock_int, base_click);
0968        set_vec(KEYBOARD_VECTOR, tty_int, base_click);
0969        set_vec(FLOPPY_VECTOR, disk_int, base_click);
0970        set_vec(PRINTER_VECTOR, lpr_int, base_click);
0971
0972        /* Put a ptr to proc table in a known place so it can be found in /dev/mem */
0973        set_vec( (BASE - 4)/4, proc, (phys_clicks) 0);
0974
0975        bill_ptr = proc_addr(HARDWARE);          /* it has to point somewhere */
0976        pick_proc();
0977
0978        /* Now go to the assembly code to start running the current process. */
0979        port_out(INT_CTLMASK, 0);     /* do not mask out any interrupts in 8259A */
0980        restart();
0981   }


0984   /*===========================================================================*
0985    *                              unexpected_int                               *
0986    *===========================================================================*/
0987   PUBLIC unexpected_int()
0988   {
0989   /* A trap or interrupt has occurred that was not expected. */
0990     panic("Unexpected trap or interrupt.  cur_proc =", cur_proc);
0991   }


0994   /*===========================================================================*
0995    *                                  trap                                     *
0996    *===========================================================================*/
0997   PUBLIC trap()
0998   {
0999   /* A trap (vector >= 16) has occurred.  It was not expected. */
```

```
1000
1001        printf("\nUnexpected trap. ");
1002        printf("This may be due to accidentally including in your program\n");
1003        printf("a non-MINIX library routine that is trying to make a system call.\n");
1004        printf("pc = 0x%x    size of program = 0x%x\n",proc_ptr->p_pcpsw.pc,
1005                                        proc_ptr->p_map[D].mem_len<<4);
1006     }


1009    /*========================================================================*
1010     *                              panic                                     *
1011     *========================================================================*/
1012    PUBLIC panic(s,n)
1013    char *s;
1014    int n;
1015    {
1016    /* The system has run aground of a fatal error.  Terminate execution.
1017     * If the panic originated in MM or FS, the string will be empty and the
1018     * file system already syncked.  If the panic originates in the kernel, we are
1019     * kind of stuck.
1020     */
1021
1022      if (*s != 0) {
1023            printf("\nKernel panic: %s",s);
1024            if (n != NO_NUM) printf(" %d", n);
1025            printf("\n");
1026      }
1027      printf("\nType space to reboot\n");
1028      wreboot();
1029
1030    }

1032    #ifdef i8088
1033    /*========================================================================*
1034     *                              set_vec                                   *
1035     *========================================================================*/
1036    PRIVATE set_vec(vec_nr, addr, base_click)
1037    int vec_nr;                        /* which vector */
1038    int (*addr)();                     /* where to start */
1039    phys_clicks base_click;            /* click where kernel sits in memory */
1040    {
1041    /* Set up an interrupt vector. */
1042
1043      unsigned vec[2];
1044      unsigned u;
1045      phys_bytes phys_b;
1046      extern unsigned sizes[8];
1047
1048      /* Build the vector in the array 'vec'. */
1049      vec[0] = (unsigned) addr;
```

```
1050        vec[1] = (unsigned) base_click;
1051        u = (unsigned) vec;
1052
1053        /* Copy the vector into place. */
1054        phys_b = ( (phys_bytes) base_click + (phys_bytes) sizes[0]) << CLICK_SHIFT;
1055        phys_b += u;
1056        phys_copy(phys_b, (phys_bytes) 4*vec_nr, (phys_bytes) 4);
1057    }
1058    #endif
```

```
1100   | This file is part of the lowest layer of the MINIX kernel.  All processing
1101   | switching and message handling is done here and in file "proc.c".  This file
1102   | is entered on every transition to the kernel, both for sending/receiving
1103   | messages and for all interrupts.  In all cases, the trap or interrupt
1104   | routine first calls save() to store the machine state in the proc table.
1105   | Then the stack is switched to k_stack.  Finally, the real trap or interrupt
1106   | handler (in C) is called.  When it returns, the interrupt routine jumps to
1107   | restart, to run the process or task whose number is in 'cur_proc'.
1108   |
1109   | The external entry points into this file are:
1110   |     s_call:    process or task wants to send or receive a message
1111   |     tty_int:   interrupt routine for each key depression and release
1112   |     lpr_int:   interrupt routine for each line printer interrupt
1113   |     disk_int:  disk interrupt routine
1114   |     clock_int: clock interrupt routine (HZ times per second)
1115   |     surprise:  all other interrupts < 16 are vectored here
1116   |     trp:       all traps with vector >= 16 are vectored here
1117   |     restart:   start running a task or process
1118
1119   #include "const.h"
1120   #include "../h/const.h"
1121   #include "../h/com.h"
1122
1123   | The following procedures are defined in this file and called from outside it.
1124   .globl _tty_int, _lpr_int, _clock_int, _disk_int
1125   .globl _s_call, _surprise, _trp, _restart
1126
1127   | The following external procedures are called in this file.
1128   .globl _main, _sys_call, _interrupt, _keyboard, _panic, _unexpected_int, _trap
1129   .globl _pr_char
1130
1131   | Variables and data structures.
1132   .globl _cur_proc, _proc_ptr, _scan_code, _int_mess, _k_stack, splimit
1133   .globl _sizes
1134
1135   | The following constants are offsets into the proc table.
1136   esreg = 14
1137   dsreg = 16
1138   csreg = 18
1139   ssreg = 20
1140   SP    = 22
1141   PC    = 24
1142   PSW   = 28
1143   SPLIM = 50
1144   OFF   = 18
1145   ROFF  = 12
1146
1147   .text
1148
1149
```

```
1150        |*=============================================================================*
1151        |*                          MINIX                                              *
1152        |*=============================================================================*
1153    MINIX:                          | this is the entry point for the MINIX kernel.
1154            jmp M.0                 | skip over the next few bytes
1155            .word 0,0               | build puts DS at kernel text address 4
1156    M.0:    cli                     | disable interrupts
1157            mov ax,cs               | set up segment registers
1158            mov ds,ax               | set up ds
1159            mov ax,4                | build has loaded this word with ds value
1160            mov ds,ax               | ds now contains proper value
1161            mov ss,ax               | ss now contains proper value
1162            mov _scan_code,bx       | save scan code for '=' key from bootstrap
1163            mov sp,#_k_stack        | set sp to point to the top of the
1164            add sp,#K_STACK_BYTES   |        kernel stack
1165
1166            call _main              | start the main program of MINIX
1167    M.1:    jmp M.1                 | this should never be executed
1168
1169
1170        |*=============================================================================*
1171        |*                          s_call                                             *
1172        |*=============================================================================*
1173    _s_call:                        | System calls are vectored here.
1174            call save               | save the machine state
1175            mov bp,_proc_ptr        | use bp to access sys call parameters
1176            push 2(bp)              | push(pointer to user message) (was bx)
1177            push (bp)               | push(src/dest) (was ax)
1178            push _cur_proc          | push caller
1179            push 4(bp)              | push(SEND/RECEIVE/BOTH) (was cx)
1180            call _sys_call          | sys_call(function, caller, src_dest, m_ptr)
1181            jmp _restart            | jump to code to restart proc/task running
1182
1183
1184        |*=============================================================================*
1185        |*                          tty_int                                            *
1186        |*=============================================================================*
1187    _tty_int:                       | Interrupt routine for terminal input.
1188            call save               | save the machine state
1189            call _keyboard          | process a keyboard interrupt
1190            jmp _restart            | continue execution
1191
1192
1193        |*=============================================================================*
1194        |*                          lpr_int                                            *
1195        |*=============================================================================*
1196    _lpr_int:                       | Interrupt routine for terminal input.
1197            call save               | save the machine state
1198            call _pr_char           | process a line printer interrupt
1199            jmp _restart            | continue execution
```

```
1200     |*===========================================================================*
1201     |*                              disk_int                                      *
1202     |*===========================================================================*
1203     _disk_int:                      | Interrupt routine for the floppy disk.
1204           call save                 | save the machine state
1205           mov _int_mess+2,*DISKINT  | build message for disk task
1206           mov ax,#_int_mess         | prepare to call interrupt(FLOPPY, &intmess)
1207           push ax                   | push second parameter
1208           mov ax,*FLOPPY            | prepare to push first parameter
1209           push ax                   | push first parameter
1210           call _interrupt           | this is the call
1211           jmp _restart              | continue execution
1212
1213
1214     |*===========================================================================*
1215     |*                              clock_int                                     *
1216     |*===========================================================================*
1217     _clock_int:                     | Interrupt routine for the clock.
1218           call save                 | save the machine state
1219           mov _int_mess+2,*CLOCK_TICK   | build message for clock task
1220           mov ax,#_int_mess         | prepare to call interrupt(CLOCK, &intmess)
1221           push ax                   | push second parameter
1222           mov ax,*CLOCK             | prepare to push first parameter
1223           push ax                   | push first parameter
1224           call _interrupt           | this is the call
1225           jmp _restart              | continue execution
1226
1227
1228     |*===========================================================================*
1229     |*                              surprise                                      *
1230     |*===========================================================================*
1231     _surprise:                      | This is where unexpected interrupts come.
1232           call save                 | save the machine state
1233           call _unexpected_int      | go panic
1234           jmp _restart              | never executed
1235
1236
1237     |*===========================================================================*
1238     |*                              trp                                           *
1239     |*===========================================================================*
1240     _trp:                           | This is where unexpected traps come.
1241           call save                 | save the machine state
1242           call _trap                | print a message
1243           jmp _restart              | this error is not fatal
1244
1245
1246     |*===========================================================================*
1247     |*                              save                                          *
1248     |*===========================================================================*
1249     save:                           | save the machine state in the proc table.
```

```
1250              push ds               | stack: psw/cs/pc/ret addr/ds
1251              push cs               | prepare to restore ds
1252              pop ds                | ds has now been set to cs
1253              mov ds,4              | word 4 in kernel text space contains ds value
1254              pop ds_save           | stack: psw/cs/pc/ret addr
1255              pop ret_save          | stack: psw/cs/pc
1256              mov bx_save,bx        | save bx for later ; we need a free register
1257              mov bx,_proc_ptr      | start save set up; make bx point to save area
1258              add bx,*OFF           | bx points to place to store cs
1259              pop PC-OFF(bx)        | store pc in proc table
1260              pop csreg-OFF(bx)     | store cs in proc table
1261              pop PSW-OFF(bx)       | store psw
1262              mov ssreg-OFF(bx),ss  | store ss
1263              mov SP-OFF(bx),sp     | sp as it was prior to interrupt
1264              mov sp,bx             | now use sp to point into proc table/task save
1265              mov bx,ds             | about to set ss
1266              mov ss,bx             | set ss
1267              push ds_save          | start saving all the registers, sp first
1268              push es               | save es between sp and bp
1269              mov es,bx             | es now references kernel memory too
1270              push bp               | save bp
1271              push di               | save di
1272              push si               | save si
1273              push dx               | save dx
1274              push cx               | save cx
1275              push bx_save          | save original bx
1276              push ax               | all registers now saved
1277              mov sp,#_k_stack      | temporary stack for interrupts
1278              add sp,#K_STACK_BYTES | set sp to top of temporary stack
1279              mov splimit,#_k_stack | limit for temporary stack
1280              add splimit,#8        | splimit checks for stack overflow
1281              mov ax,ret_save       | ax = address to return to
1282              jmp (ax)              | return to caller; Note: sp points to saved ax
1283
1284
1285      |*===========================================================================*
1286      |*                              restart                                      *
1287      |*===========================================================================*
1288  _restart:                         | This routine sets up and runs a proc or task.
1289              cmp _cur_proc,#IDLE    | restart user; if cur_proc = IDLE, go idle
1290              je idle               | no user is runnable, jump to idle routine
1291              cli                   | disable interrupts
1292              mov sp,_proc_ptr      | return to user, fetch regs from proc table
1293              pop ax                | start restoring registers
1294              pop bx                | restore bx
1295              pop cx                | restore cx
1296              pop dx                | restore dx
1297              pop si                | restore si
1298              pop di                | restore di
1299              mov lds_low,bx        | lds_low contains bx
```

```
1300            mov bx,sp                  | bx points to saved bp register
1301            mov bp,SPLIM-ROFF(bx)      | splimit = p_splimit
1302            mov splimit,bp             | ditto
1303            mov bp,dsreg-ROFF(bx)      | bp = ds
1304            mov lds_low+2,bp           | lds_low+2 contains ds
1305            pop bp                     | restore bp
1306            pop es                     | restore es
1307            mov sp,SP-ROFF(bx)         | restore sp
1308            mov ss,ssreg-ROFF(bx)      | restore ss using the value of ds
1309            push PSW-ROFF(bx)          | push psw
1310            push csreg-ROFF(bx)        | push cs
1311            push PC-ROFF(bx)           | push pc
1312            lds bx,lds_low             | restore ds and bx in one fell swoop
1313            iret                       | return to user or task
1314
1315
1316    |*===========================================================================*
1317    |*                              idle                                        *
1318    |*===========================================================================*
1319    idle:                              | executed when there is no work
1320            sti                        | enable interrupts
1321    L3:     wait                       | just idle while waiting for interrupt
1322            jmp L3                     | loop until interrupt
1323
1324
1325
1326    |*===========================================================================*
1327    |*                              data                                        *
1328    |*===========================================================================*
1329    .data
1330    _sizes: .word 0x526F               | this must be the first data entry (magic #)
1331            .zerow 7                   | build table uses prev word and this space
1332    bx_save: .word 0                   | storage for bx
1333    ds_save: .word 0                   | storage for ds
1334    ret_save:.word 0                   | storage for return address
1335    lds_low: .word 0,0                 | storage used for restoring bx
1336    ttyomess: .asciz "RS232 interrupt"
1337
1338    .bss
1339    begbss:
```

```
1350     | This file contains a number of assembly code utility routines needed by the
1351     | kernel.  They are:
1352     |
1353     |    phys_copy:  copies data from anywhere to anywhere in memory
1354     |    cp_mess:    copies messages from source to destination
1355     |    port_out:   outputs data on an I/O port
1356     |    port_in:    inputs data from an I/O port
1357     |    lock:       disable interrupts
1358     |    unlock:     enable interrupts
1359     |    restore:    restore interrupts (enable/disabled) as they were before lock()
1360     |    build_sig:  build 4 word structure pushed onto stack for signals
1361     |    csv:        procedure prolog to save the registers
1362     |    cret:       procedure epilog to restore the registers
1363     |    get_chrome: returns 0 is display is monochrome, 1 if it is color
1364     |    vid_copy:   copy data to video ram (on color display during retrace only)
1365     |    get_byte:   reads a byte from a user program and returns it as value
1366     |    reboot:     reboot for CTRL-ALT-DEL
1367     |    wreboot:    wait for character then reboot
1368     |
1369     | The following procedures are defined in this file and called from outside it.
1370     .globl _phys_copy, _cp_mess, _port_out, _port_in, _lock, _unlock, _restore
1371     .globl _build_sig, csv, cret, _get_chrome, _vid_copy, _get_byte, _reboot
1372     .globl _wreboot
1373
1374     | The following external procedure is called in this file.
1375     .globl _panic
1376
1377     | Variables and data structures
1378     .globl _color, _cur_proc, _proc_ptr, splimit, _vec_table
1379
1380
1381     |*===========================================================================*
1382     |*                              phys_copy                                     *
1383     |*===========================================================================*
1384     | This routine copies a block of physical memory.  It is called by:
1385     |     phys_copy( (long) source, (long) destination, (long) bytecount)
1386
1387     _phys_copy:
1388            pushf                    | save flags
1389            cli                      | disable interrupts
1390            push bp                  | save the registers
1391            push ax                  | save ax
1392            push bx                  | save bx
1393            push cx                  | save cx
1394            push dx                  | save dx
1395            push si                  | save si
1396            push di                  | save di
1397            push ds                  | save ds
1398            push es                  | save es
1399            mov bp,sp                | set bp to point to saved es
```

```
1400
1401    L0:     mov ax,28(bp)           ax = high-order word of 32-bit destination
1402            mov di,26(bp)           di = low-order word of 32-bit destination
1403            mov cx,*4               start extracting click number from dest
1404    L1:     rcr ax,*1               click number is destination address / 16
1405            rcr di,*1               it is used in segment register for copy
1406            loop L1                 4 bits of high-order word are used
1407            mov es,di               es = destination click
1408
1409            mov ax,24(bp)           ax = high-order word of 32-bit source
1410            mov si,22(bp)           si = low-order word of 32-bit source
1411            mov cx,*4               start extracting click number from source
1412    L2:     rcr ax,*1               click number is source address / 16
1413            rcr si,*1               it is used in segment register for copy
1414            loop L2                 4 bits of high-order word are used
1415            mov ds,si               ds = source click
1416
1417            mov di,26(bp)           di = low-order word of dest address
1418            and di,*0x000F          di = offset from paragraph # in es
1419            mov si,22(bp)           si = low-order word of source address
1420            and si,*0x000F          si = offset from paragraph # in ds
1421
1422            mov dx,32(bp)           dx = high-order word of byte count
1423            mov cx,30(bp)           cx = low-order word of byte count
1424
1425            test cx,#0x8000         if bytes >= 32768, only do 32768
1426            jnz L3                  per iteration
1427            test dx,#0xFFFF         check high-order 17 bits to see if bytes
1428            jnz L3                  if bytes >= 32768 then go to L3
1429            jmp L4                  if bytes < 32768 then go to L4
1430    L3:     mov cx,#0x8000          0x8000 is unsigned 32768
1431    L4:     mov ax,cx               save actual count used in ax; needed later
1432
1433            test cx,*0x0001         should we copy a byte or a word at a time?
1434            jz L5                   jump if even
1435            rep                     copy 1 byte at a time
1436            movb                    byte copy
1437            jmp L6                  check for more bytes
1438
1439    L5:     shr cx,*1               word copy
1440            rep                     copy 1 word at a time
1441            movw                    word copy
1442
1443    L6:     mov dx,32(bp)           decr count, incr src & dst, iterate if needed
1444            mov cx,30(bp)           dx || cx is 32-bit byte count
1445            xor bx,bx               bx || ax is 32-bit actual count used
1446            sub cx,ax               compute bytes - actual count
1447            sbb dx,bx               dx || cx is # bytes not yet processed
1448            or cx,cx                see if it is 0
1449            jnz L7                  if more bytes then go to L7
```

```
1450                  or dx,dx               | keep testing
1451                  jnz L7                 | if loop done, fall through
1452
1453                  pop es                 | restore all the saved registers
1454                  pop ds                 | restore ds
1455                  pop di                 | restore di
1456                  pop si                 | restore si
1457                  pop dx                 | restore dx
1458                  pop cx                 | restore cx
1459                  pop bx                 | restore bx
1460                  pop ax                 | restore ax
1461                  pop bp                 | restore bp
1462                  popf                   | restore flags
1463                  ret                    | return to caller
1464
1465      L7:         mov 32(bp),dx          | store decremented byte count back in mem
1466                  mov 30(bp),cx          | as a long
1467                  add 26(bp),ax          | increment destination
1468                  adc 28(bp),bx          | carry from low-order word
1469                  add 22(bp),ax          | increment source
1470                  adc 24(bp),bx          | carry from low-order word
1471                  jmp L0                 | start next iteration
1472
1473
1474      |*===============================================================*
1475      |*                          cp_mess                              *
1476      |*===============================================================*
1477      | This routine is makes a fast copy of a message from anywhere in the address
1478      | space to anywhere else.  It also copies the source address provided as a
1479      | parameter to the call into the first word of the destination message.
1480      | It is called by:
1481      |    cp_mess(src, src_clicks, src_offset, dst_clicks, dst_offset)
1482      | where all 5 parameters are shorts (16-bits).
1483      |
1484      | Note that the message size, 'Msize' is in WORDS (not bytes) and must be set
1485      | correctly.  Changing the definition of message the type file and not changing
1486      | it here will lead to total disaster.
1487      | This routine destroys ax.  It preserves the other registers.
1488
1489      Msize = 12                          | size of a message in 16-bit words
1490      _cp_mess:
1491                  push bp                 | save bp
1492                  push es                 | save es
1493                  push ds                 | save ds
1494                  mov bp,sp               | index off bp because machine can't use sp
1495                  pushf                   | save flags
1496                  cli                     | disable interrupts
1497                  push cx                 | save cx
1498                  push si                 | save si
1499                  push di                 | save di
```

```
1500
1501          mov ax,8(bp)              | ax = process number of sender
1502          mov di,16(bp)             | di = offset of destination buffer
1503          mov es,14(bp)             | es = clicks of destination
1504          mov si,12(bp)             | si = offset of source message
1505          mov ds,10(bp)             | ds = clicks of source message
1506          seg es                    | segment override prefix
1507          mov (di),ax               | copy sender's process number to dest message
1508          add si,*2                 | don't copy first word
1509          add di,*2                 | don't copy first word
1510          mov cx,*Msize-1           | remember, first word doesn't count
1511          rep                       | iterate cx times to copy 11 words
1512          movw                      | copy the message
1513
1514          pop di                    | restore di
1515          pop si                    | restore si
1516          pop cx                    | restore cs
1517          popf                      | restore flags
1518          pop ds                    | restore ds
1519          pop es                    | restore es
1520          pop bp                    | restore bp
1521          ret                       | that's all folks!
1522
1523
1524  |*===========================================================================*
1525  |*                              port_out                                     *
1526  |*===========================================================================*
1527  | port_out(port, value) writes 'value' on the I/O port 'port'.
1528
1529  _port_out:
1530          push bx                   | save bx
1531          mov bx,sp                 | index off bx
1532          push ax                   | save ax
1533          push dx                   | save dx
1534          mov dx,4(bx)              | dx = port
1535          mov ax,6(bx)              | ax = value
1536          out                       | output 1 byte
1537          pop dx                    | restore dx
1538          pop ax                    | restore ax
1539          pop bx                    | restore bx
1540          ret                       | return to caller
1541
1542
1543  |*===========================================================================*
1544  |*                              port_in                                      *
1545  |*===========================================================================*
1546  | port_in(port, &value) reads from port 'port' and puts the result in 'value'.
1547  _port_in:
1548          push bx                   | save bx
1549          mov bx,sp                 | index off bx
```

```
1550            push ax             | save ax
1551            push dx             | save dx
1552            mov dx,4(bx)        | dx = port
1553            in                  | input 1 byte
1554            xorb ah,ah          | clear ah
1555            mov bx,6(bx)        | fetch address where byte is to go
1556            mov (bx),ax         | return byte to caller in param
1557            pop dx              | restore dx
1558            pop ax              | restore ax
1559            pop bx              | restore bx
1560            ret                 | return to caller
1561
1562
1563    |*===========================================================================*
1564    |*                               lock                                        *
1565    |*===========================================================================*
1566    | Disable CPU interrupts.
1567    _lock:
1568            pushf               | save flags on stack
1569            cli                 | disable interrupts
1570            pop lockvar         | save flags for possible restoration later
1571            ret                 | return to caller
1572
1573
1574    |*===========================================================================*
1575    |*                               unlock                                      *
1576    |*===========================================================================*
1577    | Enable CPU interrupts.
1578    _unlock:
1579            sti                 | enable interrupts
1580            ret                 | return to caller
1581
1582
1583    |*===========================================================================*
1584    |*                               restore                                     *
1585    |*===========================================================================*
1586    | Restore enable/disable bit to the value it had before last lock.
1587    _restore:
1588            push lockvar        | push flags as they were before previous lock
1589            popf                | restore flags
1590            ret                 | return to caller
1591
1592
1593    |*===========================================================================*
1594    |*                               build_sig                                   *
1595    |*===========================================================================*
1596    | Build a structure that is pushed onto the stack for signals.  It contains
1597    | pc, psw, etc., and is machine dependent. The format is the same as generated
1598    | by hardware interrupts, except that after the "interrupt", the signal number
1599    | is also pushed.  The signal processing routine within the user space first
```

```
1600    | * pops the signal number, to see which function to call.  Then it calls the
1601    | * function.  Finally, when the function returns to the low-level signal
1602    | * handling routine, control is passed back to where it was prior to the signal
1603    | * by executing a return-from-interrupt instruction, hence the need for using
1604    | * the hardware generated interrupt format on the stack.  The call is:
1605    | *     build_sig(sig_stuff, rp, sig)
1606    |
1607    | | Offsets within proc table
1608    | PC   = 24
1609    | csreg = 18
1610    | PSW  = 28
1611    |
1612    | _build_sig:
1613    |         push bp                  | save bp
1614    |         mov bp,sp                | set bp to sp for accessing params
1615    |         push bx                  | save bx
1616    |         push si                  | save si
1617    |         mov bx,4(bp)             | bx points to sig_stuff
1618    |         mov si,6(bp)             | si points to proc table entry
1619    |         mov ax,8(bp)             | ax = signal number
1620    |         mov (bx),ax              | put signal number in sig_stuff
1621    |         mov ax,PC(si)            | ax = signalled process' PC
1622    |         mov 2(bx),ax             | put pc in sig_stuff
1623    |         mov ax,csreg(si)         | ax = signalled process' cs
1624    |         mov 4(bx),ax             | put cs in sig_stuff
1625    |         mov ax,PSW(si)           | ax = signalled process' PSW
1626    |         mov 6(bx),ax             | put psw in sig_stuff
1627    |         pop si                   | restore si
1628    |         pop bx                   | restore bx
1629    |         pop bp                   | restore bp
1630    |         ret                      | return to caller
1631    |
1632    |
1633    | *===========================================================================*
1634    | *                              csv & cret                                    *
1635    | *===========================================================================*
1636    | This version of csv replaces the standard one.  It checks for stack overflow
1637    | within the kernel in a simpler way than is usually done. cret is standard.
1638    | csv:
1639    |         pop bx                   | bx = return address
1640    |         push bp                  | stack old frame pointer
1641    |         mov bp,sp                | set new frame pointer to sp
1642    |         push di                  | save di
1643    |         push si                  | save si
1644    |         sub sp,ax                | ax = # bytes of local variables
1645    |         cmp sp,splimit           | has kernel stack grown too large
1646    |         jbe csv.1                | if sp is too low, panic
1647    |         jmp (bx)                 | normal return: copy bx to program counter
1648    |
1649    | csv.1:
```

```
1650              mov  splimit,#0         | prevent call to panic from aborting in csv
1651              mov  bx,_proc_ptr       | update rp->p_splimit
1652              mov  50(bx),#0          | rp->sp_limit = 0
1653              push _cur_proc          | task number
1654              mov  ax,#stkoverrun     | stack overran the kernel stack area
1655              push ax                 | push first parameter
1656              call _panic             | call is: panic(stkoverrun, cur_proc)
1657              jmp  csv.1              | this should not be necessary
1658
1659
1660      cret:
1661              lea  sp,*-4(bp)         | set sp to point to saved si
1662              pop  si                 | restore saved si
1663              pop  di                 | restore saved di
1664              pop  bp                 | restore bp
1665              ret                     | end of procedure
1666
1667      |*=========================================================================*
1668      |*                            get_chrome                                   *
1669      |*=========================================================================*
1670      | This routine calls the BIOS to find out if the display is monochrome or
1671      | color.  The drivers are different, as are the video ram addresses, so we
1672      | need to know.
1673      _get_chrome:
1674              int  0x11              | call the BIOS to get equipment type
1675              andb al,#0x30          | isolate color/mono field
1676              cmpb al,*0x30          | 0x30 is monochrome
1677              je   getchr1           | if monochrome then go to getchr1
1678              mov  ax,#1             | color = 1
1679              ret                    | color return
1680      getchr1: xor ax,ax             | mono = 0
1681              ret                    | monochrome return
1682
1683
1684      |*=========================================================================*
1685      |*                            vid_copy                                     *
1686      |*=========================================================================*
1687      | This routine takes a string of (character, attribute) pairs and writes them
1688      | onto the screen.  For a color display, the writing only takes places during
1689      | the vertical retrace interval, to avoid displaying garbage on the screen.
1690      | The call is:
1691      |     vid_copy(buffer, videobase, offset, words)
1692      | where
1693      |     'buffer'   is a pointer to the (character, attribute) pairs
1694      |     'videobase' is 0xB800 for color and 0xB000 for monochrome displays
1695      |     'offset'   tells where within video ram to copy the data
1696      |     'words'    tells how many words to copy
1697      | if buffer is zero, the fill char (BLANK) is used
1698
1699      BLANK = 0x0700               | controls color of cursor on blank screen
```

```
1700
1701    _vid_copy:
1702            push bp                    we need bp to access the parameters
1703            mov bp,sp                  set bp to sp for indexing
1704            push si                    save the registers
1705            push di                    save di
1706            push cx                    save cx
1707            push dx                    save dx
1708            push es                    save es
1709            mov si,4(bp)               si = pointer to data to be copied
1710            mov di,8(bp)               di = offset within video ram
1711            mov cx,10(bp)              cx = word count for copy loop
1712            mov dx,#0x3DA              prepare to see if color display is retracing
1713
1714            test _color,*1             skip vertical retrace test if display is mono
1715            jz vid.3                   if monochrome then go to vid.2
1716
1717    vid.1:  in                         with a color display, you can only copy to
1718            test al,*010               the video ram during vertical retrace, so
1719            jnz vid.1                  wait for start of retrace period.  Bit 3 of
1720    vid.2:  in                         0x3DA is set during retrace.  First wait
1721            testb al,*010              until it is off (no retrace), then wait
1722            jz vid.2                   until it comes on (start of retrace)
1723
1724    vid.3:  pushf                      copying may now start; save flags
1725            cli                        interrupts just get in the way: disable them
1726            mov es,6(bp)               load es now: int routines may ruin it
1727
1728            cmp si,#0                  si = 0 means blank the screen
1729            je vid.5                   jump for blanking
1730            lock                       this is a trick for the IBM PC simulator only
1731            nop                        'lock' indicates a video ram access
1732            rep                        this is the copy loop
1733            movw                       ditto
1734
1735    vid.4:  popf                       restore flags
1736            pop es                     restore registers
1737            pop dx                     restore dx
1738            pop cx                     restore cx
1739            pop di                     restore di
1740            pop si                     restore si
1741            pop bp                     restore bp
1742            ret                        return to caller
1743
1744    vid.5:  mov ax,#BLANK              ax = blanking character
1745            rep                        copy loop
1746            stow                       blank screen
1747            jmp vid.4                  done
1748
1749
```

```
1750        |*===========================================================================*
1751        |*                              get_byte                                     *
1752        |*===========================================================================*
1753        | This routine is used to fetch a byte from anywhere in memory.
1754        | The call is:
1755        |     c = get_byte(seg, off)
1756        | where
1757        |     'seg' is the value to put in es
1758        |     'off' is the offset from the es value
1759        _get_byte:
1760              push bp                   | save bp
1761              mov bp,sp                 | we need to access parameters
1762              push es                   | save es
1763              mov es,4(bp)              | load es with segment value
1764              mov bx,6(bp)              | load bx with offset from segment
1765              seg es                    | go get the byte
1766              movb al,(bx)              | al = byte
1767              xorb ah,ah                | ax = byte
1768              pop es                    | restore es
1769              pop bp                    | restore bp
1770              ret                       | return to caller
1771
1772
1773
1774
1775        |*===========================================================================*
1776        |*                           reboot & wreboot                                *
1777        |*===========================================================================*
1778        | This code reboots the PC
1779
1780        _reboot:
1781              cli                       | disable interrupts
1782              mov ax,#0x20              | re-enable interrupt controller
1783              out 0x20
1784              call resvec               | restore the vectors in low core
1785              int 0x19                  | reboot the PC
1786
1787        _wreboot:
1788              cli                       | disable interrupts
1789              mov ax,#0x20              | re-enable interrupt controller
1790              out 0x20
1791              call resvec               | restore the vectors in low core
1792              xor ax,ax                 | wait for character before continuing
1793              int 0x16                  | get char
1794              int 0x19                  | reboot the PC
1795
1796        | Restore the interrupt vectors in low core.
1797        resvec: cld
1798              mov cx,#2*65
1799              mov si,#_vec_table
```

```
1800              xor di,di
1801              mov es,di
1802              rep
1803              movw
1804              ret
1805
1806     .data
1807     lockvar:      .word 0       | place to store flags for lock()/restore()
1808     splimit:      .word 0       | stack limit for current task (kernel only)
1809     stkoverrun:   .asciz "Kernel stack overrun, task = "
1810     _vec_table:   .zerow 130    | storage for interrupt vectors
```

```
1850    /* This file contains essentially all of the process and message handling.
1851     * It has two main entry points from the outside:
1852     *
1853     *   sys_call:   called when a process or task does SEND, RECEIVE or SENDREC
1854     *   interrupt: called by interrupt routines to send a message to task
1855     *
1856     * It also has five minor entry points:
1857     *
1858     *   ready:     put a process on one of the ready queues so it can be run
1859     *   unready:   remove a process from the ready queues
1860     *   sched:     a process has run too long; schedule another one
1861     *   mini_send: send a message (used by interrupt signals, etc.)
1862     *   pick_proc: pick a process to run (used by system initialization)
1863     */
1864
1865    #include "../h/const.h"
1866    #include "../h/type.h"
1867    #include "../h/callnr.h"
1868    #include "../h/com.h"
1869    #include "../h/error.h"
1870    #include "const.h"
1871    #include "type.h"
1872    #include "glo.h"
1873    #include "proc.h"
1874
1875    /*===========================================================================*
1876     *                              interrupt                                     *
1877     *===========================================================================*/
1878    PUBLIC interrupt(task, m_ptr)
1879    int task;                           /* number of task to be started */
1880    message *m_ptr;                     /* interrupt message to send to the task */
1881    {
1882    /* An interrupt has occurred.  Schedule the task that handles it. */
1883
1884      int i, n, old_map, this_bit;
1885
1886    #ifdef i8088
1887      /* Re-enable the 8259A interrupt controller. */
1888      port_out(INT_CTL, ENABLE);     /* this re-enables the 8259A controller chip */
1889    #endif
1890
1891      /* Try to send the interrupt message to the indicated task. */
1892      this_bit = 1 << (-task);
1893      if (mini_send(HARDWARE, task, m_ptr) != OK) {
1894          /* The message could not be sent to the task; it was not waiting. */
1895          old_map = busy_map;          /* save original map of busy tasks */
1896          if (task == CLOCK) {
1897                  lost_ticks++;
1898          } else {
1899                  busy_map |= this_bit;                /* mark task as busy */
```

```
1900                        task_mess[-task] = m_ptr;        /* record message pointer */
1901                }
1902        } else {
1903                /* Hardware interrupt was successfully sent as a message. */
1904                busy_map &= ~this_bit;  /* turn off the bit in case it was on */
1905                old_map = busy_map;
1906        }
1907
1908        /* See if any tasks that were previously busy are now listening for msgs. */
1909        if (old_map != 0) {
1910                for (i = 2; i <= NR_TASKS; i++) {
1911                        /* Check each task looking for one with a pending interrupt. */
1912                        if ( (old_map>>i) & 1) {
1913                                /* Task 'i' has a pending interrupt. */
1914                                n = mini_send(HARDWARE, -i, task_mess[i]);
1915                                if (n == OK) busy_map &= ~(1 << i);
1916                        }
1917                }
1918        }
1919
1920        /* If a task has just been readied and a user is running, run the task. */
1921        if (rdy_head[TASK_Q] != NIL_PROC && (cur_proc >= 0 || cur_proc == IDLE))
1922                pick_proc();
1923 }


1926 /*===========================================================================*
1927  *                              sys_call                                     *
1928  *===========================================================================*/
1929 PUBLIC sys_call(function, caller, src_dest, m_ptr)
1930 int function;                    /* SEND, RECEIVE, or BOTH */
1931 int caller;                      /* who is making this call */
1932 int src_dest;                    /* source to receive from or dest to send to */
1933 message *m_ptr;                  /* pointer to message */
1934 {
1935 /* The only system calls that exist in MINIX are sending and receiving
1936  * messages.  These are done by trapping to the kernel with an INT instruction.
1937  * The trap is caught and sys_call() is called to send or receive a message (or
1938  * both).
1939  */
1940
1941   register struct proc *rp;
1942   int n;
1943
1944   /* Check for bad system call parameters. */
1945   rp = proc_addr(caller);
1946   if (src_dest < -NR_TASKS || (src_dest >= NR_PROCS && src_dest != ANY) ) {
1947         rp->p_reg[RET_REG] = E_BAD_SRC;
1948         return;
1949   }
```

```
1950          if (function != BOTH && caller >= LOW_USER) {
1951                  rp->p_reg[RET_REG] = E_NO_PERM; /* users only do BOTH */
1952                  return;
1953          }
1954
1955          /* The parameters are ok. Do the call. */
1956          if (function & SEND) {
1957                  n = mini_send(caller, src_dest, m_ptr); /* func = SEND or BOTH */
1958                  if (function == SEND || n != OK) rp->p_reg[RET_REG] = n;
1959                  if (n != OK) return;      /* SEND failed */
1960          }
1961
1962          if (function & RECEIVE) {
1963                  n = mini_rec(caller, src_dest, m_ptr);        /* func = RECEIVE or BOTH */
1964                  rp->p_reg[RET_REG] = n;
1965          }
1966    }
1967
1968    /*===========================================================================*
1969     *                              mini_send                                     *
1970     *===========================================================================*/
1971    PUBLIC int mini_send(caller, dest, m_ptr)
1972    int caller;                           /* who is trying to send a message? */
1973    int dest;                             /* to whom is message being sent? */
1974    message *m_ptr;                       /* pointer to message buffer */
1975    {
1976    /* Send a message from 'caller' to 'dest'.  If 'dest' is blocked waiting for
1977     * this message, copy the message to it and unblock 'dest'.  If 'dest' is not
1978     * waiting at all, or is waiting for another source, queue 'caller'.
1979     */
1980
1981      register struct proc *caller_ptr, *dest_ptr, *next_ptr;
1982      vir_bytes vb;                       /* message buffer pointer as vir_bytes */
1983      vir_clicks vlo, vhi;                /* virtual clicks containing message to send */
1984      vir_clicks len;                     /* length of data segment in clicks */
1985
1986      /* User processes are only allowed to send to FS and MM.  Check for this. */
1987      if (caller >= LOW_USER && (dest != FS_PROC_NR && dest != MM_PROC_NR))
1988              return(E_BAD_DEST);
1989      caller_ptr = proc_addr(caller);        /* pointer to source's proc entry */
1990      dest_ptr = proc_addr(dest);    /* pointer to destination's proc entry */
1991      if (dest_ptr->p_flags & P_SLOT_FREE) return(E_BAD_DEST);        /* dead dest */
1992
1993      /* Check for messages wrapping around top of memory or outside data seg. */
1994      len = caller_ptr->p_map[D].mem_len;
1995      vb = (vir_bytes) m_ptr;
1996      vlo = vb >> CLICK_SHIFT;        /* vir click for bottom of message */
1997      vhi = (vb + MESS_SIZE - 1) >> CLICK_SHIFT;   /* vir click for top of message */
1998      if (vhi < vlo || vhi - caller_ptr->p_map[D].mem_vir >= len)return(E_BAD_ADDR);
1999
```

```
2000          /* Check to see if 'dest' is blocked waiting for this message. */
2001          if ( (dest_ptr->p_flags & RECEIVING) &&
2002                          (dest_ptr->p_getfrom == ANY || dest_ptr->p_getfrom == caller) )
2003              /* Destination is indeed waiting for this message. */
2004              cp_mess(caller, caller_ptr->p_map[D].mem_phys, m_ptr,
2005                                      dest_ptr->p_map[D].mem_phys, dest_ptr->p_messbuf
2006              dest_ptr->p_flags &= ~RECEIVING;        /* deblock destination */
2007              if (dest_ptr->p_flags == 0) ready(dest_ptr);
2008          } else {
2009              /* Destination is not waiting.  Block and queue caller. */
2010              if (caller == HARDWARE) return(E_OVERRUN);
2011              caller_ptr->p_messbuf = m_ptr;
2012              caller_ptr->p_flags |= SENDING;
2013              unready(caller_ptr);
2014
2015              /* Process is now blocked.  Put in on the destination's queue. */
2016              if ( (next_ptr = dest_ptr->p_callerq) == NIL_PROC) {
2017                      dest_ptr->p_callerq = caller_ptr;
2018              } else {
2019                      while (next_ptr->p_sendlink != NIL_PROC)
2020                              next_ptr = next_ptr->p_sendlink;
2021                      next_ptr->p_sendlink = caller_ptr;
2022              }
2023              caller_ptr->p_sendlink = NIL_PROC;
2024          }
2025      return(OK);
2026      }


2029      /*===========================================================================*
2030       *                              mini_rec                                      *
2031       *===========================================================================*/
2032      PRIVATE int mini_rec(caller, src, m_ptr)
2033      int caller;                        /* process trying to get message */
2034      int src;                           /* which message source is wanted (or ANY) */
2035      message *m_ptr;                     /* pointer to message buffer */
2036      {
2037      /* A process or task wants to get a message.  If one is already queued,
2038       * acquire it and deblock the sender.  If no message from the desired source
2039       * is available, block the caller.  No need to check parameters for validity.
2040       * Users calls are always sendrec(), and mini_send() has checked already.
2041       * Calls from the tasks, MM, and FS are trusted.
2042       */
2043
2044        register struct proc *caller_ptr, *sender_ptr, *prev_ptr;
2045        int sender;
2046
2047        caller_ptr = proc_addr(caller);          /* pointer to caller's proc structure */
2048
2049        /* Check to see if a message from desired source is already available. */
```

```
2050          sender_ptr = caller_ptr->p_callerq;
2051          while (sender_ptr != NIL_PROC) {
2052                  sender = sender_ptr - proc - NR_TASKS;
2053                  if (src == ANY || src == sender) {
2054                          /* An acceptable message has been found. */
2055                          cp_mess(sender, sender_ptr->p_map[D].mem_phys, sender_ptr->p_messbuf,
2056                                              caller_ptr->p_map[D].mem_phys, m_ptr);
2057                          sender_ptr->p_flags &= ~SENDING;        /* deblock sender */
2058                          if (sender_ptr->p_flags == 0) ready(sender_ptr);
2059                          if (sender_ptr == caller_ptr->p_callerq)
2060                                  caller_ptr->p_callerq = sender_ptr->p_sendlink;
2061                          else
2062                                  prev_ptr->p_sendlink = sender_ptr->p_sendlink;
2063                          return(OK);
2064                  }
2065                  prev_ptr = sender_ptr;
2066                  sender_ptr = sender_ptr->p_sendlink;
2067          }
2068
2069          /* No suitable message is available.  Block the process trying to receive. */
2070          caller_ptr->p_getfrom = src;
2071          caller_ptr->p_messbuf = m_ptr;
2072          caller_ptr->p_flags |= RECEIVING;
2073          unready(caller_ptr);
2074
2075          /* If MM has just blocked and there are kernel signals pending, now is the
2076           * time to tell MM about them, since it will be able to accept the message.
2077           */
2078          if (sig_procs > 0 && caller == MM_PROC_NR && src == ANY) inform(MM_PROC_NR);
2079          return(OK);
2080  }


2083  /*===========================================================================*
2084   *                              pick_proc                                     *
2085   *===========================================================================*/
2086  PUBLIC pick_proc()
2087  {
2088  /* Decide who to run now. */
2089
2090    register int q;                       /* which queue to use */
2091
2092    if (rdy_head[TASK_Q] != NIL_PROC) q = TASK_Q;
2093    else if (rdy_head[SERVER_Q] != NIL_PROC) q = SERVER_Q;
2094    else q = USER_Q;
2095
2096    /* Set 'cur_proc' and 'proc_ptr'. If system is idle, set 'cur_proc' to a
2097     * special value (IDLE), and set 'proc_ptr' to point to an unused proc table
2098     * slot, namely, that of task -1 (HARDWARE), so save() will have somewhere to
2099     * deposit the registers when a interrupt occurs on an idle machine.
```

```
2100          * Record previous process so that when clock tick happens, the clock task
2101          * can find out who was running just before it began to run.  (While the
2102          * clock task is running, 'cur_proc' = CLOCKTASK. In addition, set 'bill_ptr'
2103          * to always point to the process to be billed for CPU time.
2104          */
2105         prev_proc = cur_proc;
2106         if (rdy_head[q] != NIL_PROC) {
2107                 /* Someone is runnable. */
2108                 cur_proc = rdy_head[q] - proc - NR_TASKS;
2109                 proc_ptr = rdy_head[q];
2110                 if (cur_proc >= LOW_USER) bill_ptr = proc_ptr;
2111         } else {
2112                 /* No one is runnable. */
2113                 cur_proc = IDLE;
2114                 proc_ptr = proc_addr(HARDWARE);
2115                 bill_ptr = proc_ptr;
2116         }
2117     }


2119     /*===========================================================================*
2120      *                              ready                                         *
2121      *===========================================================================*/
2122     PUBLIC ready(rp)
2123     register struct proc *rp;        /* this process is now runnable */
2124     {
2125     /* Add 'rp' to the end of one of the queues of runnable processes. Three
2126      * queues are maintained:
2127      *    TASK_Q   - (highest priority) for runnable tasks
2128      *    SERVER_Q - (middle priority) for MM and FS only
2129      *    USER_Q   - (lowest priority) for user processes
2130      */
2131
2132       register int q;                   /* TASK_Q, SERVER_Q, or USER_Q */
2133       int r;
2134
2135       lock();                           /* disable interrupts */
2136       r = (rp - proc) - NR_TASKS;       /* task or proc number */
2137       q = (r < 0 ? TASK_Q : r < LOW_USER ? SERVER_Q : USER_Q);
2138
2139       /* See if the relevant queue is empty. */
2140       if (rdy_head[q] == NIL_PROC)
2141             rdy_head[q] = rp;           /* add to empty queue */
2142       else
2143             rdy_tail[q]->p_nextready = rp;  /* add to tail of nonempty queue */
2144       rdy_tail[q] = rp;                 /* new entry has no successor */
2145       rp->p_nextready = NIL_PROC;
2146       restore();                        /* restore interrupts to previous state */
2147     }
```

```
2150      /*===========================================================================*
2151       *                              unready                                      *
2152       *===========================================================================*/
2153      PUBLIC unready(rp)
2154      register struct proc *rp;        /* this process is no longer runnable */
2155      {
2156      /* A process has blocked. */
2157
2158        register struct proc *xp;
2159        int r, q;
2160
2161        lock();                          /* disable interrupts */
2162        r = rp - proc - NR_TASKS;
2163        q = (r < 0 ? TASK_Q : r < LOW_USER ? SERVER_Q : USER_Q);
2164        if ( (xp = rdy_head[q]) == NIL_PROC) return;
2165        if (xp == rp) {
2166            /* Remove head of queue */
2167            rdy_head[q] = xp->p_nextready;
2168            pick_proc();
2169        } else {
2170            /* Search body of queue.  A process can be made unready even if it is
2171             * not running by being sent a signal that kills it.
2172             */
2173            while (xp->p_nextready != rp)
2174                    if ( (xp = xp->p_nextready) == NIL_PROC) return;
2175            xp->p_nextready = xp->p_nextready->p_nextready;
2176            while (xp->p_nextready != NIL_PROC) xp = xp->p_nextready;
2177            rdy_tail[q] = xp;
2178        }
2179        restore();                       /* restore interrupts to previous state */
2180      }


2183      /*===========================================================================*
2184       *                              sched                                        *
2185       *===========================================================================*/
2186      PUBLIC sched()
2187      {
2188      /* The current process has run too long.  If another low priority (user)
2189       * process is runnable, put the current process on the end of the user queue,
2190       * possibly promoting another user to head of the queue.
2191       */
2192
2193        lock();                          /* disable interrupts */
2194        if (rdy_head[USER_Q] == NIL_PROC) {
2195            restore();                   /* restore interrupts to previous state */
2196            return;
2197        }
2198
2199        /* One or more user processes queued. */
```

```
2200        rdy_tail[USER_Q]->p_nextready = rdy_head[USER_Q];
2201        rdy_tail[USER_Q] = rdy_head[USER_Q];
2202        rdy_head[USER_Q] = rdy_head[USER_Q]->p_nextready;
2203        rdy_tail[USER_Q]->p_nextready = NIL_PROC;
2204        pick_proc();
2205        restore();                              /* restore interrupts to previous state */
2206    }
```

```
2250    /* This file contains the drivers for four special files:
2251     *      /dev/null       - null device (data sink)
2252     *      /dev/mem        - absolute memory
2253     *      /dev/kmem       - kernel virtual memory
2254     *      /dev/ram        - RAM disk
2255     * It accepts three messages, for reading, for writing, and for
2256     * control. All use message format m2 and with these parameters:
2257     *
2258     *    m_type     DEVICE    PROC_NR    COUNT    POSITION ADRRESS
2259     * ----------------------------------------------------------------
2260     * | DISK_READ  | device | proc nr | bytes  | offset | buf ptr |
2261     * |------------+--------+---------+--------+--------+---------|
2262     * | DISK_WRITE | device | proc nr | bytes  | offset | buf ptr |
2263     * |------------+--------+---------+--------+--------+---------|
2264     * | DISK_IOCTL | device |         | blocks | ram org |        |
2265     * ----------------------------------------------------------------
2266     *
2267     *
2268     * The file contains one entry point:
2269     *
2270     *    mem_task:  main entry when system is brought up
2271     *
2272     */
2273
2274    #include "../h/const.h"
2275    #include "../h/type.h"
2276    #include "../h/callnr.h"
2277    #include "../h/com.h"
2278    #include "../h/error.h"
2279    #include "const.h"
2280    #include "type.h"
2281    #include "proc.h"
2282
2283    #define NR_RAMS             4      /* number of RAM-type devices */
2284
2285    PRIVATE message mess;                  /* message buffer */
2286    PRIVATE phys_bytes ram_origin[NR_RAMS]; /* origin of each RAM disk  */
2287    PRIVATE phys_bytes ram_limit[NR_RAMS];  /* limit of RAM disk per minor dev. */
2288
2289    /*===========================================================================*
2290     *                              mem_task                                      *
2291     *===========================================================================*/
2292    PUBLIC mem_task()
2293    {
2294    /* Main program of the disk driver task. */
2295
2296      int r, caller, proc_nr;
2297      extern unsigned sizes[8];
2298      extern phys_clicks get_base();
2299
```

```
2300
2301        /* Initialize this task. */
2302        ram_origin[KMEM_DEV] = (phys_bytes) get_base() << CLICK_SHIFT;
2303        ram_limit[KMEM_DEV] = (sizes[0] + sizes[1]) << CLICK_SHIFT;
2304        ram_limit[MEM_DEV] = MEM_BYTES;
2305
2306        /* Here is the main loop of the memory task.  It waits for a message, carries
2307         * it out, and sends a reply.
2308         */
2309        while (TRUE) {
2310                /* First wait for a request to read or write. */
2311                receive(ANY, &mess);
2312                if (mess.m_source < 0)
2313                        panic("mem task got message from ", mess.m_source);
2314                caller = mess.m_source;
2315                proc_nr = mess.PROC_NR;
2316
2317                /* Now carry out the work.  It depends on the opcode. */
2318                switch(mess.m_type) {
2319                    case DISK_READ:    r = do_mem(&mess);    break;
2320                    case DISK_WRITE:   r = do_mem(&mess);    break;
2321                    case DISK_IOCTL:   r = do_setup(&mess);  break;
2322                    default:           r = EINVAL;           break;
2323                }
2324
2325                /* Finally, prepare and send the reply message. */
2326                mess.m_type = TASK_REPLY;
2327                mess.REP_PROC_NR = proc_nr;
2328                mess.REP_STATUS = r;
2329                send(caller, &mess);
2330        }
2331    }


2334    /*===========================================================================*
2335     *                              do_mem                                        *
2336     *===========================================================================*/
2337    PRIVATE int do_mem(m_ptr)
2338    register message *m_ptr;         /* pointer to read or write message */
2339    {
2340    /* Read or write /dev/null, /dev/mem, /dev/kmem, or /dev/ram. */
2341
2342      int device, count;
2343      phys_bytes mem_phys, user_phys;
2344      struct proc *rp;
2345      extern phys_clicks get_base();
2346      extern phys_bytes umap();
2347
2348      /* Get minor device number and check for /dev/null. */
2349      device = m_ptr->DEVICE;
```

```
2350        if (device < 0 || device >= NR_RAMS) return(ENXIO);   /* bad minor device */
2351        if (device == NULL_DEV) return(m_ptr->m_type == DISK_READ ? 0 : m_ptr->COUNT);
2352
2353        /* Set up 'mem_phys' for /dev/mem, /dev/kmem, or /dev/ram. */
2354        if (m_ptr->POSITION < 0) return(ENXIO);
2355        mem_phys = ram_origin[device] + m_ptr->POSITION;
2356        if (mem_phys > ram_limit[device]) return(0);
2357        count = m_ptr->COUNT;
2358        if(mem_phys + count > ram_limit[device]) count = ram_limit[device] - mem_phys;
2359
2360        /* Determine address where data is to go or to come from. */
2361        rp = proc_addr(m_ptr->PROC_NR);
2362        user_phys = umap(rp, D, (vir_bytes) m_ptr->ADDRESS, (vir_bytes) count);
2363        if (user_phys == 0) return(E_BAD_ADDR);
2364
2365        /* Copy the data. */
2366        if (m_ptr->m_type == DISK_READ)
2367              phys_copy(mem_phys, user_phys, (long) count);
2368        else
2369              phys_copy(user_phys, mem_phys, (long) count);
2370        return(count);
2371    }


2374    /*===========================================================================*
2375     *                              do_setup                                      *
2376     *===========================================================================*/
2377    PRIVATE int do_setup(m_ptr)
2378    message *m_ptr;                    /* pointer to read or write message */
2379    {
2380    /* Set parameters for one of the disk RAMs. */
2381
2382        int device;
2383
2384        device = m_ptr->DEVICE;
2385        if (device < 0 || device >= NR_RAMS) return(ENXIO);   /* bad minor device */
2386        ram_origin[device] = m_ptr->POSITION;
2387        ram_limit[device] = m_ptr->POSITION + (long) m_ptr->COUNT * BLOCK_SIZE;
2388        return(OK);
2389    }
```

```
2400   /* This file contains a driver for a Floppy Disk Controller (FDC) using the
2401    * NEC PD765 chip.  The driver supports two operations: read a block and
2402    * write a block.  It accepts two messages, one for reading and one for
2403    * writing, both using message format m2 and with the same parameters:
2404    *
2405    *    m_type      DEVICE    PROC_NR    COUNT    POSITION  ADRRESS
2406    * ------------------------------------------------------------------
2407    * | DISK_READ  | device  | proc nr  | bytes  | offset | buf ptr |
2408    * |------------+---------+----------+--------+--------+---------|
2409    * | DISK_WRITE | device  | proc nr  | bytes  | offset | buf ptr |
2410    * ------------------------------------------------------------------
2411    *
2412    * The file contains one entry point:
2413    *
2414    *    floppy_task:      main entry when system is brought up
2415    *
2416    */
2417
2418   #include "../h/const.h"
2419   #include "../h/type.h"
2420   #include "../h/callnr.h"
2421   #include "../h/com.h"
2422   #include "../h/error.h"
2423   #include "const.h"
2424   #include "type.h"
2425   #include "proc.h"
2426
2427   /* I/O Ports used by floppy disk task. */
2428   #define DOR             0x3F2    /* motor drive control bits */
2429   #define FDC_STATUS      0x3F4    /* floppy disk controller status register */
2430   #define FDC_DATA        0x3F5    /* floppy disk controller data register */
2431   #define DMA_ADDR        0x004    /* port for low 16 bits of DMA address */
2432   #define DMA_TOP         0x081    /* port for top 4 bits of 20-bit DMA addr */
2433   #define DMA_COUNT       0x005    /* port for DMA count (count = bytes - 1) */
2434   #define DMA_M2          0x00C    /* DMA status port */
2435   #define DMA_M1          0x00B    /* DMA status port */
2436   #define DMA_INIT        0x00A    /* DMA init port */
2437
2438   /* Status registers returned as result of operation. */
2439   #define ST0             0x00     /* status register 0 */
2440   #define ST1             0x01     /* status register 1 */
2441   #define ST2             0x02     /* status register 2 */
2442   #define ST3             0x00     /* status register 3 (return by DRIVE_SENSE) */
2443   #define ST_CYL          0x03     /* slot where controller reports cylinder */
2444   #define ST_HEAD         0x04     /* slot where controller reports head */
2445   #define ST_SEC          0x05     /* slot where controller reports sector */
2446   #define ST_PCN          0x01     /* slot where controller reports present cyl */
2447
2448   /* Fields within the I/O ports. */
2449   #define MASTER          0x80     /* used to see who is master */
```

```
2450    #define DIRECTION      0x40      /* is FDC trying to read or write? */
2451    #define CTL_BUSY       0x10      /* used to see when controller is busy */
2452    #define CTL_ACCEPTING  0x80      /* bit pattern FDC gives when idle */
2453    #define MOTOR_MASK     0xF0      /* these bits control the motors in DOR */
2454    #define ENABLE_INT     0x0C      /* used for setting DOR port */
2455    #define ST0_BITS       0xF8      /* check top 5 bits of seek status */
2456    #define ST3_FAULT      0x80      /* if this bit is set, drive is sick */
2457    #define ST3_WR_PROTECT 0x40      /* set when diskette is write protected */
2458    #define ST3_READY      0x20      /* set when drive is ready */
2459    #define TRANS_ST0      0x00      /* top 5 bits of ST0 for READ/WRITE */
2460    #define SEEK_ST0       0x20      /* top 5 bits of ST0 for SEEK */
2461    #define BAD_SECTOR     0x05      /* if these bits are set in ST1, recalibrate */
2462    #define BAD_CYL        0x1F      /* if any of these bits are set, recalibrate */
2463    #define WRITE_PROTECT  0x02      /* bit is set if diskette is write protected */
2464    #define CHANGE         0xC0      /* value returned by FDC after reset */
2465
2466    /* Floppy disk controller command bytes. */
2467    #define FDC_SEEK        0x0F     /* command the drive to seek */
2468    #define FDC_READ        0xE6     /* command the drive to read */
2469    #define FDC_WRITE       0xC5     /* command the drive to write */
2470    #define FDC_SENSE       0x08     /* command the controller to tell its status */
2471    #define FDC_RECALIBRATE 0x07     /* command the drive to go to cyl 0 */
2472    #define FDC_SPECIFY     0x03     /* command the drive to accept params */
2473
2474    /* DMA channel commands. */
2475    #define DMA_READ        0x46     /* DMA read opcode */
2476    #define DMA_WRITE       0x4A     /* DMA write opcode */
2477
2478    /* Parameters for the disk drive. */
2479    #define SECTOR_SIZE     512      /* physical sector size in bytes */
2480    #define NR_SECTORS      0x09     /* number of sectors per track */
2481    #define NR_HEADS        0x02     /* two heads (i.e., two tracks/cylinder) */
2482    #define GAP             0x2A     /* intersector gap size */
2483    #define DTL             0xFF     /* determines data length (sector size) */
2484    #define SPEC1           0xDF     /* first parameter to SPECIFY */
2485    #define SPEC2           0x02     /* second parameter to SPECIFY */
2486
2487    #define MOTOR_OFF       3*HZ     /* how long to wait before stopping motor */
2488    #define MOTOR_START     HZ/4     /* how long does it take motor to start up? */
2489
2490    /* Error codes */
2491    #define ERR_SEEK         -1      /* bad seek */
2492    #define ERR_TRANSFER     -2      /* bad transfer */
2493    #define ERR_STATUS       -3      /* something wrong when getting status */
2494    #define ERR_RECALIBRATE  -4      /* recalibrate didn't work properly */
2495    #define ERR_WR_PROTECT   -5      /* diskette is write protected */
2496    #define ERR_DRIVE        -6      /* something wrong with a drive */
2497
2498    /* Miscellaneous. */
2499    #define MOTOR_RUNNING   0xFF     /* message type for clock interrupt */
```

```
2500   #define MAX_ERRORS       10    /* how often to try rd/wt before quitting */
2501   #define MAX_RESULTS       8    /* max number of bytes controller returns */
2502   #define NR_DRIVES         2    /* maximum number of drives */
2503   #define DIVISOR         128    /* used for sector size encoding */
2504   #define MAX_FDC_RETRY   100    /* max # times to try to output to FDC */
2505   #define NR_BLOCKS       720    /* number of blocks on 9 sector diskette */
2506
2507   /* Variables. */
2508   PRIVATE struct floppy {        /* main drive struct, one entry per drive */
2509     int fl_opcode;               /* DISK_READ or DISK_WRITE */
2510     int fl_curcyl;               /* current cylinder */
2511     int fl_procnr;               /* which proc wanted this operation? */
2512     int fl_drive;                /* drive number addressed */
2513     int fl_cylinder;             /* cylinder number addressed */
2514     int fl_sector;               /* sector addressed */
2515     int fl_head;                 /* head number addressed */
2516     int fl_count;                /* byte count */
2517     vir_bytes fl_address;        /* user virtual address */
2518     char fl_results[MAX_RESULTS]; /* the controller can give lots of output */
2519     char fl_calibration;         /* CALIBRATED or UNCALIBRATED */
2520   } floppy[NR_DRIVES];
2521
2522   #define UNCALIBRATED      0    /* drive needs to be calibrated at next use */
2523   #define CALIBRATED        1    /* no calibration needed */
2524
2525   PRIVATE int motor_status;      /* current motor status is in 4 high bits */
2526   PRIVATE int motor_goal;        /* desired motor status is in 4 high bits */
2527   PRIVATE int prev_motor;        /* which motor was started last */
2528   PRIVATE int need_reset;        /* set to 1 when controller must be reset */
2529   PRIVATE int initialized;       /* set to 1 after first successful transfer */
2530   PRIVATE int steps_per_cyl = 1; /* # pulses to give stepping motor per cyl */
2531
2532   PRIVATE message mess;          /* message buffer for in and out */
2533
2534   PRIVATE char len[] = {-1,0,1,-1,2,-1,-1,3,-1,-1,-1,-1,-1,-1,-1,4};
2535   PRIVATE char interleave[] = {1,2,3,4,5,6,7,8,9};
2536
2537   /*===========================================================================*
2538    *                              floppy_task                                  *
2539    *===========================================================================*/
2540   PUBLIC floppy_task()
2541   {
2542   /* Main program of the floppy disk driver task. */
2543
2544     int r, caller, proc_nr;
2545
2546     /* Here is the main loop of the disk task.  It waits for a message, carries
2547      * it out, and sends a reply.
2548      */
2549     while (TRUE) {
```

```
2550                /* First wait for a request to read or write a disk block. */
2551                receive(ANY, &mess);     /* get a request to do some work */
2552                if (mess.m_source < 0)
2553                        panic("disk task got message from ", mess.m_source);
2554                caller = mess.m_source;
2555                proc_nr = mess.PROC_NR;
2556
2557                /* Now carry out the work. */
2558                switch(mess.m_type) {
2559                    case DISK_READ:    r = do_rdwt(&mess);      break;
2560                    case DISK_WRITE:   r = do_rdwt(&mess);      break;
2561                    default:           r = EINVAL;             break;
2562                }
2563
2564                /* Finally, prepare and send the reply message. */
2565                mess.m_type = TASK_REPLY;
2566                mess.REP_PROC_NR = proc_nr;
2567                mess.REP_STATUS = r;     /* # of bytes transferred or error code */
2568                send(caller, &mess);     /* send reply to caller */
2569          }
2570      }


2573      /*===========================================================================*
2574       *                              do_rdwt                                       *
2575       *===========================================================================*/
2576      PRIVATE int do_rdwt(m_ptr)
2577      message *m_ptr;                      /* pointer to read or write message */
2578      {
2579      /* Carry out a read or write request from the disk. */
2580        register struct floppy *fp;
2581        int r, drive, errors, stop_motor();
2582        long block;
2583
2584        /* Decode the message parameters. */
2585        drive = m_ptr->DEVICE;
2586        if (drive < 0 || drive >= NR_DRIVES) return(EIO);
2587        fp = &floppy[drive];                /* 'fp' points to entry for this drive */
2588        fp->fl_drive = drive;               /* save drive number explicitly */
2589        fp->fl_opcode = m_ptr->m_type;          /* DISK_READ or DISK_WRITE */
2590        if (m_ptr->POSITION % BLOCK_SIZE != 0) return(EINVAL);
2591        block = m_ptr->POSITION/SECTOR_SIZE;
2592        if (block >= NR_BLOCKS) return(0);
2593        fp->fl_cylinder = (int) (block / (NR_HEADS * NR_SECTORS));
2594        fp->fl_sector = (int) interleave[block % NR_SECTORS];
2595        fp->fl_head = (int) (block % (NR_HEADS*NR_SECTORS) )/NR_SECTORS;
2596        fp->fl_count = m_ptr->COUNT;
2597        fp->fl_address = (vir_bytes) m_ptr->ADDRESS;
2598        fp->fl_procnr = m_ptr->PROC_NR;
2599        if (fp->fl_count != BLOCK_SIZE) return(EINVAL);
```

```
2600
2601        errors = 0;
2602
2603        /* This loop allows a failed operation to be repeated. */
2604        while (errors <= MAX_ERRORS) {
2605
2606              /* If a lot of errors occur when 'initialized' is 0, it probably
2607               * means that we are trying at the wrong density.  Try another one.
2608               * Increment 'errors' here since loop is aborted on error.
2609               */
2610              errors++;                  /* increment count once per loop cycle */
2611              if (initialized == 0 && errors == MAX_ERRORS && fp->fl_cylinder > 0) {
2612                    if (steps_per_cyl > 1) {
2613                          panic("Unreadable diskette (drive density?)", NO_NUM);
2614                    } else {
2615                          steps_per_cyl++;
2616                          errors = 0;
2617                    }
2618              }
2619
2620              /* First check to see if a reset is needed. */
2621              if (need_reset) reset();
2622
2623              /* Now set up the DMA chip. */
2624              dma_setup(fp);
2625
2626              /* See if motor is running; if not, turn it on and wait */
2627              start_motor(fp);
2628
2629              /* If we are going to a new cylinder, perform a seek. */
2630              r = seek(fp);
2631              if (r != OK) continue;  /* if error, try again */
2632
2633              /* Perform the transfer. */
2634              r = transfer(fp);
2635              if (r == OK) break;       /* if successful, exit loop */
2636              if (r == ERR_WR_PROTECT) break; /* retries won't help */
2637
2638        }
2639
2640        /* Start watch_dog timer to turn motor off in a few seconds */
2641        motor_goal = ENABLE_INT;        /* when timer goes off, kill all motors */
2642        clock_mess(MOTOR_OFF, stop_motor);
2643        if (r == OK && fp->fl_cylinder > 0) initialized = 1;  /* seek works */
2644        return(r == OK ? BLOCK_SIZE : EIO);
2645  }
```

```
2650     /*===========================================================================*
2651      *                              dma_setup                                     *
2652      *===========================================================================*/
2653     PRIVATE dma_setup(fp)
2654     struct floppy *fp;                    /* pointer to the drive struct */
2655     {
2656     /* The IBM PC can perform DMA operations by using the DMA chip.  To use it,
2657      * the DMA (Direct Memory Access) chip is loaded with the 20-bit memory address
2658      * to by read from or written to, the byte count minus 1, and a read or write
2659      * opcode.  This routine sets up the DMA chip.  Note that the chip is not
2660      * capable of doing a DMA across a 64K boundary (e.g., you can't read a
2661      * 512-byte block starting at physical address 65520).
2662      */
2663
2664       int mode, low_addr, high_addr, top_addr, low_ct, high_ct, top_end;
2665       vir_bytes vir, ct;
2666       phys_bytes user_phys;
2667       extern phys_bytes umap();
2668
2669       mode = (fp->fl_opcode == DISK_READ ? DMA_READ : DMA_WRITE);
2670       vir = (vir_bytes) fp->fl_address;
2671       ct = (vir_bytes) fp->fl_count;
2672       user_phys = umap(proc_addr(fp->fl_procnr), D, vir, ct);
2673       low_addr  = (int) (user_phys >>  0) & BYTE;
2674       high_addr = (int) (user_phys >>  8) & BYTE;
2675       top_addr  = (int) (user_phys >> 16) & BYTE;
2676       low_ct  = (int) ( (ct - 1) >> 0) & BYTE;
2677       high_ct = (int) ( (ct - 1) >> 8) & BYTE;
2678
2679       /* Check to see if the transfer will require the DMA address counter to
2680        * go from one 64K segment to another.  If so, do not even start it, since
2681        * the hardware does not carry from bit 15 to bit 16 of the DMA address.
2682        * Also check for bad buffer address.  These errors mean FS contains a bug.
2683        */
2684       if (user_phys == 0) panic("FS gave floppy disk driver bad addr", (int) vir);
2685       top_end = (int) (((user_phys + ct - 1) >> 16) & BYTE);
2686       if (top_end != top_addr) panic("Trying to DMA across 64K boundary", top_addr);
2687
2688       /* Now set up the DMA registers. */
2689       lock();
2690       port_out(DMA_M2, mode);       /* set the DMA mode */
2691       port_out(DMA_M1, mode);       /* set it again */
2692       port_out(DMA_ADDR, low_addr); /* output low-order 8 bits */
2693       port_out(DMA_ADDR, high_addr);/* output next 8 bits */
2694       port_out(DMA_TOP, top_addr);  /* output highest 4 bits */
2695       port_out(DMA_COUNT, low_ct);  /* output low 8 bits of count - 1 */
2696       port_out(DMA_COUNT, high_ct); /* output high 8 bits of count - 1 */
2697       unlock();
2698       port_out(DMA_INIT, 2);        /* initialize DMA */
2699     }
```

```
2700   /*===========================================================================*
2701    *                              start_motor                                  *
2702    *===========================================================================*/
2703   PRIVATE start_motor(fp)
2704   struct floppy *fp;                    /* pointer to the drive struct */
2705   {
2706   /* Control of the floppy disk motors is a big pain.  If a motor is off, you
2707    * have to turn it on first, which takes 1/2 second.  You can't leave it on
2708    * all the time, since that would wear out the diskette.  However, if you turn
2709    * the motor off after each operation, the system performance will be awful.
2710    * The compromise used here is to leave it on for a few seconds after each
2711    * operation.  If a new operation is started in that interval, it need not be
2712    * turned on again.  If no new operation is started, a timer goes off and the
2713    * motor is turned off.  I/O port DOR has bits to control each of 4 drives.
2714    * Interrupts must be disabled temporarily to prevent clock interrupt from
2715    * turning off motors while we are testing the bits.
2716    */
2717
2718     int motor_bit, running, send_mess();
2719
2720     lock();                             /* no interrupts while checking out motor */
2721     motor_bit = 1 << (fp->fl_drive + 4);  /* bit mask for this drive */
2722     motor_goal = motor_bit | ENABLE_INT | fp->fl_drive;
2723     if (motor_status & prev_motor) motor_goal |= prev_motor;
2724     running = motor_status & motor_bit;    /* nonzero if this motor is running */
2725     port_out(DOR, motor_goal);
2726     motor_status = motor_goal;
2727     prev_motor = motor_bit;             /* record motor started for next time */
2728     unlock();
2729
2730     /* If the motor was already running, we don't have to wait for it. */
2731     if (running) return;                /* motor was already running */
2732     clock_mess(MOTOR_START, send_mess);  /* motor was not running */
2733     receive(CLOCK, &mess);              /* wait for clock interrupt */
2734   }


2737   /*===========================================================================*
2738    *                              stop_motor                                   *
2739    *===========================================================================*/
2740   PRIVATE stop_motor()
2741   {
2742   /* This routine is called by the clock interrupt after several seconds have
2743    * elapsed with no floppy disk activity.  It checks to see if any drives are
2744    * supposed to be turned off, and if so, turns them off.
2745    */
2746
2747     if ( (motor_goal & MOTOR_MASK) != (motor_status & MOTOR_MASK) ) {
2748         port_out(DOR, motor_goal);
2749         motor_status = motor_goal;
```

```
2750      }
2751    }


2754    /*===========================================================================*
2755     *                              seek                                         *
2756     *===========================================================================*/
2757    PRIVATE int seek(fp)
2758    struct floppy *fp;                  /* pointer to the drive struct */
2759    {
2760    /* Issue a SEEK command on the indicated drive unless the arm is already
2761     * positioned on the correct cylinder.
2762     */
2763
2764      int r;
2765
2766      /* Are we already on the correct cylinder? */
2767      if (fp->fl_calibration == UNCALIBRATED)
2768            if (recalibrate(fp) != OK) return(ERR_SEEK);
2769      if (fp->fl_curcyl == fp->fl_cylinder) return(OK);
2770
2771      /* No.  Wrong cylinder.  Issue a SEEK and wait for interrupt. */
2772      fdc_out(FDC_SEEK);                 /* start issuing the SEEK command */
2773      fdc_out( (fp->fl_head << 2) | fp->fl_drive);
2774      fdc_out(fp->fl_cylinder * steps_per_cyl);
2775      if (need_reset) return(ERR_SEEK);     /* if controller is sick, abort seek */
2776      receive(HARDWARE, &mess);
2777
2778      /* Interrupt has been received.  Check drive status. */
2779      fdc_out(FDC_SENSE);               /* probe FDC to make it return status */
2780      r = fdc_results(fp);              /* get controller status bytes */
2781      if ( (fp->fl_results[ST0] & ST0_BITS) != SEEK_ST0) r = ERR_SEEK;
2782      if (fp->fl_results[ST1] != fp->fl_cylinder * steps_per_cyl) r = ERR_SEEK;
2783      if (r != OK)
2784            if (recalibrate(fp) != OK) return(ERR_SEEK);
2785      return(r);
2786    }


2789    /*===========================================================================*
2790     *                              transfer                                     *
2791     *===========================================================================*/
2792    PRIVATE int transfer(fp)
2793    register struct floppy *fp;       /* pointer to the drive struct */
2794    {
2795    /* The drive is now on the proper cylinder.  Read or write 1 block. */
2796
2797      int r, s, op;
2798
2799      /* Never attempt a transfer if the drive is uncalibrated or motor is off. */
```

```
2800        if (fp->fl_calibration == UNCALIBRATED) return(ERR_TRANSFER);
2801        if ( ( (motor_status>>(fp->fl_drive+4)) & 1) == 0) return(ERR_TRANSFER);
2802
2803        /* The command is issued by outputing 9 bytes to the controller chip. */
2804        op = (fp->fl_opcode == DISK_READ ? FDC_READ : FDC_WRITE);
2805        fdc_out(op);                    /* issue the read or write command */
2806        fdc_out( (fp->fl_head << 2) | fp->fl_drive);
2807        fdc_out(fp->fl_cylinder);       /* tell controller which cylinder */
2808        fdc_out(fp->fl_head);           /* tell controller which head */
2809        fdc_out(fp->fl_sector);         /* tell controller which sector */
2810        fdc_out( (int) len[SECTOR_SIZE/DIVISOR]);      /* sector size */
2811        fdc_out(NR_SECTORS);            /* tell controller how big a track is */
2812        fdc_out(GAP);                   /* tell controller how big sector gap is */
2813        fdc_out(DTL);                   /* tell controller about data length */
2814
2815        /* Block, waiting for disk interrupt. */
2816        if (need_reset) return(ERR_TRANSFER); /* if controller is sick, abort op */
2817        receive(HARDWARE, &mess);
2818
2819        /* Get controller status and check for errors. */
2820        r = fdc_results(fp);
2821        if (r != OK) return(r);
2822        if ( (fp->fl_results[ST1] & BAD_SECTOR) || (fp->fl_results[ST2] & BAD_CYL) )
2823            fp->fl_calibration = UNCALIBRATED;
2824        if (fp->fl_results[ST1] & WRITE_PROTECT) {
2825            printf("Diskette in drive %d is write protected.\n", fp->fl_drive);
2826            return(ERR_WR_PROTECT);
2827        }
2828        if ((fp->fl_results[ST0] & ST0_BITS) != TRANS_ST0) return(ERR_TRANSFER);
2829        if (fp->fl_results[ST1] | fp->fl_results[ST2]) return(ERR_TRANSFER);
2830
2831        /* Compare actual numbers of sectors transferred with expected number. */
2832        s =  (fp->fl_results[ST_CYL] - fp->fl_cylinder) * NR_HEADS * NR_SECTORS;
2833        s += (fp->fl_results[ST_HEAD] - fp->fl_head) * NR_SECTORS;
2834        s += (fp->fl_results[ST_SEC] - fp->fl_sector);
2835        if (s * SECTOR_SIZE != fp->fl_count) return(ERR_TRANSFER);
2836        return(OK);
2837    }


2840    /*===========================================================================*
2841     *                              fdc_results                                  *
2842     *===========================================================================*/
2843    PRIVATE int fdc_results(fp)
2844    register struct floppy *fp;        /* pointer to the drive struct */
2845    {
2846    /* Extract results from the controller after an operation. */
2847
2848        int i, j, status;
2849
```

```
2850        /* Loop, extracting bytes from FDC until it says it has no more. */
2851        for (i = 0; i < MAX_RESULTS; i++) {
2852              port_in(FDC_STATUS, &status);
2853              if ( (status & MASTER) == 0) return(ERR_STATUS);
2854              port_in(FDC_STATUS, &status);   /* read it again */
2855              if ( (status & DIRECTION) == 0) return(ERR_STATUS);
2856              port_in(FDC_DATA, &status);
2857              fp->fl_results[i] = status & BYTE;
2858              for (j = 0; j < 5; j++) ;        /* delay loop */
2859              port_in(FDC_STATUS, &status);
2860              if ( (status & CTL_BUSY) == 0) return(OK);
2861        }
2862
2863        /* FDC is giving back too many results. */
2864        need_reset = TRUE;              /* controller chip must be reset */
2865        return(ERR_STATUS);
2866   }


2869   /*===========================================================================*
2870    *                              fdc_out                                       *
2871    *===========================================================================*/
2872   PRIVATE fdc_out(val)
2873   int val;                        /* write this byte to floppy disk controller */
2874   {
2875   /* Output a byte to the controller.  This is not entirely trivial, since you
2876    * can only write to it when it is listening, and it decides when to listen.
2877    * If the controller refuses to listen, the FDC chip is given a hard reset.
2878    */
2879
2880      int retries, r;
2881
2882      if (need_reset) return;      /* if controller is not listening, return */
2883      retries = MAX_FDC_RETRY;
2884
2885      /* It may take several tries to get the FDC to accept a command. */
2886      while (retries-- > 0) {
2887            port_in(FDC_STATUS, &r);
2888            r &= (MASTER | DIRECTION);       /* just look at bits 2 and 3 */
2889            if (r != CTL_ACCEPTING) continue;       /* FDC is not listening */
2890            port_out(FDC_DATA, val);
2891            return;
2892      }
2893
2894      /* Controller is not listening.  Hit it over the head with a hammer. */
2895      need_reset = TRUE;
2896   }
```

```
2900   /*===========================================================================*
2901    *                              recalibrate                                  *
2902    *===========================================================================*/
2903   PRIVATE int recalibrate(fp)
2904   register struct floppy *fp;      /* pointer tot he drive struct */
2905   {
2906   /* The floppy disk controller has no way of determining its absolute arm
2907    * position (cylinder).  Instead, it steps the arm a cylinder at a time and
2908    * keeps track of where it thinks it is (in software).  However, after a
2909    * SEEK, the hardware reads information from the diskette telling where the
2910    * arm actually is.  If the arm is in the wrong place, a recalibration is done,
2911    * which forces the arm to cylinder 0.  This way the controller can get back
2912    * into sync with reality.
2913    */
2914
2915     int r;
2916
2917     /* Issue the RECALIBRATE command and wait for the interrupt. */
2918     start_motor(fp);                    /* can't recalibrate with motor off */
2919     fdc_out(FDC_RECALIBRATE);           /* tell drive to recalibrate itself */
2920     fdc_out(fp->fl_drive);              /* specify drive */
2921     if (need_reset) return(ERR_SEEK);      /* don't wait if controller is sick */
2922     receive(HARDWARE, &mess);           /* wait for interrupt message */
2923
2924     /* Determine if the recalibration succeeded. */
2925     fdc_out(FDC_SENSE);                 /* issue SENSE command to see where we are */
2926     r = fdc_results(fp);               /* get results of the SENSE command */
2927     fp->fl_curcyl = -1;                /* force a SEEK next time */
2928     if (r != OK ||                     /* controller would not respond */
2929        (fp->fl_results[ST0]&ST0_BITS) != SEEK_ST0 || fp->fl_results[ST_PCN] !=0){
2930           /* Recalibration failed.  FDC must be reset. */
2931           need_reset = TRUE;
2932           fp->fl_calibration = UNCALIBRATED;
2933           return(ERR_RECALIBRATE);
2934     } else {
2935           /* Recalibration succeeded. */
2936           fp->fl_calibration = CALIBRATED;
2937           return(OK);
2938     }
2939   }


2942   /*===========================================================================*
2943    *                                 reset                                     *
2944    *===========================================================================*/
2945   PRIVATE reset()
2946   {
2947   /* Issue a reset to the controller.  This is done after any catastrophe,
2948    * like the controller refusing to respond.
2949    */
```

```
2950
2951      int i, r, status;
2952      register struct floppy *fp;
2953
2954      /* Disable interrupts and strobe reset bit low. */
2955      need_reset = FALSE;
2956      lock();
2957      motor_status = 0;
2958      motor_goal = 0;
2959      port_out(DOR, 0);              /* strobe reset bit low */
2960      port_out(DOR, ENABLE_INT);     /* strobe it high again */
2961      unlock();                      /* interrupts allowed again */
2962      receive(HARDWARE, &mess);      /* collect the RESET interrupt */
2963
2964      /* Interrupt from the reset has been received.  Continue resetting. */
2965      fp = &floppy[0];               /* use floppy[0] for scratch */
2966      fp->fl_results[0] = 0;         /* this byte will be checked shortly */
2967      fdc_out(FDC_SENSE);            /* did it work? */
2968      r = fdc_results(fp);           /* get results */
2969      if (r != OK) panic("FDC won't reset", r);
2970      status = fp->fl_results[0] & BYTE;
2971      if (status != CHANGE)
2972          panic("FDC did not become ready after reset", fp->fl_results[0]);
2973
2974      /* Reset succeeded.  Tell FDC drive parameters. */
2975      fdc_out(FDC_SPECIFY);          /* specify some timing parameters */
2976      fdc_out(SPEC1);                /* step-rate and head-unload-time */
2977      fdc_out(SPEC2);                /* head-load-time and non-dma */
2978
2979      for (i = 0; i < NR_DRIVES; i++) floppy[i].fl_calibration = UNCALIBRATED;
2980  }


2983  /*===========================================================================*
2984   *                              clock_mess                                    *
2985   *===========================================================================*/
2986  PRIVATE clock_mess(ticks, func)
2987  int ticks;                        /* how many clock ticks to wait */
2988  int (*func)();                    /* function to call upon time out */
2989  {
2990  /* Send the clock task a message. */
2991
2992    mess.m_type = SET_ALARM;
2993    mess.CLOCK_PROC_NR = FLOPPY;
2994    mess.DELTA_TICKS = ticks;
2995    mess.FUNC_TO_CALL = func;
2996    sendrec(CLOCK, &mess);
2997  }
```

```
3000    /*===========================================================================*
3001     *                              send_mess                                     *
3002     *===========================================================================*/
3003    PRIVATE send_mess()
3004    {
3005    /* This routine is called when the clock task has timed out on motor startup.*/
3006
3007      mess.m_type = MOTOR_RUNNING;
3008      send(FLOPPY, &mess);
3009    }
```

```
3050    /* This file contains the code and data for the clock task.  The clock task
3051     * has a single entry point, clock_task().  It accepts four message types:
3052     *
3053     *   CLOCK_TICK:  a clock interrupt has occurred
3054     *   GET_TIME:    a process wants the real time
3055     *   SET_TIME:    a process wants to set the real time
3056     *   SET_ALARM:   a process wants to be alerted after a specified interval
3057     *
3058     * The input message is format m6.  The parameters are as follows:
3059     *
3060     *     m_type   CLOCK_PROC   FUNC    NEW_TIME
3061     * -------------------------------------------
3062     * | SET_ALARM | proc_nr  |f to call| delta   |
3063     * |-----------+----------+---------+---------|
3064     * | CLOCK_TICK |         |         |         |
3065     * |-----------+----------+---------+---------|
3066     * | GET_TIME  |          |         |         |
3067     * |-----------+----------+---------+---------|
3068     * | SET_TIME  |          |         | newtime |
3069     * -------------------------------------------
3070     *
3071     * When an alarm goes off, if the caller is a user process, a SIGALRM signal
3072     * is sent to it.  If it is a task, a function specified by the caller will
3073     * be invoked.  This function may, for example, send a message, but only if
3074     * it is certain that the task will be blocked when the timer goes off.
3075     */
3076
3077    #include "../h/const.h"
3078    #include "../h/type.h"
3079    #include "../h/callnr.h"
3080    #include "../h/com.h"
3081    #include "../h/error.h"
3082    #include "../h/signal.h"
3083    #include "const.h"
3084    #include "type.h"
3085    #include "glo.h"
3086    #include "proc.h"
3087
3088    /* Constant definitions. */
3089    #define MILLISEC          100      /* how often to call the scheduler (msec) */
3090    #define SCHED_RATE (MILLISEC*HZ/1000)   /* number of ticks per schedule */
3091
3092    /* Clock parameters. */
3093    #define TIMER0            0x40     /* port address for timer channel 0 */
3094    #define TIMER_MODE        0x43     /* port address for timer channel 3 */
3095    #define IBM_FREQ     1193182L      /* IBM clock frequency for setting timer */
3096    #define SQUARE_WAVE       0x36     /* mode for generating square wave */
3097
3098    /* Clock task variables. */
3099    PRIVATE real_time boot_time;       /* time in seconds of system boot */
```

```
3100   PRIVATE real_time next_alarm;    /* probable time of next alarm */
3101   PRIVATE sched_ticks = SCHED_RATE;      /* counter: when 0, call scheduler */
3102   PRIVATE struct proc *prev_ptr;  /* last user process run by clock task */
3103   PRIVATE message mc;                    /* message buffer for both input and output */
3104   PRIVATE int (*watch_dog[NR_TASKS+1])(); /* watch_dog functions to call */
3105
3106   /*===========================================================================*
3107    *                              clock_task                                   *
3108    *===========================================================================*/
3109   PUBLIC clock_task()
3110   {
3111   /* Main program of clock task.  It determines which of the 4 possible
3112    * calls this is by looking at 'mc.m_type'.   Then it dispatches.
3113    */
3114
3115     int opcode;
3116
3117     init_clock();                    /* initialize clock tables */
3118
3119     /* Main loop of the clock task.  Get work, process it, sometimes reply. */
3120     while (TRUE) {
3121        receive(ANY, &mc);            /* go get a message */
3122        opcode = mc.m_type;           /* extract the function code */
3123
3124        switch (opcode) {
3125           case SET_ALARM:  do_setalarm(&mc);      break;
3126           case GET_TIME:   do_get_time();         break;
3127           case SET_TIME:   do_set_time(&mc);      break;
3128           case CLOCK_TICK: do_clocktick();        break;
3129           default: panic("clock task got bad message", mc.m_type);
3130        }
3131
3132        /* Send reply, except for clock tick. */
3133        mc.m_type = OK;
3134        if (opcode != CLOCK_TICK) send(mc.m_source, &mc);
3135     }
3136   }


3139   /*===========================================================================*
3140    *                              do_setalarm                                  *
3141    *===========================================================================*/
3142   PRIVATE do_setalarm(m_ptr)
3143   message *m_ptr;                   /* pointer to request message */
3144   {
3145   /* A process wants an alarm signal or a task wants a given watch_dog function
3146    * called after a specified interval.  Record the request and check to see
3147    * it is the very next alarm needed.
3148    */
3149
```

```
3150          register struct proc *rp;
3151          int proc_nr;                    /* which process wants the alarm */
3152          long delta_ticks;               /* in how many clock ticks does he want it? */
3153          int (*function)();              /* function to call (tasks only) */
3154
3155          /* Extract the parameters from the message. */
3156          proc_nr = m_ptr->CLOCK_PROC_NR;        /* process to interrupt later */
3157          delta_ticks = m_ptr->DELTA_TICKS;      /* how many ticks to wait */
3158          function = m_ptr->FUNC_TO_CALL;        /* function to call (tasks only) */
3159          rp = proc_addr(proc_nr);
3160          mc.SECONDS_LEFT = (rp->p_alarm == 0L ? 0 : (rp->p_alarm - realtime)/HZ );
3161          rp->p_alarm = (delta_ticks == 0L ? 0L : realtime + delta_ticks);
3162          if (proc_nr < 0) watch_dog[-proc_nr] = function;
3163
3164          /* Which alarm is next? */
3165          next_alarm = MAX_P_LONG;
3166          for (rp = &proc[0]; rp < &proc[NR_TASKS+NR_PROCS]; rp++)
3167                  if(rp->p_alarm != 0 && rp->p_alarm < next_alarm)next_alarm=rp->p_alarm;
3168
3169      }


3172      /*========================================================================*
3173       *                              do_get_time                               *
3174       *========================================================================*/
3175      PRIVATE do_get_time()
3176      {
3177      /* Get and return the current clock time in ticks. */
3178
3179        mc.m_type = REAL_TIME;           /* set message type for reply */
3180        mc.NEW_TIME = boot_time + realtime/HZ;        /* current real time */
3181      }


3184      /*========================================================================*
3185       *                              do_set_time                               *
3186       *========================================================================*/
3187      PRIVATE do_set_time(m_ptr)
3188      message *m_ptr;                    /* pointer to request message */
3189      {
3190      /* Set the real time clock.  Only the superuser can use this call. */
3191
3192        boot_time = m_ptr->NEW_TIME - realtime/HZ;
3193      }


3196      /*========================================================================*
3197       *                              do_clocktick                              *
3198       *========================================================================*/
3199      PRIVATE do_clocktick()
```

```
3200      {
3201      /* This routine called on every clock tick. */
3202
3203          register struct proc *rp;
3204          register int t, proc_nr;
3205
3206          /* To guard against race conditions, first copy 'lost_ticks' to a local
3207           * variable, add this to 'realtime', and then subtract it from 'lost_ticks'.
3208           */
3209          t = lost_ticks;                    /* 'lost_ticks' counts missed interrupts */
3210          realtime += t + 1;                 /* update the time of day */
3211          lost_ticks -= t;                   /* these interrupts are no longer missed */
3212
3213          if (next_alarm <= realtime) {
3214                  /* An alarm may have gone off, but proc may have exited, so check. */
3215                  next_alarm = MAX_P_LONG;           /* start computing next alarm */
3216                  for (rp = &proc[0]; rp < &proc[NR_TASKS+NR_PROCS]; rp++) {
3217                          if (rp->p_alarm != (real_time) 0) {
3218                                  /* See if this alarm time has been reached. */
3219                                  if (rp->p_alarm <= realtime) {
3220                                          /* A timer has gone off.  If it is a user proc,
3221                                           * send it a signal.  If it is a task, call the
3222                                           * function previously specified by the task.
3223                                           */
3224                                          proc_nr = rp - proc - NR_TASKS;
3225                                          if (proc_nr >= 0)
3226                                                  cause_sig(proc_nr, SIGALRM);
3227                                          else
3228                                                  (*watch_dog[-proc_nr])();
3229                                          rp->p_alarm = 0;
3230                                  }
3231
3232                                  /* Work on determining which alarm is next. */
3233                                  if (rp->p_alarm != 0 && rp->p_alarm < next_alarm)
3234                                          next_alarm = rp->p_alarm;
3235                          }
3236                  }
3237          }
3238
3239          accounting();                      /* keep track of who is using the cpu */
3240
3241          /* If a user process has been running too long, pick another one. */
3242          if (--sched_ticks == 0) {
3243                  if (bill_ptr == prev_ptr) sched();      /* process has run too long */
3244                  sched_ticks = SCHED_RATE;               /* reset quantum */
3245                  prev_ptr = bill_ptr;                    /* new previous process */
3246          }
3247
3248      }
```

```
3250     /*===========================================================================*
3251      *                              accounting                                   *
3252      *===========================================================================*/
3253     PRIVATE accounting()
3254     {
3255     /* Update user and system accounting times.  The variable 'bill_ptr' is always
3256      * kept pointing to the process to charge for CPU usage.  If the CPU was in
3257      * user code prior to this clock tick, charge the tick as user time, otherwise
3258      * charge it as system time.
3259      */
3260
3261      if (prev_proc >= LOW_USER)
3262             bill_ptr->user_time++;   /* charge CPU time */
3263      else
3264             bill_ptr->sys_time++;    /* charge system time */
3265     }


3268     #ifdef i8088
3269     /*===========================================================================*
3270      *                              init_clock                                   *
3271      *===========================================================================*/
3272     PRIVATE init_clock()
3273     {
3274     /* Initialize channel 2 of the 8253A timer to e.g. 60 Hz. */
3275
3276      unsigned int count, low_byte, high_byte;
3277
3278      count = (unsigned) (IBM_FREQ/HZ);        /* value to load into the timer */
3279      low_byte = count & BYTE;                 /* compute low-order byte */
3280      high_byte = (count >> 8) & BYTE;         /* compute high-order byte */
3281      port_out(TIMER_MODE, SQUARE_WAVE);       /* set timer to run continuously */
3282      port_out(TIMER0, low_byte);              /* load timer low byte */
3283      port_out(TIMER0, high_byte);             /* load timer high byte */
3284     }
3285     #endif
```

```
3300   /* This file contains the terminal driver, both for the IBM console and regular
3301    * ASCII terminals.  It is split into two sections, a device-independent part
3302    * and a device-dependent part.  The device-independent part accepts
3303    * characters to be printed from programs and queues them in a standard way
3304    * for device-dependent output.  It also accepts input and queues it for
3305    * programs. This file contains 2 main entry points: tty_task() and keyboard().
3306    * When a key is struck on a terminal, an interrupt to an assembly language
3307    * routine is generated.  This routine saves the machine state and registers
3308    * and calls keyboard(), which enters the character in an internal table, and
3309    * then sends a message to the terminal task.  The main program of the terminal
3310    * task is tty_task(). It accepts not only messages about typed input, but
3311    * also requests to read and write from terminals, etc.
3312    *
3313    * The device-dependent part interfaces with the IBM console and ASCII
3314    * terminals.  The IBM keyboard is unusual in that keystrokes yield key numbers
3315    * rather than ASCII codes, and furthermore, an interrupt is generated when a
3316    * key is depressed and again when it is released.  The IBM display is memory
3317    * mapped, so outputting characters such as line feed, backspace and bell are
3318    * tricky.
3319    *
3320    * The valid messages and their parameters are:
3321    *
3322    *    TTY_CHAR_INT: a character has been typed on a terminal (input interrupt)
3323    *    TTY_O_DONE:   a character has been output (output completed interrupt)
3324    *    TTY_READ:     a process wants to read from a terminal
3325    *    TTY_WRITE:    a process wants to write on a terminal
3326    *    TTY_IOCTL:    a process wants to change a terminal's parameters
3327    *    CANCEL:       terminate a previous incomplete system call immediately
3328    *
3329    *    m_type       TTY_LINE   PROC_NR    COUNT    TTY_SPEK  TTY_FLAGS  ADDRESS
3330    * -------------------------------------------------------------------------
3331    * | TTY_CHAR_INT|          |         |         |         |         |array ptr|
3332    * |-------------+---------+---------+---------+---------+---------+---------|
3333    * | TTY_O_DONE  |minor dev|         |         |         |         |         |
3334    * |-------------+---------+---------+---------+---------+---------+---------|
3335    * | TTY_READ    |minor dev| proc nr |  count  |         |         | buf ptr |
3336    * |-------------+---------+---------+---------+---------+---------+---------|
3337    * | TTY_WRITE   |minor dev| proc nr |  count  |         |         | buf ptr |
3338    * |-------------+---------+---------+---------+---------+---------+---------|
3339    * | TTY_IOCTL   |minor dev| proc nr |func code|erase etc|  flags  |         |
3340    * |-------------+---------+---------+---------+---------+---------+---------|
3341    * | CANCEL      |minor dev| proc nr |         |         |         |         |
3342    * -------------------------------------------------------------------------
3343    */
3344
3345   #include "../h/const.h"
3346   #include "../h/type.h"
3347   #include "../h/callnr.h"
3348   #include "../h/com.h"
3349   #include "../h/error.h"
```

```
3350    #include "../h/sgtty.h"
3351    #include "../h/signal.h"
3352    #include "const.h"
3353    #include "type.h"
3354    #include "proc.h"
3355
3356    #define NR_TTYS            1      /* how many terminals can system handle */
3357    #define TTY_IN_BYTES     200      /* input queue size */
3358    #define TTY_RAM_WORDS    320      /* ram buffer size */
3359    #define TTY_BUF_SIZE     256      /* unit for copying to/from queues */
3360    #define TAB_SIZE           8      /* distance between tabs */
3361    #define TAB_MASK          07      /* mask for tty_column when tabbing */
3362    #define MAX_OVERRUN       16      /* size of overrun input buffer */
3363
3364    #define ERASE_CHAR      '\b'      /* default erase character */
3365    #define KILL_CHAR        '@'      /* default kill character */
3366    #define INTR_CHAR (char)0177      /* default interrupt character */
3367    #define QUIT_CHAR (char) 034      /* default quit character */
3368    #define XOFF_CHAR (char) 023      /* default x-off character (CTRL-S) */
3369    #define XON_CHAR  (char) 021      /* default x-on character (CTRL-Q) */
3370    #define EOT_CHAR  (char) 004      /* CTRL-D */
3371    #define MARKER    (char) 000      /* non-escaped CTRL-D stored as MARKER */
3372    #define DEL_CODE  (char) 83       /* DEL for use in CTRL-ALT-DEL reboot */
3373    #define AT_SIGN         0220      /* code to yield for CTRL-@ */
3374
3375    #define F1                59      /* scan code for function key F1 */
3376    #define F2                60      /* scan code for function key F2 */
3377    #define F10               68      /* scan code for function key F9 */
3378    #define TOP_ROW           14      /* codes below this are shifted if CTRL */
3379
3380    PRIVATE struct tty_struct {
3381       /* Input queue.  Typed characters are stored here until read by a program. */
3382       char tty_inqueue[TTY_IN_BYTES];     /* array used to store the characters */
3383       char *tty_inhead;            /* pointer to place where next char goes */
3384       char *tty_intail;            /* pointer to next char to be given to prog */
3385       int tty_incount;             /* # chars in tty_inqueue */
3386       int tty_lfct;                /* # line feeds in tty_inqueue */
3387
3388       /* Output section. */
3389       int tty_ramqueue[TTY_RAM_WORDS];    /* buffer for video RAM */
3390       int tty_rwords;              /* number of WORDS (not bytes) in outqueue */
3391       int tty_org;                 /* location in RAM where 6845 base points */
3392       int tty_vid;                 /* current position of cursor in video RAM */
3393       char tty_esc_state;          /* O=normal, 1 = ESC seen, 2 = ESC + x seen */
3394       char tty_echar;              /* first character following an ESC */
3395       int tty_attribute;           /* current attribute byte << 8 */
3396       int (*tty_devstart)();       /* routine to start actual device output */
3397
3398       /* Terminal parameters and status. */
3399       int tty_mode;                /* terminal mode set by IOCTL */
```

```
3400          int tty_column;                /* current column number (0-origin) */
3401          int tty_row;                   /* current row (0 at bottom of screen) */
3402          char tty_busy;                 /* 1 when output in progress, else 0 */
3403          char tty_escaped;              /* 1 when '\' just seen, else 0 */
3404          char tty_inhibited;            /* 1 when CTRL-S just seen (stops output) */
3405          char tty_makebreak;            /* 1 for terminals that interrupt twice/key */
3406          char tty_waiting;              /* 1 when output process waiting for reply */
3407
3408          /* User settable characters: erase, kill, interrupt, quit, x-on; x-off. */
3409          char tty_erase;                /* char used to erase 1 char (init ^H) */
3410          char tty_kill;                 /* char used to erase a line (init @) */
3411          char tty_intr;                 /* char used to send SIGINT  (init DEL) */
3412          char tty_quit;                 /* char used for core dump   (init CTRL-\) */
3413          char tty_xon;                  /* char used to start output (init CTRL-Q)*/
3414          char tty_xoff;                 /* char used to stop output  (init CTRL-S) */
3415          char tty_eof;                  /* char used to stop output  (init CTRL-D) */
3416
3417          /* Information about incomplete I/O requests is stored here. */
3418          char tty_incaller;             /* process that made the call (usually FS) */
3419          char tty_inproc;               /* process that wants to read from tty */
3420          char *tty_in_vir;              /* virtual address where data is to go */
3421          int tty_inleft;                /* how many chars are still needed */
3422          char tty_otcaller;             /* process that made the call (usually FS) */
3423          char tty_outproc;              /* process that wants to write to tty */
3424          char *tty_out_vir;             /* virtual address where data comes from */
3425          phys_bytes tty_phys;           /* physical address where data comes from */
3426          int tty_outleft;               /* # chars yet to be copied to tty_outqueue */
3427          int tty_cum;                   /* # chars copied to tty_outqueue so far */
3428
3429          /* Miscellaneous. */
3430          int tty_ioport;                /* I/O port number for this terminal */
3431      } tty_struct[NR_TTYS];
3432
3433      /* Values for the fields. */
3434      #define NOT_ESCAPED   0    /* previous character on this line not '\' */
3435      #define ESCAPED       1    /* previous character on this line was '\' */
3436      #define RUNNING       0    /* no CRTL-S has been typed to stop the tty */
3437      #define STOPPED       1    /* CTRL-S has been typed to stop the tty */
3438      #define INACTIVE      0    /* the tty is not printing */
3439      #define BUSY          1    /* the tty is printing */
3440      #define ONE_INT       0    /* regular terminals interrupt once per char */
3441      #define TWO_INTS      1    /* IBM console interrupts two times per char */
3442      #define NOT_WAITING   0    /* no output process is hanging */
3443      #define WAITING       1    /* an output process is waiting for a reply */
3444
3445      PRIVATE char tty_driver_buf[2*MAX_OVERRUN+2]; /* driver collects chars here */
3446      PRIVATE char tty_copy_buf[2*MAX_OVERRUN];  /* copy buf used to avoid races */
3447      PRIVATE char tty_buf[TTY_BUF_SIZE];      /* scratch buffer to/from user space */
3448      PRIVATE int shift1, shift2, capslock, numlock; /* keep track of shift keys */
3449      PRIVATE int control, alt;        /* keep track of key statii */
```

```
3450    PRIVATE int olivetti;              /* flag set for Olivetti M24 keyboard */
3451    PUBLIC scan_code;                  /* scan code for '=' saved by bootstrap */
3452
3453    /* Scan codes to ASCII for unshifted keys */
3454    PRIVATE char unsh[] = {
3455      0,033,'1','2','3','4','5','6',          '7','8','9','0','-','=','\b','\t',
3456      'q','w','e','r','t','y','u','i',        'o','p','[',']',015,0202,'a','s',
3457      'd','f','g','h','j','k','l',';',        047,0140,0200,0134,'z','x','c','v',
3458      'b','n','m',',','.','/',0201,'*',       0203,' ',0204,0241,0242,0243,0244,0245,
3459      0246,0247,0250,0251,0252,0205,0210,0267,  0270,0271,0211,0264,0265,0266,0214
3460      ,0261,  0262,0263,'0',0177
3461    };
3462
3463    /* Scan codes to ASCII for shifted keys */
3464    PRIVATE char sh[] = {
3465      0,033,'!','@','#','$','%','^',          '&','*','(',')','_','+','\b','\t',
3466      'Q','W','E','R','T','Y','U','I',        'O','P','{','}',015,0202,'A','S',
3467      'D','F','G','H','J','K','L',':',        042,'~',0200,'|','Z','X','C','V',
3468      'B','N','M','<','>','?',0201,'*',       0203,' ',0204,0221,0222,0223,0224,0225,
3469      0226,0227,0230,0231,0232,0204,0213,'7',  '8','9',0211,'4','5','6',0214,'1',
3470      '2','3','0',177
3471    };
3472
3473
3474    /* Scan codes to ASCII for Olivetti M24 for unshifted keys. */
3475    PRIVATE char unm24[] = {
3476      0,033,'1','2','3','4','5','6',          '7','8','9','0','-','^','\b','\t',
3477      'q','w','e','r','t','y','u','i',        'o','p','@','[','\r',0202,'a','s',
3478      'd','f','g','h','j','k','l',';',        ':','',']',0200,'\\','z','x','c','v',
3479      'b','n','m',',','.','/',0201,'*',       0203,' ',0204,0241,0242,0243,0244,0245,
3480      0246,0247,0250,0251,0252,023,0210,'7',  '8','9',0211,'4','5','6',0214,'1',
3481      '2','3','0','.',' ',014,0212,'\r',       '\b','\n','\f',013,032,0213,' ','/',
3482      0253,0254,0255,0256,0257,0215,0216,0217
3483    };
3484
3485    /* Scan codes to ASCII for Olivetti M24 for shifted keys. */
3486    PRIVATE char m24[] = {
3487      0,033,'!','"','#','$','%','&',          047,'(',')','_','=','~','\b','\t',
3488      'Q','W','E','R','T','Y','U','I',        'O','P',0140,'{','\r',0202,'A','S',
3489      'D','F','G','H','J','K','L','+',        '*','}',0200,'|','Z','X','C','V',
3490      'B','N','M','<','>','?',0201,'*',       0203,' ',0204,0221,0222,0223,0224,0225,
3491      0226,0227,0230,0231,0232,0270,023,036,  013,037,0211,'\b',036,'\f',0214,04,
3492      '\n',037,0207,0177,0271,014,0272,'\r',   '\b','\n','\f',036,032,0273,0274,'/',
3493      0233,0234,0235,0236,0237,0275,0276,0277
3494    };
3495
3496
3497    /*========================================================================*
3498     *                            tty_task                                    *
3499     *========================================================================*/
```

```
3500    PUBLIC tty_task()
3501    {
3502    /* Main routine of the terminal task. */
3503
3504      message tty_mess;               /* buffer for all incoming messages */
3505      register struct tty_struct *tp;
3506
3507      tty_init();                     /* initialize */
3508      while (TRUE) {
3509            receive(ANY, &tty_mess);
3510            tp = &tty_struct[tty_mess.TTY_LINE];
3511            switch(tty_mess.m_type) {
3512                case TTY_CHAR_INT:  do_charint(&tty_mess);          break;
3513                case TTY_READ:      do_read(tp, &tty_mess);         break;
3514                case TTY_WRITE:     do_write(tp, &tty_mess);        break;
3515                case TTY_IOCTL:     do_ioctl(tp, &tty_mess);        break;
3516                case CANCEL   :     do_cancel(tp, &tty_mess);       break;
3517                case TTY_O_DONE:    /* reserved for future use (RS-232 terminals)*/
3518                default:            tty_reply(TASK_REPLY, tty_mess.m_source,
3519                                        tty_mess.PROC_NR, EINVAL, 0L, 0L);
3520            }
3521      }
3522    }


3525    /*===========================================================================*
3526     *                              do_charint                                    *
3527     *===========================================================================*/
3528    PRIVATE do_charint(m_ptr)
3529    message *m_ptr;                  /* message containing pointer to char(s) */
3530    {
3531    /* A character has been typed.  If a character is typed and the tty task is
3532     * not able to service it immediately, the character is accumulated within
3533     * the tty driver.  Thus multiple chars may be accumulated.  A single message
3534     * to the tty task may have to process several characters.
3535     */
3536
3537      int m, n, count, replyee, caller;
3538      char *ptr, *copy_ptr, ch;
3539      struct tty_struct *tp;
3540
3541      lock();                         /* prevent races by disabling interrupts */
3542      ptr = m_ptr->ADDRESS;           /* pointer to accumulated char array */
3543      copy_ptr = tty_copy_buf;        /* ptr to shadow array where chars copied */
3544      n = *ptr;                       /* how many chars have been accumulated */
3545      count = n;                      /* save the character count */
3546      n = n + n;                      /* each char occupies 2 bytes */
3547      ptr += 2;                       /* skip count field at start of array */
3548      while (n-- > 0)
3549            *copy_ptr++ = *ptr++;     /* copy the array to safety */
```

```
3550        ptr = m_ptr->ADDRESS;
3551        *ptr = 0;                        /* accumulation count set to 0 */
3552        unlock();                        /* re-enable interrupts */
3553
3554        /* Loop on the accumulated characters, processing each in turn. */
3555        copy_ptr = tty_copy_buf;
3556        while (count-- > 0) {
3557                ch = *copy_ptr++;        /* get the character typed */
3558                n = *copy_ptr++;         /* get the line number it came in on */
3559                in_char(n, ch);          /* queue the char and echo it */
3560
3561                /* See if a previously blocked reader can now be satisfied. */
3562                tp = &tty_struct[n];     /* pointer to struct for this character */
3563                if (tp->tty_inleft > 0 ) {       /* does anybody want input? */
3564                        m = tp->tty_mode & (CBREAK | RAW);
3565                        if (tp->tty_lfct > 0 || (m != 0 && tp->tty_incount > 0)) {
3566                                m = rd_chars(tp);
3567
3568                                /* Tell hanging reader that chars have arrived. */
3569                                replyee = (int) tp->tty_incaller;
3570                                caller = (int) tp->tty_inproc;
3571                                tty_reply(REVIVE, replyee, caller, m, 0L, 0L);
3572                        }
3573                }
3574        }
3575 }


3578 /*===========================================================================*
3579  *                              in_char                                      *
3580  *===========================================================================*/
3581 PRIVATE in_char(line, ch)
3582 int line;                                /* line number on which char arrived */
3583 char ch;                                 /* scan code for character that arrived */
3584 {
3585 /* A character has just been typed in.  Process, save, and echo it. */
3586
3587   register struct tty_struct *tp;
3588   int mode, sig;
3589   char make_break();
3590   tp = &tty_struct[line];                /* set 'tp' to point to proper struct */
3591   /* Function keys are temporarily being used for debug dumps. */
3592   if (ch >= F1 && ch <= F10) {  /* Check for function keys F1, F2, ... F10 */
3593        func_key(ch);             /* process function key */
3594        return;
3595   }
3596   if (tp->tty_incount >= TTY_IN_BYTES) return;  /* no room, discard char */
3597   mode = tp->tty_mode & (RAW | CBREAK);
3598   if (tp->tty_makebreak)
3599        ch = make_break(ch);     /* console give 2 ints/ch */
```

```
3600        else
3601                if (mode != RAW) ch &= 0177;      /* 7-bit chars except in raw mode */
3602        if (ch == 0) return;
3603
3604        /* Processing for COOKED and CBREAK mode contains special checks. */
3605        if (mode == COOKED || mode == CBREAK) {
3606                /* Handle erase, kill and escape processing. */
3607                if (mode == COOKED) {
3608                        /* First erase processing (rub out of last character). */
3609                        if (ch == tp->tty_erase && tp->tty_escaped == NOT_ESCAPED) {
3610                                chuck(tp);          /* remove last char entered */
3611                                echo(tp, '\b'); /* remove it from the screen */
3612                                echo(tp, ' ');
3613                                echo(tp, '\b');
3614                                return;
3615                        }
3616
3617                        /* Now do kill processing (remove current line). */
3618                        if (ch == tp->tty_kill && tp->tty_escaped == NOT_ESCAPED) {
3619                                while( chuck(tp) == OK) /* keep looping */ ;
3620                                echo(tp, tp->tty_kill);
3621                                echo (tp, '\n');
3622                                return;
3623                        }
3624
3625                        /* Handle EOT and the escape symbol (backslash). */
3626                        if (tp->tty_escaped == NOT_ESCAPED) {
3627                                /* Normal case: previous char was not backslash. */
3628                                if (ch == '\\') {
3629                                        /* An escaped symbol has just been typed. */
3630                                        tp->tty_escaped = ESCAPED;
3631                                        echo(tp, ch);
3632                                        return; /* do not store the '\' */
3633                                }
3634                                /* CTRL-D means end-of-file, unless it is escaped. It
3635                                 * is stored in the text as MARKER, and counts as a
3636                                 * line feed in terms of knowing whether a full line
3637                                 * has been typed already.
3638                                 */
3639                                if (ch == tp->tty_eof) ch = MARKER;
3640                        } else {
3641                                /* Previous character was backslash. */
3642                                tp->tty_escaped = NOT_ESCAPED;  /* turn escaping off */
3643                                if (ch != tp->tty_erase && ch != tp->tty_kill &&
3644                                                        ch != tp->tty_eof) {
3645                                        /* Store the escape previously skipped over */
3646                                        *tp->tty_inhead++ = '\\';
3647                                        tp->tty_incount++;
3648                                        if (tp->tty_inhead ==
3649                                                        &tp->tty_inqueue[TTY_IN_BYTES])
```

```
3650                                        tp->tty_inhead = tp->tty_inqueue;
3651                              }
3652                      }
3653              }
3654              /* Both COOKED and CBREAK modes come here; first map CR to LF. */
3655              if (ch == '\r' && (tp->tty_mode & CRMOD)) ch = '\n';
3656
3657              /* Check for interrupt and quit characters. */
3658              if (ch == tp->tty_intr || ch == tp->tty_quit) {
3659                      sig = (ch == tp->tty_intr ? SIGINT : SIGQUIT);
3660                      tp->tty_inhibited = RUNNING;     /* do implied CRTL-Q */
3661                      finish(tp, EINTR);               /* send reply */
3662                      echo(tp, '\n');
3663                      cause_sig(LOW_USER + 1 + line, sig);
3664                      return;
3665              }
3666
3667              /* Check for and process CTRL-S (terminal stop). */
3668              if (ch == tp->tty_xoff) {
3669                      tp->tty_inhibited = STOPPED;
3670                      return;
3671              }
3672
3673              /* Check for and process CTRL-Q (terminal start). */
3674              if (ch == tp->tty_xon) {
3675                      tp->tty_inhibited = RUNNING;
3676                      (*tp->tty_devstart)(tp);         /* resume output */
3677                      return;
3678              }
3679      }
3680
3681      /* All 3 modes come here. */
3682      if (ch == '\n' || ch == MARKER) tp->tty_lfct++;          /* count line feeds */
3683      *tp->tty_inhead++ = ch;          /* save the character in the input queue */
3684      if (tp->tty_inhead == &tp->tty_inqueue[TTY_IN_BYTES])
3685          tp->tty_inhead = tp->tty_inqueue;        /* handle wraparound */
3686      tp->tty_incount++;
3687      echo(tp, ch);
3688 }


3691 #ifdef i8088
3692 /*===========================================================================*
3693  *                              make_break                                   *
3694  *===========================================================================*/
3695 PRIVATE char make_break(ch)
3696 char ch;                         /* scan code of key just struck or released */
3697 {
3698 /* This routine can handle keyboards that interrupt only on key depression,
3699  * as well as keyboards that interrupt on key depression and key release.
```

```
3700        * For efficiency, the interrupt routine filters out most key releases.
3701        */
3702
3703       int c, make, code;
3704
3705
3706       c = ch & 0177;                /* high-order bit set on key release */
3707       make = (ch & 0200 ? 0 : 1);   /* 1 when key depressed, 0 when key released */
3708       if (olivetti == FALSE) {
3709            /* Standard IBM keyboard. */
3710            code = (shift1 || shift2 || capslock ? sh[c] : unsh[c]);
3711            if (control && c < TOP_ROW) code = sh[c];        /* CTRL-(top row) */
3712            if (c > 70 && numlock) code = sh[c];     /* numlock depressed */
3713       } else {
3714            /* (Olivetti M24 or AT&T 6300) with Olivetti-style keyboard. */
3715            code = (shift1 || shift2 || capslock ? m24[c] : unm24[c]);
3716            if (control && c < TOP_ROW) code = sh[c];        /* CTRL-(top row) */
3717            if (c > 70 && numlock) code = m24[c];    /* numlock depressed */
3718       }
3719       code &= BYTE;
3720       if (code < 0200 || code >= 0206) {
3721            /* Ordinary key, i.e. not shift, control, alt, etc. */
3722            if (alt) code |= 0200;  /* alt key ORs 0200 into code */
3723            if (control) code &= 037;
3724            if (code == 0) code = AT_SIGN;  /* @ is 0100, so CTRL-@ = 0 */
3725            if (make == 0) code = 0;       /* key release */
3726            return(code);
3727       }
3728
3729       /* Table entries 0200 - 0206 denote special actions. */
3730       switch(code - 0200) {
3731         case 0:     shift1 = make;          break; /* shift key on left */
3732         case 1:     shift2 = make;          break; /* shift key on right */
3733         case 2:     control = make;         break; /* control */
3734         case 3:     alt = make;             break; /* alt key */
3735         case 4:     if (make) capslock = 1 - capslock; break;    /* caps lock */
3736         case 5:     if (make) numlock  = 1 - numlock;  break;    /* num lock */
3737       }
3738       return(0);
3739   }
3740   #endif
3741
3742
3743   /*===========================================================================*
3744    *                              echo                                          *
3745    *===========================================================================*/
3746   PRIVATE echo(tp, c)
3747   register struct tty_struct *tp; /* terminal on which to echo */
3748   register char c;                /* character to echo */
3749   {
```

```
3750     /* Echo a character on the terminal. */
3751
3752       if ( (tp->tty_mode & ECHO) == 0) return;       /* if no echoing, don't echo */
3753       if (c != MARKER) out_char(tp, c);
3754       flush(tp);                      /* force character out onto the screen */
3755     }


3758     /*===========================================================================*
3759      *                            chuck                                          *
3760      *===========================================================================*/
3761     PRIVATE int chuck(tp)
3762     register struct tty_struct *tp; /* from which tty should chars be removed */
3763     {
3764     /* Delete one character from the input queue.  Used for erase and kill. */
3765
3766       char *prev;
3767
3768       /* If input queue is empty, don't delete anything. */
3769       if (tp->tty_incount == 0) return(-1);
3770
3771       /* Don't delete '\n' or '\r'. */
3772       prev = (tp->tty_inhead != tp->tty_inqueue ? tp->tty_inhead - 1 :
3773                                         &tp->tty_inqueue[TTY_IN_BYTES-1]);
3774       if (*prev == '\n' || *prev == '\r') return(-1);
3775       tp->tty_inhead = prev;
3776       tp->tty_incount--;
3777       return(OK);                     /* char erasure was possible */
3778     }


3781     /*===========================================================================*
3782      *                            do_read                                        *
3783      *===========================================================================*/
3784     PRIVATE do_read(tp, m_ptr)
3785     register struct tty_struct *tp; /* pointer to tty struct */
3786     message *m_ptr;                 /* pointer to message sent to the task */
3787     {
3788     /* A process wants to read from a terminal. */
3789
3790       int code, caller;
3791
3792       if (tp->tty_inleft > 0) {       /* if someone else is hanging, give up */
3793             tty_reply(TASK_REPLY,m_ptr->m_source,m_ptr->PROC_NR, E_TRY_AGAIN,0L,0L);
3794             return;
3795       }
3796
3797       /* Copy information from the message to the tty struct. */
3798       tp->tty_incaller = m_ptr->m_source;
3799       tp->tty_inproc = m_ptr->PROC_NR;
```

```
3800        tp->tty_in_vir = m_ptr->ADDRESS;
3801        tp->tty_inleft = m_ptr->COUNT;
3802
3803        /* Try to get chars.  This call either gets enough, or gets nothing. */
3804        code = rd_chars(tp);
3805        caller = (int) tp->tty_inproc;
3806        tty_reply(TASK_REPLY, m_ptr->m_source, caller, code, 0L, 0L);
3807   }


3810   /*===========================================================================*
3811    *                                 rd_chars                                  *
3812    *===========================================================================*/
3813   PRIVATE rd_chars(tp)
3814   register struct tty_struct *tp; /* pointer to terminal to read from */
3815   {
3816   /* A process wants to read from a terminal.  First check if enough data is
3817    * available. If so, pass it to the user.  If not, send FS a message telling
3818    * it to suspend the user.  When enough data arrives later, the tty driver
3819    * copies it to the user space directly and notifies FS with a message.
3820    */
3821
3822        int cooked, ct, user_ct, buf_ct, cum, enough, eot_seen;
3823        vir_bytes in_vir, left;
3824        phys_bytes user_phys, tty_phys;
3825        char ch, *tty_ptr;
3826        struct proc *rp;
3827        extern phys_bytes umap();
3828
3829        cooked = ( (tp->tty_mode & (RAW | CBREAK)) ? 0 : 1);   /* 1 iff COOKED mode */
3830        if (tp->tty_incount == 0 || (cooked && tp->tty_lfct == 0)) return(SUSPEND);
3831        rp = proc_addr(tp->tty_inproc);
3832        in_vir = (vir_bytes) tp-> tty_in_vir;
3833        left = (vir_bytes) tp->tty_inleft;
3834        if ( (user_phys = umap(rp, D, in_vir, left)) == 0) return(E_BAD_ADDR);
3835        tty_phys = umap(proc_addr(TTY), D, (vir_bytes) tty_buf, TTY_BUF_SIZE);
3836        cum = 0;
3837        enough = 0;
3838        eot_seen = 0;
3839
3840        /* The outer loop iterates on buffers, one buffer load per iteration. */
3841        while (tp->tty_inleft > 0) {
3842             buf_ct = MIN(tp->tty_inleft, tp->tty_incount);
3843             buf_ct = MIN(buf_ct, TTY_BUF_SIZE);
3844             ct = 0;
3845             tty_ptr = tty_buf;
3846
3847             /* The inner loop fills one buffer. */
3848             while(buf_ct-- > 0) {
3849                  ch = *tp->tty_intail++;
```

```
3850                        if (tp->tty_intail == &tp->tty_inqueue[TTY_IN_BYTES])
3851                                tp->tty_intail = tp->tty_inqueue;
3852                        *tty_ptr++ = ch;
3853                        ct++;
3854                        if (ch == '\n' || ch == MARKER) {
3855                                tp->tty_lfct--;
3856                                if (cooked && ch == MARKER) eot_seen++;
3857                                enough++;        /* exit loop */
3858                                if (cooked) break;      /* only provide 1 line */
3859                        }
3860                }
3861
3862                /* Copy one buffer to user space.  Be careful about CTRL-D.  In cooked
3863                 * mode it is not transmitted to user programs, and is not counted as
3864                 * a character as far as the count goes, but it does occupy space in
3865                 * the driver's tables and must be counted there.
3866                 */
3867                user_ct = (eot_seen ? ct - 1 : ct);      /* bytes to copy to user */
3868                phys_copy(tty_phys, user_phys, (phys_bytes) user_ct);
3869                user_phys += user_ct;
3870                cum += user_ct;
3871                tp->tty_inleft -= ct;
3872                tp->tty_incount -= ct;
3873                if (tp->tty_incount == 0 || enough) break;
3874        }
3875
3876        tp->tty_inleft = 0;
3877        return(cum);
3878  }
3879
3880
3881  /*===========================================================================*
3882   *                              finish                                       *
3883   *===========================================================================*/
3884  PRIVATE finish(tp, code)
3885  register struct tty_struct *tp; /* pointer to tty struct */
3886  int code;                       /* reply code */
3887  {
3888  /* A command has terminated (possibly due to DEL).  Tell caller. */
3889
3890    int replyee, caller;
3891
3892    tp->tty_rwords = 0;
3893    tp->tty_outleft = 0;
3894    if (tp->tty_waiting == NOT_WAITING) return;
3895    replyee = (int) tp->tty_otcaller;
3896    caller = (int) tp->tty_outproc;
3897    tty_reply(TASK_REPLY, replyee, caller, code, 0L, 0L);
3898    tp->tty_waiting = NOT_WAITING;
3899  }
```

```
3902   /*===========================================================================*
3903    *                              do_write                                     *
3904    *===========================================================================*/
3905   PRIVATE do_write(tp, m_ptr)
3906   register struct tty_struct *tp; /* pointer to tty struct */
3907   message *m_ptr;                         /* pointer to message sent to the task */
3908   {
3909   /* A process wants to write on a terminal. */
3910
3911     vir_bytes out_vir, out_left;
3912     struct proc *rp;
3913     extern phys_bytes umap();
3914
3915     /* Copy message parameters to the tty structure. */
3916     tp->tty_otcaller = m_ptr->m_source;
3917     tp->tty_outproc = m_ptr->PROC_NR;
3918     tp->tty_out_vir = m_ptr->ADDRESS;
3919     tp->tty_outleft = m_ptr->COUNT;
3920     tp->tty_waiting = WAITING;
3921     tp->tty_cum = 0;
3922
3923     /* Compute the physical address where the data is in user space. */
3924     rp = proc_addr(tp->tty_outproc);
3925     out_vir = (vir_bytes) tp->tty_out_vir;
3926     out_left = (vir_bytes) tp->tty_outleft;
3927     if ( (tp->tty_phys = umap(rp, D, out_vir, out_left)) == 0) {
3928           /* Buffer address provided by user is outside its address space. */
3929           tp->tty_cum = E_BAD_ADDR;
3930           tp->tty_outleft = 0;
3931     }
3932
3933     /* Copy characters from the user process to the terminal. */
3934     (*tp->tty_devstart)(tp);      /* copy data to queue and start I/O */
3935   }


3938   /*===========================================================================*
3939    *                              do_ioctl                                     *
3940    *===========================================================================*/
3941   PRIVATE do_ioctl(tp, m_ptr)
3942   register struct tty_struct *tp; /* pointer to tty_struct */
3943   message *m_ptr;                         /* pointer to message sent to task */
3944   {
3945   /* Perform IOCTL on this terminal. */
3946
3947     long flags, erki, erase, kill, intr, quit, xon, xoff, eof;
3948     int r;
3949
```

```
3950        r = OK;
3951        flags = 0;
3952        erki = 0;
3953        switch(m_ptr->TTY_REQUEST) {
3954            case TIOCSETP:
3955                /* Set erase, kill, and flags. */
3956                tp->tty_erase = (char) ((m_ptr->TTY_SPEK >> 8) & BYTE); /* erase  */
3957                tp->tty_kill  = (char) ((m_ptr->TTY_SPEK >> 0) & BYTE); /* kill   */
3958                tp->tty_mode  = (int) m_ptr->TTY_FLAGS; /* mode word */
3959                break;
3960
3961            case TIOCSETC:
3962                /* Set intr, quit, xon, xoff, eof (brk not used). */
3963                tp->tty_intr = (char) ((m_ptr->TTY_SPEK >> 24) & BYTE); /* interrupt */
3964                tp->tty_quit = (char) ((m_ptr->TTY_SPEK >> 16) & BYTE); /* quit */
3965                tp->tty_xon  = (char) ((m_ptr->TTY_SPEK >>  8) & BYTE); /* CTRL-S */
3966                tp->tty_xoff = (char) ((m_ptr->TTY_SPEK >>  0) & BYTE); /* CTRL-Q */
3967                tp->tty_eof  = (char) ((m_ptr->TTY_FLAGS >> 8) & BYTE); /* CTRL-D */
3968                break;
3969
3970            case TIOCGETP:
3971                /* Get erase, kill, and flags. */
3972                erase = ((long) tp->tty_erase) & BYTE;
3973                kill  = ((long) tp->tty_kill) & BYTE;
3974                erki  = (erase << 8) | kill;
3975                flags = (long) tp->tty_mode;
3976                break;
3977
3978            case TIOCGETC:
3979                /* Get intr, quit, xon, xoff, eof. */
3980                intr  = ((long) tp->tty_intr) & BYTE;
3981                quit  = ((long) tp->tty_quit) & BYTE;
3982                xon   = ((long) tp->tty_xon)  & BYTE;
3983                xoff  = ((long) tp->tty_xoff) & BYTE;
3984                eof   = ((long) tp->tty_eof)  & BYTE;
3985                erki  = (intr << 24) | (quit << 16) | (xon << 8) | (xoff << 0);
3986                flags = (eof <<8);
3987                break;
3988
3989            default:
3990                r = EINVAL;
3991        }
3992
3993        /* Send the reply. */
3994        tty_reply(TASK_REPLY, m_ptr->m_source, m_ptr->PROC_NR, r, flags, erki);
3995    }
```

```
4000   /*===========================================================================*
4001    *                              do_cancel                                    *
4002    *===========================================================================*/
4003   PRIVATE do_cancel(tp, m_ptr)
4004   register struct tty_struct *tp;  /* pointer to tty_struct */
4005   message *m_ptr;                  /* pointer to message sent to task */
4006   {
4007   /* A signal has been sent to a process that is hanging trying to read or write.
4008    * The pending read or write must be finished off immediately.
4009    */
4010
4011     /* First check to see if the process is indeed hanging.  If it is not, don't
4012      * reply (to avoid race conditions).
4013      */
4014     if (tp->tty_inleft == 0 && tp->tty_outleft == 0) return;
4015
4016     /* Kill off input and output. */
4017     tp->tty_inhead = tp->tty_inqueue;      /* discard all input */
4018     tp->tty_intail = tp->tty_inqueue;
4019     tp->tty_incount = 0;
4020     tp->tty_lfct = 0;
4021     tp->tty_inleft = 0;
4022     tp->tty_outleft = 0;
4023     tp->tty_waiting = NOT_WAITING;         /* don't send reply */
4024     tp->tty_inhibited = RUNNING;
4025     tty_reply(TASK_REPLY, m_ptr->m_source, m_ptr->PROC_NR, EINTR, 0L, 0L);
4026   }

4028   /*===========================================================================*
4029    *                              tty_reply                                    *
4030    *===========================================================================*/
4031   PRIVATE tty_reply(code, replyee, proc_nr, status, extra, other)
4032   int code;                        /* TASK_REPLY or REVIVE */
4033   int replyee;                     /* destination address for the reply */
4034   int proc_nr;                     /* to whom should the reply go? */
4035   int status;                      /* reply code */
4036   long extra;                      /* extra value */
4037   long other;                      /* used for IOCTL replies */
4038   {
4039   /* Send a reply to a process that wanted to read or write data. */
4040
4041     message tty_mess;
4042
4043     tty_mess.m_type = code;
4044     tty_mess.REP_PROC_NR = proc_nr;
4045     tty_mess.REP_STATUS = status;
4046     tty_mess.TTY_FLAGS = extra;    /* used by IOCTL for flags (mode) */
4047     tty_mess.TTY_SPEK = other;     /* used by IOCTL for erase and kill chars */
4048     send(replyee, &tty_mess);
4049   }
```

```
4050    /****************************************************************/
4051    /****************************************************************/
4052    /****************************************************************/
4053    /****************************************************************/
4054    /****************************************************************/
4055
4056    #ifdef i8088
4057    /* Now begins the code and data for the device-dependent tty drivers. */
4058
4059    /* Definitions used by the console driver. */
4060    #define COLOR_BASE      0xB800    /* video ram paragraph for color display */
4061    #define MONO_BASE       0xB000    /* video ram address for mono display */
4062    #define C_VID_MASK      0x3FFF    /* mask for 16K video RAM */
4063    #define M_VID_MASK      0x0FFF    /* mask for  4K video RAM */
4064    #define C_RETRACE       0x0300    /* how many characters to display at once */
4065    #define M_RETRACE       0x7000    /* how many characters to display at once */
4066    #define WORD_MASK       0xFFFF    /* mask for 16 bits */
4067    #define OFF_MASK        0x000F    /* mask for  4 bits */
4068    #define BEEP_FREQ       0x0533    /* value to put into timer to set beep freq */
4069    #define B_TIME          0x2000    /* how long to sound the CTRL-G beep tone */
4070    #define BLANK           0x0700    /* determines  cursor color on blank screen */
4071    #define LINE_WIDTH          80    /* # characters on a line */
4072    #define SCR_LINES           25    /* # lines on the screen */
4073    #define CTRL_S              31    /* scan code for letter S (for CRTL-S) */
4074    #define MONOCHROME           1    /* value for tty_ioport tells color vs. mono */
4075    #define CONSOLE              0    /* line number for console */
4076    #define GO_FORWARD           0    /* scroll forward */
4077    #define GO_BACKWARD          1    /* scroll backward */
4078    #define TIMER2            0x42    /* I/O port for timer channel 2 */
4079    #define TIMER3            0x43    /* I/O port for timer channel 3 */
4080    #define KEYBD             0x60    /* I/O port for keyboard data */
4081    #define PORT_B            0x61    /* I/O port for 8255 port B */
4082    #define KBIT              0x80    /* bit used to ack characters to keyboard */
4083
4084    /* Constants relating to the video RAM and 6845. */
4085    #define M_6845           0x3B0    /* port for 6845 mono */
4086    #define C_6845           0x3D0    /* port for 6845 color */
4087    #define INDEX                4    /* 6845's index register */
4088    #define DATA                 5    /* 6845's data register */
4089    #define CUR_SIZE            10    /* 6845's cursor size register */
4090    #define VID_ORG             12    /* 6845's origin register */
4091    #define CURSOR              14    /* 6845's cursor register */
4092
4093    /* Definitions used for determining if the keyboard is IBM or Olivetti type. */
4094    #define KB_STATUS         0x64    /* Olivetti keyboard status port */
4095    #define BYTE_AVAIL        0x01    /* there is something in KEYBD port */
4096    #define KB_BUSY           0x02    /* KEYBD port ready to accept a command */
4097    #define DELUXE            0x01    /* this bit is set up iff deluxe keyboard */
4098    #define GET_TYPE             5    /* command to get keyboard type */
4099    #define OLIVETTI_EQUAL      12    /* the '=' key is 12 on olivetti, 13 on IBM */
```

```
4100
4101    /* Global variables used by the console driver. */
4102    PUBLIC  int color;                /* 1 if console is color, 0 if it is mono */
4103    PUBLIC  message keybd_mess;       /* message used for console input chars */
4104    PRIVATE vid_retrace;             /* how many characters to display per burst */
4105    PRIVATE unsigned vid_base;        /* base of video ram (0xB000 or 0xB800) */
4106    PRIVATE int vid_mask;            /* 037777 for color (16K) or 07777 for mono */
4107    PRIVATE int vid_port;            /* I/O port for accessing 6845 */
4108
4109
4110    /*===========================================================================*
4111     *                               keyboard                                    *
4112     *===========================================================================*/
4113    PUBLIC keyboard()
4114    {
4115    /* A keyboard interrupt has occurred.  Process it. */
4116
4117      int val, code, k, raw_bit;
4118      char stopc;
4119
4120      /* Fetch the character from the keyboard hardware and acknowledge it. */
4121      port_in(KEYBD, &code);          /* get the scan code for the key struck */
4122      port_in(PORT_B, &val);          /* strobe the keyboard to ack the char */
4123      port_out(PORT_B, val | KBIT);   /* strobe the bit high */
4124      port_out(PORT_B, val);          /* now strobe it low */
4125
4126      /* The IBM keyboard interrupts twice per key, once when depressed, once when
4127       * released.  Filter out the latter, ignoring all but the shift-type keys.
4128       * The shift-type keys, 29, 42, 54, 56, and 69 must be processed normally.
4129       */
4130      k = code - 0200;                /* codes > 0200 mean key release */
4131      if (k > 0) {
4132          /* A key has been released. */
4133          if (k != 29 && k != 42 && k != 54 && k != 56 && k != 69) {
4134                  port_out(INT_CTL, ENABLE);      /* re-enable interrupts */
4135                  return;              /* don't call tty_task() */
4136          }
4137      } else {
4138          /* Check to see if character is CTRL-S, to stop output. Setting xoff
4139           * to anything other than CTRL-S will not be detected here, but will
4140           * be detected later, in the driver.  A general routine to detect any
4141           * xoff character here would be complicated since we only have the
4142           * scan code here, not the ASCII character.
4143           */
4144          raw_bit = tty_struct[CONSOLE].tty_mode & RAW;
4145          stopc = tty_struct[CONSOLE].tty_xoff;
4146          if (raw_bit == 0 && control && code == CTRL_S && stopc == XOFF_CHAR) {
4147                  tty_struct[CONSOLE].tty_inhibited = STOPPED;
4148                  port_out(INT_CTL, ENABLE);
4149                  return;
```

```
4150                }
4151        }
4152
4153        /* Check for CTRL-ALT-DEL, and if found, reboot the computer. */
4154        if (control && alt && code == DEL_CODE) reboot();      /* CTRL-ALT-DEL */
4155
4156        /* Store the character in memory so the task can get at it later. */
4157        if ( (k = tty_driver_buf[0]) < tty_driver_buf[1]) {
4158                /* There is room to store this character; do it. */
4159                k = k + k;                        /* each entry contains two bytes */
4160                tty_driver_buf[k+2] = code;       /* store the scan code */
4161                tty_driver_buf[k+3] = CONSOLE;    /* tell which line it came from */
4162                tty_driver_buf[0]++;              /* increment counter */
4163
4164                /* Build and send the interrupt message. */
4165                keybd_mess.m_type = TTY_CHAR_INT;
4166                keybd_mess.ADDRESS = tty_driver_buf;
4167                interrupt(TTY, &keybd_mess);      /* send a message to the tty task */
4168        } else {
4169                /* Too many characters have been buffered.  Discard excess. */
4170                port_out(INT_CTL, ENABLE);        /* re-enable 8259A controller */
4171        }
4172    }


4175    /*===========================================================================*
4176     *                              console                                       *
4177     *===========================================================================*/
4178    PRIVATE console(tp)
4179    register struct tty_struct *tp; /* tells which terminal is to be used */
4180    {
4181    /* Copy as much data as possible to the output queue, then start I/O.  On
4182     * memory-mapped terminals, such as the IBM console, the I/O will also be
4183     * finished, and the counts updated.  Keep repeating until all I/O done.
4184     */
4185
4186      int count;
4187      char c;
4188      unsigned segment, offset, offset1;
4189
4190      /* Loop over the user bytes one at a time, outputting each one. */
4191      segment = (tp->tty_phys >> 4) & WORD_MASK;
4192      offset = tp->tty_phys & OFF_MASK;
4193      offset1 = offset;
4194      count = 0;
4195
4196      while (tp->tty_outleft > 0 && tp->tty_inhibited == RUNNING) {
4197            c = get_byte(segment, offset); /* fetch 1 byte from user space */
4198            out_char(tp, c);               /* write 1 byte to terminal */
4199            offset++;                      /* advance one character in user buffer */
```

```
4200               tp->tty_outleft--;        /* decrement count */
4201          }
4202          flush(tp);                        /* clear out the pending characters */
4203
4204          /* Update terminal data structure. */
4205          count = offset - offset1;        /* # characters printed */
4206          tp->tty_phys += count;           /* advance physical data pointer */
4207          tp->tty_cum += count;            /* number of characters printed */
4208
4209          /* If all data has been copied to the terminal, send the reply. */
4210          if (tp->tty_outleft == 0) finish(tp, tp->tty_cum);
4211     }


4214     /*===========================================================================*
4215      *                              out_char                                     *
4216      *===========================================================================*/
4217     PRIVATE out_char(tp, c)
4218     register struct tty_struct *tp; /* pointer to tty struct */
4219     char c;                         /* character to be output */
4220     {
4221     /* Output a character on the console. Check for escape sequences, including
4222      *    ESC 32+x 32+y to move cursor to (x, y)
4223      *    ESC ~ 0       to clear from cursor to end of screen
4224      *    ESC ~ 1       to reverse scroll the screen 1 line
4225      *    ESC z x       to set the attribute byte to x (z is a literal here)
4226      */
4227
4228          /* Check to see if we are part way through an escape sequence. */
4229          if (tp->tty_esc_state == 1) {
4230               tp->tty_echar = c;
4231               tp->tty_esc_state = 2;
4232               return;
4233          }
4234
4235          if (tp->tty_esc_state == 2) {
4236               escape(tp, tp->tty_echar, c);
4237               tp->tty_esc_state = 0;
4238               return;
4239          }
4240
4241          switch(c) {
4242               case 007:                    /* ring the bell */
4243                    flush(tp);              /* print any chars queued for output */
4244                    beep(BEEP_FREQ);/* BEEP_FREQ gives bell tone */
4245                    return;
4246
4247               case 013:                    /* CTRL-K */
4248                    move_to(tp, tp->tty_column, tp->tty_row + 1);
4249                    return;
```

```
4250
4251            case 014:                 /* CTRL-L */
4252                    move_to(tp, tp->tty_column + 1, tp->tty_row);
4253                    return;
4254
4255            case 016:                 /* CTRL-N */
4256                    move_to(tp, tp->tty_column + 1, tp->tty_row);
4257                    return;
4258
4259            case '\b':                /* backspace */
4260                    move_to(tp, tp->tty_column - 1, tp->tty_row);
4261                    return;
4262
4263            case '\n':                /* line feed */
4264                    if (tp->tty_mode & CRMOD) out_char(tp, '\r');
4265                    if (tp->tty_row == 0)
4266                            scroll_screen(tp, GO_FORWARD);
4267                    else
4268                            tp->tty_row--;
4269                    move_to(tp, tp->tty_column, tp->tty_row);
4270                    return;
4271
4272            case '\r':                /* carriage return */
4273                    move_to(tp, 0, tp->tty_row);
4274                    return;
4275
4276            case '\t':                /* tab */
4277                    if ( (tp->tty_mode & XTABS) == XTABS) {
4278                            do {
4279                                    out_char(tp, ' ');
4280                            } while (tp->tty_column & TAB_MASK);
4281                            return;
4282                    }
4283                    /* Ignore tab is XTABS is off--video RAM has no hardware tab */
4284                    return;
4285
4286            case 033:                 /* ESC - start of an escape sequence */
4287                    flush(tp);        /* print any chars queued for output */
4288                    tp->tty_esc_state = 1;  /* mark ESC as seen */
4289                    return;
4290
4291            default:                  /* printable chars are stored in ramqueue */
4292                    if (tp->tty_column >= LINE_WIDTH) return;       /* long line */
4293                    if (tp->tty_rwords == TTY_RAM_WORDS) flush(tp);
4294                    tp->tty_ramqueue[tp->tty_rwords++] = tp->tty_attribute | c;
4295                    tp->tty_column++;         /* next column */
4296                    return;
4297    }
4298  }
```

```
4301   /*===========================================================================*
4302    *                              scroll_screen                                *
4303    *===========================================================================*/
4304   PRIVATE scroll_screen(tp, dir)
4305   register struct tty_struct *tp; /* pointer to tty struct */
4306   int dir;                        /* GO_FORWARD or GO_BACKWARD */
4307   {
4308     int amount, offset;
4309
4310     amount = (dir == GO_FORWARD ? 2 * LINE_WIDTH : -2 * LINE_WIDTH);
4311     tp->tty_org = (tp->tty_org + amount) & vid_mask;
4312     if (dir == GO_FORWARD)
4313           offset = (tp->tty_org + 2 * (SCR_LINES - 1) * LINE_WIDTH) & vid_mask;
4314     else
4315           offset = tp->tty_org;
4316
4317     /* Blank the new line at top or bottom. */
4318     vid_copy(NIL_PTR, vid_base, offset, LINE_WIDTH);
4319     set_6845(VID_ORG, tp->tty_org >> 1);  /* 6845 thinks in words */
4320   }


4323   /*===========================================================================*
4324    *                              flush                                         *
4325    *===========================================================================*/
4326   PRIVATE flush(tp)
4327   register struct tty_struct *tp; /* pointer to tty struct */
4328   {
4329   /* Have the characters in 'ramqueue' transferred to the screen. */
4330
4331     if (tp->tty_rwords == 0) return;
4332     vid_copy(tp->tty_ramqueue, vid_base, tp->tty_vid, tp->tty_rwords);
4333
4334     /* Update the video parameters and cursor. */
4335     tp->tty_vid += 2 * tp->tty_rwords;
4336     set_6845(CURSOR, tp->tty_vid >> 1);   /* cursor counts in words */
4337     tp->tty_rwords = 0;
4338   }

4340   /*===========================================================================*
4341    *                              move_to                                       *
4342    *===========================================================================*/
4343   PRIVATE move_to(tp, x, y)
4344   struct tty_struct *tp;          /* pointer to tty struct */
4345   int x;                          /* column (0 <= x <= 79) */
4346   int y;                          /* row (0 <= y <= 24, 0 at bottom) */
4347   {
4348   /* Move the cursor to (x, y). */
4349
```

```
4350        flush(tp);                      /* flush any pending characters */
4351        if (x < 0 || x >= LINE_WIDTH || y < 0 || y >= SCR_LINES) return;
4352        tp->tty_column = x;             /* set x co-ordinate */
4353        tp->tty_row = y;                /* set y co-ordinate */
4354        tp->tty_vid = (tp->tty_org + 2*(SCR_LINES-1-y)* LINE_WIDTH + 2*x);
4355        set_6845(CURSOR, tp->tty_vid >> 1);   /* cursor counts in words */
4356    }


4359    /*===========================================================================*
4360     *                              escape                                       *
4361     *===========================================================================*/
4362    PRIVATE escape(tp, x, y)
4363    register struct tty_struct *tp; /* pointer to tty struct */
4364    char x;                             /* escape sequence is ESC x y; this is x */
4365    char y;                             /* escape sequence is ESC x y; this is y */
4366    {
4367    /* Handle an escape sequence. */
4368
4369        int n, ct, vx;
4370
4371
4372        /* Check for ESC z attribute - used to change attribute byte. */
4373        if (x == 'z') {
4374            /* Set attribute byte */
4375            tp->tty_attribute = y << 8;
4376            return;
4377        }
4378        /* Check for ESC ~ n -  used for clear screen, reverse scroll. */
4379        if (x == '~') {
4380            if (y == '0') {
4381                /* Clear from cursor to end of screen */
4382                n = 2 * LINE_WIDTH * (tp->tty_row + 1) - 2 * tp->tty_column;
4383                vx = tp->tty_vid;
4384                while (n > 0) {
4385                    ct = MIN(n, vid_retrace);
4386                    vid_copy(NIL_PTR, vid_base, vx, ct/2);
4387                    vx += ct;
4388                    n -= ct;
4389                }
4390            } else if (y == '1') {
4391                /* Reverse scroll. */
4392                scroll_screen(tp, GO_BACKWARD);
4393            }
4394            return;
4395        }
4396
4397        /* Must be cursor movement (or invalid). */
4398        move_to(tp, x - 32, y - 32);
4399    }
```

```
4400   /*===========================================================================*
4401    *                              set_6845                                      *
4402    *===========================================================================*/
4403   PRIVATE set_6845(reg, val)
4404   int reg;                        /* which register pair to set */
4405   int val;                        /* 16-bit value to set it to */
4406   {
4407   /* Set a register pair inside the 6845.
4408    * Registers 10-11 control the format of the cursor (how high it is, etc).
4409    * Registers 12-13 tell the 6845 where in video ram to start (in WORDS)
4410    * Registers 14-15 tell the 6845 where to put the cursor (in WORDS)
4411    *
4412    * Note that registers 12-15 work in words, i.e. 0x0000 is the top left
4413    * character, but 0x0001 (not 0x0002) is the next character.  This addressing
4414    * is different from the way the 8088 addresses the video ram, where 0x0002
4415    * is the address of the next character.
4416    */
4417     port_out(vid_port + INDEX, reg);       /* set the index register */
4418     port_out(vid_port + DATA, (val>>8) & BYTE);   /* output high byte */
4419     port_out(vid_port + INDEX, reg + 1);   /* again */
4420     port_out(vid_port + DATA, val&BYTE);   /* output low byte */
4421   }


4424   /*===========================================================================*
4425    *                              beep                                          *
4426    *===========================================================================*/
4427   PRIVATE beep(f)
4428   int f;                          /* this value determines beep frequency */
4429   {
4430   /* Making a beeping sound on the speaker (output for CRTL-G).  The beep is
4431    * kept short, because interrupts must be disabled during beeping, and it
4432    * is undesirable to keep them off too long.  This routine works by turning
4433    * on the bits in port B of the 8255 chip that drive the speaker.
4434    */
4435
4436     int x, k;
4437
4438     lock();                       /* disable interrupts */
4439     port_out(TIMER3,0xB6);        /* set up timer channel 2 mode */
4440     port_out(TIMER2, f&BYTE);     /* load low-order bits of frequency in timer */
4441     port_out(TIMER2,(f>>8)&BYTE); /* now high-order bits of frequency in timer */
4442     port_in(PORT_B,&x);           /* acquire status of port B */
4443     port_out(PORT_B, x|3);        /* turn bits 0 and 1 on to beep */
4444     for (k = 0; k < B_TIME; k++); /* delay loop while beeper sounding */
4445     port_out(PORT_B, x);          /* restore port B the way it was */
4446     unlock();                     /* re-enable interrupts */
4447   }
```

```
4450    /*===========================================================================*
4451     *                              tty_init                                      *
4452     *===========================================================================*/
4453    PRIVATE tty_init()
4454    {
4455    /* Initialize the tty tables. */
4456
4457      register struct tty_struct *tp;
4458
4459      for (tp = &tty_struct[0]; tp < &tty_struct[NR_TTYS]; tp++) {
4460            tp->tty_inhead = tp->tty_inqueue;
4461            tp->tty_intail = tp->tty_inqueue;
4462            tp->tty_mode = CRMOD | XTABS | ECHO;
4463            tp->tty_devstart = console;
4464            tp->tty_erase = ERASE_CHAR;
4465            tp->tty_kill  = KILL_CHAR;
4466            tp->tty_intr  = INTR_CHAR;
4467            tp->tty_quit  = QUIT_CHAR;
4468            tp->tty_xon   = XON_CHAR;
4469            tp->tty_xoff  = XOFF_CHAR;
4470            tp->tty_eof   = EOT_CHAR;
4471      }
4472
4473      tty_struct[0].tty_makebreak = TWO_INTS;          /* tty 0 is console */
4474      if (color) {
4475            vid_base = COLOR_BASE;
4476            vid_mask = C_VID_MASK;
4477            vid_port = C_6845;
4478            vid_retrace = C_RETRACE;
4479      } else {
4480            vid_base = MONO_BASE;
4481            vid_mask = M_VID_MASK;
4482            vid_port = M_6845;
4483            vid_retrace = M_RETRACE;
4484      }
4485      tty_struct[0].tty_attribute = BLANK;
4486      tty_driver_buf[1] = MAX_OVERRUN;        /* set up limit on keyboard buffering */
4487      set_6845(CUR_SIZE, 31);                 /* set cursor shape */
4488      set_6845(VID_ORG, 0);                   /* use page 0 of video ram */
4489      move_to(&tty_struct[0], 0, 0);          /* move cursor to lower left corner */
4490
4491      /* Determine which keyboard type is attached.  The bootstrap program asks
4492       * the user to type an '='.  The scan codes for '=' differ depending on the
4493       * keyboard in use.
4494       */
4495      if (scan_code == OLIVETTI_EQUAL) olivetti = TRUE;
4496    }
```

```
4500    /*===========================================================================*
4501     *                              putc                                          *
4502     *===========================================================================*/
4503    PUBLIC putc(c)
4504    char c;                         /* character to print */
4505    {
4506    /* This procedure is used by the version of printf() that is linked with
4507     * the kernel itself.  The one in the library sends a message to FS, which is
4508     * not what is needed for printing within the kernel.  This version just queues
4509     * the character and starts the output.
4510     */
4511
4512      out_char(&tty_struct[0], c);
4513    }



4516    /*===========================================================================*
4517     *                              func_key                                      *
4518     *===========================================================================*/
4519    PRIVATE func_key(ch)
4520    char ch;                        /* scan code for a function key */
4521    {
4522    /* This procedure traps function keys for debugging purposes.  When MINIX is
4523     * fully debugged, it should be removed.
4524     */
4525
4526      if (ch == F1) p_dmp();        /* print process table */
4527      if (ch == F2) map_dmp();      /* print memory map */
4528    }
4529    #endif
```

```
4550    /* This task handles the interface between file system and kernel as well as
4551     * between memory manager and kernel.  System services are obtained by sending
4552     * sys_task() a message specifying what is needed.  To make life easier for
4553     * MM and FS, a library is provided with routines whose names are of the
4554     * form sys_xxx, e.g. sys_xit sends the SYS_XIT message to sys_task.  The
4555     * message types and parameters are:
4556     *
4557     *    SYS_FORK    informs kernel that a process has forked
4558     *    SYS_NEWMAP  allows MM to set up a process memory map
4559     *    SYS_EXEC    sets program counter and stack pointer after EXEC
4560     *    SYS_XIT     informs kernel that a process has exited
4561     *    SYS_GETSP   caller wants to read out some process' stack pointer
4562     *    SYS_TIMES   caller wants to get accounting times for a process
4563     *    SYS_ABORT   MM or FS cannot go on; abort MINIX
4564     *    SYS_SIG     send a signal to a process
4565     *    SYS_COPY    requests a block of data to be copied between processes
4566     *
4567     * Message type m1 is used for all except SYS_SIG and SYS_COPY, both of
4568     * which need special parameter types.
4569     *
4570     *    m_type      PROC1       PROC2       PID      MEM_PTR
4571     * -------------------------------------------------------
4572     * | SYS_FORKED | parent  | child   | pid     |         |
4573     * |------------+---------+---------+---------+---------|
4574     * | SYS_NEWMAP | proc nr |         |         | map ptr |
4575     * |------------+---------+---------+---------+---------|
4576     * | SYS_EXEC   | proc nr |         | new sp  |         |
4577     * |------------+---------+---------+---------+---------|
4578     * | SYS_XIT    | parent  | exitee  |         |         |
4579     * |------------+---------+---------+---------+---------|
4580     * | SYS_GETSP  | proc nr |         |         |         |
4581     * |------------+---------+---------+---------+---------|
4582     * | SYS_TIMES  | proc nr |         | buf ptr |         |
4583     * |------------+---------+---------+---------+---------|
4584     * | SYS_ABORT  |         |         |         |         |
4585     * -------------------------------------------------------
4586     *
4587     *
4588     *    m_type      m6_i1       m6_i2       m6_i3    m6_f1
4589     * -------------------------------------------------------
4590     * | SYS_SIG    | proc_nr | sig     |         | handler |
4591     * -------------------------------------------------------
4592     *
4593     *
4594     *    m_type      m5_c1   m5_i1   m5_l1   m5_c2   m5_i2   m5_l2   m5_l3
4595     * -----------------------------------------------------------------------
4596     * | SYS_COPY   |src seg|src proc|src vir|dst seg|dst proc|dst vir| byte ct |
4597     * -----------------------------------------------------------------------
4598     *
4599     * In addition to the main sys_task() entry point, there are three other minor
```

```
4600      * entry points:
4601      *    cause_sig: take action to cause a signal to occur, sooner or later
4602      *    inform:    tell MM about pending signals
4603      *    umap:      compute the physical address for a given virtual address
4604      */
4605
4606     #include "../h/const.h"
4607     #include "../h/type.h"
4608     #include "../h/callnr.h"
4609     #include "../h/com.h"
4610     #include "../h/error.h"
4611     #include "../h/signal.h"
4612     #include "const.h"
4613     #include "type.h"
4614     #include "glo.h"
4615     #include "proc.h"
4616
4617     #define COPY_UNIT     65534L     /* max bytes to copy at once */
4618
4619     extern phys_bytes umap();
4620
4621     PRIVATE message m;
4622     PRIVATE char sig_stuff[SIG_PUSH_BYTES]; /* used to send signals to processes */
4623
4624     /*===========================================================================*
4625      *                              sys_task                                     *
4626      *===========================================================================*/
4627     PUBLIC sys_task()
4628     {
4629     /* Main entry point of sys_task.  Get the message and dispatch on type. */
4630
4631       register int r;
4632
4633       while (TRUE) {
4634             receive(ANY, &m);
4635
4636             switch (m.m_type) {     /* which system call */
4637                 case SYS_FORKED:   r = do_fork(&m);       break;
4638                 case SYS_NEWMAP:   r = do_newmap(&m);     break;
4639                 case SYS_EXEC:     r = do_exec(&m);       break;
4640                 case SYS_XIT:      r = do_xit(&m);        break;
4641                 case SYS_GETSP:    r = do_getsp(&m);      break;
4642                 case SYS_TIMES:    r = do_times(&m);      break;
4643                 case SYS_ABORT:    r = do_abort(&m);      break;
4644                 case SYS_SIG:      r = do_sig(&m);        break;
4645                 case SYS_COPY:     r = do_copy(&m);       break;
4646                 default:           r = E_BAD_FCN;
4647             }
4648
4649             m.m_type = r;           /* 'r' reports status of call */
```

```
4650                 send(m.m_source, &m);   /* send reply to caller */
4651         }
4652    }


4655    /*===========================================================================*
4656     *                              do_fork                                       *
4657     *===========================================================================*/
4658    PRIVATE int do_fork(m_ptr)
4659    message *m_ptr;                         /* pointer to request message */
4660    {
4661    /* Handle sys_fork().  'kl' has forked.  The child is 'k2'. */
4662
4663      register struct proc *rpc;
4664      register char *sptr, *dptr;           /* pointers for copying proc struct */
4665      int kl;                               /* number of parent process */
4666      int k2;                               /* number of child process */
4667      int pid;                              /* process id of child */
4668      int bytes;                            /* counter for copying proc struct */
4669
4670      kl = m_ptr->PROC1;                    /* extract parent slot number from msg */
4671      k2 = m_ptr->PROC2;                    /* extract child slot number */
4672      pid = m_ptr->PID;                     /* extract child process id */
4673
4674      if (kl < 0 || kl >= NR_PROCS || k2 < 0 || k2 >= NR_PROCS)return(E_BAD_PROC);
4675      rpc = proc_addr(k2);
4676
4677      /* Copy parent 'proc' struct to child. */
4678      sptr = (char *) proc_addr(kl);        /* parent pointer */
4679      dptr = (char *) proc_addr(k2);        /* child pointer */
4680      bytes = sizeof(struct proc);          /* # bytes to copy */
4681      while (bytes--) *dptr++ = *sptr++;    /* copy parent struct to child */
4682
4683      rpc->p_flags |= NO_MAP;               /* inhibit the process from running */
4684      rpc->p_pid = pid;                     /* install child's pid */
4685      rpc->p_reg[RET_REG] = 0;              /* child sees pid = 0 to know it is child */
4686
4687      rpc->user_time = 0;                   /* set all the accounting times to 0 */
4688      rpc->sys_time = 0;
4689      rpc->child_utime = 0;
4690      rpc->child_stime = 0;
4691      return(OK);
4692    }


4695    /*===========================================================================*
4696     *                              do_newmap                                     *
4697     *===========================================================================*/
4698    PRIVATE int do_newmap(m_ptr)
4699    message *m_ptr;                         /* pointer to request message */
```

```
4700    {
4701    /* Handle sys_newmap().  Fetch the memory map from MM. */
4702
4703      register struct proc *rp, *rsrc;
4704      phys_bytes src_phys, dst_phys, pn;
4705      vir_bytes vmm, vsys, vn;
4706      int caller;                      /* whose space has the new map (usually MM) */
4707      int k;                           /* process whose map is to be loaded */
4708      int old_flags;                   /* value of flags before modification */
4709      struct mem_map *map_ptr;         /* virtual address of map inside caller (MM) */
4710
4711      /* Extract message parameters and copy new memory map from MM. */
4712      caller = m_ptr->m_source;
4713      k = m_ptr->PROC1;
4714      map_ptr = (struct mem_map *) m_ptr->MEM_PTR;
4715      if (k < -NR_TASKS || k >= NR_PROCS) return(E_BAD_PROC);
4716      rp = proc_addr(k);               /* ptr to entry of user getting new map */
4717      rsrc = proc_addr(caller);        /* ptr to MM's proc entry */
4718      vn = NR_SEGS * sizeof(struct mem_map);
4719      pn = vn;
4720      vmm = (vir_bytes) map_ptr;    /* careful about sign extension */
4721      vsys = (vir_bytes) rp->p_map; /* again, careful about sign extension */
4722      if ( (src_phys = umap(rsrc, D, vmm, vn)) == 0)
4723          panic("bad call to sys_newmap (src)", NO_NUM);
4724      if ( (dst_phys = umap(proc_addr(SYSTASK), D, vsys, vn)) == 0)
4725          panic("bad call to sys_newmap (dst)", NO_NUM);
4726      phys_copy(src_phys, dst_phys, pn);
4727
4728    #ifdef i8088
4729      /* On 8088, set segment registers. */
4730      rp->p_reg[CS_REG] = rp->p_map[T].mem_phys;    /* set cs */
4731      rp->p_reg[DS_REG] = rp->p_map[D].mem_phys;    /* set ds */
4732      rp->p_reg[SS_REG] = rp->p_map[D].mem_phys;    /* set ss */
4733      rp->p_reg[ES_REG] = rp->p_map[D].mem_phys;    /* set es */
4734    #endif
4735
4736      old_flags = rp->p_flags;      /* save the previous value of the flags */
4737      rp->p_flags &= ~NO_MAP;
4738      if (old_flags != 0 && rp->p_flags == 0) ready(rp);
4739      return(OK);
4740    }


4743    /*===========================================================================*
4744     *                              do_exec                                       *
4745     *===========================================================================*/
4746    PRIVATE int do_exec(m_ptr)
4747    message *m_ptr;                   /* pointer to request message */
4748    {
4749    /* Handle sys_exec().  A process has done a successful EXEC. Patch it up. */
```

```
4750
4751        register struct proc *rp;
4752        int k;                           /* which process */
4753        int *sp;                         /* new sp */
4754
4755        k = m_ptr->PROC1;                /* 'k' tells which process did EXEC */
4756        sp = (int *) m_ptr->STACK_PTR;
4757        if (k < 0 || k >= NR_PROCS) return(E_BAD_PROC);
4758        rp = proc_addr(k);
4759        rp->p_sp = sp;                   /* set the stack pointer */
4760        rp->p_pcpsw.pc = (int (*)()) 0;       /* reset pc */
4761        rp->p_alarm = 0;                 /* reset alarm timer */
4762        rp->p_flags &= ~RECEIVING;       /* MM does not reply to EXEC call */
4763        if (rp->p_flags == 0) ready(rp);
4764        return(OK);
4765   }


4768   /*===========================================================================*
4769    *                              do_xit                                       *
4770    *===========================================================================*/
4771   PRIVATE int do_xit(m_ptr)
4772   message *m_ptr;                       /* pointer to request message */
4773   {
4774   /* Handle sys_xit().  A process has exited. */
4775
4776        register struct proc *rp, *rc;
4777        struct proc *np, *xp;
4778        int parent;                      /* number of exiting proc's parent */
4779        int proc_nr;                     /* number of process doing the exit */
4780
4781        parent = m_ptr->PROC1;           /* slot number of parent process */
4782        proc_nr = m_ptr->PROC2;          /* slot number of exiting process */
4783        if (parent < 0 || parent >= NR_PROCS || proc_nr < 0 || proc_nr >= NR_PROCS)
4784            return(E_BAD_PROC);
4785        rp = proc_addr(parent);
4786        rc = proc_addr(proc_nr);
4787        rp->child_utime += rc->user_time + rc->child_utime;   /* accum child times */
4788        rp->child_stime += rc->sys_time + rc->child_stime;
4789        unready(rc);
4790        rc->p_alarm = 0;                 /* turn off alarm timer */
4791
4792        /* If the process being terminated happens to be queued trying to send a
4793         * message (i.e., the process was killed by a signal, rather than it doing an
4794         * EXIT), then it must be removed from the message queues.
4795         */
4796        if (rc->p_flags & SENDING) {
4797            /* Check all proc slots to see if the exiting process is queued. */
4798            for (rp = &proc[0]; rp < &proc[NR_TASKS + NR_PROCS]; rp++) {
4799                if (rp->p_callerq == NIL_PROC) continue;
```

```
4800                         if (rp->p_callerq == rc) {
4801                                 /* Exiting process is on front of this queue. */
4802                                 rp->p_callerq = rc->p_sendlink;
4803                                 break;
4804                         } else {
4805                                 /* See if exiting process is in middle of queue. */
4806                                 np = rp->p_callerq;
4807                                 while ( ( xp = np->p_sendlink) != NIL_PROC)
4808                                         if (xp == rc) {
4809                                                 np->p_sendlink = xp->p_sendlink;
4810                                                 break;
4811                                         } else {
4812                                                 np = xp;
4813                                         }
4814                         }
4815                 }
4816         }
4817     rc->p_flags = P_SLOT_FREE;
4818     return(OK);
4819 }


4822 /*===========================================================================*
4823  *                              do_getsp                                     *
4824  *===========================================================================*/
4825 PRIVATE int do_getsp(m_ptr)
4826 message *m_ptr;                         /* pointer to request message */
4827 {
4828 /* Handle sys_getsp().  MM wants to know what sp is. */
4829
4830   register struct proc *rp;
4831   int k;                                /* whose stack pointer is wanted? */
4832
4833   k = m_ptr->PROC1;
4834   if (k < 0 || k >= NR_PROCS) return(E_BAD_PROC);
4835   rp = proc_addr(k);
4836   m.STACK_PTR = (char *) rp->p_sp;      /* return sp here */
4837   return(OK);
4838 }


4841 /*===========================================================================*
4842  *                              do_times                                     *
4843  *===========================================================================*/
4844 PRIVATE int do_times(m_ptr)
4845 message *m_ptr;                         /* pointer to request message */
4846 {
4847 /* Handle sys_times().  Retrieve the accounting information. */
4848
4849   register struct proc *rp;
```

```
4850        int k;
4851
4852        k = m_ptr->PROC1;                  /* k tells whose times are wanted */
4853        if (k < 0 || k >= NR_PROCS) return(E_BAD_PROC);
4854        rp = proc_addr(k);
4855
4856        /* Insert the four times needed by the TIMES system call in the message. */
4857        m_ptr->USER_TIME   = rp->user_time;
4858        m_ptr->SYSTEM_TIME = rp->sys_time;
4859        m_ptr->CHILD_UTIME = rp->child_utime;
4860        m_ptr->CHILD_STIME = rp->child_stime;
4861        return(OK);
4862    }


4865    /*===========================================================================*
4866     *                            do_abort                                       *
4867     *===========================================================================*/
4868    PRIVATE int do_abort(m_ptr)
4869    message *m_ptr;                        /* pointer to request message */
4870    {
4871    /* Handle sys_abort.  MINIX is unable to continue.  Terminate operation. */
4872
4873        panic("", NO_NUM);
4874    }


4877    /*===========================================================================*
4878     *                            do_sig                                         *
4879     *===========================================================================*/
4880    PRIVATE int do_sig(m_ptr)
4881    message *m_ptr;                        /* pointer to request message */
4882    {
4883    /* Handle sys_sig(). Signal a process.  The stack is known to be big enough. */
4884
4885        register struct proc *rp;
4886        phys_bytes src_phys, dst_phys;
4887        vir_bytes vir_addr, sig_size, new_sp;
4888        int proc_nr;                       /* process number */
4889        int sig;                           /* signal number 1-16 */
4890        int (*sig_handler)();              /* pointer to the signal handler */
4891
4892        /* Extract parameters and prepare to build the words that get pushed. */
4893        proc_nr = m_ptr->PR;               /* process being signalled */
4894        sig = m_ptr->SIGNUM;               /* signal number, 1 to 16 */
4895        sig_handler = m_ptr->FUNC;    /* run time system addr for catching sigs */
4896        if (proc_nr < LOW_USER || proc_nr >= NR_PROCS) return(E_BAD_PROC);
4897        rp = proc_addr(proc_nr);
4898        vir_addr = (vir_bytes) sig_stuff;     /* info to be pushed is in 'sig_stuff' */
4899        new_sp = (vir_bytes) rp->p_sp;
```

```
4900
4901        /* Actually build the block of words to push onto the stack. */
4902        build_sig(sig_stuff, rp, sig);          /* build up the info to be pushed */
4903
4904        /* Prepare to do the push, and do it. */
4905        sig_size = SIG_PUSH_BYTES;
4906        new_sp -= sig_size;
4907        src_phys = umap(proc_addr(SYSTASK), D, vir_addr, sig_size);
4908        dst_phys = umap(rp, S, new_sp, sig_size);
4909        if (dst_phys == 0) panic("do_sig can't signal; SP bad", NO_NUM);
4910        phys_copy(src_phys, dst_phys, (phys_bytes) sig_size); /* push pc, psw */
4911
4912        /* Change process' sp and pc to reflect the interrupt. */
4913        rp->p_sp = (int *) new_sp;
4914        rp->p_pcpsw.pc = sig_handler;
4915        return(OK);
4916    }


4919    /*===========================================================================*
4920     *                              do_copy                                       *
4921     *===========================================================================*/
4922    PRIVATE int do_copy(m_ptr)
4923    message *m_ptr;                      /* pointer to request message */
4924    {
4925    /* Handle sys_copy().  Copy data for MM or FS. */
4926
4927        int src_proc, dst_proc, src_space, dst_space;
4928        vir_bytes src_vir, dst_vir;
4929        phys_bytes src_phys, dst_phys, bytes;
4930
4931        /* Dismember the command message. */
4932        src_proc = m_ptr->SRC_PROC_NR;
4933        dst_proc = m_ptr->DST_PROC_NR;
4934        src_space = m_ptr->SRC_SPACE;
4935        dst_space = m_ptr->DST_SPACE;
4936        src_vir = (vir_bytes) m_ptr->SRC_BUFFER;
4937        dst_vir = (vir_bytes) m_ptr->DST_BUFFER;
4938        bytes = (phys_bytes) m_ptr->COPY_BYTES;
4939
4940        /* Compute the source and destination addresses and do the copy. */
4941        if (src_proc == ABS)
4942            src_phys = (phys_bytes) m_ptr->SRC_BUFFER;
4943        else
4944            src_phys = umap(proc_addr(src_proc),src_space,src_vir,(vir_bytes)bytes);
4945
4946        if (dst_proc == ABS)
4947            dst_phys = (phys_bytes) m_ptr->DST_BUFFER;
4948        else
4949            dst_phys = umap(proc_addr(dst_proc),dst_space,dst_vir,(vir_bytes)bytes);
```

```
4950
4951        if (src_phys == 0 || dst_phys == 0) return(EFAULT);
4952        phys_copy(src_phys, dst_phys, bytes);
4953        return(OK);
4954    }


4957    /*===========================================================================*
4958     *                              cause_sig                                     *
4959     *===========================================================================*/
4960    PUBLIC cause_sig(proc_nr, sig_nr)
4961    int proc_nr;                      /* process to be signalled */
4962    int sig_nr;                       /* signal to be sent in range 1 - 16 */
4963    {
4964    /* A task wants to send a signal to a process.   Examples of such tasks are:
4965     *    TTY wanting to cause SIGINT upon getting a DEL
4966     *    CLOCK wanting to cause SIGALRM when timer expires
4967     * Signals are handled by sending a message to MM.  The tasks don't dare do
4968     * that directly, for fear of what would happen if MM were busy.  Instead they
4969     * call cause_sig, which sets bits in p_pending, and then carefully checks to
4970     * see if MM is free.  If so, a message is sent to it.  If not, when it becomes
4971     * free, a message is sent.  The calling task always gets control back from
4972     * cause_sig() immediately.
4973     */
4974
4975      register struct proc *rp;
4976
4977      rp = proc_addr(proc_nr);
4978      if (rp->p_pending == 0) sig_procs++;   /* incr if a new proc is now pending */
4979      rp->p_pending |= 1 << (sig_nr - 1);
4980      inform(MM_PROC_NR);               /* see if MM is free */
4981    }


4984    /*===========================================================================*
4985     *                              inform                                        *
4986     *===========================================================================*/
4987    PUBLIC inform(proc_nr)
4988    int proc_nr;                      /* MM_PROC_NR or FS_PROC_NR */
4989    {
4990    /* When a signal is detected by the kernel (e.g., DEL), or generated by a task
4991     * (e.g. clock task for SIGALRM), cause_sig() is called to set a bit in the
4992     * p_pending field of the process to signal.  Then inform() is called to see
4993     * if MM is idle and can be told about it.  Whenever MM blocks, a check is
4994     * made to see if 'sig_procs' is nonzero; if so, inform() is called.
4995     */
4996
4997      register struct proc *rp, *mmp;
4998
4999      /* If MM is not waiting for new input, forget it. */
```

```
5000          mmp = proc_addr(proc_nr);
5001          if ( ((mmp->p_flags & RECEIVING) == 0) || mmp->p_getfrom != ANY) return;
5002
5003          /* MM is waiting for new input.  Find a process with pending signals. */
5004          for (rp = proc_addr(0); rp < proc_addr(NR_PROCS); rp++)
5005                  if (rp->p_pending != 0) {
5006                          m.m_type = KSIG;
5007                          m.PROC1 = rp - proc - NR_TASKS;
5008                          m.SIG_MAP = rp->p_pending;
5009                          sig_procs--;
5010                          if (mini_send(HARDWARE, proc_nr, &m) != OK)
5011                                  panic("can't inform MM", NO_NUM);
5012                          rp->p_pending = 0;       /* the ball is now in MM's court */
5013                          return;
5014                  }
5015          }


5018  /*===========================================================================*
5019   *                              umap                                         *
5020   *===========================================================================*/
5021  PUBLIC phys_bytes umap(rp, seg, vir_addr, bytes)
5022  register struct proc *rp;      /* pointer to proc table entry for process */
5023  int seg;                       /* T, D, or S segment */
5024  vir_bytes vir_addr;            /* virtual address in bytes within the seg */
5025  vir_bytes bytes;               /* # of bytes to be copied */
5026  {
5027  /* Calculate the physical memory address for a given virtual address. */
5028    vir_clicks vc;                /* the virtual address in clicks */
5029    phys_bytes seg_base, pa;      /* intermediate variables as phys_bytes */
5030
5031    /* If 'seg' is D it could really be S and vice versa.  T really means T.
5032     * If the virtual address falls in the gap,  it causes a problem. On the
5033     * 8088 it is probably a legal stack reference, since "stackfaults" are
5034     * not detected by the hardware.  On 8088s, the gap is called S and
5035     * accepted, but on other machines it is called D and rejected.
5036     */
5037    if (bytes <= 0) return( (phys_bytes) 0);
5038    vc = (vir_addr + bytes - 1) >> CLICK_SHIFT;   /* last click of data */
5039
5040  #ifdef i8088
5041    if (seg != T)
5042          seg = (vc < rp->p_map[D].mem_vir + rp->p_map[D].mem_len ? D : S);
5043  #else
5044    if (seg != T)
5045          seg = (vc < rp->p_map[S].mem_vir ? D : S);
5046  #endif
5047
5048    if((vir_addr>>CLICK_SHIFT) >= rp->p_map[seg].mem_vir + rp->p_map[seg].mem_len)
5049          return( (phys_bytes) 0 );
```

```
5050        seg_base = (phys_bytes) rp->p_map[seg].mem_phys;
5051        seg_base = seg_base << CLICK_SHIFT;    /* segment orgin in bytes */
5052        pa = (phys_bytes) vir_addr;
5053        pa -= rp->p_map[seg].mem_vir << CLICK_SHIFT;
5054        return(seg_base + pa);
5055    }
```

```
5100    /* The object file of "table.c" contains all the data.  In the *.h files,
5101     * declared variables appear with EXTERN in front of them, as in
5102     *
5103     *    EXTERN int x;
5104     *
5105     * Normally EXTERN is defined as extern, so when they are included in another
5106     * file, no storage is allocated.  If the EXTERN were not present, but just
5107     * say,
5108     *
5109     *    int x;
5110     *
5111     * then including this file in several source files would cause 'x' to be
5112     * declared several times.  While some linkers accept this, others do not,
5113     * so they are declared extern when included normally.  However, it must
5114     * be declared for real somewhere.  That is done here, but redefining
5115     * EXTERN as the null string, so the inclusion of all the *.h files in
5116     * table.c actually generates storage for them.  All the initialized
5117     * variables are also declared here, since
5118     *
5119     * extern int x = 4;
5120     *
5121     * is not allowed.  If such variables are shared, they must also be declared
5122     * in one of the *.h files without the initialization.
5123     */
5124
5125    #include "../h/const.h"
5126    #include "../h/type.h"
5127    #include "const.h"
5128    #include "type.h"
5129    #undef   EXTERN
5130    #define  EXTERN
5131    #include "glo.h"
5132    #include "proc.h"
5133
5134    extern int sys_task(), clock_task(), mem_task(), floppy_task(),
5135                winchester_task(), tty_task(), printer_task();
5136
5137    /* The startup routine of each task is given below, from -NR_TASKS upwards.
5138     * The order of the names here MUST agree with the numerical values assigned to
5139     * the tasks in ../h/com.h.
5140     */
5141    int (*task[NR_TASKS+INIT_PROC_NR+1])() = {
5142     printer_task, tty_task, winchester_task, floppy_task, mem_task,
5143     clock_task, sys_task, 0, 0, 0, 0
5144    };
```

```
5150      /* Constants used by the Memory Manager. */
5151
5152      #define ZEROBUF_SIZE      1024      /* buffer size for erasing memory */
5153
5154      /* Size of MM's stack depends mostly on do_exec(). */
5155      #if ZEROBUF_SIZE > MAX_PATH
5156      #define MM_STACK_BYTES  MAX_ISTACK_BYTES + ZEROBUF_SIZE + 384
5157      #else
5158      #define MM_STACK_BYTES  MAX_ISTACK_BYTES + MAX_PATH + 384
5159      #endif
5160
5161      #define NO_MEM (phys_clicks)0    /* returned by alloc_mem() with mem is up */
5162
5163      #ifdef i8088
5164      #define PAGE_SIZE        16      /* how many bytes in a page */
5165      #define MAX_PAGES      4096      /* how many pages in the virtual addr space */
5166      #define HDR_SIZE         32      /* # bytes in the exec file header */
5167      #endif
5168
5169      #define printf        printk
```

```
5200    /* Global variables. */
5201    EXTERN struct mproc *mp;           /* ptr to 'mproc' slot of current process */
5202    EXTERN int dont_reply;             /* normally 0; set to 1 to inhibit reply */
5203    EXTERN int procs_in_use;           /* how many processes are marked as IN_USE */
5204
5205    /* The parameters of the call are kept here. */
5206    EXTERN message mm_in;              /* the incoming message itself is kept here. */
5207    EXTERN message mm_out;             /* the reply message is built up here. */
5208    EXTERN int who;                    /* caller's proc number */
5209    EXTERN int mm_call;                /* caller's proc number */
5210
5211    /* The following variables are used for returning results to the caller. */
5212    EXTERN int err_code;               /* temporary storage for error number */
5213    EXTERN int result2;                /* secondary result */
5214    EXTERN char *res_ptr;              /* result, if pointer */
5215
5216    EXTERN char mm_stack[MM_STACK_BYTES];    /* MM's stack */
5217
```

```
5250    /* This table has one slot per process.  It contains all the memory management
5251     * information for each process.  Among other things, it defines the text, data
5252     * and stack segments, uids and gids, and various flags.  The kernel and file
5253     * systems have tables that are also indexed by process, with the contents
5254     * of corresponding slots referring to the same process in all three.
5255     */
5256
5257    EXTERN struct mproc {
5258      struct mem_map mp_seg[NR_SEGS];        /* points to text, data, stack */
5259      char mp_exitstatus;              /* storage for status when process exits */
5260      char mp_sigstatus;               /* storage for signal # for killed processes */
5261      int mp_pid;                      /* process id */
5262      int mp_parent;                   /* index of parent process */
5263      int mp_procgrp;                  /* process group (used for signals) */
5264
5265      /* Real and effective uids and gids. */
5266      uid mp_realuid;                  /* process' real uid */
5267      uid mp_effuid;                   /* process' effective uid */
5268      gid mp_realgid;                  /* process' real gid */
5269      gid mp_effgid;                   /* process' effective gid */
5270
5271      /* Bit maps for signals. */
5272      unshort mp_ignore;               /* 1 means ignore the signal, 0 means don't */
5273      unshort mp_catch;                /* 1 means catch the signal, 0 means don't */
5274      int (*mp_func)();                /* all signals vectored to a single user fcn */
5275
5276      unsigned mp_flags;               /* flag bits */
5277    } mproc[NR_PROCS];
5278
5279    /* Flag values */
5280    #define IN_USE            001   /* set when 'mproc' slot in use */
5281    #define WAITING           002   /* set by WAIT system call */
5282    #define HANGING           004   /* set by EXIT system call */
5283    #define PAUSED            010   /* set by PAUSE system call */
5284    #define ALARM_ON          020   /* set when SIGALRM timer started */
5285    #define SEPARATE          040   /* set if file is separate I & D space */
```

```
5300      /* The following names are synonyms for the variables in the input message. */
5301      #define addr              mm_in.m1_p1
5302      #define exec_name         mm_in.m1_p1
5303      #define exec_len          mm_in.m1_i1
5304      #define func              mm_in.m6_f1
5305      #define grpid             (gid) mm_in.m1_i1
5306      #define kill_sig          mm_in.m1_i2
5307      #define namelen           mm_in.m1_i1
5308      #define pid               mm_in.m1_i1
5309      #define seconds           mm_in.m1_i1
5310      #define sig               mm_in.m6_i1
5311      #define stack_bytes       mm_in.m1_i2
5312      #define stack_ptr         mm_in.m1_p2
5313      #define status            mm_in.m1_i1
5314      #define usr_id            (uid) mm_in.m1_i1
5315
5316      /* The following names are synonyms for the variables in the output message. */
5317      #define reply_type        mm_out.m_type
5318      #define reply_i1          mm_out.m2_i1
5319      #define reply_p1          mm_out.m2_p1
```

```
5350    /* If there were any type definitions local to the Memory Manager, they would
5351     * be here.  This file is included only for symmetry with the kernel and File
5352     * System, which do have some local type definitions.
5353     */
5354
5355    #include "../h/type.h"
```

```
5400    /* This file contains the main program of the memory manager and some related
5401     * procedures.  When MINIX starts up, the kernel runs for a little while,
5402     * initializing itself and its tasks, and then it runs MM.  MM at this point
5403     * does not know where FS is in memory and how big it is.  By convention, FS
5404     * must start at the click following MM, so MM can deduce where it starts at
5405     * least.  Later, when FS runs for the first time, FS makes a pseudo-call,
5406     * BRK2, to tell MM how big it is.  This allows MM to figure out where INIT
5407     * is.
5408     *
5409     * The entry points into this file are:
5410     *   main:      starts MM running
5411     *   reply:     reply to a process making an MM system call
5412     *   do_brk2:   pseudo-call for FS to report its size
5413     */
5414
5415    #include "../h/const.h"
5416    #include "../h/type.h"
5417    #include "../h/callnr.h"
5418    #include "../h/com.h"
5419    #include "../h/error.h"
5420    #include "const.h"
5421    #include "glo.h"
5422    #include "mproc.h"
5423    #include "param.h"
5424
5425    #define ENOUGH (phys_clicks) 4096        /* any # > max(FS size, INIT size) */
5426    #define CLICK_TO_K (1024L/CLICK_SIZE)    /* convert clicks to K */
5427
5428    PRIVATE phys_clicks tot_mem;
5429    extern (*mm_callvec[])();
5430    extern char *sp_limit;                  /* stack limit register; checked on calls */
5431
5432    /*===========================================================================*
5433     *                              main                                          *
5434     *===========================================================================*/
5435    PUBLIC main()
5436    {
5437    /* Main routine of the memory manager. */
5438
5439      int error;
5440
5441      mm_init();                            /* initialize memory manager tables */
5442
5443      /* This is MM's main loop- get work and do it, forever and forever. */
5444      while (TRUE) {
5445            /* Wait for message. */
5446            get_work();                     /* wait for an MM system call */
5447            mp = &mproc[who];
5448
5449            /* Set some flags. */
```

```
5450                    error = OK;
5451                    dont_reply = FALSE;
5452                    err_code = -999;
5453
5454                    /* If the call number is valid, perform the call. */
5455                    if (mm_call < 0 || mm_call >= NCALLS)
5456                            error = E_BAD_CALL;
5457                    else
5458                            error = (*mm_callvec[mm_call])();
5459
5460                    /* Send the results back to the user to indicate completion. */
5461                    if (dont_reply) continue;          /* no reply for EXIT and WAIT */
5462                    if (mm_call == EXEC && error == OK) continue;
5463                    reply(who, error, result2, res_ptr);
5464            }
5465    }


5468    /*===========================================================================*
5469     *                              get_work                                     *
5470     *===========================================================================*/
5471    PRIVATE get_work()
5472    {
5473    /* Wait for the next message and extract useful information from it. */
5474
5475      if (receive(ANY, &mm_in) != OK) panic("MM receive error", NO_NUM);
5476      who = mm_in.m_source;             /* who sent the message */
5477      if (who < HARDWARE || who >= NR_PROCS) panic("MM called by", who);
5478      mm_call = mm_in.m_type;           /* system call number */
5479    }


5482    /*===========================================================================*
5483     *                              reply                                        *
5484     *===========================================================================*/
5485    PUBLIC reply(proc_nr, result, res2, respt)
5486    int proc_nr;                        /* process to reply to */
5487    int result;                         /* result of the call (usually OK or error #)*/
5488    int res2;                           /* secondary result */
5489    char *respt;                        /* result if pointer */
5490    {
5491    /* Send a reply to a user process. */
5492
5493      register struct mproc *proc_ptr;
5494
5495      /* To make MM robust, check to see if destination is still alive. */
5496      proc_ptr = &mproc[proc_nr];
5497      if ( (proc_ptr->mp_flags&IN_USE) == 0 || (proc_ptr->mp_flags&HANGING)) return;
5498      reply_type = result;
5499      reply_il = res2;
```

```
5500          reply_p1 = respt;
5501          if (send(proc_nr, &mm_out) != OK) panic("MM can't reply", NO_NUM);
5502        }


5505   /*===========================================================================*
5506    *                               mm_init                                     *
5507    *===========================================================================*/
5508   PRIVATE mm_init()
5509   {
5510   /* Initialize the memory manager. */
5511
5512      extern phys_clicks get_tot_mem(), alloc_mem();
5513
5514      /* Find out how much memory the machine has and set up core map.  MM and FS
5515       * are part of the map.  Tell the kernel.
5516       */
5517      tot_mem = get_tot_mem();        /* # clicks in mem starting at absolute 0 */
5518      mem_init(tot_mem);              /* initialize tables to all physical mem */
5519
5520      /* Initialize MM's tables. */
5521      mproc[MM_PROC_NR].mp_flags |= IN_USE;
5522      mproc[FS_PROC_NR].mp_flags |= IN_USE;
5523      mproc[INIT_PROC_NR].mp_flags |= IN_USE;
5524      procs_in_use = 3;
5525
5526      /* Set stack limit, which is checked on every procedure call. */
5527      sp_limit = mm_stack - 32;
5528   }


5531   /*===========================================================================*
5532    *                               do_brk2                                     *
5533    *===========================================================================*/
5534   PUBLIC do_brk2()
5535   {
5536   /* This "call" is made once by FS during system initialization and then never
5537    * again by anyone.  It contains the origin and size of INIT, and the combined
5538    * size of the 1536 bytes of unused mem, MINIX and RAM disk.
5539    *    ml_il = size of INIT text in clicks
5540    *    ml_i2 = size of INIT data in clicks
5541    *    ml_i3 = number of bytes for MINIX + RAM DISK
5542    *    ml_p1 = origin of INIT in clicks
5543    */
5544
5545      int mem1, mem2, mem3;
5546      register struct mproc *rmp;
5547      phys_clicks init_org, init_clicks, ram_base, ram_clicks, tot_clicks;
5548      phys_clicks init_text_clicks, init_data_clicks;
5549
```

```
5550          if (who != FS_PROC_NR) return(EPERM); /* only FS make do BRK2 */
5551
5552      /* Remove the memory used by MINIX and RAM disk from the memory map. */
5553      init_text_clicks = mm_in.m1_i1;       /* size of INIT in clicks */
5554      init_data_clicks = mm_in.m1_i2;       /* size of INIT in clicks */
5555      tot_clicks = mm_in.m1_i3;             /* total size of MINIX + RAM disk */
5556      init_org = (phys_clicks) mm_in.m1_p1; /* addr where INIT begins in memory */
5557      init_clicks = init_text_clicks + init_data_clicks;
5558      ram_base = init_org + init_clicks;    /* start of RAM disk */
5559      ram_clicks = tot_clicks - ram_base;   /* size of RAM disk */
5560      alloc_mem(tot_clicks);                /* remove RAM disk from map */
5561
5562      /* Print memory information. */
5563      mem1 = tot_mem/CLICK_TO_K;
5564      mem2 = (ram_base + 512/CLICK_SIZE)/CLICK_TO_K;        /* MINIX, rounded */
5565      mem3 = ram_clicks/CLICK_TO_K;
5566      printf("%c 8%c~0",033, 033);  /* go to top of screen and clear screen */
5567      printf("Memory size = %dK     ", mem1);
5568      printf("MINIX = %dK     ", mem2);
5569      printf("RAM disk = %dK     ", mem3);
5570      printf("Available = %dK\n\n", mem1 - mem2 - mem3);
5571      if (mem1 - mem2 - mem3 < 32) {
5572              printf("\nNot enough memory to run MINIX\n\n", NO_NUM);
5573              sys_abort();
5574      }
5575
5576      /* Initialize INIT's table entry. */
5577      rmp = &mproc[INIT_PROC_NR];
5578      rmp->mp_seg[T].mem_phys = init_org;
5579      rmp->mp_seg[T].mem_len  = init_text_clicks;
5580      rmp->mp_seg[D].mem_phys = init_org + init_text_clicks;
5581      rmp->mp_seg[D].mem_len  = init_data_clicks;
5582      rmp->mp_seg[S].mem_vir  = init_clicks;
5583      rmp->mp_seg[S].mem_phys = init_org + init_clicks;
5584      if (init_text_clicks != 0) rmp->mp_flags |= SEPARATE;
5585
5586      return(OK);
5587  }


5590  /*===========================================================================*
5591   *                              set_map                                      *
5592   *===========================================================================*/
5593  PRIVATE set_map(proc_nr, base, clicks)
5594  int proc_nr;                     /* whose map to set? */
5595  phys_clicks base;                /* where in memory does the process start? */
5596  phys_clicks clicks;              /* total size in clicks (sep I & D not used) */
5597  {
5598  /* Set up the memory map as part of the system initialization. */
5599
```

```
5600        register struct mproc *rmp;
5601        vir_clicks vclicks;
5602
5603        rmp = &mproc[proc_nr];
5604        vclicks = (vir_clicks) clicks;
5605        rmp->mp_seg[T].mem_vir = 0;
5606        rmp->mp_seg[T].mem_len = 0;
5607        rmp->mp_seg[T].mem_phys = base;
5608        rmp->mp_seg[D].mem_vir = 0;
5609        rmp->mp_seg[D].mem_len = vclicks;
5610        rmp->mp_seg[D].mem_phys = base;
5611        rmp->mp_seg[S].mem_vir = vclicks;
5612        rmp->mp_seg[S].mem_len = 0;
5613        rmp->mp_seg[S].mem_phys = base + vclicks;
5614        sys_newmap(proc_nr, rmp->mp_seg);
5615    }
```

```
5650     /* This file deals with creating processes (via FORK) and deleting them (via
5651      * EXIT/WAIT).  When a process forks, a new slot in the 'mproc' table is
5652      * allocated for it, and a copy of the parent's core image is made for the
5653      * child.  Then the kernel and file system are informed.  A process is removed
5654      * from the 'mproc' table when two events have occurred: (1) it has exited or
5655      * been killed by a signal, and (2) the parent has done a WAIT.  If the process
5656      * exits first, it continues to occupy a slot until the parent does a WAIT.
5657      *
5658      * The entry points into this file are:
5659      *   do_fork:   perform the FORK system call
5660      *   do_mm_exit:        perform the EXIT system call (by calling mm_exit())
5661      *   mm_exit:   actually do the exiting
5662      *   do_wait:   perform the WAIT system call
5663      */
5664
5665     #include "../h/const.h"
5666     #include "../h/type.h"
5667     #include "../h/callnr.h"
5668     #include "../h/error.h"
5669     #include "const.h"
5670     #include "glo.h"
5671     #include "mproc.h"
5672     #include "param.h"
5673
5674     #define LAST_FEW           2   /* last few slots reserved for superuser */
5675
5676     PRIVATE next_pid = INIT_PROC_NR+1;      /* next pid to be assigned */
5677
5678     /* Some C compilers require static declarations to precede their first use. */
5679
5680     /*===========================================================================*
5681      *                             do_fork                                       *
5682      *===========================================================================*/
5683     PUBLIC int do_fork()
5684     {
5685     /* The process pointed to by 'mp' has forked.  Create a child process. */
5686
5687       register struct mproc *rmp;    /* pointer to parent */
5688       register struct mproc *rmc;    /* pointer to child */
5689       int i, child_nr, t;
5690       char *sptr, *dptr;
5691       long prog_bytes;
5692       phys_clicks prog_clicks, child_base;
5693       long parent_abs, child_abs;
5694       extern phys_clicks alloc_mem();
5695
5696       /* If tables might fill up during FORK, don't even start since recovery half
5697        * way through is such a nuisance.
5698        */
5699
```

```
5700        rmp = mp;
5701        if (procs_in_use == NR_PROCS) return(EAGAIN);
5702        if (procs_in_use >= NR_PROCS - LAST_FEW && rmp->mp_effuid != 0)return(EAGAIN);
5703
5704        /* Determine how much memory to allocate. */
5705        prog_clicks = (phys_clicks) rmp->mp_seg[T].mem_len + rmp->mp_seg[D].mem_len +
5706                                                        rmp->mp_seg[S].mem_len;
5707  #ifdef i8088
5708        prog_clicks += rmp->mp_seg[S].mem_vir - rmp->mp_seg[D].mem_len; /* gap too */
5709  #endif
5710        prog_bytes = (long) prog_clicks << CLICK_SHIFT;
5711        if ( (child_base = alloc_mem(prog_clicks)) == NO_MEM) return(EAGAIN);
5712
5713        /* Create a copy of the parent's core image for the child. */
5714        child_abs = (long) child_base << CLICK_SHIFT;
5715        parent_abs = (long) rmp->mp_seg[T].mem_phys << CLICK_SHIFT;
5716        i = mem_copy(ABS, 0, parent_abs, ABS, 0, child_abs, prog_bytes);
5717        if ( i < 0) panic("do_fork can't copy", i);
5718
5719        /* Find a slot in 'mproc' for the child process.  A slot must exist. */
5720        for (rmc = &mproc[0]; rmc < &mproc[NR_PROCS]; rmc++)
5721            if ( (rmc->mp_flags & IN_USE) == 0) break;
5722
5723        /* Set up the child and its memory map; copy its 'mproc' slot from parent. */
5724        child_nr = rmc - mproc;        /* slot number of the child */
5725        procs_in_use++;
5726        sptr = (char *) rmp;           /* pointer to parent's 'mproc' slot */
5727        dptr = (char *) rmc;           /* pointer to child's 'mproc' slot */
5728        i = sizeof(struct mproc);      /* number of bytes in a proc slot. */
5729        while (i--) *dptr++ = *sptr++;/* copy from parent slot to child's */
5730
5731        rmc->mp_parent = who;          /* record child's parent */
5732        rmc->mp_seg[T].mem_phys = child_base;
5733        rmc->mp_seg[D].mem_phys = child_base + rmc->mp_seg[T].mem_len;
5734        rmc->mp_seg[S].mem_phys = rmc->mp_seg[D].mem_phys +
5735                            (rmp->mp_seg[S].mem_phys - rmp->mp_seg[D].mem_phys);
5736        rmc->mp_exitstatus = 0;
5737        rmc->mp_sigstatus = 0;
5738
5739        /* Find a free pid for the child and put it in the table. */
5740        do {
5741            t = 0;                     /* 't' = 0 means pid still free */
5742            next_pid = (next_pid < 30000 ? next_pid + 1 : INIT_PROC_NR + 1);
5743            for (rmp = &mproc[0]; rmp < &mproc[NR_PROCS]; rmp++)
5744                if (rmp->mp_pid == next_pid) {
5745                        t = 1;
5746                        break;
5747                }
5748            rmc->mp_pid = next_pid; /* assign pid to child */
5749        } while (t);
```

```
5750
5751        /* Tell kernel and file system about the (now successful) FORK. */
5752        sys_forked(who, child_nr, rmc->mp_pid);
5753        tell_fs(FORK, who, child_nr, 0);
5754
5755        /* Report child's memory map to kernel. */
5756        sys_newmap(child_nr, rmc->mp_seg);
5757
5758        /* Reply to child to wake it up. */
5759        reply(child_nr, 0, 0, NIL_PTR);
5760        return(next_pid);                    /* child's pid */
5761    }


5764    /*===========================================================================*
5765     *                              do_mm_exit                                    *
5766     *===========================================================================*/
5767    PUBLIC int do_mm_exit()
5768    {
5769    /* Perform the exit(status) system call. The real work is done by mm_exit(),
5770     * which is also called when a process is killed by a signal.
5771     */
5772
5773        mm_exit(mp, status);
5774        dont_reply = TRUE;              /* don't reply to newly terminated process */
5775        return(OK);                     /* pro forma return code */
5776    }


5779    /*===========================================================================*
5780     *                              mm_exit                                       *
5781     *===========================================================================*/
5782    PUBLIC mm_exit(rmp, exit_status)
5783    register struct mproc *rmp;      /* pointer to the process to be terminated */
5784    int exit_status;                /* the process' exit status (for parent) */
5785    {
5786    /* A process is done.  If parent is waiting for it, clean it up, else hang. */
5787
5788        /* How to terminate a process is determined by whether or not the
5789         * parent process has already done a WAIT.  Test to see if it has.
5790         */
5791        rmp->mp_exitstatus = (char) exit_status;     /* store status in 'mproc' */
5792
5793        if (mproc[rmp->mp_parent].mp_flags & WAITING)
5794            cleanup(rmp);               /* release parent and tell everybody */
5795        else
5796            rmp->mp_flags |= HANGING;        /* Parent not waiting.  Suspend proc */
5797
5798        /* If the exited process has a timer pending, kill it. */
5799        if (rmp->mp_flags & ALARM_ON) set_alarm(rmp - mproc, (unsigned) 0);
```

```
5800
5801      /* Tell the kernel that the process is no longer runnable. */
5802      sys_xit(rmp->mp_parent, rmp - mproc);
5803    }


5806    /*===========================================================================*
5807     *                              do_wait                                       *
5808     *===========================================================================*/
5809    PUBLIC int do_wait()
5810    {
5811    /* A process wants to wait for a child to terminate. If one is already waiting,
5812     * go clean it up and let this WAIT call terminate.  Otherwise, really wait.
5813     */
5814
5815      register struct mproc *rp;
5816      register int children;
5817
5818      /* A process calling WAIT never gets a reply in the usual way via the
5819       * reply() in the main loop.  If a child has already exited, the routine
5820       * cleanup() sends the reply to awaken the caller.
5821       */
5822
5823      /* Is there a child waiting to be collected? */
5824      children = 0;
5825      for (rp = &mproc[0]; rp < &mproc[NR_PROCS]; rp++) {
5826          if ( (rp->mp_flags & IN_USE) && rp->mp_parent == who) {
5827                  children++;
5828                  if (rp->mp_flags & HANGING) {
5829                          cleanup(rp);    /* a child has already exited */
5830                          dont_reply = TRUE;
5831                          return(OK);
5832                  }
5833          }
5834      }
5835
5836      /* No child has exited.  Wait for one, unless none exists. */
5837      if (children > 0) {             /* does this process have any children? */
5838          mp->mp_flags |= WAITING;
5839          dont_reply = TRUE;
5840          return(OK);                /* yes - wait for one to exit */
5841      } else
5842          return(ECHILD);            /* no - parent has no children */
5843    }


5846    /*===========================================================================*
5847     *                              cleanup                                       *
5848     *===========================================================================*/
5849    PRIVATE cleanup(child)
```

```
5850        register struct mproc *child;   /* tells which process is exiting */
5851        {
5852        /* Clean up the remains of a process.  This routine is only called if two
5853         * conditions are satisfied:
5854         *      1. The process has done an EXIT or has been killed by a signal.
5855         *      2. The process' parent has done a WAIT.
5856         *
5857         * It tells everyone about the process' demise and also releases the memory, if
5858         * that has not yet been done.  (Whether it has or has not been done depends on
5859         * the order the EXIT and WAIT were done in.)
5860         */
5861          register struct mproc *parent, *rp;
5862          int init_waiting, child_nr;
5863          unsigned int r;
5864          phys_clicks s;
5865
5866          child_nr = child - mproc;
5867          parent = &mproc[child->mp_parent];
5868
5869          /* Wakeup the parent and tell the file system that the process is dead. */
5870          r = child->mp_sigstatus & 0377;
5871          r = r | (child->mp_exitstatus << 8);
5872          reply(child->mp_parent, child->mp_pid, r, NIL_PTR);
5873          tell_fs(EXIT, child_nr, 0, 0);  /* file system can free the proc slot */
5874
5875          /* Release the memory occupied by the child. */
5876          s = (phys_clicks) child->mp_seg[S].mem_vir + child->mp_seg[S].mem_len;
5877          if (child->mp_flags & SEPARATE) s += child->mp_seg[T].mem_len;
5878          free_mem(child->mp_seg[T].mem_phys, s);         /* free the memory */
5879
5880          /* Update flags. */
5881          child->mp_flags &= ~HANGING;   /* turn off HANGING bit */
5882          parent->mp_flags &= ~WAITING; /* turn off WAITING bit */
5883          child->mp_flags &= ~IN_USE;    /* release the table slot */
5884          procs_in_use--;
5885
5886          /* If exiting process has children, disinherit them.  INIT is new parent. */
5887          init_waiting = (mproc[INIT_PROC_NR].mp_flags & WAITING ? 1 : 0);
5888          for (rp = &mproc[0]; rp < &mproc[NR_PROCS]; rp++) {
5889                  if (rp->mp_parent == child_nr) {
5890                          /* 'rp' points to a child to be disinherited. */
5891                          rp->mp_parent = INIT_PROC_NR;   /* init takes over */
5892                          if (init_waiting && (rp->mp_flags & HANGING) ) {
5893                                  /* Init was waiting. */
5894                                  cleanup(rp);    /* recursive call */
5895                                  init_waiting = 0;
5896                          }
5897                  }
5898          }
5899        }
```

```
5900     /* This file handles the EXEC system call.  It performs the work as follows:
5901      *      - see if the permissions allow the file to be executed
5902      *      - read the header and extract the sizes
5903      *      - fetch the initial args and environment from the user space
5904      *      - allocate the memory for the new process
5905      *      - copy the initial stack from MM to the process
5906      *      - read in the text and data segments and copy to the process
5907      *      - take care of setuid and setgid bits
5908      *      - fix up 'mproc' table
5909      *      - tell kernel about EXEC
5910      *
5911      *      The only entry point is do_exec.
5912      */
5913
5914     #include "../h/const.h"
5915     #include "../h/type.h"
5916     #include "../h/callnr.h"
5917     #include "../h/error.h"
5918     #include "../h/stat.h"
5919     #include "const.h"
5920     #include "glo.h"
5921     #include "mproc.h"
5922     #include "param.h"
5923
5924     #define MAGIC     0x04000301L    /* magic number with 2 bits masked off */
5925     #define SEP       0x00200000L    /* value for separate I & D */
5926     #define TEXTB             2      /* location of text size in header */
5927     #define DATAB             3      /* location of data size in header */
5928     #define BSSB              4      /* location of bss size in header */
5929     #define TOTB              6      /* location of total size in header */
5930
5931     /*===========================================================================*
5932      *                              do_exec                                       *
5933      *===========================================================================*/
5934     PUBLIC int do_exec()
5935     {
5936     /* Perform the exece(name, argv, envp) call.  The user library builds a
5937      * complete stack image, including pointers, args, environ, etc.  The stack
5938      * is copied to a buffer inside MM, and then to the new core image.
5939      */
5940
5941       register struct mproc *rmp;
5942       int m, r, fd, ft;
5943       char mbuf[MAX_ISTACK_BYTES];  /* buffer for stack and zeroes */
5944       union u {
5945             char name_buf[MAX_PATH];        /* the name of the file to exec */
5946             char zb[ZEROBUF_SIZE];  /* used to zero bss */
5947       } u;
5948       char *new_sp;
5949       vir_bytes src, dst, text_bytes, data_bytes, bss_bytes, stk_bytes, vsp;
```

```
5950        phys_bytes tot_bytes;              /* total space for program, including gap */
5951        vir_clicks sc;
5952        struct stat s_buf;
5953
5954        /* Do some validity checks. */
5955        rmp = mp;
5956        stk_bytes = (vir_bytes) stack_bytes;
5957        if (stk_bytes > MAX_ISTACK_BYTES) return(ENOMEM);      /* stack too big */
5958        if (exec_len <= 0 || exec_len > MAX_PATH) return(EINVAL);
5959
5960        /* Get the exec file name and see if the file is executable. */
5961        src = (vir_bytes) exec_name;
5962        dst = (vir_bytes) u.name_buf;
5963        r = mem_copy(who, D, (long) src, MM_PROC_NR, D, (long) dst, (long) exec_len);
5964        if (r != OK) return(r);           /* file name not in user data segment */
5965        tell_fs(CHDIR, who, 0, 0);    /* temporarily switch to user's directory */
5966        fd = allowed(u.name_buf, &s_buf, X_BIT);       /* is file executable? */
5967        tell_fs(CHDIR, 0, 1, 0);       /* switch back to MM's own directory */
5968        if (fd < 0) return(EACCES);   /* file was not executable */
5969
5970        /* Read the file header and extract the segment sizes. */
5971        sc = (stk_bytes + CLICK_SIZE - 1) >> CLICK_SHIFT;
5972        m = read_header(fd, &ft, &text_bytes, &data_bytes, &bss_bytes, &tot_bytes,sc);
5973        if (m < 0) {
5974                close(fd);                 /* something wrong with header */
5975                return(ENOEXEC);
5976        }
5977
5978        /* Fetch the stack from the user before destroying the old core image. */
5979        src = (vir_bytes) stack_ptr;
5980        dst = (vir_bytes) mbuf;
5981        r = mem_copy(who, D, (long) src, MM_PROC_NR, D, (long) dst, (long) stk_bytes);
5982        if (r != OK) {
5983                close(fd);                 /* can't fetch stack (e.g. bad virtual addr) */
5984                return(EACCES);
5985        }
5986
5987        /* Allocate new memory and release old memory.  Fix map and tell kernel. */
5988        r = new_mem(text_bytes, data_bytes, bss_bytes, stk_bytes, tot_bytes,
5989                                                u.zb, ZEROBUF_SIZE);
5990        if (r != OK) {
5991                close(fd);                 /* insufficient core or program too big */
5992                return(r);
5993        }
5994
5995        /* Patch up stack and copy it from MM to new core image. */
5996        vsp = (vir_bytes) rmp->mp_seg[S].mem_vir << CLICK_SHIFT;
5997        patch_ptr(mbuf, vsp);
5998        src = (vir_bytes) mbuf;
5999        r = mem_copy(MM_PROC_NR, D, (long) src, who, D, (long) vsp, (long) stk_bytes);
```

```
6000        if (r != OK) panic("do_exec stack copy err", NO_NUM);
6001
6002        /* Read in text and data segments. */
6003        load_seg(fd, T, text_bytes);
6004        load_seg(fd, D, data_bytes);
6005        close(fd);                      /* don't need exec file any more */
6006
6007        /* Take care of setuid/setgid bits. */
6008        if (s_buf.st_mode & I_SET_UID_BIT) {
6009             rmp->mp_effuid = s_buf.st_uid;
6010             tell_fs(SETUID, who, (int) rmp->mp_realuid, (int) rmp->mp_effuid);
6011        }
6012        if (s_buf.st_mode & I_SET_GID_BIT) {
6013             rmp->mp_effgid = s_buf.st_gid;
6014             tell_fs(SETGID, who, (int) rmp->mp_realgid, (int) rmp->mp_effgid);
6015        }
6016
6017        /* Fix up some 'mproc' fields and tell kernel that exec is done. */
6018        rmp->mp_catch = 0;              /* reset all caught signals */
6019        rmp->mp_flags &= ~SEPARATE;     /* turn off SEPARATE bit */
6020        rmp->mp_flags |= ft;            /* turn it on for separate I & D files */
6021        new_sp = (char *) vsp;
6022        sys_exec(who, new_sp);
6023        return(OK);
6024   }


6027   /*===========================================================================*
6028    *                             read_header                                   *
6029    *===========================================================================*/
6030   PRIVATE int read_header(fd, ft, text_bytes, data_bytes, bss_bytes, tot_bytes,sc)
6031   int fd;                              /* file descriptor for reading exec file */
6032   int *ft;                             /* place to return ft number */
6033   vir_bytes *text_bytes;               /* place to return text size */
6034   vir_bytes *data_bytes;               /* place to return initialized data size */
6035   vir_bytes *bss_bytes;                /* place to return bss size */
6036   phys_bytes *tot_bytes;               /* place to return total size */
6037   vir_clicks sc;                       /* stack size in clicks */
6038   {
6039   /* Read the header and extract the text, data, bss and total sizes from it. */
6040
6041      int m, ct;
6042      vir_clicks tc, dc, s_vir, dvir;
6043      phys_clicks totc;
6044      long buf[HDR_SIZE/sizeof(long)];
6045
6046      /* Read the header and check the magic number.  The standard MINIX header
6047       * consists of 8 longs, as follows:
6048       *    0: 0x04100301L (combined I & D space) or 0x04200301L (separate I & D)
6049       *    1: 0x00000020L
```

```
6050        *     2: size of text segments in bytes
6051        *     3: size of initialized data segment in bytes
6052        *     4: size of bss in bytes
6053        *     5: 0x00000000L
6054        *     6: total memory allocated to program (text, data and stack, combined)
6055        *     7: 0x00000000L
6056        * The longs are represented low-order byte first and high-order byte last.
6057        * The first byte of the header is always 0x01, followed by 0x03.
6058        * The header is followed directly by the text and data segments, whose sizes
6059        * are given in the header.
6060        */
6061
6062        if (read(fd, buf, HDR_SIZE) != HDR_SIZE) return(ENOEXEC);
6063        if ( (buf[0] & 0xFF0FFFFFL) != MAGIC) return(ENOEXEC);
6064        *ft = (buf[0] & SEP ? SEPARATE : 0);   /* separate I & D or not */
6065
6066        /* Get text and data sizes. */
6067        *text_bytes = (vir_bytes) buf[TEXTB]; /* text size in bytes */
6068        *data_bytes = (vir_bytes) buf[DATAB]; /* data size in bytes */
6069        if (*ft != SEPARATE) {
6070                /* If I & D space is not separated, it is all considered data. Text=0 */
6071                *data_bytes += *text_bytes;
6072                *text_bytes = 0;
6073        }
6074
6075        /* Get bss and total sizes. */
6076        *bss_bytes = (vir_bytes) buf[BSSB];    /* bss size in bytes */
6077        *tot_bytes = buf[TOTB];          /* total bytes to allocate for program */
6078        if (*tot_bytes == 0) return(ENOEXEC);
6079
6080        /* Check to see if segment sizes are feasible. */
6081        tc = (*text_bytes + CLICK_SHIFT - 1) >> CLICK_SHIFT;
6082        dc = (*data_bytes + *bss_bytes + CLICK_SHIFT - 1) >> CLICK_SHIFT;
6083        totc = (*tot_bytes + CLICK_SIZE - 1) >> CLICK_SHIFT;
6084        if (dc >= totc) return(ENOEXEC);        /* stack must be at least 1 click */
6085        dvir = (*ft == SEPARATE ? 0 : tc);
6086        s_vir = dvir + (totc - sc);
6087        m = size_ok(*ft, tc, dc, sc, dvir, s_vir);
6088        ct = buf[1] & BYTE;            /* header length */
6089        if (ct > HDR_SIZE) read(fd, buf, ct - HDR_SIZE);    /* skip unused hdr */
6090        return(m);
6091    }


6094    /*===========================================================================*
6095     *                              new_mem                                       *
6096     *===========================================================================*/
6097    PRIVATE int new_mem(text_bytes, data_bytes, bss_bytes,stk_bytes,tot_bytes,bf,zs)
6098    vir_bytes text_bytes;               /* text segment size in bytes */
6099    vir_bytes data_bytes;               /* size of initialized data in bytes */
```

```
6100    vir_bytes bss_bytes;            /* size of bss in bytes */
6101    vir_bytes stk_bytes;            /* size of initial stack segment in bytes */
6102    phys_bytes tot_bytes;           /* total memory to allocate, including gap */
6103    char bf[ZEROBUF_SIZE];          /* buffer to use for zeroing data segment */
6104    int zs;                         /* true size of 'bf' */
6105    {
6106    /* Allocate new memory and release the old memory.  Change the map and report
6107     * the new map to the kernel.  Zero the new core image's bss, gap and stack.
6108     */
6109
6110      register struct mproc *rmp;
6111      char *rzp;
6112      vir_bytes vzb;
6113      vir_clicks text_clicks, data_clicks, gap_clicks, stack_clicks, tot_clicks;
6114      phys_clicks new_base, old_clicks;
6115      phys_bytes bytes, base, count, bss_offset;
6116      extern phys_clicks alloc_mem();
6117      extern phys_clicks max_hole();
6118
6119      /* Acquire the new memory.  Each of the 4 parts: text, (data+bss), gap,
6120       * and stack occupies an integral number of clicks, starting at click
6121       * boundary.  The data and bss parts are run together with no space.
6122       */
6123
6124      text_clicks = (text_bytes + CLICK_SIZE - 1) >> CLICK_SHIFT;
6125      data_clicks = (data_bytes + bss_bytes + CLICK_SIZE - 1) >> CLICK_SHIFT;
6126      stack_clicks = (stk_bytes + CLICK_SIZE - 1) >> CLICK_SHIFT;
6127      tot_clicks = (tot_bytes + CLICK_SIZE - 1) >> CLICK_SHIFT;
6128      gap_clicks = tot_clicks - data_clicks - stack_clicks;
6129      if ( (int) gap_clicks < 0) return(ENOMEM);
6130
6131      /* Check to see if there is a hole big enough.  If so, we can risk first
6132       * releasing the old core image before allocating the new one, since we
6133       * know it will succeed.  If there is not enough, return failure.
6134       */
6135      if (text_clicks + tot_clicks > max_hole()) return(EAGAIN);
6136
6137      /* There is enough memory for the new core image.  Release the old one. */
6138      rmp = mp;
6139      old_clicks = (phys_clicks) rmp->mp_seg[S].mem_vir + rmp->mp_seg[S].mem_len;
6140      if (rmp->mp_flags & SEPARATE) old_clicks += rmp->mp_seg[T].mem_len;
6141      free_mem(rmp->mp_seg[T].mem_phys, old_clicks);         /* free the memory */
6142
6143      /* We have now passed the point of no return.  The old core image has been
6144       * forever lost.  The call must go through now.  Set up and report new map
6145       */
6146      new_base = alloc_mem(text_clicks + tot_clicks);       /* new core image */
6147      if (new_base == NO_MEM) panic("MM hole list is inconsistent", NO_NUM);
6148      rmp->mp_seg[T].mem_vir = 0;
6149      rmp->mp_seg[T].mem_len = text_clicks;
```

```
6150        rmp->mp_seg[T].mem_phys = new_base;
6151        rmp->mp_seg[D].mem_vir = 0;
6152        rmp->mp_seg[D].mem_len = data_clicks;
6153        rmp->mp_seg[D].mem_phys = new_base + text_clicks;
6154        rmp->mp_seg[S].mem_vir = rmp->mp_seg[D].mem_vir + data_clicks + gap_clicks;
6155        rmp->mp_seg[S].mem_len = stack_clicks;
6156        rmp->mp_seg[S].mem_phys = rmp->mp_seg[D].mem_phys + data_clicks + gap_clicks;
6157        sys_newmap(who, rmp->mp_seg); /* report new map to the kernel */
6158
6159        /* Zero the bss, gap, and stack segment. Start just above text.  */
6160        for (rzp = &bf[0]; rzp < &bf[zs]; rzp++) *rzp = 0;    /* clear buffer */
6161        bytes = (phys_bytes) (data_clicks + gap_clicks + stack_clicks) << CLICK_SHIFT;
6162        vzb = (vir_bytes) bf;
6163        base = (long) rmp->mp_seg[T].mem_phys + rmp->mp_seg[T].mem_len;
6164        base = base << CLICK_SHIFT;
6165        bss_offset = (data_bytes >> CLICK_SHIFT) << CLICK_SHIFT;
6166        base += bss_offset;
6167        bytes -= bss_offset;
6168
6169        while (bytes > 0) {
6170              count = (long) MIN(bytes, (phys_bytes) zs);
6171              if (mem_copy(MM_PROC_NR, D, (long) vzb, ABS, 0, base, count) != OK)
6172                    panic("new_mem can't zero", NO_NUM);
6173              base += count;
6174              bytes -= count;
6175        }
6176      return(OK);
6177    }


6180    /*===========================================================================*
6181     *                              patch_ptr                                     *
6182     *===========================================================================*/
6183    PRIVATE patch_ptr(stack, base)
6184    char stack[MAX_ISTACK_BYTES];    /* pointer to stack image within MM */
6185    vir_bytes base;                  /* virtual address of stack base inside user */
6186    {
6187    /* When doing an exec(name, argv, envp) call, the user builds up a stack
6188     * image with arg and env pointers relative to the start of the stack.  Now
6189     * these pointers must be relocated, since the stack is not positioned at
6190     * address 0 in the user's address space.
6191     */
6192
6193      char **ap, flag;
6194      vir_bytes v;
6195
6196      flag = 0;                      /* counts number of 0-pointers seen */
6197      ap = (char **) stack;          /* points initially to 'nargs' */
6198      ap++;                          /* now points to argv[0] */
6199      while (flag < 2) {
```

```
6200              if (ap >= (char **) &stack[MAX_ISTACK_BYTES]) return;   /* too bad */
6201              if (*ap != NIL_PTR) {
6202                      v = (vir_bytes) *ap;    /* v is relative pointer */
6203                      v += base;              /* relocate it */
6204                      *ap = (char *) v;       /* put it back */
6205              } else {
6206                      flag++;
6207              }
6208              ap++;
6209          }
6210      }


6213    /*===========================================================================*
6214     *                              load_seg                                      *
6215     *===========================================================================*/
6216    PRIVATE load_seg(fd, seg, seg_bytes)
6217    int fd;                                  /* file descriptor to read from */
6218    int seg;                                 /* T or D */
6219    vir_bytes seg_bytes;                     /* how big is the segment */
6220    {
6221    /* Read in text or data from the exec file and copy to the new core image.
6222     * This procedure is a little bit tricky.  The logical way to load a segment
6223     * would be to read it block by block and copy each block to the user space
6224     * one at a time.  This is too slow, so we do something dirty here, namely
6225     * send the user space and virtual address to the file system in the upper
6226     * 10 bits of the file descriptor, and pass it the user virtual address
6227     * instead of a MM address.  The file system copies the whole segment
6228     * directly to user space, bypassing MM completely.
6229     */
6230
6231      int new_fd, bytes;
6232      char *ubuf_ptr;
6233
6234      if (seg_bytes == 0) return;    /* text size for combined I & D is 0 */
6235      new_fd = (who << 8) | (seg << 6) | fd;
6236      ubuf_ptr = (char *) (mp->mp_seg[seg].mem_vir << CLICK_SHIFT);
6237      bytes = (int) seg_bytes;
6238      read(new_fd, ubuf_ptr, bytes);
6239      }
```

```
6250   /* The MINIX model of memory allocation reserves a fixed amount of memory for
6251    * the combined text, data, and stack segements.  The amount used for a child
6252    * process created by FORK is the same as the parent had.  If the child does
6253    * an EXEC later, the new size is taken from the header of the file EXEC'ed.
6254    *
6255    * The layout in memory consists of the text segment, followed by the data
6256    * segment, followed by a gap (unused memory), followed by the stack segment.
6257    * The data segment grows upward and the stack grows downward, so each can
6258    * take memory from the gap.  If they meet, the process must be killed.  The
6259    * procedures in this file deal with the growth of the data and stack segments.
6260    *
6261    * The entry points into this file are:
6262    *   do_brk:     BRK/SBRK system calls to grow or shrink the data segment
6263    *   adjust:     see if a proposed segment adjustment is allowed
6264    *   size_ok:    see if the segment sizes are feasible
6265    *   stack_fault: grow the stack segment
6266    */

6268   #include "../h/const.h"
6269   #include "../h/type.h"
6270   #include "../h/error.h"
6271   #include "../h/signal.h"
6272   #include "const.h"
6273   #include "glo.h"
6274   #include "mproc.h"
6275   #include "param.h"

6277   #define DATA_CHANGED      1    /* flag value when data segment size changed */
6278   #define STACK_CHANGED     2    /* flag value when stack size changed */

6280   /*===========================================================================*
6281    *                              do_brk                                        *
6282    *===========================================================================*/
6283   PUBLIC int do_brk()
6284   {
6285   /* Perform the brk(addr) system call.
6286    *
6287    * The call is complicated by the fact that on some machines (e.g., 8088),
6288    * the stack pointer can grow beyond the base of the stack segment without
6289    * anybody noticing it.   For a file not using separate I & D space,
6290    * the parameter, 'addr' is to the total size, text + data.  For a file using
6291    * separate text and data spaces, it is just the data size. Files using
6292    * separate I & D space have the SEPARATE bit in mp_flags set.
6293    */

6295     register struct mproc *rmp;
6296     int r;
6297     vir_bytes v, new_sp;
6298     vir_clicks new_clicks;
6299
```

```
6300          rmp = mp;
6301          v = (vir_bytes) addr;          /* 'addr' is the new data segment size */
6302          new_clicks = (vir_clicks) ( ((long) v + CLICK_SIZE - 1) >> CLICK_SHIFT);
6303          sys_getsp(who, &new_sp);          /* ask kernel for current sp value */
6304          r = adjust(rmp, new_clicks, new_sp);
6305          res_ptr = (r == OK ? addr : (char *) -1);
6306          return(r);                    /* return new size or -1 */
6307    }


6310    /*===========================================================================*
6311     *                              adjust                                        *
6312     *===========================================================================*/
6313    PUBLIC int adjust(rmp, data_clicks, sp)
6314    register struct mproc *rmp;        /* whose memory is being adjusted? */
6315    vir_clicks data_clicks;            /* how big is data segment to become? */
6316    vir_bytes sp;                      /* new value of sp */
6317    {
6318    /* See if data and stack segments can coexist, adjusting them if need be.
6319     * Memory is never allocated or freed.  Instead it is added or removed from the
6320     * gap between data segment and stack segment.  If the gap size becomes
6321     * negative, the adjustment of data or stack fails and ENOMEM is returned.
6322     */
6323
6324      register struct mem_map *mem_sp, *mem_dp;
6325      vir_clicks sp_click, gap_base, lower, old_clicks;
6326      int changed, r, ft;
6327      long base_of_stack, delta;       /* longs avoid certain problems */
6328
6329      mem_dp = &rmp->mp_seg[D];         /* pointer to data segment map */
6330      mem_sp = &rmp->mp_seg[S];         /* pointer to stack segment map */
6331      changed = 0;                     /* set when either segment changed */
6332
6333      /* See if stack size has gone negative (i.e., sp too close to 0xFFFF...) */
6334      base_of_stack = (long) mem_sp->mem_vir + (long) mem_sp->mem_len;
6335      sp_click = sp >> CLICK_SHIFT; /* click containing sp */
6336      if (sp_click >= base_of_stack) return(ENOMEM);          /* sp too high */
6337
6338      /* Compute size of gap between stack and data segments. */
6339      delta = (long) mem_sp->mem_vir - (long) sp_click;
6340      lower = (delta > 0 ? sp_click : mem_sp->mem_vir);
6341      gap_base = mem_dp->mem_vir + data_clicks;
6342      if (lower < gap_base) return(ENOMEM); /* data and stack collided */
6343
6344      /* Update data length (but not data orgin) on behalf of brk() system call. */
6345      old_clicks = mem_dp->mem_len;
6346      if (data_clicks != mem_dp->mem_len) {
6347            mem_dp->mem_len = data_clicks;
6348            changed |= DATA_CHANGED;
6349      }
```

```
6350
6351        /* Update stack length and origin due to change in stack pointer. */
6352        if (delta > 0) {
6353             mem_sp->mem_vir -= delta;
6354             mem_sp->mem_phys -= delta;
6355             mem_sp->mem_len += delta;
6356             changed |= STACK_CHANGED;
6357        }
6358
6359        /* Do the new data and stack segment sizes fit in the address space? */
6360        ft = (rmp->mp_flags & SEPARATE);
6361        r = size_ok(ft, rmp->mp_seg[T].mem_len, rmp->mp_seg[D].mem_len,
6362             rmp->mp_seg[S].mem_len, rmp->mp_seg[D].mem_vir, rmp->mp_seg[S].mem_vir);
6363        if (r == OK) {
6364             if (changed) sys_newmap(rmp - mproc, rmp->mp_seg);
6365             return(OK);
6366        }
6367
6368        /* New sizes don't fit or require too many page/segment registers. Restore.*/
6369        if (changed & DATA_CHANGED) mem_dp->mem_len = old_clicks;
6370        if (changed & STACK_CHANGED) {
6371             mem_sp->mem_vir += delta;
6372             mem_sp->mem_phys += delta;
6373             mem_sp->mem_len -= delta;
6374        }
6375        return(ENOMEM);
6376   }


6379   /*===========================================================================*
6380    *                              size_ok                                     *
6381    *===========================================================================*/
6382   PUBLIC int size_ok(file_type, tc, dc, sc, dvir, s_vir)
6383   int file_type;                  /* SEPARATE or 0 */
6384   vir_clicks tc;                  /* text size in clicks */
6385   vir_clicks dc;                  /* data size in clicks */
6386   vir_clicks sc;                  /* stack size in clicks */
6387   vir_clicks dvir;                /* virtual address for start of data seg */
6388   vir_clicks s_vir;               /* virtual address for start of stack seg */
6389   {
6390   /* Check to see if the sizes are feasible and enough segmentation registers
6391    * exist.  On a machine with eight 8K pages, text, data, stack sizes of
6392    * (32K, 16K, 16K) will fit, but (33K, 17K, 13K) will not, even though the
6393    * former is bigger (64K) than the latter (63K).  Even on the 8088 this test
6394    * is needed, since the data and stack may not exceed 4096 clicks.
6395    */
6396
6397     int pt, pd, ps;                /* segment sizes in pages */
6398
6399     pt = ( (tc << CLICK_SHIFT) + PAGE_SIZE - 1)/PAGE_SIZE;
```

```
6400        pd = ( (dc << CLICK_SHIFT) + PAGE_SIZE - 1)/PAGE_SIZE;
6401        ps = ( (sc << CLICK_SHIFT) + PAGE_SIZE - 1)/PAGE_SIZE;
6402
6403        if (file_type == SEPARATE) {
6404                if (pt > MAX_PAGES || pd + ps > MAX_PAGES) return(ENOMEM);
6405        } else {
6406                if (pt + pd + ps > MAX_PAGES) return(ENOMEM);
6407        }
6408
6409        if (dvir + dc > s_vir) return(ENOMEM);
6410
6411        return(OK);
6412   }


6415   /*===========================================================================*
6416    *                               stack_fault                                 *
6417    *===========================================================================*/
6418   PUBLIC stack_fault(proc_nr)
6419   int proc_nr;                    /* tells who got the stack fault */
6420   {
6421   /* Handle a stack fault by growing the stack segment until sp is inside of it.
6422    * If this is impossible because data segment is in the way, kill the process.
6423    */
6424
6425     register struct mproc *rmp;
6426     int r;
6427     vir_bytes new_sp;
6428
6429     rmp = &mproc[proc_nr];
6430     sys_getsp(rmp - mproc, &new_sp);
6431     r = adjust(rmp, rmp->mp_seg[D].mem_len, new_sp);
6432     if (r == OK) return;
6433
6434     /* Stack has bumped into data segment.  Kill the process. */
6435     rmp->mp_catch = 0;             /* don't catch this signal */
6436     sig_proc(rmp, SIGSEGV);        /* terminate process */
6437   }
```

```
6450    /* This file handles signals, which are asynchronous events and are generally
6451     * a messy and unpleasant business.  Signals can be generated by the KILL
6452     * system call, or from the keyboard (SIGINT) or from the clock (SIGALRM).
6453     * In all cases control eventually passes to check_sig() to see which processes
6454     * can be signalled.  The actual signalling is done by sig_proc().
6455     *
6456     * The entry points into this file are:
6457     *   do_signal: perform the SIGNAL system call
6458     *   do_kill:   perform the KILL system call
6459     *   do_ksig:   accept a signal originating in the kernel (e.g., SIGINT)
6460     *   sig_proc:  interrupt or terminate a signalled process
6461     *   do_alarm:  perform the ALARM system call by calling set_alarm()
6462     *   set_alarm: tell the clock task to start or stop a timer
6463     *   do_pause:  perform the PAUSE system call
6464     *   unpause:   check to see if process is suspended on anything
6465     */
6466
6467    #include "../h/const.h"
6468    #include "../h/type.h"
6469    #include "../h/callnr.h"
6470    #include "../h/com.h"
6471    #include "../h/error.h"
6472    #include "../h/signal.h"
6473    #include "../h/stat.h"
6474    #include "const.h"
6475    #include "glo.h"
6476    #include "mproc.h"
6477    #include "param.h"
6478
6479    #define DUMP_SIZE         256     /* buffer size for core dumps */
6480    #define CORE_MODE         0777    /* mode to use on core image files */
6481    #define DUMPED            0200    /* bit set in status when core dumped */
6482
6483    PRIVATE message m_sig;
6484
6485    /*===========================================================================*
6486     *                              do_signal                                    *
6487     *===========================================================================*/
6488    PUBLIC int do_signal()
6489    {
6490    /* Perform the signal(sig, func) call by setting bits to indicate that a signal
6491     * is to be caught or ignored.
6492     */
6493
6494      int mask;
6495
6496      if (sig < 1 || sig > NR_SIGS) return(EINVAL);
6497      if (sig == SIGKILL) return(OK);       /* SIGKILL may not ignored/caught */
6498      mask = 1 << (sig - 1);        /* singleton set with 'sig' bit on */
6499
```

```
6500        /* All this func does is set the bit maps for subsequent sig processing. */
6501        if (func == SIG_IGN) {
6502                mp->mp_ignore |= mask;
6503                mp->mp_catch &= ~mask;
6504        } else if (func == SIG_DFL) {
6505                mp->mp_ignore &= ~mask;
6506                mp->mp_catch &= ~mask;
6507        } else {
6508                mp->mp_ignore &= ~mask;
6509                mp->mp_catch |= mask;
6510                mp->mp_func = func;
6511        }
6512        return(OK);
6513 }


6516 /*===========================================================================*
6517  *                              do_kill                                       *
6518  *===========================================================================*/
6519 PUBLIC int do_kill()
6520 {
6521 /* Perform the kill(pid, kill_sig) system call. */
6522
6523     return check_sig(pid, kill_sig, mp->mp_effuid);
6524 }


6527 /*===========================================================================*
6528  *                              do_ksig                                       *
6529  *===========================================================================*/
6530 PUBLIC int do_ksig()
6531 {
6532 /* Certain signals, such as segmentation violations and DEL, originate in the
6533  * kernel.  When the kernel detects such signals, it sets bits in a bit map.
6534  * As soon is MM is awaiting new work, the kernel sends MM a message containing
6535  * the process slot and bit map.  That message comes here.  The File System
6536  * also uses this mechanism to signal writing on broken pipes (SIGPIPE).
6537  */
6538
6539     register struct mproc *rmp;
6540     int i, proc_id, proc_nr, id;
6541     unshort sig_map;                    /* bits 0 - 15 for sigs 1 - 16 */
6542
6543     /* Only kernel and FS may make this call. */
6544     if (who != HARDWARE && who != FS_PROC_NR) return(EPERM);
6545
6546     proc_nr = mm_in.PROC1;
6547     rmp = &mproc[proc_nr];
6548     if ( (rmp->mp_flags & IN_USE) == 0 || (rmp->mp_flags & HANGING) ) return(OK);
6549     proc_id = rmp->mp_pid;
```

```
6550        sig_map = (unshort) mm_in.SIG_MAP;
6551        mp = &mproc[0];                 /* pretend kernel signals are from MM */
6552
6553        /* Stack faults are passed from kernel to MM as pseudo-signal 16. */
6554        if (sig_map == 1 << (STACK_FAULT - 1)) {
6555            stack_fault(proc_nr);
6556            return(OK);
6557        }
6558
6559        /* Check each bit in turn to see if a signal is to be sent.  Unlike
6560         * kill(), the kernel may collect several unrelated signals for a process
6561         * and pass them to MM in one blow.  Thus loop on the bit map. For SIGINT
6562         * and SIGQUIT, use proc_id 0, since multiple processes may have to signalled.
6563         */
6564        for (i = 0; i < NR_SIGS; i++) {
6565            id = (i+1 == SIGINT || i+1 == SIGQUIT ? 0 : proc_id);
6566            if ( (sig_map >> i) & 1) check_sig(id, i + 1, SUPER_USER);
6567        }
6568
6569        dont_reply = TRUE;              /* don't reply to the kernel */
6570        return(OK);
6571    }


6574    /*===========================================================================*
6575     *                              check_sig                                     *
6576     *===========================================================================*/
6577    PRIVATE int check_sig(proc_id, sig_nr, send_uid)
6578    int proc_id;                    /* pid of process to signal, or 0 or -1 */
6579    int sig_nr;                     /* which signal to send (1-16) */
6580    uid send_uid;                   /* identity of process sending the signal */
6581    {
6582    /* Check to see if it is possible to send a signal.  The signal may have to be
6583     * sent to a group of processes.  This routine is invoked by the KILL system
6584     * call, and also when the kernel catches a DEL or other signal. SIGALRM too.
6585     */
6586
6587        register struct mproc *rmp;
6588        int count, send_sig;
6589        unshort mask;
6590        extern unshort core_bits;
6591
6592        if (sig_nr < 1 || sig_nr > NR_SIGS) return(EINVAL);
6593        count = 0;                      /* count # of signals sent */
6594        mask = 1 << (sig_nr - 1);
6595
6596        /* Search the proc table for processes to signal.  Several tests are made:
6597         *    - if proc's uid != sender's, and sender is not superuser, don't signal
6598         *    - if specific process requested (i.e., 'procpid' > 0, check for match
6599         *    - if a process has already exited, it can't receive signals
```

```
6600          *     - if 'proc_id' is 0 signal everyone in same process group except caller
6601          */
6602         for (rmp = &mproc[INIT_PROC_NR + 1]; rmp < &mproc[NR_PROCS]; rmp++ ) {
6603                 if ( (rmp->mp_flags & IN_USE) == 0) continue;
6604                 send_sig = TRUE;        /* if it's FALSE at end of loop, don't signal */
6605                 if (send_uid != rmp->mp_effuid && send_uid != SUPER_USER)send_sig=FALSE;
6606                 if (proc_id > 0 && proc_id != rmp->mp_pid) send_sig = FALSE;
6607                 if (rmp->mp_flags & HANGING) send_sig = FALSE;   /*don't wake the dead*/
6608                 if (proc_id == 0 && mp->mp_procgrp != rmp->mp_procgrp) send_sig = FALSE;
6609                 if (send_uid == SUPER_USER && proc_id == -1) send_sig = TRUE;
6610
6611                 /* SIGALARM is a little special.  When a process exits, a clock signal
6612                  * can arrive just as the timer is being turned off.  Also, turn off
6613                  * ALARM_ON bit when timer goes off to keep it accurate.
6614                  */
6615                 if (sig_nr == SIGALRM) {
6616                         if ( (rmp->mp_flags & ALARM_ON) == 0) continue;
6617                         rmp->mp_flags &= ~ALARM_ON;
6618                 }
6619
6620                 if (send_sig == FALSE || rmp->mp_ignore & mask) continue;
6621
6622                 /* If process is hanging on PAUSE, WAIT, tty, pipe, etc. release it. */
6623                 unpause(rmp - mproc);   /* check to see if process is paused */
6624                 count++;
6625
6626                 /* Send the signal or kill the process, possibly with core dump. */
6627                 sig_proc(rmp, sig_nr);
6628                 if (proc_id > 0) break; /* only one process being signalled */
6629         }
6630
6631         /* If the calling process has killed itself, don't reply. */
6632         if ((mp->mp_flags & IN_USE) == 0 || (mp->mp_flags & HANGING))dont_reply =TRUE;
6633         return(count > 0 ? OK : ESRCH);
6634 }


6637 /*===========================================================================*
6638  *                              sig_proc                                     *
6639  *===========================================================================*/
6640 PUBLIC sig_proc(rmp, sig_nr)
6641 register struct mproc *rmp;      /* pointer to the process to be signalled */
6642 int sig_nr;                      /* signal to send to process (1-16) */
6643 {
6644 /* Send a signal to a process.  Check to see if the signal is to be caught.
6645  * If so, the pc, psw, and signal number are to be pushed onto the process'
6646  * stack.  If the stack cannot grow or the signal is not to be caught, kill
6647  * the process.
6648  */
6649
```

```
6650        unshort mask;
6651        int core_file;
6652        vir_bytes new_sp;
6653        extern unshort core_bits;
6654
6655        if ( (rmp->mp_flags & IN_USE) == 0) return;   /* if already dead forget it */
6656        mask = 1 << (sig_nr - 1);
6657        if (rmp->mp_catch & mask) {
6658             /* Signal should be caught. */
6659             rmp->mp_catch &= ~mask;          /* disable further signals */
6660             sys_getsp(rmp - mproc, &new_sp);
6661             new_sp -= SIG_PUSH_BYTES;
6662             if (adjust(rmp, rmp->mp_seg[D].mem_len, new_sp) == OK) {
6663                     sys_sig(rmp - mproc, sig_nr, rmp->mp_func);
6664                     return;          /* successful signal */
6665             }
6666        }
6667
6668        /* Signal should not or cannot be caught.  Take default action. */
6669        core_file = ( core_bits >> (sig_nr - 1 )) & 1;
6670        rmp->mp_sigstatus = (char) sig_nr;
6671        mm_exit(rmp, 0);                   /* terminate process */
6672        if (core_file) dump_core(rmp); /* dump core */
6673     }


6676     /*===========================================================================*
6677      *                              do_alarm                                     *
6678      *===========================================================================*/
6679     PUBLIC int do_alarm()
6680     {
6681     /* Perform the alarm(seconds) system call. */
6682
6683        register int r;
6684        unsigned sec;
6685
6686        sec = (unsigned) seconds;
6687        r = set_alarm(who, sec);
6688        return(r);
6689     }


6692     /*===========================================================================*
6693      *                              set_alarm                                    *
6694      *===========================================================================*/
6695     PUBLIC int set_alarm(proc_nr, sec)
6696     int proc_nr;                       /* process that wants the alarm */
6697     unsigned sec;                      /* how many seconds delay before the signal */
6698     {
6699     /* This routine is used by do_alarm() to set the alarm timer.  It is also
```

```
6700        * to turn the timer off when a process exits with the timer still on.
6701        */
6702
6703        int remaining;
6704
6705        m_sig.m_type = SET_ALARM;
6706        m_sig.PROC_NR = proc_nr;
6707        m_sig.DELTA_TICKS = HZ * sec;
6708        if (sec != 0)
6709                mproc[proc_nr].mp_flags |= ALARM_ON;     /* turn ALARM_ON bit on */
6710        else
6711                mproc[proc_nr].mp_flags &= ~ALARM_ON;    /* turn ALARM_ON bit off */
6712
6713        /* Tell the clock task to provide a signal message when the time comes. */
6714        if (sendrec(CLOCK, &m_sig) != OK) panic("alarm er", NO_NUM);
6715        remaining = (int) m_sig.SECONDS_LEFT;
6716        return(remaining);
6717    }


6720    /*===========================================================================*
6721     *                              do_pause                                      *
6722     *===========================================================================*/
6723    PUBLIC int do_pause()
6724    {
6725    /* Perform the pause() system call. */
6726
6727        mp->mp_flags |= PAUSED;          /* turn on PAUSE bit */
6728        dont_reply = TRUE;
6729        return(OK);
6730    }


6733    /*===========================================================================*
6734     *                              unpause                                       *
6735     *===========================================================================*/
6736    PUBLIC unpause(pro)
6737    int pro;                            /* which process number */
6738    {
6739    /* A signal is to be sent to a process.  It that process is hanging on a
6740     * system call, the system call must be terminated with EINTR.  Possible
6741     * calls are PAUSE, WAIT, READ and WRITE, the latter two for pipes and ttys.
6742     * First check if the process is hanging on PAUSE or WAIT.  If not, tell FS,
6743     * so it can check for READs and WRITEs from pipes, ttys and the like.
6744     */
6745
6746        register struct mproc *rmp;
6747
6748        rmp = &mproc[pro];
6749
```

```
6750        /* Check to see if process is hanging on PAUSE call. */
6751        if (rmp->mp_flags & PAUSED) {
6752                rmp->mp_flags &= ~PAUSED;         /* turn off PAUSED bit */
6753                reply(pro, EINTR, 0, NIL_PTR);
6754                return;
6755        }
6756
6757        /* Check to see if process is hanging on a WAIT call. */
6758        if (rmp->mp_flags & WAITING) {
6759                rmp->mp_flags &= ~ WAITING;     /* turn off WAITING bit */
6760                reply(pro, EINTR, 0, NIL_PTR);
6761                return;
6762        }
6763
6764        /* Process is not hanging on an MM call.  Ask FS to take a look. */
6765        tell_fs(UNPAUSE, pro, 0, 0);
6766
6767        return;
6768     }
6769
6770
6771     /*===========================================================================*
6772      *                              dump_core                                    *
6773      *===========================================================================*/
6774     PRIVATE dump_core(rmp)
6775     register struct mproc *rmp;      /* whose core is to be dumped */
6776     {
6777     /* Make a core dump on the file "core", if possible. */
6778
6779        struct stat s_buf, d_buf;
6780        char buf[DUMP_SIZE];
6781        int i, r, s, erl, er2, slot;
6782        vir_bytes v_buf;
6783        long len, a, c, ct, dest;
6784        struct mproc *xmp;
6785        extern char core_name[];
6786
6787
6788        /* Change to working directory of dumpee. */
6789        slot = rmp - mproc;
6790        tell_fs(CHDIR, slot, 0, 0);
6791
6792        /* Can core file be written? */
6793        if (rmp->mp_realuid != rmp->mp_effuid) return;
6794        xmp = mp;                        /* allowed() looks at 'mp' */
6795        mp = rmp;
6796        r = allowed(core_name, &s_buf, W_BIT);        /* is core_file writable */
6797        s = allowed(".", &d_buf, W_BIT);     /* is directory writable? */
6798        mp = xmp;
6799        if (r >= 0) close(r);
```

```
6800      if (s >= 0) close(s);
6801      if (rmp->mp_effuid == SUPER_USER) r = 0;          /* su can always dump core */
6802
6803      if (r >= 0 || (r == ENOENT && s >= 0)) {
6804            /* Either file is writable or it doesn't exist & dir is writable */
6805            r = creat(core_name, CORE_MODE);
6806            tell_fs(CHDIR, 0, 1, 0);          /* go back to MM's own dir */
6807            if (r < 0) return;
6808            rmp->mp_sigstatus |= DUMPED;
6809
6810            /* First loop through segments and write each length on core file. */
6811            for (i = 0; i < NR_SEGS; i++) {
6812                  len = rmp->mp_seg[i].mem_len << CLICK_SHIFT;
6813                  if (write(r, (char *) &len, sizeof len) < 0) {
6814                        close(r);
6815                        return;
6816                  }
6817            }
6818
6819            /* Now loop through segments and write the segments themselves out. */
6820            v_buf = (vir_bytes) buf;
6821            dest = (long) v_buf;
6822            for (i = 0; i < NR_SEGS; i++) {
6823                  a = (phys_bytes) rmp->mp_seg[i].mem_vir << CLICK_SHIFT;
6824                  c = (phys_bytes) rmp->mp_seg[i].mem_len << CLICK_SHIFT;
6825
6826                  /* Loop through a segment, dumping it. */
6827                  while (c > 0) {
6828                        ct = MIN(c, DUMP_SIZE);
6829                        er1 = mem_copy(slot, i, a, MM_PROC_NR, D, dest, ct);
6830                        er2 = write(r, buf, (int) ct);
6831                        if (er1 < 0 || er2 < 0) {
6832                              close(r);
6833                              return;
6834                        }
6835                        a += ct;
6836                        c -= ct;
6837                  }
6838            }
6839      } else {
6840            tell_fs(CHDIR, 0, 1, 0);          /* go back to MM's own dir */
6841            close(r);
6842            return;
6843      }
6844
6845      close(r);
6846  }
```

```
6850     /* This file handles the 4 system calls that get and set uids and gids.
6851      * It also handles getpid().  The code for each one is so tiny that it hardly
6852      * seemed worthwhile to make each a separate function.
6853      */
6854
6855     #include "../h/const.h"
6856     #include "../h/type.h"
6857     #include "../h/callnr.h"
6858     #include "../h/error.h"
6859     #include "const.h"
6860     #include "glo.h"
6861     #include "mproc.h"
6862     #include "param.h"
6863
6864     /*===========================================================================*
6865      *                              do_getset                                    *
6866      *===========================================================================*/
6867     PUBLIC int do_getset()
6868     {
6869     /* Handle GETUID, GETGID, GETPID, SETUID, SETGID.  The three GETs return
6870      * their primary results in 'r'.  GETUID and GETGID also return secondary
6871      * results (the effective IDs) in 'result2', which is returned to the user.
6872      */
6873
6874       register struct mproc *rmp = mp;
6875       register int r;
6876
6877       switch(mm_call) {
6878           case GETUID:
6879                   r = rmp->mp_realuid;
6880                   result2 = rmp->mp_effuid;
6881                   break;
6882
6883           case GETGID:
6884                   r = rmp->mp_realgid;
6885                   result2 = rmp->mp_effgid;
6886                   break;
6887
6888           case GETPID:
6889                   r = mproc[who].mp_pid;
6890                   result2 = mproc[rmp->mp_parent].mp_pid;
6891                   break;
6892
6893           case SETUID:
6894                   if (rmp->mp_realuid != usr_id && rmp->mp_effuid != SUPER_USER)
6895                           return(EPERM);
6896                   rmp->mp_realuid = usr_id;
6897                   rmp->mp_effuid = usr_id;
6898                   tell_fs(SETUID, who, usr_id, usr_id);
6899                   r = OK;
```

```
6900                    break;
6901
6902            case SETGID:
6903                    if (rmp->mp_realgid != grpid && rmp->mp_effuid != SUPER_USER)
6904                            return(EPERM);
6905                    rmp->mp_realgid = grpid;
6906                    rmp->mp_effgid = grpid;
6907                    tell_fs(SETGID, who, grpid, grpid);
6908                    r = OK;
6909                    break;
6910        }
6911
6912        return(r);
6913    }
```

```
6950      /* This file is concerned with allocating and freeing arbitrary-size blocks of
6951       * physical memory on behalf of the FORK and EXEC system calls.  The key data
6952       * structure used is the hole table, which maintains a list of holes in memory.
6953       * It is kept sorted in order of increasing memory address. The addresses
6954       * it contains refer to physical memory, starting at absolute address 0
6955       * (i.e., they are not relative to the start of MM).  During system
6956       * initialization, that part of memory containing the interrupt vectors,
6957       * kernel, and MM are "allocated" to mark them as not available and to
6958       * remove them from the hole list.
6959       *
6960       * The entry points into this file are:
6961       *    alloc_mem: allocate a given sized chunk of memory
6962       *    free_mem:  release a previously allocated chunk of memory
6963       *    mem_init:  initialize the tables when MM start up
6964       *    max_hole:  returns the largest hole currently available
6965       */
6966
6967      #include "../h/const.h"
6968      #include "../h/type.h"
6969      #include "const.h"
6970
6971      #define NR_HOLES        128    /* max # entries in hole table */
6972      #define NIL_HOLE (struct hole *) 0
6973
6974      PRIVATE struct hole {
6975        phys_clicks h_base;              /* where does the hole begin? */
6976        phys_clicks h_len;              /* how big is the hole? */
6977        struct hole *h_next;            /* pointer to next entry on the list */
6978      } hole[NR_HOLES];
6979
6980
6981      PRIVATE struct hole *hole_head; /* pointer to first hole */
6982      PRIVATE struct hole *free_slots;         /* ptr to list of unused table slots */
6983
6984      /*===========================================================================*
6985       *                              alloc_mem                                     *
6986       *===========================================================================*/
6987      PUBLIC phys_clicks alloc_mem(clicks)
6988      phys_clicks clicks;                     /* amount of memory requested */
6989      {
6990      /* Allocate a block of memory from the free list using first fit. The block
6991       * consists of a sequence of contiguous bytes, whose length in clicks is
6992       * given by 'clicks'.  A pointer to the block is returned.  The block is
6993       * always on a click boundary.  This procedure is called when memory is
6994       * needed for FORK or EXEC.
6995       */
6996
6997        register struct hole *hp, *prev_ptr;
6998        phys_clicks old_base;
6999
```

```
7000        hp = hole_head;
7001        while (hp != NIL_HOLE) {
7002              if (hp->h_len >= clicks) {
7003                    /* We found a hole that is big enough.  Use it. */
7004                    old_base = hp->h_base;  /* remember where it started */
7005                    hp->h_base += clicks;   /* bite a piece off */
7006                    hp->h_len -= clicks;    /* ditto */
7007
7008                    /* If hole is only partly used, reduce size and return. */
7009                    if (hp->h_len != 0) return(old_base);
7010
7011                    /* The entire hole has been used up.  Manipulate free list. */
7012                    del_slot(prev_ptr, hp);
7013                    return(old_base);
7014              }
7015
7016              prev_ptr = hp;
7017              hp = hp->h_next;
7018        }
7019      return(NO_MEM);
7020    }


7023    /*===========================================================================*
7024     *                              free_mem                                      *
7025     *===========================================================================*/
7026    PUBLIC free_mem(base, clicks)
7027    phys_clicks base;                    /* base address of block to free */
7028    phys_clicks clicks;                  /* number of clicks to free */
7029    {
7030    /* Return a block of free memory to the hole list.  The parameters tell where
7031     * the block starts in physical memory and how big it is.  The block is added
7032     * to the hole list.  If it is contiguous with an existing hole on either end,
7033     * it is merged with the hole or holes.
7034     */
7035
7036      register struct hole *hp, *new_ptr, *prev_ptr;
7037
7038      if ( (new_ptr = free_slots) == NIL_HOLE) panic("Hole table full", NO_NUM);
7039      new_ptr->h_base = base;
7040      new_ptr->h_len = clicks;
7041      free_slots = new_ptr->h_next;
7042      hp = hole_head;
7043
7044      /* If this block's address is numerically less than the lowest hole currently
7045       * available, or if no holes are currently available, put this hole on the
7046       * front of the hole list.
7047       */
7048      if (hp == NIL_HOLE || base <= hp->h_base) {
7049            /* Block to be freed goes on front of hole list. */
```

```
7050                new_ptr->h_next = hp;
7051                hole_head = new_ptr;
7052                merge(new_ptr);
7053                return;
7054        }
7055
7056        /* Block to be returned does not go on front of hole list. */
7057        while (hp != NIL_HOLE && base > hp->h_base) {
7058                prev_ptr = hp;
7059                hp = hp->h_next;
7060        }
7061
7062        /* We found where it goes.  Insert block after 'prev_ptr'. */
7063        new_ptr->h_next = prev_ptr->h_next;
7064        prev_ptr->h_next = new_ptr;
7065        merge(prev_ptr);                 /* sequence is 'prev_ptr', 'new_ptr', 'hp' */
7066   }


7069   /*===========================================================================*
7070    *                              del_slot                                     *
7071    *===========================================================================*/
7072   PRIVATE del_slot(prev_ptr, hp)
7073   register struct hole *prev_ptr; /* pointer to hole entry just ahead of 'hp' */
7074   register struct hole *hp;        /* pointer to hole entry to be removed */
7075   {
7076   /* Remove an entry from the hole list.  This procedure is called when a
7077    * request to allocate memory removes a hole in its entirety, thus reducing
7078    * the numbers of holes in memory, and requiring the elimination of one
7079    * entry in the hole list.
7080    */
7081
7082        if (hp == hole_head)
7083                hole_head = hp->h_next;
7084        else
7085                prev_ptr->h_next = hp->h_next;
7086
7087        hp->h_next = free_slots;
7088        free_slots = hp;
7089   }


7092   /*===========================================================================*
7093    *                              merge                                        *
7094    *===========================================================================*/
7095   PRIVATE merge(hp)
7096   register struct hole *hp;        /* ptr to hole to merge with its successors */
7097   {
7098   /* Check for contiguous holes and merge any found.  Contiguous holes can occur
7099    * when a block of memory is freed, and it happens to abut another hole on
```

```
7100        * either or both ends.  The pointer 'hp' points to the first of a series of
7101        * three holes that can potentially all be merged together.
7102        */
7103
7104        register struct hole *next_ptr;
7105
7106        /* If 'hp' points to the last hole, no merging is possible.  If it does not,
7107         * try to absorb its successor into it and free the successor's table entry.
7108         */
7109        if ( (next_ptr = hp->h_next) == NIL_HOLE) return;
7110        if (hp->h_base + hp->h_len == next_ptr->h_base) {
7111                hp->h_len += next_ptr->h_len;   /* first one gets second one's mem */
7112                del_slot(hp, next_ptr);
7113        } else {
7114                hp = next_ptr;
7115        }
7116
7117        /* If 'hp' now points to the last hole, return; otherwise, try to absorb its
7118         * succesor into it.
7119         */
7120        if ( (next_ptr = hp->h_next) == NIL_HOLE) return;
7121        if (hp->h_base + hp->h_len == next_ptr->h_base) {
7122                hp->h_len += next_ptr->h_len;
7123                del_slot(hp, next_ptr);
7124        }
7125    }


7128    /*===========================================================================*
7129     *                              max_hole                                      *
7130     *===========================================================================*/
7131    PUBLIC phys_clicks max_hole()
7132    {
7133    /* Scan the hole list and return the largest hole. */
7134
7135        register struct hole *hp;
7136        register phys_clicks max;
7137
7138        hp = hole_head;
7139        max = 0;
7140        while (hp != NIL_HOLE) {
7141                if (hp->h_len > max) max = hp->h_len;
7142                hp = hp->h_next;
7143        }
7144        return(max);
7145    }
```

```
7150    /*===========================================================================*
7151     *                              mem_init                                      *
7152     *===========================================================================*/
7153    PUBLIC mem_init(clicks)
7154    phys_clicks clicks;                /* amount of memory available */
7155    {
7156    /* Initialize hole lists.  There are two lists: 'hole_head' points to a linked
7157     * list of all the holes (unused memory) in the system; 'free_slots' points to
7158     * a linked list of table entries that are not in use.  Initially, the former
7159     * list has one entry, a single hole encompassing all of memory, and the second
7160     * list links together all the remaining table slots.  As memory becomes more
7161     * fragmented in the course of time (i.e., the initial big hole breaks up into
7162     * many small holes), new table slots are needed to represent them.  These
7163     * slots are taken from the list headed by 'free_slots'.
7164     */
7165
7166      register struct hole *hp;
7167
7168      for (hp = &hole[0]; hp < &hole[NR_HOLES]; hp++) hp->h_next = hp + 1;
7169      hole[0].h_next = NIL_HOLE;      /* only 1 big hole initially */
7170      hole[NR_HOLES-1].h_next = NIL_HOLE;
7171      hole_head = &hole[0];
7172      free_slots = &hole[1];
7173      hole[0].h_base = 0;
7174      hole[0].h_len = clicks;
7175    }
```

```
7200   /* This file contains some useful utility routines used by MM.
7201    *
7202    * The entries into the file are:
7203    *   allowed:    see if an access is permitted
7204    *   mem_copy:   copy data from somewhere in memory to somewhere else
7205    *   no_sys:     this routine is called for invalid system call numbers
7206    *   panic:      MM has run aground of a fatal error and cannot continue
7207    */
7208
7209   #include "../h/const.h"
7210   #include "../h/type.h"
7211   #include "../h/callnr.h"
7212   #include "../h/com.h"
7213   #include "../h/error.h"
7214   #include "../h/stat.h"
7215   #include "const.h"
7216   #include "glo.h"
7217   #include "mproc.h"
7218
7219   PRIVATE message copy_mess;
7220
7221   /*===========================================================================*
7222    *                              allowed                                       *
7223    *===========================================================================*/
7224   PUBLIC int allowed(name_buf, s_buf, mask)
7225   char *name_buf;                  /* pointer to file name to be EXECed */
7226   struct stat *s_buf;              /* buffer for doing and returning stat struct */
7227   int mask;                        /* R_BIT, W_BIT, or X_BIT */
7228   {
7229   /* Check to see if file can be accessed.  Return EACCES or ENOENT if the access
7230    * is prohibited.  If it is legal open the file and return a file descriptor.
7231    */
7232
7233     register int fd, shift;
7234     int mode;
7235     extern errno;
7236
7237     /* Open the file and stat it. */
7238     if ( (fd = open(name_buf, 0)) < 0) return(-errno);
7239     if (fstat(fd, s_buf) < 0) panic("allowed: fstat failed", NO_NUM);
7240
7241     /* Only regular files can be executed. */
7242     mode = s_buf->st_mode & I_TYPE;
7243     if (mask == X_BIT && mode != I_REGULAR) {
7244         close(fd);
7245         return(EACCES);
7246     }
7247     /* Even for superuser, at least 1 X bit must be on. */
7248     if (mp->mp_effuid == 0 && mask == X_BIT &&
7249         (s_buf->st_mode & (X_BIT << 6 | X_BIT << 3 | X_BIT))) return(fd);
```

```
7250
7251        /* Right adjust the relevant set of permission bits. */
7252        if (mp->mp_effuid == s_buf->st_uid) shift = 6;
7253        else if (mp->mp_effgid == s_buf->st_gid) shift = 3;
7254        else shift = 0;
7255
7256        if (s_buf->st_mode >> shift & mask)    /* test the relevant bits */
7257                return(fd);                 /* permission granted */
7258        else {
7259                close(fd);                  /* permission denied */
7260                return(EACCES);
7261        }
7262    }


7265    /*===========================================================================*
7266     *                              mem_copy                                      *
7267     *===========================================================================*/
7268    PUBLIC int mem_copy(src_proc,src_seg, src_vir, dst_proc,dst_seg, dst_vir, bytes)
7269    int src_proc;                  /* source process */
7270    int src_seg;                   /* source segment: T, D, or S */
7271    long src_vir;                  /* source virtual address (clicks for ABS) */
7272    int dst_proc;                  /* dest process */
7273    int dst_seg;                   /* dest segment: T, D, or S */
7274    long dst_vir;                  /* dest virtual address (clicks for ABS) */
7275    long bytes;                    /* how many bytes (clicks for ABS) */
7276    {
7277    /* Transfer a block of data.  The source and destination can each either be a
7278     * process (including MM) or absolute memory, indicate by setting 'src_proc'
7279     * or 'dst_proc' to ABS.
7280     */
7281
7282      if (bytes == 0L) return(OK);
7283      copy_mess.SRC_SPACE = (char) src_seg;
7284      copy_mess.SRC_PROC_NR = src_proc;
7285      copy_mess.SRC_BUFFER = src_vir;
7286
7287      copy_mess.DST_SPACE = (char) dst_seg;
7288      copy_mess.DST_PROC_NR = dst_proc;
7289      copy_mess.DST_BUFFER = dst_vir;
7290
7291      copy_mess.COPY_BYTES = bytes;
7292      sys_copy(&copy_mess);
7293      return(copy_mess.m_type);
7294    }
7295    /*===========================================================================*
7296     *                              no_sys                                        *
7297     *===========================================================================*/
7298    PUBLIC int no_sys()
7299    {
```

```
7300    /* A system call number not implemented by MM has been requested. */
7301
7302      return(EINVAL);
7303    }


7306    /*===========================================================================*
7307     *                              panic                                        *
7308     *===========================================================================*/
7309    PUBLIC panic(format, num)
7310    char *format;                        /* format string */
7311    int num;                             /* number to go with format string */
7312    {
7313    /* Something awful has happened.  Panics are caused when an internal
7314     * inconsistency is detected, e.g., a programm_ing error or illegal value of a
7315     * defined constant.
7316     */
7317
7318      printf("Memory manager panic: %s ", format);
7319      if (num != NO_NUM) printf("%d",num);
7320      printf("\n");
7321      tell_fs(SYNC, 0, 0, 0);            /* flush the cache to the disk */
7322      sys_abort();
7323    }
```

```
7350     /* MM must occasionally print some message.  It uses the standard library
7351      * routine prink().  (The name "printf" is really a macro defined as "printk").
7352      * Printing is done by calling the TTY task directly, not going through FS.
7353      */
7354
7355     #include "../h/const.h"
7356     #include "../h/type.h"
7357     #include "../h/com.h"
7358
7359     #define STD_OUTPUT          1    /* file descriptor for standard output */
7360     #define BUF_SIZE          100    /* print buffer size */
7361
7362     PRIVATE int buf_count;          /* # characters in the buffer */
7363     PRIVATE char print_buf[BUF_SIZE];      /* output is buffered here */
7364     PRIVATE message putch_msg;      /* used for message to TTY task */
7365
7366     /*===========================================================================*
7367      *                              putc                                         *
7368      *===========================================================================*/
7369     PUBLIC putc(c)
7370     char c;
7371     {
7372
7373       /* Accumulate another character.  If '\n' or buffer full, print it. */
7374       print_buf[buf_count++] = c;
7375       if (buf_count == BUF_SIZE) F_l_u_s_h();
7376       if (c == '\n')  F_l_u_s_h();
7377     }
7378

7380     /*===========================================================================*
7381      *                              F_l_u_s_h                                    *
7382      *===========================================================================*/
7383     PRIVATE F_l_u_s_h()
7384     {
7385     /* Flush the print buffer by calling TTY task. */
7386
7387       if (buf_count == 0) return;
7388       putch_msg.m_type = TTY_WRITE;
7389       putch_msg.PROC_NR  = 0;
7390       putch_msg.TTY_LINE = 0;
7391       putch_msg.ADDRESS  = print_buf;
7392       putch_msg.COUNT = buf_count;
7393       sendrec(TTY, &putch_msg);
7394       buf_count = 0;
7395     }
```

```
7400    /* This file contains the table used to map system call numbers onto the
7401     * routines that perform them.
7402     */
7403
7404    #include "../h/const.h"
7405    #include "../h/type.h"
7406    #include "const.h"
7407
7408    #undef EXTERN
7409    #define EXTERN
7410
7411    #include "../h/callnr.h"
7412    #include "glo.h"
7413    #include "mproc.h"
7414    #include "param.h"
7415
7416    /* Miscellaneous */
7417    char core_name[] = {"core"};    /* file name where core images are produced */
7418    unshort core_bits = 0xOEFC;     /* which signals cause core images */
7419
7420    extern char mm_stack[];
7421    char *stackpt = &mm_stack[MM_STACK_BYTES];        /* initial stack pointer */
7422
7423    extern do_mm_exit(), do_fork(), do_wait(), do_brk(), do_getset(), do_exec();
7424    extern do_signal(), do_kill(), do_pause(), do_alarm();
7425    extern no_sys(), unpause(), do_ksig(), do_brk2();
7426
7427    int (*mm_callvec[NCALLS])() = {
7428            no_sys,         /*  0 = unused  */
7429            do_mm_exit,     /*  1 = exit    */
7430            do_fork,        /*  2 = fork    */
7431            no_sys,         /*  3 = read    */
7432            no_sys,         /*  4 = write   */
7433            no_sys,         /*  5 = open    */
7434            no_sys,         /*  6 = close   */
7435            do_wait,        /*  7 = wait    */
7436            no_sys,         /*  8 = creat   */
7437            no_sys,         /*  9 = link    */
7438            no_sys,         /* 10 = unlink  */
7439            no_sys,         /* 11 = exec    */
7440            no_sys,         /* 12 = chdir   */
7441            no_sys,         /* 13 = time    */
7442            no_sys,         /* 14 = mknod   */
7443            no_sys,         /* 15 = chmod   */
7444            no_sys,         /* 16 = chown   */
7445            do_brk,         /* 17 = break   */
7446            no_sys,         /* 18 = stat    */
7447            no_sys,         /* 19 = lseek   */
7448            do_getset,      /* 20 = getpid  */
7449            no_sys,         /* 21 = mount   */
```

```
7450          no_sys,          /* 22 = umount  */
7451          do_getset,       /* 23 = setuid  */
7452          do_getset,       /* 24 = getuid  */
7453          no_sys,          /* 25 = stime   */
7454          no_sys,          /* 26 = (ptrace)*/
7455          do_alarm,        /* 27 = alarm   */
7456          no_sys,          /* 28 = fstat   */
7457          do_pause,        /* 29 = pause   */
7458          no_sys,          /* 30 = utime   */
7459          no_sys,          /* 31 = (stty)  */
7460          no_sys,          /* 32 = (gtty)  */
7461          no_sys,          /* 33 = access  */
7462          no_sys,          /* 34 = (nice)  */
7463          no_sys,          /* 35 = (ftime) */
7464          no_sys,          /* 36 = sync    */
7465          do_kill,         /* 37 = kill    */
7466          no_sys,          /* 38 = unused  */
7467          no_sys,          /* 39 = unused  */
7468          no_sys,          /* 40 = unused  */
7469          no_sys,          /* 41 = dup     */
7470          no_sys,          /* 42 = pipe    */
7471          no_sys,          /* 43 = times   */
7472          no_sys,          /* 44 = (prof)  */
7473          no_sys,          /* 45 = unused  */
7474          do_getset,       /* 46 = setgid  */
7475          do_getset,       /* 47 = getgid  */
7476          do_signal,       /* 48 = sig     */
7477          no_sys,          /* 49 = unused  */
7478          no_sys,          /* 50 = unused  */
7479          no_sys,          /* 51 = (acct)  */
7480          no_sys,          /* 52 = (phys)  */
7481          no_sys,          /* 53 = (lock)  */
7482          no_sys,          /* 54 = ioctl   */
7483          no_sys,          /* 55 = unused  */
7484          no_sys,          /* 56 = (mpx)   */
7485          no_sys,          /* 57 = unused  */
7486          no_sys,          /* 58 = unused  */
7487          do_exec,         /* 59 = exece   */
7488          no_sys,          /* 60 = umask   */
7489          no_sys,          /* 61 = chroot  */
7490          no_sys,          /* 62 = unused  */
7491          no_sys,          /* 63 = unused  */
7492
7493          do_ksig,         /* 64 = KSIG: signals originating in the kernel */
7494          no_sys,          /* 65 = UNPAUSE */
7495          do_brk2,         /* 66 = BRK2 (used to tell MM size of FS,INIT) */
7496          no_sys,          /* 67 = REVIVE  */
7497          no_sys           /* 68 = TASK_REPLY     */
7498    };
```

```
7500    /* Tables sizes */
7501    #define NR_ZONE_NUMS        9       /* # zone numbers in an inode */
7502    #define NR_BUFS            30       /* # blocks in the buffer cache */
7503    #define NR_BUF_HASH        32       /* size of buf hash table; MUST BE POWER OF 2*/
7504    #define NR_FDS             20       /* max file descriptors per process */
7505    #define NR_FILPS           64       /* # slots in filp table */
7506    #define I_MAP_SLOTS         4       /* max # of blocks in the inode bit map */
7507    #define ZMAP_SLOTS          6       /* max # of blocks in the zone bit map */
7508    #define NR_INODES          32       /* # slots in "in core" inode table */
7509    #define NR_SUPERS           3       /* # slots in super block table */
7510    #define NAME_SIZE          14       /* # bytes in a directory component */
7511    #define FS_STACK_BYTES    512       /* size of file system stack */
7512
7513    /* Miscellaneous constants */
7514    #define SUPER_MAGIC     0x137F      /* magic number contained in super-block */
7515    #define SU_UID      (uid) 0         /* super_user's uid */
7516    #define SYS_UID     (uid) 0         /* uid for processes MM and INIT */
7517    #define SYS_GID     (gid) 0         /* gid for processes MM and INIT */
7518    #define NORMAL            0         /* forces get_block to do disk read */
7519    #define NO_READ           1         /* prevents get_block from doing disk read */
7520
7521    #define XPIPE             0         /* used in fp_task when suspended on pipe */
7522    #define NO_BIT     (bit_nr) 0       /* returned by alloc_bit() to signal failure */
7523    #define DUP_MASK       0100         /* mask to distinguish dup2 from dup */
7524
7525    #define LOOK_UP           0         /* tells search_dir to lookup string */
7526    #define ENTER             1         /* tells search_dir to make dir entry */
7527    #define DELETE            2         /* tells search_dir to delete entry */
7528
7529    #define CLEAN             0         /* disk and memory copies identical */
7530    #define DIRTY             1         /* disk and memory copies differ */
7531
7532    #define BOOT_BLOCK (block_nr) 0 /* block number of boot block */
7533    #define SUPER_BLOCK (block_nr)1 /* block number of super block */
7534    #define ROOT_INODE (inode_nr) 1 /* inode number for root directory */
7535
7536    /* Derived sizes */
7537    #define ZONE_NUM_SIZE      sizeof(zone_nr)            /* # bytes in zone nr*/
7538    #define NR_DZONE_NUM       (NR_ZONE_NUMS-2)           /* # zones in inode */
7539    #define DIR_ENTRY_SIZE     sizeof(dir_struct)         /* # bytes/dir entry */
7540    #define INODES_PER_BLOCK   (BLOCK_SIZE/INODE_SIZE)    /* # inodes/disk blk */
7541    #define INODE_SIZE         (sizeof (d_inode))         /* bytes in disk inode*/
7542    #define NR_DIR_ENTRIES     (BLOCK_SIZE/DIR_ENTRY_SIZE) /* # dir entries/blk*/
7543    #define NR_INDIRECTS       (BLOCK_SIZE/ZONE_NUM_SIZE) /* # zones/indir blk */
7544    #define INTS_PER_BLOCK     (BLOCK_SIZE/sizeof(int))   /* # integers/blk */
7545    #define SUPER_SIZE         sizeof(struct super_block) /* super_block size */
7546    #define PIPE_SIZE          (NR_DZONE_NUM*BLOCK_SIZE)  /* pipe size in bytes*/
7547    #define MAX_ZONES (NR_DZONE_NUM+NR_INDIRECTS+(long)NR_INDIRECTS*NR_INDIRECTS)
7548                                                /* max # of zones in a file */
7549    #define printf printk
```

```
7550     /* Buffer (block) cache.  To acquire a block, a routine calls get_block(),
7551      * telling which block it wants.  The block is then regarded as "in use"
7552      * and has its 'b_count' field incremented.  All the blocks, whether in use
7553      * or not, are chained together in an LRU list, with 'front' pointing
7554      * to the least recently used block, and 'rear' to the most recently used
7555      * block.  A reverse chain, using the field b_prev is also maintained.
7556      * Usage for LRU is measured by the time the put_block() is done.  The second
7557      * parameter to put_block() can violate the LRU order and put a block on the
7558      * front of the list, if it will probably not be needed soon.  If a block
7559      * is modified, the modifying routine must set b_dirt to DIRTY, so the block
7560      * will eventually be rewritten to the disk.
7561      */
7562
7563     EXTERN struct buf {
7564       /* Data portion of the buffer. */
7565       union {
7566         char   b__data[BLOCK_SIZE];          /* ordinary user data */
7567         dir_struct b__dir[NR_DIR_ENTRIES];   /* directory block */
7568         zone_nr b__ind[NR_INDIRECTS];        /* indirect block */
7569         d_inode b__inode[INODES_PER_BLOCK];  /* inode block */
7570         int    b__int[INTS_PER_BLOCK];       /* block full of integers */
7571       } b;
7572
7573       /* Header portion of the buffer. */
7574       struct buf *b_next;             /* used to link bufs in a chain */
7575       struct buf *b_prev;             /* used to link bufs the other way */
7576       struct buf *b_hash;             /* used to link bufs on hash chains */
7577       block_nr b_blocknr;             /* block number of its (minor) device */
7578       dev_nr b_dev;                   /* major | minor device where block resides */
7579       char   b_dirt;                  /* CLEAN or DIRTY */
7580       char   b_count;                 /* number of users of this buffer */
7581     } buf[NR_BUFS];
7582
7583     /* A block is free if b_dev == NO_DEV. */
7584
7585     #define NIL_BUF (struct buf *) 0        /* indicates absence of a buffer */
7586
7587     /* These defs make it possible to use to bp->b_data instead of bp->b.b__data */
7588     #define b_data   b.b__data
7589     #define b_dir    b.b__dir
7590     #define b_ind    b.b__ind
7591     #define b_inode  b.b__inode
7592     #define b_int    b.b__int
7593
7594     EXTERN struct buf *buf_hash[NR_BUF_HASH];        /* the buffer hash table */
7595
7596     EXTERN struct buf *front;       /* points to least recently used free block */
7597     EXTERN struct buf *rear;        /* points to most recently used free block */
7598     EXTERN int bufs_in_use;         /* # bufs currently in use (not on free list) */
7599
```

```
7600    /* When a block is released, the type of usage is passed to put_block(). */
7601    #define WRITE_IMMED        0100 /* block should be written to disk now */
7602    #define ONE_SHOT           0200 /* set if block not likely to be needed soon */
7603    #define INODE_BLOCK        0 + WRITE_IMMED                /* inode block */
7604    #define DIRECTORY_BLOCK    1 + WRITE_IMMED                /* directory block */
7605    #define INDIRECT_BLOCK     2 + WRITE_IMMED                /* pointer block */
7606    #define I_MAP_BLOCK        3 + WRITE_IMMED + ONE_SHOT     /* inode bit map */
7607    #define ZMAP_BLOCK         4 + WRITE_IMMED + ONE_SHOT     /* free zone map */
7608    #define ZUPER_BLOCK        5 + WRITE_IMMED + ONE_SHOT     /* super block */
7609    #define FULL_DATA_BLOCK    6                              /* data, fully used */
7610    #define PARTIAL_DATA_BLOCK 7                              /* data, partly used */
```

```
7650    /* Device table.  This table is indexed by major device number.  It provides
7651     * the link between major device numbers and the routines that process them.
7652     */
7653
7654    EXTERN struct dmap {
7655      int (*dmap_open)();
7656      int (*dmap_rw)();
7657      int (*dmap_close)();
7658      int dmap_task;
7659    } dmap[];
7660
```

```
7700    /* This is the filp table.  It is an intermediary between file descriptors and
7701     * inodes.  A slot is free if filp_count == 0.
7702     */
7703
7704    EXTERN struct filp {
7705      mask_bits filp_mode;          /* RW bits, telling how file is opened */
7706      int filp_count;               /* how many file descriptors share this slot? */
7707      struct inode *filp_ino;       /* pointer to the inode */
7708      file_pos filp_pos;            /* file position */
7709    } filp[NR_FILPS];
7710
7711    #define NIL_FILP (struct filp *) 0      /* indicates absence of a filp slot */
```

```
7750    /* This is the per-process information.  A slot is reserved for each potential
7751     * process. Thus NR_PROCS must be the same as in the kernel. It is not possible
7752     * or even necessary to tell when a slot is free here.
7753     */
7754
7755    EXTERN struct fproc {
7756      mask_bits fp_umask;               /* mask set by umask system call */
7757      struct inode *fp_workdir;         /* pointer to working directory's inode */
7758      struct inode *fp_rootdir;         /* pointer to current root dir (see chroot) */
7759      struct filp *fp_filp[NR_FDS];     /* the file descriptor table */
7760      uid fp_realuid;                   /* real user id */
7761      uid fp_effuid;                    /* effective user id */
7762      gid fp_realgid;                   /* real group id */
7763      gid fp_effgid;                    /* effective group id */
7764      dev_nr fs_tty;                    /* major/minor of controlling tty */
7765      int fp_fd;                        /* place to save fd if rd/wr can't finish */
7766      char *fp_buffer;                  /* place to save buffer if rd/wr can't finish */
7767      int  fp_nbytes;                   /* place to save bytes if rd/wr can't finish */
7768      char fp_suspended;                /* set to indicate process hanging */
7769      char fp_revived;                  /* set to indicate process being revived */
7770      char fp_task;                     /* which task is proc suspended on */
7771    } fproc[NR_PROCS];
7772
7773    /* Field values. */
7774    #define NOT_SUSPENDED    0          /* process is not suspended on pipe or task */
7775    #define SUSPENDED        1          /* process is suspended on pipe or task */
7776    #define NOT_REVIVING     0          /* process is not being revived */
7777    #define REVIVING         1          /* process is being revived from suspension */
```

```
7800   /* File System global variables */
7801   EXTERN struct fproc *fp;          /* pointer to caller's fproc struct */
7802   EXTERN int super_user;            /* 1 if caller is super_user, else 0 */
7803   EXTERN int dont_reply;            /* normally 0; set to 1 to inhibit reply */
7804   EXTERN int susp_count;            /* number of procs suspended on pipe */
7805   EXTERN int reviving;              /* number of pipe processes to be revived */
7806   EXTERN file_pos rdahedpos;        /* position to read ahead */
7807   EXTERN struct inode *rdahed_inode;     /* pointer to inode to read ahead */
7808
7809   /* The parameters of the call are kept here. */
7810   EXTERN message m;                 /* the input message itself */
7811   EXTERN message m1;                /* the output message used for reply */
7812   EXTERN int who;                   /* caller's proc number */
7813   EXTERN int fs_call;               /* system call number */
7814   EXTERN char user_path[MAX_PATH];/* storage for user path name */
7815
7816   /* The following variables are used for returning results to the caller. */
7817   EXTERN int err_code;              /* temporary storage for error number */
7818
7819   EXTERN char fstack[FS_STACK_BYTES];     /* the File System's stack. */
```

```
7850    /* Inode table.  This table holds inodes that are currently in use.  In some
7851     * cases they have been opened by an open() or creat() system call, in other
7852     * cases the file system itself needs the inode for one reason or another,
7853     * such as to search a directory for a path name.
7854     * The first part of the struct holds fields that are present on the
7855     * disk; the second part holds fields not present on the disk.
7856     * The disk inode part is also declared in "type.h" as 'd_inode'.
7857     */
7858
7859    EXTERN struct inode {
7860      unshort i_mode;                    /* file type, protection, etc. */
7861      uid i_uid;                         /* user id of the file's owner */
7862      file_pos i_size;                   /* current file size in bytes */
7863      real_time i_modtime;               /* when was file data last changed */
7864      gid i_gid;                         /* group number */
7865      links i_nlinks;                    /* how many links to this file */
7866      zone_nr i_zone[NR_ZONE_NUMS];      /* zone numbers for direct, ind, and dbl ind */
7867
7868      /* The following items are not present on the disk. */
7869      dev_nr i_dev;                      /* which device is the inode on */
7870      inode_nr i_num;                    /* inode number on its (minor) device */
7871      short int i_count;                 /* # times inode used; 0 means slot is free */
7872      char i_dirt;                       /* CLEAN or DIRTY */
7873      char i_pipe;                       /* set to I_PIPE if pipe */
7874      char i_mount;                      /* this bit is set if file mounted on */
7875      char i_seek;                       /* set on LSEEK, cleared on READ/WRITE */
7876    } inode[NR_INODES];
7877
7878
7879    #define NIL_INODE (struct inode *) 0     /* indicates absence of inode slot */
7880
7881    /* Field values.  Note that CLEAN and DIRTY are defined in "const.h" */
7882    #define NO_PIPE           0      /* i_pipe is NO_PIPE if inode is not a pipe */
7883    #define I_PIPE            1      /* i_pipe is I_PIPE if inode is a pipe */
7884    #define NO_MOUNT          0      /* i_mount is NO_MOUNT if file not mounted on */
7885    #define I_MOUNT           1      /* i_mount is I_MOUNT if file mounted on */
7886    #define NO_SEEK           0      /* i_seek = NO_SEEK if last op was not SEEK */
7887    #define ISEEK             1      /* i_seek = ISEEK if last op was SEEK */
```

```
7900  /* The following names are synonyms for the variables in the input message. */
7901  #define acc_time     m.m2_l1
7902  #define addr         m.m1_i3
7903  #define buffer       m.m1_p1
7904  #define cd_flag      m.m1_i2
7905  #define child        m.m1_i2
7906  #define co_mode      m.m1_i1
7907  #define eff_grp_id   m.m1_i3
7908  #define eff_user_id  m.m1_i3
7909  #define erki         m.m1_p1
7910  #define fd           m.m1_i1
7911  #define fd2          m.m1_i2
7912  #define ioflags      m.m1_i3
7913  #define group        m.m1_i3
7914  #define real_grp_id  m.m1_i2
7915  #define ls_fd        m.m2_i1
7916  #define mk_mode      m.m1_i2
7917  #define mode         m.m3_i2
7918  #define name         m.m3_p1
7919  #define name1        m.m1_p1
7920  #define name2        m.m1_p2
7921  #define name_length  m.m3_i1
7922  #define name1_length m.m1_i1
7923  #define name2_length m.m1_i2
7924  #define nbytes       m.m1_i2
7925  #define offset       m.m2_l1
7926  #define owner        m.m1_i2
7927  #define parent       m.m1_i1
7928  #define pathname     m.m3_ca1
7929  #define pro          m.m1_i1
7930  #define rd_only      m.m1_i3
7931  #define real_user_id m.m1_i2
7932  #define request      m.m1_i2
7933  #define sig          m.m1_i2
7934  #define slot1        m.m1_i1
7935  #define tp           m.m2_l1
7936  #define update_time  m.m2_l2
7937  #define utime_file   m.m2_p1
7938  #define utime_length m.m2_i1
7939  #define whence       m.m2_i2
7940
7941  /* The following names are synonyms for the variables in the output message. */
7942  #define reply_type   m1.m_type
7943  #define reply_l1     m1.m2_l1
7944  #define reply_i1     m1.m1_i1
7945  #define reply_i2     m1.m1_i2
7946  #define reply_t1     m1.m4_l1
7947  #define reply_t2     m1.m4_l2
7948  #define reply_t3     m1.m4_l3
7949  #define reply_t4     m1.m4_l4
```

```
7950    /* Super block table.  The root file system and every mounted file system
7951     * has an entry here.  The entry holds information about the sizes of the bit
7952     * maps and inodes.  The s_ninodes field gives the number of inodes available
7953     * for files and directories, including the root directory.  Inode 0 is
7954     * on the disk, but not used.  Thus s_ninodes = 4 means that 5 bits will be
7955     * used in the bit map, bit 0, which is always 1 and not used, and bits 1-4
7956     * for files and directories.  The disk layout is:
7957     *
7958     *        Item          # blocks
7959     *     boot block        1
7960     *     super block       1
7961     *     inode map        s_imap_blocks
7962     *     zone map         s_zmap_blocks
7963     *     inodes           (s_ninodes + 1 + INODES_PER_BLOCK - 1)/INODES_PER_BLOCK
7964     *     unused           whatever is needed to fill out the current zone
7965     *     data zones       (s_nzones - s_firstdatazone) << s_log_zone_size
7966     *
7967     * A super_block slot is free if s_dev == NO_DEV.
7968     */
7969
7970
7971    EXTERN struct super_block {
7972      inode_nr s_ninodes;              /* # usable inodes on the minor device */
7973      zone_nr s_nzones;               /* total device size, including bit maps etc */
7974      unshort s_imap_blocks;          /* # of blocks used by inode bit map */
7975      unshort s_zmap_blocks;          /* # of blocks used by zone bit map */
7976      zone_nr s_firstdatazone;        /* number of first data zone */
7977      short int s_log_zone_size;      /* log2 of blocks/zone */
7978      file_pos s_max_size;            /* maximum file size on this device */
7979      int s_magic;                    /* magic number to recognize super-blocks */
7980
7981      /* The following items are only used when the super_block is in memory. */
7982      struct buf *s_imap[I_MAP_SLOTS]; /* pointers to the in-core inode bit map */
7983      struct buf *s_zmap[ZMAP_SLOTS]; /* pointers to the in-core zone bit map */
7984      dev_nr s_dev;                   /* whose super block is this? */
7985      struct inode *s_isup;           /* inode for root dir of mounted file sys */
7986      struct inode *s_imount;         /* inode mounted on */
7987      real_time s_time;               /* time of last update */
7988      char s_rd_only;                 /* set to 1 iff file sys mounted read only */
7989      char s_dirt;                    /* CLEAN or DIRTY */
7990    } super_block[NR_SUPERS];
7991
7992    #define NIL_SUPER (struct super_block *) 0
```

```
8000    /* Type definitions local to the File System. */
8001
8002    typedef struct {                    /* directory entry */
8003      inode_nr d_inum;                  /* inode number */
8004      char d_name[NAME_SIZE];           /* character string */
8005    } dir_struct;
8006
8007    /* Declaration of the disk inode used in rw_inode(). */
8008    typedef struct {                    /* disk inode.  Memory inode is in "inotab.h" */
8009      mask_bits i_mode;                 /* file type, protection, etc. */
8010      uid i_uid;                        /* user id of the file's owner */
8011      file_pos i_size;                  /* current file size in bytes */
8012      real_time i_modtime;              /* when was file data last changed */
8013      gid i_gid;                        /* group number */
8014      links i_nlinks;                   /* how many links to this file */
8015      zone_nr i_zone[NR_ZONE_NUMS];     /* block nums for direct, ind, and dbl ind */
8016    } d_inode;
```

```
8050    /* The file system maintains a buffer cache to reduce the number of disk
8051     * accesses needed.  Whenever a read or write to the disk is done, a check is
8052     * first made to see if the block is in the cache.  This file manages the
8053     * cache.
8054     *
8055     * The entry points into this file are:
8056     *   get_block:    request to fetch a block for reading or writing from cache
8057     *   put_block:    return a block previously requested with get_block
8058     *   alloc_zone:   allocate a new zone (to increase the length of a file)
8059     *   free_zone:    release a zone (when a file is removed)
8060     *   rw_block:     read or write a block from the disk itself
8061     *   invalidate:   remove all the cache blocks on some device
8062     */
8063
8064    #include "../h/const.h"
8065    #include "../h/type.h"
8066    #include "../h/error.h"
8067    #include "const.h"
8068    #include "type.h"
8069    #include "buf.h"
8070    #include "file.h"
8071    #include "fproc.h"
8072    #include "glo.h"
8073    #include "inode.h"
8074    #include "super.h"
8075
8076    /*===========================================================================*
8077     *                              get_block                                     *
8078     *===========================================================================*/
8079    PUBLIC struct buf *get_block(dev, block, only_search)
8080    register dev_nr dev;            /* on which device is the block? */
8081    register block_nr block;        /* which block is wanted? */
8082    int only_search;                /* if NO_READ, don't read, else act normal */
8083    {
8084    /* Check to see if the requested block is in the block cache.  If so, return
8085     * a pointer to it.  If not, evict some other block and fetch it (unless
8086     * 'only_search' is 1).  All blocks in the cache, whether in use or not,
8087     * are linked together in a chain, with 'front' pointing to the least recently
8088     * used block and 'rear' to the most recently used block.  If 'only_search' is
8089     * 1, the block being requested will be overwritten in its entirety, so it is
8090     * only necessary to see if it is in the cache; if it is not, any free buffer
8091     * will do.  It is not necessary to actually read the block in from disk.
8092     * In addition to the LRU chain, there is also a hash chain to link together
8093     * blocks whose block numbers end with the same bit strings, for fast lookup.
8094     */
8095
8096      register struct buf *bp, *prev_ptr;
8097
8098      /* Search the list of blocks not currently in use for (dev, block). */
8099      bp = buf_hash[block & (NR_BUF_HASH - 1)];     /* search the hash chain */
```

```
8100        if (dev != NO_DEV) {
8101                while (bp != NIL_BUF) {
8102                        if (bp->b_blocknr == block && bp->b_dev == dev) {
8103                                /* Block needed has been found. */
8104                                if (bp->b_count == 0) bufs_in_use++;
8105                                bp->b_count++;  /* record that block is in use */
8106                                return(bp);
8107                        } else {
8108                                /* This block is not the one sought. */
8109                                bp = bp->b_hash; /* move to next block on hash chain */
8110                        }
8111                }
8112        }
8113
8114        /* Desired block is not on available chain.  Take oldest block ('front').
8115         * However, a block that is aready in use (b_count > 0) may not be taken.
8116         */
8117        if (bufs_in_use == NR_BUFS) panic("All buffers in use", NR_BUFS);
8118        bufs_in_use++;                  /* one more buffer in use now */
8119        bp = front;
8120        while (bp->b_count > 0 && bp->b_next != NIL_BUF) bp = bp->b_next;
8121        if (bp == NIL_BUF || bp->b_count > 0) panic("No free buffer", NO_NUM);
8122
8123        /* Remove the block that was just taken from its hash chain. */
8124        prev_ptr = buf_hash[bp->b_blocknr & (NR_BUF_HASH - 1)];
8125        if (prev_ptr == bp) {
8126            buf_hash[bp->b_blocknr & (NR_BUF_HASH - 1)] = bp->b_hash;
8127        } else {
8128                /* The block just taken is not on the front of its hash chain. */
8129                while (prev_ptr->b_hash != NIL_BUF)
8130                        if (prev_ptr->b_hash == bp) {
8131                                prev_ptr->b_hash = bp->b_hash;  /* found it */
8132                                break;
8133                        } else {
8134                                prev_ptr = prev_ptr->b_hash;     /* keep looking */
8135                        }
8136        }
8137
8138        /* If the  block taken is dirty, make it clean by rewriting it to disk. */
8139        if (bp->b_dirt == DIRTY && bp->b_dev != NO_DEV) rw_block(bp, WRITING);
8140
8141        /* Fill in block's parameters and add it to the hash chain where it goes. */
8142        bp->b_dev = dev;                /* fill in device number */
8143        bp->b_blocknr = block;          /* fill in block number */
8144        bp->b_count++;                  /* record that block is being used */
8145        bp->b_hash = buf_hash[bp->b_blocknr & (NR_BUF_HASH - 1)];
8146        buf_hash[bp->b_blocknr & (NR_BUF_HASH - 1)] = bp;       /* add to hash list */
8147
8148        /* Go get the requested block, unless only_search = NO_READ. */
8149        if (dev != NO_DEV && only_search == NORMAL) rw_block(bp, READING);
```

```
8150        return(bp);                    /* return the newly acquired block */
8151    }


8154    /*===========================================================================*
8155     *                              put_block                                     *
8156     *===========================================================================*/
8157    PUBLIC put_block(bp, block_type)
8158    register struct buf *bp;        /* pointer to the buffer to be released */
8159    int block_type;                 /* INODE_BLOCK, DIRECTORY_BLOCK, or whatever */
8160    {
8161    /* Return a block to the list of available blocks.   Depending on 'block_type'
8162     * it may be put on the front or rear of the LRU chain.  Blocks that are
8163     * expected to be needed again shortly (e.g., partially full data blocks)
8164     * go on the rear; blocks that are unlikely to be needed again shortly
8165     * (e.g., full data blocks) go on the front.  Blocks whose loss can hurt
8166     * the integrity of the file system (e.g., inode blocks) are written to
8167     * disk immediately if they are dirty.
8168     */
8169
8170      register struct buf *next_ptr, *prev_ptr;
8171
8172      if (bp == NIL_BUF) return;     /* it is easier to check here than in caller */
8173
8174      /* If block is no longer in use, first remove it from LRU chain. */
8175      bp->b_count--;                  /* there is one use fewer now */
8176      if (bp->b_count > 0) return;   /* block is still in use */
8177
8178      bufs_in_use--;                  /* one fewer block buffers in use */
8179      next_ptr = bp->b_next;          /* successor on LRU chain */
8180      prev_ptr = bp->b_prev;          /* predecessor on LRU chain */
8181      if (prev_ptr != NIL_BUF)
8182            prev_ptr->b_next = next_ptr;
8183      else
8184            front = next_ptr;        /* this block was at front of chain */
8185
8186      if (next_ptr != NIL_BUF)
8187            next_ptr->b_prev = prev_ptr;
8188      else
8189            rear = prev_ptr;         /* this block was at rear of chain */
8190
8191      /* Put this block back on the LRU chain.  If the ONE_SHOT bit is set in
8192       * 'block_type', the block is not likely to be needed again shortly, so put
8193       * it on the front of the LRU chain where it will be the first one to be
8194       * taken when a free buffer is needed later.
8195       */
8196      if (block_type & ONE_SHOT) {
8197            /* Block probably won't be needed quickly. Put it on front of chain.
8198             * It will be the next block to be evicted from the cache.
8199             */
```

```
8200                    bp->b_prev = NIL_BUF;
8201                    bp->b_next = front;
8202                    if (front == NIL_BUF)
8203                            rear = bp;          /* LRU chain was empty */
8204                    else
8205                            front->b_prev = bp;
8206                    front = bp;
8207            } else {
8208                    /* Block probably will be needed quickly.  Put it on rear of chain.
8209                     * It will not be evicted from the cache for a long time.
8210                     */
8211                    bp->b_prev = rear;
8212                    bp->b_next = NIL_BUF;
8213                    if (rear == NIL_BUF)
8214                            front = bp;
8215                    else
8216                            rear->b_next = bp;
8217                    rear = bp;
8218            }
8219
8220            /* Some blocks are so important (e.g., inodes, indirect blocks) that they
8221             * should be written to the disk immediately to avoid messing up the file
8222             * system in the event of a crash.
8223             */
8224            if ((block_type & WRITE_IMMED) && bp->b_dirt==DIRTY && bp->b_dev != NO_DEV)
8225                    rw_block(bp, WRITING);
8226
8227            /* Super blocks must not be cached, lest mount use cached block. */
8228            if (block_type == ZUPER_BLOCK) bp->b_dev = NO_DEV;
8229    }


8232    /*===========================================================================*
8233     *                              alloc_zone                                    *
8234     *===========================================================================*/
8235    PUBLIC zone_nr alloc_zone(dev, z)
8236    dev_nr dev;                             /* device where zone wanted */
8237    zone_nr z;                              /* try to allocate new zone near this one */
8238    {
8239    /* Allocate a new zone on the indicated device and return its number. */
8240
8241      bit_nr b, bit;
8242      struct super_block *sp;
8243      int major, minor;
8244      extern bit_nr alloc_bit();
8245      extern struct super_block *get_super();
8246
8247      /* Note that the routine alloc_bit() returns 1 for the lowest possible
8248       * zone, which corresponds to sp->s_firstdatazone.  To convert a value
8249       * between the bit number, 'b', used by alloc_bit() and the zone number, 'z',
```

```
8250          * stored in the inode, use the formula:
8251          *     z = b + sp->s_firstdatazone - 1
8252          * Alloc_bit() never returns 0, since this is used for NO_BIT (failure).
8253          */
8254         sp = get_super(dev);             /* find the super_block for this device */
8255         bit = (bit_nr) z - (sp->s_firstdatazone - 1);
8256         b = alloc_bit(sp->s_zmap, (bit_nr) sp->s_nzones - sp->s_firstdatazone + 1,
8257                                                 sp->s_zmap_blocks, bit);
8258         if (b == NO_BIT) {
8259                 err_code = ENOSPC;
8260                 major = (int) (sp->s_dev >> MAJOR) & BYTE;
8261                 minor = (int) (sp->s_dev >> MINOR) & BYTE;
8262                 if (sp->s_dev == ROOT_DEV)
8263                         printf("No space on root device (RAM disk)\n");
8264                 else
8265                         printf("No space on device %d/%d\n", major, minor);
8266                 return(NO_ZONE);
8267         }
8268         return(sp->s_firstdatazone - 1 + (zone_nr) b);
8269     }


8272     /*================================================================*
8273      *                         free_zone                              *
8274      *================================================================*/
8275     PUBLIC free_zone(dev, numb)
8276     dev_nr dev;                              /* device where zone located */
8277     zone_nr numb;                            /* zone to be returned */
8278     {
8279     /* Return a zone. */
8280
8281       register struct super_block *sp;
8282       extern struct super_block *get_super();
8283
8284       if (numb == NO_ZONE) return;  /* checking here easier than in caller */
8285
8286       /* Locate the appropriate super_block and return bit. */
8287       sp = get_super(dev);
8288       free_bit(sp->s_zmap, (bit_nr) numb - (sp->s_firstdatazone - 1) );
8289     }


8292     /*================================================================*
8293      *                          rw_block                              *
8294      *================================================================*/
8295     PUBLIC rw_block(bp, rw_flag)
8296     register struct buf *bp;            /* buffer pointer */
8297     int rw_flag;                        /* READING or WRITING */
8298     {
8299     /* Read or write a disk block. This is the only routine in which actual disk
```

```
8300      * I/O is invoked.  If an error occurs, a message is printed here, but the error
8301      * is not reported to the caller.  If the error occurred while purging a block
8302      * from the cache, it is not clear what the caller could do about it anyway.
8303      */
8304
8305       int r;
8306       long pos;
8307       dev_nr dev;
8308
8309       if (bp->b_dev != NO_DEV) {
8310             pos = (long) bp->b_blocknr * BLOCK_SIZE;
8311             r = dev_io(rw_flag, bp->b_dev, pos, BLOCK_SIZE, FS_PROC_NR, bp->b_data);
8312             if (r < 0) {
8313                   dev = bp->b_dev;
8314                   printf("Unrecoverable disk error on device %d/%d, block %d\n",
8315                         (dev>>MAJOR)&BYTE, (dev>>MINOR)&BYTE, bp->b_blocknr);
8316             }
8317       }
8318
8319       bp->b_dirt = CLEAN;
8320    }


8323    /*===========================================================================*
8324     *                              invalidate                                   *
8325     *===========================================================================*/
8326    PUBLIC invalidate(device)
8327    dev_nr device;                        /* device whose blocks are to be purged */
8328    {
8329    /* Remove all the blocks belonging to some device from the cache. */
8330
8331       register struct buf *bp;
8332
8333       for (bp = &buf[0]; bp < &buf[NR_BUFS]; bp++)
8334             if (bp->b_dev == device) bp->b_dev = NO_DEV;
8335    }
```

```
8350     /* This file manages the inode table.  There are procedures to allocate and
8351      * deallocate inodes, acquire, erase, and release them, and read and write
8352      * them from the disk.
8353      *
8354      * The entry points into this file are
8355      *   get_inode:    search inode table for a given inode; if not there, read it
8356      *   put_inode:    indicate that an inode is no longer needed in memory
8357      *   alloc_inode:  allocate a new, unused inode
8358      *   wipe_inode:   erase some fields of a newly allocated inode
8359      *   free_inode:   mark an inode as available for a new file
8360      *   rw_inode:     read a disk block and extract an inode, or corresp. write
8361      *   dup_inode:    indicate that someone else is using an inode table entry
8362      */
8363
8364     #include "../h/const.h"
8365     #include "../h/type.h"
8366     #include "../h/error.h"
8367     #include "const.h"
8368     #include "type.h"
8369     #include "buf.h"
8370     #include "file.h"
8371     #include "fproc.h"
8372     #include "glo.h"
8373     #include "inode.h"
8374     #include "super.h"
8375
8376     /*===========================================================================*
8377      *                              get_inode                                     *
8378      *===========================================================================*/
8379     PUBLIC struct inode *get_inode(dev, numb)
8380     dev_nr dev;                      /* device on which inode resides */
8381     inode_nr numb;                   /* inode number */
8382     {
8383     /* Find a slot in the inode table, load the specified inode into it, and
8384      * return a pointer to the slot.  If 'dev' == NO_DEV, just return a free slot.
8385      */
8386
8387       register struct inode *rip, *xp;
8388
8389       /* Search the inode table both for (dev, numb) and a free slot. */
8390       xp = NIL_INODE;
8391       for (rip = &inode[0]; rip < &inode[NR_INODES]; rip++) {
8392             if (rip->i_count > 0) { /* only check used slots for (dev, numb) */
8393                     if (rip->i_dev == dev && rip->i_num == numb) {
8394                             /* This is the inode that we are looking for. */
8395                             rip->i_count++;
8396                             return(rip);    /* (dev, numb) found */
8397                     }
8398             } else
8399                     xp = rip;       /* remember this free slot for later */
```

```
8400            }
8401
8402            /* Inode we want is not currently in use.  Did we find a free slot? */
8403            if (xp == NIL_INODE) {           /* inode table completely full */
8404                    err_code = ENFILE;
8405                    return(NIL_INODE);
8406            }
8407
8408            /* A free inode slot has been located.  Load the inode into it. */
8409            xp->i_dev = dev;
8410            xp->i_num = numb;
8411            xp->i_count = 1;
8412            if (dev != NO_DEV) rw_inode(xp, READING);       /* get inode from disk */
8413
8414            return(xp);
8415    }


8418    /*===========================================================================*
8419     *                              put_inode                                     *
8420     *===========================================================================*/
8421    PUBLIC put_inode(rip)
8422    register struct inode *rip;         /* pointer to inode to be released */
8423    {
8424    /* The caller is no longer using this inode.  If no one else is using it either
8425     * write it back to the disk immediately.  If it has no links, truncate it and
8426     * return it to the pool of available inodes.
8427     */
8428
8429            if (rip == NIL_INODE) return; /* checking here is easier than in caller */
8430            if (--rip->i_count == 0) {     /* i_count == 0 means no one is using it now */
8431                    if ((rip->i_nlinks & BYTE) == 0) {
8432                            /* i_nlinks == 0 means free the inode. */
8433                            truncate(rip);   /* return all the disk blocks */
8434                            rip->i_mode = I_NOT_ALLOC;       /* clear I_TYPE field */
8435                            rip->i_pipe = NO_PIPE;
8436                            free_inode(rip->i_dev, rip->i_num);
8437                    }
8438
8439                    if (rip->i_dirt == DIRTY) rw_inode(rip, WRITING);
8440            }
8441    }


8443    /*===========================================================================*
8444     *                              alloc_inode                                   *
8445     *===========================================================================*/
8446    PUBLIC struct inode *alloc_inode(dev, bits)
8447    dev_nr dev;                         /* device on which to allocate the inode */
8448    mask_bits bits;                     /* mode of the inode */
8449    {
```

```
8450        /* Allocate a free inode on 'dev', and return a pointer to it. */
8451
8452        register struct inode *rip;
8453        register struct super_block *sp;
8454        int major, minor;
8455        inode_nr numb;
8456        bit_nr b;
8457        extern bit_nr alloc_bit();
8458        extern struct inode *get_inode();
8459        extern struct super_block *get_super();
8460
8461        /* Acquire an inode from the bit map. */
8462        sp = get_super(dev);             /* get pointer to super_block */
8463        b=alloc_bit(sp->s_imap, (bit_nr)sp->s_ninodes+1, sp->s_imap_blocks,(bit_nr)0);
8464        if (b == NO_BIT) {
8465                err_code = ENFILE;
8466                major = (int) (sp->s_dev >> MAJOR) & BYTE;
8467                minor = (int) (sp->s_dev >> MINOR) & BYTE;
8468                if (sp->s_dev == ROOT_DEV)
8469                        printf("Out of i-nodes on root device (RAM disk)\n");
8470                else
8471                        printf("Out of i-nodes on device %d/%d\n", major, minor);
8472                return(NIL_INODE);
8473        }
8474        numb = (inode_nr) b;
8475
8476        /* Try to acquire a slot in the inode table. */
8477        if ( (rip = get_inode(NO_DEV, numb)) == NIL_INODE) {
8478                /* No inode table slots available.  Free the inode just allocated. */
8479                free_bit(sp->s_imap, b);
8480        } else {
8481                /* An inode slot is available.  Put the inode just allocated into it. */
8482                rip->i_mode = bits;
8483                rip->i_nlinks = (links) 0;
8484                rip->i_uid = fp->fp_effuid;
8485                rip->i_gid = fp->fp_effgid;
8486                rip->i_dev = dev;        /* was provisionally set to NO_DEV */
8487
8488                /* The fields not cleared already are cleared in wipe_inode().  They have
8489                 * been put there because truncate() needs to clear the same fields if
8490                 * the file happens to be open while being truncated.  It saves space
8491                 * not to repeat the code twice.
8492                 */
8493                wipe_inode(rip);
8494        }
8495
8496        return(rip);
8497    }
```

```
8500    /*================================================================*
8501     *                          wipe_inode                            *
8502     *================================================================*/
8503    PUBLIC wipe_inode(rip)
8504    register struct inode *rip;     /* The inode to be erased. */
8505    {
8506    /* Erase some fields in the inode.  This function is called from alloc_inode()
8507     * when a new inode is to be allocated, and from truncate(), when an existing
8508     * inode is to be truncated.
8509     */
8510
8511      register int i;
8512      extern real_time clock_time();
8513
8514      rip->i_size = 0;
8515      rip->i_modtime = clock_time();
8516      rip->i_dirt = DIRTY;
8517      for (i = 0; i < NR_ZONE_NUMS; i++)
8518            rip->i_zone[i] = NO_ZONE;
8519    }


8522    /*================================================================*
8523     *                          free_inode                            *
8524     *================================================================*/
8525    PUBLIC free_inode(dev, numb)
8526    dev_nr dev;                     /* on which device is the inode */
8527    inode_nr numb;                  /* number of inode to be freed */
8528    {
8529    /* Return an inode to the pool of unallocated inodes. */
8530
8531      register struct super_block *sp;
8532      extern struct super_block *get_super();
8533
8534      /* Locate the appropriate super_block. */
8535      sp = get_super(dev);
8536    ' free_bit(sp->s_imap, (bit_nr) numb);
8537    }


8540    /*================================================================*
8541     *                          rw_inode                              *
8542     *================================================================*/
8543    PUBLIC rw_inode(rip, rw_flag)
8544    register struct inode *rip;     /* pointer to inode to be read/written */
8545    int rw_flag;                    /* READING or WRITING */
8546    {
8547    /* An entry in the inode table is to be copied to or from the disk. */
8548
8549      register struct buf *bp;
```

```
8550        register d_inode *dip;
8551        register struct super_block *sp;
8552        block_nr b;
8553        extern struct buf *get_block();
8554        extern struct super_block *get_super();
8555
8556        /* Get the block where the inode resides. */
8557        sp = get_super(rip->i_dev);
8558        b = (block_nr) (rip->i_num - 1)/INODES_PER_BLOCK +
8559                                    sp->s_imap_blocks + sp->s_zmap_blocks + 2;
8560        bp = get_block(rip->i_dev, b, NORMAL);
8561        dip = bp->b_inode + (rip->i_num - 1) % INODES_PER_BLOCK;
8562
8563        /* Do the read or write. */
8564        if (rw_flag == READING) {
8565            copy((char *)rip, (char *) dip, INODE_SIZE); /* copy from blk to inode */
8566        } else {
8567            copy((char *)dip, (char *) rip, INODE_SIZE); /* copy from inode to blk */
8568            bp->b_dirt = DIRTY;
8569        }
8570
8571        put_block(bp, INODE_BLOCK);
8572        rip->i_dirt = CLEAN;
8573    }


8576    /*===========================================================================*
8577     *                              dup_inode                                     *
8578     *===========================================================================*/
8579    PUBLIC dup_inode(ip)
8580    struct inode *ip;                  /* The inode to be duplicated. */
8581    {
8582    /* This routine is a simplified form of get_inode() for the case where
8583     * the inode pointer is already known.
8584     */
8585
8586        ip->i_count++;
8587    }
```

```
8600    /* This file manages the super block table and the related data structures,
8601     * namely, the bit maps that keep track of which zones and which inodes are
8602     * allocated and which are free.  When a new inode or zone is needed, the
8603     * appropriate bit map is searched for a free entry.
8604     *
8605     * The entry points into this file are
8606     *    load_bit_maps:    get the bit maps for the root or a newly mounted device
8607     *    unload_bit_maps:  write the bit maps back to disk after an UMOUNT
8608     *    alloc_bit:        somebody wants to allocate a zone or inode; find one
8609     *    free_bit:         indicate that a zone or inode is available for allocation
8610     *    get_super:        search the 'superblock' table for a device
8611     *    mounted:          tells if file inode is on mounted (or ROOT) file system
8612     *    scale_factor:     get the zone-to-block conversion factor for a device
8613     *    rw_super:         read or write a superblock
8614     */
8615
8616    #include "../h/const.h"
8617    #include "../h/type.h"
8618    #include "../h/error.h"
8619    #include "const.h"
8620    #include "type.h"
8621    #include "buf.h"
8622    #include "inode.h"
8623    #include "super.h"
8624
8625    #define INT_BITS (sizeof(int)<<3)
8626    #define BIT_MAP_SHIFT    13      /* (log2 of BLOCK_SIZE) + 3; 13 for 1k blocks */
8627
8628    /*===========================================================================*
8629     *                              load_bit_maps                                 *
8630     *===========================================================================*/
8631    PUBLIC int load_bit_maps(dev)
8632    dev_nr dev;                      /* which device? */
8633    {
8634    /* Load the bit map for some device into the cache and set up superblock. */
8635
8636      register int i;
8637      register struct super_block *sp;
8638      block_nr zbase;
8639      extern struct buf *get_block();
8640      extern struct super_block *get_super();
8641
8642      sp = get_super(dev);           /* get the superblock pointer */
8643      if (bufs_in_use + sp->s_imap_blocks + sp->s_zmap_blocks >= NR_BUFS - 3)
8644          return(ERROR);             /* insufficient buffers left for bit maps */
8645      if (sp->s_imap_blocks > I_MAP_SLOTS || sp->s_zmap_blocks > ZMAP_SLOTS)
8646          panic("too many map blocks", NO_NUM);
8647
8648      /* Load the inode map from the disk. */
8649      for (i = 0; i < sp->s_imap_blocks; i++)
```

```
8650                sp->s_imap[i] = get_block(dev, SUPER_BLOCK + 1 + i, NORMAL);
8651
8652        /* Load the zone map from the disk. */
8653        zbase = SUPER_BLOCK + 1 + sp->s_imap_blocks;
8654        for (i = 0; i < sp->s_zmap_blocks; i++)
8655                sp->s_zmap[i] = get_block(dev, zbase + i, NORMAL);
8656
8657        /* inodes 0 and 1, and zone 0 are never allocated.  Mark them as busy. */
8658        sp->s_imap[0]->b_int[0] |= 3;  /* inodes 0, 1 busy */
8659        sp->s_zmap[0]->b_int[0] |= 1;  /* zone 0 busy */
8660        bufs_in_use += sp->s_imap_blocks + sp->s_zmap_blocks;
8661        return(OK);
8662    }



8666    /*===========================================================================*
8667     *                              unload_bit_maps                              *
8668     *===========================================================================*/
8669    PUBLIC unload_bit_maps(dev)
8670    dev_nr dev;                      /* which device is being unmounted? */
8671    {
8672    /* Unload the bit maps so a device can be unmounted. */
8673
8674        register int i;
8675        register struct super_block *sp;
8676        struct super_block *get_super();
8677
8678        sp = get_super(dev);             /* get the superblock pointer */
8679        bufs_in_use -= sp->s_imap_blocks + sp->s_zmap_blocks;
8680        for (i = 0; i < sp->s_imap_blocks; i++) put_block(sp->s_imap[i], I_MAP_BLOCK);
8681        for (i = 0; i < sp->s_zmap_blocks; i++) put_block(sp->s_zmap[i], ZMAP_BLOCK);
8682        return(OK);
8683    }



8686    /*===========================================================================*
8687     *                              alloc_bit                                     *
8688     *===========================================================================*/
8689    PUBLIC bit_nr alloc_bit(map_ptr, map_bits, bit_blocks, origin)
8690    struct buf *map_ptr[];            /* pointer to array of bit block pointers */
8691    bit_nr map_bits;                 /* how many bits are there in the bit map? */
8692    unshort bit_blocks;              /* how many blocks are there in the bit map? */
8693    bit_nr origin;                   /* number of bit to start searching at */
8694    {
8695    /* Allocate a bit from a bit map and return its bit number. */
8696
8697        register unsigned k;
8698        register int *wptr, *wlim;
8699        int i, a, b, w, o, block_count;
```

```
8700        struct buf *bp;
8701
8702        /* Figure out where to start the bit search (depends on 'origin'). */
8703        if (origin >= map_bits) origin = 0;    /* for robustness */
8704        b = origin >> BIT_MAP_SHIFT;
8705        o = origin - (b << BIT_MAP_SHIFT);
8706        w = o/INT_BITS;
8707        block_count = (w == 0 ? bit_blocks : bit_blocks + 1);
8708
8709        /* The outer while loop iterates on the blocks of the map.  The inner
8710         * while loop iterates on the words of a block.  The for loop iterates
8711         * on the bits of a word.
8712         */
8713        while (block_count--) {
8714                /* If need be, loop on all the blocks in the bit map. */
8715                bp = map_ptr[b];
8716                wptr = &bp->b_int[w];
8717                wlim = &bp->b_int[INTS_PER_BLOCK];
8718                while (wptr != wlim) {
8719                        /* Loop on all the words of one of the bit map blocks. */
8720                        if ((k = (unsigned) *wptr) != (unsigned) ~0) {
8721                                /* This word contains a free bit.  Allocate it. */
8722                                for (i = 0; i < INT_BITS; i++)
8723                                        if (((k >> i) & 1) == 0) {
8724                                                a = i + (wptr - &bp->b_int[0])*INT_BITS
8725                                                        + (b << BIT_MAP_SHIFT);
8726                                                /* If 'a' beyond map check other blks*/
8727                                                if (a >= map_bits) {
8728                                                        wptr = wlim - 1;
8729                                                        break;
8730                                                }
8731                                                *wptr |= 1 << i;
8732                                                bp->b_dirt = DIRTY;
8733                                                return( (bit_nr) a);
8734                                        }
8735                        }
8736                        wptr++;         /* examine next word in this bit map block */
8737                }
8738                if (++b == bit_blocks) b = 0;    /* we have wrapped around */
8739                w = 0;
8740        }
8741        return(NO_BIT);                 /* no bit could be allocated */
8742 }

8744 /*===========================================================================*
8745  *                              free_bit                                     *
8746  *===========================================================================*/
8747 PUBLIC free_bit(map_ptr, bit_returned)
8748 struct buf *map_ptr[];          /* pointer to array of bit block pointers */
8749 bit_nr bit_returned;            /* number of bit to insert into the map */
```

```
8750    {
8751    /* Return a zone or inode by turning on its bitmap bit. */
8752
8753      int b, r, w, bit;
8754      struct buf *bp;
8755
8756      b = bit_returned >> BIT_MAP_SHIFT;      /* 'b' tells which block it is in */
8757      r = bit_returned - (b << BIT_MAP_SHIFT);
8758      w = r/INT_BITS;                         /* 'w' tells which word it is in */
8759      bit = r % INT_BITS;
8760      bp = map_ptr[b];
8761      if (((bp->b_int[w] >> bit)& 1)== 0)
8762           panic("trying to free unused block--check file sys", (int)bit_returned);
8763      bp->b_int[w] &= ~(1 << bit);  /* turn the bit on */
8764      bp->b_dirt = DIRTY;
8765    }


8768    /*===========================================================================*
8769     *                            get_super                                      *
8770     *===========================================================================*/
8771    PUBLIC struct super_block *get_super(dev)
8772    dev_nr dev;                      /* device number whose super_block is sought */
8773    {
8774    /* Search the superblock table for this device.  It is supposed to be there. */
8775
8776      register struct super_block *sp;
8777
8778      for (sp = &super_block[0]; sp < &super_block[NR_SUPERS]; sp++)
8779           if (sp->s_dev == dev) return(sp);
8780
8781      /* Search failed.  Something wrong. */
8782      panic("can't find superblock for device", (int) dev);
8783    }


8786    /*===========================================================================*
8787     *                            mounted                                        *
8788     *===========================================================================*/
8789    PUBLIC int mounted(rip)
8790    register struct inode *rip;      /* pointer to inode */
8791    {
8792    /* Report on whether the given inode is on a mounted (or ROOT) file system. */
8793
8794      register struct super_block *sp;
8795      register dev_nr dev;
8796
8797      dev = rip->i_dev;
8798      if (dev == ROOT_DEV) return(TRUE);      /* inode is on root file system */
8799
```

```
8800        for (sp = &super_block[0]; sp < &super_block[NR_SUPERS]; sp++)
8801              if (sp->s_dev == dev) return(TRUE);
8802
8803        return(FALSE);
8804    }


8807    /*===========================================================================*
8808     *                              scale_factor                                 *
8809     *===========================================================================*/
8810    PUBLIC int scale_factor(ip)
8811    struct inode *ip;                    /* pointer to inode whose superblock needed */
8812    {
8813    /* Return the scale factor used for converting blocks to zones. */
8814      register struct super_block *sp;
8815      extern struct super_block *get_super();
8816
8817      sp = get_super(ip->i_dev);
8818      return(sp->s_log_zone_size);
8819    }


8821    /*===========================================================================*
8822     *                              rw_super                                     *
8823     *===========================================================================*/
8824    PUBLIC rw_super(sp, rw_flag)
8825    register struct super_block *sp; /* pointer to a superblock */
8826    int rw_flag;                         /* READING or WRITING */
8827    {
8828    /* Read or write a superblock. */
8829
8830      register struct buf *bp;
8831      dev_nr dev;
8832      extern struct buf *get_block();
8833
8834      /* Check if this is a read or write, and do it. */
8835      if (rw_flag == READING) {
8836            dev = sp->s_dev;            /* save device; it will be overwritten by copy*/
8837            bp = get_block(sp->s_dev, (block_nr) SUPER_BLOCK, NORMAL);
8838            copy( (char *) sp, bp->b_data, SUPER_SIZE);
8839            sp->s_dev = dev;           /* restore device number */
8840      } else {
8841            /* On a write, it is not necessary to go read superblock from disk. */
8842            bp = get_block(sp->s_dev, (block_nr) SUPER_BLOCK, NO_READ);
8843            copy(bp->b_data, (char *) sp, SUPER_SIZE);
8844            bp->b_dirt = DIRTY;
8845      }
8846
8847      sp->s_dirt = CLEAN;
8848      put_block(bp, ZUPER_BLOCK);
8849    }
```

```
8850    /* This file contains the procedures that manipulate file descriptors.
8851     *
8852     * The entry points into this file are
8853     *   get_fd:    look for free file descriptor and free filp slots
8854     *   get_filp:  look up the filp entry for a given file descriptor
8855     *   find_filp: find a filp slot that points to a given inode
8856     */
8857
8858    #include "../h/const.h"
8859    #include "../h/type.h"
8860    #include "../h/error.h"
8861    #include "const.h"
8862    #include "type.h"
8863    #include "file.h"
8864    #include "fproc.h"
8865    #include "glo.h"
8866    #include "inode.h"
8867
8868    /*===========================================================================*
8869     *                              get_fd                                       *
8870     *===========================================================================*/
8871    PUBLIC int get_fd(bits, k, fpt)
8872    mask_bits bits;                      /* mode of the file to be created (RWX bits) */
8873    int *k;                              /* place to return file descriptor */
8874    struct filp **fpt;                   /* place to return filp slot */
8875    {
8876    /* Look for a free file descriptor and a free filp slot.  Fill in the mode word
8877     * in the latter, but don't claim either one yet, since the open() or creat()
8878     * may yet fail.
8879     */
8880
8881      register struct filp *f;
8882      register int i;
8883
8884      *k = -1;                           /* we need a way to tell if file desc found */
8885
8886      /* Search the fproc table for a free file descriptor. */
8887      for (i = 0; i < NR_FDS; i++) {
8888            if (fp->fp_filp[i] == NIL_FILP) {
8889                    /* A file descriptor has been located. */
8890                    *k = i;
8891                    break;
8892            }
8893      }
8894
8895      /* Check to see if a file descriptor has been found. */
8896      if (*k < 0) return(EMFILE);     /* this is why we initialized k to -1 */
8897
8898      /* Now that a file descriptor has been found, look for a free filp slot. */
8899      for (f = &filp[0]; f < &filp[NR_FILPS]; f++) {
```

```
8900                if (f->filp_count == 0) {
8901                        f->filp_mode = bits;
8902                        f->filp_pos = 0L;
8903                        *fpt = f;
8904                        return(OK);
8905                }
8906        }
8907
8908        /* If control passes here, the filp table must be full.  Report that back. */
8909        return(ENFILE);
8910    }


8913    /*===========================================================================*
8914     *                              get_filp                                      *
8915     *===========================================================================*/
8916    PUBLIC struct filp *get_filp(fild)
8917    int fild;                       /* file descriptor */
8918    {
8919    /* See if 'fild' refers to a valid file descr.  If so, return its filp ptr. */
8920
8921        err_code = EBADF;
8922        if (fild < 0 || fild >= NR_FDS ) return(NIL_FILP);
8923        return(fp->fp_filp[fild]);     /* may also be NIL_FILP */
8924    }


8927    /*===========================================================================*
8928     *                              find_filp                                     *
8929     *===========================================================================*/
8930    PUBLIC struct filp *find_filp(rip, bits)
8931    register struct inode *rip;     /* inode referred to by the filp to be found */
8932    int bits;                       /* mode of the filp to be found (RWX bits) */
8933    {
8934    /* Find a filp slot that refers to the inode 'rip' in a way as described
8935     * by the mode bit 'bits'. Used for determining whether somebody is still
8936     * interested in either end of a pipe; other applications are conceivable.
8937     * Like 'get_fd' it performs its job by linear search through the filp table.
8938     */
8939
8940        register struct filp *f;
8941
8942        for (f = &filp[0]; f < &filp[NR_FILPS]; f++) {
8943                if (f->filp_count != 0 && f->filp_ino == rip && (f->filp_mode & bits))
8944                        return(f);
8945        }
8946
8947        /* If control passes here, the filp wasn't there.  Report that back. */
8948        return(NIL_FILP);
8949    }
```

```
8950     /* This file contains the main program of the File System.  It consists of
8951      * a loop that gets messages requesting work, carries out the work, and sends
8952      * replies.
8953      *
8954      * The entry points into this file are
8955      *   main:      main program of the File System
8956      *   reply:     send a reply to a process after the requested work is done
8957      */
8958
8959     #include "../h/const.h"
8960     #include "../h/type.h"
8961     #include "../h/callnr.h"
8962     #include "../h/com.h"
8963     #include "../h/error.h"
8964     #include "const.h"
8965     #include "type.h"
8966     #include "buf.h"
8967     #include "file.h"
8968     #include "fproc.h"
8969     #include "glo.h"
8970     #include "inode.h"
8971     #include "param.h"
8972     #include "super.h"
8973
8974     #define M64K      0xFFFF0000L    /* 16 bit mask for DMA check */
8975     #define INFO             2      /* where in data_org is info from build */
8976
8977     /*===========================================================================*
8978      *                              main                                         *
8979      *===========================================================================*/
8980     PUBLIC main()
8981     {
8982     /* This is the main program of the file system.  The main loop consists of
8983      * three major activities: getting new work, processing the work, and sending
8984      * the reply.  This loop never terminates as long as the file system runs.
8985      */
8986       int error;
8987       extern int (*call_vector[NCALLS])();
8988
8989       fs_init();
8990
8991       /* This is the main loop that gets work, processes it, and sends replies. */
8992       while (TRUE) {
8993             get_work();                /* sets who and fs_call */
8994
8995             fp = &fproc[who];          /* pointer to proc table struct */
8996             super_user = (fp->fp_effuid == SU_UID ? TRUE : FALSE);   /* su? */
8997             dont_reply = FALSE;        /* in other words, do reply is default */
8998
8999             /* Call the internal function that does the work. */
```

```
9000              if (fs_call < 0 || fs_call >= NCALLS)
9001                      error = E_BAD_CALL;
9002              else
9003                      error = (*call_vector[fs_call])();
9004
9005              /* Copy the results back to the user and send reply. */
9006              if (dont_reply) continue;
9007              reply(who, error);
9008              if (rdahed_inode != NIL_INODE) read_ahead(); /* do block read ahead */
9009      }
9010  }


9013  /*===========================================================================*
9014   *                              get_work                                     *
9015   *===========================================================================*/
9016  PRIVATE get_work()
9017  {
9018    /* Normally wait for new input.  However, if 'reviving' is
9019     * nonzero, a suspended process must be awakened.
9020     */
9021
9022    register struct fproc *rp;
9023
9024    if (reviving != 0) {
9025            /* Revive a suspended process. */
9026            for (rp = &fproc[0]; rp < &fproc[NR_PROCS]; rp++)
9027                    if (rp->fp_revived == REVIVING) {
9028                            who = rp - fproc;
9029                            fs_call = rp->fp_fd & BYTE;
9030                            fd = (rp->fp_fd >>8) & BYTE;
9031                            buffer = rp->fp_buffer;
9032                            nbytes = rp->fp_nbytes;
9033                            rp->fp_suspended = NOT_SUSPENDED; /* no longer hanging*/
9034                            rp->fp_revived = NOT_REVIVING;
9035                            reviving--;
9036                            return;
9037                    }
9038            panic("get_work couldn't revive anyone", NO_NUM);
9039    }
9040
9041    /* Normal case.  No one to revive. */
9042    if (receive(ANY, &m) != OK) panic("fs receive error", NO_NUM);
9043
9044    who = m.m_source;
9045    fs_call = m.m_type;
9046  }
```

```
9050    /*===========================================================================*
9051     *                              reply                                        *
9052     *===========================================================================*/
9053    PUBLIC reply(whom, result)
9054    int whom;                          /* process to reply to */
9055    int result;                        /* result of the call (usually OK or error #) */
9056    {
9057    /* Send a reply to a user process. It may fail (if the process has just
9058     * been killed by a signal, so don't check the return code.  If the send
9059     * fails, just ignore it.
9060     */
9061
9062      reply_type = result;
9063      send(whom, &m1);
9064    }


9066    /*===========================================================================*
9067     *                              fs_init                                      *
9068     *===========================================================================*/
9069    PRIVATE fs_init()
9070    {
9071    /* Initialize global variables, tables, etc. */
9072
9073      register struct inode *rip;
9074      int i;
9075      extern struct inode *get_inode();
9076
9077      buf_pool();                       /* initialize buffer pool */
9078      load_ram();                       /* Load RAM disk from root diskette. */
9079      load_super();                     /* Load super block for root device */
9080
9081      /* Initialize the 'fproc' fields for process 0 and process 2. */
9082      for (i = 0; i < 3; i+= 2) {
9083            fp = &fproc[i];
9084            rip = get_inode(ROOT_DEV, ROOT_INODE);
9085            fp->fp_rootdir = rip;
9086            dup_inode(rip);
9087            fp->fp_workdir = rip;
9088            fp->fp_realuid = (uid) SYS_UID;
9089            fp->fp_effuid = (uid) SYS_UID;
9090            fp->fp_realgid = (gid) SYS_GID;
9091            fp->fp_effgid = (gid) SYS_GID;
9092            fp->fp_umask = ~0;
9093      }
9094
9095      /* Certain relations must hold for the file system to work at all. */
9096      if (ZONE_NUM_SIZE != 2) panic("ZONE_NUM_SIZE != 2", NO_NUM);
9097      if (SUPER_SIZE > BLOCK_SIZE) panic("SUPER_SIZE > BLOCK_SIZE", NO_NUM);
9098      if(BLOCK_SIZE % INODE_SIZE != 0)panic("BLOCK_SIZE % INODE_SIZE != 0", NO_NUM);
9099      if (NR_FDS > 127) panic("NR_FDS > 127", NO_NUM);
```

```
9100        if (NR_BUFS < 6) panic("NR_BUFS < 6", NO_NUM);
9101        if (sizeof(d_inode) != 32) panic("inode size != 32", NO_NUM);
9102    }


9104    /*===========================================================================*
9105     *                              buf_pool                                      *
9106     *===========================================================================*/
9107    PRIVATE buf_pool()
9108    {
9109    /* Initialize the buffer pool.  On the IBM PC, the hardware DMA chip is
9110     * not able to cross 64K boundaries, so any buffer that happens to lie
9111     * across such a boundary is not used.  This is not very elegant, but all
9112     * the alternative solutions are as bad, if not worse.  The fault lies with
9113     * the PC hardware.
9114     */
9115      register struct buf *bp;
9116      vir_bytes low_off, high_off;
9117      phys_bytes org;
9118      extern phys_clicks get_base();
9119
9120      bufs_in_use = 0;
9121      front = &buf[0];
9122      rear = &buf[NR_BUFS - 1];
9123
9124      for (bp = &buf[0]; bp < &buf[NR_BUFS]; bp++) {
9125            bp->b_blocknr = NO_BLOCK;
9126            bp->b_dev = NO_DEV;
9127            bp->b_next = bp + 1;
9128            bp->b_prev = bp - 1;
9129      }
9130      buf[0].b_prev = NIL_BUF;
9131      buf[NR_BUFS - 1].b_next = NIL_BUF;
9132
9133      /* Delete any buffers that span a 64K boundary. */
9134    #ifdef i8088
9135      for (bp = &buf[0]; bp < &buf[NR_BUFS]; bp++) {
9136            org = get_base() << CLICK_SHIFT;          /* phys addr where FS is */
9137            low_off = (vir_bytes) bp->b_data;
9138            high_off = low_off + BLOCK_SIZE - 1;
9139            if (((org + low_off) & M64K) != ((org + high_off) & M64K)) {
9140                    if (bp == &buf[0]) {
9141                            front = &buf[1];
9142                            buf[1].b_prev = NIL_BUF;
9143                    } else if (bp == &buf[NR_BUFS - 1]) {
9144                            rear = &buf[NR_BUFS - 2];
9145                            buf[NR_BUFS - 2].b_next = NIL_BUF;
9146                    } else {
9147                            /* Delete a buffer in the middle. */
9148                            bp->b_prev->b_next = bp + 1;
9149                            bp->b_next->b_prev = bp - 1;
```

```
9150                          }
9151                  }
9152          }
9153     #endif
9154
9155        for (bp = &buf[0]; bp < &buf[NR_BUFS]; bp++) bp->b_hash = bp->b_next;
9156        buf_hash[NO_BLOCK & (NR_BUF_HASH - 1)] = front;
9157     }


9160     /*===========================================================================*
9161      *                              load_ram                                     *
9162      *===========================================================================*/
9163     PRIVATE load_ram()
9164     {
9165     /* The root diskette contains a block-by-block image of the root file system
9166      * starting at 0.  Go get it and copy it to the RAM disk.
9167      */
9168
9169        register struct buf *bp, *bp1;
9170        int count;
9171        long k_loaded;
9172        struct super_block *sp;
9173        block_nr i;
9174        phys_clicks ram_clicks, init_org, init_text_clicks, init_data_clicks;
9175        extern phys_clicks data_org[INFO + 2];
9176        extern struct buf *get_block();
9177
9178        /* Get size of INIT by reading block on diskette where 'build' put it. */
9179        init_org = data_org[INFO];
9180        init_text_clicks = data_org[INFO + 1];
9181        init_data_clicks = data_org[INFO + 2];
9182
9183        /* Get size of RAM disk by reading root file system's super block */
9184        bp = get_block(BOOT_DEV, SUPER_BLOCK, NORMAL);  /* get RAM super block */
9185        copy(super_block, bp->b_data, sizeof(struct super_block));
9186        sp = &super_block[0];
9187        if (sp->s_magic != SUPER_MAGIC)
9188            panic("Diskette in drive 0 is not root file system", NO_NUM);
9189        count = sp->s_nzones << sp->s_log_zone_size;  /* # blocks on root dev */
9190        ram_clicks = count * (BLOCK_SIZE/CLICK_SIZE);
9191        put_block(bp, FULL_DATA_BLOCK);
9192
9193        /* Tell MM the origin and size of INIT, and the amount of memory used for the
9194         * system plus RAM disk combined, so it can remove all of it from the map.
9195         */
9196        m1.m_type = BRK2;
9197        m1.m1_i1 = init_text_clicks;
9198        m1.m1_i2 = init_data_clicks;
9199        m1.m1_i3 = init_org + init_text_clicks + init_data_clicks + ram_clicks;
```

```
9200          ml.ml_p1 = (char *) init_org;
9201          if (sendrec(MM_PROC_NR, &ml) != OK) panic("FS Can't report to MM", NO_NUM);
9202
9203          /* Tell RAM driver where RAM disk is and how big it is. */
9204          ml.m_type = DISK_IOCTL;
9205          ml.DEVICE = RAM_DEV;
9206          ml.POSITION = (long) init_org + (long) init_text_clicks + init_data_clicks;
9207          ml.POSITION = ml.POSITION << CLICK_SHIFT;
9208          ml.COUNT = count;
9209          if (sendrec(MEM, &ml) != OK) panic("Can't report size to MEM", NO_NUM);
9210
9211          /* Copy the blocks one at a time from the root diskette to the RAM */
9212          printf("Loading RAM disk from root diskette.     Loaded:   OK ");
9213          for (i = 0; i < count; i++) {
9214                  bp = get_block(BOOT_DEV, (block_nr) i, NORMAL);
9215                  bp1 = get_block(ROOT_DEV, i, NO_READ);
9216                  copy(bp1->b_data, bp->b_data, BLOCK_SIZE);
9217                  bp1->b_dirt = DIRTY;
9218                  put_block(bp, I_MAP_BLOCK);
9219                  put_block(bp1, I_MAP_BLOCK);
9220                  k_loaded = ( (long) i * BLOCK_SIZE)/1024L;       /* K loaded so far */
9221                  if (k_loaded % 5 == 0) printf("\b\b\b\b%3DK %c", k_loaded, 0);
9222          }
9223
9224      printf("\rRAM disk loaded.  Please remove root diskette.          \n\n");
9225    }


9228    /*===========================================================================*
9229     *                              load_super                                   *
9230     *===========================================================================*/
9231    PRIVATE load_super()
9232    {
9233      register struct super_block *sp;
9234      register struct inode *rip;
9235      extern struct inode *get_inode();
9236
9237    /* Initialize the super_block table. */
9238
9239        for (sp = &super_block[0]; sp < &super_block[NR_SUPERS]; sp++)
9240                sp->s_dev = NO_DEV;
9241
9242        /* Read in super_block for the root file system. */
9243        sp = &super_block[0];
9244        sp->s_dev = ROOT_DEV;
9245        rw_super(sp,READING);
9246        rip = get_inode(ROOT_DEV, ROOT_INODE);             /* inode for root dir */
9247
9248        /* Check super_block for consistency (is it the right diskette?). */
9249        if ( (rip->i_mode & I_TYPE) != I_DIRECTORY || rip->i_nlinks < 3 ||
```

```
9250                                              sp->s_magic != SUPER_MAGIC)
9251          panic("Root file system corrupted.  Possibly wrong diskette.", NO_NUM);
9252
9253     sp->s_imount = rip;
9254     dup_inode(rip);
9255     sp->s_isup = rip;
9256     sp->s_rd_only = 0;
9257     if (load_bit_maps(ROOT_DEV) != OK)
9258          panic("init: can't load root bit maps", NO_NUM);
9259   }
```

```
9300    /* This file contains the table used to map system call numbers onto the
9301     * routines that perform them.
9302     */
9303
9304    #include "../h/const.h"
9305    #include "../h/type.h"
9306    #include "../h/stat.h"
9307    #include "const.h"
9308    #include "type.h"
9309    #include "dev.h"
9310
9311    #undef EXTERN
9312    #define EXTERN
9313
9314    #include "../h/callnr.h"
9315    #include "../h/com.h"
9316    #include "../h/error.h"
9317    #include "buf.h"
9318    #include "file.h"
9319    #include "fproc.h"
9320    #include "glo.h"
9321    #include "inode.h"
9322    #include "super.h"
9323
9324    extern do_access(), do_chdir(), do_chmod(), do_chown(), do_chroot();
9325    extern do_close(), do_creat(), do_dup(), do_exit(), do_fork(), do_fstat();
9326    extern do_ioctl(), do_link(), do_lseek(), do_mknod(), do_mount(), do_open();
9327    extern do_pipe(), do_read(), do_revive(), do_set(), do_stat(), do_stime();
9328    extern do_sync(), do_time(), do_tims(), do_umask(), do_umount(), do_unlink();
9329    extern do_unpause(), do_utime(), do_write(), no_call(), no_sys();
9330
9331    extern char fstack[];
9332    char *stackpt = &fstack[FS_STACK_BYTES];          /* initial stack pointer */
9333
9334    int (*call_vector[NCALLS])() = {
9335            no_sys,         /*  0 = unused */
9336            do_exit,        /*  1 = exit   */
9337            do_fork,        /*  2 = fork   */
9338            do_read,        /*  3 = read   */
9339            do_write,       /*  4 = write  */
9340            do_open,        /*  5 = open   */
9341            do_close,       /*  6 = close  */
9342            no_sys,         /*  7 = wait   */
9343            do_creat,       /*  8 = creat  */
9344            do_link,        /*  9 = link   */
9345            do_unlink,      /* 10 = unlink */
9346            no_sys,         /* 11 = exec   */
9347            do_chdir,       /* 12 = chdir  */
9348            do_time,        /* 13 = time   */
9349            do_mknod,       /* 14 = mknod  */
```

```
9350            do_chmod,        /* 15 = chmod   */
9351            do_chown,        /* 16 = chown   */
9352            no_sys,          /* 17 = break   */
9353            do_stat,         /* 18 = stat    */
9354            do_lseek,        /* 19 = lseek   */
9355            no_sys,          /* 20 = getpid  */
9356            do_mount,        /* 21 = mount   */
9357            do_umount,       /* 22 = umount  */
9358            do_set,          /* 23 = setuid  */
9359            no_sys,          /* 24 = getuid  */
9360            do_stime,        /* 25 = stime   */
9361            no_sys,          /* 26 = (ptrace)*/
9362            no_sys,          /* 27 = alarm   */
9363            do_fstat,        /* 28 = fstat   */
9364            no_sys,          /* 29 = pause   */
9365            do_utime,        /* 30 = utime   */
9366            no_sys,          /* 31 = (stty)  */
9367            no_sys,          /* 32 = (gtty)  */
9368            do_access,       /* 33 = access  */
9369            no_sys,          /* 34 = (nice)  */
9370            no_sys,          /* 35 = (ftime) */
9371            do_sync,         /* 36 = sync    */
9372            no_sys,          /* 37 = kill    */
9373            no_sys,          /* 38 = unused  */
9374            no_sys,          /* 39 = unused  */
9375            no_sys,          /* 40 = unused  */
9376            do_dup,          /* 41 = dup     */
9377            do_pipe,         /* 42 = pipe    */
9378            do_tims,         /* 43 = times   */
9379            no_sys,          /* 44 = (prof)  */
9380            no_sys,          /* 45 = unused  */
9381            do_set,          /* 46 = setgid  */
9382            no_sys,          /* 47 = getgid  */
9383            no_sys,          /* 48 = sig     */
9384            no_sys,          /* 49 = unused  */
9385            no_sys,          /* 50 = unused  */
9386            no_sys,          /* 51 = (acct)  */
9387            no_sys,          /* 52 = (phys)  */
9388            no_sys,          /* 53 = (lock)  */
9389            do_ioctl,        /* 54 = ioctl   */
9390            no_sys,          /* 55 = unused  */
9391            no_sys,          /* 56 = (mpx)   */
9392            no_sys,          /* 57 = unused  */
9393            no_sys,          /* 58 = unused  */
9394            no_sys,          /* 59 = exece   */
9395            do_umask,        /* 60 = umask   */
9396            do_chroot,       /* 61 = chroot  */
9397            no_sys,          /* 62 = unused  */
9398            no_sys,          /* 63 = unused  */
9399
```

```
9400            no_sys,         /* 64 = KSIG: signals originating in the kernel */
9401            do_unpause,     /* 65 = UNPAUSE */
9402            no_sys,         /* 66 = BRK2 (used to tell MM size of FS,INIT)  */
9403            do_revive,      /* 67 = REVIVE  */
9404            no_sys          /* 68 = TASK_REPLY       */
9405    };
9406
9407
9408    extern rw_dev(), rw_dev2();
9409
9410    /* The order of the entries here determines the mapping between major device
9411     * numbers and tasks.  The first entry (major device 0) is not used.  The
9412     * next entry is major device 1, etc.  Character and block devices can be
9413     * intermixed at random.  If this ordering is changed, BOOT_DEV and ROOT_DEV
9414     * must be changed to correspond to the new values.
9415     */
9416    struct dmap dmap[] = {
9417    /*  Open         Read/Write     Close      Task #       Device File
9418        ----         ----------     -----      -------      ------ ----     */
9419        0,           0,             0,         0,           /* 0 = not used */
9420        no_call,     rw_dev,        no_call,   MEM,         /* 1 = /dev/mem */
9421        no_call,     rw_dev,        no_call,   FLOPPY,      /* 2 = /dev/fd0 */
9422        no_call,     rw_dev,        no_call,   WINCHESTER,  /* 3 = /dev/hd0 */
9423        no_call,     rw_dev,        no_call,   TTY,         /* 4 = /dev/tty0 */
9424        no_call,     rw_dev2,       no_call,   TTY,         /* 5 = /dev/tty */
9425        no_call,     rw_dev,        no_call,   PRINTER      /* 6 = /dev/lp  */
9426    };
9427
9428    int max_major = sizeof(dmap)/sizeof(struct dmap);
```

```
9450      /* This file contains the procedures for creating, opening, closing, and
9451       * seeking on files.
9452       *
9453       * The entry points into this file are
9454       *   do_creat:   perform the CREAT system call
9455       *   do_mknod:   perform the MKNOD system call
9456       *   do_open:    perform the OPEN system call
9457       *   do_close:   perform the CLOSE system call
9458       *   do_lseek:   perform the LSEEK system call
9459       */
9460
9461      #include "../h/const.h"
9462      #include "../h/type.h"
9463      #include "../h/callnr.h"
9464      #include "../h/error.h"
9465      #include "const.h"
9466      #include "type.h"
9467      #include "buf.h"
9468      #include "file.h"
9469      #include "fproc.h"
9470      #include "glo.h"
9471      #include "inode.h"
9472      #include "param.h"
9473
9474      PRIVATE char mode_map[] = {R_BIT, W_BIT, R_BIT|W_BIT, 0};
9475
9476      /*===========================================================================*
9477       *                              do_creat                                     *
9478       *===========================================================================*/
9479      PUBLIC int do_creat()
9480      {
9481      /* Perform the creat(name, mode) system call. */
9482
9483        register struct inode *rip;
9484        register int r;
9485        register mask_bits bits;
9486        struct filp *fil_ptr;
9487        int file_d;
9488        extern struct inode *new_node();
9489
9490        /* See if name ok and file descriptor and filp slots are available. */
9491        if (fetch_name(name, name_length, M3) != OK) return(err_code);
9492        if ( (r = get_fd(W_BIT, &file_d, &fil_ptr)) != OK) return(r);
9493
9494        /* Create a new inode by calling new_node(). */
9495        bits = I_REGULAR | (mode & ALL_MODES & fp->fp_umask);
9496        rip = new_node(user_path, bits, NO_ZONE);
9497        r = err_code;
9498        if (r != OK && r != EEXIST) return(r);
9499
```

```
9500        /* At this point two possibilities exist: the given path did not exist
9501         * and has been created, or it pre-existed. In the later case, truncate
9502         * if possible, otherwise return an error.
9503         */
9504        if (r == EEXIST) {
9505                /* File exists already. */
9506                switch (rip->i_mode & I_TYPE) {
9507                    case I_REGULAR:                /* truncate regular file */
9508                        if ( (r = forbidden(rip, W_BIT, 0)) == OK) truncate(rip);
9509                        break;
9510
9511                    case I_DIRECTORY:   /* can't truncate directory */
9512                        r = EISDIR;
9513                        break;
9514
9515                    case I_CHAR_SPECIAL:          /* special files are special */
9516                    case I_BLOCK_SPECIAL:
9517                        if ( (r = forbidden(rip, W_BIT, 0)) != OK) break;
9518                        r = dev_open( (dev_nr) rip->i_zone[0], W_BIT);
9519                        break;
9520                }
9521        }
9522
9523        /* If error, return inode. */
9524        if (r != OK) {
9525                put_inode(rip);
9526                return(r);
9527        }
9528
9529        /* Claim the file descriptor and filp slot and fill them in. */
9530        fp->fp_filp[file_d] = fil_ptr;
9531        fil_ptr->filp_count = 1;
9532        fil_ptr->filp_ino = rip;
9533        return(file_d);
9534   }



9538   /*===========================================================================*
9539    *                              do_mknod                                      *
9540    *===========================================================================*/
9541   PUBLIC int do_mknod()
9542   {
9543   /* Perform the mknod(name, mode, addr) system call. */
9544
9545     register mask_bits bits;
9546
9547     if (!super_user) return(EPERM);        /* only super_user may make nodes */
9548     if (fetch_name(name1, name1_length, M1) != OK) return(err_code);
9549     bits = (mode & I_TYPE) | (mode  & ALL_MODES & fp->fp_umask);
```

```
9550          put_inode(new_node(user_path, bits, (zone_nr) addr));
9551          return(err_code);
9552    }


9554    /*===========================================================================*
9555     *                              new_node                                     *
9556     *===========================================================================*/
9557    PRIVATE struct inode *new_node(path, bits, z0)
9558    char *path;                     /* pointer to path name */
9559    mask_bits bits;                 /* mode of the new inode */
9560    zone_nr z0;                     /* zone number 0 for new inode */
9561    {
9562    /* This function is called by do_creat() and do_mknod().  In both cases it
9563     * allocates a new inode, makes a directory entry for it on the path 'path',
9564     * and initializes it.  It returns a pointer to the inode if it can do this;
9565     * err_code is set to OK or EEXIST. If it can't, it returns NIL_INODE and
9566     * 'err_code' contains the appropriate message.
9567     */

9569      register struct inode *rlast_dir_ptr, *rip;
9570      register int r;
9571      char string[NAME_SIZE];
9572      extern struct inode *alloc_inode(), *advance(), *last_dir();

9574      /* See if the path can be opened down to the last directory. */
9575      if ((rlast_dir_ptr = last_dir(path, string)) == NIL_INODE) return(NIL_INODE);

9577      /* The final directory is accessible. Get final component of the path. */
9578      rip = advance(rlast_dir_ptr, string);
9579      if ( rip == NIL_INODE && err_code == ENOENT) {
9580              /* Last path component does not exist.  Make new directory entry. */
9581              if ( (rip = alloc_inode(rlast_dir_ptr->i_dev, bits)) == NIL_INODE) {
9582                      /* Can't creat new inode: out of inodes. */
9583                      put_inode(rlast_dir_ptr);
9584                      return(NIL_INODE);
9585              }

9587              /* Force inode to the disk before making directory entry to make
9588               * the system more robust in the face of a crash: an inode with
9589               * no directory entry is much better than the opposite.
9590               */
9591              rip->i_nlinks++;
9592              rip->i_zone[0] = z0;
9593              rw_inode(rip, WRITING);          /* force inode to disk now */

9595              /* New inode acquired.  Try to make directory entry. */
9596              if ((r = search_dir(rlast_dir_ptr, string, &rip->i_num,ENTER)) != OK) {
9597                      put_inode(rlast_dir_ptr);
9598                      rip->i_nlinks--;         /* pity, have to free disk inode */
9599                      rip->i_dirt = DIRTY;     /* dirty inodes are written out */
```

```
9600                        put_inode(rip); /* this call frees the inode */
9601                        err_code = r;
9602                        return(NIL_INODE);
9603                  }
9604
9605            } else {
9606                  /* Either last component exists, or there is some problem. */
9607                  if (rip != NIL_INODE)
9608                        r = EEXIST;
9609                  else
9610                        r = err_code;
9611            }
9612
9613      /* Return the directory inode and exit. */
9614      put_inode(rlast_dir_ptr);
9615      err_code = r;
9616      return(rip);
9617  }

9619  /*===========================================================================*
9620   *                              do_open                                       *
9621   *===========================================================================*/
9622  PUBLIC int do_open()
9623  {
9624  /* Perform the open(name, mode) system call. */
9625
9626      register struct inode *rip;
9627      struct filp *fil_ptr;
9628      register int r;
9629      register mask_bits bits;
9630      int file_d;
9631      extern struct inode *eat_path();
9632
9633      /* See if file descriptor and filp slots are available.  The variable
9634       * 'mode' is 0 for read, 1 for write, 2 for read+write.  The variable
9635       * 'bits' needs to be R_BIT, W_BIT, and R_BIT|W_BIT respectively.
9636       */
9637      if (mode < 0 || mode > 2) return(EINVAL);
9638      if (fetch_name(name, name_length, M3) != OK) return(err_code);
9639      bits = (mask_bits) mode_map[mode];
9640      if ( (r = get_fd(bits, &file_d, &fil_ptr)) != OK) return(r);
9641
9642      /* Scan path name. */
9643      if ( (rip = eat_path(user_path)) == NIL_INODE) return(err_code);
9644
9645      if ((r = forbidden(rip, bits, 0)) != OK) {
9646            put_inode(rip);                 /* can't open: protection violation */
9647            return(r);
9648      }
9649
```

```
9650          /* Opening regular files, directories and special files are different. */
9651          switch (rip->i_mode & I_TYPE) {
9652             case I_DIRECTORY:
9653                if (bits & W_BIT) {
9654                        put_inode(rip);
9655                        return(EISDIR);
9656                }
9657                break;
9658
9659             case I_CHAR_SPECIAL:
9660                /* Assume that first open of char special file is controlling tty. */
9661                if (fp->fs_tty == 0) fp->fs_tty = (dev_nr) rip->i_zone[0];
9662                dev_open((dev_nr) rip->i_zone[0], (int) bits);
9663                break;
9664
9665             case I_BLOCK_SPECIAL:
9666                dev_open((dev_nr) rip->i_zone[0], (int) bits);
9667                break;
9668          }
9669
9670          /* Claim the file descriptor and filp slot and fill them in. */
9671          fp->fp_filp[file_d] = fil_ptr;
9672          fil_ptr->filp_count = 1;
9673          fil_ptr->filp_ino = rip;
9674          return(file_d);
9675       }

9677       /*===========================================================================*
9678        *                              do_close                                      *
9679        *===========================================================================*/
9680       PUBLIC int do_close()
9681       {
9682       /* Perform the close(fd) system call. */
9683
9684          register struct filp *rfilp;
9685          register struct inode *rip;
9686          int rw;
9687          int mode_word;
9688          extern struct filp *get_filp();
9689
9690          /* First locate the inode that belongs to the file descriptor. */
9691          if ( (rfilp = get_filp(fd)) == NIL_FILP) return(err_code);
9692          rip = rfilp->filp_ino;          /* 'rip' points to the inode */
9693
9694          /* Check to see if the file is special. */
9695          mode_word = rip->i_mode & I_TYPE;
9696          if (mode_word == I_CHAR_SPECIAL || mode_word == I_BLOCK_SPECIAL) {
9697                if (mode_word == I_BLOCK_SPECIAL) {
9698                        /* Invalidate cache entries unless special is mounted or ROOT.*/
9699                        do_sync();       /* purge cache */
```

```
9700                     if (mounted(rip) == FALSE) invalidate((dev_nr) rip->i_zone[0]);
9701               }
9702             dev_close((dev_nr) rip->i_zone[0]);
9703         }
9704
9705     /* If the inode being closed is a pipe, release everyone hanging on it. */
9706     if (rfilp->filp_ino->i_pipe) {
9707             rw = (rfilp->filp_mode & R_BIT ? WRITE : READ);
9708             release(rfilp->filp_ino, rw, NR_PROCS);
9709     }
9710
9711     /* If a write has been done, the inode is already marked as DIRTY. */
9712     if (--rfilp->filp_count == 0) put_inode(rfilp->filp_ino);
9713
9714     fp->fp_filp[fd] = NIL_FILP;
9715     return(OK);
9716   }
9717
9718   /*===========================================================================*
9719    *                              do_lseek                                      *
9720    *===========================================================================*/
9721   PUBLIC int do_lseek()
9722   {
9723   /* Perform the lseek(ls_fd, offset, whence) system call. */
9724
9725     register struct filp *rfilp;
9726     register file_pos pos;
9727     extern struct filp *get_filp();
9728
9729     /* Check to see if the file descriptor is valid. */
9730     if ( (rfilp = get_filp(ls_fd)) == NIL_FILP) return(err_code);
9731
9732     /* No lseek on pipes. */
9733     if (rfilp->filp_ino->i_pipe == I_PIPE) return(ESPIPE);
9734
9735     /* The value of 'whence' determines the algorithm to use. */
9736     switch(whence) {
9737           case 0: pos = offset;   break;
9738           case 1: pos = rfilp->filp_pos + offset; break;
9739           case 2: pos = rfilp->filp_ino->i_size + offset; break;
9740           default: return(EINVAL);
9741     }
9742     if (pos < (file_pos) 0) return(EINVAL);
9743
9744     rfilp->filp_ino->i_seek = ISEEK;        /* inhibit read ahead */
9745     rfilp->filp_pos = pos;
9746
9747     reply_l1 = pos;                         /* insert the long into the output message */
9748     return(OK);
9749   }
```

```
9750    /* This file contains the heart of the mechanism used to read (and write)
9751     * files.  Read and write requests are split up into chunks that do not cross
9752     * block boundaries.  Each chunk is then processed in turn.  Reads on special
9753     * files are also detected and handled.
9754     *
9755     * The entry points into this file are
9756     *   do_read:    perform the READ system call by calling read_write
9757     *   read_write: actually do the work of READ and WRITE
9758     *   read_map:   given an inode and file position, lookup its zone number
9759     *   rw_user:    call the kernel to read and write user space
9760     *   read_ahead: manage the block read ahead business
9761     */

9763    #include "../h/const.h"
9764    #include "../h/type.h"
9765    #include "../h/com.h"
9766    #include "../h/error.h"
9767    #include "const.h"
9768    #include "type.h"
9769    #include "buf.h"
9770    #include "file.h"
9771    #include "fproc.h"
9772    #include "glo.h"
9773    #include "inode.h"
9774    #include "param.h"
9775    #include "super.h"

9777    #define FD_MASK          077    /* max file descriptor is 63 */

9779    PRIVATE message umess;          /* message for asking SYSTASK for user copy */

9781    /*===========================================================================*
9782     *                              do_read                                       *
9783     *===========================================================================*/
9784    PUBLIC int do_read()
9785    {
9786      return(read_write(READING));
9787    }



9791    /*===========================================================================*
9792     *                              read_write                                    *
9793     *===========================================================================*/
9794    PUBLIC int read_write(rw_flag)
9795    int rw_flag;                    /* READING or WRITING */
9796    {
9797    /* Perform read(fd, buffer, nbytes) or write(fd, buffer, nbytes) call. */

9799      register struct inode *rip;
```

```
9800        register struct filp *f;
9801        register file_pos bytes_left, f_size;
9802        register unsigned off, cum_io;
9803        file_pos position;
9804        int r, chunk, virg, mode_word, usr, seg;
9805        struct filp *wf;
9806        extern struct super_block *get_super();
9807        extern struct filp *find_filp(), *get_filp();
9808        extern real_time clock_time();
9809
9810        /* MM loads segments by putting funny things in upper 10 bits of 'fd'. */
9811        if (who == MM_PROC_NR && (fd & (~BYTE)) ) {
9812                usr = (fd >> 8) & BYTE;
9813                seg = (fd >> 6) & 03;
9814                fd &= FD_MASK;              /* get rid of user and segment bits */
9815        } else {
9816                usr = who;                  /* normal case */
9817                seg = D;
9818        }
9819
9820        /* If the file descriptor is valid, get the inode, size and mode. */
9821        if (nbytes == 0) return(0);    /* so char special files need not check for 0*/
9822        if (who != MM_PROC_NR && nbytes < 0) return(EINVAL);  /* only MM > 32K */
9823        if ( (f = get_filp(fd)) == NIL_FILP) return(err_code);
9824        if ( ((f->filp_mode) & (rw_flag == READING ? R_BIT : W_BIT)) == 0)
9825                return(EBADF);
9826        position = f->filp_pos;
9827        if (position < (file_pos) 0) return(EINVAL);
9828        rip = f->filp_ino;
9829        f_size = rip->i_size;
9830        r = OK;
9831        cum_io = 0;
9832        virg = TRUE;
9833        mode_word = rip->i_mode & I_TYPE;
9834
9835        /* Check for character special files. */
9836        if (mode_word == I_CHAR_SPECIAL) {
9837                if ((r = dev_io(rw_flag, (dev_nr) rip->i_zone[0], (long) position,
9838                                                nbytes, who, buffer)) >= 0) {
9839                        cum_io = r;
9840                        position += r;
9841                        r = OK;
9842                }
9843        } else {
9844                if (rw_flag == WRITING && mode_word != I_BLOCK_SPECIAL) {
9845                        /* Check in advance to see if file will grow too big. */
9846                        if (position > get_super(rip->i_dev)->s_max_size - nbytes )
9847                                return(EFBIG);
9848
9849                        /* Clear the zone containing present EOF if hole about
```

```
9850                         * to be created.  This is necessary because all unwritten
9851                         * blocks prior to the EOF must read as zeros.
9852                         */
9853                        if (position > f_size) clear_zone(rip, f_size, 0);
9854                }
9855
9856                /* Pipes are a little different.  Check. */
9857                if (rip->i_pipe && (r = pipe_check(rip, rw_flag, virg,
9858                                        nbytes, &position)) <= 0) return(0);
9859
9860                /* Split the transfer into chunks that don't span two blocks. */
9861                while (nbytes != 0) {
9862                        off = position % BLOCK_SIZE;     /* offset within a block */
9863                        chunk = MIN(nbytes, BLOCK_SIZE - off);
9864                        if (chunk < 0) chunk = BLOCK_SIZE - off;
9865
9866                        if (rw_flag == READING) {
9867                                if ((bytes_left = f_size - position) <= 0)
9868                                        break;
9869                                else
9870                                        if (chunk > bytes_left) chunk = bytes_left;
9871                        }
9872
9873                        /* Read or write 'chunk' bytes. */
9874                        r=rw_chunk(rip, position, off, chunk, rw_flag, buffer, seg,usr);
9875                        if (r != OK) break;     /* EOF reached */
9876
9877                        /* Update counters and pointers. */
9878                        buffer += chunk;        /* user buffer address */
9879                        nbytes -= chunk;        /* bytes yet to be read */
9880                        cum_io += chunk;        /* bytes read so far */
9881                        position += chunk;      /* position within the file */
9882                        virg = FALSE; /* tells pipe_check() that data has been copied */
9883                }
9884        }
9885
9886        /* On write, update file size and access time. */
9887        if (rw_flag == WRITING) {
9888                if (mode_word != I_CHAR_SPECIAL && mode_word != I_BLOCK_SPECIAL &&
9889                                                        position > f_size)
9890                        rip->i_size = position;
9891                rip->i_modtime = clock_time();
9892                rip->i_dirt = DIRTY;
9893        } else {
9894                if (rip->i_pipe && position >= rip->i_size) {
9895                        /* Reset pipe pointers. */
9896                        rip->i_size = 0;        /* no data left */
9897                        position = 0;           /* reset reader(s) */
9898                        if ( (wf = find_filp(rip, W_BIT)) != NIL_FILP) wf->filp_pos = 0;
9899                }
```

```
9900         }
9901         f->filp_pos = position;
9902
9903         /* Check to see if read-ahead is called for, and if so, set it up. */
9904         if (rw_flag == READING && rip->i_seek == NO_SEEK && position % BLOCK_SIZE == 0
9905                     && (mode_word == I_REGULAR || mode_word == I_DIRECTORY)) {
9906                 rdahed_inode = rip;
9907                 rdahedpos = position;
9908         }
9909         if (mode_word == I_REGULAR) rip->i_seek = NO_SEEK;
9910
9911         return(r == OK ? cum_io : r);
9912     }



9916     /*===========================================================================*
9917      *                              rw_chunk                                     *
9918      *===========================================================================*/
9919     PRIVATE int rw_chunk(rip, position, off, chunk, rw_flag, buff, seg, usr)
9920     register struct inode *rip;     /* pointer to inode for file to be rd/wr */
9921     file_pos position;              /* position within file to read or write */
9922     unsigned off;                   /* off within the current block */
9923     int chunk;                      /* number of bytes to read or write */
9924     int rw_flag;                    /* READING or WRITING */
9925     char *buff;                     /* virtual address of the user buffer */
9926     int seg;                        /* T or D segment in user space */
9927     int usr;                        /* which user process */
9928     {
9929     /* Read or write (part of) a block. */
9930
9931       register struct buf *bp;
9932       register int r;
9933       int dir, n, block_spec;
9934       block_nr b;
9935       dev_nr dev;
9936       extern struct buf *get_block(), *new_block();
9937       extern block_nr read_map();
9938
9939       block_spec = (rip->i_mode & I_TYPE) == I_BLOCK_SPECIAL;
9940       if (block_spec) {
9941             b = position/BLOCK_SIZE;
9942             dev = (dev_nr) rip->i_zone[0];
9943       } else {
9944             b = read_map(rip, position);
9945             dev = rip->i_dev;
9946       }
9947
9948       if (!block_spec && b == NO_BLOCK) {
9949             if (rw_flag == READING) {
```

```
9950                         /* Reading from a nonexistent block.  Must read as all zeros. */
9951                         bp = get_block(NO_DEV, NO_BLOCK, NORMAL);      /* get a buffer */
9952                         zero_block(bp);
9953                 } else {
9954                         /* Writing to a nonexistent block. Create and enter in inode. */
9955                         if ((bp = new_block(rip, position)) == NIL_BUF)return(err_code);
9956                 }
9957         } else {
9958                 /* Normally an existing block to be partially overwritten is first read
9959                  * in.  However, a full block need not be read in.  If it is already in
9960                  * the cache, acquire it, otherwise just acquire a free buffer.
9961                  */
9962                 n = (rw_flag == WRITING && chunk == BLOCK_SIZE ? NO_READ : NORMAL);
9963                 if(rw_flag == WRITING && off == 0 && position >= rip->i_size) n=NO_READ;
9964                 bp = get_block(dev, b, n);
9965         }
9966
9967         /* In all cases, bp now points to a valid buffer. */
9968         if (rw_flag == WRITING && chunk != BLOCK_SIZE && !block_spec &&
9969                                         position >= rip->i_size && off == 0)
9970                 zero_block(bp);
9971         dir = (rw_flag == READING ? TO_USER : FROM_USER);
9972         r = rw_user(seg, usr, (vir_bytes)buff, (vir_bytes)chunk, bp->b_data+off, dir);
9973         if (rw_flag == WRITING) bp->b_dirt = DIRTY;
9974         n = (off + chunk == BLOCK_SIZE ? FULL_DATA_BLOCK : PARTIAL_DATA_BLOCK);
9975         put_block(bp, n);
9976         return(r);
9977 }



9981 /*===========================================================================*
9982  *                              read_map                                     *
9983  *===========================================================================*/
9984 PUBLIC block_nr read_map(rip, position)
9985 register struct inode *rip;      /* ptr to inode to map from */
9986 file_pos position;               /* position in file whose blk wanted */
9987 {
9988 /* Given an inode and a position within the corresponding file, locate the
9989  * block (not zone) number in which that position is to be found and return it.
9990  */
9991
9992   register struct buf *bp;
9993   register zone_nr z;
9994   register block_nr b;
9995   register long excess, zone, block_pos;
9996   register int scale, boff;
9997   extern struct buf *get_block();
9998
9999   scale = scale_factor(rip);      /* for block-zone conversion */
```

```
10000        block_pos = position/BLOCK_SIZE;        /* relative blk # in file */
10001        zone = block_pos >> scale;      /* position's zone */
10002        boff = block_pos - (zone << scale);    /* relative blk # within zone */
10003
10004        /* Is 'position' to be found in the inode itself? */
10005        if (zone < NR_DZONE_NUM) {
10006                if ( (z = rip->i_zone[zone]) == NO_ZONE) return(NO_BLOCK);
10007                b = ((block_nr) z << scale) + boff;
10008                return(b);
10009        }
10010
10011        /* It is not in the inode, so it must be single or double indirect. */
10012        excess = zone - NR_DZONE_NUM; /* first NR_DZONE_NUM don't count */
10013
10014        if (excess < NR_INDIRECTS) {
10015                /* 'position' can be located via the single indirect block. */
10016                z = rip->i_zone[NR_DZONE_NUM];
10017        } else {
10018                /* 'position' can be located via the double indirect block. */
10019                if ( (z = rip->i_zone[NR_DZONE_NUM+1]) == NO_ZONE) return(NO_BLOCK);
10020                excess -= NR_INDIRECTS;                        /* single indir doesn't count *
10021                b = (block_nr) z << scale;
10022                bp = get_block(rip->i_dev, b, NORMAL);  /* get double indirect block */
10023                z = bp->b_ind[excess/NR_INDIRECTS];        /* z is zone # for single ind *
10024                put_block(bp, INDIRECT_BLOCK);             /* release double ind block */
10025                excess = excess % NR_INDIRECTS;             /* index into single ind blk */
10026        }
10027
10028        /* 'z' is zone number for single indirect block; 'excess' is index into it. *
10029        if (z == NO_ZONE) return(NO_BLOCK);
10030        b = (block_nr) z << scale;
10031        bp = get_block(rip->i_dev, b, NORMAL);             /* get single indirect block */
10032        z = bp->b_ind[excess];
10033        put_block(bp, INDIRECT_BLOCK);                     /* release single indirect blk
10034        if (z == NO_ZONE) return(NO_BLOCK);
10035        b = ((block_nr) z << scale) + boff;
10036        return(b);
10037 }

10039 /*===========================================================================*
10040  *                              rw_user                                     *
10041  *===========================================================================*/
10042 PUBLIC int rw_user(s, u, vir, bytes, buff, direction)
10043 int s;                          /* D or T space (stack is also D) */
10044 int u;                          /* process number to r/w (usually = 'who') */
10045 vir_bytes vir;                  /* virtual address to move to/from */
10046 vir_bytes bytes;                /* how many bytes to move */
10047 char *buff;                     /* pointer to FS space */
10048 int direction;                  /* TO_USER or FROM_USER */
10049 {
```

```
10050      /* Transfer a block of data.  Two options exist, depending on 'direction':
10051       *      TO_USER:      Move from FS space to user virtual space
10052       *      FROM_USER:    Move from user virtual space to FS space
10053       */
10054
10055        if (direction == TO_USER ) {
10056              /* Write from FS space to user space. */
10057              umess.SRC_SPACE   = D;
10058              umess.SRC_PROC_NR = FS_PROC_NR;
10059              umess.SRC_BUFFER = (long) buff;
10060              umess.DST_SPACE   = s;
10061              umess.DST_PROC_NR = u;
10062              umess.DST_BUFFER = (long) vir;
10063        } else {
10064              /* Read from user space to FS space. */
10065              umess.SRC_SPACE   = s;
10066              umess.SRC_PROC_NR = u;
10067              umess.SRC_BUFFER = (long) vir;
10068              umess.DST_SPACE   = D;
10069              umess.DST_PROC_NR = FS_PROC_NR;
10070              umess.DST_BUFFER = (long) buff;
10071        }
10072
10073        umess.COPY_BYTES = (long) bytes;
10074        sys_copy(&umess);
10075        return(umess.m_type);
10076      }


10079      /*===========================================================================*
10080       *                           read_ahead                                      *
10081       *===========================================================================*/
10082      PUBLIC read_ahead()
10083      {
10084      /* Read a block into the cache before it is needed. */
10085
10086        register struct inode *rip;
10087        struct buf *bp;
10088        block_nr b;
10089        extern struct buf *get_block();
10090
10091        rip = rdahed_inode;            /* pointer to inode to read ahead from */
10092        rdahed_inode = NIL_INODE;      /* turn off read ahead */
10093        if ( (b = read_map(rip, rdahedpos)) == NO_BLOCK) return;     /* at EOF */
10094        bp = get_block(rip->i_dev, b, NORMAL);
10095        put_block(bp, PARTIAL_DATA_BLOCK);
10096      }
```

```
10100   /* This file is the counterpart of "read.c".  It contains the code for writing
10101    * insofar as this is not contained in read_write().
10102    *
10103    * The entry points into this file are
10104    *   do_write:     call read_write to perform the WRITE system call
10105    *   write_map:    add a new zone to an inode
10106    *   clear_zone:   erase a zone in the middle of a file
10107    *   new_block:    acquire a new block
10108    */
10109
10110   #include "../h/const.h"
10111   #include "../h/type.h"
10112   #include "../h/error.h"
10113   #include "const.h"
10114   #include "type.h"
10115   #include "buf.h"
10116   #include "file.h"
10117   #include "fproc.h"
10118   #include "glo.h"
10119   #include "inode.h"
10120   #include "super.h"
10121
10122   /*===========================================================================*
10123    *                              do_write                                      *
10124    *===========================================================================*/
10125   PUBLIC int do_write()
10126   {
10127   /* Perform the write(fd, buffer, nbytes) system call. */
10128     return(read_write(WRITING));
10129   }
10132   /*===========================================================================*
10133    *                              write_map                                     *
10134    *===========================================================================*/
10135   PRIVATE int write_map(rip, position, new_zone)
10136   register struct inode *rip;      /* pointer to inode to be changed */
10137   file_pos position;               /* file address to be mapped */
10138   zone_nr new_zone;                /* zone # to be inserted */
10139   {
10140   /* Write a new zone into an inode. */
10141     int scale;
10142     zone_nr z, *zp;
10143     register block_nr b;
10144     long excess, zone;
10145     int index;
10146     struct buf *bp;
10147     int new_ind, new_dbl;
10148
10149     extern zone_nr alloc_zone();
```

```
10150          extern struct buf *get_block();
10151          extern real_time clock_time();
10152
10153          rip->i_dirt = DIRTY;              /* inode will be changed */
10154          bp = NIL_BUF;
10155          scale = scale_factor(rip);    /* for zone-block conversion */
10156          zone = (position/BLOCK_SIZE) >> scale;       /* relative zone # to insert */
10157
10158          /* Is 'position' to be found in the inode itself? */
10159          if (zone < NR_DZONE_NUM) {
10160                  rip->i_zone[zone] = new_zone;
10161                  rip->i_modtime = clock_time();
10162                  return(OK);
10163          }
10164
10165          /* It is not in the inode, so it must be single or double indirect. */
10166          excess = zone - NR_DZONE_NUM; /* first NR_DZONE_NUM don't count */
10167          new_ind = FALSE;
10168          new_dbl = FALSE;
10169
10170          if (excess < NR_INDIRECTS) {
10171                  /* 'position' can be located via the single indirect block. */
10172                  zp = &rip->i_zone[NR_DZONE_NUM];
10173          } else {
10174                  /* 'position' can be located via the double indirect block. */
10175                  if ( (z = rip->i_zone[NR_DZONE_NUM+1]) == NO_ZONE) {
10176                          /* Create the double indirect block. */
10177                          if ( (z = alloc_zone(rip->i_dev, rip->i_zone[0])) == NO_ZONE)
10178                                  return(err_code);
10179                          rip->i_zone[NR_DZONE_NUM+1] = z;
10180                          new_dbl = TRUE; /* set flag for later */
10181                  }
10182
10183                  /* Either way, 'z' is zone number for double indirect block. */
10184                  excess -= NR_INDIRECTS; /* single indirect doesn't count */
10185                  index = excess / NR_INDIRECTS;
10186                  excess = excess % NR_INDIRECTS;
10187                  if (index >= NR_INDIRECTS) return(EFBIG);
10188                  b = (block_nr) z << scale;
10189                  bp = get_block(rip->i_dev, b, (new_dbl ? NO_READ : NORMAL));
10190                  if (new_dbl) zero_block(bp);
10191                  zp= &bp->b_ind[index];
10192          }
10193
10194          /* 'zp' now points to place where indirect zone # goes; 'excess' is index. */
10195          if (*zp == NO_ZONE) {
10196                  /* Create indirect block. */
10197                  *zp = alloc_zone(rip->i_dev, rip->i_zone[0]);
10198                  new_ind = TRUE;
10199                  if (bp != NIL_BUF) bp->b_dirt = DIRTY;  /* if double ind, it is dirty */
```

```
10200                     if (*zp == NO_ZONE) {
10201                             put_block(bp, INDIRECT_BLOCK); /* release dbl indirect blk */
10202                             return(err_code);         /* couldn't create single ind */
10203                     }
10204             }
10205             put_block(bp, INDIRECT_BLOCK);            /* release double indirect blk */
10206
10207             /* 'zp' now points to indirect block's zone number. */
10208             b = (block_nr) *zp << scale;
10209             bp = get_block(rip->i_dev, b, (new_ind ? NO_READ : NORMAL) );
10210             if (new_ind) zero_block(bp);
10211             bp->b_ind[excess] = new_zone;
10212             rip->i_modtime = clock_time();
10213             bp->b_dirt = DIRTY;
10214             put_block(bp, INDIRECT_BLOCK);
10215
10216             return(OK);
10217     }
10218
10219     /*===========================================================================*
10220      *                              clear_zone                                    *
10221      *===========================================================================*/
10222     PUBLIC clear_zone(rip, pos, flag)
10223     register struct inode *rip;     /* inode to clear */
10224     file_pos pos;                    /* points to block to clear */
10225     int flag;                        /* 0 if called by read_write, 1 by new_block */
10226     {
10227     /* Zero a zone, possibly starting in the middle.  The parameter 'pos' gives
10228      * a byte in the first block to be zeroed.  Clearzone() is called from
10229      * read_write and new_block().
10230      */
10231
10232       register struct buf *bp;
10233       register block_nr b, blo, bhi;
10234       register file_pos next;
10235       register int scale;
10236       register zone_type zone_size;
10237       extern struct buf *get_block();
10238       extern block_nr read_map();
10239
10240       /* If the block size and zone size are the same, clear_zone() not needed. */
10241       if ( (scale = scale_factor(rip)) == 0) return;
10242
10243
10244       zone_size = (zone_type) BLOCK_SIZE << scale;
10245       if (flag == 1) pos = (pos/zone_size) * zone_size;
10246       next = pos + BLOCK_SIZE - 1;
10247
10248       /* If 'pos' is in the last block of a zone, do not clear the zone. */
10249       if (next/zone_size != pos/zone_size) return;
```

```
10250        if ( (blo = read_map(rip, next)) == NO_BLOCK) return;
10251        bhi = (  ((blo>>scale)+1) << scale)   - 1;
10252
10253        /* Clear all the blocks between 'blo' and 'bhi'. */
10254        for (b = blo; b <= bhi; b++) {
10255              bp = get_block(rip->i_dev, b, NO_READ);
10256              zero_block(bp);
10257              put_block(bp, FULL_DATA_BLOCK);
10258        }
10259   }


10262   /*===========================================================================*
10263    *                              new_block                                     *
10264    *===========================================================================*/
10265   PUBLIC struct buf *new_block(rip, position)
10266   register struct inode *rip;       /* pointer to inode */
10267   file_pos position;                /* file pointer */
10268   {
10269   /* Acquire a new block and return a pointer to it.  Doing so may require
10270    * allocating a complete zone, and then returning the initial block.
10271    * On the other hand, the current zone may still have some unused blocks.
10272    */
10273
10274     register struct buf *bp;
10275     block_nr b, base_block;
10276     zone_nr z;
10277     zone_type zone_size;
10278     int scale, r;
10279     struct super_block *sp;
10280     extern struct buf *get_block();
10281     extern struct super_block *get_super();
10282     extern block_nr read_map();
10283     extern zone_nr alloc_zone();
10284
10285     /* Is another block available in the current zone? */
10286     if ( (b = read_map(rip, position)) == NO_BLOCK) {
10287           /* Choose first zone if need be. */
10288           if (rip->i_size == 0) {
10289                 sp = get_super(rip->i_dev);
10290                 z = sp->s_firstdatazone;
10291           } else {
10292                 z = rip->i_zone[0];
10293           }
10294           if ( (z = alloc_zone(rip->i_dev, z)) == NO_ZONE) return(NIL_BUF);
10295           if ( (r = write_map(rip, position, z)) != OK) {
10296                 free_zone(rip->i_dev, z);
10297                 err_code = r;
10298                 return(NIL_BUF);
10299           }
```

```
10300
10301                /* If we are not writing at EOF, clear the zone, just to be safe. */
10302                if ( position != rip->i_size) clear_zone(rip, position, 1);
10303                scale = scale_factor(rip);
10304                base_block = (block_nr) z << scale;
10305                zone_size = (zone_type) BLOCK_SIZE << scale;
10306                b = base_block + (block_nr)((position % zone_size)/BLOCK_SIZE);
10307          }
10308
10309          bp = get_block(rip->i_dev, b, NO_READ);
10310          zero_block(bp);
10311          return(bp);
10312    }


10315    /*===========================================================================*
10316     *                            zero_block                                      *
10317     *===========================================================================*/
10318    PUBLIC zero_block(bp)
10319    register struct buf *bp;          /* pointer to buffer to zero */
10320    {
10321    /* Zero a block. */
10322
10323      register int n;
10324      register int *zip;
10325
10326      n = INTS_PER_BLOCK;              /* number of integers in a block */
10327      zip = bp->b_int;                 /* where to start clearing */
10328
10329      do { *zip++ = 0;}  while (--n);
10330      bp->b_dirt = DIRTY;
10331    }
```

```
10350      /* This file deals with the suspension and revival of processes.  A process can
10351       * be suspended because it wants to read or write from a pipe and can't, or
10352       * because it wants to read or write from a special file and can't.  When a
10353       * process can't continue it is suspended, and revived later when it is able
10354       * to continue.
10355       *
10356       * The entry points into this file are
10357       *   do_pipe:      perform the PIPE system call
10358       *   pipe_check:   check to see that a read or write on a pipe is feasible now
10359       *   suspend:      suspend a process that cannot do a requested read or write
10360       *   release:      check to see if a suspended process can be released and do it
10361       *   revive:       mark a suspended process as able to run again
10362       *   do_unpause:   a signal has been sent to a process; see if it suspended
10363       */

10365      #include "../h/const.h"
10366      #include "../h/type.h"
10367      #include "../h/callnr.h"
10368      #include "../h/com.h"
10369      #include "../h/error.h"
10370      #include "../h/signal.h"
10371      #include "const.h"
10372      #include "type.h"
10373      #include "file.h"
10374      #include "fproc.h"
10375      #include "glo.h"
10376      #include "inode.h"
10377      #include "param.h"

10379      PRIVATE message mess;

10381      /*===========================================================================*
10382       *                              do_pipe                                       *
10383       *===========================================================================*/
10384      PUBLIC int do_pipe()
10385      {
10386      /* Perform the pipe(fil_des) system call. */

10388        register struct fproc *rfp;
10389        register struct inode *rip;
10390        int r;
10391        dev_nr device;
10392        struct filp *fil_ptr0, *fil_ptr1;
10393        int fil_des[2];                   /* reply goes here */
10394        extern struct inode *alloc_inode();

10396        /* Acquire two file descriptors. */
10397        rfp = fp;
10398        if ( (r = get_fd(R_BIT, &fil_des[0], &fil_ptr0)) != OK) return(r);
10399        rfp->fp_filp[fil_des[0]] = fil_ptr0;
```

```
10400        fil_ptr0->filp_count = 1;
10401        if ( (r = get_fd(W_BIT, &fil_des[1], &fil_ptr1)) != OK) {
10402              rfp->fp_filp[fil_des[0]] = NIL_FILP;
10403              fil_ptr0->filp_count = 0;
10404              return(r);
10405        }
10406        rfp->fp_filp[fil_des[1]] = fil_ptr1;
10407        fil_ptr1->filp_count = 1;
10408
10409        /* Make the inode in the current working directory. */
10410        device = rfp->fp_workdir->i_dev;      /* inode dev is same as working dir */
10411        if ( (rip = alloc_inode(device, I_REGULAR)) == NIL_INODE) {
10412              rfp->fp_filp[fil_des[0]] = NIL_FILP;
10413              fil_ptr0->filp_count = 0;
10414              rfp->fp_filp[fil_des[1]] = NIL_FILP;
10415              fil_ptr1->filp_count = 0;
10416              return(err_code);
10417        }
10418
10419        rip->i_pipe = I_PIPE;
10420        fil_ptr0->filp_ino = rip;
10421        dup_inode(rip);                  /* for double usage */
10422        fil_ptr1->filp_ino = rip;
10423        rw_inode(rip, WRITING);          /* mark inode as allocated */
10424        reply_i1 = fil_des[0];
10425        reply_i2 = fil_des[1];
10426        return(OK);
10427   }


10430   /*===========================================================================*
10431    *                              pipe_check                                    *
10432    *===========================================================================*/
10433   PUBLIC int pipe_check(rip, rw_flag, virgin, bytes, position)
10434   register struct inode *rip;      /* the inode of the pipe */
10435   int rw_flag;                     /* READING or WRITING */
10436   int virgin;                      /* 1 if no data transferred yet, else 0 */
10437   register int bytes;              /* bytes to be read or written (all chunks) */
10438   register file_pos *position;     /* pointer to current file position */
10439   {
10440   /* Pipes are a little different.  If a process reads from an empty pipe for
10441    * which a writer still exists, suspend the reader.  If the pipe is empty
10442    * and there is no writer, return 0 bytes.  If a process is writing to a
10443    * pipe and no one is reading from it, give a broken pipe error.
10444    */
10445
10446     extern struct filp *find_filp();
10447
10448     /* If reading, check for empty pipe. */
10449     if (rw_flag == READING) {
```

```
10450                    if (*position >= rip->i_size) {
10451                            /* Process is reading from an empty pipe. */
10452                            if (find_filp(rip, W_BIT) != NIL_FILP) {
10453                                    /* Writer exists; suspend rdr if no data already read.*/
10454                                    if (virgin) suspend(XPIPE);      /* block reader */
10455
10456                                    /* If need be, activate sleeping writer. */
10457                                    if (susp_count > 0) release(rip, WRITE, 1);
10458                            }
10459                            return(0);
10460                    }
10461            } else {
10462                    /* Process is writing to a pipe. */
10463                    if (find_filp(rip, R_BIT) == NIL_FILP) {
10464                            /* Tell MM to generate a SIGPIPE signal. */
10465                            mess.m_type = KSIG;
10466                            mess.PROC1 = fp - fproc;
10467                            mess.SIG_MAP = 1 << (SIGPIPE - 1);
10468                            send(MM_PROC_NR, &mess);
10469                            return(EPIPE);
10470                    }
10471
10472                    if (*position + bytes > PIPE_SIZE) {
10473                            suspend(XPIPE); /* stop writer -- pipe full */
10474                            return(0);
10475                    }
10476
10477                    /* Writing to an empty pipe.  Search for suspended reader. */
10478                    if (*position == 0) release(rip, READ, 1);
10479            }
10480
10481        return(1);
10482    }


10485    /*===========================================================================*
10486     *                              suspend                                       *
10487     *===========================================================================*/
10488    PUBLIC suspend(task)
10489    int task;                          /* who is proc waiting for? (PIPE = pipe) */
10490    {
10491    /* Take measures to suspend the processing of the present system call.
10492     * Store the parameters to be used upon resuming in the process table.
10493     * (Actually they are not used when a process is waiting for an I/O device,
10494     * but they are needed for pipes, and it is not worth making the distinction.)
10495     */
10496
10497        if (task == XPIPE) susp_count++;        /* count procs suspended on pipe */
10498        fp->fp_suspended = SUSPENDED;
10499        fp->fp_fd = fd << 8 | fs_call;
```

```
10500        fp->fp_buffer = buffer;
10501        fp->fp_nbytes = nbytes;
10502        fp->fp_task = -task;
10503        dont_reply = TRUE;              /* do not send caller a reply message now */
10504    }


10507  /*===========================================================================*
10508   *                              release                                       *
10509   *===========================================================================*/
10510  PUBLIC release(ip, call_nr, count)
10511  register struct inode *ip;        /* inode of pipe */
10512  int call_nr;                      /* READ or WRITE */
10513  int count;                        /* max number of processes to release */
10514  {
10515  /* Check to see if any process is hanging on the pipe whose inode is in '-ip'.
10516   * If one is, and it was trying to perform the call indicated by 'call_nr'
10517   * (READ or WRITE), release it.
10518   */
10519
10520    register struct fproc *rp;
10521
10522    /* Search the proc table. */
10523    for (rp = &fproc[0]; rp < &fproc[NR_PROCS]; rp++) {
10524          if (rp->fp_suspended == SUSPENDED && (rp->fp_fd & BYTE) == call_nr &&
10525                          rp->fp_filp[rp->fp_fd>>8]->filp_ino == ip) {
10526                  revive(rp - fproc, 0);
10527                  susp_count--;    /* keep track of who is suspended */
10528                  if (--count == 0) return;
10529          }
10530    }
10531  }


10534  /*===========================================================================*
10535   *                              revive                                        *
10536   *===========================================================================*/
10537  PUBLIC revive(proc_nr, bytes)
10538  int proc_nr;                      /* process to revive */
10539  int bytes;                        /* if hanging on task, how many bytes read */
10540  {
10541  /* Revive a previously blocked process. When a process hangs on tty, this
10542   * is the way it is eventually released.
10543   */
10544
10545    register struct fproc *rfp;
10546
10547    if (proc_nr < 0 || proc_nr >= NR_PROCS) panic("revive err", proc_nr);
10548    rfp = &fproc[proc_nr];
10549    if (rfp->fp_suspended == NOT_SUSPENDED) return;
```

```
10550
10551          /* The 'reviving' flag only applies to pipes. Processes waiting for TTY get
10552           * a message right away.  The revival process is different for TTY and pipes.
10553           * For TTY revival, the work is already done, for pipes it is not: the proc
10554           * must be restarted so it can try again.
10555           */
10556          if (rfp->fp_task == XPIPE) {
10557                  /* Revive a process suspended on a pipe. */
10558                  rfp->fp_revived = REVIVING;
10559                  reviving++;                 /* process was waiting on pipe */
10560          } else {
10561                  /* Revive a process suspended on TTY or other device. */
10562                  rfp->fp_suspended = NOT_SUSPENDED;
10563                  rfp->fp_nbytes = bytes; /* pretend it only wants what there is */
10564                  reply(proc_nr, bytes);  /* unblock the process */
10565          }
10566  }


10569  /*===========================================================================*
10570   *                              do_unpause                                   *
10571   *===========================================================================*/
10572  PUBLIC int do_unpause()
10573  {
10574  /* A signal has been sent to a user who is paused on the file system.
10575   * Abort the system call with the EINTR error message.
10576   */
10577
10578    register struct fproc *rfp;
10579    int proc_nr, task;
10580    struct filp *f;
10581    dev_nr dev;
10582    extern struct filp *get_filp();
10583
10584    if (who > MM_PROC_NR) return(EPERM);
10585    proc_nr = pro;
10586    if (proc_nr < 0 || proc_nr >= NR_PROCS) panic("unpause err 1", proc_nr);
10587    rfp = &fproc[proc_nr];
10588    if (rfp->fp_suspended == NOT_SUSPENDED) return(OK);
10589    task = -rfp->fp_task;
10590
10591    if (task != XPIPE) {
10592          f = get_filp(rfp->fp_fd);
10593          dev = f->filp_ino->i_zone[0];   /* device on which proc is hanging */
10594          mess.TTY_LINE = (dev >> MINOR) & BYTE;
10595          mess.PROC_NR = proc_nr;
10596          mess.m_type = CANCEL;
10597          if (sendrec(task, &mess) != OK) panic("unpause err 2", NO_NUM);
10598          while (mess.REP_PROC_NR != proc_nr) {
10599                  revive(mess.REP_PROC_NR, mess.REP_STATUS);
```

```
10600                    if (receive(task, &m) != OK) panic("unpause err 3", NO_NUM);
10601            }
10602            revive(proc_nr, EINTR); /* signal interrupted call */
10603        }
10604
10605    return(OK);
10606  }
```

```
10650      /* This file contains the procedures that look up path names in the directory
10651       * system and determine the inode number that goes with a given path name.
10652       *
10653       *  The entry points into this file are
10654       *   eat_path:   the 'main' routine of the path-to-inode conversion mechanism
10655       *   last_dir:   find the final directory on a given path
10656       *   advance:    parse one component of a path name
10657       *   search_dir: search a directory for a string and return its inode number
10658       */

10660      #include "../h/const.h"
10661      #include "../h/type.h"
10662      #include "../h/error.h"
10663      #include "const.h"
10664      #include "type.h"
10665      #include "buf.h"
10666      #include "file.h"
10667      #include "fproc.h"
10668      #include "glo.h"
10669      #include "inode.h"
10670      #include "super.h"

10672      /*===========================================================================*
10673       *                              eat_path                                     *
10674       *===========================================================================*/
10675      PUBLIC struct inode *eat_path(path)
10676      char *path;                          /* the path name to be parsed */
10677      {
10678      /* Parse the path 'path' and put its inode in the inode table.  If not
10679       * possible, return NIL_INODE as function value and an error code in 'err_code'.
10680       */

10682        register struct inode *ldip, *rip;
10683        char string[NAME_SIZE];            /* hold 1 path component name here */
10684        extern struct inode *last_dir(), *advance();

10686        /* First open the path down to the final directory. */
10687        if ( (ldip = last_dir(path, string)) == NIL_INODE)
10688             return(NIL_INODE);           /* we couldn't open final directory */

10690        /* The path consisting only of "/" is a special case, check for it. */
10691        if (string[0] == '\0') return(ldip);

10693        /* Get final component of the path. */
10694        rip = advance(ldip, string);
10695        put_inode(ldip);
10696        return(rip);
10697      }
```

```
10700   /*===========================================================================*
10701    *                              last_dir                                     *
10702    *===========================================================================*/
10703   PUBLIC struct inode *last_dir(path, string)
10704   char *path;                     /* the path name to be parsed */
10705   char string[NAME_SIZE];         /* the final component is returned here */
10706   {
10707   /* Given a path, 'path', located in the fs address space, parse it as
10708    * far as the last directory, fetch the inode for the last directory into
10709    * the inode table, and return a pointer to the inode.  In
10710    * addition, return the final component of the path in 'string'.
10711    * If the last directory can't be opened, return NIL_INODE and
10712    * the reason for failure in 'err_code'.
10713    */
10714
10715     register struct inode *rip;
10716     register char *new_name;
10717     register struct inode *new_ip;
10718     extern struct inode *advance();
10719     extern char *get_name();
10720
10721     /* Is the path absolute or relative?  Initialize 'rip' accordingly. */
10722     rip = (*path == '/' ? fp->fp_rootdir : fp->fp_workdir);
10723     dup_inode(rip);                 /* inode will be returned with put_inode */
10724
10725     /* Scan the path component by component. */
10726     while (TRUE) {
10727             /* Extract one component. */
10728             if ( (new_name = get_name(path, string)) == (char*) 0) {
10729                     put_inode(rip); /* bad path in user space */
10730                     return(NIL_INODE);
10731             }
10732             if (*new_name == '\0') return(rip);     /* normal exit */
10733
10734             /* There is more path.  Keep parsing. */
10735             new_ip = advance(rip, string);
10736             put_inode(rip);                 /* rip either obsolete or irrelevant */
10737             if (new_ip == NIL_INODE) return(NIL_INODE);
10738
10739             /* The call to advance() succeeded.  Fetch next component. */
10740             path = new_name;
10741             rip = new_ip;
10742     }
10743   }


10746   /*===========================================================================*
10747    *                              get_name                                     *
10748    *===========================================================================*/
10749   PRIVATE char *get_name(old_name, string)
```

```
10750        char *old_name;                 /* path name to parse */
10751        char string[NAME_SIZE];         /* component extracted from 'old_name' */
10752     {
10753     /* Given a pointer to a path name in fs space, 'old_name', copy the next
10754      * component to 'string' and pad with zeros.  A pointer to that part of
10755      * the name as yet unparsed is returned.  Roughly speaking,
10756      * 'get_name' = 'old_name' - 'string'.
10757      *
10758      * This routine follows the standard convention that /usr/ast, /usr//ast,
10759      * //usr///ast and /usr/ast/ are all equivalent.
10760      */
10761
10762        register int c;
10763        register char *np, *rnp;
10764
10765        np = string;                    /* 'np' points to current position */
10766        rnp = old_name;                 /* 'rnp' points to unparsed string */
10767        while ( (c = *rnp) == '/') rnp++;     /* skip leading slashes */
10768
10769        /* Copy the unparsed path, 'old_name', to the array, 'string'. */
10770        while ( rnp < &user_path[MAX_PATH]  &&  c != '/'   && c != '\0') {
10771              if (np < &string[NAME_SIZE]) *np++ = c;
10772              c = *++rnp;               /* advance to next character */
10773        }
10774
10775        /* To make /usr/ast/ equivalent to /usr/ast, skip trailing slashes. */
10776        while (c == '/' && rnp < &user_path[MAX_PATH]) c = *++rnp;
10777
10778        /* Pad the component name out to NAME_SIZE chars, using 0 as filler. */
10779        while (np < &string[NAME_SIZE]) *np++ = '\0';
10780
10781        if (rnp >= &user_path[MAX_PATH]) {
10782              err_code = E_LONG_STRING;
10783              return((char *) 0);
10784        }
10785        return(rnp);
10786     }


10789     /*===========================================================================*
10790      *                              advance                                      *
10791      *===========================================================================*/
10792     PUBLIC struct inode *advance(dirp, string)
10793     struct inode *dirp;             /* inode for directory to be searched */
10794     char string[NAME_SIZE];         /* component name to look for */
10795     {
10796     /* Given a directory and a component of a path, look up the component in
10797      * the directory, find the inode, open it, and return a pointer to its inode
10798      * slot.  If it can't be done, return NIL_INODE.
10799      */
```

```
10800
10801        register struct inode *rip;
10802        register struct super_block *sp;
10803        register int r;
10804        dev_nr mnt_dev;
10805        inode_nr numb;
10806        extern struct inode *get_inode();
10807
10808        /* If 'string' is empty, yield same inode straight away. */
10809        if (string[0] == '\0') return(get_inode(dirp->i_dev, dirp->i_num));
10810
10811        /* If 'string' is not present in the directory, signal error. */
10812        if ( (r = search_dir(dirp, string, &numb, LOOK_UP)) != OK) {
10813                err_code = r;
10814                return(NIL_INODE);
10815        }
10816
10817        /* The component has been found in the directory.  Get inode. */
10818        if ( (rip = get_inode(dirp->i_dev, numb)) == NIL_INODE) return(NIL_INODE);
10819
10820        if (rip->i_num == ROOT_INODE)
10821                if (dirp->i_num == ROOT_INODE) {
10822                        if (string[1] == '.') {
10823                                for (sp = &super_block[1]; sp < &super_block[NR_SUPERS]; sp++)
10824                                        if (sp->s_dev == rip->i_dev) {
10825                                                /* Release the root inode.  Replace by the
10826                                                 * inode mounted on.
10827                                                 */
10828                                                put_inode(rip);
10829                                                mnt_dev = sp->s_imount->i_dev;
10830                                                rip = get_inode(mnt_dev, sp->s_imount->i_num);
10831                                                rip = advance(rip, string);
10832                                                break;
10833                                        }
10834                        }
10835                }
10836        }
10837        /* See if the inode is mounted on.  If so, switch to root directory of the
10838         * mounted file system.  The super_block provides the linkage between the
10839         * inode mounted on and the root directory of the mounted file system.
10840         */
10841        while (rip->i_mount == I_MOUNT) {
10842                /* The inode is indeed mounted on. */
10843                for (sp = &super_block[0]; sp < &super_block[NR_SUPERS]; sp++) {
10844                        if (sp->s_imount == rip) {
10845                                /* Release the inode mounted on.  Replace by the
10846                                 * inode of the root inode of the mounted device.
10847                                 */
10848                                put_inode(rip);
10849                                rip = get_inode(sp->s_dev, ROOT_INODE);
```

```
10850                              break;
10851                      }
10852              }
10853      }
10854      return(rip);              /* return pointer to inode's component */
10855  }


10858  /*===========================================================================*
10859   *                              search_dir                                   *
10860   *===========================================================================*/
10861  PUBLIC int search_dir(ldir_ptr, string, numb, flag)
10862  register struct inode *ldir_ptr;        /* ptr to inode for dir to search */
10863  char string[NAME_SIZE];          /* component to search for */
10864  inode_nr *numb;                  /* pointer to inode number */
10865  int flag;                        /* LOOK_UP, ENTER, or DELETE */
10866  {
10867  /* This function searches the directory whose inode is pointed to by 'ldip':
10868   * if (flag == LOOK_UP) search for 'string' and return inode # in 'numb';
10869   * if (flag == ENTER)   enter 'string' in the directory with inode # '*numb';
10870   * if (flag == DELETE) delete 'string' from the directory;
10871   */
10872
10873    register dir_struct *dp;
10874    register struct buf *bp;
10875    register int r;
10876    mask_bits bits;
10877    file_pos pos;
10878    unsigned new_slots, old_slots;
10879    block_nr b;
10880    int e_hit;
10881    extern struct buf *get_block(), *new_block();
10882    extern block_nr read_map();
10883    extern real_time clock_time();
10884
10885    /* If 'ldir_ptr' is not a pointer to a searchable dir inode, error. */
10886    if ( (ldir_ptr->i_mode & I_TYPE) != I_DIRECTORY) return(ENOTDIR);
10887    bits = (flag == LOOK_UP ? X_BIT : W_BIT|X_BIT);
10888    if ( (r = forbidden(ldir_ptr, bits, 0)) != OK)
10889            return(r);
10890
10891    /* Step through the directory one block at a time. */
10892    old_slots = ldir_ptr->i_size/DIR_ENTRY_SIZE;
10893    new_slots = 0;
10894    e_hit = FALSE;
10895    for (pos = 0; pos < ldir_ptr->i_size; pos += BLOCK_SIZE) {
10896            b = read_map(ldir_ptr, pos);     /* get block number */
10897
10898            /* Since directories don't have holes, 'b' cannot be NO_BLOCK. */
10899            bp = get_block(ldir_ptr->i_dev, b, NORMAL);     /* get a dir block */
```

```
10900
10901                 /* Search a directory block. */
10902                 for (dp = &bp->b_dir[0]; dp < &bp->b_dir[NR_DIR_ENTRIES]; dp++) {
10903                         if (++new_slots > old_slots) { /* not found, but room left */
10904                                 if (flag == ENTER) e_hit = TRUE;
10905                                 break;
10906                         }
10907                         if (flag != ENTER && dp->d_inum != 0
10908                                         && cmp_string(dp->d_name, string, NAME_SIZE)) {
10909                                 /* LOOK_UP or DELETE found what it wanted. */
10910                                 if (flag == DELETE) {
10911                                         dp->d_inum = 0; /* erase entry */
10912                                         bp->b_dirt = DIRTY;
10913                                         ldir_ptr->i_modtime = clock_time();
10914                                 } else
10915                                         *numb = dp->d_inum;     /* 'flag' is LOOK_UP */
10916                                 put_block(bp, DIRECTORY_BLOCK);
10917                                 return(OK);
10918                         }
10919
10920                         /* Check for free slot for the benefit of ENTER. */
10921                         if (flag == ENTER && dp->d_inum == 0) {
10922                                 e_hit = TRUE;   /* we found a free slot */
10923                                 break;
10924                         }
10925                 }
10926
10927                 /* The whole block has been searched or ENTER has a free slot. */
10928                 if (e_hit) break;        /* e_hit set if ENTER can be performed now */
10929                 put_block(bp, DIRECTORY_BLOCK); /* otherwise, continue searching dir */
10930         }
10931
10932         /* The whole directory has now been searched. */
10933         if (flag != ENTER) return(ENOENT);
10934
10935         /* This call is for ENTER.  If no free slot has been found so far, try to
10936          * extend directory.
10937          */
10938         if (e_hit == FALSE) { /* directory is full and no room left in last block */
10939                 new_slots ++;           /* increase directory size by 1 entry */
10940                 if (new_slots == 0) return(EFBIG); /* dir size limited by slot count */
10941                 if ( (bp = new_block(ldir_ptr, ldir_ptr->i_size)) == NIL_BUF)
10942                         return(err_code);
10943                 dp = &bp->b_dir[0];
10944         }
10945
10946         /* 'bp' now points to a directory block with space. 'dp' points to slot. */
10947         copy(dp->d_name, string, NAME_SIZE);
10948         dp->d_inum = *numb;
10949         bp->b_dirt = DIRTY;
```

```
10950          put_block(bp, DIRECTORY_BLOCK);
10951          ldir_ptr->i_modtime = clock_time();
10952          ldir_ptr->i_dirt = DIRTY;
10953          if (new_slots > old_slots)
10954                  ldir_ptr->i_size = (file_pos) new_slots * DIR_ENTRY_SIZE;
10955          return(OK);
10956      }
```

```
11000   /* This file performs the MOUNT and UMOUNT system calls.
11001    *
11002    * The entry points into this file are
11003    *   do_mount:  perform the MOUNT system call
11004    *   do_umount: perform the UMOUNT system call
11005    */
11006
11007   #include "../h/const.h"
11008   #include "../h/type.h"
11009   #include "../h/error.h"
11010   #include "const.h"
11011   #include "type.h"
11012   #include "buf.h"
11013   #include "file.h"
11014   #include "fproc.h"
11015   #include "glo.h"
11016   #include "inode.h"
11017   #include "param.h"
11018   #include "super.h"
11019
11020   /*===========================================================================*
11021    *                              do_mount                                     *
11022    *===========================================================================*/
11023   PUBLIC int do_mount()
11024   {
11025   /* Perform the mount(name, mfile, rd_only) system call. */
11026
11027     register struct inode *rip, *root_ip;
11028     register struct super_block *xp, *sp;
11029     register dev_nr dev;
11030     register mask_bits bits;
11031     register int r;
11032     int found;
11033     extern struct inode *get_inode(), *eat_path();
11034     extern dev_nr name_to_dev();
11035
11036     /* Only the super-user may do MOUNT. */
11037     if (!super_user) return(EPERM);
11038
11039     /* If 'name' is not for a block special file, return error. */
11040     if (fetch_name(name1, name1_length, M1) != OK) return(err_code);
11041     if ( (dev = name_to_dev(user_path)) == NO_DEV) return(err_code);
11042
11043     /* Scan super block table to see if dev already mounted & find a free slot.*/
11044     sp = NIL_SUPER;
11045     found = FALSE;
11046     for (xp = &super_block[0]; xp < &super_block[NR_SUPERS]; xp++) {
11047           if (xp->s_dev == dev) found = TRUE;      /* is it mounted already? */
11048           if (xp->s_dev == NO_DEV) sp = xp;        /* record free slot */
11049     }
```

```
11050        if (found) return(EBUSY);       /* already mounted */
11051        if (sp == NIL_SUPER) return(ENFILE);  /* no super block available */
11052
11053        /* Fill in the super block. */
11054        sp->s_dev = dev;                /* rw_super() needs to know which dev */
11055        rw_super(sp, READING);
11056        sp->s_dev = dev;                /* however, rw_super() overwrites s_dev */
11057
11058        /* Make a few basic checks to see if super block looks reasonable. */
11059        if (sp->s_magic != SUPER_MAGIC || sp->s_ninodes < 1 || sp->s_nzones < 1 ||
11060                          sp->s_imap_blocks < 1 || sp->s_zmap_blocks < 1) {
11061                sp->s_dev = NO_DEV;
11062                return(EINVAL);
11063        }
11064
11065        /* Now get the inode of the file to be mounted on. */
11066        if (fetch_name(name2, name2_length, M1) != OK) {
11067                sp->s_dev = NO_DEV;
11068                return(err_code);
11069        }
11070        if ( (rip = eat_path(user_path)) == NIL_INODE) {
11071                sp->s_dev = NO_DEV;
11072                return(err_code);
11073        }
11074
11075        /* It may not be busy. */
11076        r = OK;
11077        if (rip->i_count > 1) r = EBUSY;
11078
11079        /* It may not be special. */
11080        bits = rip->i_mode & I_TYPE;
11081        if (bits == I_BLOCK_SPECIAL || bits == I_CHAR_SPECIAL) r = ENOTDIR;
11082
11083        /* Get the root inode of the mounted file system. */
11084        root_ip = NIL_INODE;            /* if 'r' not OK, make sure this is defined */
11085        if (r == OK) {
11086                if ( (root_ip = get_inode(dev, ROOT_INODE)) == NIL_INODE) r = err_code;
11087        }
11088
11089        /* Load the i-node and zone bit maps from the new device. */
11090        if (r == OK) {
11091                if (load_bit_maps(dev) != OK) r = ENFILE;       /* load bit maps */
11092        }
11093
11094        /* If error, return the super block and the inodes. */
11095        if (r != OK) {
11096                sp->s_dev = NO_DEV;
11097                put_inode(rip);
11098                put_inode(root_ip);
11099                return(r);
```

```
11100          }
11101
11102          /* File types of 'rip' and 'root_ip' may not conflict. */
11103          if ( (rip->i_mode & I_TYPE) == I_DIRECTORY &&
11104                  (root_ip->i_mode & I_TYPE) != I_DIRECTORY) r = ENOTDIR;
11105
11106          /* If error, return the super block and both inodes. */
11107          if (r != OK) {
11108                  sp->s_dev = NO_DEV;
11109                  put_inode(rip);
11110                  put_inode(root_ip);
11111                  return(r);
11112          }
11113
11114          /* Nothing else can go wrong.  Perform the mount. */
11115          rip->i_mount = I_MOUNT;          /* this bit says the inode is mounted on */
11116          sp->s_imount = rip;
11117          sp->s_isup = root_ip;
11118          sp->s_rd_only = rd_only;
11119          return(OK);
11120          }
11121
11122
11123          /*===========================================================================*
11124           *                              do_umount                                    *
11125           *===========================================================================*/
11126          PUBLIC int do_umount()
11127          {
11128          /* Perform the umount(name) system call. */
11129
11130            register struct inode *rip;
11131            struct super_block *sp, *sp1;
11132            dev_nr dev;
11133            int count;
11134            extern dev_nr name_to_dev();
11135
11136
11137            /* Only the super-user may do UMOUNT. */
11138            if (!super_user) return(EPERM);
11139
11140            /* If 'name' is not for a block special file, return error. */
11141            if (fetch_name(name, name_length, M3) != OK) return(err_code);
11142            if ( (dev = name_to_dev(user_path)) == NO_DEV) return(err_code);
11143
11144            /* See if the mounted device is busy.  Only 1 inode using it should be
11145             * open -- the root inode -- and that inode only 1 time.
11146             */
11147            count = 0;
11148            for (rip = &inode[0]; rip< &inode[NR_INODES]; rip++)
11149                    if (rip->i_count > 0 && rip->i_dev == dev) count += rip->i_count;
```

```
11150        if (count > 1) return(EBUSY); /* can't umount a busy file system */
11151
11152        /* Find the super block. */
11153        sp = NIL_SUPER;
11154        for (sp1 = &super_block[0]; sp1 < &super_block[NR_SUPERS]; sp1++) {
11155            if (sp1->s_dev == dev) {
11156                    sp = sp1;
11157                    break;
11158            }
11159        }
11160        if (sp == NIL_SUPER) return(EINVAL);
11161
11162        /* Release the bit maps, sync the disk, and invalidate cache. */
11163        if (unload_bit_maps(dev) != OK) panic("do_umount", NO_NUM);
11164        do_sync();                        /* force any cached blocks out of memory */
11165        invalidate(dev);                  /* invalidate cache entries for this dev */
11166
11167        /* Finish off the unmount. */
11168        sp->s_imount->i_mount = NO_MOUNT;     /* inode returns to normal */
11169        put_inode(sp->s_imount);         /* release the inode mounted on */
11170        put_inode(sp->s_isup);           /* release the root inode of the mounted fs */
11171        sp->s_imount = NIL_INODE;
11172        sp->s_dev = NO_DEV;
11173        return(OK);
11174    }


11177    /*===========================================================================*
11178     *                            name_to_dev                                    *
11179     *===========================================================================*/
11180    PRIVATE dev_nr name_to_dev(path)
11181    char *path;                          /* pointer to path name */
11182    {
11183    /* Convert the block special file 'path' to a device number.  If 'path'
11184     * is not a block special file, return error code in 'err_code'.
11185     */
11186
11187        register struct inode *rip;
11188        register dev_nr dev;
11189        extern struct inode *eat_path();
11190
11191        /* If 'path' can't be opened, give up immediately. */
11192        if ( (rip = eat_path(path)) == NIL_INODE) return(NO_DEV);
11193
11194        /* If 'path' is not a block special file, return error. */
11195        if ( (rip->i_mode & I_TYPE) != I_BLOCK_SPECIAL) {
11196            err_code = ENOTBLK;
11197            put_inode(rip);
11198            return(NO_DEV);
11199        }
```

```
11200
11201        /* Extract the device number. */
11202        dev = (dev_nr) rip->i_zone[0];
11203        put_inode(rip);
11204        return(dev);
11205    }
```

```
11250   /* This file handles the LINK and UNLINK system calls.  It also deals with
11251    * deallocating the storage used by a file when the last UNLINK is done to a
11252    * file and the blocks must be returned to the free block pool.
11253    *
11254    * The entry points into this file are
11255    *   do_link:   perform the LINK system call
11256    *   do_unlink: perform the UNLINK system call
11257    *   truncate:  release all the blocks associated with an inode
11258    */
11259
11260   #include "../h/const.h"
11261   #include "../h/type.h"
11262   #include "../h/error.h"
11263   #include "const.h"
11264   #include "type.h"
11265   #include "buf.h"
11266   #include "file.h"
11267   #include "fproc.h"
11268   #include "glo.h"
11269   #include "inode.h"
11270   #include "param.h"
11271
11272   /*===========================================================================*
11273    *                              do_link                                       *
11274    *===========================================================================*/
11275   PUBLIC int do_link()
11276   {
11277   /* Perform the link(name, name2) system call. */
11278
11279     register struct inode *ip, *rip;
11280     register int r;
11281     char string[NAME_SIZE];
11282     struct inode *new_ip;
11283     extern struct inode *advance(), *last_dir(), *eat_path();
11284
11285     /* See if 'name' (file to be linked) exists. */
11286     if (fetch_name(name1, name1_length, M1) != OK) return(err_code);
11287     if ( (rip = eat_path(user_path)) == NIL_INODE) return(err_code);
11288
11289     /* Check to see if the file has maximum number of links already. */
11290     r = OK;
11291     if ( (rip->i_nlinks & BYTE) == MAX_LINKS) r = EMLINK;
11292
11293     /* Only super_user may link to directories. */
11294     if (r == OK)
11295           if ( (rip->i_mode & I_TYPE) == I_DIRECTORY && !super_user) r = EPERM;
11296
11297     /* If error with 'name', return the inode. */
11298     if (r != OK) {
11299           put_inode(rip);
```

```
11300              return(r);
11301        }
11302
11303        /* Does the final directory of 'name2' exist? */
11304        if (fetch_name(name2, name2_length, M1) != OK) return(err_code);
11305        if ( (ip = last_dir(user_path, string)) == NIL_INODE) r = err_code;
11306
11307        /* If 'name2' exists in full (even if no space) set 'r' to error. */
11308        if (r == OK) {
11309              if ( (new_ip = advance(ip, string)) == NIL_INODE) {
11310                    r = err_code;
11311                    if (r == ENOENT) r = OK;
11312              } else {
11313                    put_inode(new_ip);
11314                    r = EEXIST;
11315              }
11316        }
11317
11318        /* Check for links across devices. */
11319        if (r == OK)
11320              if (rip->i_dev != ip->i_dev) r = EXDEV;
11321
11322        /* Try to link. */
11323        if (r == OK)
11324              r = search_dir(ip, string, &rip->i_num, ENTER);
11325
11326        /* If success, register the linking. */
11327        if (r == OK) {
11328              rip->i_nlinks++;
11329              rip->i_dirt = DIRTY;
11330        }
11331
11332        /* Done.  Release both inodes. */
11333        put_inode(rip);
11334        put_inode(ip);
11335        return(r);
11336    }


11339    /*===========================================================================*
11340     *                              do_unlink                                     *
11341     *===========================================================================*/
11342    PUBLIC int do_unlink()
11343    {
11344    /* Perform the unlink(name) system call. */
11345
11346        register struct inode *rip, *rlast_dir_ptr;
11347        register int r;
11348        inode_nr numb;
11349        char string[NAME_SIZE];
```

```
11350        extern struct inode *advance(), *last_dir();
11351
11352        /* Get the last directory in the path. */
11353        if (fetch_name(name, name_length, M3) != OK) return(err_code);
11354        if ( (rlast_dir_ptr = last_dir(user_path, string)) == NIL_INODE)
11355             return(err_code);
11356
11357        /* The last directory exists.  Does the file also exist? */
11358        r = OK;
11359        if ( (rip = advance(rlast_dir_ptr, string)) == NIL_INODE) r = err_code;
11360
11361        /* If error, return inode. */
11362        if (r != OK) {
11363             put_inode(rlast_dir_ptr);
11364             return(r);
11365        }
11366
11367        /* See if the file is a directory. */
11368        if ( (rip->i_mode & I_TYPE) == I_DIRECTORY && !super_user)
11369             r = EPERM;                      /* only super_user can unlink directory */
11370        if (r == OK)
11371             r = search_dir(rlast_dir_ptr, string, &numb, DELETE);
11372
11373        if (r == OK) {
11374             rip->i_nlinks--;
11375             rip->i_dirt = DIRTY;
11376        }
11377
11378        /* If unlink was possible, it has been done, otherwise it has not. */
11379        put_inode(rip);
11380        put_inode(rlast_dir_ptr);
11381        return(r);
11382   }


11385   /*==============================================================================*
11386    *                              truncate                                        *
11387    *==============================================================================*/
11388   PUBLIC truncate(rip)
11389   register struct inode *rip;     /* pointer to inode to be truncated */
11390   {
11391   /* Remove all the zones from the inode 'rip' and mark it dirty. */
11392
11393      register file_pos position;
11394      register zone_type zone_size;
11395      register block_nr b;
11396      register zone_nr z, *iz;
11397      register int scale;
11398      register struct buf *bp;
11399      register dev_nr dev;
```

```
11400        extern struct buf *get_block();
11401        extern block_nr read_map();

11403        dev = rip->i_dev;                   /* device on which inode resides */
11404        scale = scale_factor(rip);
11405        zone_size = (zone_type) BLOCK_SIZE << scale;
11406        if (rip->i_pipe == I_PIPE) rip->i_size = PIPE_SIZE;    /* pipes can shrink */

11408        /* Step through the file a zone at a time, finding and freeing the zones. */
11409        for (position = 0; position < rip->i_size; position += zone_size) {
11410              if ( (b = read_map(rip, position)) != NO_BLOCK) {
11411                    z = (zone_nr) b >> scale;
11412                    free_zone(dev, z);
11413              }
11414        }

11416        /* All the data zones have been freed.  Now free the indirect zones. */
11417        free_zone(dev, rip->i_zone[NR_DZONE_NUM]);      /* single indirect zone */
11418        if ( (z = rip->i_zone[NR_DZONE_NUM+1]) != NO_ZONE) {
11419              b = (block_nr) z << scale;
11420              bp = get_block(dev, b, NORMAL); /* get double indirect zone */
11421              for (iz = &bp->b_ind[0]; iz < &bp->b_ind[NR_INDIRECTS]; iz++) {
11422                    free_zone(dev, *iz);
11423              }

11425              /* Now free the double indirect zone itself. */
11426              put_block(bp, INDIRECT_BLOCK);
11427              free_zone(dev, z);
11428        }

11430        /* The inode being truncated might currently be open, so certain fields must
11431         * be cleared immediately, even though these fields are also cleared by
11432         * alloc_inode(). The function wipe_inode() does the dirty work in both cases
11433         */
11434        wipe_inode(rip);
11435 }
```

```
11450       /* This file contains the code for performing four system calls relating to
11451        * status and directories.
11452        *
11453        * The entry points into this file are
11454        *   do_chdir:  perform the CHDIR system call
11455        *   do_chroot: perform the CHROOT system call
11456        *   do_stat:   perform the STAT system call
11457        *   do_fstat:  perform the FSTAT system call
11458        */
11459
11460       #include "../h/const.h"
11461       #include "../h/type.h"
11462       #include "../h/error.h"
11463       #include "../h/stat.h"
11464       #include "const.h"
11465       #include "type.h"
11466       #include "file.h"
11467       #include "fproc.h"
11468       #include "glo.h"
11469       #include "inode.h"
11470       #include "param.h"
11471
11472       /*===========================================================================*
11473        *                              do_chdir                                      *
11474        *===========================================================================*/
11475       PUBLIC int do_chdir()
11476       {
11477       /* Change directory.  This function is  also called by MM to simulate a chdir
11478        * in order to do EXEC, etc.
11479        */
11480
11481         register struct fproc *rfp;
11482
11483         if (who == MM_PROC_NR) {
11484              rfp = &fproc[slot1];
11485              put_inode(fp->fp_workdir);
11486              fp->fp_workdir = (cd_flag ? fp->fp_rootdir : rfp->fp_workdir);
11487              dup_inode(fp->fp_workdir);
11488              fp->fp_effuid = (cd_flag ? SUPER_USER : rfp->fp_effuid);
11489              return(OK);
11490         }
11491
11492       /* Perform the chdir(name) system call. */
11493         return change(&fp->fp_workdir, name, name_length);
11494       }
11495
11496
11497       /*===========================================================================*
11498        *                              do_chroot                                     *
11499        *===========================================================================*/
```

```
11500   PUBLIC int do_chroot()
11501   {
11502   /* Perform the chroot(name) system call. */
11503
11504     register int r;
11505
11506     if (!super_user) return(EPERM);        /* only su may chroot() */
11507     r = change(&fp->fp_rootdir, name, name_length);
11508     return(r);
11509   }


11512   /*===========================================================================*
11513    *                              change                                       *
11514    *===========================================================================*/
11515   PRIVATE int change(iip, name_ptr, len)
11516   struct inode **iip;              /* pointer to the inode pointer for the dir */
11517   char *name_ptr;                 /* pointer to the directory name to change to */
11518   int len;                        /* length of the directory name string */
11519   {
11520   /* Do the actual work for chdir() and chroot(). */
11521
11522     struct inode *rip;
11523     register int r;
11524     extern struct inode *eat_path();
11525
11526     /* Try to open the new directory. */
11527     if (fetch_name(name_ptr, len, M3) != OK) return(err_code);
11528     if ( (rip = eat_path(user_path)) == NIL_INODE) return(err_code);
11529
11530     /* It must be a directory and also be searchable. */
11531     if ( (rip->i_mode & I_TYPE) != I_DIRECTORY)
11532             r = ENOTDIR;
11533     else
11534             r = forbidden(rip, X_BIT, 0);   /* check if dir is searchable */
11535
11536     /* If error, return inode. */
11537     if (r != OK) {
11538             put_inode(rip);
11539             return(r);
11540     }
11541
11542     /* Everything is OK.  Make the change. */
11543     put_inode(*iip);                /* release the old directory */
11544     *iip = rip;                     /* acquire the new one */
11545     return(OK);
11546   }
```

```
11550      /*===========================================================================*
11551       *                              do_stat                                      *
11552       *===========================================================================*/
11553      PUBLIC int do_stat()
11554      {
11555      /* Perform the stat(name, buf) system call. */
11556
11557        register struct inode *rip;
11558        register int r;
11559        extern struct inode *eat_path();
11560
11561        /* Both stat() and fstat() use the same routine to do the real work.  That
11562         * routine expects an inode, so acquire it temporarily.
11563         */
11564        if (fetch_name(name1, name1_length, M1) != OK) return(err_code);
11565        if ( (rip = eat_path(user_path)) == NIL_INODE) return(err_code);
11566        r = stat_inode(rip, NIL_FILP, name2); /* actually do the work.*/
11567        put_inode(rip);                    /* release the inode */
11568        return(r);
11569      }


11572      /*===========================================================================*
11573       *                              do_fstat                                     *
11574       *===========================================================================*/
11575      PUBLIC int do_fstat()
11576      {
11577      /* Perform the fstat(fd, buf) system call. */
11578
11579        register struct filp *rfilp;
11580        extern struct filp *get_filp();
11581
11582        /* Is the file descriptor valid? */
11583        if ( (rfilp = get_filp(fd)) == NIL_FILP) return(err_code);
11584
11585        return(stat_inode(rfilp->filp_ino, rfilp, buffer));
11586      }


11589      /*===========================================================================*
11590       *                              stat_inode                                   *
11591       *===========================================================================*/
11592      PRIVATE int stat_inode(rip, fil_ptr, user_addr)
11593      register struct inode *rip;     /* pointer to inode to stat */
11594      struct filp *fil_ptr;           /* filp pointer, supplied by 'fstat' */
11595      char *user_addr;                        /* user space address where stat buf goes */
11596      {
11597      /* Common code for stat and fstat system calls. */
11598
11599        register struct stat *stp;
```

```
11600          struct stat statbuf;
11601          int r;
11602          vir_bytes v;
11603
11604          /* Fill in the statbuf struct. */
11605          stp = &statbuf;                    /* set up pointer to the buffer */
11606          stp->st_dev = (int) rip->i_dev;
11607          stp->st_ino = rip->i_num;
11608          stp->st_mode = rip->i_mode;
11609          stp->st_nlink = rip->i_nlinks & BYTE;
11610          stp->st_uid = rip->i_uid;
11611          stp->st_gid = rip->i_gid & BYTE;
11612          stp->st_rdev = rip->i_zone[0];
11613          stp->st_size = rip->i_size;
11614          if (  (rip->i_pipe == I_PIPE) &&        /* IF it is a pipe */
11615                (fil_ptr != NIL_FILP) &&         /* AND it was fstat */
11616                (fil_ptr->filp_mode == R_BIT))   /* on the reading end, */
11617                  stp->st_size -= fil_ptr->filp_pos; /* adjust the visible size. */
11618          stp->st_atime = rip->i_modtime;
11619          stp->st_mtime = rip->i_modtime;
11620          stp->st_ctime = rip->i_modtime;
11621
11622          /* Copy the struct to user space. */
11623          v = (vir_bytes) user_addr;
11624          r = rw_user(D, who, v, (vir_bytes) sizeof statbuf, (char *) stp, TO_USER);
11625          return(r);
11626        }
```

```
11650    /* This file deals with protection in the file system.  It contains the code
11651     * for four system calls that relate to protection.
11652     *
11653     * The entry points into this file are
11654     *   do_chmod:  perform the CHMOD system call
11655     *   do_chown:  perform the CHOWN system call
11656     *   do_umask:  perform the UMASK system call
11657     *   do_access: perform the ACCESS system call
11658     *   forbidden: check to see if a given access is allowed on a given inode
11659     */
11660
11661    #include "../h/const.h"
11662    #include "../h/type.h"
11663    #include "../h/error.h"
11664    #include "const.h"
11665    #include "type.h"
11666    #include "buf.h"
11667    #include "file.h"
11668    #include "fproc.h"
11669    #include "glo.h"
11670    #include "inode.h"
11671    #include "param.h"
11672    #include "super.h"
11673
11674    /*===========================================================================*
11675     *                              do_chmod                                      *
11676     *===========================================================================*/
11677    PUBLIC int do_chmod()
11678    {
11679    /* Perform the chmod(name, mode) system call. */
11680
11681      register struct inode *rip;
11682      register int r;
11683      extern struct inode *eat_path();
11684
11685      /* Temporarily open the file. */
11686      if (fetch_name(name, name_length, M3) != OK) return(err_code);
11687      if ( (rip = eat_path(user_path)) == NIL_INODE) return(err_code);
11688
11689      /* Only the owner or the super_user may change the mode of a file.
11690       * No one may change the mode of a file on a read-only file system.
11691       */
11692      if (rip->i_uid != fp->fp_effuid && !super_user)
11693            r = EPERM;
11694      else
11695            r = read_only(rip);
11696
11697      /* If error, return inode. */
11698      if (r != OK) {
11699            put_inode(rip);
```

```
11700              return(r);
11701      }
11702
11703      /* Now make the change. */
11704      rip->i_mode = (rip->i_mode & ~ALL_MODES) | (mode & ALL_MODES);
11705      rip->i_dirt = DIRTY;
11706
11707      put_inode(rip);
11708      return(OK);
11709  }


11712  /*===========================================================================*
11713   *                              do_chown                                     *
11714   *===========================================================================*/
11715  PUBLIC int do_chown()
11716  {
11717  /* Perform the chown(name, owner, group) system call. */
11718
11719    register struct inode *rip;
11720    register int r;
11721    extern struct inode *eat_path();
11722
11723    /* Only the super_user may perform the chown() call. */
11724    if (!super_user) return(EPERM);
11725
11726    /* Temporarily open the file. */
11727    if (fetch_name(namel, namel_length, M1) != OK) return(err_code);
11728    if ( (rip = eat_path(user_path)) == NIL_INODE) return(err_code);
11729
11730    /* Not permitted to change the owner of a file on a read-only file sys. */
11731    r = read_only(rip);
11732    if (r == OK) {
11733            rip->i_uid = owner;
11734            rip->i_gid = group;
11735            rip->i_dirt = DIRTY;
11736    }
11737
11738    put_inode(rip);
11739    return(r);
11740  }


11743  /*===========================================================================*
11744   *                              do_umask                                     *
11745   *===========================================================================*/
11746  PUBLIC int do_umask()
11747  {
11748  /* Perform the umask(co_mode) system call. */
11749    register mask_bits r;
```

```
11750
11751        r = ~fp->fp_umask;                /* set 'r' to complement of old mask */
11752        fp->fp_umask = ~(co_mode & RWX_MODES);
11753        return(r);                       /* return complement of old mask */
11754    }


11757    /*===========================================================================*
11758     *                              do_access                                    *
11759     *===========================================================================*/
11760    PUBLIC int do_access()
11761    {
11762    /* Perform the access(name, mode) system call. */
11763
11764        struct inode *rip;
11765        register int r;
11766        extern struct inode *eat_path();
11767
11768        /* Temporarily open the file whose access is to be checked. */
11769        if (fetch_name(name, name_length, M3) != OK) return(err_code);
11770        if ( (rip = eat_path(user_path)) == NIL_INODE) return(err_code);
11771
11772        /* Now check the permissions. */
11773        r = forbidden(rip, (mask_bits) mode, 1);
11774        put_inode(rip);
11775        return(r);
11776    }


11779    /*===========================================================================*
11780     *                              forbidden                                    *
11781     *===========================================================================*/
11782    PUBLIC int forbidden(rip, access_desired, real_uid)
11783    register struct inode *rip;       /* pointer to inode to be checked */
11784    mask_bits access_desired;         /* RWX bits */
11785    int real_uid;                     /* set iff real uid to be tested */
11786    {
11787    /* Given a pointer to an inode, 'rip', and the accessed desired, determine
11788     * if the access is allowed, and if not why not.  The routine looks up the
11789     * caller's uid in the 'fproc' table.  If the access is allowed, OK is returned
11790     * if it is forbidden, EACCES is returned.
11791     */
11792
11793        register mask_bits bits, perm_bits, xmask;
11794        int r, shift, test_uid, test_gid;
11795
11796        /* Isolate the relevant rwx bits from the mode. */
11797        bits = rip->i_mode;
11798        test_uid = (real_uid ? fp->fp_realuid : fp->fp_effuid);
11799        test_gid = (real_uid ? fp->fp_realgid : fp->fp_effgid);
```

```
11800          if (super_user) {
11801                  perm_bits = 07;
11802          } else {
11803                  if (test_uid == rip->i_uid) shift = 6;          /* owner */
11804                  else if (test_gid == rip->i_gid ) shift = 3;    /* group */
11805                  else shift = 0;                                 /* other */
11806                  perm_bits = (bits >> shift) & 07;
11807          }
11808
11809          /* If access desired is not a subset of what is allowed, it is refused. */
11810          r = OK;
11811          if ((perm_bits | access_desired) != perm_bits) r = EACCES;
11812
11813          /* If none of the X bits are on, not even the super-user can execute it. */
11814          xmask = (X_BIT << 6) | (X_BIT << 3) | X_BIT;  /* all 3 X bits */
11815          if ( (access_desired & X_BIT) && (bits & xmask) == 0) r = EACCES;
11816
11817          /* Check to see if someone is trying to write on a file system that is
11818           * mounted read-only.
11819           */
11820          if (r == OK)
11821                  if (access_desired & W_BIT) r = read_only(rip);
11822
11823      return(r);
11824    }


11827    /*===========================================================================*
11828     *                              read_only                                    *
11829     *===========================================================================*/
11830    PRIVATE int read_only(ip)
11831    struct inode *ip;                /* ptr to inode whose file sys is to be cked */
11832    {
11833    /* Check to see if the file system on which the inode 'ip' resides is mounted
11834     * read only.  If so, return EROFS, else return OK.
11835     */
11836
11837      register struct super_block *sp;
11838      extern struct super_block *get_super();
11839
11840      sp = get_super(ip->i_dev);
11841      return(sp->s_rd_only ? EROFS : OK);
11842    }
```

```
11850      /* This file takes care of those system calls that deal with time.
11851       *
11852       * The entry points into this file are
11853       *   do_utime:  perform the UTIME system call
11854       *   do_time:   perform the TIME system call
11855       *   do_stime:  perform the STIME system call
11856       *   do_tims:   perform the TIMES system call
11857       */
11858
11859      #include "../h/const.h"
11860      #include "../h/type.h"
11861      #include "../h/callnr.h"
11862      #include "../h/com.h"
11863      #include "../h/error.h"
11864      #include "const.h"
11865      #include "type.h"
11866      #include "file.h"
11867      #include "fproc.h"
11868      #include "glo.h"
11869      #include "inode.h"
11870      #include "param.h"
11871
11872      PRIVATE message clock_mess;
11873
11874      /*===========================================================================*
11875       *                              do_utime                                      *
11876       *===========================================================================*/
11877      PUBLIC int do_utime()
11878      {
11879      /* Perform the utime(name, timep) system call. */
11880
11881        register struct inode *rip;
11882        register int r;
11883        extern struct inode *eat_path();
11884
11885        /* Temporarily open the file. */
11886        if (fetch_name(utime_file, utime_length, M1) != OK) return(err_code);
11887        if ( (rip = eat_path(user_path)) == NIL_INODE) return(err_code);
11888
11889        /* Only the owner of a file or the super_user can change its time. */
11890        r = OK;
11891        if (rip->i_uid != fp->fp_effuid && !super_user) r = EPERM;
11892        if (r == OK) {
11893              rip->i_modtime = update_time;
11894              rip->i_dirt = DIRTY;
11895        }
11896
11897        put_inode(rip);
11898        return(r);
11899      }
```

```
11902    /*===========================================================================*
11903     *                              do_time                                       *
11904     *===========================================================================*/
11905    PUBLIC int do_time()
11906
11907    {
11908    /* Perform the time(tp) system call. */
11909
11910      extern real_time clock_time();
11911
11912      reply_l1 = clock_time();        /* return time in seconds */
11913      return(OK);
11914    }


11917    /*===========================================================================*
11918     *                              do_stime                                      *
11919     *===========================================================================*/
11920    PUBLIC int do_stime()
11921    {
11922    /* Perform the stime(tp) system call. */
11923
11924      register int k;
11925
11926      if (!super_user) return(EPERM);
11927      clock_mess.m_type = SET_TIME;
11928      clock_mess.NEW_TIME = (long) tp;
11929      if ( (k = sendrec(CLOCK, &clock_mess)) != OK) panic("do_stime error", k);
11930      return (OK);
11931    }


11934    /*===========================================================================*
11935     *                              do_tims                                       *
11936     *===========================================================================*/
11937    PUBLIC int do_tims()
11938    {
11939    /* Perform the times(buffer) system call. */
11940
11941      real_time t[4];
11942
11943      sys_times(who, t);
11944      reply_t1 = t[0];
11945      reply_t2 = t[1];
11946      reply_t3 = t[2];
11947      reply_t4 = t[3];
11948      return(OK);
11949    }
```

```
11950      /* This file contains a collection of miscellaneous procedures.  Some of them
11951       * perform simple system calls.  Some others do a little part of system calls
11952       * that are mostly performed by the Memory Manager.
11953       *
11954       * The entry points into this file are
11955       *   do_dup:    perform the DUP system call
11956       *   do_sync:   perform the SYNC system call
11957       *   do_fork:   adjust the tables after MM has performed a FORK system call
11958       *   do_exit:   a process has exited; note that in the tables
11959       *   do_set:    set uid or gid for some process
11960       *   do_revive: revive a process that was waiting for something (e.g. TTY)
11961       */
11962
11963      #include "../h/const.h"
11964      #include "../h/type.h"
11965      #include "../h/callnr.h"
11966      #include "../h/com.h"
11967      #include "../h/error.h"
11968      #include "const.h"
11969      #include "type.h"
11970      #include "buf.h"
11971      #include "file.h"
11972      #include "fproc.h"
11973      #include "glo.h"
11974      #include "inode.h"
11975      #include "param.h"
11976      #include "super.h"
11977
11978      /*===========================================================================*
11979       *                              do_dup                                       *
11980       *===========================================================================*/
11981      PUBLIC int do_dup()
11982      {
11983      /* Perform the dup(fd) or dup(fd,fd2) system call. */
11984
11985        register int rfd;
11986        register struct fproc *rfp;
11987        struct filp *dummy;
11988        int r;
11989        extern struct filp *get_filp();
11990
11991        /* Is the file descriptor valid? */
11992        rfd = fd & ~DUP_MASK;          /* kill off dup2 bit, if on */
11993        rfp = fp;
11994        if (get_filp(rfd) == NIL_FILP) return(err_code);
11995
11996        /* Distinguish between dup and dup2. */
11997        if (fd == rfd) {                       /* bit not on */
11998              /* dup(fd) */
11999              if ( (r = get_fd(0, &fd2, &dummy)) != OK) return(r);
```

```
12000        } else {
12001            /* dup2(fd, fd2) */
12002            if (fd2 < 0 || fd2 >= NR_FDS) return(EBADF);
12003            if (rfd == fd2) return(fd2);     /* ignore the call: dup2(x, x) */
12004            fd = fd2;                  /* prepare to close fd2 */
12005            do_close();                /* cannot fail */
12006        }
12007
12008        /* Success. Set up new file descriptors. */
12009        rfp->fp_filp[fd2] = rfp->fp_filp[rfd];
12010        rfp->fp_filp[fd2]->filp_count++;
12011        return(fd2);
12012    }


12015    /*===========================================================================*
12016     *                              do_sync                                       *
12017     *===========================================================================*/
12018    PUBLIC int do_sync()
12019    {
12020    /* Perform the sync() system call.  Flush all the tables. */
12021
12022        register struct inode *rip;
12023        register struct buf *bp;
12024        register struct super_block *sp;
12025        extern real_time clock_time();
12026        extern struct super_block *get_super();
12027
12028        /* The order in which the various tables are flushed is critical.  The
12029         * blocks must be flushed last, since rw_inode() and rw_super() leave their
12030         * results in the block cache.
12031         */
12032
12033        /* Update the time in the root super_block. */
12034        sp = get_super(ROOT_DEV);
12035        sp->s_time = clock_time();
12036        sp->s_dirt = DIRTY;
12037
12038        /* Write all the dirty inodes to the disk. */
12039        for (rip = &inode[0]; rip < &inode[NR_INODES]; rip++)
12040            if (rip->i_count > 0 && rip->i_dirt == DIRTY) rw_inode(rip, WRITING);
12041
12042        /* Write all the dirty super_blocks to the disk. */
12043        for (sp = &super_block[0]; sp < &super_block[NR_SUPERS]; sp++)
12044            if (sp->s_dev != NO_DEV && sp->s_dirt == DIRTY) rw_super(sp, WRITING);
12045
12046        /* Write all the dirty blocks to the disk. */
12047        for (bp = &buf[0]; bp < &buf[NR_BUFS]; bp++)
12048            if (bp->b_dev != NO_DEV && bp->b_dirt == DIRTY) rw_block(bp, WRITING);
12049
```

```
12050       return(OK);              /* sync() can't fail */
12051    }


12054    /*===========================================================================*
12055     *                              do_fork                                       *
12056     *===========================================================================*/
12057    PUBLIC int do_fork()
12058    {
12059    /* Perform those aspects of the fork() system call that relate to files.
12060     * In particular, let the child inherit its parents file descriptors.
12061     * The parent and child parameters tell who forked off whom. The file
12062     * system uses the same slot numbers as the kernel.  Only MM makes this call.
12063     */
12064
12065      register struct fproc *cp;
12066      register char *sptr, *dptr;
12067      int i;
12068
12069      /* Only MM may make this call directly. */
12070      if (who != MM_PROC_NR) return(ERROR);
12071
12072      /* Copy the parent's fproc struct to the child. */
12073      sptr = (char *) &fproc[parent];      /* pointer to parent's 'fproc' struct */
12074      dptr = (char *) &fproc[child];       /* pointer to child's 'fproc' struct */
12075      i = sizeof(struct fproc);            /* how many bytes to copy */
12076      while (i--) *dptr++ = *sptr++;       /* fproc[child] = fproc[parent] */
12077
12078      /* Increase the counters in the 'filp' table. */
12079      cp = &fproc[child];
12080      for (i = 0; i < NR_FDS; i++)
12081          if (cp->fp_filp[i] != NIL_FILP) cp->fp_filp[i]->filp_count++;
12082
12083      /* Record the fact that both root and working dir have another user. */
12084      dup_inode(cp->fp_rootdir);
12085      dup_inode(cp->fp_workdir);
12086      return(OK);
12087    }


12090    /*===========================================================================*
12091     *                              do_exit                                       *
12092     *===========================================================================*/
12093    PUBLIC int do_exit()
12094    {
12095    /* Perform the file system portion of the exit(status) system call. */
12096
12097      register int i;
12098
12099      /* Only MM may do the EXIT call directly. */
```

```
12100        if (who != MM_PROC_NR) return(ERROR);
12101
12102        /* Nevertheless, pretend that the call came from the user. */
12103        fp = &fproc[slot1];              /* get_filp() needs 'fp' */
12104
12105        /* Loop on file descriptors, closing any that are open. */
12106        for (i=0; i < NR_FDS; i++) {
12107                fd = i;
12108                do_close();
12109        }
12110
12111        /* Release root and working directories. */
12112        put_inode(fp->fp_rootdir);
12113        put_inode(fp->fp_workdir);
12114
12115        if (fp->fp_suspended == SUSPENDED && fp->fp_task == XPIPE) susp_count--;
12116        fp->fp_suspended = NOT_SUSPENDED;
12117        return(OK);
12118 }


12121 /*===========================================================================*
12122  *                              do_set                                       *
12123  *===========================================================================*/
12124 PUBLIC int do_set()
12125 {
12126 /* Set uid or gid field. */
12127
12128   register struct fproc *tfp;
12129
12130   /* Only MM may make this call directly. */
12131   if (who != MM_PROC_NR) return(ERROR);
12132
12133   tfp = &fproc[slot1];
12134   if (fs_call == SETUID) {
12135         tfp->fp_realuid = (uid) real_user_id;
12136         tfp->fp_effuid =  (uid) eff_user_id;
12137   }
12138   if (fs_call == SETGID) {
12139         tfp->fp_effgid =  (gid) eff_grp_id;
12140         tfp->fp_realgid = (gid) real_grp_id;
12141   }
12142   return(OK);
12143 }


12146 /*===========================================================================*
12147  *                              do_revive                                    *
12148  *===========================================================================*/
12149 PUBLIC int do_revive()
```

```
12150    {
12151    /* A task, typically TTY, has now gotten the characters that were needed for a
12152     * previous read.  The process did not get a reply when it made the call.
12153     * Instead it was suspended.  Now we can send the reply to wake it up.  This
12154     * business has to be done carefully, since the incoming message is from
12155     * a task (to which no reply can be sent), and the reply must go to a process
12156     * that blocked earlier.  The reply to the caller is inhibited by setting the
12157     * 'dont_reply' flag, and the reply to the blocked process is done explicitly
12158     * in revive().
12159     */
12160
12161      if (who > 0) return(EPERM);
12162      revive(m.REP_PROC_NR, m.REP_STATUS);
12163      dont_reply = TRUE;              /* don't reply to the TTY task */
12164      return(OK);
12165    }
```

```
12200   /* When a needed block is not in the cache, it must be fetched from the disk.
12201    * Special character files also require I/O.  The routines for these are here.
12202    *
12203    * The entry points in this file are:
12204    *   dev_open:   called when a special file is opened
12205    *   dev_close: called when a special file is closed
12206    *   dev_io:     perform a read or write on a block or character device
12207    *   do_ioctl:   perform the IOCTL system call
12208    *   rw_dev:     procedure that actually calls the kernel tasks
12209    *   rw_dev2:    procedure that actually calls task for /dev/tty
12210    *   no_call:    dummy procedure (e.g., used when device need not be opened)
12211    */
12212
12213   #include "../h/const.h"
12214   #include "../h/type.h"
12215   #include "../h/com.h"
12216   #include "../h/error.h"
12217   #include "const.h"
12218   #include "type.h"
12219   #include "dev.h"
12220   #include "file.h"
12221   #include "fproc.h"
12222   #include "glo.h"
12223   #include "inode.h"
12224   #include "param.h"
12225
12226   PRIVATE message dev_mess;
12227   PRIVATE major, minor, task;
12228   extern max_major;
12229
12230   /*===========================================================================*
12231    *                              dev_open                                      *
12232    *===========================================================================*/
12233   PUBLIC int dev_open(dev, mod)
12234   dev_nr dev;                          /* which device to open */
12235   int mod;                             /* how to open it */
12236   {
12237   /* Special files may need special processing upon open. */
12238
12239     find_dev(dev);
12240     (*dmap[major].dmap_open)(task, &dev_mess);
12241     return(dev_mess.REP_STATUS);
12242   }


12245   /*===========================================================================*
12246    *                              dev_close                                     *
12247    *===========================================================================*/
12248   PUBLIC dev_close(dev)
12249   dev_nr dev;                          /* which device to close */
```

```
12250    {
12251    /* This procedure can be used when a special file needs to be closed. */
12252
12253      find_dev(dev);
12254      (*dmap[major].dmap_close)(task, &dev_mess);
12255    }


12258    /*===========================================================================*
12259     *                              dev_io                                       *
12260     *===========================================================================*/
12261    PUBLIC int dev_io(rw_flag, dev, pos, bytes, proc, buff)
12262    int rw_flag;                        /* READING or WRITING */
12263    dev_nr dev;                         /* major-minor device number */
12264    long pos;                           /* byte position */
12265    int bytes;                          /* how many bytes to transfer */
12266    int proc;                           /* in whose address space is buff? */
12267    char *buff;                         /* virtual address of the buffer */
12268    {
12269    /* Read or write from a device.  The parameter 'dev' tells which one. */
12270
12271      find_dev(dev);
12272
12273      /* Set up the message passed to task. */
12274      dev_mess.m_type   = (rw_flag == READING ? DISK_READ : DISK_WRITE);
12275      dev_mess.DEVICE   = (dev >> MINOR) & BYTE;
12276      dev_mess.POSITION = pos;
12277      dev_mess.PROC_NR  = proc;
12278      dev_mess.ADDRESS  = buff;
12279      dev_mess.COUNT    = bytes;
12280
12281      /* Call the task. */
12282      (*dmap[major].dmap_rw)(task, &dev_mess);
12283
12284      /* Task has completed.  See if call completed. */
12285      if (dev_mess.REP_STATUS == SUSPEND) suspend(task);    /* suspend user */
12286
12287      return(dev_mess.REP_STATUS);
12288    }


12291    /*===========================================================================*
12292     *                              do_ioctl                                     *
12293     *===========================================================================*/
12294    PUBLIC do_ioctl()
12295    {
12296    /* Perform the ioctl(ls_fd, request, argx) system call (uses m2 fmt). */
12297
12298      struct filp *f;
12299      register struct inode *rip;
```

```
12300      extern struct filp *get_filp();
12301
12302      if ( (f = get_filp(ls_fd)) == NIL_FILP) return(err_code);
12303      rip = f->filp_ino;              /* get inode pointer */
12304      if ( (rip->i_mode & I_TYPE) != I_CHAR_SPECIAL) return(ENOTTY);
12305      find_dev(rip->i_zone[0]);
12306
12307      dev_mess.m_type  = TTY_IOCTL;
12308      dev_mess.PROC_NR = who;
12309      dev_mess.TTY_LINE = minor;
12310      dev_mess.TTY_REQUEST = m.TTY_REQUEST;
12311      dev_mess.TTY_SPEK = m.TTY_SPEK;
12312      dev_mess.TTY_FLAGS = m.TTY_FLAGS;
12313
12314      /* Call the task. */
12315      (*dmap[major].dmap_rw)(task, &dev_mess);
12316
12317      /* Task has completed.  See if call completed. */
12318      if (dev_mess.m_type == SUSPEND) suspend(task);  /* User must be suspended. */
12319      m1.TTY_SPEK = dev_mess.TTY_SPEK;        /* erase and kill */
12320      m1.TTY_FLAGS = dev_mess.TTY_FLAGS;      /* flags */
12321      return(dev_mess.REP_STATUS);
12322    }


12325  /*===========================================================================*
12326   *                              find_dev                                     *
12327   *===========================================================================*/
12328  PRIVATE find_dev(dev)
12329  dev_nr dev;                       /* device */
12330  {
12331  /* Extract the major and minor device number from the parameter. */
12332
12333    major = (dev >> MAJOR) & BYTE;          /* major device number */
12334    minor = (dev >> MINOR) & BYTE;          /* minor device number */
12335    if (major == 0 || major >= max_major) panic("bad major dev", major);
12336    task = dmap[major].dmap_task; /* which task services the device */
12337    dev_mess.DEVICE = minor;
12338    }


12341  /*===========================================================================*
12342   *                              rw_dev                                       *
12343   *===========================================================================*/
12344  PUBLIC rw_dev(task_nr, mess_ptr)
12345  int task_nr;                      /* which task to call */
12346  message *mess_ptr;                /* pointer to message for task */
12347  {
12348  /* All file system I/O ultimately comes down to I/O on major/minor device
12349   * pairs.  These lead to calls on the following routines via the dmap table.
```

```
12350      */
12351
12352      int proc_nr;
12353
12354      proc_nr = mess_ptr->PROC_NR;
12355
12356      if (sendrec(task_nr, mess_ptr) != OK) panic("rw_dev: can't send", NO_NUM);
12357      while (mess_ptr->REP_PROC_NR != proc_nr) {
12358            /* Instead of the reply to this request, we got a message for an
12359             * earlier request.  Handle it and go receive again.
12360             */
12361            revive(mess_ptr->REP_PROC_NR, mess_ptr->REP_STATUS);
12362            receive(task_nr, mess_ptr);
12363      }
12364   }


12367   /*===========================================================================*
12368    *                            rw_dev2                                        *
12369    *===========================================================================*/
12370   PUBLIC rw_dev2(dummy, mess_ptr)
12371   int dummy;                        /* not used - for compatibility with rw_dev() */
12372   message *mess_ptr;                /* pointer to message for task */
12373   {
12374   /* This routine is only called for one device, namely /dev/tty.  It's job
12375    * is to change the message to use the controlling terminal, instead of the
12376    * major/minor pair for /dev/tty itself.
12377    */
12378
12379      int task_nr, major_device;
12380
12381      major_device = (fp->fs_tty >> MAJOR) & BYTE;
12382      task_nr = dmap[major_device].dmap_task;      /* task for controlling tty */
12383      mess_ptr->DEVICE = (fp->fs_tty >> MINOR) & BYTE;
12384      rw_dev(task_nr, mess_ptr);
12385   }


12388   /*===========================================================================*
12389    *                            no_call                                        *
12390    *===========================================================================*/
12391   PUBLIC int no_call(task_nr, m_ptr)
12392   int task_nr;                      /* which task */
12393   message *m_ptr;                   /* message pointer */
12394   {
12395   /* Null operation always succeeds. */
12396
12397      m_ptr->REP_STATUS = OK;
12398   }
```

```
12400    /* This file contains a few general purpose utility routines.
12401     *
12402     * The entry points into this file are
12403     *   clock_time:  ask the clock task for the real time
12404     *   cmp_string:  compare two strings (e.g., while searching directory)
12405     *   copy:        copy a string
12406     *   fetch_name:  go get a path name from user space
12407     *   no_sys:      reject a system call that FS does not handle
12408     *   panic:       something awful has occurred;  MINIX cannot continue
12409     */
12410
12411    #include "../h/const.h"
12412    #include "../h/type.h"
12413    #include "../h/com.h"
12414    #include "../h/error.h"
12415    #include "const.h"
12416    #include "type.h"
12417    #include "buf.h"
12418    #include "file.h"
12419    #include "fproc.h"
12420    #include "glo.h"
12421    #include "inode.h"
12422    #include "param.h"
12423    #include "super.h"
12424
12425    PRIVATE int panicking;              /* inhibits recursive panics during sync */
12426    PRIVATE message clock_mess;
12427
12428    /*===========================================================================*
12429     *                              clock_time                                    *
12430     *===========================================================================*/
12431    PUBLIC real_time clock_time()
12432    {
12433    /* This routine returns the time in seconds since 1.1.1970. */
12434
12435      register int k;
12436      register struct super_block *sp;
12437      extern struct super_block *get_super();
12438
12439      clock_mess.m_type = GET_TIME;
12440      if ( (k = sendrec(CLOCK, &clock_mess)) != OK) panic("clock_time err", k);
12441
12442      /* Since we now have the time, update the super block.  It is almost free. */
12443      sp = get_super(ROOT_DEV);
12444      sp->s_time = clock_mess.NEW_TIME;     /* update super block time */
12445      sp->s_dirt = DIRTY;
12446
12447      return (real_time) clock_mess.NEW_TIME;
12448    }
```

```
12451    /*===========================================================================*
12452     *                              cmp_string                                   *
12453     *===========================================================================*/
12454    PUBLIC int cmp_string(rsp1, rsp2, n)
12455    register char *rsp1, *rsp2;      /* pointers to the two strings */
12456    register int n;                  /* string length */
12457    {
12458    /* Compare two strings of length 'n'.  If they are the same, return 1. .
12459     * If they differ, return 0.
12460     */
12461
12462      do {
12463            if (*rsp1++ != *rsp2++) return(0);
12464      } while (--n);
12465
12466      /* The strings are identical. */
12467      return(1);
12468    }


12472    /*===========================================================================*
12473     *                                 copy                                      *
12474     *===========================================================================*/
12475    PUBLIC copy(dest, source, bytes)
12476    char *dest;                      /* destination pointer */
12477    char *source;                    /* source pointer */
12478    int bytes;                       /* how much data to move */
12479    {
12480    /* Copy a byte string of length 'bytes' from 'source' to 'dest'.
12481     * If all three parameters are exactly divisible by the integer size, copy them
12482     * an integer at a time.  Otherwise copy character-by-character.
12483     */
12484
12485      if (bytes <= 0) return;                /* makes test-at-the-end possible */
12486
12487      if (bytes % sizeof(int) == 0 && (int) dest % sizeof(int) == 0 &&
12488                                             (int) source % sizeof(int) == 0) {
12489            /* Copy the string an integer at a time. */
12490            register int n = bytes/sizeof(int);
12491            register int *dpi = (int *) dest;
12492            register int *spi = (int *) source;
12493
12494            do { *dpi++ = *spi++; } while (--n);
12495
12496      } else {
12497
12498            /* Copy the string character-by-character. */
12499            register int n = bytes;
```

```
12500            register char *dpc = (char *) dest;
12501            register char *spc = (char *) source;
12502
12503            do { *dpc++ = *spc++; } while (--n);
12504
12505      }
12506  }


12509  /*===========================================================================*
12510   *                              fetch_name                                   *
12511   *===========================================================================*/
12512  PUBLIC int fetch_name(path, len, flag)
12513  char *path;                      /* pointer to the path in user space */
12514  int len;                         /* path length, including 0 byte */
12515  int flag;                        /* M3 means path may be in message */
12516  {
12517  /* Go get path and put it in 'user_path'.
12518   * If 'flag' = M3 and 'len' <= M3_STRING, the path is present in 'message'.
12519   * If it is not, go copy it from user space.
12520   */
12521
12522    register char *rpu, *rpm;
12523    vir_bytes vpath;
12524
12525    if (flag == M3 && len <= M3_STRING) {
12526            /* Just copy the path from the message to 'user_path'. */
12527            rpu = &user_path[0];
12528            rpm = pathname;          /* contained in input message */
12529            do { *rpu++ = *rpm++; } while (--len);
12530            return(OK);
12531    }
12532
12533    /* String is not contained in the message.  Go get it from user space. */
12534    if (len > MAX_PATH) {
12535            err_code = E_LONG_STRING;
12536            return(ERROR);
12537    }
12538    vpath = (vir_bytes) path;
12539    err_code = rw_user(D, who, vpath, (vir_bytes) len, user_path, FROM_USER);
12540    return(err_code);
12541  }


12544  /*===========================================================================*
12545   *                              no_sys                                       *
12546   *===========================================================================*/
12547  PUBLIC int no_sys()
12548  {
12549  /* Somebody has used an illegal system call number */
```

```
12550
12551      return(EINVAL);
12552    }


12555    /*===========================================================================*
12556     *                              panic                                         *
12557     *===========================================================================*/
12558    PUBLIC panic(format, num)
12559    char *format;                       /* format string */
12560    int num;                            /* number to go with format string */
12561    {
12562    /* Something awful has happened.  Panics are caused when an internal
12563     * inconsistency is detected, e.g., a programming error or illegal value of a
12564     * defined constant.
12565     */
12566
12567      if (panicking) return;            /* do not panic during a sync */
12568      panicking = TRUE;                 /* prevent another panic during the sync */
12569      printf("File system panic: %s ", format);
12570      if (num != NO_NUM) printf("%d",num);
12571      printf("\n");
12572      do_sync();                        /* flush everything to the disk */
12573      sys_abort();
12574    }
```

```
12600   /* FS must occasionally print some message.  It uses the standard library
12601    * routine printf(), which calls putc() and flush(). Library
12602    * versions of these routines do printing by sending messages to FS.  Here
12603    * we obviously can't do that, so FS calls the TTY task directly.
12604    */
12605
12606   #include "../h/const.h"
12607   #include "../h/type.h"
12608   #include "../h/com.h"
12609
12610   #define STDOUTPUT           1     /* file descriptor for standard output */
12611   #define BUFSIZE           100     /* print buffer size */
12612
12613   PRIVATE int bufcount;             /* # characters in the buffer */
12614   PRIVATE char printbuf [BUFSIZE];         /* output is buffered here */
12615   PRIVATE message putchmsg;         /* used for message to TTY task */
12616
12617   /*===========================================================================*
12618    *                              putc                                         *
12619    *===========================================================================*/
12620   PUBLIC putc(c)
12621   char c;
12622   {
12623
12624     if (c == 0) {
12625           flush();
12626           return;
12627     }
12628     printbuf[bufcount++] = c;
12629     if (bufcount == BUFSIZE) flush();
12630     if (c == '\n')  flush();
12631   }


12634   /*===========================================================================*
12635    *                              flush                                        *
12636    *===========================================================================*/
12637   PRIVATE flush()
12638   {
12639   /* Flush the print buffer. */
12640
12641     if (bufcount == 0) return;
12642     putchmsg.m_type = TTY_WRITE;
12643     putchmsg.PROC_NR  = 1;
12644     putchmsg.TTY_LINE = 0;
12645     putchmsg.ADDRESS  = printbuf;
12646     putchmsg.COUNT = bufcount;
12647     sendrec(TTY, &putchmsg);
12648     bufcount = 0;
12649   }
```

F

MINIX CROSS REFERENCE LISTING

This appendix lists the principal procedure names, global variables, defined constants, and other macros present in the listing of Appendix E. Local variables and structure members are not listed, as this would have increased the length of this appendix substantially. The **boldface** entries show the lines on which the symbols are defined.

ABS	**0049** 4941 4946 5716 6171
ACCESS	**0130**
ADDRESS	**0211** 2362 2597 3542 3550 3800 3918 4166 7391 12278 12645
ALARM	**0126**
ALARM_ON	**5284** 5799 6616 6617 6709 6711
ALL_MODES	**0072** 9495 9549 11704
ANY	**0154** 1946 2002 2053 2078 2311 2551 3121 3509 4634 5001 5475 9042
AT_SIGN	**3373** 3724
BAD_CYL	**2462** 2822
BAD_SECTOR	**2461** 2822
BASE	**0874** 0903 0973
BEEP_FREQ	**4068** 4244
BIT_MAP_SHIFT	**8626** 8704 8705 8725 8756 8757
BLANK	**4070** 1697 1699 1744 4485
BLOCK_SIZE	**0018** 2387 2590 2599 2644 7540 7542 7543 7544 7546 7566 8310 8311 9097 9098 9138 9190 9216 9220 9862 9863 9864

687

CRMOD   **0372** 3655 4264 4462
CS_REG   **0664** 0941 4730
CTL_ACCEPTING **2452** 2889
CTL_BUSY   **2451** 2860
CTRL_S   **4073** 4146
CURSOR   **4091** 4336 4355
CUR_SIZE   **4089** 4487
C_6845   **4086** 4477
C_RETRACE   **4064** 4478
C_VID_MASK   **4062** 4476
D   **0028** 0924 0925 0934 0935 0937 0942 0943 0944 0960 1005
                          1994 1998 2004 2005 2055 2056 2362 2672 3467 3489 3834
                          3835 3927 4722 4724 4731 4732 4733 4907 5042 5045 5580
                          5581 5608 5609 5610 5705 5708 5733 5734 5735 5963 5981
                          5999 6004 6151 6152 6153 6154 6156 6171 6329 6361 6362
                          6431 6662 6829 9817 10057 10068 11624 12539
DATA   **4088** 4418 4420
DATAB   **5927** 6068
DATA_CHANGED **6277** 6348 6369
DELETE   **7527** 10910 11371
DELTA_TICKS   **0200** 2994 3157 6707
DELUXE   **4097**
DEL_CODE   **3372** 4154
DEVICE   **0207** 2349 2384 2585 9205 12275 12337 12383
DIRECTION   **2450** 2855 2888
DIRECTORY_BLO **7604** 10916 10929 10950
DIRTY   **7530** 8139 8224 8439 8516 8568 8732 8764 8844 9217 9599
                          9892 9973 10153 10199 10213 10330 10912 10949 10952 11329 11375
                          11705 11735 11894 12036 12040 12044 12048 12445
DIR_ENTRY_SIZE **7539** 7542 10892 10954
DISKINT   **0185** 1205
DISK_IOCTL   **0188** 2321 9204
DISK_READ   **0186** 2319 2351 2366 2559 2669 2804 12274
DISK_WRITE   **0187** 2320 2560 12274
DIVISOR   **2503** 2810
DMA_ADDR   **2431** 2692 2693
DMA_COUNT   **2433** 2695 2696
DMA_INIT   **2436** 2698
DMA_M1   **2435** 2691
DMA_M2   **2434** 2690
DMA_READ   **2475** 2669
DMA_TOP   **2432** 2694
DMA_WRITE   **2476** 2669
DOR   **2428** 2725 2748 2959 2960
DST_BUFFER   **0229** 4937 4947 7289 10062 10070
DST_PROC_NR   **0228** 4933 7288 10061 10069
DST_SPACE   **0227** 4935 7287 10060 10068
DS_REG   **0663** 0942 4731

DTL	**2483** 2813	
DUMPED	**6481** 6808	
DUMP_SIZE	**6479** 6780 6828	
DUP	**0133**	
DUP_MASK	**7523** 11992	
E2BIG	**0263**	
EACCES	**0269** 5968 5984 7245 7260 11811 11815	
EAGAIN	**0267** 5701 5702 5711 6135	
EBADF	**0265** 8921 9825 12002	
EBUSY	**0272** 11050 11077 11150	
ECHILD	**0266** 5842	
ECHO	**0373** 3752 4462	
EDOM	**0289**	
EEXIST	**0273** 9498 9504 9608 11314	
EFAULT	**0270** 4951	
EFBIG	**0283** 9847 10187 10940	
EINTR	**0260** 3661 4025 6753 6760 10602	
EINVAL	**0278** 2322 2561 2590 2599 3519 3990 5958 6496 6592 7302	
	9637 9740 9742 9822 9827 11062 11160 12551	
EIO	**0261** 2586 2644	
EISDIR	**0277** 9512 9655	
EMFILE	**0280** 8896	
EMLINK	**0287** 11291	
ENABLE	**0680** 1888 4134 4148 4170	
ENABLE_INT	**2454** 2641 2722 2960	
ENFILE	**0279** 8404 8465 8909 11051 11091	
ENODEV	**0275**	
ENOENT	**0258** 6803 9579 10933 11311	
ENOEXEC	**0264** 5975 6062 6063 6078 6084	
ENOMEM	**0268** 5957 6129 6336 6342 6375 6404 6406 6409	
ENOSPC	**0284** 8259	
ENOTBLK	**0271** 11196	
ENOTDIR	**0276** 10886 11081 11104 11532	
ENOTTY	**0281** 12304	
ENOUGH	**5425**	
ENTER	**7526** 9596 10904 10907 10921 10933 11324	
ENXIO	**0262** 2350 2354 2385	
EOT_CHAR	**3370** 4470	
EPERM	**0257** 5550 6544 6895 6904 9547 10584 11037 11138 11295 11369	
	11506 11693 11724 11891 11926 12161	
EPIPE	**0288** 10469	
ERANGE	**0290**	
ERASE_CHAR	**3364** 4464	
EROFS	**0286** 11841	
ERROR	**0256** 8644 12070 12100 12131 12536	
ERR_DRIVE	**2496**	
ERR_RECALIBRA	**2494** 2933	
ERR_SEEK	**2491** 2768 2775 2781 2782 2784 2921	

ERR_STATUS   **2493** 2853 2855 2865
ERR_TRANSFER   **2492** 2800 2801 2816 2828 2829 2835
ERR_WR_PROTEC **2495** 2636 2826
ESCAPED   **3435** 3630
ESPIPE   **0285** 9733
ESRCH   **0259** 6633
ES_REG   **0662** 0944 4733
ETXTBSY   **0282**
EXDEV   **0274** 11320
EXEC   **0140** 5462
EXIT   **0102** 5873
EXTERN   **0009 7409 9312**
E_BAD_ADDR   **0306** 1998 2363 3834 3929
E_BAD_BUF   **0301**
E_BAD_CALL   **0293** 5456 9001
E_BAD_DEST   **0297** 1988 1991
E_BAD_FCN   **0305** 4646
E_BAD_PROC   **0307** 4674 4715 4757 4784 4834 4853 4896
E_BAD_SRC   **0298** 1947
E_LOCKED   **0292**
E_LONG_STRING   **0294** 10782 12535
E_NO_MESSAGE   **0303**
E_NO_PERM   **0304** 1951
E_OVERRUN   **0300** 2010
E_TASK   **0302**
E_TRY_AGAIN   **0299** 3793
F1   **3375** 3592 4526
F10   **3377** 3592
F2   **3376** 4527
FALSE   **0015** 2955 3708 5451 6605 6606 6607 6608 6620 8803 8996
                    8997 9700 9882 10167 10168 10894 10938 11045
FDC_DATA   **2430** 2856 2890
FDC_READ   **2468** 2804
FDC_RECALIBRA **2471** 2919
FDC_SEEK   **2467** 2772
FDC_SENSE   **2470** 2779 2925 2967
FDC_SPECIFY   **2472** 2975
FDC_STATUS   **2429** 2852 2854 2859 2887
FDC_WRITE   **2469** 2804
FD_MASK   **9777** 9814
FLOPPY   **0183** 1206 1208 2993 3008 9421
FLOPPY_VECTOR **0673** 0969
FORK   **0103** 5753
FORWARD   **0012**
FROM_USER   **0046** 9971 12539
FSTAT   **0127**
FS_PROC_NR   **0039** 1987 5522 5550 6544 8311 10058 10069
FS_STACK_BYTES **7511** 7819 9332

MESS_SIZE	**0567** 1997
MILLISEC	**3089** 3090
MIN	**0502** 3842 3843 4385 6170 6828 9863
MINIX	**1153** 1100 1151 1166
MINOR	**0022** 8261 8315 8467 10594 12275 12334 12383
MKNOD	**0114**
MM_PROC_NR	**0038** 1987 2078 4980 5521 5963 5981 5999 6171 6829 9201 9811 9822 10468 10584 11483 12070 12100 12131
MM_STACK_BYT	**5156** 5158 5216 7421
MONOCHROME	**4074**
MONO_BASE	**4061** 4480
MOTOR_MASK	**2453** 2747
MOTOR_OFF	**2487** 2642
MOTOR_RUNNIN	**2499** 3007
MOTOR_START	**2488** 2732
MOUNT	**0121**
M_6845	**4085** 4482
M_RETRACE	**4065** 4483
M_VID_MASK	**4063** 4481
NAME_SIZE	**7510** 8004 9571 10683 10705 10751 10771 10779 10794 10863 10908 10947 11281 11349
NCALLS	**0100** 5455 7427 8987 9000 9334
NERROR	**0254**
NEW_TIME	**0202** 3180 3192 11928 12444 12447
NIL_BUF	**7585** 8101 8120 8121 8129 8172 8181 8186 8200 8202 8212 8213 9130 9131 9142 9145 9955 10154 10199 10294 10298 10941
NIL_FILP	**7711** 8888 8922 8948 9691 9714 9730 9823 9898 10402 10412 10414 10452 10463 11566 11583 11615 11994 12081 12302
NIL_HOLE	**6972** 7001 7038 7048 7057 7109 7120 7140 7169 7170
NIL_INODE	**7879** 8390 8403 8405 8429 8472 8477 9008 9575 9579 9581 9584 9602 9607 9643 10092 10411 10687 10688 10730 10737 10814 10818 11070 11084 11086 11171 11192 11287 11305 11309 11354 11359 11528 11565 11687 11728 11770 11887
NIL_MESS	**0568**
NIL_PROC	**0788** 1921 2016 2019 2023 2051 2092 2093 2106 2140 2145 2164 2174 2176 2194 2203 4799 4807
NIL_PTR	**0053** 4318 4386 5759 5872 6201 6753 6760
NIL_SUPER	**7992** 11044 11051 11153 11160
NORMAL	**7518** 8149 8560 8650 8655 8837 9184 9214 9951 9962 10022 10031 10094 10189 10209 10899 11420
NOT_ESCAPED	**3434** 3609 3618 3626 3642
NOT_REVIVING	**7776** 9034
NOT_SUSPENDED	**7774** 9033 10549 10562 10588 12116
NOT_WAITING	**3442** 3894 3898 4023
NO_BIT	**7522** 8258 8464 8741
NO_BLOCK	**0507** 9125 9156 9948 9951 10006 10019 10029 10034 10093 10250 10286 11410
NO_DEV	**0524** 8100 8139 8149 8224 8228 8309 8334 8412 8477 9126

```
                   12397
RET_REG            0686 1947 1951 1958 1964 4685
REVIVE             0148 3571
REVIVING           7777 9027 10558
ROOT_DEV           0061 8262 8468 8798 9084 9215 9244 9246 9257 12034 12443
ROOT_INODE         7534 9084 9246 10820 10821 10849 11086
RUNNING            3436 3660 3675 4024 4196
RWX_MODES          0073 11752
R_BIT              0074 9474 9707 9824 10398 10463 11616
S                  0029 0926 0927 0928 0931 0936 0937 3466 3488 4908 5042
                   5045 5582 5583 5611 5612 5613 5706 5708 5734 5735 5876
                   5996 6139 6154 6155 6156 6330 6362
SAFETY             0872 0913 0951
SCHED_RATE         3090 3101 3244
SCR_LINES          4072 4313 4351 4354
SECONDS_LEFT       0204 3160 6715
SECTOR_SIZE        2479 2591 2810 2835
SEEK_ST0           2460 2781 2929
SEND               0151 1179 1956 1958
SENDING            0784 2012 2057 4796
SEP                5925 6064
SEPARATE           5285 5584 5877 6019 6064 6069 6085 6140 6360 6403
SERVER_Q           0692 2093 2137 2163
SETGID             0136 6014 6902 6907 12138
SETUID             0123 6010 6893 6898 12134
SET_ALARM          0171 2992 3125 6705
SET_TIME           0174 3127 11927
SIGALRM            0415 3226 6615
SIGBUS             0411
SIGEMT             0408
SIGFPE             0409
SIGHUP             0402
SIGILL             0405
SIGINT             0403 3659 6565
SIGIOT             0407
SIGKILL            0410 6497
SIGNAL             0138
SIGNUM             0243 4894
SIGPIPE            0414 10467
SIGQUIT            0404 3659 6565
SIGSEGV            0412 6436
SIGSYS             0413
SIGTERM            0416
SIGTRAP            0406
SIG_DFL            0421 6504
SIG_IGN            0422 6501
SIG_MAP            0247 5008 6550 10467
SIG_PUSH_BYTES     0057 4622 4905 6661
```

SIZES	**0875**
SPEC1	**2484** 2976
SPEC2	**2485** 2977
SQUARE_WAVE	**3096** 3281
SRC_BUFFER	**0226** 4936 4942 7285 10059 10067
SRC_PROC_NR	**0225** 4932 7284 10058 10066
SRC_SPACE	**0224** 4934 7283 10057 10065
SS_REG	**0665** 0943 4732
ST0	**2439** 2781 2828 2929
ST0_BITS	**2455** 2781 2828 2929
ST1	**2440** 2782 2822 2824 2829
ST2	**2441** 2822 2829
ST3	**2442**
ST3_FAULT	**2456**
ST3_READY	**2458**
ST3_WR_PROTEC	**2457**
STACK_CHANGE	**6278** 6356 6370
STACK_FAULT	**0418** 6554
STACK_PTR	**0241** 4756 4836
STAT	**0118**
STDOUTPUT	**12610**
STD_OUTPUT	**7359**
STIME	**0125**
STOPPED	**3437** 3669 4147
ST_CYL	**2443** 2832
ST_HEAD	**2444** 2833
ST_PCN	**2446** 2929
ST_SEC	**2445** 2834
SUPER_BLOCK	**7533** 8650 8653 8837 8842 9184
SUPER_MAGIC	**7514** 9187 9250 11059
SUPER_SIZE	**7545** 8838 8843 9097
SUPER_USER	**0019** 6566 6605 6609 6801 6894 6903 11488
SUSPEND	**0197** 3830 12285 12318
SUSPENDED	**7775** 10498 10524 12115
SU_UID	**7515** 8996
SYNC	**0131** 7321
SYSTASK	**0159** 4724 4907
SYSTEM_TIME	**0234** 4858
SYS_ABORT	**0168** 4643
SYS_COPY	**0165** 4645
SYS_EXEC	**0166** 4639
SYS_FORKED	**0163** 4637
SYS_GETSP	**0161** 4641
SYS_GID	**7517** 9090 9091
SYS_NEWMAP	**0164** 4638
SYS_SIG	**0162** 4644
SYS_TIMES	**0167** 4642
SYS_UID	**7516** 9088 9089

alloc_zone	**8235** 10149 10177 10197 10283 10294
allowed	**7224** 5966 6796 6797
alt	**3449** 3722 3734 4154
b_data	**7588** 8311 8838 8843 9137 9185 9216 9972
b_dir	**7589** 10902 10943
b_ind	**7590** 10023 10032 10191 10211 11421
b_inode	**7591** 8561
b_int	**7592** 8658 8659 8716 8717 8724 8761 8763 10327
beep	**4427** 4244
begbss	**1339**
block	**1384** 2582 2591 2592 2593 2594 2595 8079 8081 8099 8102 8143
boot_time	**3099** 3180 3192
buf_count	**7362** 7374 7375 7387 7392 7394
buf_pool	**9107** 9077
bufcount	**12613** 12628 12629 12641 12646 12648
buffer	**7903** 1502 1691 1693 1697 9031 9838 9874 9878 10500 11585
bufs_in_use	**7598** 8104 8117 8118 8178 8643 8660 8679 9120
build_sig	**1612** 1360 1371 1594 1605 1612 4902
busy_map	**0795** 1895 1899 1904 1905 1915
capslock	**3448** 3710 3715 3735
cause_sig	**4960** 3226 3663
cd_flag	**7904** 11486 11488
change	**11515** 11493 11507
check_sig	**6577** 6523 6566
child	**7905** 5849 5850 5866 5867 5870 5871 5872 5876 5877 5878 5881 5883 12074 12079
chuck	**3761** 3610 3619
cleanup	**5849** 5794 5829 5894
clear_zone	**10222** 9853 10302
clock_int	**1217** 0891 0967 1114 1124 1215 1217
clock_mess	**2986** 2642 2732 11872 11927 11928 11929 12426 12439 12440 12444 12447
clock_task	**3109** 5134 5143
clock_time	**12431** 8512 8515 9808 9891 10151 10161 10212 10883 10913 10951 11910 11912 12025 12035
cmp_string	**12454** 10908
co_mode	**7906** 11752
color	**4102** 0890 0957 1363 1364 1378 1671 1675 1678 1679 1688 1694 1699 1712 1714 1717 4474
console	**4178** 4463
control	**3449** 1602 3711 3716 3723 3733 4146 4154
copy	**12475** 1364 1405 1413 1433 1435 1436 1439 1440 1441 1477 1507 1508 1509 1511 1512 1647 1695 1696 1711 1717 1732 1745 8565 8567 8838 8843 9185 9216 10947
copy_mess	**7219** 7283 7284 7285 7287 7288 7289 7291 7292 7293
cp_mess	**1490** 1354 1370 1475 1481 1490 2004 2055
cret	**1660** 1362 1371 1634 1637

mode_map **9474** 9639
motor_goal **2526** 2641 2722 2723 2725 2726 2747 2748 2749 2958
motor_status **2525** 2723 2724 2726 2747 2749 2801 2957
mounted **8789** 9700
move_to **4343** 4248 4252 4256 4260 4269 4273 4398 4489
name **7918** 9491 9638 11141 11353 11493 11507 11686 11769
name1 **7919** 9548 11040 11286 11564 11727
name1_length **7922** 9548 11040 11286 11564 11727
name2 **7920** 11066 11304 11566
name2_length **7923** 11066 11304
name_length **7921** 9491 9638 11141 11353 11493 11507 11686 11769
name_to_dev **11180** 11034 11041 11134 11142
namelen **5307**
nbytes **7924** 9032 9821 9822 9838 9846 9858 9861 9863 9879 10501
need_reset **2528** 2621 2775 2816 2864 2882 2895 2921 2931 2955
new_block **10265** 9936 9955 10881 10941
new_mem **6097** 5988
new_node **9557** 9488 9496 9550
next_alarm **3100** 3165 3167 3213 3215 3233 3234
next_pid **5676** 5742 5744 5748 5760
no_call **12391** 9329 9420 9421 9422 9423 9424 9425
no_sys **7298 12547** 7425 7428 7431 7432 7433 7434 7436 7437 7438
7439 7440 7441 7442 7443 7444 7446 7447 7449 7450 7453
7454 7456 7458 7459 7460 7461 7462 7463 7464 7466 7467
7468 7469 7470 7471 7472 7473 7477 7478 7479 7480 7481
7482 7483 7484 7485 7486 7488 7489 7490 7491 7494 7496
7497 9329 9335 9342 9346 9352 9355 9359 9361 9362 9364
9366 9367 9369 9370 9372 9373 9374 9375 9379 9380 9382
9383 9384 9385 9386 9387 9388 9390 9391 9392 9393 9394
9397 9398 9400 9402 9404
numlock **3448** 3712 3717 3736
offset **7925** 1418 1420 1502 1504 1691 1695 1710 1758 1764 4188
4192 4193 4197 4199 4205 4308 4313 4315 4318 9737 9738
9739
olivetti **3450** 3708 4495
out_char **4217** 3753 4198 4264 4279 4512
owner **7926** 11733
panic **1012 7309 12558** 0990 1128 1233 1375 1646 1650 1656 2313
2553 2613 2684 2686 2969 2972 3129 4723 4725 4873 4909
5011 5475 5477 5501 5717 6000 6147 6172 6714 7038 7239
8117 8121 8646 8762 8782 9038 9042 9096 9097 9098 9099
9100 9101 9188 9201 9209 9251 9258 10547 10586 10597 10600
11163 11929 12335 12356 12440
panicking **12425** 12567 12568
parent **7927** 4778 4781 4783 4785 5861 5867 5882 12073
patch_ptr **6183** 5997
pathname **7928** 12528
phys_copy **1387** 0961 1056 1353 1370 1382 1385 1387 2367 2369 3868

	4726 4910 4952
pick_proc	**2086** 0976 1922 2168 2204
pid	**5308** 4667 4672 4684 6523
pipe_check	**10433** 9857
port_in	**1547** 1356 1370 1544 1546 1547 2852 2854 2856 2859 2887
	4121 4122 4442
port_out	**1529** 0979 1355 1370 1525 1527 1529 1888 2690 2691 2692
	2693 2694 2695 2696 2698 2725 2748 2890 2959 2960 3281
	3282 3283 4123 4124 4134 4148 4170 4417 4418 4419 4420
	4439 4440 4441 4443 4445
prev_motor	**2527** 2723 2727
prev_proc	**0708** 2105 3261
prev_ptr	**3102** 2044 2062 2065 3243 3245 6997 7012 7016 7036 7058
	7063 7064 7065 7072 7073 7085 8096 8124 8125 8129 8130
	8131 8134 8170 8180 8181 8182 8187 8189
print_buf	**7363** 7374 7391
printbuf	**12614** 12628 12645
printf	**0695 5169 7549** 1001 1002 1003 1004 1023 1024 1025 1027
	2825 5566 5567 5568 5569 5570 5572 7318 7319 7320 8263
	8265 8314 8469 8471 9212 9221 9224 12569 12570 12571
pro	**7929** 6736 6737 6748 6753 6760 6765 10585
proc_addr	**0787** 0953 0960 0975 1945 1989 1990 2047 2114 2361 2672
	3159 3831 3835 3924 4675 4678 4679 4716 4717 4724 4758
	4785 4786 4835 4854 4897 4907 4944 4949 4977 5000 5004
procs_in_use	**5203** 5524 5701 5702 5725 5884
put_block	**8157** 8571 8680 8681 8848 9191 9218 9219 9975 10024 10033
	10095 10201 10205 10214 10257 10916 10929 10950 11426
put_inode	**8421** 9525 9550 9583 9597 9600 9614 9646 9654 9712 10695
	10729 10736 10828 10848 11097 11098 11109 11110 11169 11170
	11197 11203 11299 11313 11333 11334 11363 11379 11380 11485
	11538 11543 11567 11699 11707 11738 11774 11897 12112 12113
putc	**4503 7369 12620**
putch_msg	**7364** 7388 7389 7390 7391 7392 7393
putchmsg	**12615** 12642 12643 12644 12645 12646 12647
ram_limit	**2287** 2303 2304 2356 2358 2387
ram_origin	**2286** 2302 2355 2386
rd_chars	**3813** 3566 3804
rd_only	**7930** 11118
rdahedpos	**7806** 9907 10093
read_ahead	**10082** 9008
read_header	**6030** 5972
read_map	**9984** 9937 9944 10093 10238 10250 10282 10286 10882 10896 11401
	11410
read_only	**11830** 11695 11731 11821
read_write	**9794** 9786 10128
ready	**2122** 0915 2007 2058 4738 4763
real_grp_id	**7914** 12140
real_user_id	**7931** 12135

realtime	**0703** 3160 3161 3180 3192 3210 3213 3219
reboot	**1780** 1366 1367 1371 1776 1780 1785 1794 4154
recalibrate	**2903** 2768 2784
release	**10510** 1111 9708 10457 10478
reply	**5485 9053** 5463 5759 5872 6753 6760 9007 10564
reply_i1	**5318 7944** 5499 10424
reply_i2	**7945** 10425
reply_l1	**7943** 9747 11912
reply_p1	**5319** 5500
reply_t1	**7946** 11944
reply_t2	**7947** 11945
reply_t3	**7948** 11946
reply_t4	**7949** 11947
reply_type	**5317 7942** 5498 9062
request	**7932**
res_ptr	**5214** 5463 6305
reset	**2945** 2621
restart	**1288** 0980 1107 1117 1125 1181 1190 1199 1211 1225 1234 1243 1286 1288 1289
restore	**1587** 1251 1294 1295 1296 1297 1298 1305 1306 1307 1308 1312 1359 1362 1370 1453 1454 1455 1456 1457 1458 1459 1460 1461 1462 1514 1515 1516 1517 1518 1519 1520 1537 1538 1539 1557 1558 1559 1584 1587 1589 1627 1628 1629 1662 1663 1664 1735 1736 1737 1738 1739 1740 1741 1768 1769 1784 1791 1807 2146 2179 2195 2205
result2	**5213** 5463 6880 6885 6890
resvec	**1797** 1784 1791
revive	**10537** 10526 10599 10602 12162 12361
reviving	**7805** 9024 9035 10559
rw_block	**8295** 8139 8149 8225 12048
rw_chunk	**9919** 9874
rw_dev	**12344** 9408 9420 9421 9422 9423 9425 12384
rw_dev2	**12370** 9408 9424
rw_inode	**8543** 8412 8439 9593 10423 12040
rw_super	**8824** 9245 11055 12044
rw_user	**10042** 9972 11624 12539
s_call	**1173** 0891 0966 1110 1125 1171 1173
save	**1249** 1104 1162 1174 1188 1197 1204 1218 1232 1241 1247 1256 1257 1264 1268 1270 1271 1272 1273 1274 1275 1361 1388 1390 1391 1392 1393 1394 1395 1396 1397 1398 1431 1491 1492 1493 1495 1497 1498 1499 1530 1532 1533 1548 1550 1551 1568 1570 1613 1615 1616 1642 1643 1704 1705 1706 1707 1708 1724 1760 1762
scale_factor	**8810** 9999 10155 10241 10303 11404
scan_code	**3451** 1132 1162 4495
sched	**2186** 3243
sched_ticks	**3101** 3242 3244
scroll_screen	**4304** 4266 4392

search_dir	**10861** 9596 10812 11324 11371
seconds	**5309** 6686
seek	**2757** 2630
send_mess	**3003** 2718 2732
set_6845	**4403** 4319 4336 4355 4487 4488
set_alarm	**6695** 5799 6687
set_map	**5593**
set_vec	**1036** 0964 0965 0966 0967 0968 0969 0970 0973
sh	**3464** 3710 3711 3712 3716
shift1	**3448** 3710 3715 3731
shift2	**3448** 3710 3715 3732
sig	**5310** **7933** 1605 3588 3659 3663 4889 4894 4902 6496 6497 6498
sig_proc	**6640** 6436 6627
sig_procs	**0709** 2078 4978 5009
sig_stuff	**4622** 1605 1617 1620 1622 1624 1626 4898 4902
size_ok	**6382** 6087 6361
sizes	**1330** 0889 0904 0925 0927 0928 0932 0934 0935 0936 0937 1046 1054 1133 1330 2297 2303
slot1	**7934** 11484 12103 12133
stack_bytes	**5311** 5956
stack_fault	**6418** 6555
stack_ptr	**5312** 5979
start_motor	**2703** 2627 2918
stat_inode	**11592** 11566 11585
status	**5313** 2848 2852 2853 2854 2855 2856 2857 2859 2860 2951 2970 2971 4031 4035 4045 5773
steps_per_cyl	**2530** 2612 2615 2774 2782
stop_motor	**2740** 2581 2642
super_user	**7802** 8996 9547 11037 11138 11295 11368 11506 11692 11724 11800 11891 11926
surprise	**1231** 0892 0964 1115 1125 1229 1231
susp_count	**7804** 10457 10497 10527 12115
suspend	**10488** 10454 10473 12285 12318
sys_call	**1929** 1128 1180
sys_task	**4627** 5134 5143
task	**12227** 0890 0914 1107 1110 1117 1181 1205 1219 1264 1288 1313 1653 1808 1878 1879 1892 1893 1896 1900 5141 10488 10489 10497 10502 10579 10589 10591 10597 10600 12240 12254 12282 12285 12315 12318 12336
task_mess	**0796** 1900 1914
tot_mem	**5428** 5517 5518 5563
tp	**7935** 11928
transfer	**2792** 2634
trap	**0997** 1103 1105 1128 1242
trp	**1240** 0892 0965 1116 1125 1238 1240
truncate	**11388** 8433 9508
tty_buf	**3447** 3835 3845

INDEX

N

O